...gments

...f detailed recommendations comes par...
...tes and mainly from those of a great nu...
...ds. Without the generous help and coop...
...ble winemakers, merchants, and critics...
...t. I particularly want to thank the follow...
...earch or in the areas of their special kn...

...asset MW
...Borden
...Péter Botos
... Bowden
...Cass
...el Cooper
...t Dean
...ael Edwards
...ueline Friedrich
...is Gastin
...semary George MW
...bert Gorjak
...mes Halliday

Shirley Nelson
Dr Annie Kay
Chandra Kurt
Gabriel Lachmann
Gareth Lawrence
James Lawther MW
John Livingstone-
  Learmonth
Nico Manessis
Richard Mayson
Adam Montefiore
Jasper Morris MW
Vladimir Moskva...

...pecial thanks to Margaret Rand who t...

Hugh Johnson's Pocket Wine B...

Edited and designed by Mitchell Beazl...
Group Limited, 2-4 Heron Quays, Lon...

© Octopus Publishing Group Limited...

First edition published 1977
Revised editions published 1978, 19...
1987, 1988, 1989, 1990, 1991, 1992, 199...
2001, 2002(twice), 2003.

A CIP record for this book is...

ISBN 1 84000 731 1

The author and publisher...
assist them in keeping fu...
care has been taken in t...
nor the author can acce...
use thereof, or from th...

Commissioning Editor...
Editor: Emma Rice
Executive Art Editor:...
Design: Fiona Know...
Production: Julie Y...

Printed and boun...

Hugh Johnson

Pocket Wine Book

2004

Acknowle...
This store
my own n...
kind frien...
innumera...
attempt ...
with res...

Gerard B...
Charles ...
Dr Ernö...
Gregor...
Bruce ...
Micha...
Rupe...
Mich...
Jac...
De...
Ro...
Ro...
Ja...

MITCHELL BEAZLEY

Contents

Agenda 2004

When I wrote the first edition of this book in 1977 I did most of it from my own notes and my then-nimble memory. It had less than half the number of pages and had a spacious, almost leisurely feel.

Today's editions (this is the 27th revision) are a different matter. Keeping abreast in the modern wine world is like taking a census in a rabbit warren. Wines world-wide are getting steadily better – if more alike. Competition is getting stiffer; prices are coming down. We have never had anything like the choice – which makes selection harder. What, then, should we be looking out for? What are the themes for 2004?

Theme one is the growing number of grape varieties trying to catch your attention. The stranglehold of Chardonnay and Cabernet is at an end. Whether out of ambition, curiosity, or boredom, winemakers have moved on from the Surefire Five international varieties. They are exploring the staples of the Rhône, Tuscany, Rioja... European growers are busy taking stock of indigenous grapes they have ignored or taken for granted in the past, from Agiorgitiko in the Aegean via Negroamaro in Puglia and Nero d'Avola in Sicily to Garo in Catalonia and Touriga in Portugal. Syrah/Shiraz is now a standard quality red grape for warm regions (inspired as much by its key place in Australia as its historic role on the Rhône). Mourvèdre from Provence, Tuscany's Sangiovese, and Spain's Tempranillo are being planted with high hopes to add to the palette of California and Australia, South America and South Africa. Meanwhile the old wine cultures of South America are dining out on the old French varieties they had previously relegated: Malbec in Argentina, Carmenère in Chile and Tannat in Uruguay. Each brings something original and special to the feast. South Africa parades its Pinotage with perhaps rather less conviction. And of course California has its Zinfandel.

These are all red wine varieties. The range of white grapes with star potential is more limited. Sauvignon Blanc has an obvious slot as an aromatically fresh grape to complement the weight of Chardonnay. We all love to refresh ourselves with it, without holding our breath for great qualities of depth or ageability. Riesling is the white grape to play the serious lead role opposite Chardonnay. No wine is so adaptable, from dynamically dry to featherweight fruity to celestially sweet, or so durable.

In 2003 there are signs of a Riesling renaissance. The evidence comes from as far apart as Germany and Australia, with important contributions from Austria, Alsace and New Zealand. What else is competing? The fragrant Viognier has had some exposure. Marsanne and Verdelho make good wine in warm climates. Greco and Vermentino can be attractive in Italy, and Alvarinho and Verdejo in Portugal and Spain. Grüner Veltliner is seriously good in Austria and Chenin Blanc is a sleeper to remember, but the only other white with anything like universal application is Pinot Gris, a Chardonnay cousin whose profile is on the rise. It is not aromatic. Its qualities are (or can be) power and vitality. Watch out for it.

Grapes are fundamental. So is the question of age. In a world that likes to push new products through the system as rapidly as possible, wines which progress to maturity with measured tread are inconvenient. The time it takes can be reduced – up to a point. New understanding of the ripening process, methods of cultivation and cellar techniques can give wines with less rough edges. But isn't something lost en route? In Bordeaux the argument centres on whether the "garage" tendency of

dense, powerful, and oaky wines, popular (and drunk young) in America
will ever mature to classic Bordeaux flavours. High prices are traditionally
justified by investment potential. If wines peak quickly they are poor
investments. It seems reasonable to have both fast-track and slow-track
wines – so long as we know which is which. Time will tell.

It is the business of this book to spell out clearly which wines to
drink this year and which to keep. Please read the explanations of the
vintage symbols on the jacket flap and page 6 carefully. The star system
has also been slightly revised this year to keep in step with the 5th
edition of my Wine Companion – just out – giving more emphasis to
current quality as opposed to producers' established reputations.

Certain agenda items don't go away. One is too much oak, still a fault
of many aspirant wines. Another is too much alcohol in wines trying to
taste more important than their intrinsic quality merits. Wines with good
flavour concentration and balance of acidity and tannins (harder to
achieve in warm climates) need no more than 12° to 13° alcohol. More
just makes them heady. If refreshment rather than headaches is what you
seek check the alcoholic degree on the label. Over 14 is too much.

The question of faulty corks is still very much in the air, with the
threat of a screwcap revolution concentrating minds in the cork industry
as only a view of the scaffold can. As more alternatives to corks are
proposed and adopted we may arrive at the best of both worlds: perfect
corks to end the nuisance of mouldy taint and perfect screwcaps for the
great majority of wines that need only to be kept fresh for a year or two.

Last year I referred to the absurd April rush to judgment of the new
vintage in Bordeaux. The events of spring 2003, when prices retreated,
took some of the pressure off. The buyers' market has arrived – except,
it seems, in restaurants, where mark-ups are as outrageous as ever.
Where the customer is charged five or six times the cost of the wine
the wine-drinker is subsidising the diner. The moral is to drink interesting
but modest wines in such restaurants and top wines at home.

Laying aside the broader issues, though, this micro-encyclopedia
looks closely at the present position in this fast-changing world.
Even readers who bought the last edition (others, I'm afraid, only
come back to the well at intervals of two or three) will find
thousands of changes of detail, emphasis, and evaluation.

This is intended to be a practical guide; theory has no place
here. It compresses all the useful information you can't possibly
carry in your head – and neither can I. You are faced with a daunting
restaurant wine list, or mind-numbing shelves of bottles in a store.
Your mind goes blank; out comes your little book. You can start with
what you propose to eat, see pp 17–31, or where you are by turning
up a national section, or a grape variety. Establish which country a
wine comes from, then look up the principal words on the label in
that country's section. You should find enough information to guide
your choice – and often a great deal more. Even after 27 editions I
can browse for hours...

How to use this book

The top line of most entries consists of the following information:

①

Aglianico del Vulture Bas | r dr (s/sw sp) | ★★★ | 88 90' **91 92** 93' 94' 95 96 (98)

② ... **③** ... **④**

① Wine name and the region the wine comes from.

② Whether it is red, rosé or white (or brown/amber), dry, sweet or
sparkling, or several of these (and which is most important):

r	red
p	rosé
w	white
br	brown
dr	dry*
sw	sweet
s/sw	semi-sweet
sp	sparkling

( ) brackets here denote a less important wine
*assume wine is dry when **dr** or **sw** are not indicated

③ Its general standing as to quality: a necessarily rough-and-ready
guide based on its current reputation as reflected in its prices:

★	plain, everyday quality
★★	above average
★★★	well known, highly reputed
★★★★	grand, prestigious, expensive

So much is more or less objective. Additionally there is a subjective rating:

★ etc   Stars are coloured for any wine which in my experience is usually
especially good within its price range. There are good everyday wines
as well as good luxury wines. This system helps you find them.

④ Vintage information: which of the recent vintages can be recommended; of
these, which are ready to drink this year, and which will probably improve
with keeping. Your choice for current drinking should be one of the vintage
years printed in **bold** type. Buy light-type years for further maturing.

95 etc   recommended years which may be currently available
90'etc   vintage regarded as particularly successful for the property in
question
87 etc   years in **bold** should be ready for drinking (the others should
be kept)
89 etc   vintages in colour are those recommended first for drinking in
2004. (See also Bordeaux introduction, page 80.)
(98) etc   provisional rating

The German vintages work on a different principle again: see page 134.

Other abbreviations

DYA	drink the youngest available
NV	vintage not normally shown on label; in Champagne, means a blend of several vintages for continuity
CHABLIS	properties, areas or terms cross-referred within the section

A quick-reference vintage chart appears on pages 286-7

Vintage report 2002

The vintage of 2002 was defined, in much of Europe, by rain. Usually there was too much of it: local newspapers in the south of France had photographs of villages turned to lakes, and there were stories of whole vineyards washed away. The southern Rhône was manning the pumps; so was Tuscany; so was Navarra; so was Penedes; so was Ribera del Duero; so was the Mosel. In Bordeaux faces grew longer and longer as August wore on and the weather showed no sign of improvement, though here it was relentless chill and cloud rather than heavy rain that was the problem. It looked like being the wash-out vintage to end all wash-out vintages.

And yet, in the end, it wasn't. Much depended on when the rain fell, and when it stopped: rain at or around harvest-time certainly took its toll of quality in the northern and southern Rhône, the Midi, Tuscany and Piedmont, much of Spain, Austria (for Grüner Veltliner) and the north of Portugal. Here good wines were only made if producers were super-selective, and lucky with it. But even so, some grape varieties got through: Austria made some super Rieslings, and dessert wines too. The Mosel somehow not only survived but had a very good vintage. And in Bordeaux the weather changed in the nick of time (the beginning of September, in fact) and while the wines are certainly patchy they are a hundred times better than anyone would have predicted back in August.

Those parts of Europe that did not get rained on may feel somewhat, as it were, overshadowed. Burgundy had a very successful vintage (though Beaujolais was damper) and so did Alsace, and it will be a vintage year in Champagne. Rioja suffered from too little rain, though probably received little sympathy on that count from its neighbours. It was, in fact, the regions most beloved of British journalists on holiday that were the wettest. This may prove to be the crucial factor in colouring impressions of the year.

The rest of the wine world had mixed experiences in 2002. California had a fairly cool summer but a dry one, and quality looks very promising; the states of the Pacific Northwest are also reporting good, focused, balanced wines. In Australia temperatures were unusually cool, which produced great wines in many places. In Victoria yields were right down, quality right up; yields were down, too, in South Australia, but not in Riverland, which managed that sought-after combination of quality and quantity. In New South Wales rain was the problem in most areas – and when it rains here it really rains. In Western Australia it was a case of nice weather for swans: the Swan District had the best vintage for nearly 20 years. In New Zealand a rather dismal summer turned into a warm, sunny autumn; it's not the greatest of vintages, though Hawkes Bay Chardonnay looks very good, but it's certainly perfectly respectable.

Chile's 2002 vintage was good in the areas around Santiago, but rainier further south; and Argentina had the sort of uneventful weather that growers love: not too hot, not too wet, and no hail to speak of. A long warm spell in South Africa produced good, well-balanced reds of mercifully not over-high alcohol. Well-tempered weather for well-tempered wines.

A closer look at 2001...

It may not have had the glamour of 2000, but in many cases 2001 had more solid worth. But that lack of glamour has meant that the 2001 vintage in many places was overlooked by wine lovers still nursing the damage done to their wallets by the previous vintage: 2001 red Bordeaux found very few takers in Germany, for example, and high stocks in Bordeaux should mean plenty of choice once the wines are in bottle in 2003. It's also a vintage for drinking, not for investment.

Bordeaux produced some remarkably good wines, although mostly in a more classic mould than 2000, without the flashiness that many of the 2000s display. It was, however, a much less homogeneous year than 2000, both in wine quality and in critical opinion, with some asserting that it is a Merlot year, and that the Right Bank came off best, while others retort that Margaux, St-Julien and Pauillac are excellent, along with St-Emilion, but that Pomerol has some decidedly green tannins. This greenness is the most frequent problem of the vintage, since sugar ripeness surged ahead while tannic ripeness often lagged behind. Painstaking viticulture was the only preventative; patience and good luck helped, too. The dry whites, though, have been almost universally successful, with tense, elegant fruit – 2001 is definitely a year to buy white Graves and Pessac-Léognan – and the sweet whites are superb, with plentiful botrytis and high acidity.

Things were rather more homogeneous in Burgundy, with the Côte d'Or giving good reds pretty well everywhere. First tastings show them to be pretty wines, with very good balance, seductive fruit, and silky, though often quite substantial, tannins. Not wines to lay down for the long term, but certainly wines to buy for tremendous enjoyment. If anything the whites are better, with crisp, zesty acidity and good weight. It's a year in which village and vineyard differences show particularly clearly.

In Champagne, rain caused huge problems with rot and unripeness. Luck and severe selection will have produced enough non-vintage wines to tide the producers over, but it will be very surprising if any makes a vintage wine.

There was some September rain in the Rhône, too, but far less catastrophic than in Champagne. The wines, both north and south, red and white, are less consistent than the 2000s, but often with greater weight. In the south, Châteauneuf-du-Pape looks outstanding; in the north, Cornas and St-Joseph stand out. This was also the last of a run of excellent vintages in the Rhône: 2002 was, to put it mildly, a wash-out, and some domaines are unlikely to release any wine at all.

The Loire did well at its western end, with Muscadet looking pretty well perfect (a good year for a Muscadet revival?), pretty good in Anjou and Touraine, with some botrytis on the sweet wines, and distinctly mixed in Sancerre and Pouilly. As always in difficult years, success came to those who deserved it. Good viticulture throughout the year, and low yields, enabled good growers to wait for ripeness and pick late.

Alsace produced nicely balanced wines, in spite of the

September rain that plagued much of France. There were problems of rot, but these seem to have been overcome: first tastings show wines of elegance and good concentration.

The most concentrated of all French wines in 2001 seem to have come from the South. Here there was no rain, plenty of sun and a good drying wind. Languedoc-Roussillon has made wines with plenty of alcohol and deep colour. Some Syrah suffered from drought, but the Grenache, Mourvèdre, Cinsaut and Carignan did very well.

2001 is unlikely to be a classic vintage year in the Douro, if only because 2000 was so widely declared. But there are some very good wines, as indeed there are in Spain. In Rioja 2001 looks substantially better than 2000, with more even ripeness and richer flavours; Ribero del Duero, likewise, produced big, concentrated, well balanced wines, but in some regions the drought and heat led to uneven ripening.

Italy managed to combine both rain and hail in Piedmont with heat and dryness in Tuscany and the South. Piedmont survived its brush with autumn rain well, however, and quality seems unaffected, at least for Nebbiolo and Barbera. The earlier-ripening Dolcetto is not quite as good. Quality in Tuscany is irregular but generally quite good to very good: Montalcino seems the most consistant, with some very good Rosso on the way.

Germany had a tremendously good year in 2001; the best vintage for a generation, according to some producers. The Mosel seems to be the most consistent, with a good crop of Spätlesen and Auslesen.

In California, spring frosts cut the size of the crop in Carneros, but cool autumn weather in much of the state meant longer hangtimes, and thus better, more complex flavours. Cabernet and Zinfandel seem to have succeeded best. The Pacific Northwest had equally erratic, though different, conditions, and high alcohol levels can sit uneasily with less concentration than in 2000. The best, however, are appealing for early drinking. New York State had more consistent weather and has produced generally good quality.

In South America, Chile had low yields and made wines of good balance and concentration, and Argentina was more variable, though with mostly good reds.

The Australian summer heat reached extremes in 2001, with Western Australia, especially Great Southern, suffering least from the heat. South Australia had winter rains to help it through, and Clare Valley Riesling in particular looks good. New South Wales was patchier, with Hunter Valley Semillon doing remarkably well. In Victoria the results were only fairly good. New Zealand combined dry weather in the South Island with rain in the North. Pinot Noir looks very good indeed, Marlborough Sauvignon Blanc good to very good, but the reds of the North Island look patchier.

In South Africa low yields produced concentrated flavours from healthy fruit with good colours. A very promising vintage, with reds that should keep well.

Grape varieties

In the past two decades a radical change has come about in all except the most long-established wine countries: the names of a handful of grape varieties have become the ready reference to wine. In senior wine countries, above all France and Italy (between them producing nearly half the world's wine), more complex traditions prevail. All wine of old prestige is known by its origin, more or less narrowly defined, not just the particular fruit-juice that fermented.

For the present the two notions are in rivalry. Eventually the primacy of place over fruit will become obvious, at least for wines of quality. But for now, for most people, grape tastes are the easy reference-point – despite the fact that they are often confused by the added taste of oak. If grape flavours were really all that mattered this would be a very short book.

But of course they do matter, and a knowledge of them both guides you to flavours you enjoy and helps comparisons between regions. Hence the originally Californian term "varietal wine" – meaning, in principle, from one grape variety.

At least seven varieties – Cabernet Sauvignon, Pinot Noir, Riesling, Sauvignon Blanc, Chardonnay, Gewürztraminer, and Muscat – have tastes and smells distinct and memorable enough to form international categories of wine. To these you can add Merlot, Malbec, Syrah, Sémillon, Chenin Blanc, Pinots Blanc and Gris, Sylvaner, Viognier, Nebbiolo, Sangiovese, Tempranillo… The following are the best and/or most popular wine grapes.

Grapes for red wine

Agiorgitiko (St George) Versatile Greek (Nemea) variety with juicy damson fruit, velvety tannins. Sufficient structure for serious ageing.

Baga Bairrada (Portugal) grape. Dark, tannic; great potential; hard to grow.

Barbera Widely grown in Italy, at its best in Piedmont, giving dark, fruity, sharp wine. Fashionable in California, Australia; promising in Argentina.

Blaufränkisch Mostly Austrian; can be light and juicy but at best (in Burgenland) a considerable red. LEMBERGER in Germany, KEKFRANKOS in Hungary.

Brunello Alias for SANGIOVESE, splendid at Montalcino.

Cabernet Franc, alias Bouchet (Cab F) The lesser of two sorts of Cab grown in Bordeaux but dominant (as "Bouchet") in St-Emilion. The Cab of the Loire, making Chinon, Saumur, etc, and rosé. Used for blending with CAB S, etc, or increasingly, alone, in California, Australia.

Cabernet Sauvignon (Cab S) Grape of great character: spicy, herby, tannic, with characteristic blackcurrant aroma. The first grape of the Médoc; also makes most of the best California, S American, E European reds. Vies with Shiraz in Australia. Its wine almost always needs ageing; usually benefits from blending with eg MERLOT, CAB F, SYRAH, TEMPRANILLO, SANGIOVESE etc. Makes aromatic rosé.

Cannonau GRENACHE in its Sardinian manifestation: can be v fine, potent.

Carignan In decline in France. Needs low yields, old vines; best in Corbières. Otherwise dull but harmless. Common in N Africa, Spain, California.

Carmènere An old Bordeaux variety now virtually extinct in France. Widely used in Chile where until recently it was often mistaken for MERLOT.

Cinsault / Cinsaut Usually bulk-producing grape of S France; in S Africa crossed with PINOT N to make PINOTAGE. Pale wine, but quality potential.

Dolcetto Source of soft seductive dry red in Piedmont. Now high fashion.

Gamay The Beaujolais grape: light, very fragrant wines, at their best young. Makes even lighter wine in the Loire Valley, in central France, and in Switzerland and Savoie. Known as "Napa Gamay" in California.

Grenache, alias Garnacha, Cannonau Useful grape for strong fruity but pale wine: good rosé and vin doux naturel, esp in S France, Spain, California, but also the mainstay of beefy Priorato. Old-vine versions are prized in S Australia. Usually blended (eg in Châteauneuf-du-Pape).

Grignolino Makes one of the good everyday table wines of Piedmont.

Kadarka, alias Gamza Makes healthy, sound, agreeable reds in E Europe.

Kékfrankos Hungarian BLAUFRANKISCH; similar lightish reds.

Lambrusco Productive grape of the lower Po Valley, giving quintessentially Italian, cheerful sweet and fizzy red.

Lemberger See Blaufränkisch. Württemberg's red.

Malbec, alias Cot Minor in Bordeaux, major in Cahors (alias Auxerrois) and esp Argentina. Dark, dense, tannic wine capable of real quality.

Merlot Adaptable grape making the great fragrant and plummy wines of Pomerol and (with CAB F) St-Emilion, an important element in Médoc reds, soft and strong (and à la mode) in California, Washington, Chile, Australia. Lighter but often good in N Italy, Italian Switzerland, Slovenia, Argentina, S Africa, NZ etc. Grassy when not fully ripe.

Montepulciano A good central-eastern Italian grape, and a Tuscan town.

Morellino Alias for Sangiovese in Scansano, S Tuscany.

Mourvèdre, alias Mataro Excellent dark aromatic tannic grape used mainly for blending in Provence (but solo in Bandol) and the Midi. Enjoying new interest in eg S Australia, California.

Nebbiolo, alias Spanna and Chiavennasca One of Italy's best red grapes; makes Barolo, Barbaresco, Gattinara, Valtellina. Intense, nobly fruity, perfumed wine but v tannic: improves for years.

Periquita Ubiquitous in Portugal for firm-flavoured reds. Often blended with CABERNET S and also known as Castelão.

Petit Verdot Excellent but awkward Médoc grape now found lgely elsewhere.

Pinot Noir (Pinot N) The glory of Burgundy's Côte d'Or, with scent, flavour, and texture unmatched anywhere. Makes light wines rarely of much distinction in Germany, Switzerland, Austria, Hungary. But now splendid results in California's Sonoma, Carneros and Central Coast, Oregon, Ontario, Yarra Valley, Adelaide Hills, Tasmania, and NZ.

Pinotage Singular S African grape (PINOT N x CINSAUT). Can be very fruity and can age interestingly, but often jammy.

Primitivo S Italian grape making big, rustic wines, now fashionable because genetically identical to ZINFANDEL.

Refosco Possibly a synomym for Mondeuse of Savoie. Produces deep, flavoursome age-worthy wines, esp in warmer climates.

Sagrantino Italian grape found in Umbria for powerful cherry-flavoured wines.

St-Laurent Dark, smooth and full-flavoured Austrian speciality. Also in the Pfalz.

Sangiovese (or Sangioveto) Main red grape of Chianti and much of central Italy. Aliases inc. BRUNELLO , MORELLINO. Interesting in Australia.

Saperavi Makes good sharp very long-lived wine in Georgia, Ukraine etc. Blends very well with CABERNET S (eg in Moldova).

Spätburgunder German for PINOT N .Quality is variable, seldom wildly exciting.

Syrah, alias Shiraz The great Rhône red grape: tannic purple peppery wine which matures superbly. V imp as Shiraz in Australia, and under either name in California, Washington State, S Africa, Chile; also Switzerland, Austria, NZ.

Tannat Raspberry-perfumed, highly tannic force behind Madiran, Tursan, and other firm-structured reds from SW France. Also for rosé. Now star of Uruguay.

Tempranillo Aromatic fine Rioja grape, called Ull de Llebre in Catalonia, Cencibel in La Mancha, Tinto Fino in Ribera del Duero, Tinta Roriz in Douro, Aragonez in S Portugal. Now Australia, too. Very fashionable; elegant in cool climates, beefy in warm. Early ripening.

Touriga Nacional Top Port and Douro grape, & full-bodied reds in S Portugal.

Zinfandel (Zin) Fruity adaptable grape of California (though identical to PRIMITIVO) with blackberry-like, and sometimes metallic, flavour. Can be gloriously lush, but also makes "blush" white wine.

Grapes for white wine

Albariño The Spanish name for N Portugal's Alvarinho, making excellently fresh and fragrant wine in Galicia. Both fashionable and expensive in Spain.

Aligoté Burgundy's second-rank white grape. Crisp (often sharp) wine, needs drinking in 1–3 yrs. Perfect for mixing with cassis (blackcurrant liqueur) to make a "Kir". Widely planted in E Europe, esp Russia.

Arinto White central Portuguese grape for crisp, fragrant dry whites.

Arneis Aromatic, high-priced grape, DOC in Roero, Piedmont.

Blanc Fumé Occasional alias (in New World)of SAUV BL, referring to its "smoky" smell, particularly from the Loire (Sancerre and Pouilly). In California used for oak-aged Sauv and reversed to "Fumé Blanc". (The smoke is oak.)

Bourboulenc This and the rare Rolle make some of the Midi's best wines.

Bual Makes top-quality sw Madeira wines, not quite so rich as Malmsey.

Chardonnay (Chard) The white burgundy grape, the white Champagne grape, and the white grape of the New World, partly because it is one of the easiest to grow and vinify. All regions are trying it, mostly aged (or, better, fermented) in oak to reproduce the flavours of burgundy. Australia and California make classics (but also much dross). Those of Italy, Spain, New Zealand, South Africa, New York State, Chile, Argentina, Hungary and the Midi are all coming on strong. Called Morillon in Austria.

Chasselas Prolific early-ripening grape with little aroma, mainly grown for eating. AKA Fendant in Switzerland (where it is supreme), Gutedel in Germany.

Chenin Blanc (Chenin Bl) Great white grape of the middle Loire (Vouvray, Layon, etc). Wine can be dry or sweet (or very sweet), but with plenty of acidity. Bulk wine in California, but increasingly serious in S Africa. See also STEEN.

Clairette A low-acid grape, part of many S French blends.

Colombard Slightly fruity, nicely sharp grape,makes everyday wine in S Africa, California, SW France.

Fendant See Chasselas.

Fiano High quality grape giving peachy, spicey wine in Campania.

Folle Blanche High acid/little flavour make this ideal for brandy. Called Gros Plant in Brittany, Picpoul in Armagnac. Respectable in California.

Fumé Blanc (Fumé Bl) See Blanc Fumé.

Furmint A grape of great character: the trademark of Hungary both as the principal grape in Tokay and as vivid, vigorous table wine with an appley flavour. Called Sipon in Slovenia. Some grown in Austria.

Garganega The best grape in the Soave blend; top, esp sweet ones age well.

Gewürztraminer, alias Traminer (Gewürz) One of the most pungent grapes, distinctively spicy with aromas like rose petals and grapefruit. Wines are often rich and soft, even when fully dry. Best in Alsace; also good in Germany, E Europe, Australia, California, Pacific NW, NZ.

Grauburgunder See Pinot Gris.

Grechetto or Greco Ancient grape of central and S Italy noted for the vitality and stylishness of its wine.

Grüner Veltliner Austria's favourite (planted in almost half her vineyards). Around Vienna and in the Wachau and Weinviertel (also in Moravia) it can be delicious: light but dry, peppery and lively. Excellent young, but the best age 5 years or so.

Hárslevelü Other main grape of Tokay (with FURMINT). Adds softness and body.

Kéknyelü Low-yielding, flavourful grape giving one of Hungary's best whites. Has the potential for fieriness and spice. To be watched.

Kerner The most successful of recent German varieties, mostly RIESLING X SILVANER, but in this case Riesling x (red) Trollinger. Early-ripening flowery (but often too blatant) wine with good acidity. Popular in Pfalz, Rheinhessen, etc.

Laski Rizling Grown in Northern Italy and Eastern Europe. Much inferior to Rhine RIES, with lower acidity, best in sweet wines. Alias Welschriesling, Riesling Italico, Olaszrizling (no longer legally labelled simply "Riesling").

Loureiro The best and most fragrant Vinho Verde variety in Portugal.

Macabeo The workhorse white grape of N Spain, widespread in Rioja (alias Viura) and in Catalan cava country. Good quality potential.

Malvasia A family of grapes rather than a single variety, found all over Italy and Iberia. May be red, white or pink. Usually plump, soft wine. Malvoisie in France is unrelated.

Marsanne Principal white grape (with ROUSSANNE) of the N Rhône (eg in Hermitage, St-Joseph, St-Péray). Also good in Australia, California and (as Ermitage Blanc) the Valais. Soft full wines that age v well.

Moschofilero Good, aromatic pink Greek grape. Makes white or pink wine.

Müller-Thurgau (Müller-T) Dominant in Germany's Rheinhessen and Pfalz and too common on the Mosel; it is thought to be a cross between RIESLING and CHASSELAS DE COURTELLIER but recent studies suggest otherwise. Soft aromatic wines for drinking young. Makes good sweet wines but usually dull, often coarse, dry ones. Should have no place in top vineyards.

Muscadelle Adds aroma to white B'x, esp Sauternes. In Victoria called Tokay and used (as well as Muscat, to which it is unrelated) for Rutherglen Muscat.

Muscadet, alias Melon de Bourgogne Makes light, refreshing, v dry wines with a seaside tang round Nantes in Brittany.

Muscat (Many varieties; the best is Muscat Blanc à Petits Grains.) Widely grown, easily recognized, pungent grapes, mostly made into perfumed sweet wines, often fortified (as in France's vins doux naturels). Superb in Australia. The third element in Tokay Aszú. Rarely (eg Alsace) made dry.

Palomino, alias Listán Makes all the best sherry but poor table wine.

Pedro Ximénez, alias PX Makes very strong wine in Montilla and Málaga. Used in blending sweet sherries. Also grown in Argentina, the Canaries, Australia, California, South Africa.

Petit (and Gros) Manseng The secret weapon of the French Basque country: vital for Jurançon; increasingly blended elsewhere in the SW.

Pinot Blanc (Pinot Bl) A cousin of PINOT NOIR, similar to but milder than Chardonnay: light, fresh, fruity, not aromatic, to drink young; eg good for Italian spumante. Grown in Alsace, Northern Italy, Southern Germany, and Eastern Europe. Weissburgunder in Germany. See also Muscadet.

Pinot Gris (Pinot Gr) At best makes rather heavy, even "thick", full-bodied whites with a certain spicy style. Can be alias Ruländer (sweet) or Grauburgunder (dry) in Germany; Pinot Grigio in Italy. Also found in Hungary, Slovenia, Canada, Oregon, NZ...

> ### Riesling
> It is a strange irony that Riesling is making its re-entrance on the world-stage through, as it were, the back door. No serious commentator disagrees that Riesling stands level with Chardonnay. They are the world's best white wine grapes, in diametrically opposite styles. While Chardonnay gives full-bodied but aromatically discreet wines, Riesling offers a range from steely to voluptuous, always positively perfumed, and with ageing potential far beyond any Chardonnay. Germany is the great Riesling protagonist and makes the greatest Riesling in all styles. Yet its popularity is being revived, of all places, South Australia, where this cool-climate grape does its best, in body at least, to ape Chardonnay. Holding the middle ground, with forceful but still steely wines, is Austria. Meanwhile lovers of light and fragrant, often piercingly refreshing Rieslings have the Mosel as their exclusive playground. Also grown in Alsace (but absurdly grown nowhere else in France), Pacific NW, Ontario, California, and South Africa.

Pinot Noir (Pinot N) Superlative black grape (See "Grapes for red wine") used in Champagne and elsewhere (eg California, Australia) for making white, sparkling, or very pale pink "vin gris"

Roussanne Rhône grape of great finesse, now popping up in California, Australia. Can age well.

Ruländer Obsolescent German name for PINOT G used for sweeter wines.

Sauvignon Blanc (Sauv Bl) Makes very distinctive aromatic grassy wines, pungent in NZ, often mineral in Sancerre, riper in Australia; also good in Rueda, Austria, N Italy, S Africa. Historically confused with less aromatic Sauvignonasse in Chile. Blended with SEMILLON in Bordeaux. Can be austere or buxom. May be called FUME BLANC or vice versa.

Savagnin The grape of Vin Jaune of Savoie: related to TRAMINER?

Scheurebe Spicy-flavoured German RIES x SILVANER (possibly), very successful in Pfalz, esp for Auslesen. Can be weedy in dry wines: must be very ripe to be good.

Sémillon (Sém) Contributes the lusciousness to Sauternes and increasingly important for Graves and other dry white Bordeaux. Grassy if not fully ripe, but can make soft dry wine of great ageing potential. Superb in Australia: old Hunter Valley Semillon can be great wine. Promising in NZ.

Sercial Makes the driest Madeira (where myth used to identify it with RIESLING).

Seyval Blanc (Seyval Bl) French-made hybrid of French and American vines. V hardy and attractively fruity. Popular and reasonably successful in eastern States and England but dogmatically banned by EU from "quality" wines.

Steen S African alias for Chenin Blanc, not used for better examples.

Silvaner, alias Sylvaner Germany's former workhorse grape: wine rarely fine ex in Franken – savoury and ages admirably –and in Rheinhessen & Pfalz, where it is enjoying a renaissance. Gd in the Italian Tyrol; now declining in popularity in Alsace. Vg (and powerful) as "Johannisberg" in the Valais, Switzerland.

Tocai Friulano N Italian grape with a flavour best described as "subtle". No relation to TOKAY, but could be same as Sauvignonasse (see Sauvignon Bl).

Tokay See Pinot Gris. Also a table grape in California & supposedly Hungarian grape in Australia. The wine Tokay (Tokáji) is FURMINT, HARSLEVELU and MUSCAT.

Torrontes Strongly aromatic, MUSCAT-like Argentine speciality, usually dry.

Traminer See Gewürztraminer.

Trebbiano Important but mediocre grape of central Italy (Orvieto, Soave etc). Also grown in S France as Ugni Blanc, and Cognac as St-Emilion. Mostly thin, bland wine; needs blending (and more careful growing).

Ugni Blanc (Ugni Bl) See Trebbiano.

Verdejo The grape of Rueda in Castile, potentially fine and long-lived.

Verdelho Madeira grape making excellent medium-sweet wine; in Australia, fresh soft dry wine of great character.

Verdicchio Potentially good dry wine in central-eastern Italy.

Vermentino Italian, sprightly with satisfying texture and ageing capacity.

Vernaccia Name given to many unrelated grapes in Italy. Vernaccia di San Gimignano is crisp, lively; Vernaccia di Oristano is sherry-like.

Viognier Ultra-fashionable Rhône grape, finest in Condrieu, less fine but still aromatic in the Midi. Good examples (and less good) from California, Australia.

Viura See Macabeo.

Weissburgunder See Pinot Blanc.

Welschriesling See Laski Rizling.

Wine & food

The dilemma is most acute in restaurants. Four people have chosen
different dishes. The host calculates. A bottle of white and then one of red
is conventional, regardless of the food. The formula works up to a point.
But it can be refined – or replaced with something more original,
something to really bring out the flavours of both food and wine.

Remarkably little ink has been spilt on this byway of knowledge, but
25 years of experimentation and the ideas of many friends have gone into
making this list. It is perhaps most useful for menu-planning at home. But
used with the rest of the book, it may ease menu-stress in restaurants,
too. At the very least, it will broaden your mind.

Before the meal – aperitifs

The conventional aperitif wines are either sparkling (epitomized by
Champagne) or fortified (epitomized by sherry in Britain, Port in France,
vermouth in Italy, etc). A glass of white or rosé (or in France red) table
wine before eating is presently in vogue. It calls for something light and
stimulating, fairly dry but not acidic, with a degree of character; rather
Riesling or Chenin Blanc than Chardonnay.

Warning: Avoid peanuts; they destroy wine flavours.

Olives are also too piquant for many wines; they need sherry or a
Martini. Eat almonds, pistachios or walnuts, plain crisps or cheese
straws instead.

First courses

Aïoli A thirst-quencher is needed for its garlic heat. Rhône, sparkling
dry white; Provence rosé, Verdicchio. And marc, too, for courage.

Antipasti Dry or med white: Italian (Arneis, Soave, Pinot Grigio, Prosecco,
Vermentino); light red (Dolcetto, Franciacorta, young Chianti).

Artichoke vinaigrette An incisive dry white, eg NZ Sauv Bl; Côtes de
Gascogne or a modern Greek; young red: Bordeaux, Côtes du Rhône.
With hollandaise Full-bodied slightly crisp dry white: Pouilly-Fuissé,
Pfalz Spätlese, or a Carneros or Yarra Valley Chardonnay.

Asparagus A difficult flavour for wine, being slightly bitter, so the wine
needs plenty of its own. Sauv echoes the flavour. Sém beats Chard, esp
Australian, but Chard works well with melted butter or hollandaise. Alsace
Pinot G, even dry Muscat is gd, or Jurançon Sec.

Aubergine purée (Melitzanosalata) Crisp New World Sauv Bl eg from S
Africa or NZ, or modern Greek or Sicilian dry white. Or Bardolino red or
Chiaretto.

Avocado with seafood Dry to med or slightly sharp white: Rheingau or
Pfalz Kabinett, Grüner Veltliner, Wachau Riesling, Sancerre, Pinot Grigio;
Sonoma or Aus Chard or Sauv, or dry rosé. Or Chablis Premier Cru.
With vinaigrette Manzanilla sherry.

Bisques Dry white with plenty of body: Pinot Gris, Chard, G Veltliner.
Fino or dry amontillado sherry, or Montilla. West Australian Sem.

Boudin Noir (blood sausage) Local Sauv Bl or Chenin – esp in the Loire. Or Beaujolais Cru, esp Morgon.

Bouillabaisse Savoury dry white, Marsanne from the Midi or Rhône, Corsican or Spanish rosé, or Cassis, Verdicchio, S African Sauvignon Blanc.

Caesar Salad Spanish or S. French rosé; neutral, crisp whites, preferably from near Rome.

Carpaccio, beef Seems to work well with the flavour of most wines, incl reds. Top Tuscan is appropriate, but fine Chards are good. So are vintage and pink Champagnes. (See also Carpaccio under fish.)
Salmon Chardonnay, or Champagne.

Caviar Iced vodka. Champagne, if you must, full-bodied (eg Bollinger, Krug).

Ceviche Australian Riesling or Verdelho, S. African or NZ Sauvignon Bl.

Charcuterie Young Beaujolais-Villages or Bordeaux Blanc, Loire reds such as Saumur, Swiss or Oregon Pinot N. Young Argentine or Italian reds.

Cheese fondue Dry white: Valais Fendant or any other Swiss Chasselas, Roussette de Savoie, Grüner Veltliner, Alsace Ries or Pinot Gris. Or a Beaujolais Cru.

chowders Big-scale white, not necessarily bone dry: Pinot Gris, Rhine Spätlese, Albariño, Australian Sem, buttery Chard. Or fino sherry.

Consommé Medium-dry amontillado sherry, Sercial Madeira.

Crostini Morellino di Scansano, Montepulciano d'Abruzzo, Valpolicella, or a dry Italian white eg. Verdicchio, Orvieto.

Crudités Light red or rosé: Côtes du Rhône, Minervois, Chianti, Pinot Noir; or fino sherry. Or Alsace Sylvaner or Pinot Blanc.

Dim-Sum Classically, China tea. For fun: Pinot Grigio or Riesling; light red (Bardolino or Sancerre). Or NV Champagne or good New World fizz.

Eggs See also Soufflés. These present difficulties: they clash with most wines and spoil good ones. But local wine with local egg dishes is a safe bet. So *→** of whatever is going. Try Pinot Bl or straightforward not too oaky Chardonnay. As a last resort I can bring myself to drink Champagne with scrambled eggs.
Quail's eggs Blanc de Blancs Champagne.
Seagull's (or gull's) eggs Mature white burgundy or vintage Champagne.

Escargots Rhône reds (Gigondas, Vacqueyras), or St-Véran or Aligoté. In the Midi, vg Petits-Gris go with local white, rosé or red. In Alsace, Pinot Bl or Muscat.

Fish terrine Pfalz Riesling Spätlese Trocken, Grüner Veltliner, Chablis Premier Cru, Clare Valley Ries, Sonoma Chard; or manzanilla.

Foie gras White. In Bordeaux they drink Sauternes. Others prefer a late-harvest Pinot Gris, Riesling (incl New World), Vouvray, Montlouis, Jurançon Moelleux or Gewürz. Tokay Aszú 5 puttonyos is a Lucullan choice. Old dry amontillado can be sublime. With hot, mature vintage Champagne. But not on any account Chard or Sauv Bl.

Gazpacho A glass of fino before and after. Or Sauvignon Bl.

Goat's cheese, grilled or fried (warm salad) Sancerre, Pouilly-Fumé or New World Sauv Bl. Chilled Chinon or Saumur-Champigny or Provence rosé. Or strong red: Ch Musar, Greek, Turkish, Australian sparkling Shiraz.

Gravadlax Akvavit or iced sake. Or Grand Cru Chablis, orCalifornia, Washington, or Margaret River Chard, or Mosel Spätlese (not Trocken).

Guacamole California Chardonnay, Sauvignon Blanc, dry Muscat or NV Champagne. Or Mexican beer.

Haddock, smoked, mousse or brandade A wonderful dish for showing off any stylish full-bodied white, incl Grand Cru Chablis or Sonoma or NZ Chardonnay.

Ham, raw or cured See also Prosciutto. Alsace Grand Cru Pinot Gris or good, crisp Italian Collio white with Spanish Pata Negra or Jamon, fino sherry or tawny port.

Herrings, raw or pickled Dutch gin (young, not aged) or Scandinavian akvavit, and cold beer. If wine essential, try Muscadet.

Hors d'oeuvres See also Antipasti. Clean, fruity, sharp white: Sancerre or any Sauvignon Bl, Grüner Veltliner, Hungarian Leanyka, English white wine; or young light red Bordeaux, Rhône or Corbières. Or fino sherry.

Houmous Pungent, spicy dry white, eg Furmint or modern Greek white.

Mackerel, smoked An oily wine-destroyer. Manzanilla sherry, proper dry Vinho Verde or Schnapps, peppered or bison-grass vodka. Or good lager.

Mayonnaise Adds richness that calls for a contrasting bite in the wine. Côte Chalonnaise whites (eg Rully) are good. Try NZ Sauvignon Bl, Verdicchio or a Spätlese Trocken from the Pfalz.

Melon Strong sweet wine (if any): port, Bual Madeira, Muscat de Frontignan or vin doux naturel; or dry, perfumed Viognier, Fiano di Avellino or Australian Marsanne.

Minestrone Red: Chianti, Zin, Teroldego, Rhône Syrah, etc. Or fino.

Omelettes See Eggs.

Oysters Raw White: NV Champagne, Chablis Premier Cru, Muscadet, white Graves, Sancerre or Guinness.
Cooked Puligny-Montrachet, or good New World Chardonnay. Champagne is good with both.

Pasta Red or white according to the sauce or trimmings:
cream sauce Orvieto, Frascati, Alto Adige Chardonnay.
meat sauce Montepulciano d'Abruzzo, Salice Salentino, Merlot.
pesto (basil) sauce Barbera, Ligurian Vermentino, NZ Sauv Bl, Hungarian Hárslevelü or Furmint
seafood sauce (eg vongole) Verdicchio, Soave, top white Rioja, Cirò, Sauvignon Blanc.
tomato sauce Sauv Bl, Barbera, S Italian red, Zin, S Australian Grenache.

Pastrami Alsace Riesling, young Sangiovese or Cabernet Franc.

Pâté
chicken livers Calls for pungent white (Alsace Pinot Gris or Marsanne), a smooth red like a light Pomerol or Volnay, or even amontillado sherry.
Pâté de campagne A dry white **: Good vin de pays, Graves, Fumé Blanc.

duck pâté Ch'neuf-du-Pape, Cornas, Chianti Classico, Franciacorta.
fish pâté Muscadet, Mâcon-Villages, Australian Chard (unoaked).

Peperonata Dry Australian Ries, WA Sem or NZ Sauv Bl. Tempranillo or Grenache.

Pipérade Navarra rosado, Provence or S'th'n French rosés. Or dry Australian Ries.

Pimentos, roasted NZ Sauvignon, Spanish Chardonnay, or Valdepeñas.

Pizza Any dry Italian red ** or Rioja, Australian Shiraz, S French red or Douro red.

Prawns, shrimps or langoustines Fine dry white: burgundy, Graves, NZ Chard, Washington Riesling – even fine mature Champagne.
Indian-, Thai- or Chinese-style rich Australian Hunter Valley Chardonnay. ('Cocktail sauce' kills wine, and in time, people.)

Prosciutto (also with melon, pears or figs) Full dry or medium white: Orvieto, Lugana, Sauv Bl, Grüner Veltliner, Tokay Furmint, w Rioja, Australian Sem or Jurançon Sec.

Quiches Dry full-bodied white: Alsace, Graves, Sauv, dry Rheingau; or young red (Tempranillo, Periquita), according to ingredients.

Risotto Pinot Gr from Friuli, Gavi, youngish Sém, Dolcetto or Barbera d'Alba.
with mushrooms Cahors, Madiran, Barbera or New World Pinot Noir.
with fungi porcini Finest mature Barolo or Barbaresco

Ravioli See Pasta.
with wild mushrooms Dolcetto or Nebbiolo d'Alba, Oregon Pinot N, red Rioja crianza.

Salade niçoise Very dry, **, not too light or flowery white or rosé: Provençal, Rhône or Corsican; Catalan white; Fernão Pires, Sauv Bl.

Salads As a first course, especially with blue cheese dressing, any dry and appetizing white wine.
NB Vinegar in salad dressings destroys the flavour of wine. If you want salad at a meal with fine wine, dress the salad with wine or a little lemon juice instead of vinegar.

Salami Barbera, top Valpolicella, genuine Lambrusco, young Zinfandel, Tavel or Ajaccio rosé, Vacqueyras, young Bordeaux, Chilean Cab S.

Salmon, smoked A dry but pungent white: fino sherry, Alsace Pinot Gris, Chablis Grand Cru, Pouilly-Fumé, Pfalz Ries Spätlese, vintage Champagne. If you must have red try a lighter one such as Barbera. Vodka, schnapps or akvavit.

Seafood salad Fresh N Italian Chard or Pinot Grigio. Australian Verdelho or Clare Ries.

Shark's fin soup Add a teaspoon of Cognac. Sip amontillado.

Shrimps, potted Fino sherry, Chablis, white Rioja or Long Island Chard.

Soufflés As show dishes these deserve *** wines.
fish Dry white: *** Burgundy, Bordeaux, Alsace, Chardonnay, etc.
cheese Red burgundy or B'dx, Cab S (not Chilean or Australian), etc.

spinach (tougher on wine) Mâcon-Villages, St-Véran, Valpolicella. Champagne can also be good with all textures of soufflé.

Spinach A challenge here. Can make reds taste of rust. Good Cabs usually survive, as do neutral whites like unoaked Chard.

Tapenade Manzanilla or fino, or any sharpish dry white or rosé.

Taramasalata A rustic southern white with personality; not necessarily Retsina. Fino sherry works well. Try white Rioja or a Rhône Marsanne. The bland supermarket version goes well with fine delicate whites or Champagne.

Terrine As for pâté, or similar r: Mercurey, St-Amour, youngish St-Emilion, Tempranillo, Sangiovese; or Chilean Cab.

Tortilla Rioja crianza, fino sherry or white Mâcon-Villages.

Trout, smoked Sancerre, California or S African Sauv Bl. Rully or Bourgogne Aligoté, Chablis or Champagne.

Vegetable terrine Not a great help to fine wine, but California, Chilean or S African Chards make a fashionable marriage, Chenin Blanc such as Vouvray a lasting one.

Whitebait Crisp dry whites: Greek, Touraine Sauvignon Bl, Verdicchio or fino sherry.

Fish

Abalone Dry or medium w: Sauvignon Blanc, Côte de Beaune blanc, Pinot Grigio, Grüner Veltliner. Chinese style: vintage Champagne.

Anchovies A robust wine: red, white or rosé – try Rioja.

Bass, sea Weissburgunder from Baden or Pfalz. Vg for any fine/delicate white, eg Clare dry Riesling, Chablis, white Châteauneuf-du-Pape.

Beurre blanc, fish with A top-notch Muscadet-sur-lie, a Sauvignon/ Sém blend, Chablis Premier Cru, Vouvray or a Rheingau Riesling.

Brandade Chablis Premier Cru or Sancerre Rouge.

Bream (esp baked in a salt crust) Full-bodied white or rosé; Rioja, Albariño, Sicily, Côtes de Lubéron or Minervois.

Brill Very delicate: hence a top fish for fine old Puligny and the like.

Carpaccio of salmon or tuna See also First courses. Puligny-Montrachet, Condrieu, California Chardonnay or NZ Sauvignon Blanc.

Cod If roast, a good neutral background for fine dry/medium whites: Chablis, Meursault, Corton-Charlemagne, cru classé Graves, Grüner Veltliner, German Kabinett or dry Spätlesen, or a gd light red, eg Beaune.

Crab, cioppino Sauv Bl; but West Coast friends say Zinfandel. Also California sp wine.
cold, with salad Alsace, Austrian or Rhine Riesling, dry Australian Riesling, or Condrieu.
softshell Chardonnay or top-quality German Riesling Spätlese.

Chinese, baked with ginger and onion German Riesling Kabinett or Spätlese Halbtrocken. Tokay Furmint, Gewürz.
with Black Bean sauce A big Barossa Shiraz or Syrah.

Eel, jellied NV Champagne or a nice cup of (Ceylon) tea.
smoked Strong/sharp wine: fino sherry, Bourgogne Aligoté. Schnapps.

Fish and chips, fritto misto (or tempura) Chablis, white Bordeaux, Sauv Bl, Pinot Blanc, Gavi, Fino, Montilla, Koshu, tea or NV Champ and Cava.

Fish pie (with creamy sauce) Albariño, Soave Classico, Pinot Gr d'Alsace.

Haddock Rich dr w: Meursault, Calif or NZ Chard, Marsanne or Albariño.

Hake Sauv Bl or any fresh fruity white: Pacherenc, Tursan, white Navarra.

Halibut As turbot.

Herrings Need a white with some acidity to cut their richness. Rully, Bourgogne Aligoté, Greek, dry Sauvignon Bl. Or cider.

Kedgeree Full white, still or sparkling: Mâcon-Villages, South African Chard or (at breakfast) Champagne.

Kippers A good cup of tea, preferably Ceylon (milk, no sugar). Scotch? Dry oloroso sherry is surprisingly good.

Lamproie à la Bordelaise 5-yr-old St-Emilion or Fronsac. Or Douro reds with Portuguese lampreys.

Lobster, richly sauced Vintage Champagne, fine white burgundy, cru classé Graves, California Chard or Australian Ries, Pfalz Spätlese.
salad White: NV Champagne, Alsace Riesling, Chablis Premier Cru, Condrieu, Mosel Spätlese, Penedès Chard or Cava.

Mackerel Hard or sharp white: Sauvignon Blanc from Touraine, Gaillac, Vinho Verde, white Rioja, English white wine. Or Guinness.

Monkfish Often roasted, which suggests fuller rather than leaner wines. Try NZ Chard or NZ/Oregon Pinot Noir, Chilean Merlot.

Mullet, red A chameleon, adaptable to good white or red, esp Pinot N.

Mullet, grey Verdicchio, Terret.

Mussels Muscadet sur lie, Chablis Premier Cru, Chardonnay.
stuffed, with garlic See Escargots.

Perch, sandre Exquisite fishes for finest wines: top white burgundy, Alsace Riesling Grand Cru or noble Mosels. Or try top Swiss Fendant or Johannisberg.

Salmon, seared or grilled Fine white burgundy: Puligny- or Chassagne-Montrachet, Meursault, Corton-Charlemagne, Chablis Grand Cru; Grüner Veltliner, Condrieu, California, Idaho or NZ Chard, Rheingau Kabinett/Spätlese, Australian Ries. Young Pinot N can be good; Merlot or light claret not bad. Salmon fishcakes call for similar, but less grand, wines.

Sand-dabs This sublime fish can handle your fullest Chardonnay (but not oaky).

Sardines, fresh grilled Very dry white: Vinho Verde, Soave, Muscadet, modern Greek.

Sashimi If you are prepared to forego the wasabi, sp wines will go, or Washington or Tasmanian Chard, Chablis Grand Cru, Rheingau Riesling,

English Seyval Bl. Otherwise, iced sake, fino sherry or beer. Recent trials have matched 5-putt Tokáji with fat tuna, sea urchin, and anago (eel).

Scallops An inherently slightly sweet dish, best with med-dry whites.
in cream sauces German Spätlese, Montrachet, or top Australian Chard.
grilled or seared Hermitage Blanc, Grüner Veltliner, Entre-Deux-Mers, vintage Champagne or Pinot Noir.
with Asian seasoning NZ, S Africa Sauv Bl, Verdelho, Australian Ries, Gewürz.

Shellfish Dry white with plain boiled shellfish, richer wines with richer sauces. Crab and Riesling are part of the Creator's plan. With plateaux de fruits de mer: Muscadet, Picpoul de Pinet, Alto Adige Pinot Blanc.

Skate with brown butter White with some pungency (eg Pinot Gris d'Alsace), or a clean straightforward one like Muscadet or Verdicchio.

Snapper Sauvignon Blanc if cooked with Oriental flavours, white Rhône with Mediterranean flavours.

Sole, plaice, etc: plain, grilled or fried Perfect with fine wines: white burgundy, or its equivalent.
with sauce Depending on the ingredients: sharp dry wine for tomato sauce, fairly rich for sole véronique, etc.

Sushi Hot wasabi is usually hidden in every piece. German QbA trocken wines or simple Chablis or NV brut Champ. Or, of course, sake or beer.

Swordfish Full-bodied dry white of the country. Nothing grand.

Trout Delicate white wine, eg Mosel (especially Saar or Ruwer), Alsace Pinot Blanc.
smoked See First courses.

Tuna, grilled or seared White, red or rosé of fairly fruity character; a top St-Véran or white Hermitage, or Côtes du Rhône would be fine. Pinot Noir and Merlot are the best reds to try.

Turbot Your best rich dry white: Meursault or Chassagne-Montrachet, mature Chablis or its California, Australian or NZ equivalent. Condrieu. Mature Rheingau, Mosel or Nahe Spätlese or Auslese (not trocken).

Meat, poultry, etc

Barbecues The local wine would be Australian. Or S. Italian, Tempranillo, Zinfandel, Argentine Malbec. Bandol for a real treat.

Beef, boiled Red: Bordeaux (Bourg or Fronsac), Roussillon, Gevrey-Chambertin, Côte-Rôtie. Medium-ranking white Burgundy is good, eg. Auxey-Duresses. Or top-notch beer. Mustard is softens tannic reds, horseradish kills everything – but can be worth the sacrifice.
roast An ideal partner for fine red wine of any kind.

Beef stew Sturdy red: Pomerol or St-Emilion, Hermitage, Cornas, Barbera, Shiraz, Napa Cabernet, Ribera del Duero, Douro red.

Beef Stroganoff Dramatic red: Barolo, Valpolicella Amarone, Cahors, Hermitage, late-harvest Zin – even Moldovan Negru de Purkar.

Boudin Blanc Loire Chenin Bl esp when served with apples: dry Vouvray, Saumur, Savennières. Mature red Côtes de Beaune, if without apple.

Cabbage, stuffed Hungarian Cab Franc/Kadarka; village Rhônes; Salice Salentino, Primitivo and other spicy S Italian reds. Or Argentine Malbec.

Cajun food Fleurie, Brouilly, or Sauv Bl. With gumbo: amontillado or Mexican beer.

Cassoulet Red from SW France (Gaillac, Minervois, Corbières, St-Chinian or Fitou), or Shiraz. But best of all Beaujolais Cru or young Tempranillo.

Chicken/turkey/guinea fowl, roast Virtually any wine, incl very best bottles of dry/med white and finest old reds (esp burgundy). The meat of fowl can be adapted with sauces to match almost any fine wine (eg coq au vin with red or white burgundy). Try sparkling Shiraz with strong, sweet or spicy stuffings and trimmings.
Chicken Kiev Alsace Riesling, Collio, Chardonnay, Bergerac Rouge.

Chilli con carne Young red: Beauj, Tempranillo, Zin, Argentine Malbec.

Chinese food, Canton or Peking style Dry to med-dry white – Mosel Ries Kabinett or Spätlese trocken – can be good throughout a Chinese banquet. Gewürz, often suggested but rarely works (but brilliant with ginger) yet Chasselas and Pinot Gris are attractive alternatives. Dry or off-dry sparkling (esp cava) cuts the oil and matches sweetness. Eschew sweet/sour dishes but try St-Emilion ** (or Le Pin?), New World Pinot N, or Châteauneuf-du-Pape with duck. I often serve both white and red wines concurrently during Chinese meals.
Szechuan style Verdicchio, Alsace Pinot Blanc or v cold beer.

Choucroute garni Alsace, Pinot Blanc, Pinot Gris or Riesling or beer.

Cold meats Generally better with full-flavoured white than red. Mosel Spätlese or Hochheimer and Côte Chalonnaise are very good, as is Beaujolais. Leftover cold beef with leftover Champagne is bliss.

Confit d'oie/de canard Young tannic red B'x Cru Bourgeois, Calif Cab and Merlot, Priorato cut richness. Alsace Pinot Gris or Gewürz match it.

Coq au vin Red burgundy. In an ideal world, one bottle of Chambertin in the dish, two on the table.

Curry see Indian food

Duck or goose Rather rich white: Pfalz Spätlese or off-dry Alsace Grand Cru; or mature gamey red: Morey-St-Denis or Côte-Rôtie or Bordeaux or burgundy. With oranges or peaches, the Sauternais propose drinking Sauternes, others Monbazillac or Riesling Auslese.
Peking See Chinese food.
wild duck Big-scale red: Hermitage, Bandol, California or S African Cab, Australian Shiraz – Grange if you can find it.
with olives Top-notch Chianti or other Tuscan.

Frankfurters German, NY Riesling, Beaujolais, light Pinot Noir. Or Budweiser (Budwar).

Game birds, young birds plain-roasted The best red wine you can afford.
older birds in casseroles Red (Gevrey-Chambertin, Pommard, Santenay or Grand Cru St-Emilion, Napa Valley Cabernet or Rhône.
well-hung game Vega Sicilia, great red Rhône, Château Musar.
cold game Mature vintage Champagne.

Game pie
hot Red: Oregon Pinot Noir.
cold Good quality white Burgundy, cru Beaujolais or Champagne.

Goulash Flavoursome young red: Zinfandel, Uruguayan Tannat, Morellino di Scansano, young Australian Shiraz.

Grouse See Game birds – but push the boat right out.

Haggis Fruity red, eg young claret, New World Cabernet or Châteauneuf-du-Pape. Or of course malt whisky.

Ham Softer red burgundies: Volnay, Savigny, Beaune; Chinon or Bourgueil; sweetish German white (Rhine Spätlese); Czech Frankovka; lightish Cabernet (eg Chilean), or California Pinot Noir. And don't forget the heaven-made match of ham and sherry (or ham and Chablis).

Hamburger Young red: Beaujolais or Australian Cabernet, Chianti, Zinfandel. Or Coke or Pepsi (not 'Diet', but 'Max').

Hare Jugged hare calls for flavourful red: not-too-old burgundy or Bordeaux, Rhône (eg Gigondas), Bandol, Barbaresco, Rib del Duero, Rioja Reserva. The same for saddle. Australia's Grange would be an experience.

Indian food Medium-sw w, very cold: Orvieto abboccato, S African Chenin Bl, Alsace Pinot Bl, Indian sp, cava and NV Champagne. Or emphasize the heat with a tannic Barolo or Barbaresco, or deep-flavoured reds such as Chât'neuf-du-Pape, Cornas, Australian Grenache or Mourvèdre, or Valpolicella Amarone.

Kebabs Vigorous red: modern Greek, Corbières, Chilean Cabernet, Zinfandel or Barossa Shiraz. Sauvignon Blanc, if lots of garlic.

Kidneys Red: St-Emilion or Fronsac: Nuits-St-Georges, Cornas, Barbaresco, Rioja, Spanish or Australian Cabernet, top Alentejo.

Lamb, cutlets or chops As for roast lamb, but a little less grand. **roast** One of the traditional and best partners for very good red Bordeaux – or its Cabernet equivalents from the New World. In Spain, the partner of the finest old Rioja and Ribera del Duero Reservas.

Liver Young red: Beaujolais-Villages, St-Joseph, Médoc, Italian Merlot, Breganze Cabernet, Zinfandel, Portuguese Bairrada.
Calf's Red Rioja crianza, Salice Salentino Riserva, Fleurie.

Meatballs Tangy medium-bodied red: Mercurey, Crozes-Hermitage, Madiran, Morellino di Scansano, Langhe Nebbiolo, Zinfandel, Cabernet. **Spicy Middle-Eastern style** Simple, crisp dry white or rustic red.

Moussaka Red or rosé: Naoussa from Greece, Sangiovese, Corbières, Côtes de Provence, Ajaccio, NZ Pinot Noir.

Osso buco Low tannin, supple red, eg Dolcetto d'Alba, Pinot Noir; dry Italian white such as Soave, Lugana.

Oxtail Rather rich red: St-Emilion, Pomerol, Pommard, Nuits-St-Georges, Barolo or Rioja Reserva, Ribera del Duero, California or Coonawarra Cabernet, Châteauneuf-du-Pape.

Paella Yng Spanish r, dry w or rosé: Penedès, Somontano, Navarra, Rioja.

Pigeons Lively reds: Savigny, Chambolle-Musigny; Crozes-Hermitage, Chianti Classico or California Pinot. Or try Franken Silvaner Spätlese.

Pork, roast A good rich neutral background to a fairly light red or rich white. It deserves ** treatment – Médoc is fine. Portugal's sucking pig is eaten with Bairrada Garrafeira, Chinese is good with Pinot Noir.

Pot au feu, bollito misto, cocido Rustic red wines from the region of origin; Sangiovese di Romagna, Chusclan, Lirac, Rasteau, Portuguese Alentejo and Yecla and Jumilla from Spain.

Quail As for squab. Carmignano, Rioja Reserva, mature claret, Pinot N.

Rabbit Lively medium-bodied young Italian red or Aglianico del Vulture; Chiroubles, Chinon, Saumur-Champigny or Rhône rosé. Le Pin in France.

Satay Australia's McLaren Vale Shiraz or Alsace or NZ Gewürztraminer.

Sauerkraut (German) Lager or Pils. (But see also Choucroute garni.)

Sausages See also Frankfurters, Salami. The British banger requires a young Malbec from Argentina (a red wine, anyway), or a traditional British ale.

Shepherd's pie Rough-and-ready red seems most appropriate, eg Sangiovese di Romagna, but beer or dry cider is the real McCoy.

Squab Fine white or red Burgundy, Alsace Ries Grand Cru or mature claret.

Steak, au poivre A fairly young Rhône red or Cabernet.
tartare Vodka or light young red: Beaujolais, Bergerac, Valpolicella.
Korean Yuk Whe (the world's best steak tartare) Sake.
filet or tournedos Any red (but not old wines with Béarnaise sauce: top Californian Chard is better).
T-bone Reds of similar bone structure: Barolo, Hermitage, Australian Cabernet or Shiraz.
fiorentina (bistecca) Chianti Classico Riserva or Brunello.

Steak and kidney pie or pudding Red Rioja Reserva, Douro red or mature Bordeaux.

Stews and casseroles Burgundy such as Chambolle-Musigny or Bonnes-Mares if fairly simple; otherwise lusty full-flavoured red: young Côtes du Rhône, Toro, Corbières, Barbera, Shiraz, Zinfandel, etc.

Sweetbreads A grand dish, so grand wine: Rhine Ries or Franken Silvaner Spätlese, Alsace Grand Cru Pinot Gr, or Condrieu, depending on sauce.

Tagine These vary enormously, but fruity young reds are a good bet: Beaujolais, Tempranillo, Sangiovese, Merlot, Shiraz.

Tandoori chicken Sauvignon Blanc, or young red Bordeaux or light N Italian red served cool. Also cava and NV Champagne.

Thai food Ginger and lemongrass call for pungent Sauvignon Bl (Loire, Australia, NZ, South Africa) or Riesling (Spätlese or Australian).
coconut milk Hunter Valley and other ripe, oaked Chards; Alsace Pinot Bl for refreshment; Gewürz or Verdelho. And of course cava or NV Champagne.

Tongue Good for any red or white of abundant character, esp Italian. Also Beaujolais, Loire reds and full dry rosés.

Tripe Red, eg Corbières, Roussillon or rather sweet white (eg German Spätlese). Better: W Australian Sem-Chard, or cut with pungent dry white such as Pouilly-Fumé or fresh red eg Saumur-Champigny.

Veal, roast A good neutral background dish for any fine old red which may have faded with age (eg a Rioja Reserva) or a German or Austrian Riesling or Vouvray or Alsace Pinot Gris.

Venison Big-scale red incl Mourvèdre, solo as in Bandol, or in blends, Rhône, Bordeaux or California Cab of a mature vintage; or rather rich white (Pfalz Spätlese or Alsace Pinot Gr).

Vitello tonnato Full-bodied white esp Chard; light red (eg Valpolicella) served cool.

Vegetarian dishes

Baked pasta dishes Pasticcio, lasagne and cannelloni with elaborate vegetarian fillings and sauces: an occasion to show off a grand wine esp finest Tuscan red, but also claret and burgundy. Also Gavi from Italy.

Bubble-and-squeak Beer, stout, or Beaujolais Nouveau.

Cauliflower cheese Crisp aromatic white: Sancerre, Ries Spätlese, Muscat, English Seyval Bl or Schönburger

Couscous with vegetables Young red with a bite: Shiraz, Corbières, Minervois or well chilled rosé from Navarra or Somontano, or a robust Moroccan red.

Fennel-based dishes Sauv Bl: Pouilly-Fumé or one from NZ; English Schönburger or Seyval Blanc or a Beaujolais.

Grilled Mediterranean vegetables Brouilly, Barbera, or Shiraz .

'Meaty' aubergine, lentil or mushroom bakes Corbières, Zinfandel, Shiraz.

Mezze Hot and cold vegetable dishes. Sparkling is a good all-purpose choice as is rosé from Languedoc or Provence.

Mushrooms (in most contexts) Fleshy red; eg Pomerol, California Merlot, Rioja Reserva, top Burgundy or Vega Sicilia.
on toast Your best claret.
wild mushroom risotto (ceps/porcinis are best for wine) Ribera del Duero, Barolo or Chianti Rufina, or top claret: Pauillac or St-Estèphe.

Onion/leek tart Fruity off-dry or dry w: Alsace Pinot Gr or Gewürz, Canadian or NZ Ries, English whites, Jurançon, Australian Ries. Or Beaujolais or Loire red.

Peppers or aubergines (eggplant), stuffed Vigorous red wine: Nemea, Italian Chianti or Dolcetto, California Zinfandel, Bandol, Vacqueyras.

Pies Depending on filling, lighter styles of Chard or Côtes du Rhône.

Pumpkin/Squash ravioli or risotto Full-bodied fruity dry or off-dry white: Viognier or Marsanne, demi-sec Vouvray, Gavi, or South African Chenin.

Ratatouille Vigorous young red: Chianti, NZ Cabernet or Merlot; young red Bordeaux or Gigondas or Coteaux du Languedoc.

Spiced vegetarian dishes See under Indian food, Thai Food.

Spinach, ricotta and pasta bake/Spanacopitta Valpolicella (its bitterness helps); Greco di Molise, or w Sicilian/Sardinian.

Desserts

Apple pie, strudel or tarts Sweet German, Austrian, Loire white, Tokáji Aszú or Canadian Ice Wine.

Apples, Cox's Orange Pippins Vintage port (55 60 63 66 70 75 82 +?).

Bread-and-butter pudding Fine 10-yr-old Barsac, Tokáji Azsú or Australian botrytized Sem.

Cakes and gâteaux see also Chocolate, Coffee, Ginger, Rum. Bual or Malmsey Madeira, oloroso or cream sherry.

Cheesecake Sweet white: Vouvray or Anjou or fizz, refreshing but nothing special.

Chocolate flavours Generally only powerful flavours can compete. Bual, California Orange Muscat, Tokay Azsú, Australian Liqueur Muscat, 10-yr-old tawny port; Asti for light, fluffy mousses. Experiment with rich, ripe reds: Syrah, Zinfandel, even sparkling Shiraz. Banyuls for a weightier partnership. Médoc can match bitter black choc. Or a tot of good rum.

Christmas pudding, mince pies Tawny port, cream sherry, or liquid Christmas pudding itself, Pedro Ximénez sherry. Asti or Banyuls.

Coffee flavours Sw Muscat incl Australia Liqueur Muscats or Tokáji Aszú.

Creams, custards, fools, syllabubs see also Chocolate, Coffee, Ginger, Rum. Sauternes, Loupiac, Ste-Croix-du-Mont, Monbazillac.

Crème brûlée Sauternes or Rhine Beerenauslese, best Madeira or Tokáji. (With concealed fruit, a more modest sweet wine.)

Crêpes Suzette Sweet Champagne, Orange Muscat or Asti spumante.

Fruit
fresh Sweet Coteaux du Layon, light sweet Muscat.
poached, ie apricots, pears, etc Sweet Muscatel: try Muscat de Beaumes-de-Venise, Moscato di Pantelleria or Spanish dessert Tarragona.
dried fruit (and compotes) Banyuls, Rivesaltes, Maury.
flans and tarts Sauternes, Monbazillac or sweet Vouvray or Anjou.
salads, orange salad A fine sweet sherry, or any Muscat-based wine.

Ginger flavours Sweet Muscats, New World botrytized Ries and Sém.

Ice-cream and sorbet Fortified wine (Australian liqueur Muscat, Banyuls); sweet Asti spumante or sparkling Moscato. Amaretto liqueur with vanilla; rum with chocolate.

Lemon flavours For dishes like Tarte au Citron, try sw Riesling from Germany or Austria, or Tokay Aszú; very sw if lemon is very tart.

Meringues Recioto di Soave, Asti or Champagne doux.

Mille-feuille Delicate sweet sparkling white, eg Moscato d'Asti, demi-sec Champagne.

Nuts Finest oloroso sherry, Madeira, vintage or tawny port (nature's match for walnuts), Vin Santo, Setúbal Moscatel.

Orange flavours Experiment with old Sauternes, Tokáji Aszú or California Orange Muscat.

Panettone Jurançon moelleux, late-harvest Riesling, Barsac, Tokáji Aszú.

Pears in red wine A pause before the port. Or try Rivesaltes, Banyuls or Ries Beerenauslese.

Pecan pie Orange Muscat or liqueur Muscat.

Raspberries (no cream, little sugar) Excellent with fine reds that themselves taste of raspberries: young Juliénas, Regnié.

Rum flavours (baba, mousses, ice-cream) Muscat – from Asti to Australian liqueur, according to weight of dish.

Strawberries, wild (no cream) Serve with red Bordeaux (most exquisitely Margaux) poured over.

Strawberries and cream Sauternes or similar sweet Bordeaux, Vouvray Moelleux (90) or Jurançon Vendange Tardive.

Summer pudding Fairly young Sauternes of a good vintage (89 90 95 96 97).

Sweet soufflés Sauternes or Vouvray moelleux. Sw (or rich) Champagne.

Tiramisú Vin Santo, young tawny port, Muscat de Beaumes-de-Venise or Sauternes and Australian Liqueur Muscats.

Trifle Should be sufficiently vibrant with its internal sherry.

Zabaglione Light-gold Marsala or Australian botrytized Semillon or Asti.

Wine & cheese

The notion that wine and cheese were married in heaven is not born out by experience. Fine red wines are slaughtered by strong cheeses: only sharp or sweet white wines survive.

Principles to remember, despite exceptions, are first: the harder the cheese the more tannin the wine can have. And the creamier it is the more acidity is needed in the wine. The main exception constitutes a third principle: wines and cheeses of a region usually sympathize.

Cheese is classified by its texture and the nature of its rind, so its appearance is a guide to the type of wine to match it. Individual cheeses mentioned below are only examples taken from the hundreds sold in good cheese shops.

Fresh, no rind – cream cheese, crème fraîche, Mozzarella
Light crisp white – Simple Bordeaux Blanc, Bergerac, English unoaked whites; or pink – Anjou, Rhône; or very light, v young, v fresh red Bordeaux, Bardolino or Beaujolais.

Hard cheeses, waxed or oiled, often showing marks from cheesecloth –
Gruyère family, Manchego and other Spanish cheeses, Parmesan, Cantal, Comté, old Gouda, Cheddar and most 'traditional' English cheeses
Particularly hard to generalize here; Gouda, Gruyère, some Spanish, and a few English cheeses complement fine claret or Cab and great Shiraz/Syrah wines, but strong cheeses need less refined wines, preferably local. Sugary, granular old Dutch red Mimolette or Beaufort are good for finest mature Bordeaux. Also for Tokáji Aszú.

Blue cheeses Roquefort can be wonderful with Sauternes, but don't extend the idea to other blues. It is the sweetness of Sauternes, especially old, which complements the saltiness. Stilton and port, preferably tawny, is a classic. Intensely flavoured old oloroso, amontillado, Madeira, Marsala, and other fortified wines go with most blues.

Natural rind (mostly goat's cheese) with bluish-grey mould (the rind becomes wrinkled when mature), s'times dusted with ash – St-Marcellin Sancerre, Valençay, light fresh Sauvignon, Jurançon, Savoie, Soave, Italian Chard, lightly oaked English whites.

Bloomy rind soft cheeses, pure white rind if pasteurized, or dotted with red: Brie, Camembert, Chaource, Bougon (goat's milk 'Camembert') Full dry white burgundy or Rhône if cheese is white, immature; powerful, fruity St-Emilion, young Australian (or Rhône) Shiraz/ Syrah or Grenache if mature.

Washed-rind soft cheeses, with rather sticky orange-red rind – Langres, mature Epoisses, Maroilles, Carré de l'Est, Milleens, Munster Local reds, especially for Burgundy cheeses; vigorous Languedoc, Cahors, Côtes du Frontonnais, Corsican, southern Italian, Sicilian, Bairrada. Also powerful whites, esp Alsace Gewurztraminer and Muscat.

Semi-soft cheeses, grey-pink thickish rind – Livarot, Pont l'Evêque, Reblochon, Tomme de Savoie, St-Nectaire Powerful w Bordeaux, Chard, Alsace Pinot G, dryish Riesling, southern Italian and Sicilian w, aged w Rioja, dry oloroso sherry. But the strongest of these cheeses kill most wines.

Food & finest wine

With very special bottles, the wine sometimes guides the choice of food rather than the usual way around. The following suggestions are based largely on the gastronomic conventions of the wine regions producing these treasures, plus much diligent research. They should help bring out the best in your best wines.

Red wines

Red Bordeaux and other Cabernet Sauvignon-based wines (very old, light and delicate: eg pre-59, with exceptions such as 45) Leg or rack of young lamb, roast with a hint of herbs (but not garlic); entrecôte; roast partridge or grouse, sweetbreads; or cheese soufflé after the meat has been served.

Fully mature great vintages (eg Bordeaux 59 61) Shoulder or saddle of lamb, roast with a touch of garlic, roast ribs or grilled rump of beef.

Mature but still vigorous (eg 82 70 66) Shoulder or saddle of lamb (incl kidneys) with rich sauce. Fillet of beef marchand de vin (with wine and bone-marrow). Avoid Beef Wellington: pastry dulls the palate.

Merlot-based Bordeaux (Pomerol, St-Emilion) Beef as above (fillet is richest) or venison.

Côte d'Or red burgundy (Consider the weight and texture, which grow lighter/more velvety with age. Also the character of the wine: Nuits is earthy, Musigny flowery, great Romanées can be exotic, Pommard renowned for its four-squareness, etc.) Roast chicken, or better, capon, is a safe standard with red burgundy; guinea-fowl for slightly stronger wines, then partridge, grouse or woodcock for those progressively more rich and pungent. Hare and venison (chevreuil) are alternatives.

Great old reds The classic Burgundian formula is cheese: Epoisses (unfermented). A fabulous cheese but a terrible waste of fine old wines.

Vigorous younger burgundy Duck or goose roasted to minimize fat.

Great Syrahs: Hermitage, Côte-Rôtie, Grange; or Vega Sicilia Beef, venison, well-hung game; bone-marrow on toast; English cheese (esp best farm Cheddar) but also the newer hard goat's milk and ewe's milk cheese such as Berkswell and Ticklemore.

Rioja Gran Reserva, Pesquera... Richly flavoured roasts: wild boar, mutton, saddle of hare, whole suckling pig.

Barolo, Barbaresco Risotto with white truffles; pasta with game sauce (eg pappardelle alle lepre); porcini mushrooms; Parmesan.

White wines

Very good Chablis, white burgundy, other top quality Chardonnays White fish simply grilled or meunière. Dover sole, turbot, halibut are best; brill, drenched in butter, can be excellent. (Sea-bass is too delicate; salmon passes but does little for the finest wine.)

Supreme white burgundy (Le Montrachet, Corton-Charlemagne) or equivalent Graves Roast veal, organic chicken stuffed with truffles or herbs under the skin, or sweetbreads; richly sauced white fish or scallops as above. Or lobster or wild salmon.

Condrieu, Château-Grillet or Hermitage Blanc Very light pasta scented with herbs and tiny peas or broad beans.

Grand Cru Alsace, Riesling Truite au bleu, smoked salmon or choucroute garni.

Pinot Gris Roast or grilled veal.

Gewurztraminer Cheese soufflé (Münster cheese).

Vendange Tardive Foie gras or Tarte Tatin.

Sauternes Simple crisp buttery biscuits (eg Langue-de-Chat), white peaches, nectarines, strawberries (without cream). Not tropical fruit. Pan- seared foie-gras. Experiment with blue(?) cheeses.

Supreme Vouvray moelleux, etc Buttery biscuits, apples, apple tart.

Beerenauslese/TBA Biscuits, peaches, greengages. Desserts made from rhubarb, gooseberries, quince or apples.

Tokay Aszú (4–6 putts) Foie gras is thoroughly recommended. Fruit desserts, cream desserts, even chocolate can be wonderful.

Great vintage port or Madeira Walnuts or pecans. A Cox's Orange Pippin and a digestive biscuit is a classic English accompaniment.

Old vintage Champagne (not Blanc de Blancs) As an aperitif, or with cold partridge, grouse or woodcock.

France

More heavily shaded areas
are the wine growing regions

The following abbreviations
of regional names
are used in the text:

Al	Alsace
Beauj	Beaujolais
Burg	Burgundy
B'x	Bordeaux
Champ	Champagne
Lo	Loire
Prov	Provence
Pyr	Pyrenees
N/S Rh	North/South Rhône
SW	Southwest

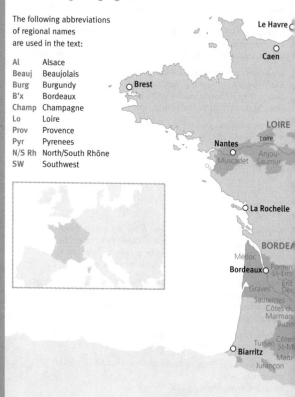

Le Havre

Caen

Brest

LOIRE

Nantes

Loire

Muscadet

Anjou-Saumur

La Rochelle

BORDEA

Médoc

Bordeaux

Pomerol
St-Émil

Graves

Ent
Deu

Sauternes

Côtes du
Marman
Buze

Biarritz

Tursan
Madi
Jurançon

Côtes
St-M

France is beginning to realize that she can afford to rest on her laurels no longer. It is not just Australia she has to watch but Chile, Argentina, New Zealand, the USA, and South Africa. Quality and value are uppermost in the mind of the 21st century wine consumer. Former loyalties cannot be relied upon.

The New World emulates the best of France at almost all levels. However sublime her best wines, the *fonctionnaires* who run the system of Appellations Contrôlées must abandon nit-picking restrictions and apply their minds to quality. The danger of fossilization combined with commercialization is a sombre prospect. The French genius for taste and style is on trial.

Appellations remain the key to French wine. An appellation defines a type. It may apply to a single small vineyard or to a large district.

Burgundy, on the whole, has the most precise and smallest
appellations, Bordeaux the widest and most general. An appellation
is the first thing to look for on a label, but more important still is the
name of the winemaker. The best growers' and merchants' names are
a vital ingredient of these pages. Regions without the overall quality
and traditions required for an appellation can be ranked as *vins
délimités de qualité supérieure* (VDQS), a shrinking category as its
members gain AC status. Their place is being taken by the relatively
new and highly successful *vins de pays. Vins de pays* are almost
always worth trying. They include some brilliant originals and often
offer France's best value for money – which still, despite all the
competition, can mean the world's.

Recent vintages of the French classics

Red Bordeaux

Médoc/red Graves For some wines bottle-age is optional: for these it is indispensable. Minor châteaux from light vintages need only 2 or 3 yrs, but even modest wines of great years can improve for 15 or so, and the great châteaux of these years need double that time.

2002 Saved by a dry, sunny Sept. The later-ripening Cabernet Sauvignon benefited most. Yields down. Some very good wines if selective.

2001 A cool September and rain at vintage meant Cabernet Sauvignon had difficulty in ripening fully. Some good wines but overall quality variable.

2000 Late flowering and a somewhat damp start to the summer looked worrying but the final product is outstanding – superb wines throughout. Keep.

1999 Vintage rain again diluted ripe juice, useful wines to drink 2004-2015.

1998 Rain at vintage *again*. But August heat ripened (even roasted) grapes. Good to very good. 2006–2015.

1997 Uneven flowering and summer rain were a double challenge. Cabernet Sauvignon ripened best. Some good wines for the canny. Now–2010.

1996 Cool summer, fine harvest, esp Cabernet. Good to excellent. 2006–2020.

1995 Heatwave and drought; saved by rain. Good to excellent. Now–2020+.

1994 Hopes of a supreme year; then heavy vintage rain. The best good, but be careful. Now–2010.

1993 Ripe grapes but a wet vintage. Attractive drinking now – 2008.

1992 Rain at flowering, in August and at vintage. A huge crop; light wines, but some easy-drinking. Now–2005.

1991 Frost in April halved crop and rain interrupted vintage. The northern Médoc did best. Drink soon. Now–2010?

1990 A paradox: a drought year with a threat of over-production. Self-discipline was essential. Its results are magnificent. To 2020+.

1989 Early spring, splendid summer. The top wines will be classics of the ripe, dark kind with elegance and length. Small ch'x are uneven. To 2020.

1988 Generally vg; tannic, balanced, beginning to open, keep top wines. To 2010.

1987 Much more enjoyable than seemed likely. Drink up.

1986 Another splendid, huge, heatwave harvest. Better than 85 in Pauillac and St-Julien; a long-term prospect. Now–2020.

1985 Vg vintage, in a heatwave. V fine wines now accessible. Now–2010.

1984 Poor. Originally overpriced. Avoid.

1983 A classic vintage, esp in Margaux: abundant tannin with fruit to balance it. But many wines need drinking. To 2010 for the best.

1982 Made in a heatwave. Huge, rich, strong wines which promise a long life but are developing unevenly. Top châteaux will run to 2015.

1981 Admirable despite rain. Not rich, now a touch austere. Now–2005.

1980 Small late harvest: ripe but rained-on. Drink up.

Older fine vintages: 75 70 66 62 61 59 55 53 49 48 47 45 29 28.

St-Emilion/Pomerol

2002 Sunny Sept but problems with rot and ripeness. Modest to good.

2001 Less rain than Médoc during vintage. Some powerful Merlot but variable.

2000 Similar conditions to Médoc less kind to Merlot but still a v gd vintage.

1999 Careful, lucky growers made excellent wines but rain was again a problem.

1998 Earlier ripening Merlot largely escaped the rain. Some excellent wines.

1997 The Merlot vintage suffered in the rain. But growers are getting better at handling problems. Good for supple wines. Now–2010.

1996 Cool, fine summer. Vintage rain. Less consistent than Médoc. Now–2015.

1995 Perhaps even better than Médoc/Graves. Now–2015.

1994 Less compromised by rain than Médoc. Vg, esp Pomerol. Now–2015.

1993 As Médoc, but better, esp in Pomerol; gd despite terrible vintage weather.

1992 Very dilute but some charming wines to drink quickly. Drink up.

1991 A sad story. Many wines not released.

1990 Another chance to make great wine or a lot of wine. Now–2020.

1989 Large, ripe, early harvest; an overall triumph. To 2020.

1988 Generally excellent; ideal conditions. But some chx over-produced. Pomerol best. Now–2005.

1987 Some v adequate wines (esp in Pomerol). Drink up.

1986 A prolific vintage; but top St-Emilions have long life ahead.

1985 One of the great yrs, with a long future. To 2010+.

1984 A sad story. Most of the crop wiped out in spring. Avoid.

1983 Less impressive than it seemed. Drink soon.

1982 Enormously rich and concentrated wines, most excellent. Now–2005.

1981 A vg vintage, though not as great as it first seemed. Now or soon.

1979 A rival to 78, but not developing as well as hoped. Drink now.

1978 Fine wines, but some lack flesh. Drink soon.

Older fine vintages: 71 70 67 66 64 61 59 53 52 49 47 45.

Red burgundy

Côte d'Or Côte de Beaune reds generally mature sooner than the bigger wines of the Côte de Nuits. Earliest drinking dates are for lighter commune wines, eg Volnay, Beaune; latest for the biggest wines of eg Chambertin, Romanée. But even the best burgundies are much more attractive young than the equivalent red Bordeaux.

2002 Avoided the rains of southern France. Promises to be very exciting.

2001 A cool damp September took the edge off; should still be good though.

2000 Difficult. Fragile grapes in Côte de Beaune. Much better in Côte de Nuits.

1999 Big ripe vintage; good colour, bags of fruit, silky tannins. Wines to keep.

1998 Ripe fruit but dry tannins. Those in balance need keeping.

1997 Again the gods smiled. Very ripe grapes, with low acidity the main potential problem. Lovely wines mostly ready soon.

1996 Fine summer and vintage. Fine ripe wines for keeping. Now–2020.

1995 Small, excellent crop, despite vintage rains. Grapes were very ripe.

1994 Compromised by vintage rain. Generally lean, but exceptions in Côte de Nuits. Drink up.

1993 An excellent vintage – concentrated. Now–2010.

1992 Ripe, plump, pleasing. No great concentration. Drink up.

1991 Very small harvest; some wines v tannic. Côte de Nuits best. Now–2010.

1990 Great vintage: perfect weather compromised only by touches of drought and some over-production. Long life ahead but start to enjoy. To 2020.

1989 Year of great charm, not necessarily for long maturing. Drink up all but best.

1988 Very good but tannic. Now–2015 (but only the best).

Older fine vintages: 85 78 71 69 66 64 62 61 59 (all mature).

White burgundy

Côte de Beaune Well-made wines of good vintages with plenty of acidity as well as fruit will improve and gain depth and richness for some years – anything up to 10. Lesser wines from lighter vintages are ready for drinking after 2 or 3 years.

2002 Ripe healthy grapes; medium-sized crop of great promise.

2001 Generally good results despite lower sugar levels.

2000 Looks very exciting. A big crop of ripe, healthy grapes.

1999 A generous vintage of good, fresh, well-balanced wines.

1998 Difficult year for white. Chassagne was successful. Drink soon
1997 Overall excellent: forward and charming.
1996 A great vintage to lay down top wines. Often awkward now. 2007–2015.
1995 A potentially great vintage, diluted in places. Now–2010.
1994 Patchy; top growers: v fine potent wines but not for keeping. Now or soon.
1993 Sept rain on under-ripe grapes. Easy & pleasant; far behind reds. Soon.
1992 Ripe, aromatic and charming. Mostly ready. Drink up.
1991 Mostly lack substance. Frost problems. Drink up.
1990 Starting to lose balance. Some excellent wines. Drink up.
1989 At best ripe, tense, structured, and long. Now–2010.

The white wines of the Mâconnais (Pouilly-Fuissé, St-Véran, Mâcon-Villages) follow a similar pattern, but do not last as long. They are more appreciated for their freshness than their richness.

Chablis Grand cru Chablis of vintages with both strength and acidity can age superbly for up to 10 years; Premiers crus proportionally less.
2002 Excellent; may be the equal of 2000.
2001 Too much rain. Relatively weak.
2000 Fine weather for harvesting ripe grapes – excellent.
1999 Another ripe vintage, some of it compromised by rain.
1998 Cool weather and some hail. Wines fair to good: not for long keeping.
1997 Another fine vintage; perhaps drink before the 96s.
1996 Ideal harvest but hail on top v'yds. Classic keeping Chablis. Now–2010.
1995 Very good to very, very good. Now–2006.
1994 Downpours on a ripe vintage. Easy wines; drink up.
1993 Fair to good quality; nothing great. Drink up.
1992 Ripe and charming wines. Grands crus splendid. Drink soon.
1991 Generally better than Côte d'Or. Useful wines. Now.
1990 Grands crus magnificent; others lack intensity and acidity. Now–2005.

Beaujolais 02: too much rain for top quality. 01: vg if picked before the rain. 00: excellent. 99: splendid, rich and deep. 98: v gd, if patchy. Best Crus will keep. 97: v gd. 95: excellent. Older wines should be finished.

Southwest France

2002 Indian summer saved late-picking vineyards (Madiran, Cahors, Jurançon). Otherwise disappointing.
2001 Hot summer & perfect vintage conditions. Perhaps too much sugar/alcohol.
2000 Better than forecast despite heavy rain in Sept. Better red wines should keep, perhaps longer than 2001.
1999 Patchy weather spoiled the vintage for some, but far from disastrous.
1998 Outstanding everywhere. The reds should be at peak in 2004.
1997 Dismally wet, but sweet whites excellent after brilliant autumn. Otherwise patchy. Madiran good, will keep.
1996 Good "commercial year" in most areas. Madirans will still keep.
1995 & 1990 Fabulous for long-lived reds – Cahors, Pécharmants, Madirans.

The Midi

2002 Not an easy year with heavy rain in early September causing problems. Varies widely from AC to AC and grower to grower.
2001 Quantity lower than average. Quality generally very good with a hot summer making for ripe concentrated wines.
2000 A warm summer throughout giving ripe fruity wines in Roussillon and Provence, and healthy grapes and balanced wines in Languedoc.

1999 Bad weather failed to ruin vintage in Roussillon, patchy in Languedoc (gd in La Clape – not in Pic St Loup). Gd weather & results in Provence.

1998 Drought in Roussillon meant small crop of conc'd wines. Wonderful vintage in Languedoc made ripe, fruity wines with great potential. Well-balanced fruity wines in Provence.

1997 Problematic in Roussillon and Languedoc – light but fruity wines. Small crop in Provence with concentration and ageing potential. To drink.

Northern Rhône

2002 Poor Sept weather. Cornas did well. Try before you buy. Best growers abandoned half their crop. Pretty gd year for whites, notably Condrieu.

2001 Good, lively year if picked before September rain. Fresh fruit, good acidity. Top year at Côte-Rôtie Often v gd whites.

2000 Good density and tannic structure. Warm and rich. Hermitage will age well, more tannin there. Good Condrieu, sumptuous. Reds more simple than 1999/2001.

1999 V successful. Full, ripe fruit. Delicious, likely to live long. More balance than the 98s. Harmony a key word. Ace Côte-Rôties. Sound whites.

1998 V gd. Big, robust vintage. More overt tannins than 99, but now fusing well. Will need time to soften. Gd Marsanne-based whites.

1997 Gd/v gd. Fat, fleshy wines that will evolve fast. Lower acidity means rich, smooth flavours. Drinking well now. Good vintage for restaurants.

1996 Potential if left to age. Early discord with fruit, tannin, acidity. Can be complex – track progress for right moment. Drink top wines 2006–08.

1995 Lots of full, ample flavour. Lesser names like Crozes delicious now. Top names need more time, maybe 2004–06. Some have firm tannins.

1994 Gd in general, v gd in Côte-Rôtie. Well-framed wines with sound core. More mineral than the '95s. Top wines showing well now.

1991 V gd in Côte-Rôtie, gd in Hermitage. Underestimated due to typical unfair linking with other parts of France. V gd whites.

Southern Rhône

2002 Nature's payback. Rainstorms flooded the South around Châteauneuf. At best, dilute reds and acceptable whites. No super-cuvées this year!

2001 Smaller crop than 2000. Gd density and lively fruit in the villages reds. Best villages: Séguret, Rasteau, Beaumes de Venise, Cairanne.

2000 Tasty wines, led by fruit, juicy and fat. Not a very long-lived year. Go for leading names. Gigondas may edge Châteauneuf in quality.

1999 V gd overall. Ripe, open fruit with correct structure in the best wines. Châteauneuf: Gd harmony 2007+. Vacqueyras: V gd. Lirac: Gd form.

1998 Excellent. A triumph for Grenache. Warm wines hiding their true power and tannin. Some can be too potent, fiery. Others evolving already.

1997 Undemanding. Fruit can be cooked, rather jammy. Drink within max 10 years, unless top name and low yields. Some whites interesting.

1996 Uneven. Tannins are brusque. The best will age for 10+ years.

1995 Sweet, succulent, fruity wines. Evolving with speed, esp if growers went for extreme ripeness. The best will live to 2010–14.

1994 Good at Châteauneuf. Good extract with noticeable tannins. Good at Lirac as well. Gigondas showing well now.

Champagne

2002 Ideal harvest yielded rich complex wines, esp Pinots. Potentially great.

2000 The sun shone through harvest to produce wines of good natural sugar and acidity. Likely to be a vintage year for all producers.

1999 Sporadic rain at harvest changed a great vintage into a good one. Some ripe expressive wines from Chardonnay.

1998 Well constituted, sound wines from both Pinot Noir and Chardonnay. Probable vintage year.

1997 Brilliant Sept weather saved vintage. Ripe, low-acid wines for easy early drinking. Drink before the 96s.

1996 Champagnes of monumental structure, high in alcohol and acidity, real keepers. Drink 2004–2015.

1995 Classic, finely balanced wines; a Chardonnay year *par excellence*. For most producers the current available vintage.

1993 The best vintage in the lean period 1991–5. Aromatic, delicate, and clean flavours. Excellent wines from Pol Roger and Jaccquesson.

The Loire

2002 Best since 1997. Vivid fruit and vibrant acidity in the dry whites. Some fine sweet Chenins. Where yields were kept low, the reds are juicy and deeply coloured. (Beware a whiff of rot in many of the Gamay-based wines.)

2001 Warm, wet winter left soils gorged with water. Best wines are from those who harvested late. But Muscadet perfect. Taste before buying.

2000 Warm rainy year, with lack of sunshine. Muscadet, Sancerre, and Touraine – satisfactory to gd. The Cab F wines are deeply coloured but not rich. Drink within 6 years. Vouvray: good for sec and demi-sec.

1999 Looked to rival the great 89 when the rains came. Cab F marked by musky "animal" aromas. Vouvray: gd for secs and demi-secs

1998 End of the Loire's luck. Episodes of frost, hail, drought, and heavy rain during harvest. Wines are light, some Cab-based reds are overly tannic.

1997 Warm and sunny with a beautful "arrière saison". The third excellent vintage. Supple reds and dry whites, and spectacular sweet wines.

1996 Excellent, though not as flattering as the 97s. The Cab-based reds need time but will age beautifully (ultimately surpassing the 97s).

1995 An excellent vintage across the board. Long-lived, well-structured, delicious wines in every appellation.

Alsace

2002 Better than most of France. Late-picked wines are good to very good. (Especially VENDANGE TARDIVE and SÉLECTIONS DES GRAINS NOBLES.)

2001 After very unsettled weather in Sept, vintage was saved by an Indian Summer. Generally well-balanced wines, good but not great.

2000 Superb – probably best since 90. Very good for Vendanges Tardives and Sélections des Grains Nobles.

1999 A difficult growing season saved by dry, sunny period mid-Aug to mid-Sept. Growers who kept yields down made gd, well-balanced wines.

1998 Unusually the 4th fine vintage in a row. Gd wines despite heatwave Aug – mid-Sept and harvest rain. More Gewurz than previous years.

1997 Almost perfect growing season ending with dry sunny conditions produced concentrated dry wines and outstanding sweet ones.

1996 Harsh winter and late spring followed by hot July and August. Ideal conditions in October gave a ripe harvest. Fine dry wines, little Gewürz.

1995 Thanks to an Indian summer the late ripening varieties were particularly successful (Pinot Gris, Gewurztraminer, and especially Riesling). Good sweet wines too.

To decipher codes, please refer to "Key to symbols" on front flap of jacket, or to "How to use this book" on page 6.

Abelé Small Reims CHAMPAGNE house with vg NV.

Abel-Lepitre Middle-rank CHAMP house. Vg Brut Millésimé (96).

Abymes Savoie w ★ DYA Hilly area nr Chambéry; light, mild Vin de Savoie AC from Jacquère grape has alpine charm. SAVOIE has many such crus for local pleasure.

Agenais SW France r p (w) ★ DYA VDP of Lot-et-Garonne, mostly from coops at Goulens, Donzac, Monflanquin and Mézin. Also from Marmandais coops.

Ajaccio Corsica r p w ★ →★★ 95 96 97 98 99 00 01 The capital of CORSICA. AC for some vg Sciacarello reds. Top-grower: Peraldi (try his Vermentino). Also Clos Capitoro, Jean Courrèges (Dom de Pratavone).

Aligoté Second-rank burgundy white grape and its wine. Should be pleasantly tart and fruity with local character when young. BOUZERON is the one commune to have an all-Aligoté appellation. The shining example is de Villaine's, but try others from good growers. NB PERNAND-VERGELESSES.

Alliet, Philippe Lo r ★★★ 85 86 87 88 89 90 93 95 96 97 98 99 00 01 02 Top-notch producer of long-lived, barrel-aged Chinons: esp Coteau du Noire CUVÉE.

Aloxe-Corton Burg r w ★★→★★★ 88' 89 90' 91 93' 95 96' 97 98 99' 01 02 Village at N end of COTE DE BEAUNE famous for two GRANDS CRUS: CORTON (red), CORTON-CHARLEMAGNE (white). Village wines are lighter but to try.

Alsace Al w (r sp) ★★→★★★ 93 95 96 97 98 99 00 01 Region comprising eastern foothills of Vosges mountains, esp Strasbourg-Mulhouse. Unique wines: aromatic, fruity, full-strength, usually dry and expressive of grape variety, but often sweeter these days. See Vendange Tardive, Sélection des Grains Nobles. Mostly sold by grape variety (PINOT Bl, Ries, GEWÜRZ etc). Matures well (except Pinot Bl, MUSCAT) up to 5, even 10 yrs; GRAND CRU even longer. Good-quality and value CREMANT. PINOT N can have good varietal character but is not widely sold outside the region.

Alsace Grand Cru W ★★★ →★★★★ 85 88 89' 90 93 95 96 97 98 99 00 01 AC restricted to 50 of the best named v'yds (approx 4,000 acres, 2025 in production) and four noble grapes (Ries, PINOT Gr, GEWÜRZ, MUSCAT) mainly dry, some sw. Not without controversy but generally vg and expressive of terroir.

> **Alsace: Wines to look for in 2004**
>
> **Muscat** (always dry in Alsace) DYA. Meyer-Fonné's vibrant Katzenthal or, for a real treat, Jean Becker's Grand Cru Froehn.
>
> **Pinot Blanc** (The Alsace alternative to Chardonnay) Willm's 2000 or Josmeyer's Pinot Blanc H Vieilles Vignes 98 (from Grand Cru Hengst, but not officially!)
>
> **Riesling** (greatest Alsacien variety) Schlumberger's Princes Abbés 99 has benchmark varietal character. At a higher level Hugel Riesling Jubilee 98 or Beyer's Comtes d'Eguisheim 97.
>
> **Pinot Gris** Clos Rebberg 99 or Grand Cru Moenchberg 99 from Marc Kreydenweiss. Or very rare SGN Cuvée Clarisse 98 from Schlumberger.
>
> **Gewürztraminer** Bruno Sorg's 2000 has lovely rich spice. Wolfberger's L'Art d'un Grand 2000 or in a sweeter style Paul Zinck's Grand Cru Pfersigbreg 2000.

Ampeau, Robert Burg ★★★ Exceptional grower and specialist in MEURSAULT & VOLNAY; also POMMARD. Perhaps unique in releasing only long-matured bottles.

André, Pierre Burg ★ NEGOCIANT at Ch Corton-André, ALOXE-CORTON; 95 acres of v'yds in CORTON (Gd. C-Charlemagne, Corton Blanc), SAVIGNY, GEVREY-CHAMBERTIN, etc. Also owns REINE PEDAUQUE.

d'Angerville, Marquis Burg ★★★ Top grower with immaculate 35-acre estate all in VOLNAY. Top wines: Champans and intense, potent CLOS des Ducs.

Anjou Lo p r w (sw dr sp) ★ →★★★★ Both region and Loire AC. Wide spectrum of styles: light reds incl AC Anjou GAMAY; improving dry whites. Gd red (CAB) ANJOU-VILLAGES; strong usually dry SAVENNIÈRES; luscious C'TX DU LAYON whites of CHENIN BL.

Anjou-Coteaux de la Loire Lo w s/sw sw ★★→★★★ 89' 90' 93 94 95' 96 97 98 99 00 01 02 Tiny AC for forceful CHENIN whites. DEMI-SEC or sw not as rich as C'TX DU LAYON, esp Musset-Roullier, Ch de Putille, Doms du Fresche, de Putille.

Anjou-Villages Lo r ★→★★★ 89 90 93 95 96 97 98 99 00 01 02 Superior central ANJOU AC for r's (mainly CAB F, some CAB S). Juicy, tannic young; good value esp Bablut, RICHOU, Rochelles, PIERRE-BISE, Ogereau, Montigilet, Ch'x de Coulaine, de Tigné (Gérard Dépardieu's). New sub-AC to watch: Anjou-Villages-Brissac.

Appellation Contrôlée (AC or AOC) Government control of origin and production (*not* quality) of all the best French wines (see Introduction).

Apremont Savoie w ★★ DYA One of the best villages of SAVOIE for pale, delicate whites, mainly from Jacquère grapes, but recently incl CHARD.

Arbin Savoie r ★★ Deep-coloured lively red from MONDEUSE grapes, rather like a good Loire CABERNET. Ideal après-ski. Drink at 1–2 yrs.

Arbois Jura r p w (sp) ★★→★★★ Various good and original light but tasty wines; speciality is VIN JAUNE. On the whole, DYA except excellent Vin Jaune.

l'Ardèche, Coteaux de Central France r p (w) ★→★★ Hilly area W of Rhône starting to buzz. New domaines, mix of fresh and oaked reds and Viognier/Marsanne whites. Best from pure SYRAH, GAMAY, CAB (NB Serret). Powerful, almost burgundian CHARD "Ardèche" by LOUIS LATOUR (keep 1–2 yrs); "Grand Ardèche" is v oaked. Also Dom du Colombier, Mazel.

Ariège SW ★ New VDP from 1998 plantings of Cabernets, Merlot, Cot, and Tannat under leadership of DOM DE RIBONNET now starting to be marketed. Will keep.

l'Arlot, Domaine de ★★★ Outstanding producer of excellent NUITS-ST-GEORGES, esp CLOS de l'Arlot, red and white. Owned by AXA Insurance.

Armagnac SW The alternative brandy; more tasty, rustic, and peppery than COGNAC. Table wines: CÔTES DE GASCOGNE, GERS, TERROIRS LANDAIS.

Armand, Comte Burg ★★★ Excellent POMMARD wines, esp Clos des Epéneaux.

Aube Southern extension of CHAMP. Now known as Côte des Bar.

Aujoux, J-M Beauj Substantial grower/merchant of BEAUJOLAIS. Swiss-owned.

Auxey-Duresses Burg r w ★★→★★★ 90' 93 95 96' 97 98 99' 02 2nd-rank (but v pretty) COTE DE BEAUNE village: affinities with VOLNAY, MEURSAULT. Best estates: Diconne, HOSPICES DE BEAUNE (Cuvée Boillot), LEROY, M Prunier. Drink whites in 3–4 yrs. Top white: Leroy's Les Boutonniers.

Avize Champ One of the top Côte des Blancs villages. All CHARDONNAY.

Aÿ Champ. One of the best PINOT N-growing villages of CHAMP.

Ayala Champ Once-famous AY-based old-style CHAMP firm. Deserves more notice for its Pinot-based blends (not its BLANC DE BLANCS).

Bandol Prov r p (w) ★★★ 85' 86 87 88 89 90 91 92 93 94 95 96 97 98 99 00 01 02 Little coastal region near Toulon producing Provence's best wines; splendid, vigorous, tannic reds predominantly from MOURVÈDRE; esp Dom de Pibarnon, Ch Pradeaux, Mas de la Rouvière, DOM TEMPIER.

Banyuls Pyr br sw ★★→★★★ One of best VINS DOUX NATURELS, chiefly from GRENACHE (Banyuls GRAND CRU: over 75% Grenache, aged for 2 yrs+): a distant relation of port. The best are RANCIOS, eg those from Doms la Rectorie, du Mas Blanc (★★★), Vial Magnères, at 10–15 yrs old. Cheap NV wines end up in bars.

Barancourt One of many CHAMP marques bought by the acquisitive Paul-François VRANKEN. PINOT N-led Champagnes, esp Cuvée des Fondateurs. Gd BOUZY ROUGE.

Barrique The Bordeaux (and Cognac) term for an oak barrel holding 225l (300 bottles). Barrique-ageing to flavour almost any wine with oak was craze of late 80s, with some sad results. Current price of oak should enjoin discretion.

Barsac B'x sw ★★→★★★★ 70 71' 75 76' 79' 81 83' 85 86' 88' 89' 90' 95 96 97 98 99 01' 02 Neighbour of SAUTERNES with similar superb golden wines from different soil; generally less rich and more racy. Richly repays long ageing. Top ch'x: CLIMENS, COUTET, DOISY-DAENE, DOISY-VEDRINES.

Barthod-Noëllat, Ghislaine Burg ★★★ Impressive range of CHAMBOLLE-MUSIGNY.

Barton & Guestier BORDEAUX shipper since 18th C, now owned by Seagram.

Bâtard-Montrachet Burg w ★★★★ 79 85 86' 88 89' 90' 92 93 94 95 96' 97' 98 99 00 Larger (55-acre) n'bour of M'RACHET. Should be v long-lived: intense flavours, rich texture. Bienvenues-B-M: separate adjacent 9-acre GRAND CRU, 15 owners, thus no substantial bottlings; v rare. Criots-Bâtard-Montrachet (4 acres) even rarer. Seek out: BOUCHARD PÈRE, J-M BOILLOT, CARILLON, DROUHIN, Gagnard, L LATOUR, LEFLAIVE, MOREY, Pernot, RAMONET, SAUZET.

Baudry, Domaine Bernard Lo r p w ★★→★★★ 85 86 87 88 89 90 93 95 96 97 98 99 00 01 02 Impeccable CHINONS in a range of styles from CHENIN-based whites to rosés to several excellent cuvées of red, including Les Grezeaux, Clos Guillot, and Les Croix Boissées. Look for new Cabernet Fr from 2002.

Baumard, Domaine des Lo ★★→★★★★ 75 76 78 81 85 86 88 89 90 93 94 95 96 97 98 99 00 01 02 Leading grower of ANJOU wine, esp SAVENNIÈRES, COTEAUX DU LAYON (CLOS Ste-Catherine), and QUARTS DE CHAUME. Baumard is making a tasty vin de table from VERDELHO. Get it while it lasts.

Baux-en-Provence, Coteaux des Prov r p ★★→★★★ 95 96 97 98 99 00 01 02 Formerly joined with C'TX D'AIX, now AC in its own right (not for w). Best wine: DOM DE TREVALLON (CAB-SYRAH) is VDP: no GRENACHE in v'yd so doesn't conform to AC (!) Also Mas Gourgonnier, Romanin, Mas Ste Berthe, Dom Hauvette.

Béarn SW France r p w ★→★★ w p DYA r 98 00 01 Low-key Basque AC centred on coop at Bellocq. Also ★★ Dom de Guilhémas. JURANCON red (esp Dom Nigri) and MADIRAN rosé must be sold as Béarn or VDP PYRENEES-ATLANTIQUES.

Beaujolais Beauj r (p w) ★ DYA Simple AC of the v big Beaujolais region: light short-lived fruity red of GAMAY grapes. Beaujolais Supérieur is little different.

Beaujolais de l'année The BEAUJOLAIS of the latest vintage, until the next.

Beaujolais Primeur (or Nouveau) Same as above, made in a hurry (often only 4–5 days fermenting) for release at midnight on the third Wednesday in November. Ideally soft, pungent, fruity and tempting; too often crude, sharp, too alcoholic. BEAUJ-VILLAGES should be a better bet.

Beaujolais-Villages Beauj r ★★ 99 00 01 Wines from better (N) half of BEAUJOLAIS; should be much tastier than plain BEAUJOLAIS. The 10 (easily) best villages are the CRUS: FLEURIE, ST-AMOUR, JULIÉNAS, CHÉNAS, MOULIN-À-VENT, CHIROUBLES, MORGON, REGNIÉ, CÔTE DE BROUILLY, BROUILLY. Of the 30 others the best lie around Beaujeu. Crus cannot be released EN PRIMEUR before December 15th. Best kept until spring (or considerably longer).

Beaumes-de-Venise S Rh br r (r p) ★★→★★★ DYA Widely regarded as France's best dessert MUSCAT, from S COTES DU RHONE; can be highly flavoured, subtle, lingering (eg Ch St Sauveur, Doms Coyeux, Durban, JABOULET, Pigeade, VIDAL-FLEURY). Mid-weight reds (Ch Redortier, Dom du Fenouillet, Cassan, co-op) gd.

Beaune Burg r (w) ★★★ 90' 91 93' 95 96' 97 98 99' 01 02 Historic wine capital of Burgundy: walled town hollow with cellars. Wines: classic burgundy – but no GRAND CRU. Many fine growers. NEGOCIANTS' CLOS wines (usually PREMIER CRU) often best; eg DROUHIN's superb Clos des Mouches (esp white), JADOT's Clos des Ursules. Beaune du Château is a BOUCHARD PERE brand. Best v'yds: Bressandes, Fèves, Grèves, Marconnets, Teurons.

Becker, Caves J ★→★★★ Proud old family firm at Zellenberg, ALSACE now making even finer wines. Classic RIESLING Hagenschlauf and GRAND CRU Froehn MUSCAT. Second label: Gaston Beck.

Bellet Prov p r w ★★★ Fashionable, much-above-average local (Rolle grape) wines from Nice. Serious producers: Ch de Bellet, Dom de la Source. Pricey.

Bergerac Dordogne r w p dr sw ★→★★★ (r) 95 98 99 00 01' Effectively, but not politically, an eastward extension of B'x with no clear break in style/quality. Top properties incl ★★★ La Tour des Gendres, Clos de la Colline, Clos des Verdots.

Otherwise ★★ Dom l'Ancienne Cure, Haut Montlong, Les Marnières, Ch'x Belingard-Chayne, de la Colline, Grinou, de la Jaubertie, du Constant, les Eyssards, Jonc Blanc, de la Mallevieille, les Marais, Les Miaudoux, le Paradis, le Raz, See also MONBAZILLAC, ROSETTE, SAUSSIGNAC, PECHARMANT, MONTRAVEL.

Besserat de Bellefon Champ Grande Tradition NV; Cuvée des Moines Brut and Rosé NV; Grande Cuvée NV; Brut and Rosé (**90 95 96**). Now in Epernay, CHAMP house known for lightish wines, not to keep. Owned by MARNE ET CHAMPAGNE.

Beyer, Léon ★★→★★★ Ancient ALSACE firm at Eguisheim. Forceful dry wines needing 5–10 yrs, esp Comtes d'Eguisheim GEWURZ, Comtes d'Eguisheim RIES from GRAND CRU Pfersigberg. Beyer is militant against GRAND CRU restrictions.

Bichot, Maison Albert Burg One of BEAUNE's lgst growers/merchants. V'yds (32-acre Dom du CLOS Frantin (★★): excellent): CHAMBERTIN, RICHEBOURG, CLOS DE VOUGEOT; Dom Long-Depaquit (★★) in CHABLIS; also many other brand names.

Billecart-Salmon NV; Rosé NV; Nicolas François Billecart (**90 95 96 97**); Bl de Blancs (**95 97**); Elizabeth Salmon Rosé (**97**). One of the best CHAMP houses, founded in 1818, still family-owned. Exquisite fresh-flavoured wines age beautifully. Part oak-fermented vintages from 2000. New single v'yd Clos St-Hilaire BLANC DE NOIRS (**95**).

Bize, Simon Burg ★★★ Admirable red burgundy grower with 35 acres at SAVIGNY-LES-BEAUNE. Usually model wines in the racy and elegant Savigny style.

Blagny Burg r w ★★→★★★ (w) **89** 92 95 **96'** 97 **99'** 00' 01 02 Hamlet between MEURSAULT and PULIGNY-M'RACHET: whites have affinities with both (and sold under both ACS), reds with VOLNAY (sold as AC Blagny). Good ones need age; esp AMPEAU, JOBARD, LATOUR, LEFLAIVE, MATROT, G Thomas.

Blanc de Blancs Any white wine made from white grapes only, esp CHAMP. Not an indication of quality but should be of style.

Blanc de Noirs White (or slightly pink or "blush") wine from red grapes.

Blanck, Paul et Fils Beyer, Léon Al ★★★ Versatile grower at Kientzheim. Gd PINOT Bl, and GRANDS CRUS Furstentum (GEWURZ, Pinot Gr, esp RIES), SCHLOSSBERG (Ries).

Blanquette de Limoux Midi w sp ★★ Gd-value fizz from nr Carcassonne with long local history. V dry, clean, increasingly tasty: CHARD and Chenin added to basic Mauzac, esp in newer AC CREMANT de Limoux.

Blaye B'x r w ★→★★★ DYA Simple dry whites from E of the Gironde and as of 2000 designation for region's top reds (lower yields, etc).

Boillot, J-M ★★★ POMMARD-based domaine: though best known for v fine, oaky whites from PULIGNY-M'RACHET, BATARD and remarkable MONTAGNY.

Boisset, Jean-Claude Burg Far and away the biggest burgundy merchant based in NUITS-ST-GEORGES. Owner of Bouchard-Aîné, Lionel Bruck, F Chauvenet, Delaunay, Jaffelin, Morin Père et Fils, de Marcilly, Pierre Ponnelle, Thomas-Bassot, Vienot, CELLIER DES SAMSONS (BEAUJOLAIS), MOREAU (CHABLIS) and a share in MOMMESSIN. Predictable commercial standards. From 99 own v'yds separated as DOM DE LA VOUGERAIE (★★★). Potentially vg.

Boizel Quality Epernay family CHAMP house; brilliant, aged BLANC DE BLANCS NV and prestige Joyau de France (**95**) at keen prices. Part of Boizel Chanoine.

Bollinger NV 'Special Cuvée'; Grande Année (**95 96**); Rosé (**96**). Top CHAMP house at AY with a distinct winey style. Luxury wines: RD (**85 88 90**), VIEILLES VIGNES Françaises (**96**) from ungrafted Pinot vines, La Côte aux Enfants, Ay.

Bonneau du Martray, Domaine Burg ★★★★ (w) ★★ (r) Biggest grower (22 acres) of CORTON-CHARLEMAGNE of highest quality; also red GRAND CRU CORTON all on a high since 90. Cellars at PERNAND-VERGELESSES. Whites have often outlived reds.

Bonnes-Mares Burg r ★★★→★★★★ 78' 85' **88'** 89 **90'** 91 **93** 95 96' 97 98 99' 00 01 02 37-acre GRAND CRU between CHAMBOLLE-MUSIGNY and MOREY-ST-DENIS. V sturdy long-lived wines, less fragrant than MUSIGNY; can rival CHAMBERTIN. Top growers: DUJAC, GROFFIER, JADOT, ROUMIER, DOM DES VAROILLES, DE VOGUE, VOUGERAIE.

Bonnezeaux Lo w sw ★★★→★★★★ 76' 78 **85' 86 88' 89' 90' 93' 94** 95' 96 **97 98 99 00** 01 Velvety, structured, complex sw CHENIN, potentially best of CTX DU LAYON. Esp Angeli, Ch de Fesles, Dom du Petit Val. Ages well, but v tempting young.

Bordeaux B'x r w (p) ★→★★ **90 94 95 96 98 00'** (for ch'x see pp 80–105) Catch-all AC for low-strength B'x. Often despised: it may be light but it still cannot be imitated. If I had to choose one simple daily wine, gd B'x would be it.

Bordeaux Supérieur ★→★★ As above, with more alcohol and ageing potential.

Borie-Manoux Admirable B'x shipper, château-owner owned by Castéja family. Ch'x incl BATAILLEY, BEAU-SITE, DOM DE L'EGLISE, HAUT-BAGES-MONPELOU, TROTTEVIEILLE.

Bouchard Père et Fils Important burgundy shipper (est 1731) and grower; excellent v'yds (232 acres), mainly COTE DE BEAUNE; cellars at Ch de Beaune. Fine quality since 1996: often poor before.

Bouches-du-Rhône Prov r p w ★ VINS DE PAYS from Marseille environs. Warming reds from southern varieties, plus CAB S, SYRAH and Merlot.

Bourg B'x r (w) ★★ **86' 88' 89' 90'** 94 95 96 **98 99** 00' 01 Un-fancy claret from E of the Gironde. For ch'x see Côtes de Bourg.

Bourgeois, Henri ★★→★★★ Lo **89 90** 93 95 96 97 98 99 **00 01 02** Leading SANCERRE grower/ merchant in Chavignol; also owns Laporte. Also POUILLY-FUME, MENETOU-SALON, and QUINCY. Top wines incl: Etienne Henri, MD de Bourgeois, La Bourgeoise, D'Antan Sancerrois, Sancerre Jadis Le Chêne Etienne. Recently bought a v'yd in New Zealand.

Bourgogne Burg r w (p) ★★ **00** 01 02 Catch-all Burgundy AC, with higher standards than basic B'x. Light often gd flavour, best at 2–4 yrs. Top growers make bargain beauties from fringes of COTE D'OR villages; do not despise. BEAUJOLAIS CRUS can also be labelled Bourgogne.

> Bourgogne is the generic word for the cheaper end of Burgundy. As well as some indifferent mass-produced wines, it also covers out-lying areas which have their own subdivisions within the AC Bourgogne.
> Coulanges-la-Vineuse, Epineuil, and Vézélay (Yonne département) Hautes Côtes de Beaune and Hautes Côtes de Nuits (Côte d'Or) Côte Chalonnaise and Couchois (Saône et Loire). The best tip is to buy Bourgogne Rouge or Blanc from good growers in the famous villages of the Côte d'Or – they will be delicious simple wines with more style than négociant bottlings.

Bourgogne Grand Ordinaire Burg r (w) ★ DYA Lowest B'y AC, also allowing GAMAY. Rare. White may incl ALIGOTE, PINOT Bl, Melon de Bourgogne.

Bourgogne Passe-Tout-Grains Burg r (p) ★ Age 1–2 yrs, junior burgundy: min 33% PINOT N, the balance GAMAY, mixed in vat. Often enjoyable. Not as heady as BEAUJ.

Bourgueil Lo r (p) ★★→★★★(★) 76' 85 86' **88 89'** 90' **95'** 96 97 98 99 01 **02** Brawny, fruity TOURAINE (mainly CAB F). Deep-flavoured, ageing like B'x in top yrs. ST-NICOLAS-DE-B'GUEIL often lighter. Esp Amirault, Audebert, Billet, Breton, Caslot, Cognard, Delaunay, Druet, Gambier, Lamé-Delisle-Boucard, Mailloches.

Bouvet-Ladubay Lo ★→★★★ Major sp SAUMUR house, TAITTINGER-controlled. Wines incl vintage BRUT Saphir, CREMANT Excellence, oak-fermented deluxe Trésor (white, rosé), with 2 yrs age, and Instinct. Also still wines (Les Nonpareils); gd sw Grand Vin de Dessert. CUVÉES: Brut Zero, Trésor Rouge.

Bouzeron Burg w ★ COTE CHALONNAISE AC specifically for ALIGOTE. Age 1–2 years. Top grower: de Villaine. Also NB BOUCHARD PERE.

Bouzy Rouge Champ r ★★★ **89 90** 95 96 **97** 98 99 Still red of famous CHAMP PINOT village. Like v light burgundy, but can last well in sunny vintages.

Bricout BRUT NV (Rés, Prestige, CUVEE Spéciale Arthur Bricout **90** 95 96); Rosé NV; Brut (**90 95** 96). AVIZE CHAMP house bought by P Martin and O Giraudière in 99. First-rate CUVEE Prestige.

Brocard, J-M Burg ★★ CHABLIS grower to note for fine value, crisp and typical wines, incl Montmains, Montée de Tonnerre. Expanding into new terroir.

Brouilly Beauj r ★★ 99 00 **01 02** Biggest of the 10 CRUS of BEAUJOLAIS: fruity, round, refreshing wine, can age 3–4 yrs. CH DE LA CHAIZE is largest estate. Top growers: Michaud, Dom de Combillaty, Dom des Grandes Vignes.

Brumont, Alain SW ★★★ Best known, but now expensive, producer in MADIRAN and one of the first to introduce oak-ageing & 100% Tannat wines. Revived the Coop at Castelnau-Rivière-Basse. Flagship wines: Ch MONTUS, Dom Bouscassé, and gd-value MADIRAN Domaine Meinjarre.

Brut Term for the dry classic wines of CHAMP. Brut Ultra/Zéro: for bone-dry wines.

Buisse, Paul ★→★★ Quality Montrichard merchant: range of, esp TOURAINE, wines.

Bugey Savoie r p w sp ★→★★ DYA VDQS for light sparkling, still or half-sparkling wines from Roussette (or Altesse) and CHARDONNAY (gd). Best from Montagnieu; also Rosé de Cerdon, mainly GAMAY.

Burguet, Alain Burg ★★→★★★ Superb GEVREY-CHAMB; esp VIEILLES VIGNES village wine.

Buxy Burg w Village in AC MONTAGNY with good coop for CHARD & PINOT.

Buzet SW France r (w p) ★★ **98'** 99 00 (01) Region SE of B'DX; similar wines, s'times a bit pruney. Dynamic co-op has bulk of production, including some single properties (eg Châteaux de Gueyze, Mazelières). More local character from (independent) Dom de Pech, Ch'x du Frandat, Sauvagnères and Tournelles.

Cabardès Midi r (p w) ★→★★ 95 96 **97 98** 99 00 01 02 New AC NW of Carcassonne. MIDI and B'X grapes show promise at Ch'x Pennautier, des Hautes-Caunettes, Ventenac, Dom de Cabrol, Co-op de Conques sur Orbiel.

Cabernet See Grapes for red wine (pages 10–13).

Cabernet d'Anjou Lo p s/sw ★ DYA Delicate, grapey, med-sw rosé. Traditionally sw, age-worthy; a few venerable bottles survive. Esp from Bablut.

Cabrières Midi p (r) ★★ DYA COTEAUX DU LANGUEDOC.

Cahors SW France r ★→★★★ 85 89 90' 95 98 (99) 00 (01') Fast-reviving v'yd mostly from Malbec (here called Auxerrois). Now range from conc, tannic, to atypical quick-drinking.

Leading Cahors Producers

★★★ CLOS DE GAMOT, du Cèdre, Lamastine. ★★ Clos Coutale, Reysséguier Ch'x du Cayrou, La Coustarelle, La Caminade, Garinet, Gaydou, La Hauts d'Aglan, La Reyne, Les Ifs, Les Lacquets, Latuc, De Lauze, Les Rigalets. Doms de la Bérangeraie, de Cause, Paillas, Pineraie, Savarines, Eugénie. Ch Lagrezette owned by Cartier and priced accordingly.

Cairanne S Rh r p w ★★ 90' 94 95' 96' 97 98'99' **00'** 01' One of best COTES DU RHONE-VILLAGES: solid, robust esp from Doms Alary, Ameillaud, Brusset, l'Oratoire St-Martin, Rabasse-Charavin, Richaud. Some improving whites.

Canard-Duchêne CHAMP house connected with VEUVE CLICQUOT. Fair prices for lively, PINOT-tasting wines. Improved quality recently. Vg Charles VII prestige CUVÉE both BRUT and ROSÉ.

Canon-Fronsac B'x r ★★→★★★ **85' 86 88 89' 90' 94 95 96** 98 00' 01 Full tannic reds of increasing quality from small area W of POMEROL. Need less age than formerly. Eg Ch'x: Barrabaque, CANON-DE-BREM, Cassagne Haut-Canon, Gaby, Lamarche Canon Candelaire, Pavillon, La Fleur Caillou, Grand-Renouil, Mazeris, Moulin-Pey-Labrie, Vraye-Canon-Boyer. See also Fronsac.

Cantenac B'x r ★★★ Village of HAUT-MEDOC entitled to the AC MARGAUX. Top ch'x include BRANE-CANTENAC, PALMER, etc.

Cap Corse Corsica w br ★★→★★★ CORSICA's wild N cape. Splendid MUSCAT from CLOS Nicrosi (Rogliano), & rare, soft, dry Vermentino w. Vaut le détour, if not le voyage.

Caramany Pyr r (w) ★ 95 96 97 **98 99** 00 01 02 Notionally superior AC for single-village COTES DU ROUSSILLON-VILLAGES.

Carillon, Louis Burg ★★★ Leading PULIGNY-M domaine now in top league. Esp PREMIER CRU Referts, Perrières and tiny amount of GRAND CRU Bienvenues-Bâtard.

Cassis Prov w (r p) ★★ DYA Seaside village E of Marseille known for dry white wines with a certain character, drunk with bouillabaisse (eg Dom de la Ferme Blanche, Clos Ste Magdeleine, Clos d'Albizzi). Not to be confused with cassis: blackcurrant liqueur made in Dijon.

Cave Cellar, or any wine establishment.

Cave coopérative Wine-growers' co-op winery; over ½ of all French production. Usually well-run, well-equipped and their wine reasonable value for money.

Cellier des Samsons ★ BEAUJOLAIS/MACONNAIS co-op at Quincié with 2,000 grower-members. Wines widely distributed; now owned by BOISSET.

Cépage Variety of vine, eg CHARD, Merlot.

Cérons B'x w dr sw ★★ **83' 85' 86' 88' 89' 90 95 96 97 98** 99 01 Neighbour of SAUTERNES with some good sweet wine, eg Ch'x de Cérons et de Calvimont, Chantegrive, Grand Enclos. Ch Archambeau makes vg dry GRAVES.

> ### Chablis
> There is no better expression of the all-conquering Chardonnay than the full but tense, limpid but stony wines it makes on the heavy limestone soils of Chablis. Chablis terroir divides into 4 quality levels (4 including Petit Chablis) with great consistency. Best makers use little or no new oak to mask the precise definition of variety and terroir. They incl: Barat, Bessin*, Billaud-Simon, Boudin*, J-M Brocard, J Collet *, D Dampt, R & V Dauvissat*, J Dauvissat, B, D et E, and J Defaix, Droin, Drouhin*, Durup, Fèvre, Geoffroy, J-P Grossot*, Laroche, Long-Depaquit, Dom des Malandes, L Michel*, Picq*, Pupillon, Raveneau*, G Robin*, Servin, Tribut, Vocoret. Simple unqualified "Chablis" may be thin; best is premier or grand cru (see below). The co-op, La Chablisienne, has high standards (esp Grenouille*) and many different labels (it makes 1 in every 3 bottles). (* = outstanding)

Chablis Burg w ★★–★★★ 95 **96' 97** 99 00' 02 Unique, flavoursome, dry minerally wine of N Burgundy, CHARD only; a total of 10,000 acres for all levels.

Chablis Grand Cru Burg w ★★★–★★★★ **83 88 89 90'** 92 **93 95'** 96' **97** 98 99 00' 02 In maturing a match for great w burgundy: often dumb in youth, at best with age combines mineral cut with hint of SAUTERNES. 7 v'yds: Blanchots, Bougros, CLOS, Grenouilles, Preuses, Valmur, Vaudésir. See also MOUTONNE.

Chablis Premier Cru Burg w ★★★ **88 89** 90' **92** 95' **96'** 97 98 99 00' 02 Technically second-rank but at best excellent, more typical of CHABLIS than its GRANDS CRUS. Can outclass more expensive MEURSAULT and other COTE DE BEAUNE. Best vineyards incl Côte de Léchet, Fourchaume, Mont de Milieu, Montée de Tonnerre, Montmains, Vaillons. See above for producers.

Chai Building for storing and maturing wine, esp in BORDEAUX.

Chambertin Burg r ★★★★ 78' 85' **88** 89 **90'** 91 **92 93** 95 96' 98 99' 00 01 02 32-acre GRAND CRU; some of the meatiest, most enduring, best red burgundy, 20 growers, including BOUCHARD, Charlopin, Damoy, DROUHIN, LEROY, MORTET, PONSOT, Rebourseau, Rossignol-Trapet, ROUSSEAU, Trapet.

Chambertin-Clos de Bèze Burg r ★★★★ 78' 85 **88** 89 **90'** 91 **92 93** 95 96'98 99' 00 01 02 37-acre neighbour of CHAMBERTIN. Similarly splendid wines. May legally be sold as Chambertin. 15 growers, incl B CLAIR, Damoy, DROUHIN, Drouhin-Laroze, FAIVELEY, GROFFIER, JADOT, ROUSSEAU.

Chambolle-Musigny Burg r ★★★ –★★★★ 88 **89** 90' 91 92 **93 95 96' 97** 98 99 00 01 02 420-acre COTE DE NUITS village: fabulously fragrant, complex, but never heavy wine. Best vineyards: Les Amoureuses, part of BONNES-MARES, Les Charmes, MUSIGNY. Growers to note: BARTHOD-NOELLAT, DROUHIN, FAIVELEY, GROFFIER, HUDELOT-NOELLAT, JADOT, MUGNERET, MUGNIER, RION, ROUMIER, Serveau, DE VOGUE.

Champagne Sparkling wine of PINOTS Noir and Meunier and/or CHARD, and its region (70,000+ acres 90 miles E of Paris); made by METHODE TRADITIONELLE. Bubbles from elsewhere, however good, cannot be Champagne.

Champagne: growers to watch in 2004

Alain Robert – perfectionist Le Mesnil grower-maker; superlative Cuvée Mesnil Sélection and Tête de Cuvée.

Richard Cheurlin – one of best grower/winemakers of the Aube. Rich but balanced Carte d'Or and vintage-dated Cuvée Jeanne.

Egly-Ouriet – first-rate grower/winemaker in Ambonnay. Superb expressions of great Pinot, esp. Blanc de Noirs Vielles Vignes.

Franck Bonville – one of the great unsung estates of the Côte des Blancs. Exquisite Blanc de blancs from Grand Cru v'yds culminate in Brut Prestige.

Jacques Selosse – Pre-eminent Avize domaine; natural non-interventionist methods; superb barrique-fermented all Chardonnay Cuvée Substance.

José Michel – Doyen of Côte d'Epernay making fresh yet mature Carte Blanche NV. Also excellent Blanc de Blanc (97 98) and vintage (96).

Pierre Gimmonet – leading Côte des Blancs grower at Cuis. Delicate, dry Cuvée Gastronome is ideal with oysters.

Henri Mandois – Pierry. Elegant wines from Meunier and Chard blends.

Larmandier-Bernier – Vertus; top-flight Blanc de Blancs grower-maker, esp Cramant Grand Cru.

Jean-Marie Tarlant – great grower in Marne valley at Oeuilly. Excellent vintage wines (esp. 96) and outstanding Krug-like Cuvée Louis fermented in oak.

Vilmart – exceptional eco-friendly estate at Rilly la Montagne. Lovely barrique-fermented Coeur de Cuvée.

Champy Père et Cie Burg ★★→★★★ Oldest NEGOCIANT, in BEAUNE, rejuvenated by Meurgey family (also brokers "DIVA"). Range of very well-chosen wines.

Chandon de Briailles, Domaine Burg ★★★ Small burgundy estate at SAVIGNY. Makes wonderful CORTON (and Corton Blanc) and vg PERNAND-VERGELESSES.

Chanson Père et Fils Burg ★→★★★ Old grower-NEGOCIANT at BEAUNE (110 acres), now owned by BOLLINGER. Esp BEAUNE CLOS des Fèves, SAVIGNY, PERNAND-VERGELESSES, CORTON. Expect better quality now.

Chapelle-Chambertin Burg r ★★★ 85 88 89' 90' 91 92 95 96' 97 98 99' 00 01 02 13-acre neighbour of CHAMBERTIN. Wine more "nervous", not so meaty. Top producers: Damoy, JADOT, Rossignol-Trapet, Trapet.

Chapoutier Rh ★★→★★★★★ Long-est'd grower and trader of full Rhônes; bio-dynamic principles. Best: special CUVEES CH'NEUF Barbe Rac (GRENACHE), HERMITAGE: L'Hermite, Le Pavillon (red), Cuvée d'Orée (white, late-picked Marsanne), also CROZES red Les Varonniers. Sound Meysonniers Crozes. New holdings in BANYULS, COLLIOURE, CTX DU TRICASTIN, and CTX D'AIX-EN-PROVENCE promising.

Chardonnay See Grapes for white wine (pages 12–16). Also the name of a MACON-VILLAGES commune. Hence Mâcon-Chardonnay.

Charlopin, Philippe Burg ★★★ Modern-style GEVREY-CHAMBERTIN estate. To watch.

Charmes-Chambertin Burg r ★★★ 85' 88 89' 90' 91 93 95 96' 97 98 99' 00 01 02 CHAMBERTIN n'bour, incl AC MAZOYERES-C. Suppler, rounder wines; esp Bachelet, Dugat, DROUHIN, DUJAC, LEROY, Perrot-Minot, ROTY, ROUMIER, ROUSSEAU, VOUGERAIE.

Chassagne-Montrachet Burg w r ★★★→★★★★ r (★★★) 90' 93 95 96' 97 98 99' 01 02; w 89' 90 92 95 96 97 98 99 00' 01 02 750-acre COTE DE BEAUNE village. Sterling hefty r; excellent rich dry w rarely with quite the finesse of

PULIGNY next door but often costs less. Best vineyards incl part of M'RACHET, BATARD-M, Boudriottes (r w), Caillerets, CRIOTS-BATARD-M, Morgeot (r w), Ruchottes, CLOS ST-JEAN (r). Growers incl Amiot-Bonfils, Blain-Gagnard, COLIN-DELEGER, DROUHIN, Fontaine-Gagnard, J N Gagnard, GAGNARD-DELAGRANGE, Lamy-Pillot, Ch de la Maltroye, MOREY, Niellon, Pillot, RAMONET.

> **Château**
> Means an estate, big or small, good or indifferent, particularly in Bordeaux (see pages 80–105). Elsewhere in France château tends to mean, literally, castle or great house, as in most of the following entries. In Burgundy, "domaine" is the usual term.

FRANCE

Château d'Arlay ★→★★ Major JURA estate; 160 acres in skilful hands with wines inc very good VIN JAUNE, VIN DE PAILLE, PINOT N and MACVIN.

Château de Beaucastel S Rh r w ★★★ 78' 79 81' 83 85 86' **88 90'** 92 93' **94'** 95' 96' 98' 99' 00' (01) One of biggest, best-run CH'NEUF-DU-PAPE estates. Deep-hued, complex wines; unusual varietal mix incl ⅓ MOURVEDRE. Drink well young, too. Sm amount of wonderful Roussanne w: keep 5–14 yrs. Also leading COTES DU RHONE Coudoulet de Beaucastel (r and w – part Viognier). Vg organic Perrin Nature CÔTES DU RHÔNE plus NEGOCIANT RASTEAU, VACQUEYRAS. Also Tablas Creek, Paso Robles, Calif.

Château du Cèdre SW r ★★★ 93 **96 98** (00') (01) Fashionable excellent CAHORS estate. Also delicious white VDP.

Château de la Chaize Beauj r ★★★ Best-known BROUILLY estate.

Château Fortia S Rh (r w) ★★ 78' 81' 83 85 88 **90 95'** 96' **97** 98' 99 00' 01 Trad 72-acre CHATEAUNEUF property. Owner's father, Baron Le Roy, also fathered the AC system in 20s. Not at top form, but signs of revival, inc whites.

Château Fuissé Burg w ★★→★★★ Now being challenged as the top estate in Pouilly-Fuissé. Numerous cuvées, made to mature more rapidly than before.

Château de Meursault Burg r w ★★★ 150-acre estate owned by PATRIARCHE, with good v'yds and wines in BEAUNE, MEURSAULT, POMMARD, VOLNAY. Splendid cellars open to the public for tasting.

Château de Mont-Redon S Rh r w ★★★ 78 88 89 **90'** 93' **94'** 95' **97'** 98' 99' 00 01 Outstanding CH'NEUF-DU-PAPE estate. Fine complex r; vg aromatic, s'times substantial w (eg 96/00). Also gd wines from Cantegril v'yd (LIRAC).

Château de Montaigne Dordogne w (sw) ★★ Home of great philosopher Michel de M, now making sw COTES DE MONTRAVEL; part-owns CH PALMER (MARGAUX).

Château Montus ★★★ SW France **89** 90' **94** 95' 96 97' 98 (00) (01) Top MADIRAN estate. Some 100% Tannat, long vinification, slow-maturing. Owner: A BRUMONT.

Château La Nerthe S Rh r (w) ★★★ 78' 81' 85 86 88 **89' 90'** 93 **94** 95' 96' 97 98' 99' 00 01 High quality 222-acre CHATEAUNEUF estate. Solid modern-style wines, esp special CUVEES Cadettes (r) and oaked Beauvenir (w). Take 5 yrs to show.

Château de Pierre-Bise Loire r w ★★→★★★★ **85 86 88 89 90 93** 95 **96 97 98** 99 00 01 02 Superb producer of ANJOU, esp C'TX DE LAYON, incl QUARTS DE CHAUME, vinifed and bottled by terroir. Also SAVENNIERES under label Clos de Coulaine.

Château Rayas S Rh r (w) ★★★ **78'** 79 **81'** 83 85 86 **88' 89** 90' 93 94' 95' 96' 98 99 00 Famous old-style 37–acre estate in CH'NEUF. Usually conc'd wines entirely GRENACHE, yet age superbly. Trad w Rayas can be vg. Pignan is gd value 2nd label. Vg Ch Fonsalette, COTES DU RHONE (NB CUVEE SYRAH & w). All benefit from decanting.

Château Routas Prov r p w ★★ Estate making its mark in COTEAUX VAROIS. Wines including SYRAH, CAB S, CHARD-Viognier, both AC and VDP.

Château de Selle Prov r p w ★★→★★★ 100-acre estate of OTT family nr Cotignac, Var. The original pace-setters for PROVENCE. Cuvée Spéciale is largely CAB S.

Château Simone Prov r p w ★★→★★★ Age 2–6 yrs or longer. Famous old property synonymous with AC PALETTE, nr Aix-en-Provence. The red is smooth but herby and spicy. White repays bottle age. Rosé exceptional.

Château de Villeneuve Loire r w ★★→★★★ 89 90 93 94 95 96 97 98 99 00 01 02 Dynamic SAUMUR estate. Exciting SAUMUR Blanc (especially Les Cormiers) and S-CHAMPIGNY (esp VIEILLES VIGNES, Grand Clos).

Château-Chalon Jura w ★★★ Not a CHATEAU but AC and village. Unique dry yellow sherry-like wine (Savagnin grape). Develops flor while ageing in barrels for min 6 yrs. Ready to drink when when bottled (62cl "Clavelin" bottle), but ages almost forever. A curiosity.

Château-Grillet N Rh w ★★ 94' 95 98 99 9-acre terraced vineyard of Viognier; one of France's smallest ACS. Absurdly over-expensive, inconsistent quality. Always cask-reared. Less floral aromas than CONDRIEU. Drink around 5 years old – or drink Condrieu.

Châteaumeillant Lo r p ★→★★ DYA A tiny VDQS area near SANCERRE. GAMAY and PINOT NOIR for light reds and rosés. Top producers: Lanoix and Cave des Vins de Châteaumeillant.

Châteauneuf-du-Pape S Rh r (w) ★★★ 78' 79 80 81' 83 85 86 88 89' 90' 93 94 95' 96 98' 99' 00' 01 8,200 acres near Avignon with core of 30 or so domaines for v fine wines (quality more variable over remaining 90). Mix of up to 13 varieties led by GRENACHE, SYRAH, MOURVEDRE. The best are dark, strong, exceptionally long-lived. Whites either fruity and zesty or rather heavy: many now "DYA". Top growers incl Ch'x DE BEAUCASTEL, FORTIA, Gardine, MONT REDON, LA NERTHE, RAYAS; Doms de Beaurenard, Bosquet des Papes, Les Cailloux, Font-de-Michelle, Pegaü, VIEUX TELEGRAPHE, Villeneuve, Henri Bonneau, Clos du Mont-Olivet, CLOS DES PAPES, Clos St-Jean, Jean Versino, Vieux Donjon, etc.

Châtillon-en-Diois Rh r p w ★ DYA Small AC of mid-Rhône. Adequate largely GAMAY reds; white (some ALIGOTE) mostly made into CLAIRETTE DE DIE.

Chave, Gérard Rh ★★★ To many the superstar grower (with his son Jean-Louis) of HERMITAGE, with 25 acres red, 12 acres white – spread over 9 hillside sites. Fleshy, v long-lived red and white (inc good red ST-JOSEPH), and also VIN DE PAILLE. Very fruity new J-L Chave brand St-Joseph bought from growers.

Chavignol Picturesque SANCERRE village with famous v'yd, Les Monts Damnés. Chalky soil gives vivid wines that age 4–5 yrs (or longer); esp from BOURGEOIS and Cotat. (Produces goats' cheese of same name.)

Chénas Beauj r ★★★ 99 00 01 02 Smallest BEAUJOLAIS CRU and one of the weightiest; n'bour to MOULIN-A-VENT and JULIENAS. Growers incl Benon, Champagnon, Charvet, Ch Chèvres, DUBOEUF, Lapierre, Robin, Trichard, co-op.

Chenin Blanc See Grapes for white wine (pages 10–16).

Chenonceau, Ch de Lo ★→★★ DYA Architectural jewel of Loire makes gd to v gd AC TOURAINE SAUV BL, CAB and CHENIN, still and sparkling. See vintages for CHEVERNY.

Chéreau-Carré ★→★★★ 85 87 88 89 90 93 95 96 97 98 99 00 01 02 Makers of some of top domaine MUSCADETS (esp Ch'x du Chasseloir, du Coing, Comte Leloup de Chasseloir). A name to follow.

Chevalier-Montrachet Burg w ★★★★ 85' 89' 90 92 95 96' 97 98 99 00 01 02 17-acre neighbour of M'RACHET making similar luxurious wine, perhaps less powerful. Incl 2.5-acre Les Demoiselles. Growers incl LATOUR, JADOT, BOUCHARD PERE, COLIN-DELEGER, LEFLAIVE, Niellon, PRIEUR.

Cheverny Lo r p w ★→★★ 95 96 97 98 99 00 01 02 Loire AC nr Chambord. Dry crisp whites from SAUV BL and CHARD. Also GAMAY, PINOT N or CAB; usually light but tasty. "Cour-Cheverny" uses the local Romorantin grape. Sp wines use CREMANT DE LOIRE and TOURAINE AC. Esp Cazin, Clos Tue-Boeuf, Huards, OISLY ET THESEE, Dom de la Desoucherie, Domaine du Moulin (Herve Villemade).

Chevillon, R ★★★ 32-acre estate at NUITS-ST-GEORGES; soft and juicy wines.

Chidaine, Francois Lo dr sw w sp ★★ Serious young Montlouis producer who has recently taken over the v'yds of Clos Baudoin (formerly Prince Poniatowski) in Vouvray. Biodynamic principles followed in both domaines.

Chignin Savoie w ★ DYA Light, soft white from Jacquère grapes for alpine summers. Chignin-Bergeron (with Roussanne grapes) is best and liveliest.

Chinon Lo r (p w) ★★→★★★ 85 86' 87 88 89' 90' 93' 95' 96 97 98 99 00 01 02 Juicy, variably rich TOURAINE CAB F. Drink cool, young; treat very good yrs like B'X. Sml quantity crisp dry CHENIN. Top growers: Bernard Baudry, Alliet, Crespin, Ch de Coulaine, COULY-DUTHEIL (CLOS de l'Echo), Druet, Ch Grille, Joguet, Lambert, Loup, Raffault.

Chiroubles Beauj r ★★★ 99 00 01 02 Good but tiny BEAUJOLAIS CRU next to FLEURIE; freshly fruity silky wine for early drinking (1–3 years). Growers incl Bouillard, Cheysson, DUBOEUF, Fourneau, Passot, Raousset, co-op.

Chorey-lès-Beaune Burg r (w) ★★ 93 95 96' 97 98 99' 01 02 Minor AC N of BEAUNE. 3 fine growers: Arnoux, Germain (Ch de Chorey), and esp TOLLOT-BEAUT.

Chusclan S Rh r p w ★→★★ 95' 96' 98' 99' 00' 01 COTES DU RHONE-VILLAGES with able co-op. Soft reds. Labels incl Cuvée de Marcoule, Les Genets, Seigneurie de Gicon. Also Ch Signac and special CUVEES from André Roux. Drink young.

Cissac HAUT-MEDOC village just west of PAUILLAC.

Clair, Bruno Burg ★★→★★★ Leading MARSANNAY estate. Vg wines from there and GEVREY-CHAMBERTIN (esp CLOS DE BEZE), FIXIN, MOREY-ST-DENIS, SAVIGNY.

Clairet Very light red wine, almost rosé. Bordeaux Clairet is an AC.

Clairette Traditional white grape of the MIDI. Its low-acid wine was a vermouth base. Revival by Terrasses de Landoc is full and zesty.

Clairette de Bellegarde Midi w ★ DYA Small AC nr Nîmes: plain neutral white.

Clairette de Die Rh w dr s/sw sp ★★ NV Popular dry or (better) semi-sweet Tradition MUSCAT-flavoured sparkling wine from pre-Alps in E Rhône; or straight dry CLAIRETTE, can age 3–4 yrs. Worth trying. Co-op, Achard-Vincent.

Clairette du Languedoc Midi w ★ DYA Nr Montpellier. Neutral dry white AC, more interest for late-harvest grapes, barrel ageing. Ch'x La Condamine Bertrand, St-André, and Cave d'Adissan looking good.

Clape, La Midi r p w ★★→★★★ CRU to note of AC COTEAUX DU LANGUEDOC. Full-bodied wines from limestone hills between Narbonne and sea. Red gains character after 2–3 yrs, whites can last even longer. Esp from Châteaux Rouquette-sur-Mer, Mire l'Etang, Pech-Céléyran, Pech-Redon, Dom de l'Hospitalet.

Claret Traditional English term for all red BORDEAUX.

Climat Burgundian word for individually named v'yd, eg BEAUNE Grèves.

Clos A term carrying some prestige, reserved for distinct (walled) v'yds, often in one ownership (esp Burgundy and ALSACE). Les Clos is CHABLIS' Grandest Cru.

Clos de Bèze See Chambertin-Clos de Bèze.

Clos de Gamot SW France ★★★ 82 83' 85 89 90' 95 96 98 (00') (01) One of the most famous CAHORS estates. Ultra-traditional, long-lived benchmark wines. New top Cuvée "Clos St. Jean" outstanding.

Clos des Lambrays Burg r ★★★ 15-acre GRAND CRU vineyard at MOREY-ST-DENIS. Great potential here, now at last being realized.

Clos des Mouches Burg r w ★★★ Splendid PREMIER CRU BEAUNE v'yd, largely owned by DROUHIN. White and red wines, spicy and memorable – and consistent.

Clos des Papes S Rh r w ★★★ Vg 79-acre (18 plots) CH'NEUF estate. Usually long-lived, stylish reds (mainly GRENACHE, MOURVEDRE) and whites (5–10 yrs).

Clos de la Roche Burg r ★★★ 78' 85' 88 89' 90' 91 93' 95 96' 97 98 99' 00 01 02 MOREY-ST-DENIS GRAND CRU (38-acres). Powerful and complex like CHAMBERTIN. Esp Amiot, BOUCHARD PERE, Bourée, DUJAC, LEROY, G. Lignier, PONSOT, REMY, ROUSSEAU.

France entries also cross-refer to Châteaux of Bordeaux section, pages 80–105.

Clos du Roi Burg r ★★★ Part of GRAND CRU CORTON. Also a BEAUNE PREMIER CRU.

Clos Rougeard Lo r (SW) ★★★ 85 86 87 88 89 90 93 94 95 96 97 98 99 00 01 02Controversial SAUMUR-CHAMPIGNY; cult following. Intense wines aged in new (or nearly new) B'x barrels. Also tiny amount of luscious COTEAUX DE SAUMUR.

Clos St-Denis Burg r ★★★ 78 85' 88 89' 90' 91 93' 95 96' 97 98 99' 00 01 02 16-acre GRAND CRU at MOREY-ST-DENIS. Splendid sturdy wine growing silky with age. Growers incl Bertagna, DUJAC, G. Lignier, PONSOT.

Clos Ste-Hune Al w ★★★★ V fine austere RIES from TRIMBACH; perhaps ALSACE'S best. Needs 5$^+$ yrs age; doesn't need GRAND CRU status.

Clos St-Jacques Burg r ★★★ 78' 85' 88 89' 90' 91 93' 95 96' 97 98 99' 00 01 02 17-acre GEVREY-CHAMBERTIN PREMIER CRU. Excellent powerful velvety long-ager, often better (and dearer) than some GRANDS CRUS, esp by ESMONIN and ROUSSEAU.

Clos St-Jean Burg r (w) ★★ 88 89' 90' 91 95 96' 97 98 99' 01 02 36-acre PREMIER CRU of CHASSAGNE-M. Vg red, more solid than subtle, eg Ch de la Maltroye. NB RAMONET.

Clos de Tart Burg r ★★★ 85' 88' 89' 90' 93 95 96' 97 98 99' 00 01 02 GRAND CRU at MOREY-ST-DENIS, owned by MOMMESSIN. At best wonderfully fragrant, young or old.

Clos de Vougeot Burg r ★★★ 78' 85' 88 89' 90' 91 92 93' 95 96' 97 98 99' 00 01 02 124-acre COTE DE NUITS GRAND CRU with many owners. Variable, occasionally sublime. Maturity depends on the grower's philosophy, technique, and position. Top growers incl CH DE LA TOUR, DROUHIN, ENGEL, FAIVELEY, GRIVOT, GROS, HUDELOT-NOELLAT, JADOT, LEROY, Chantal Lescure, MEO-CAMUZET, MUGNERET, VOUGERAIE.

Coche-Dury Burg ★★★★ 21-acre MEURSAULT dom (& 1 acre+ of CORTON-CHARLEMAGNE) with the highest reputation for oak-perfumed wines. Even MEURSAULT Villages is great (with age). Also vg ALIGOTE and reds.

Cognac Town and region of the Charentes, W France, and its brandy.

Colin-Deléger Burg ★★★ Leading CHASSAGNE-MONTRACHET estate. Superb, but rare PULIGNY-MONTRACHET Les Caillerets.

Collines Rhodaniennes S Rh r w p ★ Popular, lively Rhône VDP. Also young vine CÔTE-RÔTIE Mainly reds: Merlot, SYRAH, GAMAY. Some Viognier & CHARD.

Collioure Pyr r ★★ 95 96 97 98 99 00 01 02 Strong dry red from BANYULS area. Tiny production. Top growers incl Le CLOS des Paulilles, Doms du Mas Blanc, de la Rectorie, La Tour Vieille, Vial-Magnères.

Comté Tolosan SW r p w ★ DYA Vin de Pays. Covers multitude of sins and whole of Southwest. Mostly co-op wines. Pioneering ★★ DOM DE RIBONNET (Christian Gerber, S of Toulouse) for range of varietal wines, some long keepers.

Condrieu N Rh w ★★★ 99' 00 01 Soft fragrant white of great character (and price) from Viognier. Can be outstanding but rapid growth of v'yd (now 250 acres worked by 90 growers) has made quality more variable. Increased use of young oak (eg GUIGAL's Doriane CUVEE, Cuilleron, Villard) is a doubtful move. Best growers: Y Cuilleron, DELAS, Dumazet, Gangloff, GUIGAL, JABOULET, André Perret, Niéro, Vernay (esp long-lived Coteau de Vernon), Verzier. CHATEAU-GRILLET: similar. Dubious move to VENDANGE TARDIVE by some growers.

Confuron, J-J Burg r ★★★ Tiny NUITS-S-G estate to follow. Modern-style, full of fruit.

Corbières Midi r (p w) ★★ →★★★ 90 91 92 93 94 95 96 97 98 99 00 01 02 Vigorous bargain reds from warm stony AC. Best: Ch'x Aiguilloux, Lastours, des Ollieux, Les Palais, de la Voulte Gasparet, Doms de Fontsainte, du Vieux Parc, de Villemajou. Co-ops: Embrès-et-Castelmaure, Camplong, St-Laurent-Cabrerisse.

Cordier, Ets D Important BORDEAUX shipper and château-owner with wonderful track-record, now owned by Groupe Val d'Orbieu-Listel. Over 600 acres. Incl Ch'x CANTEMERLE, LAFAURIE-PEYRAGUEY, MEYNEY, etc.

Cornas N Rh r ★★→★★★ 83' 85' 86 88' 89' 90' 91' 93 94' 95' 96 97' 98' 99' 00' 01' 02 Sturdy, mineral-edged v dark SYRAH wine from 215-acre steep granite v'yds S of HERMITAGE. Needs to age 5–15 yrs but always keeps its rustic character. Top: Allemand, Colombo (beware: new oak), Clape, Courbis,

DELAS, Dumien-Serrette, Juge, Lionnet, JABOULET (esp St-Pierre CUVÉE), Tardieu-Laurent (modern, expensive), N Verset, Voge.

Corrèze Dordogne r ★ DYA VDP from Co-op of Branceilles, between Brive and Beaulieu. Also Dom de la Mégénie.

Corsica (Vin de Corse) Strong wines of all colours. ACS are: AJACCIO and PATRIMONIO and better crus Cap Corse and Calvi. VIN DE PAYS: ILE DE BEAUTE.

Corton Burg r ★★★ 78' 85' 88 89' 90' 91 93 95 96' 97 98 99' 00 01 02 The only GRAND CRU red of the CÔTE DE BEAUNE. 200 acres in ALOXE-C incl CLOS DU ROI, Les Bressandes. Rich & powerful, should age well. Many good growers.

Corton-Charlemagne Burg w ★★★★ 85' 86 88 89' 90' 92' 95 96' 97 98 99' 00' 01 02 White section (½) of CORTON. Rich, spicy, lingering, the Grand Cru Chablis of the Côte d'Or; ages like a red. Top growers: BONNEAU DU MARTRAY, Chapuis, COCHE-DURY, Delarche, Dubreuil-Fontaine, FAIVELEY, HOSPICES DE BEAUNE, JADOT, LATOUR, Rapet, Rollin, Javillier, VOUGERAIE.

Costières de Nîmes S Rh r p w ★→★★ 95 96 97 98' 99 00' 01' 02 Rhône delta AC; fast-improving quality, from best names (best reds: 6-8 yrs). Formerly Costières du Gard. Ch'x de Campuget, Grande Cassagne, Mourgues-du-Grès, de Nages (esp Joseph Torres), de la Tuilerie, Mas des Bressades, Dom du Vieux Relais.

> **Côte(s)** Means hillside; generally a superior vineyard to those on the plain. Many ACs are prefixed by "Côtes" or "Coteaux", meaning the same. In St-Emilion, distinguishes valley slopes from higher plateaus.

Côte de Beaune Burg r w ★★→★★★★ Used geographically: the southern half of the COTE D'OR. Applies as an AC only to parts of BEAUNE itself.

Côte de Beaune-Villages Burg r ★★ 95 96' 97 98 99' 01 02 Regional APPELLATION for lesser wines of classic area. Cannot be labelled "Côte de Beaune" without either "-Villages" or village name added.

Côte de Brouilly Beauj r ★★ 98 99 00 01 Fruity rich BEAUJ CRU. One of best. Esp from: Dom de Chavanne, G Cotton, Ch Delachanel, J-C Nesme, Ch Thivin.

Côte Chalonnaise Burg r w sp ★★ V'yd area between BEAUNE and MACON. See also BOUZERON, GIVRY, MERCUREY, MONTAGNY, RULLY. Alias "Région de Mercurey".

Côte de Nuits Burg r (w) ★★→★★★★ N half of COTE D'OR. Mostly red wine.

Côte de Nuits-Villages Burg r (w) ★★ 93 95 96' 97 98 99' 00 01 02 A junior AC for extreme N and S ends of COTE DE N; well worth investigating for bargains.

Côte d'Or Département name applied to the central and principal Burgundy v'yd slopes: COTE DE BEAUNE and COTE DE NUITS. The name is not used on labels.

Côte Roannaise Central France r p ★→★★ 95 96 97 98 99 00 01 02 AC W of Lyon. Silky, focused GAMAY. Doms Demon, Lapandéry, du Pavillon, des Millets.

Côte-Rôtie N Rh r ★★★→★★★★ 78' 83' 85' 88' 89' 90' 91' 94' 95' 96' 97 98' 99' 00' 01 Finest Rhône red, from south of Vienne, mainly SYRAH; can achieve rich, complex softness and finesse with age (especially 5 to 10[+] years). Top growers include Barge, Bernard, Burgaud, Champet, CHAPOUTIER, Clusel-Roch (improving fast), DELAS, Gaillard, J-M Gérin, GUIGAL (long oak-ageing, different and fuller), JABOULET, Jamet, Jasmin, Ogier, ROSTAING (oak here, too), VIDAL-FLEURY.

Coteaux d'Affreux Aspiring to VDP status. Should perhaps use grapes as base.

Coteaux d'Aix-en-Provence Prov r p w ★→★★★ AC on the move. Top properties incl Ch'x Bas, Revelette, Calissanne and Domaine des Béates (CHAPOUTIER-owned). See also Baux-en-Provence.

Coteaux d'Ancenis Lo r p w (sw) ★ DYA VDQS E Of Nantes. Light GAMAY r's and p's, sharpish dry w's (CHENIN). Semi-sw from Malvoisie (ages well) – esp Guindon.

Coteaux de l'Ardèche See l'Ardèche.

Coteaux de l'Aubance Lo w sw ★★→★★★★ 88' 89' 90' **93'** 94' **95'** 96 97 98 99 **00 01** 02 Similar to C'x DU LAYON, nervy sw wines from CHENIN. A few SELECTION DES GRAINS NOBLES. Esp from Bablut, Haute-Perche, Montgilet, RICHOU, Rochelles.

Coteaux des Baronnies S Rh r p w ★ DYA Rhône VIN DE PAYS near Nyons. SYRAH, Merlot, CAB S, CHARD, plus trad grapes. Promising. Dom du Rieu-Frais (incl gd Viognier) and Dom Rosière (incl gd Syrah) worth noting.

Côteaux de Chalosse SW France r p w ★ DYA. Good country wines from co-op at Mugron (Landes).

Coteaux Champenois Champ r w (p) ★★★ DYA (whites) AC for non-sp CHAMP. Vintages (if mentioned) follow those for Champ. Not worth inflated prices.

Coteaux du Giennois Lo r p w ★ DYA Sm area N of POUILLY promoted to AC in 98. Light red: blend of GAMAY and PINOT; SAUV à la SANCERRE. Top grower: Paulat.

Coteaux de Glanes SW France r ★ DYA Lively VDP from nr Bretenoux (Lot). Co-op only producer. Mostly drunk in local restaurants.

Coteaux du Languedoc Midi r p w ★★→★★★ 95 96 97 **98 99** 00 01 Scattered well-above-ordinary MIDI AC areas. Best reds (eg LA CLAPE, FAUGERES, St-Georges-d'Orques, Quatourze, ST-CHINIAN, Montpeyroux, PIC ST-LOUP) age for 2–4 yrs. Now also some good whites. Standards rising dizzily.

Coteaux du Layon Lo w s/sw sw ★★→★★★★ 75 76 **85'** 86 88' **89'** 90' **93'** 94 95 96 **97 98 99** 00 01 02 The heart of ANJOU, S of Angers: sw CHENIN; admirable acidity, ageing almost forever. New SELECTION DES GRAINS NOBLES; cf ALSACE. 7 villages can add name to AC. Top ACs: BONNEZEAUX, C du LAYON-Chaume (1ST GRAND CRU), QUARTS DE CHAUME. Growers incl Badouin, BAUMARD, Dom de la Bergerie, Cady, Delhumeau (Dme de Brize) Delesvaux, des Forges, Dme de Juchepie, Ogereau, Papin (CH DE PIERRE-BISE), Jo Pithon, Yves Soulez (Genaiserie), P-Y Tijou (Soucherie), du Breuil.

Coteaux du Loir Lo r p w dr sw ★→★★★ 76 85 88' 89' 90' **92** 93' **95 96** 97 98 99 **00 01** 02 Small region N of Tours, incl JASNIERES. Sometimes fine CHENIN, GAMAY, Pineau d'Aunis, CAB. Top growers: Chaussard, de Rycke, Fresneau, Gigou, Nicolas, Robinot. The Loir is a tributary of the Loire.

Coteaux de la Loire See Anjou-Coteaux de la Loire.

Coteaux du Lyonnais Beauj r p (w) ★ DYA Junior BEAUJOLAIS. Best EN PRIMEUR.

Coteaux de Peyriac Midi r p ★ DYA One of the most-used VIN DE PAYS names of the Aude département. Huge quantities.

Coteaux de Pierrevert S Rh r p w sp ★ Gd, early drinking co-op reds, rosés, fresh whites from nr Manosque. Dom la Blaque, Ch Régusse Ch Rousset: fuller reds. Promoted to AC 98.

Coteaux du Quercy SW France r ★→★★ **96** 98 99 00 (01) S of CAHORS promoted to VDQS and now queuing for AC. Private growers working alongside vg co-op near Monpezat incl Doms de la Combarade, la Garde, d'Aries, de Guyot, de Lafage, de Merchien.

Coteaux de Saumur Lo w sw ★★→★★★ **89 90 93** 95' 96 **97 98 99** 02 Rare potentially fine s/sw CHENIN. VOUVRAY-like sw (MOELLEUX) best. Esp CLOS ROUGEARD, Lavigne, Legrand.

Coteaux et Terrasses de Montauban SW France r p ★→★★ Dominated by co-op at LAVILLEDIEU-LE-TEMPLE. Better from Doms de Biarnès and de Montels.

Coteaux du Tricastin S Rh r p w ★★ 95' 97 98' **99' 00'** 01' Fringe mid-RHONE AC of increasing quality. Attractively spiced red can age 8 yrs. Dom de Grangeneuve, Dom de Montine, Dom St-Luc, Ch La Décelle among best.

Coteaux Varois Prov r p w ★→★★ Substantial AC zone: California-style Dom de St-Jean de Villecroze makes vg red, also CHX ROUTAS, la Calisse, Doms les Alysses, du Defends.

Coteaux du Vendômois Lo r p w ★→★★ DYA Fringe Loire VDQS west of Vendôme. Pineau d'Aunis is the key grape alone or with others, in rosés, reds and with CHENIN in whites. Promoted to AC in 2000. Producers incl Dom du Four à Chaux, Cave du Vendôme-Villiers, Patrice Colin, Emile Heredia.

Côtes d'Auvergne Central Fr r p (w) ★→★★ DYA Flourishing small VDQS. Mainly GAMAY; also PINOT NOIR, CHARDONNAY. Producers include Boulin-Constant, Bellard, Cave St-Verny, Dom de Peyra.

Côtes de Blaye B'x w ★ DYA Run-of-the-mill B'x white from BLAYE.

Côtes de Bordeaux St-Macaire B'x w dr sw ★ DYA From E of SAUTERNES.

Côtes de Bourg B'x r ★→★★ 89' 94 95 96 **98 99** 00' 01 APPELLATION used for many of the better reds of BOURG. Ch'x incl DE BARBE, DU BOUSQUET, Brûlesécaille, Bujan, Falfas, Fougas, Grand-Jour, Guerry, Haut-Guirand, Haut-Maco, Haut-Mondésir, Mercier, Nodoz, Peychaud, Roc de Cambes, Rousset, Sociondo, Tayac.

Côtes du Brulhois SW France r p (w) ★→★★ **98 99 00** 01 Nr Agen. Mostly centred on Goulens and Donzac coops. Also Dom de Coujétou-Peyret.

Côtes de Castillon B'x r ★→★★ **89** 90' 94 95' **96' 98 99** 00' 01 Flourishing region just E of ST-EMILION; similar, often lighter wines. Best CHX incl de l'A, d'Aiguilhe, de Belcier, Cap de Faugères, La Clarière-Laithwaite, Clos l'Eglise, PITRAY, Robin, Ste-Colombe, Veyry, Vieux Château Champs de Mars.

Côtes de Duras Dordogne r w p ★→★★ **98 99 00** (01) B'x satellite; mostly lighter wines. Top producers incl Doms de Laulan (gd SAUV), de Durand (bio), de la Solle, du Vieux Bourg, Amblard, Petit Malrome, Clos du Cadaret, Ch La Grave Béchade. Gd co-op.

Côtes de Forez Lo r p (sp) ★ DYA Uppermost Loire VDQS (GAMAY), around Boën, N of St-Etienne. Promoted to AC 00, but hardly worth bothering with.

Côtes de Francs B'x r w ★★ **89' 90' 94 95 96** 97 98 00' 01 Fringe BORDEAUX from E of ST-EMILION. Increasingly attractive tasty wines, esp from Châteaux Charmes-Godard, Laclaverie, de Francs, Marsau, PUYGUERAUD, La Prade.

Côtes du Frontonnais SW France r p ★★ **98 99** 00 01' S'times called the "BEAUJOLAIS of Toulouse". DYA but reds with CAB need longer. Gd growers Doms de Caze, Joliet, du Roc, and Ch'x Bellevue-la-Forêt, Boujac, Bouissel, Cahuzac, Coutinel, Plaisance, and St-Guilhem give the gd co-op a hard time keeping up.

Côtes de Gascogne SW w (r p) ★ DYA VDP branch of ARMAGNAC. Remarkably popular, led by Plaimont co-op and Grassa family (Ch de Tariquet etc). Best-known for fresh fruity whites based on the Colombard grape, often with some Gros Manseng. Variable from dull to zingy: Domaines de Joy, Papolle, Bergerayre, Maubet, Sancet, and Château Monluc, and many others.

Côtes du Jura r p w (sp) ★ DYA Many light tints/tastes. ARBOIS more substantial.

Côtes du Lubéron S Rh r p w ★→★★ 97 98' **99'** 00' 01 02 Spectacularly improved country wines from S RHONE. A proliferation of new producers including actors and media-magnates. Star is Château de la Canorgue, with very good largely SYRAH red, and whites (especially Viognier) as well. Others include Chx Val-Joanis, La Verrerie, de l'Isolette, Dom de la Citadelle, Verget, Vieille Ferme (white) and reliable co-ops Cellier de Marrenon, Cave de Bonnieux.

Côtes de la Malepère Midi r ★ DYA Rising star VDQS on frontier of MIDI and SW, nr Limoux using grape varieties from both. Watch for fresh eager reds.

Côtes du Marmandais Dordogne r p w ★→★★ **98 99** 00' 01 Improving, ever more serious AC. Cocumont co-op better than Beaupuy. Chante Coucou Clos Bacqueys, La Verrerie, Ch de Beaulieu, and Dom des Geais better still, weightier and need more ageing.

Côtes de Montravel Dordogne w dr sw ★★ dr DYA sw 97 **98 99** 01 Part of BERGERAC; traditionally med-sw, now often drier. Gd from Ch'x de Montaigne, Pique-Sègue, La Raye, La Resssaudie, Doms de Golse, de Perreau. Montravel SEC is dry, HAUT-MONTRAVEL sw.

Côtes de Provence Prov r p w ★→★★★ Revolutionized by new attitudes and investment. Castel Roubine, Commanderie de Peyrassol, Doms Bernarde, de la Courtade, OTT, des Planes, Rabiéga, Richeaume, Ch Ste Rosaline are leaders. 75% rosé, 20% red, 5% white. See also Coteaux d'Aix, Bandol, etc.

Côtes du Rhône S Rh r p w ★ 95' 98' 99 00' 01' Basic Rhône AC. Best drunk young – even as PRIMEUR. Wide variations of quality: some heavy over-production. Look for estate bottlings. See Côtes du Rhône-Villages.

Côtes du Rhône-Villages S Rh r p w ★→★★ 89' 90' 95' 96' 97' 98' 99' 00' 01' Wine of the 17 best S Rhône villages. Substantial and mainly reliable; s'times delicious. Red base is GRENACHE; but more SYRAH and MOURVEDRE now used. Growing white quality, often with Viognier, Roussanne. See Beaumes-de-Venise, Cairanne, Chusclan, Laudun, Rasteau, Sablet, Séguret, St-Gervais, etc. Sub-category with non-specified village name: gd value eg Ch. Signac, Doms Cabotte, Grand Veneur, Montbayon, Rabasse-Charavin, Renjarde, Romarins, Ste-Anne, St Siffrein, Cave Estézargues.

> Top Côtes du Rhône producers: Ch'x Courac, La Couranςonne, l'Estagnol, Fonsalette, Grand Moules, Hugues, Montfaucon, St-Esteve and Trignon (incl Viognier); Clos Simian; Co-ops Chantecotes (Ste-Cécile-les-Vignes), Villedieu (esp white); Doms La Bouvade, Charvin, Coudoulet de Beaucastel (red & white), Cros de la Mûre, Gourget, Gramenon (Grenache, Viognier), Janasse, Jaume, Perrin, Réméjeanne, St-Georges, Vieille Julienne, Vieux Chêne; Guigal, Jaboulet.

Côtes du Roussillon Pyr r p w ★→★★ 95 96 97 **98** 99 00 01 E Pyrenees AC. Hefty Carignan r best, can be v tasty (eg Gauby). Some whites.

Côtes du Roussillon-Villages Pyr r ★★ 95 96 97 **98** 99 00 01 02 Region's best reds, 28 communes incl CARAMANY, LATOUR DE FRANCE, LESQUERDE, Tautavel. Best labels: Co-op Baixas, Cazes Frères, Doms des Chênes, la Cazenove, Gauby (incl full, exotic white), Ch de Jau, Co-op Lesquerde, Dom Piquemal, Co-op Les Vignerons Catalans. Some now renounce AC status to make varietal VDP's.

Côtes de St-Mont SW France r w p ★★ (r) **98** 99 00' 01' Highly successful Gers VDQS still seeking AC status, imitating MADIRAN, PACHERENC. Co-op Plaimont all-powerful (Vihnes Retrouvées and Hauts de Bergelle ranges, Ch de Sabazan) sw Cuvée Saint-Albert (★★★) outstanding. Growers incl Ch de Bergalasse, Dom de Bartat, Dom Maouries.

Côtes du Tarn SW France VDP r p w ★ DYA overlaps GAILLAC; from same growers esp co-ops, Ch de Vigné-Lourac, Doms de Labarthe and d'Escausses.

Côtes de Thongue Midi r w ★ DYA Popular VDP from HERAULT. Dynamic area with some good wines esp Doms Arjolle, les Chemins de Bassac, Coussergues, Croix Belle, Magellan, Montmarin.

Côtes de Toul E France (Lorraine) p r w ★ DYA V light wines; mainly VIN GRIS.

Côtes du Ventoux S Rh r p (w) ★★ 95' 96 97 98' 99' 00' **01'** Booming (15,000-acre) AC between Rhône and PROVENCE for tasty reds (from café-style to much deeper flavours), easy rosés, and some decent whites. NB. La Vieille Ferme (only red), owned by J-P Perrin of CH DE BEAUCASTEL; Co-op Bedoin, Goult, St-Didier, domaine Anges, Brusset, Fondrèche, Font-Sane, Murmuriem, Verrière, Ch'x La Croix des Pins, Pesquié, Valcombe, and PAUL JABOULET are gd too.

Côtes du Vivarais S Rh r p w ★ 98' **99' 00'** 01' DYA 2,500 acres across several villages W of Montélimar; promoted to AC 99. Improving simple CUVEES; more substantial oak-aged reds. Best producers: Boulle, Gallety, Dom de Belvezet.

Coulée de Serrant Lo w dr sw ★★★★ 76' 78 79' 81 82 83' 85' 86 88 89' 90' 91 92 **93** 95' **96 97 98 99** 00 01 02 16-acre CHENIN v'yd on Loire's N bank at SAVENNIERES run on ferociously biodynamic principles. Intense strong fruity/sharp wine, good aperitif and with fish. Ages almost for ever.

Couly-Dutheil Lo r p w ★★→★★★ 85 86 87 88 **89** 90 **93** 95 96 97 **98** 99 00 01 02 Major CHINON grower/merchant; range of reliable wines – CLOS d'Olive and l'Echo: top wines. New CUVEE, Crescendo (oak-aged).

Courcel, Dom ★★★ Leading POMMARD estate – top PREMIER CRU Rugiens.

Crémant In CHAMP meant "creaming" (half-sparkling). Since 75, an AC for quality classic-method sparkling from ALSACE, Loire, BOURGOGNE and most recently LIMOUX – often a bargain. Term no longer used in Champagne.

Crémant de Loire Lo w sp ★★ →★★★ NV High quality sp, esp SAUMUR and TOURAINE. BAUMARD Berger, Delhumeau (Dme de Brizel), LANGLOIS-CHATEAU, Nerleux, Passavant.

Crépy Savoie w ★★ DYA Light, soft, Swiss-style white from S shore of Lake Geneva. "Crépitant" has been coined for its faint fizz.

Crozes-Hermitage N Rh r (w) ★★ 85' 88 89' 90' 91' 94 95' **96'** 97' 98' 99' **00'** Nr HERMITAGE: larger v'yds, SYRAH wine with fewer dimensions. Some is fruity, early-drinking (2^+ yrs); some cask-aged (wait 4–8 yrs). Gd examples from Belle, B Chave, Ch Curson, Desmeure, Doms du Colombier, des Entrefaux, du Pavillon-Mercurol, de Thalabert of JABOULET, CHAPOUTIER, Fayolle, Alain Graillot. Drink whites (mostly Marsanne) young.

Cruse et Fils Frères Historic BORDEAUX shipper. Now owned by Pernod-Ricard. The Cruse family (not the company) owns CH D'ISSAN.

Cunac SW France ★ r DYA Part of GAILLAC area. Light, fruity, quaffable reds.

Cussac Village S of ST-JULIEN. (AC HAUT-MEDOC.) Top ch'x: BEAUMONT, LANESSAN.

Cuve Close Short-cut method of making sparkling wine in a tank. Sparkle dies away in glass much quicker than with METHODE TRADITIONELLE wine.

Cuvée Wine contained in a cuve, or vat. A word of many uses, including synonym for "blend" and first-press wines (as in CHAMPAGNE); in Burgundy interchangeable with "cru". Often just refers to a "lot" of wine.

Dagueneau, Didier Lo ★★★ 88 89 90 91 92 93 94 95 96 97 98 99 **00 01 02** Top POUILLY-FUME producer. Pouilly's *enfant terrible* has created new benchmarks for the AC and for SAUV. Top CUVEE is barrel-fermented Silex. Serge D, another top producer, is Didier's uncle.

Daumas Gassac See Mas de Daumas Gassac.

De Castellane Brut NV; Blanc de Blancs; Brut (**95** 96 96); Cuvée Commodore Brut (**90** 95); Prestige Florens de Castellane (**90** 95 96). Trad Epernay CHAMP house linked with LAURENT-P. Best for vintage wines; esp Commodore.

Degré alcoolique Degrees of alcohol, ie percent by volume.

Deiss, Domaine Marcel Fine ALSACE grower at Bergheim with 50 acres, wide range incl splendid RIES (GRAND CRU Schoenenberg), GEWÜRZ (Altenburg de Bergheim), good SELECTION DES GRAINS NOBLES and VIN DE PAILLE.

Delamotte Brut; Bl de Blancs (**95** 96 98); Cuvée Nicolas Delamotte Fine sml CHARDY-dominated CHAMPAGNE house at Le Mesnil, owned by LAURENT-PERRIER.

Delas Frères ★→★★★★ Old, worthy firm of Rhône specialists with v'yds at CONDRIEU, COTE-ROTIE, HERMITAGE. Top wines: Condrieu, Hermitage, Marquise de Tourette (red/white), St Joseph Challeys gd values. Owned by ROEDERER. Quality rising.

Delbeck Small fine CHAMP house revitalized by Martin/Giraudière partners since 95. Plenty of PINOT N in blend. Excellent vintage wines (**90** 95 96) and Grand Cru Ay, Cramant and Bouzy. Also owns Bricout.

Delorme, André ★★ Leading COTE CHALONNAISE merchants and growers. Specialists in vg CREMANT DE BOURGOGNE and excellent RULLY, etc.

Demi-Sec Half-dry: in practice more than half sweet (eg of CHAMP).

Des Guelasses, Dom Source of much restaurant house wine, most in pubs and theatre bars.

Deutz Brut Classic NV; Rosé NV; Brut (**95** 96 98); Rosé (97); Bl de Bls (**95** 96). One of top small CHAMP houses, ROEDERER-owned. V dry, classic wines. Superb CUVEE William Deutz (**90** 95 96).

Dirler, J-P Al ★★→★★★ Producer of GRAND CRUS Kessler, Saering. Spiegel; esp RIES.

Dom Pérignon, Cuvée 85 88 90 92 93 95 96; Rosé 90 95 96 Luxury CUVÉE of MOET & CHANDON (launched 1936), named after the legendary abbey cellarmaster who first blended CHAMP. Astonishing consistent quality and creamy character, esp with 10–15 yrs bottle-age. New limited release of five recently disgorged vintages (93 85 80 73).

Domaine Property, particularly in Burgundy and rural France.

Dopff & Irion ★→★★ Famous Riquewihr (ALSACE) business. Esp MUSCAT les Amandiers, RIES Les Murailles, GEWÜRZ Les Sorcières, PINOT Gr Les Maquisards: long-lived. Good CREMANT d'Alsace. Now part of PFAFFENHEIM co-op.

Dopff au Moulin ★★ Ancient top-class family wine house at Riquewihr, ALSACE. Best: GEWÜRZ: GRAND CRUS BRAND and Sporen, RIES SCHOENENBOURG, Sylvaner de Riquewihr. Pioneers of Alsace sp wine; good CUVÉES: Bartholdi and Julien.

Dourthe Frères B'X merchant with wide range: good CRUS BOURGEOIS, incl BELGRAVE, MAUCAILLOU, TRONQUOY-LALANDE. Beau-Mayne is well-made brand.

Doux Sweet.

Drappier, André Leading AUBE region CHAMP house. Family-run. Vinous NV, Brut Zéro, Rosé Saignée, Carte d'Or (95 96 98), Signature Bl de Bl (95 96 98), Sumptuous prestige CUVÉE Grande Sendrée (90 95 96).

Drouhin, J & Cie Burg ★★★→★★★★ Deservedly prestigious grower (150 acres) and merchant with highest standards. Cellars in BEAUNE; v'yds in Beaune, CHABLIS, CLOS DE VOUGEOT, MUSIGNY, etc, and Oregon, USA. Top wines incl (esp) (w) BEAUNE-CLOS DES MOUCHES, CHABLIS LES CLOS, CORTON-CHARLEMAGNE, PULIGNY-M'RACHET, Les Folatières (r) GRIOTTE-CHAMBERTIN, MUSIGNY.

Duboeuf, Georges ★★ →★★★ The Grand Fromage of BEAUJOLAIS. Top-class merchant at Romanèche-Thorin. Region's leader in every sense; huge range of admirable wines. Also MOULIN-A-VENT atypically aged in new oak, white MACONNAIS, etc.

Dubos High-level BORDEAUX NEGOCIANT.

Duclot BORDEAUX NEGOCIANT; top-growth specialist. Linked with J-P MOUEIX.

Dugat Burg ★★★ Cousins Claude and Bernard both make excellent, deep coloured wines in GEVREY CHAMBERTIN under their respective labels.

Dujac, Domaine ★★★ Burg grower (Jacques Seysses) at MOREY-ST-DENIS with v'yds in that village and BONNES-MARES, ECHEZEAUX, GEVREY-CHAMBERTIN, etc. Splendidly vivid and long-lived wines. Now also buying grapes in MEURSAULT, and venture with other grapes in COTEAUX VAROIS.

Dulong Highly competent BORDEAUX merchant. Breaking all the rules with unorthodox Rebelle blends. Also VINS DE PAYS.

Durup, Jean Burg ★★ One of the biggest CHABLIS growers with 375 acres, including Domaine de l'Eglantière and admirable Ch de Maligny.

Duval-Leroy Fleur de Champagne Brut NV and vg Rosé de Saignée NV; Extra Brut; Brut 95 96; Bl de Bls 95 96; Prestige Cuvée des Rois 95 96. Rising Côte des Bl house; fine quality, gd value. Many other labels.

Echézeaux Burg r ★★★ 78' 85' 88 89' 90' 91 93 95 96' 97 98 99' 00 01 02 74-acre GRAND CRU between VOSNE-ROMANEE and CLOS DE VOUGEOT. Can be superlative, fragrant, without great weight, eg Confuron-Cotetidot, DUJAC ENGEL, GOuroux, GRIVOT, A F GROS, MUGNERET, DRC, RION, ROUGET.

Ecu, Dom de l' Lo dr w r ★★★ 85 86 87 88 89 90 93 95 96 97 98 99 00 01 02 Outstanding producer of MUSCADET DE SEVRE ET MAINE as well as delicious GROS PLANT DU PAYS NANTAIS. Cab rivals many SAUMUR-CHAMPIGNY. Biodynamic.

Edelzwicker Alsace w ★ DYA Modest blended light white.

d'Eguisheim, Cave Vinicole ★ Very good ALSACE co-op: fine GRAND CRUS Hatschbourg, Hengst, Ollwiller and Spiegel. Owns Willm. Top label: WOLFBERGER (65% of production). Best ranges: Grande Réserve, Sigillé and Armorié. Good CREMANT and PINOT.

Engel, R ★★★ Top-class grower of CL DE VOUGEOT, ECHEZEAUX, GRANDS-ECH'X, VOSNE-ROM.

Entraygues SW France r p w DYA ★ Fragrant country VDQS. Esp F Avallon's dry w.

Entre-Deux-Mers B'x w ★→★★ DYA Improving dry white B'x from between Rivers Garonne and Dordogne (aka E-2-M). Esp Ch'x BONNET, Fontenille, Moulin de Launay, Sainte-Marie, Tour de Mirambeau, Toutigeac, Turcaud, etc.

Esmonin, Sylvie Burg ★★★ V classy GEVREY-CHAMBERTIN esp CLOS ST-JACQUES.

Estaing SW France r p w ★ DYA Neighbour of ENTRAYGUES and similar in style.

L'Estandon Brand name of everyday wine of Nice (AC COTES DE PROVENCE): all colours.

l'Etoile Jura w dr sp (sw) ★★ Subregion of the JURA known for stylish whites, incl VIN JAUNE, similar to CHATEAU-CHALON; good sparkling.

Faiveley, J Burg ★★→★★★★ Family-owned growers and merchants at NUITS-ST-GEORGES, with v'yds (270 acres) in CHAMBERTIN-CLOS DE BEZE, CHAMBOLLE-MUSIGNY, CORTON, MERCUREY, NUITS (74 acres). Consistent high quality (rather than charm).

Faller, Théo/Domaine Weinbach Top ALSACE grower (Kaysersberg) run by Mme Colette Faller and her two daughters. Concentrated wines needing long ageing, up to 10 yrs. Esp GRAND CRUS SCHLOSSBERG (RIES), Furstentum (GEWÜRZ).

Faugères Midi r (p w) ★★ 95 96 97 **98 99** 00 01 Isolated C'TX DU LANGUEDOC village with above-average wine and exceptional terroir. Gained AC status 82. Esp Dom Alquier, Dom Barral de Météore, Dom des Estanilles, Ch La Liquière.

Fesles, de Lo r w sw p ★★→★★★ **93 94 95 96 97 98 00** 02 Historic estate in Bonnezeaux producing the entire range of Anjou wines. Encompasses Coteaux de Layon Chateau la Guimonière and la Roulerie.

Fessy, Sylvain Beauj ★★ Dynamic BEAUJOLAIS merchant with wide range.

Fèvre, William Burg ★★★ CHABLIS grower with the biggest GRAND CRU holding, Dom de la Maladière (45 acres). Bought 98 by HENRIOT, with immediate improvement.

Fiefs Vendéens Lo r p w ★ DYA Up-and-coming VDQS for light wines from the Vendée, just S of MUSCADET on the Atlantic coast. Wines from CHARD, CHENIN, Colombard, Grolleau, Melon (whites), CAB, PINOT N and GAMAY for reds and rosés. Esp Coirier, Ferme des Ardillers, Michon.

Filliatreau, Domaine Lo r ★★→★★★ 89 90 93 95 96 97 98 **00 01** 02 Paul Filliatreau put SAUMUR-CHAMPIGNY on map and in Paris restaurants. Supple, fruity, drinkable Jeunes Vignes. Other CUVEES aged 2–5 yrs (Vieille Vignes & La Grande Vignolle).

Fitou Midi r ★★ 95 96 97 **98 99** 00 01 02 Superior CORBIERES-style red wines; powerful, ageing well. Best from co-ops at Cascastel, Paziols and Tuchan. Interesting experiments with MOURVEDRE grapes in Leucate. Good estates, incl Ch Nouvelles, Dom Lérys, Rolland.

Fixin Burg r ★★★ **89'** 90' **91** 93 95 **96'** 97 98 99 01 02 Worthy and under-valued northern neighbour of GEVREY-CHAMBERTIN. Often splendid reds. Best v'yds: CLOS du Chapitre, Les Hervelets, Clos Napoléon. Growers incl Bertheau, R Bouvier, CLAIR, FAIVELEY, Gelin, Gelin-Molin, Guyard.

Fleurie Beauj r ★★★ 99 00 01 02 The epitome of a BEAUJOLAIS CRU: fruity, scented, silky, racy wines. Esp from Chapelle des Bois, Chignard, Depardon, Després, DUBOEUF, Ch de Fleurie, Métras, the co-op.

Floc de Gascogne SW France r p w ARMAGNAC's answer to PINEAU DES CHARENTES. Aperitif from unfermented grape juice blended with Armagnac.

Fortant de France Midi r p w ★→★★ VDP D'OC brand (dressed to kill) of reliable quality single-grape wines from Sète neighbourhood. See Skalli.

Frais Fresh or cool.

Frappé Ice-cold.

Froid Cold.

Fronsac B'x r ★→★★★ **85' 86' 88'** 89' 90' **94 95 96** 98 00' **01** Picturesque area; increasingly fine, often tannic r just W of ST-EM. Ch'x incl de Carles, DALEM, LA DAUPHINE, Fontenil, La Grave, Mayne-Vieil, Moulin-Haut-Laroque, LA RIVIERE, La Rousselle, La Vieille Cure, Villars. Give them time. See also Canon-Fronsac.

Frontignan Midi golden sw ★★ NV Strong, sweet, liquorous MUSCAT of ancient repute. Quality steadily improving, esp from Ch'x Stony and La Peyrade.

Furstentum (ALSACE) GRAND CRU at Kientzheim and Sigolsheim renowned for superb ripening ability. See FALLER DOM WEINBACH and PAUL BLANCK.

Gagnard, Jean-Noel Burg ★★★ Jean Noel's daughter, Caroline l'Estimé, has pushed this domaine to the top of the Gagnard clan. Beautifully expressive GRAND CRU, PREMIER CRU, and village wines in CHASSAGNE-MONTRACHET.

Gagnard-Delagrange, Jacques Burg ★★★ Estimable small (12-acre) grower of CHASSAGNE-MONTRACHET, cinluding some MONTRACHET. Most wines now made by next generation, Doms Blain-Gagnard and Fontaine-Gagnard.

A Guide to Gaillac

Good all-rounders Mas Pignou, Mas d'Aurel, Doms de Barreau, Labarthe, and d'Escausses, Ch de Mayragues, co-op at Técou (esp. "Passion" range).
Reds Doms de Cailloutis, Larroque, Pialentou, Salvy and La Chanade.
Local varieties Robert Plageoles, Doms de Ramaye, Causse-Marines (all ★★★).
Sweet whites Doms de Causse-Marines, Rotier, Long Pech, Mas de Bicary.
Dry whites Dom de Caussez, Marine, Chx d'Arlus, Vigné-Lourac.
Sparkling Doms Réné Rieux, La Tronque and Canto Perlic.
Vins de pays Dom Borie-Vieille (Muscadelle) Perlé Dom de Salmes

---

Gaillac SW France r p w dr sw sp ★→★★★ Mostly DYA except oaked reds **95** 98 **99** 00' (01), sw whites (97' **98 99 00'** 01').

Gamay See Grapes for red wine (pages 10–12).

Garage Vins de Garage are (usually) Bordeaux made on such a small scale that your garage would be big enough. Each bottle costs much the same as a full service.

Gard, Vin de Pays du Languedoc ★ The Gard département at the mouth of the Rhône is a centre of gd VDP production, incl Coteaux Flaviens, Pont du Gard, Cévennes, SABLES DU GOLFE DU LION, Salavès, Uzège and Vaunage.

Gers r w p ★ DYA Indistinguishable from nearby COTES DE GASCOGNE.

Gevrey-Chambertin Burg r ★★★ **85'** 88 **89'** 90' 91 93 **95** 96' **97** 98 99' 00 01 Village containing the great CHAMBERTIN, its GRAND CRU cousins and many other noble vineyards (eg PREMIERS CRUS Cazetiers, Combe aux Moines, CLOS ST-JACQUES, Clos des Varoilles), as well as much more commonplace land. Growers include Bachelet, L. Boillot, Damoy, DROUHIN, DUGAT, ESMONIN, FAIVELEY, Harmand-Geoffroy, JADOT, Leclerc, LEROY, MORTET, ROTY, ROUSSEAU, Serafin, TRAPET, VAROILLES.

Gewürztraminer Speciality grape of ALSACE: one of 4 allowed for specified GRAND CRU wines. The most aromatic of Alsace grapes: at best like rose-petals to smell, grapefruit and/or lychees to taste.

Gigondas S Rh r p ★★→★★★★ 78 81' 83 85 86 88 **89'** 90' 93 **94** 95' **96 97** 98' 99' 00' 01' Worthy neighbour to CH'NEUF-DU-PAPE. Strong, full-bodied, s'times peppery, largely GRENACHE; eg Ch de Montmirail, Redortier, Saint-Cosme, Clos du Joncuas, Dom Boussière du Cayron, Font-Sane, Goubert, Gour de Chaulé, Grapillon d'Or, Les Hauts de Montmirail, Pesquier, les Pallières, Raspail-Äy, Sta-Duc, St-Gayan, des Travers, du Trignon.

Ginestet Long-established B'X NEGOCIANT now owned by Bernard Taillan, said to be second in turnover.

Girardin, Vincent Burg r w ★★→★★★ Quality grower in SANTENAY has become dynamic merchant, specializing in C' DE BEAUNE ACs. Modern, oak and fruit style.

Givry Burg r w ★★ **95** 96' **97 98** 99 00 02 Underrated COTE CHALONNAISE village: light but tasty and typical burgundy from eg DELORME, Dom Joblot, L LATOUR, T Lespinasse, CLOS Salomon, Sarrazin, BARON THENARD.

Gorges et Côtes de Millau SW France r p w ★ DYA Locally popular country wines. Reds best. Co-op at Aguessac dominant .

Gosset V old small CHAMP house at AY. Excellent full-bodied wine (esp Grand Millésime 96). Gosset Celebris (**90** 95 96) is prestige CUVÉE, with Celebris Rosé (**95** 96), launched 95 by owners, Cointreau family of COGNAC Frapin.

Gouges, Henri ★★★ Reinvigorated estate for rich, complex NUITS-ST-GEORGES.

Goût Taste, eg goût anglais: as the English like it (ie dry for CHAMP, or well-aged).

Grand Cru One of top Burgundy v'yds with its own APPELLATION CONTROLEE. In ALSACE one of the 50 top v'yds covered by Alsace Grand Cru AC, but more vague elsewhere. In ST-EMILION the third rank of ch'x, incl about 200 properties.

Grande Champagne The AC of the best area of COGNAC. Nothing fizzy about it.

Grande Rue, La Burg r ★★★ 89' 90' **91 93** 95 96' **97** 98 99' 00 01 02 VOSNE-R GRAND CRU, neighbour to ROMANEE-CONTI. Owned by Dom Lamarche.

Grands-Echézeaux Burg r ★★★★ 78' 85' 88' 89' 90' 91' **92 93** 95 96' 97 98 99' 00 01 02 Superlative 22-acre GRAND CRU next to CLOS DE VOUGEOT. Wines not weighty but aromatic. Viz: DROUHIN, ENGEL, DRC, GROS.

Gratien, Alfred and Gratien & Meyer ★→★★ Brut NV; Brut **95** 96; Prestige Cuvée Paradis Brut and Rosé (96). Excellent smaller family-run CHAMP house. Fine, v dry, long-lasting wine is still fermented in barrels. Gratien & Meyer is counterpart at SAUMUR. (Vg Cuvée Flamme.) Both now owned by large German co but no lessening of standards.

Graves B'x r w ★★→★★★★ Region S of B'DX city with excellent soft earthy reds, dry whites (SAUV-SÉM) reasserting star status. PESSAC-LEOGNAN is inner zone.

Graves de Vayres B'x r w ★ 95 96 98 99 00' DYA ENTRE-D-M; no special character.

Grenache See grapes for red and white wine (pages 10–16).

Griotte-Chambertin Burg r ★★★★ 85' 88' 89' **90' 91 93** 95 96' **97** 98 99' 00 01 02 14-acre GRAND CRU adjoining CHAMBERTIN. Similar wine, but less masculine, more "tender". Growers incl DUGAT, DROUHIN, PONSOT.

Grivot, Jean Burg ★★★→★★★★ 35-acre COTE DE NUITS domaine, in 5 ACS incl RICHEBOURG, Nuits PREMIERS CRUS, VOSNE-ROMANEE, CLOS DE VOUGEOT. Top quality.

Groffier, Robert Burg ★★★ Pure, elegant GEVREY-CHAMBERTIN, CHAMBOLLE-MUSIGNY, esp Les Amoureuses.

Gros, Domaines Burg ★★★→★★★★ An excellent family of vignerons in VOSNE-ROMANEE comprising (at least) Domaines Jean, Michel, Anne et François, Anne-François Gros and Gros Frère et Soeur.

Gros Plant du Pays Nantais Lo w ★ DYA Junior VDQS cousin of MUSCADET, sharper, lighter; from the COGNAC grape, aka Folle Blanche, Ugni Bl, etc.

Guffens-Heynen Burg ★★★ Belgian POUILLY-FUISSE grower. Tiny quantity, top quality. Heady GAMAY and COTE D'OR wines (bought-in grapes) – also VERGET.

Guigal, Ets E Celebrated grower (22-ha COTE-ROTIE) Hermitage, St-Joseph, and merchant of CONDRIEU, Côte-Rôtie, HERMITAGE. Owner of VIDAL-FLEURY, de Vallouit & Dom J-L Grippat. By ageing single-v'yd Côte-Rôtie (La Mouline, La Landonne and La Turque) for 42 months in new oak, Guigal (plus Ch d'Ampuis: 38 months oak) breaks local tradition to please (esp) American palates. His standard wines are gd value and reliable, esp red COTES DU RHONE. Special CONDRIEU La Doriane (since 94) – full, oaky sweet Luminescence (since 99).

Guy Saget Lo ★★ Family firm with v'yds in the Pouilly-Fume and Pouilly sur Loire appellations (Domaine Saget), gradually buying up estates throughout the Loire to become one of the region's biggest proprietors. Saget's négociant line accounts for half the firm's annual production of 5 million bottles.

Haut-Poitou Lo w r ★→★★ DYA Up-and-coming VDQS S of ANJOU. Vg whites (CHARD, SAUV, CHENIN) from CAVE linked with DUBOEUF. Reds: GAMAY, CAB, best age 4–5 yrs. Has rejected restrictions of AC status for freedom of choice.

Haut-Benauge B'x w ★ DYA AC for a limited area in ENTRE-DEUX-MERS.

Haut-Médoc B'x r ★★→★★★ **82' 83' 85' 86' 88' 89' 90'** 95 96 98 00 01'
Big AC incl best parts of MEDOC. Most of zone has communal ACS (eg MARGAUX,
PAUILLAC). Some excellent ch'x (eg LA LAGUNE): simply AC HAUT-MEDOC.

Haut-Montravel Dordogne w sw ★★ 90' **94** 95' **96** 97' **98** (99) Rare MONTRAVEL SW
white; rather like MONBAZILLAC. Look for Ch'x Le Bondieu, Moulin Caresse, Puy-
Servain-Terrement, Roque-Peyre, also Dom de Libarde and Dom. de Grouyat.

Hautes-Côtes de Beaune Burg ★★ r **96 98** 99' **00** 01 02 w 99' 00' 01 02 AC for a
dozen villages in the hills behind the COTE DE BEAUNE. Light wines, worth
investigating. Top growers: Cornu, Devevey, Jacob, Mazilly.

Hautes-Côtes de Nuits Burg ★★ r **96 98** 99' **00** 01 02 w 99' 00' 01 02 As above,
for COTE DE NUITS. An area on the way up. Top growers: Duband, C Cornu,
Jayer-Gilles, M GROS. Also has large BEAUNE co-op.

Heidsieck, Charles Brut Réserve NV; Brut **90** 95 96; Rosé **95** 96 Major Reims
CHAMP house, now controlled by Rémy Martin Blanc des Millénaires (**90 95
96**). Fine quality recently esp new innovative Mis en Cave range range of NV
cuvées showing year of bottling. NV: real bargain. See also Piper-Heidsèck.

Heidsieck, Monopole Brut NV Blue Top; Red Top; Gold Top (96 98). Once
illustrious CHAMP house now owned by VRANKEN group. Red Top CUVEE
virtually BL DE NOIRS. Luxury brand Diamant Bleu (90 95 96) is excellent.

Hengst Wintzenheim (ALSACE) GRAND CRU. Excels with top-notch GEWÜRZ from
Albert Mann; also Pinot-Auxerrois, Chasselas (esp JOSMEYER'S) and PINOT
Noir (esp A Mann's) with no GRAND CRU status.

Henriot Brut Souverain NV; Blanc de Blancs de CHARD NV; Brut 90 **95**; Brut Rosé
95 **96**; Luxury Cuvée: Cuvée des Enchanteleurs 88 **90** 95. Old family CHAMP
house; regained independence in '94. Very fine, fresh, creamy style. Joseph
H. also owns BOUCHARD PERE (since 95) and FEVRE.

Hérault Midi Biggest v'yd département: 263,000 acres of vines. Some vg AC
COTEAUX DU LANGUEDOC and pioneering VDP de l'Hérault, as well as VIN DE TABLE.

Hermitage N Rh r w ★★★→★★★★ 61' 66 72 **78'** 79 82 83' **85' 88 89' 90'** 91' **94**
95' 96' 97' 98' 99' 00' 01' By tradition, the "manliest" wine of France: dark,
powerful and profound. Truest example of SYRAH from 309 hillside acres on E
bank of Rhône, granite plus clay-chalk. Needs long ageing. White (Marsanne,
some Roussanne) is heady and golden; now usually made for early drinking,
though best mature for up to 25 yrs; can be better red. Top makers:
Belle, CHAPOUTIER, CHAVE, Dom du Colombier, DELAS, Desmeure, Faurie, GUIGAL,
JABOULET, M Sorrel, Tardieu-Laurent. TAIN co-op also useful and improving.

Hospices de Beaune Burg Historic hospital and charitable institution in BEAUNE,
with excellent v'yds (known by "CUVEE" names) in BEAUNE, CORTON, MEURSAULT,
POMMARD, VOLNAY. Wines are auctioned on the third Sunday of each November.

Hudelot-Noëllat, Alain ★★★ Under-appreciated VOUGEOT estate producing some
excellent wines, in a light but fine style.

Huët L'Echansonne Lo ★★→★★★★ 47' 59' 76' **85' 88' 89' 90'** 93 95' 96 97 98
99 00 01 (SEC and DEMI-SEC) 02 Leading top-quality estate in VOUVRAY, run
on biodynamic principles. Wines for long ageing. Single-v'yard wines
best: Le Haut Lieu, Le Mont, Clos du Bourg.

Hugel et Fils ★→★★★ The best-known ALSACE co; founded at Riquewihr in 1639
and still in the family. "Johnny" H (ret'd '97) is the region's beloved
spokesman (Jean-Philippe and Etienne are in charge with Marc as
winemaker). Quality escalates with Tradition and Jubilee ranges. Hugels are
militantly against Alsace GRAND CRU system. SELECTIONS DES GRAINS NOBLES: Hugel
pioneered this style and still makes some of finest examples. Also
occasionally VIN DE PAILLE.

Ile de Beauté Name given to VINS DE PAYS from CORSICA. Mostly red.

Impériale BORDEAUX bottle holding 8.5 normal bottles (6.4 litres).

Irancy ("Bourgogne Irancy") Burg r (p) ★★ 96' **98** 99' **00** 02 Good light red made nr CHABLIS from PINOT N and the local César. The best vintages mature well. To watch. Growers incl Colinot.

Irouléguy SW France r p (w) ★★ **95'** 96 **97** 98 **99** 00 (01') Improving local wines of Basque country with a rustic twang. Dark dense Tannat/CAB reds to keep 5 yrs+. Gd from Doms Ilarria, Brana, Arretxea, Etchegaraya and Abotia and good co-op. Rivalling MADIRAN.

Jaboulet Aîné, Paul Old family firm at TAIN, leading grower of HERMITAGE (esp La Chapelle ★★★★), CORNAS St-Pierre, CROZES Thalabert (vg value), Roure; merchant of other Rhône wines – esp COTES DU RHONE Parallèle 45, COTES DU VENTOUX. Whites now more fat than before, so drink young.

Jacquart Brut NV, Brut Rosé NV (Carte Blanche and Cuvée Spéciale); Brut **90** 95 **96** Co-op-based CHAMP marque; in quantity the sixth-largest. Fair quality. Luxury brands: CUVÉE Nominée Blanc **90** 95 96, CN Rosé 95 **96** Vg Mosaïque BL DE BLANCS **95** 96 Mosaïque Rosé 96

Jacquesson Excellent small Dizy CHAMP house. Vg vintage BL DE BLANCS (95 96); exquisite barrel-fermented "Grand Vin" luxury CUVÉES: both w (88 95 96) and rosé (90 95 96). Also Dégorgement Tardif (75 85) and Vigneron de L'Année 2002.

Jadot, Louis Burg ★★→★★★★ Top-quality merchant house with v'yds (155 acres) in BEAUNE, CORTON, Magenta, Ch des Jacques (MOULIN A VENT), etc. Wines to bank on.

Jardin de la France Lo w r p DYA One of France's four regional VINS DE PAYS. Covers Loire Valley: mostly single grape (esp CHARD, GAMAY, SAUV).

Jasnières Lo w dr (sw) ★★★ 76 78 79 83 85 86 88' **89'** 90' 93' **95'** 96 97 98 **99** 00 01 02 Rare and almost immortal dry VOUVRAY-like wine (CHENIN) of N TOURAINE. Esp Aubert la Chapelle, Chaussard, Gigou, Nicolas, Robinot.

Jayer, Henri Near-legendary Burgundy figure. See Rouget, Emmanuel.

Jeroboam In BORDEAUX, a 6-bottle bottle (holding 4.5 litres) or triple MAGNUM; in CHAMPAGNE, a double magnum.

Jobard, François Burg ★★★ Small MEURSAULT domaine; classic, slow-evolving wines. Look out also for nephew Remi Jobard's more modern-style wines.

Jolivet, Pascal Lo ★★→★★★ Considerable producer of good Sancerre and Pouilly-Fumé at several levels.

Joseph Perrier CUVÉE Royale BRUT NV; Cuvée Royale Bl de Blancs NV; Cuvée Royale Rosé NV; Brut **90** 95 96. Excellent smaller CHAMP house at Chalons with gd v'yds in Marne Valley. Supple fruity style; vg prestige Cuvée Joséphine **89** 90. Part-owned since 98 by ALAIN THIENOT.

Josmeyer ★★→★★★ Family house at Wintzenheim, ALSACE. Vg long-ageing wines, esp GEWÜRZ and Pinot Bl. Fine RIES from GRAND CRU Hengst. Wide range.

Juliénas Beauj r ★★★ **99** 00 01 Leading CRU of BEAUJOLAIS: vigorous fruity wine to keep 2–3 yrs. Growers incl Ch'x du Bois de la Salle, des Capitans, de Juliénas, des Vignes; Doms Bottière, R Monnet, Michel Tête, co-op.

Jura See Côtes du Jura.

Jurançon SW France w sw dr ★→★★★ **89'** 90' **94** 95' 96 97' 98 **00** (01') Racy long-lived speciality of Pau in Pyrenean foothills. Not to be missed. At best like wildflower SAUTERNES. Sw better than dry esp as aperitif. Top growers: Doms du Bellegarde, Barrère, Bordenave, Capdevielle, Castéra, de Souch, du Cinquau, Dom Cauhapé, Gaillot, Guirouilh, Jolys, Lamouroux, Lapeyre, Larredya, Nigri, de Rousse, Uroulat, Bousquet, and (esp dry) Bellevue, Cabarrouy. Also co-op's dry Grain Sauvage, BRUT d'Ocean and Peyre d'Or.

Kaefferkopf Alsace w dr sw ★★★ Ammerschwihr v'yd famous for blends rather than single-variety wines and denied GRAND CRU status for this reason.

Kientzheim-Kayserberg, Cave Vinicole de ★→★★ Important ALSACE co-op now back to top quality. Esp GEWÜRZ, RIES GRAND CRU Schlossberg and CREMANT.

Kientzler, André ★★→★★★ ALSACE RIESLING specialist in Geisburg GRAND CRU, esp VENDANGE TARDIVE and SGN. Equally good from GCs Kirchberg de Ribeauvillé for GEWURZ, Osterberg for occasional "vins de glaces" (Eisweins). Also very good Auxerrois, Chasselas.

Kreydenweiss Marc ★★→★★★ Fine ALSACE grower: 30 acres at Andlau, esp for PINOT Gr (vg GRAND CRU Moenchberg), Pinot Bl and RIES. Top wine: Grand Cru Kastelberg (ages 20 yrs); also fine Auxerrois "Kritt Klevner" and gd VENDANGE TARDIVE. One of first in Alsace to use new oak. Good Ries-Pinot Gr blend "Clos du Val d'Eléon". Great believer in terroir and in biodynamic viticulture.

Kriter Popular sparkler processed in Burgundy by PATRIARCHE. See the fountain on the Autoroute du Soleil.

Krug Grande CUVÉE; Vintage **85 88 89** 90; Rosé; CLOS du Mesnil (BL DE BLANCS) **85 86 88 89** 90; Krug Collection **62 64 66 69 71 73** 76 79 81 Small and supremely prestigious CHAMP house. Dense full-bodied v dry wines: long ageing, superlative quality. Owned since 99 by MOET-Hennessy.

Kuentz-Bas ★→★★★ Top-quality ALSACE grower/merchant at Husseren-les-Châteaux, esp for PINOT Gr, GEWÜRZ. Also good VENDANGES TARDIVES.

Labouré-Roi Burg ★★→★★★ Reliable, dynamic merchant at NUITS. Mostly whites. Many fine dom wines, esp René Manuel's MEURSAULT, Chantal Lescure's NUITS.

Ladoix-Serrigny Burg r (w) ★★ 95 96' 97 98 99' 01 02 Northernmost village of COTE DE BEAUNE below hills of CORTON. To watch for bargains.

Ladoucette, de ★★→★★★ 89 90 93 94 95 96 97 98 99 00 01 Leading producer of POUILLY-FUME, based at Ch de Nozet. Luxury brand Baron de L can be wonderful. Also SANCERRE Comte Lafond, La Poussie, Marc Brédif (and PIC, CHABLIS).

Lafarge, Michel ★★★★ 25-acre COTE DE BEAUNE estate with excellent VOLNAYS.

Lafon, Domaine des Comtes Burg ★★★★ Top estate in MEURSAULT, LE M'RACHET, VOLNAY. Glorious intense ws; extraordinary dark rs. Now also in the Maconnais.

Laguiche, Marquis de Burg ★★★★ Largest owner of LE MONTRACHET. Superb DROUHIN-made wines.

Lalande de Pomerol B'x r ★★→★★★ 88' 89' 90' 94 95 **96 98** 99 00' 01' Neighbour to POMEROL. Wines similar, but less mellow. General improvement in quality from 99. New investors and younger generation taking over. Top ch'x: Les Annereaux, DE BEL-AIR, Belles-Graves, Bertineau-St-Vincent, La Croix-St-André, La Fleur de Boüard, Garraud, Perron, La Sergue, SIAURAC, TOURNEFEUILLE. To try.

Lamartine, Château SW France r ★★★ One of top new CAHORS estates. Powerful reds which also achieve some elegance and finesse.

Landron (Domaines) Lo dr w (also Dom de la Louvetrie) Excellent organic producer of MUSCADET DE SÈVRE ET MAINE with several CUVÉES, bottled by terroir, incl Fief du Breuil and Amphibolite.

Langlois-Château Lo ★→★★★One of top SAUMUR sp houses (esp CREMANT). Controlled by BOLLINGER. Also range of still wines, esp Saumur Bl VIEILLES VIGNES.

Lanson Père & Fils Black Label NV; Rosé NV; BRUT 95 96 **97** Imp'ting improving CHAMP house; cellars at Reims. Long-lived luxury brand: Noble CUVEE (89 **95** 96). Black Label improved by longer ageing. New cuvée: BL DE BLS **94** 95 95.

Laroche ★★→★★★ Important grower (190 acres) and dynamic CHABLIS merchant, incl Domaines La Jouchère and Laroche. Top wines: Blanchots (esp Réserve de l'Obédiencerie ★★★) and CLOS VIEILLE VIGNES. Also blends gd non-regional CHARD and now ambitious MIDI range, Dom La Chevalière.

Latour, Louis Burg ★★→★★★ Famous merchant and grower with v'yds (120 acres) in BEAUNE, CORTON, etc. Very good white: CHEVALIER-M'RACHET Les Demoiselles, CORTON-CHARLEMAGNE, M'RACHET, gd-value MONTAGNY and ARDECHE CHARD etc. Ch de Corton Grancey. Also PINOT N Valmoissine from the Var.

Latour de France r (w) ★→★★★ 95 96 97 **98 99** 00 01 02 Supposedly superior village in AC COTES DE ROUSSILLON-VILLAGES.

Latricières-Chambertin Burg r ★★★ 85' **88'** 89' **90'** 91 **93** 95 96' **97** 98 99' 00 01 02 17-acre GRAND CRU neighbour of CHAMBERTIN. Similar wine but lighter and "prettier", eg from FAIVELEY, LEROY, PONSOT, TRAPET.

Laudun S Rh w r p ★ Village of COTES DU RHONE-VILLAGES (west bank). Red style is soft. Attractive wines from Serre de Bernon co-op incl fresh whites. Dom Pelaquié is best, esp white, also Ch. Courac, Duseigneur, Prieuré St-Pierre.

Laurent-Perrier BRUT NV; Rosé NV; Brut **95** 96 98 Dynamic successful family-owned CHAMP house at Tours-sur-Marne. Vg minerally NV; excellent luxury brands: Grand Siècle La Cuvée Lumière du Millésime (90), CGS Alexandra Brut Rosé (90 **95** 96). Also Ultra Brut. Owns SALON, DELAMOTTE, DE CASTELLANE.

Lavilledieu-du-Temple SW France r p w ★ DYA Fruity wines mostly from co-op nr Montauban. Also Doms de Gazanias and de Rouch.

Leflaive, Domaine Burg ★★★★ Once again among the best w burgundy growers, at PULIGNY-M. Best v'yds: Bienvenues-, CHEVALIER-M'TRACHET, Clavoillons, Pucelles and (since 91) Le M'rachet. Ever-finer wines on biodynamic principles.

Leflaive, Olivier Burg ★★★ High-quality NEGOCIANT at PULIGNY-M'RACHET, cousin of the above. Reliable wines, mostly white, but drink them young.

Léognan B'x r w ★★★→★★★★ Top village of GRAVES with its own AC: PESSAC-LEOGNAN. Best ch'x: DOM DE CHEVALIER, HAUT-BAILLY.

Leroy, Domaine Burg ★★★★ Domaine built around purchase of Noellat in VOSNE ROMANÉE in 1988 & Leroy family holdings (known as d'Auvenay). Extraordinary quality from tiny (biodynamic) yields; equally extraordinary prices.

Leroy, Maison Burg ★★★★ The ultimate NEGOCIANT-ELEVEUR at AUXEY-DURESSES with sky-high standards and the finest stocks of expensive old wine in Burgundy.

Lesquerde ★★ 95 96 97 **98 99** 00 01 02 New superior AC village of COTES DU ROUSSILLON-VILLAGES.

Lichine, Alexis & Cie BORDEAUX merchants (once of the late Alexis Lichine). No connection now with CH PRIEURE-LICHINE.

Lie, sur On the lees. MUSCADET is often bottled straight from the vat, for maximum zest and character.

Limoux Pyr r w ★★ Burgeoning AC for sp BLANQUETTE DE LIMOUX or better CREMANT de Limoux, oak-aged CHARD for Limoux AC PINOT N for VDP as well as traditional grapes (Pinot N is now allowed in blend for Crémant). Growers incl Doms de Fourn, des Martinolles; gd co-op. Also new AC for red from 2003; MERLOT based with CABERNET but not Pinot N.

Liquoreux Term for a very sweet wine: eg SAUTERNES, top VOUVRAY, JURANCON, etc.

Lirac S Rh r p w ★★ 89' 90' 94' 95' 96 **98' 99' 00'** 01' Next to TAVEL. Approachable, often soft r (can age 5+ yrs). Red overtaking rosé, esp Doms Cantegril, Devoy-Martine, Joncier, Maby (Fermade), André Méjan, de la Mordorée, Sabon, Ch d'Aquéria, de Bouchassy, Ségriès. Greater use of MOURVEDRE firming some reds. Gd whites.

Listel Midi r p w ★→★★ DYA Vast (4,000-acre⁺) historic estate on Golfe du Lion. Owned by VAL D'ORBIEU. Pleasant light "vins des sables" incl sp. Dom du Bosquet-Canet: fruity CAB; Dom de Villeroy: fresh BL DE BLCS SUR LIE; rosé Gris de Gris; and CHARD. Also fruity, almost non-alcoholic PETILLANT, Ch de Malijay: COTES DU RHONE; Abbaye de Ste-Hilaire: CTX VAROIS; Ch La Gordonne: COTES DE PROVENCE.

Listrac-Médoc B'x r ★★→★★★ **90' 95 96** 98 00' 01 Village of HAUT-MEDOC next to MOULIS. Grown-up clarets with tannic grip Best ch'x: CLARKE, FONREAUD, FOURCAS-DUPRE, FOURCAS-HOSTEN, Mayne-Lalande, and good co-op.

Livinière, La See Minervois-La Livinière.

Long-Depaquit Burg Vg CHABLIS domaine (esp MOUTONNE), owned by BICHOT.

Lorentz, Gustave ★★ ALSACE grower and merchant at Bergheim. Esp GEWÜRZ, RIES from GRAND CRUS Altenberg de Bergheim, Kanzlerberg. Also owns Jerome Lorentz. Equally good for top estate and volume wines.

Loron & Fils ★→★★ Big-scale grower and merchant at Pontanevaux; specialist in BEAUJOLAIS and sound VINS DE TABLE.

Loupiac B'x w sw ★★ 86' 88' **89** 90 95 **96 97 98** 99 01' 01 Across River Garonne from SAUTERNES and by no means to be despised. Top ch'x: CLOS-Jean, LOUPIAC-GAUDIET, Mémoires, Noble, RICAUD, Les Roques.

Lugny See Mâcon-Lugny.

Lussac-St-Emilion B'x r ★★ **85 86' 88'** 89' 90' 94 95 **96 98** 00' 01 NE neighbour to ST-EMILION. Top ch'x incl Barbe Blanche, BEL AIR, Bellevue, de la Grenière, Mayne-Blanc, DU LYONNAT, Co-op (at PUISSEGUIN) makes pleasant Roc de Lussac.

Macération carbonique Traditional fermentation technique: whole bunches of unbroken grapes in a closed vat. Fermentation inside each grape eventually bursts it, giving vivid fruity mild wine, not for ageing. Esp in BEAUJOLAIS; now much used in the MIDI and elsewhere, even CHATEAUNEUF-DU-PAPE.

The Mâconnais

The hilly zone just north of Beaujolais has outcrops of limestone where Chardonnay gives full, if not often fine, wines. The village of Chardonnay here may (or may not) be the home of the variety. Granite soils give light Gamay reds. The top Mâconnais AC is Pouilly-Fuissé, followed by Pouilly Vinzelles, St Véran and Viré-Clessé, then Mâcon-Villages with a village name. The potential is here to produce lower-priced, richly typical Chardonnays to out-do the New World (and indeed the S of France). Currently, most wines are less than extraordinary but things are looking up.

Mâcon Burg r w (p) DYA Sound, usually unremarkable reds (GAMAY best), tasty dry (CHARD) whites. Also Macon Superieur (similar).

Mâcon-Lugny Burg (r) w sp ★★ 99 00' 01 Village next to VIRE with huge and vg co-op (4M bottles). Les Genevrières is sold by LOUIS LATOUR.

Mâcon-Villages Burg w ★★ →★★★ **99** 00' **01 02** Increasingly well-made (when not over-produced). Named for their villages, eg M-Lugny, -Prissé, -Uchizy. Best co-op Prissé, Lugny. Top growers: Vincent (Fuissé), THEVENET, Bonhomme, Guillemot-Michel, Merlin (La Roche Vineuse). See also Viré-Clessé.

Macvin Jura w sw ★★ AC for "traditional" MARC and grape-juice aperitif.

Madiran SW France r ★★→★★★ 89' 90' 94 95' **96** 97 98' 99 (00) (01) Dark vigorous Gascon red, like tough fruity MEDOC mainly from Tannat grape. Needs age. Try MONTUS, Bouscassé, Chapelle Lenclos, Labranche-Laffont, Laffont, Peyros, Pichard, Laffitte-Teston, Capmartin, and Barréjat. Good co-ops Crouseilles, Plaimont, Castelnau-Rivière-Basse. White is AC PACHERENC DU VIC BILH.

Magnum A double bottle (1.5 litres).

Mähler-Besse First-class Dutch NEGOCIANT in B'x. Has share in CH PALMER and owns Ch Michel de Montaigne. Brands incl Cheval Noir. (Total: 250 acres.)

Mailly-Champagne Top CHAMP co-op. Luxury wine: CUVEE des Echansons.

Maire, Henri ★→★★ The biggest grower/merchant of JURA wines, with half of the entire AC. Some top wines, many cheerfully commercial. Fun to visit.

Mann, Albert ★→★★★ Growers at Wettolsheim admired for their rich elegant wines. Excellent Pinot Bl Auxerrois, Pinot N. Fine Riesling and Gewürz from Grands Crus Schlossberg and Hengst respectively.

Maranges Burg r (w) ★★ 96 **97 98** 99' 01 02 AC for 600-odd acres of S COTE DE BEAUNE, beyond SANTENAY: ⅓ PREMIER CRU. Top NEGOCIANTS: DROUHIN, Givardin.

Marc Grape skins after pressing; also the strong-smelling brandy made from them (the equivalent of Italian "Grappa").

Marcillac SW France r p ★→★★ DYA AC from 90. Violet-hued with grassy red-fruit character. Gd co-op at Valady. J-L Matha, Doms du Cros, Costes, and Laurens.

Margaux B'x r ★★→★★★★ 78 81 82' 83' 85 86' 87 88' 89 90' 95 96 98 99 00' 01 Village of HAUT-MEDOC. Some of most elegant and fragrant red BORDEAUX. AC incl CANTENAC and several other villages. Top ch'x incl MARGAUX, RAUZAN-SEGLA, BRANE-CANTENAC etc.

Marionnet, Henry Lo ★→★★★ 95 96 97 98 99 00 01 **02** Leading TOURAINE property specializing in GAMAY and SAUV. Top CUVEE Le M de Marionnet. Other cuvées include Provignage, Vinifera (both ungrafted vines), Première Vendange, Cepages Oubliés. Some wildflowers here.

Marne et Champagne Recent but huge-scale CHAMP house, owner (since 91) of LANSON and many smaller brands, incl BESSERAT DE BELLEFON. Alfred Rothschild brand v gd CHARD-based wines.

Marque déposée Trademark.

Marsannay Burg p r (w) ★★ 96' **97 98** 99' **00 01** 02 (rosé DYA) Village with fine light red and delicate PINOT N rosé. Incl villages of Chenôve, Couchey. Growers: Charlopin, CLAIR, Dijon University, JADOT, ROTY, TRAPET.

Mas de Daumas Gassac Midi r w p ★★★ 82 93 94' 95 96 97 98 99 00 01 The first "first-growth" estate of the LANGUEDOC (there are now other contenders), producing potent largely CAB S on apparently unique soil. Extraordinary quality – recently celebrated 25 vintages. Also Rosé Frisant and a rich fragrant white of blended CHARD, Viognier, Petit Manseng etc to drink at 2–3 yrs. Also quick-drinking red, Les Terrasses de Guilhem, from nearby co-op and trad Languedoc varietals (Clairette, Cinsault, Aramon etc) from old vines under Terrasses de Landoc label. VIN DE PAYS status. From 98 intriguing new sw wine: Vin de Laurence (Sém, Muscats and Sercial!).

Maury Pyr r sw ★★ NV Red VIN DOUX NATUREL of GRENACHE from ROUSSILLON. Taste the schist terroir. Much recent improvement, esp at Mas Amiel.

Mazis (or Mazy) Chambertin Burg r ★★★ 78' 85' 88' 89' 90' 91 93 95 96' **97** 98 99' 00 01 02 30-acre GRAND CRU neighbour of CHAMBERTIN, s'times equally potent. Best from FAIVELEY, HOSPICES DE BEAUNE, LEROY, Maume, ROTY.

Mazoyères-Chambertin See Charmes-Chambertin.

Médoc B'x r ★★ 85 86' 88' 89' 90' 95 96 98 00' 01 AC for reds of the less-good (northern) part of BORDEAUX's biggest top-quality district. Flavours tend to earthiness. HAUT-MEDOC is much better. Top ch'x include LA CARDONNE, GREYSAC, LOUDENNE, LES ORMES-SORBET, POTENSAC, LA TOUR-DE-BY.

Meffre, Gabriel ★★ The biggest S Rhône estate, based at GIGONDAS. Variable quality, recent progress. Often in French supermarkets. Also bottles and sells for small CHATEAUNEUF-DU-PAPE domaines, eg Guy Jullian, Dom de Baban.

Mellot, Alphonse Lo ★★→★★★ 88 89 90 91 92 93 94 95 96 97 98 99 00 01 **02** Leading SANCERRE grower. Especially for La Moussière and wood-aged CUVEE Edmond, Génération XIX.

Menetou-Salon Lo r p w ★★ DYA Highly attractive similar wines from W of SANCERRE: SAUV BL white full of charm, PINOT N light red. Top growers: Henri Pellé, Jean-Max Roger. Reds from Clément can age.

Méo-Camuzet ★★★★ V fine domaine in CLOS DE VOUGEOT, NUITS-ST-GEORGES, RICHEBOURG, VOSNE-ROMANEE. HENRI JAYER inspired. Esp V-R Cros Parantoux.

Mercier & Cie, Champagne BRUT NV; Brut Rosé NV; Brut **97 98** One of biggest CHAMP houses at Epernay. Controlled by MOET & CHANDON. Fair commercial quality, sold mainly in France. Good powerful PINOT-led CUVEE Eugene Mercier.

Mercurey Burg r w ★★→★★★ 90' 93 95 96' 97 98 99' 01 02 (Vintages are for reds). Leading red- wine village of COTE CHALONNAISE. Gd middle-rank burgundy incl improving w's. Try Ch de Chamirey, FAIVELEY, M Juillot, Lorenzon, Raquillet, Dom de Suremain.

Mercurey, Région de The alternative name for the COTE CHALONNAISE.

Mérode, Domaine Prince de ★★★ A top domaine for CORTON and POMMARD.

Mesnil-sur-Oger, Le Champ ★★★★ One of top Côte des Blancs villages; Structured CHARD for v long ageing.

Métaireau, Louis Loire w ★★→★★★ 89 90 **91 92** 93 **94** 95 96 97 **98 99** 00 01 02 A key figure in the MUSCADET quality revolution. Expensive well-finished wines: Number One, CUVEES Grand Mouton, and LM.

Méthode champenoise Traditional laborious method of putting bubbles into CHAMP by refermenting wine in its bottle. Must use terms "classic method" or "méthode traditionnelle" outside region. Not mentioned on Champ labels.

Méthode traditionnelle See entry above.

Meursault Burg w (r) ★★★→★★★★ 89' **90 91** 92 95 96' 97 99 00' 01 02 COTE DE BEAUNE village with some of world's greatest w's: savoury, dry but nutty and mellow. Best v'yds: Charmes, Genevrières, Perrières; also: Goutte d'Or, Meursault-Blagny, Poruzots, Narvaux, Tesson, Tillets. Producers incl AMPEAU, J-M BOILLOT, M Bouzereau, Boyer-Martenot, CH DE MEURSAULT, COCHE-DURY, Ente, Fichet, Grivault, P Javillier, JOBARD, LAFON, LATOUR, O LEFLAIVE, LEROY, Manuel, Matrot, Michelot-Buisson, P MOREY, G ROULOT. See also neighbouring Blagny.

Meursault-Blagny See Blagny.

Michel, Louis ★★★ CHABLIS domaine with model unoaked, v long-lived wines, incl superb LES CLOS, vg Montmains, MONTEE DE TONNERRE.

Midi General term for S of Fr, W of Rhône. Improving; brilliant promise. Top wines often based on variety (best tend to be blends). A melting-pot.

Minervois Midi r (p w) br sw ★ →★★★ **90 91** 92 93 94 95 96 97 **98 99** 00 01 Hilly AC region; good, lively wines, esp Ch du Donjon, Fabas, Dom Laurent Fabre, CO-OPS LA LIVINIERE, de Peyriac, Pouzols; La Tour Boisée, de Violet, CLOS Centeilles. Sw Minervois Noble being developed. See St-Jean de Minervois.

Minervois-La Livinière, La Midi r (p w) ★ →★★ Quality village (see last entry) the only sub-appellation or cru in Minervois. Best growers: Abbaye de Tholomies, Borie de Maurel, Combe Blanche, Ch de Gourgazaud, Clos Centeilles, Laville-Bertrou, Doms Maris, Ste-Eulalie, Co-op La Livinière, Vipur.

Mis en bouteille au château/domaine Bottled at the CHATEAU, property or estate. NB "dans nos caves" (in our cellars) or "dans la région de production" (in the area of production) are often used but mean little.

Mittnacht Freres, Domaine Rising ALSACE star with v'yds in Riquewihr and Hunawihr. Lovely Pinot Bl, fine Ries (Grand Cru ROSACKER), excellent Pinot Gr.

Moelleux "With marrow": creamy sweet. ie. sw wines of VOUVRAY, COT' DU LAYON.

Moët & Chandon Brut NV; Rosé 95 96 98; Brut Imperial 95 96 98 Lgst CHAMP merchant/grower with cellars in Epernay; branches in Argentina, Australia, Brazil, California, Germany, Spain. Consistent high quality, esp vintage wines. Coteaux Champenois Saran: still wine. Prestige CUVEE: DOM PERIGNON. Impressive multi-vintage Esprit du Siècle. Links with CLICQUOT, MERCIER, POMMERY, RUINART, KRUG.

Moillard Burg ★★→★★★ Big family firm (DOMAINE THOMAS-MOILLARD) in NUITS-ST-GEORGES, making full range, incl dark and v tasty wines.

Mommessin, J ★→★★ Major BEAUJOLAIS merchant, merged with THORIN, now owned by BOISSET. Owner of CLOS DE TART. White wines less successful than red.

Monbazillac Dordogne w sw ★★→★★★★ **76' 85' 89** 90' 94 95' 97' 98 99' (01') Golden SAUTERNES-style wine from BERGERAC, now back on top form. At best can equal Sauternes as at Tirecul-la-Gravière. Top producers: L'Ancienne Cure, Ch'x de Belingard-Chayne, Bellevue, La Borderie, Treuil-de-Nailhac, Le Fagé, Haut-Bernasse, Petit Paris, Poulvère, Theulet, Dom de la Haute-Brie et du Caillou, Clos Fontindoule and La Grande Maison stand out among 120 growers. Also Co-op de Monbazillac (Ch'x de Monbazillac & Septy).

Mondeuse Savoie r ★★ DYA Red grape of SAVOIE. Potentially gd vigorous deep-coloured wine. Possibly same as NE Italy's Refosco. Don't miss a chance.

Monopole V'yd under single ownership.

Montagne-St-Emilion B'x r ★★ 85 86' 88' 89' 90' 94 95 96 98 00' 01 North East neighbour and largest satellite of ST-EMILION: similar wines and APPELLATION regulations; becoming more important each year. Top ch'x: Calon, Faizeau, Maison Blanche, Montaiguillon, Roudier, Teyssier, DES TOURS, VIEUX-CH-ST-ANDRE.

Montagny Burg w ★★ 97 99' 00 01 02 COTE CHALONNAISE village. Between MACON and MEURSAULT, both geographically and gastronomically. Top producers: Aladame, J-M BOILLOT, Cave de Buxy, LOUIS , Michel, Ch de la Saule.

Montée de Tonnerre Burg w ★★★ 90 93 95 96' 97 98 99 00' 02 Famous excellent CHABLIS 1ER CRU. Esp BROCARD, Duplessis, L MICHEL, Raveneau, Robin.

Monthelie Burg r (w) ★★→★★★ 93 95 96' 97 98 99' 00 01 02 Little-known VOLNAY neighbour, s'times almost equal. Excellent fragrant reds, esp BOUCHARD PERE, COCHE-DURY, LAFON, DROUHIN, Garaudet, Ch de Monthelie (Suremain).

Montille, Hubert de Burg ★★★ VOLNAY and POMMARD domaine to note.

Montlouis Lo w dr sw (sp) ★★→★★★ 85' 88' 89 90' 93' 95' 96 97 98 99 00 01 02 (sec) N'bour of VOUVRAY. Similar sw, or long-lived dry wines; also sp. Top growers: Berger, Chidaine, Deletang, Moyer, Frantz Saumon, Taille aux Loups.

Montrachet Burg w ★★★★ 78 79 82 85' 86 88 89' 90 91 92' 93 94 95 96' 97 98 99 00' 01 02 (Both 't's in the name are silent.) 19-acre GRAND CRU v'yd in both PULIGNY- and CHASSAGNE-M'RACHET. Potentially the greatest white burgundy: strong, perfumed, intense, dry yet luscious. Top wines from LAFON, LAGUICHE (DROUHIN), LEFLAIVE, RAMONET, DOM DE LA ROMANEE-CONTI, THENARD.

Montravel Dordogne ★★ p dr w DYA r 00' (01) Now AC for all three colours. Similar to BERGERAC. Good examples from Doms de Krevel, Gouyat, Perreau, ch'x du Fouga, Masburel, Laulerie, Péchaurieux, Pique-Sègue. Separate ACS for semi-sw COTES DE MONTRAVEL and sw HAUT-MONTRAVEL.

Morey, Domaines Burg ★★★ 50 acres in CHASSAGNE-M'RACHET. Vg wines made by family members, esp Bernard, incl BATARD-M'RACHET. Also Pierre M in MEURSAULT.

Morey-St-Denis Burg r ★★★ 85' 88 89' 90' 91 93 95 96' 97 98 99' 00 01 02 Small village with four GRANDS CRUS between GEVREY-CHAMBERTIN and CHAMBOLLE-MUSIGNY. Glorious wine often overlooked. Incl Amiot, DUJAC, H Lignier, Moillard-Grivot, Perrot-Minot, PONSOT, ROUMIER, ROUSSEAU, Serveau.

Morgon Beauj r ★★★ 95 96 97 98 99 00 01 02 The firmest cru of BEAUJOLAIS, needing time to develop its rich savoury flavour. Growers incl Aucoeur, Ch de Bellevue, Desvignes, J Foillard, Lapièrre, Ch de Pizay. DUBOEUF excellent.

Mortet, Denis ★★★ Splendid perfectionist GEVREY domaine. Super wines since 93, incl a range of village Gevreys and excellent 1ER CRU Lavaux St-Jacques.

Moueix, J-P et Cie B'x ★★★ Legendary proprietor and merchant of ST-EM and POM Ch'x incl LA FLEUR-PETRUS, MAGDELAINE and PETRUS. Also in Calif: see DOMINUS.

Moulin-à-Vent Beauj r ★★★ 91 93 95 96' 97 98 99 00 01 02 The biggest and potentially best wine of BEAUJOLAIS; can be powerful, meaty, and long-lived, can even taste like fine Rhône or burgundy. Many gd growers, esp Ch du Moulin-à-Vent, Ch des Jacques, Dom des Hospices, Janodet, JADOT, Merlin.

Moulis B'x r ★★ →★★★ 90 94 95 96 98 00' 01 H-MEDOC village with several Crus Exceptionnels: CHASSE-SPLEEN, MAUCAILLOU, POUJEAUX (THEIL). Gd hunting ground.

Mourvèdre See Grapes for red wine pages 10–12.

Mousseux Sparkling.

Mouton Cadet Popular brand of blended r and w B'x. Not a quality leader.

Moutonne ★★★ CHABLIS GRAND CRU honoris causa (between VAUDESIR and Preuses), owned by BICHOT.

Mugneret/Mugneret-Gibourg Burg ★★★ Superb reds from top COTE DE NUITS sites.

Mugnier, J-F Burg ★★★→★★★★ 10-acre Ch de Chambolle estate with first-class delicate CHAMBOLLE-MUSIGNY Les Amoureuses and MUSIGNY. Also BONNES-MARES.

Mumm, G H & Cie Cordon Rouge NV; Mumm de Cramant NV; Cordon Rouge 95 96; Rosé NV Major CHAMP grower and merchant. NV much improved by new winemaker; very fair vintages. Also in Napa, California; Chile, Argentina, South Africa ("Cape Mumm").

Muré, Clos St-Landelin ★★→★★★ V fine ALSACE grower and merchant at Rouffach with v'yds in GRAND CRU Vorbourg. Full-bodied wines: ripe (unusual) PINOT N, big RIES and MUSCAT VENDANGES TARDIVES.

Muscadet Lo w ★→★★★ DYA (but see below) Popular, good-value, often delicious very dry wine from near Nantes at the mouth of the Loire. Should never be sharp but should have a faint iodine tang. Perfect with fish and seafood. Best are from zonal ACS: COTEAUX DE LA LOIRE, M COTES DE GRAND LIEU, SEVRE-ET-MAINE. Choose a SUR LIE.

Muscadet Côtes de Grand Lieu ★→★★ 88 89 90 93 95 96 97 98 99 00 01 **02** Recent zonal AC ('95) for MUSCADET named after the Lac de Grand Lieu in the middle of the zone. Best are SUR LIE, from eg Bâtard, Luc Choblet, Malidain.

Muscadet Coteaux de la Loire Lo w ★→★★ 88 89 90 93 95 96 97 98 99 00 01 **02** Small MUSCADET zone E of Nantes, best are SUR LIE, esp Guindon, Luneau-Papin, Les Vignerons de la Noëlle.

Muscadet de Sèvre-et-Maine ★→★★★ 88 89 90 93 95 96 97 **98 99 00 01** 02 Wine from central (best) part of area. Top growers incl Guy Bossard (DOME DE L'ECU), CHEREAU-CARRE, Bruno Cormerai, Dom de la Haute Fevrie, Michel Delhomeau, Douillard, Landron, Luneau-Papin, METAIREAU. 2001 vintage can be perfection.

Muscat Distinctively perfumed and usually sweet wine, often fortified as VIN DOUX NATUREL. Made dry and not fortified in ALSACE where it is the main aperitif wine. For Muscat grape, see Grapes for white wine, pp 12-16.

Muscat de Beaumes-de-Venise See Beaumes-de-Venise.

Muscat de Frontignan See Frontignan.

Muscat de Lunel Midi golden sw ★★ NV Ditto. A small area but good, making real recent progress. Look for Dom CLOS Bellevue, Lacoste.

Muscat de Mireval Midi sw ★★ NV Ditto, from nr Montpellier. Dom La Capelle.

Muscat de Rivesaltes Midi golden sw ★★ NV Sweet MUSCAT wine from large zone near Perpignan. Especially good from Cazes Frères, CH de Jau.

Musigny Burg r (w) ★★★★ 85' 88' 89' 90' 91 **92 93** 95 96' **97** 98 **99'** 00 01 02 25-acre GRAND CRU in CHAMBOLLE-MUSIGNY. Can be the most beautiful, if not the most powerful, of all red burgundies (and a little white). Best growers: DROUHIN, JADOT, LEROY, MUGNIER, PRIEUR, ROUMIER, DE VOGUE, Vougeraie.

Napoléon Brand name of family-owned Prieur CHAMPAGNE house at Vertus. Excellent Carte d'Or NV and first-rate vintages, esp **95 96**.

Nature Natural or unprocessed – esp of still CHAMP.

Négociant-éleveur Merchant who "brings up" (ie matures) the wine.

Nicolas, Ets Paris-based wholesale and retail wine merchant controlled by Castel Frères. One of the biggest in France.

Nuits-St-Georges Burg r ★★→★★★★ 85' 88' **89'** 90' 91 93 **95** 96' **97** 98 99' 00 01 02 Important wine town: wines of all qualities, typically sturdy, tannic, needing time. Name often shortened to "Nuits". Best v'yds incl Les Cailles, CLOS des Corvées, Les Pruliers, Les St-Georges, Vaucrains, etc. Many growers and merchants esp DOM DE L'ARLOT, Ambroise, J Chauvenet, R. Chevillon, CONFURON, FAIVELEY, GOUGES, GRIVOT, Lechéneaut, LEROY, Machard de Gramont, Michelot, RION, THOMAS-MOILLARD.

d'Oc (Vin de Pays d'Oc) Midi r p w ★→★★ Regional VIN DE PAYS for Languedoc and ROUSSILLON. Esp single-grape wines and VINS DE PAYS PRIMEURS. Tremendous technical advances recently. Top producers: VAL D'ORBIEU, SKALLI, Jeanjean and numerous small growers.

Oisly & Thesée, Vignerons de ★★ 89 90 93 95 96 97 98 99 **00 01 02** Go-ahead co-op in E TOURAINE (Loire), with gd SAUV BL (esp Cuvée Excellence), CAB, GAMAY, Cot, and CHARD. Blends labelled Baronnie d'Aignan and gd domaine wines.

Orléanais, Vin de l' Lo r p w ★ DYA Small VDQS for light but fruity wines, based on Pinots Meunier and Noir, CAB and CHARD. Esp CLOS St-Fiacre.

Ostertag ★★ Sm ALSACE domaine at Epfig. Uses new oak for gd PINOT N; best RIES, Pinot Gr of GRAND CRU Muenchberg. GEWÜRZ from lieu-dit Fronholz worth ageing.

Ott, Domaines Producer of PROVENCE, incl CH DE SELLE (rosé, red), CLOS Mireille (white), BANDOL Ch de Romassan.

Pacherenc du Vic-Bilh SW Fr w dr sw ★★ The white wine of MADIRAN Dry DYA and (better) sw (age up to 5 yrs for oaked versions). For growers see Madiran.

Paillard, Bruno Brut Première Cuvée NV; Rosé Première Cuvée; CHARD Réserve Privée, Brut **90** 95 **90**. Superb Nec Plus Ultra Prestige Cuvée (90). Small prestigious young CHAMP house; very high standard. Also owns Château de Sarrin in Provence.

Palette Prov r p w ★★ Tiny AC near Aix-en-Provence. Full reds, fragrant rosés and whites from CH SIMONE.

Pasquier-Desvignes Beauj ★→★★ V old firm of BEAUJ merchants nr BROUILLY.

Patriarche Burg ★→★★ One of the bigger burgundy merchants. Cellars in BEAUNE; also owns CH DE MEURSAULT (150 acres), sparkling KRITER etc.

Patrimonio Corsica r w p ★★ →★★★ 95 96 97 **98 99** 00 01 02 Wide range from dramatic chalk hills in N CORSICA. Corsica's best. Fragrant reds from Nielluccio, characterful whites. Top growers: Gentile, Leccia, Arena.

Pauillac B'x r ★★★→★★★★ 66' 70' 75 **78' 79** 81' 82' **83' 85' 86' 88' 89'** 90' 93 94 **95'** 96' 98 99 00' 01 B'x (HAUT-MEDOC) village with 3 1st growths (LAFITE, LATOUR, MOUTON) and many other fine CH'X, famous for high flavour; varied in style.

Pécharmant Dordogne r ★★→★★★ **90'** 95' 98 99 (01') (02) Inner AC for top BERGERAC r, for ageing. Best: La Métairie, Doms du Haut-Pécharmant, des Costes, des Bertranoux; CHX Champarel, Terre Vieille, Les Grangettes, and de Tiregand. Also (from Bergerac co-op) Doms Brisseau-Belloc, du Vieux Sapin, Ch le Charmeil.

Pelure d'oignon "Onion skin" – tawny tint of certain rosés.

Perlant or Perlé Very slightly sparkling.

Pernand-Vergelesses Burg r (w) ★★★ 90 **93** 95 **96'** 97 98 99' 00 01 Village next to ALOXE-CORTON containing part of the great CORTON and C-CHARLEMAGNE v'yds and one other top v'yd: Ile des Vergelesses. Growers incl CHANDON DE BRIAILLES, CHANSON, Delarche, Dubreuil-Fontaine, JADOT, LATOUR, Rapet.

Perrier-Jouët Brut NV; Blason de France NV; Blason de France Rosé NV; BRUT **90** 95 97 Excellent CHAMP grower at Epernay, the first to make dry Champagne and once the smartest name of all; now best for vintage wines. Luxury brands: Belle Epoque (88 **90** 95 96) in a painted bottle. Also Belle Epoque Rosé (**90** 97).

Pessac-Léognan B'x r w ★★★→★★★★ **90'** 95 **96** 98 00' 01 AC for the best part of N GRAVES, incl area of most of the GRANDS CRUS, HAUT-BRION, PAPE CLÉMENT etc.

Pétillant Normally means slightly sparkling; but half-sparkling speciality in TOURAINE esp VOUVRAY and MONTLOUIS.

Petit Chablis Burg w ★ DYA Wine from fourth-rank CHABLIS v'yds. Not much character but can be pleasantly fresh. Best: co-op La Chablisienne.

Pfaffenheim ★★ Top ALSACE co-op with 580 acres. Strongly individual wines incl good Sylvaner and vg PINOTS (N, Gr, Bl). GRANDS CRUS: Goldert, Steinert and Hatschbourg. Hartenberger CREMANT d'Alsace is vg. Also owns DOPFF & IRION.

Pfersigberg Eguisheim (ALSACE) GRAND CRU with two parcels; v aromatic wines. GEWÜRZ does v well. RIES esp Paul Ginglinger, BRUNO SORG and LEON BEYER Comtes d'Eguisheim. Top grower: KUENTZ-BAS.

Philipponnat NV; Rosé NV; Réserve Spéciale **93** 95 **96**; CLOS des Goisses **88** 90 95 96 Small family-run CHAMP house for well-structured wines. Remarkable single-v'yd CLOS des Goisses and charming rosé. Also Le Reflet BRUT NV.

Piat Père & Fils ★ Big-scale merchant of BEAUJ and MACON, controlled by Diageo.

Pic St-Loup Midi ★→★★ r (p) Notable COTEAUX DU L'DOC cru. Top growers: Ch'x de Cazeneuve, Clos Marie, de Lancyre, Lascaux, Mas Bruguière, Dom de l'Hortus.

Picpoul de Pinet Midi w ★→★★ Improving AC exclusively for the old variety Picpoul. Best growers: Dom Gaujal, Co-op Pomérols, Félines-Jourdan.

Pineau des Charentes Strong sweet aperitif: white grape juice and COGNAC.

Pinot See Grapes for white and red wine (pages 10–16).

Piper-Heidsieck BRUT NV; Brut Rosé NV; Brut **90** 95 CHAMP-makers of old repute at Reims. Rare (**90** 95 96) and Brut Sauvage (**90** 96) are best, but non-vintage CUVÉES much improved. See also Piper Sonoma, California.

Plageoles, Robert The arch-priest of GAILLAC and defender of the lost grape varieties of the Tarn. Amazingly eccentric wines include a *vin jaune* left to oxidize like sherry, an ultra-sweet dessert wine from Ondenc grapes left to dry in the sun. Also Muscadelle, Duras, and Prunelar.

Pol Roger BRUT White Foil NV; Brut 88 **90** 93 95 96; Rosé 95 96; Blanc de CHARD 88 **90** 93 95 **96** Top-ranking family-owned CHAMP house at Epernay, much loved in Britain. Esp gd silky NV White Foil, Rosé, Réserve PR (88) and CHARD. Sumptuous CUVÉE: Sir Winston Churchill (90 93). New chef de CAVES Dominique Petit, ex KRUG.

Pomerol B'x r ★★★→★★★★ 70 75' **81'** 82' **83** 85 86 88 89' 90' **94 95 96** 98' 00' Next village to ST-EM: similar but more plummy, creamy wines, often maturing sooner, reliable, delicious. Top ch'x incl: CERTAN-DE-MAY, L'EVANGILE, LA FLEUR, LA FLEUR-PETRUS, LATOUR-A-POMEROL, PETRUS, LE PIN, TROTANOY, VIEUX CH CERTAN etc.

Pommard Burg r ★★★ 85' **88'** 89' **90** 91 **93** 95 96' **97** 98 99' 01 02 The biggest COTE D'OR village. Few superlative wines, but many potent and often tannic ones to age 10 yrs⁺. Best v'yds: Epenots, HOSPICES DE BEAUNE CUVÉES, Rugiens. Growers incl COMTE ARMAND, Billard-Gonnet, J-M BOILLOT, DE COURCEL, Gaunoux, LEROY, Machard de Gramont, DE MONTILLE, Ch de Pommard, Pothier-Rieusset.

Pommery Brut NV; Rosé NV; Brut **85 87 90 91 95** 96 V big CHAMP house at Reims, much improved. Sold to VRANKEN 02. Outstanding luxury CUVÉE Louise (82 85 90 95). Cuvée Louise Rosé (**88 90** 95).

Ponsot ★★★★ Controversial 25-acre MOREY-ST-DENIS estate. Many idiosyncratic high-quality GRANDS CRUS, incl CHAMBERTIN, CHAPELLE-C, CLOS DE LA ROCHE, CLOS ST-DENIS.

Portes de la Mediterranée New regional VDP from S RHÔNE/PROVENCE. Easy reds and interesting whites, including Viognier.

Potel, Nicolas Burg ★★→★★★★ M. Potel founded a small négociant after his father's DOM DE LA POUSSE D'OR was sold. Impressive reds, especially BOURGOGNE ROUGE, VOLNAY, NUITS-ST-GEORGES.

Pouilly-Fuissé Burg w ★★→★★★ 92' 95 **96** 97 **98** 99 00 01 02 The best white of the MACON region, potent and dense. At its best (eg Ch Fuissé VIEILLES VIGNES) outstanding, but usually over-priced compared with (eg) CHABLIS. Top growers: Ferret, Forest, VERGET, Luquet, Merlin, Noblet, Valette, Vincent.

Pouilly-Fumé Lo w ★★→★★★ 90' 91' 92' 93' 94 95' 96 97 98 99 00 **01 02** "Gun-flinty", fruity, often sharp white from upper Loire, nr SANCERRE. Grapes must be SAUV BL. Best CUVÉES can improve 5–6 yrs. Top growers incl Cailbourin, Chatelain, DAGUENEAU, Ch de Favray, Edmond and André Figeat, LADOUCETTE, Masson-Blondelet, Ch de Tracy, Tinel Blondelet, CAVE de Pouilly-sur-Loire, Redde. Sancerre is currently more consistent.

Pouilly-Loché Burg w ★★ 99 00' **01** 02 POUILLY-FUISSE's neighbour. Similar, cheaper; scarce. Can be sold as POUILLY-VINZELLES.

Pouilly-sur-Loire Lo w ★ DYA Neutral wine from the same v'yds as POUILLY-FUME but different grapes (Chasselas). Rarely seen today, ever-diminishing.

Pouilly-Vinzelles Burg w ★★ 99 00' **01** 02 Neighbour of POUILLY-FUISSE. Similar wine, worth looking for. Value. Best: Soufrandière.

Pousse d'Or, Domaine de la Burg ★★★ 32-acre estate in POMMARD, SANTENAY and esp VOLNAY, where its MONOPOLES Bousse d'Or and CLOS des 60 Ouvrées are powerful, tannic, and were justly famous under Gérard Potel (manager 1964-96). Unproven under new ownership.

Premier Cru First growth in B'X; second rank of v'yds (after GRAND CRU) in Burgundy.

Premières Côtes de Blaye B'X r w ★→★★ 88' 89' 90' **93 94 95 96 98** 00' 01 Restricted AC for better BLAYE wines; greater emphasis on r. Ch'x incl, Bel Air la Royère, Bertinerie, Côtes de Bourg Charron, Haut-Sociando, Jonqueyres, Loumède, Segonzac, des Toutes, La Tonnelle.

Premières Côtes de Bordeaux B'X r w (p) dr sw ★→★★ **94 95 96 98 00'** 01 Large hilly area east of GRAVES across the River Garonne: gd bet for quality and value, upgrading sharply. Largely Merlot. Ch'x incl Carignan, Carsin, Chelivette, Fayau, Grand-Mouëys, du Juge, Lamothe de Haux, Plaisance, Puy Bardens, REYNON, Suau, Tanesse. To watch, esp in gd vintages.

Prieur, Domaine Jacques Burg ★★★ Splendid 40-acre estate all in top Burgundy sites, incl PREMIER CRU MEURSAULT, VOLNAY, PULIGNY- and even LE M'RACHET. Now 50% owned by RODET. Quality could still improve.

Primeur "Early" wine for refreshment and uplift; esp from BEAUJOLAIS; VINS DE PAYS too. Wine sold "En Primeur" is still in barrel for delivery when bottled.

Prissé See Mâcon-Villages.

Propriétaire-récoltant Owner-manager.

Provence See Côtes de Provence, Cassis, Bandol, Palette, Coteaux des Baux-en-Provence, Bouches-du-Rhône, Coteaux d'Aix-en-Provence, Coteaux Varois.

Puisseguin St-Emilion B'X r ★★ 88' 89' 90' **94 95 96 98** 00' 01 Satellite neighbour of ST-EMILION; wines similar – not so fine or weighty but often value. Ch'x incl Bel Air, Durand-Laplagne, Fongaban, LAURETS, Soleil, Vieux-Ch-Guibeau. Also Roc de Puisseguin from co-operative.

Puligny-Montrachet Burg w (r) ★★★→★★★★ 89' 92 95 **96' 97 99** 00 01 02 Smaller neighbour of CHASSAGNE-M: potentially even finer, more vital and complex rich, dry wine. (But apparent finesse can be result of over-production.) Best v'yds: BATARD-M, Bienvenues-Bâtard-M, Caillerets, CHEVALIER-M, Clavoillon, Les Combettes, M'RACHET, Pucelles etc. Top growers incl AMPEAU, J-M BOILLOT, BOUCHARD PERE, L CARILLON, CHARTRON, Chavy, DROUHIN, JADOT, LATOUR, DOM LEFLAIVE, O LEFLAIVE, Pernot, SAUZET.

Pyrénées-Atlantiques SW France DYA VDP for wines not qualifying for local ACS MADIRAN, PACHERENC DU VIC BILH or JURANCON.

Quarts de Chaume Lo w SW ★★★→★★★★ 75 76 78' 79' 82 **85' 86 88' 89' 90' 91 92 93' 94** 95 96 97 98 99 00 01 02 Famous COTEAUX DU LAYON plot. CHENIN grapes grown for immensely long-lived intense rich golden wine. Esp from BAUMARD, Bellerive, Claude Papin (CH DE PIERRE-BISE), Suronde.

Quatourze Midi r w (p) ★ **95 96 97 98 99 00** 01 02 Minor cru of C'TX DE LANGUEDOC. Best wines: Dom Notre Dame du Quatourze (virtually sole producer).

Quincy Lo w ★→★★ DYA Sml area: v dry SANCERRE-style SAUV BL. Worth trying. Growers: Domaine Mardon, Sorbe, Domaine de Silice (whose wines can age).

Ramonet, Domaine Burg ★★→★★★★ Leading (legendary) estate in CHASSAGNE-M'RACHET with 42 acres, incl some M'RACHET. Vg whites, & red CLOS ST-JEAN.

Rancio The delicious nutty tang of brown wood-aged fortified wine eg VDN, esp BANYULS. Indicates exposure to oxygen and/or heat: a fault in table wine.

Rangen High-class ALSACE GRAND CRU in Thann and Vieux Thann. Owes reputation to ZIND-HUMBRECHT. SCHOFFIT is other main grower. Esp for PINOT Gr, GEWÜRZ, RIES.

Rasteau S Rh r br sw (p w dr) ★★ 90' 94 95' 96 **98' 99' 00'** 01 Village for sound, robust reds, especially Beaurenard, CAVE des Vignerons, CH du Trignon, Doms Didier Charavin, Rabasse-Charavin, Girasols, Gourt de Mautens, St-Gayan, Soumade, Perrin. Strong sweet GRENACHE dessert wine is (declining) speciality.

Ratafia de Champagne Sweet aperitif made in CHAMP of 67% grape juice and 33% brandy. Not unlike PINEAU DES CHARENTES.

Récolte Crop or vintage.

Regnié Beauj r ** 99 00 **01** 02 Village between MORGON and BROUILLY, promoted to cru in '88. About 1,800 acres. Try DUBOEUF, Aucoeur, or Rampon.

Reine Pédauque, La Burg ★ Long-est'd grower-merchant at ALOXE-CORTON. V'yds in ALOXE-CORTON, SAVIGNY, etc., and COTES DU RHONE. Owned by PIERRE ANDRE.

Remoissenet Père & Fils Burg ★★ Merchant (esp for whites and THENARD wines) with a tiny BEAUNE estate (5 acres). Give red time. Also broker for NICOLAS.

Rémy Pannier Important Loire wine merchant at SAUMUR.

Reuilly Lo w (r p) ★★ N'bour of QUINCY. Similar whites; rising reputation. Also rosés (PINOTS N, Gr), reds (PN). Esp Claude Lafond, Beurdin, Sorbe, Vincent.

Ribonnet, Domaine de SW France ★★ Christian Gerber makes pioneering range of varietals (r p w) without benefit of APPELLATION in Haute Garonne and ARIÉGE.

Riceys, Rosé des Champ p ★★★ DYA Minute AC in AUBE for a notable PINOT N rosé. Principal producers: A Bonnet, Jacques Defrance.

Richeaume, Domaine Côte de Prov r ★★ Notable Cab/Syrah; organic; a model.

Richebourg Burg r ★★★★ 78' 85' **88'** 89' 90' 91 **93'** 95 96' **97** 98 99' 00 01 02 19-acre VOSNE-ROMANEE GRAND CRU. Powerful, perfumed, fabulously expensive wine, among Burg's best. Top growers: GRIVOT, J GROS, A GROS, LEROY, MEO-CAMUZET, DRC.

Richou, Dom Lo ★→★★ 88 89 90 95 96 97 98 99 **00 01** 02 Long-est'd, quality ANJOU estate for wide range of wines, esp ANJOU-VILLAGES VIEILLES VIGNES, COTEAUX DE L'AUBANCE Les Trois Demoiselles.

Riesling See Grapes for white wine (pages 12–16).

Rion, Daniel et Fils Burg ★★★ 48-acre domaine in Prémeaux (NUITS). Excellent VOSNE-ROMANEE (Les Chaumes, Les Beaumonts), Nuits PREMIER CRU Les Vignes Rondes and ECHEZEAUX. Former winemaker Patrice Rion now has his own domaine and négociant label.

Rivesaltes Midi r w br dr sw ★★ NV Fortified wine of east Pyrenees. A tradition v much alive, if struggling these days. Top producers: Doms Cazes, Sarda-Malet, Vaquer, des Schistes, CH de Jau. See Muscat de Rivesaltes.

Up and coming producers from the Touraine appellations:

Bourgueil Domaine des Ouches

Cheverny Herve Villemade, Clos de Tue-Boeuf, Daridan/Cellier de la Marigonnerie

Chinon Jean-Pierre Crespin, Coulaine, Dme de Bel Air.

Jasnières Eric Nicolas/Domaine de Belliviere, Jean-Pierre Robinot, Christian Chaussard.

Touraine Domaine de la Garreliere, Domaine des Cailloux du Paradis

Vin de Pays de la Vienne: Ampelidae

Roche-aux-Moines, La Lo w SW ★★★ 76' 78 79 82 85 86 88' **89' 90'** **93' 94** 95' 96 **97 98 99** 00 01 02 Sixty-acre v'yd in SAVENNIERES, ANJOU. Intense strong fruity/sharp wine, needs long ageing or drinking fresh.

Rodet, Antonin Burg ★★→★★★ Substantial quality merchant with large (332-acre) estate, esp in MERCUREY (Ch de Chamirey) and Domaine d l'Aigle, nr Limoux. See also Prieur.

Roederer, Louis Brut Premier NV; Rich NV; BRUT **85 89 90 93** 95 96 97; BLANC DE BLANCS 91 93 95 96; Brut Rosé **91 95 96** 97. Top-drawer family-owned CHAMP-grower and merchant at Reims. Vanilla-rich NV with plenty of flavour. Sumptuous Cristal (may be greatest of all prestige CUVEES) and Cristal Rosé (**85 89 90 95** 96 97). Also owns Champ house DEUTZ, DELAS in Rhône, and CH DE PEZ in B'DX. See also Roederer Estate, California.

Rolly Gassmann ★ Distinguished ALSACE grower at Rorschwihr, esp for Auxerrois and MUSCAT from lieu-dit Moenchreben. House style is usually off-dry.

Romanée, La Burg r ★★★★ 78' 85' 88' 89' 90' 91 93 95 96' 97 98 99' 00 01 02 2-acre GRAND CRU in VOSNE-ROMANEE, just uphill from ROMANEE-CONTI. MONOPOLE of Liger-Belair, sold by BOUCHARD PERE. L-B making wine for themselves from 02.

Romanée-Conti Burg r ★★★★ 66' 76 78' 80' 82 83 85' 88' 89' 90' 91 93' 95 96' 97 98 99' 00 01 02 4.3-acre MONOPOLE GRAND CRU in VOSNE-ROMANEE; 450 cases per annum. The most celebrated and expensive red wine in the world, with reserves of flavour beyond imagination. See next entry.

Romanée-Conti, Domaine de la (DRC) Burg ★★★★ The grandest estate in Burgundy. Incl the whole of ROMANEE-C and LA TACHE and major parts of ECHEZEAUX, GRANDS ECH'X, RICHEBOURG and ROMANEE-ST-VIVANT. Also tiny part of M'RACHET. Crown-jewel prices (if you can buy them at all). Keep top DRC vintages for decades.

Romanée-St-Vivant Burg r ★★★★ 85' 88' 89' 90' 91 93' 95 96' 97 98 99' 00 01 02 23-acre GRAND CRU in VOSNE-ROMANEE. Similar to ROMANEE-CONTI but lighter and less sumptuous. Top growers: DRC, DROUHIN, HUDELOT-NOËLLAT, LEROY.

Rosacker (ALSACE) GRAND CRU of 26ha at Hunwihr. Produces best Riesling in Alsace (see CLOS STE. HUNE, SIPP-MACK and MITTNACHT)

Rosé d'Anjou Lo p ★ DYA Pale slightly sw rosé. CAB D'ANJOU should be better.

Rosé de Loire Lo p ★→★★ DYA Wide-ranging AC for dr Loire rosé (ANJOU is sw).

Rosette Dordogne w s/sw ★★ DYA Pocket-sized AC for charming aperitif wines, eg CLOS Romain, CH Puypezat-Rosette and Dom de la Cardinolle.

Rostaing, René ★★★ N Rh Growing COTE-ROTIE estate with prime plots, notably La Blonde (soft, elegant wines) & fuller, firmer La Viaillère and La Landonne (15–20 years). Style is normally polished, accomplished, some new oak. Also CONDRIEU and Languedoc.

Roty, Joseph Burg ★★★ Small grower of classic GEVREY-CHAMBERTIN, esp CHARMES- and MAZIS-CHAMBERTIN. Long-lived wines.

Rouget, Emmanuel Burg ★★★★ Inheritor of the legendary estate of Henri Jayer in ECHEZEAUX, NUITS-ST-G, and VOSNE-ROMANEE. Top wine: Vosne-R-Cros Parantoux.

Roulot, Domaine G Burg ★★★ Excellent range of 7 (2 1ER CRU) distinctive MEURSAULTS.

Roumier, Georges Burg ★★★★ Christophe R makes exceptional long-lived wines in BONNES-MARES, CHAMBOLLE-MUSIGNY-Amoureuses, MUSIGNY etc. V high standards.

Rousseau, Domaine A Burg ★★★★ Grower famous for CHAMBERTIN etc, of highest quality. Wines are intense (not deep-coloured), long-lived & mostly GRAND CRU.

Roussette de Savoie w ★★ DYA The tastiest fresh white from S of Lake Geneva.

Roussillon Midi Top region for VINS DOUX NATURELS (eg MAURY, RIVESALTES, BANYULS). Lighter MUSCATS and younger vintage wines are taking over from darker heavier wines. See Côtes du Roussillon for table wines.

Ruchottes-Chambertin Burg r ★★★★ 85' 88' 89' 90' 91 93' 95 96' 97 98 99' 00 01 02 7.5-acre GRAND CRU neighbour of CHAMBERTIN. Similar splendid lasting wine of great finesse. Top growers: LEROY, MUGNERET, ROUMIER, ROUSSEAU.

Ruinart "R" de Ruinart BRUT NV; Ruinart Rosé NV; "R" de Ruinart Brut (**88 90 93** 95 96). Oldest CHAMP house, owned by MOET-Hennessy, with elegant wines, esp luxury brands: Dom Ruinart (88 **90** 93 95), Dom Ruinart Rosé (**81 83 86** 88 90). Minerally Bl de Bls NV since 2001. Also L'Exclusive de Ruinart.

Rully Burg r w (sp) ★★ (r) **99 01** 02 (w) 99 00 **01 02** COTE CHALONNAISE village. Still white and red are light but tasty, good value, esp whites. Growers incl DELORME, FAIVELEY, Dom de la Folie, Jacquesson, A RODET.

Sables du Golfe du Lion Midi p r w ★ DYA VIN DE PAYS from Mediterranean sand-dunes: esp Gris de Gris from Carignan, GRENACHE, Cinsault. Dominated by LISTEL.

Sablet S Rh r w (p) ★★ 90' 94 95' 96 **98' 99'** 00' Admirable, improving COTES DU RHONE village, esp Dom de Boissan, Les Goubert, Piaugier, CH du Trignon, Dom de Verquière. Nicely full whites to try, too.

St-Amour Beauj r ** 99 00 **01** 02 Northernmost CRU of BEAUJOLAIS: light, fruity, irresistible (esp. on Feb 14th). Growers to try: Janin, Patissier, Revillon.

St-Aubin Burg w r **★** (w) **96' 99** 00 **01** 02 (r) **96' 97 98 99' 01** 02 Understated n'bour of CHASSAGNE-M, up a side-valley. Several 1ERS CRUS: light firm quite stylish wines; fair prices. Also sold as COTE DE BEAUNE-VILLAGES. Top growers incl JADOT, J Lamy, Lamy-Pillot, H Prudhon, RAMONET, Roux, Thomas.

St-Bris Burg w ★ DYA See Sauvignon de St Bris.

St-Chinian Midi r ★→★★ 95 96 97 **98 99** 00 01 02 Hilly area of growing reputation in COTEAUX DU LANGUEDOC. AC since 82. Tasty southern reds, esp co-op Roquebrun, and from CH de Viranel, Dom Canet Valette.

St-Emilion B'x r ★★→★★★★ 70' 75 79' 81 82' **83' 85'** 86' 88 89' 90' **94 95 96** 98' 00' 01 Biggest quality B'x district (13,300 acres); solid rich tasty wines from many CHX, incl AUSONE, CANON, CHEVAL BLANC, FIGEAC, MAGDELAINE, etc. And gd co-op.

St-Estèphe B'x r ★★→★★★★ 78' **81** 82' **83'** 85' 86 **88'** 89' 90' **94 95'** 96 98 00' 01 N village of HAUT-MEDOC. Solid, structured, sometimes superlative wines. Top CHX: COS D'ESTOURNEL, MONTROSE, CALON-SEGUR, etc, and more notable CRUS BOURGEOIS than any other HAUT-MEDOC commune.

St-Gall BRUT NV; Extra Brut NV; Brut BLANC DE BLANCS NV; Brut Rosé NV; Brut Blanc de Blancs 90 95 96; CUVEE Orpale Blanc de Blancs **88** 90 95 96 Brand name used by Union-Champagne: top CHAMP growers' co-op at AVIZE. Cuvée Orpale exceptionally gd value.

St-Georges-St-Emilion B'x r ★★ 82 **83' 85'** 86' 88' 89' 90' **94 95 96 98** 00' 01 Part of MONTAGNE-ST-EM with high standards. Best ch'x: Belair-Montaiguillon, Maquin-St-G, ST-GEORGES, Tour du Pas-St-G, Griffe de Cap d'Or.

St-Gervais S Rh r (w) ★ West bank S Rhône village. Sound co-op, excellent Dom Ste-Anne reds (marked MOURVEDRE flavours); whites incl a Viognier.

St-Jean de Minervois Min w sw ★★ Perhaps top French MUSCAT: sw and fine. Much recent progress esp Dom de Barroubio, Michel Sigé, co-op.

St-Joseph N Rh r w ★★ 89 90' 91 94' 95' 96 97' **98'** 99' **00'** 01' AC stretching whole length of N Rhône (40 miles). Delicious, fruit-packed wines at its core, around Tournon; elsewhere quality variable. Often better, more structure than CROZES-HERMITAGE, esp from CHAPOUTIER (Les Granits) B Gripa, Guigal's Grippat; also CHAVE, Chèze, Coursodon, Cuilleron, DELAS, Faury, Gaillard, Gonon, JABOULET, Marsanne, Paret, Perret (esp Grisières), Trollat. Gd aromatic whites, too (mainly Marsanne grape).

St-Julien B'x r ★★★→★★★★ 70' 75 78' 81' 82' **83'** 85' 86' 88' 89' 90' 93 94 95' 96 98 99 00' 01 Mid-MEDOC village with a dozen of BORDEAUX's best ch'x, incl three LEOVILLES, BEYCHEVELLE, DUCRU-BEAUCAILLOU, GRUAUD-LAROSE, etc. The epitome of harmonious, fragrant and savoury red wine.

St-Nicolas-de-Bourgueil Lo r p ★★ 88 89' 90' 95' 96 97 **98** 00 01 02 Next to BOURGUEIL: same lively, fruity CAB F. Growers: Amirault, Cognard, Mabileau, Taluau.

St-Péray N Rh w sp ★★ **99'** 00 **01'** W Rhône (mainly Marsanne grape), some of it sp. Curiosity worth trying. Top names: S Chaboud, B Gripa, Lionnet, J-L Thiers, TAIN co-op. Jaboulet planting here.

St-Pourçain-sur-Sioule Central France r p w ★→★★ DYA Niche wine. Light red and rosé from GAMAY and/or PINOT NOIR, white from Tressalier and/or CHARDONNAY (increasingly popular) or SAUVIGNON BLANC. Recent vintages improved. Growers include: Ray, Dom de Bellevue, Pétillat, and gd co-op.

St-Romain Burg w r ★★ (w) 99 00' 01 02 Overlooked village just behind COTE DE BEAUNE. Value, esp for firm fresh whites. Reds have a clean cut. Top growers: De Chassorney, FEVRE, Jean Germain, Gras, LATOUR, LEROY.

St-Véran Burg w ★★ 99 00' **01** 02 Next door AC to POUILLY-FUISSE. Best nearly as good; others on unsuitable soil. Try DUBOEUF, Doms Corsin, des Deux Roches, des Valanges, Demessey, CH FUISSE.

Ste-Croix-du-Mont B'x w sw ★★ 83 86' 88' 89 90 **95' 96 97 98** 99 01 N'bour to SAUTERNES with similar golden wine. No superlatives but well worth trying, esp CH Loubens, Ch Lousteau Vieil, Ch du Mont. Often a bargain, esp with age.

Salon 71 73 76 82 83 85 88 90 The original BLANC DE BLANCS CHAMP, from Le Mesnil in the Côte des Blancs. Intense v dry wine with long keeping qualities. Tiny quantities. Bought in 88 by LAURENT-PERRIER.

Sancerre Lo w (r p) ★★→★★★ 96 97 98 99 00 01 02 The world's model for fragrant SAUV BL, almost indistinguishable from POUILLY-FUME, its neighbour across River Loire. Top wines can age 5 yrs⁺. Also generally light PINOT N red (best drunk at 2–3 yrs) and rosé (do not over-chill). Occasional vg VENDANGES TARDIVES. Top growers incl BOURGEOIS, Cotat Frères, Lucien Crochet, André Dezat, Jolivet, MELLOT, Vincent Pinard, Roger, Vacheron.

Santenay Burg r (w) ★★★ 88' 89' 90' 93 95 96' 97 98 99' 01 02 Sturdy reds from village S of CHASSAGNE. Best v'yds: La Comme, Les Gravières, CLOS de Tavannes. Top growers: GIRARDIN, Lequin-Roussot, Muzard, POUSSE D'OR.

Saumur Lo r w p sp ★→★★★ 89 90 93 95 97 98 **00 01 02** Fresh fruity whites plus a few more serious, vg CREMANT and Saumur MOUSSEUX (producers incl BOUVET-LADUBAY, CAVE des Vignerons de Saumur, GRATIEN ET MEYER, LANGLOIS-CHATEAU), pale rosés and increasingly good CAB F (see next entry).

Saumur-Champigny Lo r ★★→★★★ 88 89' 90' 93' **95' 96** 97 98 **00 01** 02 Flourishing 9-commune AC for fresh CAB F ageing remarkably in sunny years. Look for CH DU HUREAU, CH DE VILLENEUVE, domaines FILLIATREAU, Legrand, Nerleux, Roches Neuves, Val Brun, CLOS ROUGEARD, co-op St-Cyr.

Saussignac Dordogne w sw ★★→★★★ 95' 96 97' 98 99 (01') MONBAZILLAC-style age-worthy wines. Producers of new ultra-sw style incl Dom de Richard, CHX les Miaudoux, Tourmentine, le Payral, le Chabrier and Clos d'Yvigne.

Sauternes B'x w sw ★★→★★★★★ 67' 71' 75 76' 79' **81** 83' 85 86' 88' 89' 90' 95' **96** 97 98 99 01' 02 District of 5 villages (incl BARSAC) which make France's best sw wine, strong (14%⁺ alcohol), luscious and golden, demanding to be aged 10 yrs. Top CHX are D'YQUEM, CLIMENS, COUTET, GUIRAUD, SUDUIRAUT, etc. Dry wines cannot be sold as Sauternes.

Sauvignon Blanc See Grapes for white wine (pages 12–16).

Sauvignon de St-Bris Burg w ★★ DYA A new AC, cousin of SANCERRE, from nr CHABLIS. To try. "Dom Saint Prix" from Dom Bersan is good. Goisot best.

Sauzet, Etienne Burg ★★★ Top-quality white burgundy estate and merchant at PULIGNY-M'RACHET. Clearly-defined, well-bred wines, better drunk young.

Savennières Lo w dr sw ★★★→★★★★ 75 76' 78' **85** 86' **88 89' 90'** 93 95' 96 97 98 99 00 01 02 Small ANJOU district of pungent long-lived whites, incl Baumard, CH de Chamboureau, Ch de Coulaine, Closel, Ch d'Epiré. Top sites: COULEE DE SERRANT, ROCHE-AUX-MOINES, CLOS du Papillon.

Savigny-lès-Beaune Burg r (w) ★★★ 90' 93 95 96' 97 98 99' **00 01** 02 Important village next to BEAUNE; similar mid-weight wines, often deliciously lively, fruity. Top v'yds: Dominode, Guettes, Lavières, Marconnets, Vergelesses; growers: BIZE, Camus, CHANDON DE BRIAILLES, CLAIR, Ecard, Girard, LEROY, Pavelot, TOLLOT-BEAUT.

Savoie E France r w sp ★★ DYA Alpine area with light dry wines like some Swiss or minor Loires. APREMONT, CREPY and SEYSSEL are best-known whites, ROUSSETTE is more interesting. Also good MONDEUSE red.

Schlossberg V successful ALSACE GRAND CRU for RIES in two parts: Kientzheim and small section at Kaysersberg. Top growers: FALLER/DOM WEINBACH & PAUL BLANCK.

Schlumberger, Domaines ★→★★★ ALSACE growers at Guebwiller & lgst v'yd owners in region. Unusually rich wines incl luscious GEWURZ GRAND CRUS Kessler & Kitterlé (also SGN & VT). Fine RIES from GRAND CRUS Kitterlé, Saering. Also gd PINOT GR.

Schlumberger, Robert de Lo SAUMUR sparkling wine made by Austrian method: fruity and delicate.

Schoffit, Domaine ★★→★★★ Colmar ALSACE house with GRAND CRU RANGEN PINOT Gr, GEWÜRZ of top-quality. Chasselas is unusual everyday delight.

Schröder & Schÿler Old BORDEAUX merchant, co-owner of CH KIRWAN.

Schoenenbourg V rich successful Riquewihr GRAND CRU (ALSACE): RIES, Tokay-PINOT Gr, v fine VT and SGN. Esp from MARCEL DEISS and DOPFF AU MOULIN. Also vg MUSCAT.

Sciacarello Original grape of CORSICA for red and rosé, eg AJACCIO, Sartène.

Sec Literally means dry, though CHAMP so-called is medium-sweet (and better at breakfast, tea-time, and weddings than BRUT).

Séguret S Rh r w ★★ Good, improving S Rhône village nr GIGONDAS. Peppery, quite full red; rounded clean white. Esp CH La Courançonne, Dom de Cabasse, Garancière, Mourchon.

Sélection des Grains Nobles (SGN) Term coined by HUGEL for ALSACE equivalent to German Beerenauslese and since 1984 subject to v strict regulations. Grains nobles are individual grapes with "noble rot".

Serafin Burg ★★★ Christian S has gained a cult following for his intense GEVREY CHAMBERTIN VIEILLES VIGNES and CHARMES CHAMBERTIN GRAND CRU.

Sèvre-et-Maine The delimited zone containing the best v'yds of MUSCADET.

Seyssel Savoie w sp ★★ NV Delicate pale w, pleasant sp. NB. Mollex-Corbonod.

Sichel & Co One of B's most respected merchant houses. Peter A Sichel died in 98; his five sons continue with the family's interests in CHX D'ANGLUDET and PALMER, in CORBIERES, and as B'x merchants.

Silvaner See Grapes for white wine (pages 12–16).

Sipp, Jean and Louis ALSACE growers in Ribeauvillé (Louis is also a NEGOCIANT). Both produce vg RIES GRAND CRU Kirchberg. Jean's: youthful elegance (smaller v'yd, own vines only); Louis': firmer when mature. Louis also makes vg GEWÜRZ, esp Grand Cru Osterberg.

Sipp-Mack Great Riesling specialist at Hunawihr (est'd 1698). Outstanding Ries from Grands Crus rosacker and Osterberg (vg Pinot Gr from the latter).

Sirius Serious oak-aged blended BORDEAUX from Maison SICHEL.

Skalli ★→★★ Revolutionary producer of VINS DE PAYS D'OC from CAB S, Merlot, CHARD etc, at Sète in the LANGUEDOC, inspired by Mondavi. FORTANT DE FRANCE is standard brand. Style and value. Now Midi ACS as well.

Sorg, Bruno ★★ ·★★★ First-class small ALSACE grower at Eguisheim for GRAND CRUS Florimont (RIES) and PFERSIGBERG (MUSCAT). Also v good Auxerrois.

Sur Lie See Lie and Muscadet.

Syrah See Grapes for red wine (pages 10–12).

Tâche, La Burg r ★★★★ 78' **80'** 85' **88' 89'** 90' 93' 95 96' 97 98 99' 00 **01** 02 15-acre (1,500-case) GRAND CRU of VOSNE-ROMANEE and one of best v'yds on earth: big perfumed luxurious wine. See DOMAINE DE LA ROMANEE-CONTI.

Tain, Cave Co-opérative de, 425-members in N Rhône ACS; owns ¼ HERMITAGE. Making increasingly gd red Hermitage since 91 & sound Crozes. Good value.

Taittinger BRUT NV; Rosé NV; Brut **85 88 90 95** 96 98; Collection Brut **78 81 82 83 85 86 88** 90 Fashionable (and excellent) Reims CHAMP grower and merchant; wines have distinctive silky flowery touch. Luxury brand: Comtes de Champagne BLANC DE BLANCS (82 **85 88 90 91 94 95** 96), also vg rich Pinot Prestige Rosé NV. See also Domaine Carneros, California.

Tastevin, Confrèrie des Chevaliers du Burgundy's cheerful and colourful promotion society. Wine with the Tastevinage label has been approved by it and is usually of a fair standard. A "tastevin" is the traditional shallow silver wine-tasting cup of Burgundy.

Tavel Rh p ★★ DYA France's most famous, though not her best, rosé: strong, very full, & dry. Best growers: CH d'Aquéria, Dom Corne-Loup, GUIGAL, Maby, Dom de la Mordorée, Prieuré de Montézargues, Lafond, Ch de Trinquevedel.

Tempier, Domaine ★★★★ The top grower of BANDOL: noble reds & also rosé.

FRANCE

Terroirs Landais Gascony r p w ★ VDP an extension in the département of Landes of the COTES DE GASCOGNE. Domaine de Laballe is most seen example.

Thénard, Domaine Burg The major grower of the GIVRY appellation, but best known for his substantial portion (4⁺ acres) of LE MONTRACHET. Could still try much harder with this jewel.

Thevenet, Jean Burg ★★★ Dom de la Bongran at Clessé stands out for rich concentrated (even sweet!) white MACON.

Thézac-Perricard SW Fr r p ★ 98' 99 00' (01) VDP W of CAHORS. Same grapes but lighter style. Made by co-op at Thézac.

Thiénot, Alain Broker-turned-merchant; dynamic force for gd in CHAMP. Grande Cuvée **85 88** 90 95 96: could become one of best luxury CUVEES. Also owns Marie Stuart CHAMP, Ch Ricaud in LOUPIAC.

Thomas-Moillard Burg ★★★ Underrated NUITS-ST-GEORGES estate for slow-emerging wines; sister co is Moillard-Grivot NEGOCIANT house.

Thorin, J Beauj ★ Grower and major merchant of BEAUJOLAIS.

Thouarsais, Vin de Lo w r p ★ DYA Light CHENIN (20% CHARD permitted), GAMAY and CAB from tiny VDQS S of SAUMUR. Esp Gigon.

Tokay d'Alsace Old name for PINOT Gris in ALSACE in imitation of Hungarian Tokay. Now changed to Tokay-Pinot-Gris. Will be just Pinot Gris from 2007.

Tollot-Beaut ★★★ Stylish and consistent burgundy grower with 50 acres in the COTE DE BEAUNE, including v'yds at Beaune Grèves, CORTON, SAVIGNY- (Les Champs Chevrey) and at their CHOREY-LES-BEAUNE base.

Touraine Lo r p w dr sw sp ★→★★★ 89 95 97 **98 99** 00 01 02 Big mid-Loire region; immense range, incl dry white SAUVIGNON BLANC, dry and sweet CHENIN (eg VOUVRAY), red CHINON and BOURGUEIL. Also large AC with light CABERNET FRANC, GAMAYS, gutsy Cot, or increasingly a blend of these; grassy Sauvignon Blanc and MOUSSEUX; often bargains. Producers MARIONNET, Dehelly, Puzelat/Clos de Tue-Boeuf, Courtois, Oisly-Thesée, Ch de Petit Thouars, Jacky Marteau, Dom des Corbillieres, Clos Roche Blanche, Dom de la Presle.

Touraine-Amboise Lo r w p ★→★★ Touraine subappellation. "François 1er" is engaging local blend of GAMAY, Cot (MALBEC), & CAB F. Dutertre, Xavier Frissant.

Touraine-Azay-le-Rideau Lo dr w p ★→★★ CHENIN-based dry & off-dry whites, Grolleau-dominated rosés. Crespin, Ch de la Roche, James Paget, Pibaleau Pere et Fils.

Touraine-Mesland Lo r w p ★→★★ Best represented by its user-friendly red blends (Gamay, Cot, and Cab F). Ch Gaillard, Clos de la Briderie.

Touraine-Noble Joué Loire p ★→★★ DYA Ancient but recently revived rosé from three PINOTS (Gris, Meunier, Noir) just S of Tours. Esp from Rousseau and Sard. Granted AOC status (Touraine-Noble Joué) in 2000.

Trévallon, Domaine de Provence r w ★★★ 88 89 90 91 92 **93 94** 95 **96'** 97 98 99 00 01 Highly fashionable estate at Les Baux. Rich intense CABERNET-SYRAH blend to age.

Trimbach, F E ★★★ →★★★★ Distinguished ALSACE grower and merchant at Ribeauvillé; supremely elegant if at times austere house style. Best wines incl RIES CLOS STE-HUNE, CUVEE Frédéric-Emile (grapes mostly from GRAND CRU Osterberg). Also GEWÜRZ. Opposed to GRAND CRU system like HUGEL.

Turckheim, Cave Vinicole de ★★ Important co-op in ALSACE. Large range of wines, incl GRANDS CRUS from 790 acres. Less exciting recently.

Tursan SW France r p w ★→★★★ VDQS aspiring to AOC. Easy drinking holiday-style wines. Mostly from co-operative at Geaune, but Château de Bachen (★★★) belongs to master-chef Michel Guérard. The white is excellent; super-ripe oak-aged Sauvignon Blanc. Also ★★ Domaine de Perchade-Pourrouchet.

Vacqueyras S Rh r (w) ✶✶ 89' 90' 93 94 **95'** 96' **97** 98' **99'** 00' 01' Full, peppery GRENACHE-based neighbour to GIGONDAS – finer structure and often cheaper. Try JABOULET'S, Armouriers, Chx de Montmirail, des Tours, Doms Archimbaud-Vache, Charbonnière, Couroulu, Font de Papier, Fourmone, Garrigue, Grapillon d'Or, Monardière, Montvac, Pascal Frères, Le Sang des Cailloux.

Val d'Orbieu, Vignerons du Association of some 200 top growers and co-ops in CORBIERES, COTEAUX DU LANGUEDOC, MINERVOIS, ROUSSILLON etc, marketing a first-class range of selected MIDI AC and VDP wines.

Valençay Lo r p w ✶ DYA VDQS in E TOURAINE; light easy-drinking sometimes sharp wines from similar range of grapes as Touraine, especially SAUV BL.

Vallée du Paradis Midi r w p ✶ Popular VDP of local red varieties in CORBIERES.

Valmagne, Abbaye de Glorious Cistercian abbey nr Sète converted to cellar.

Valréas S Rh r (p w) ✶✶ 95' 96 **98' 99 00'** 01 COTES DU RHONE village with big co-op. Gd mid-weight reds (more sap than CAIRANNE, RASTEAU), improving whites. Esp Emmanuel Bouchard, Dom des Grands Devers, Ch la Décelle.

Varichon & Clerc Principal makers and shippers of SAVOIE sparkling wines.

Vaudésir Burg w ✶✶✶✶ 85' **88** 89' 90 **92 93 95** 96' **97 98** 99 00' 01 02 Arguably the best of seven CHABLIS GRANDS CRUS (but then so are the others).

VDQS Vin Délimité de Qualité Supérieure (see page 33).

Vendange Harvest. **Vendange Tardive** Late harvest. ALSACE equivalent to German Auslese, but usually higher alcohol.

Verget Burg ✶✶→✶✶✶ The NEGOCIANT business of J-M GUFFENS-HEYNEN with mixed range from MACON to MONTRACHET. Intense wines, often models, bought-in grapes. Chablis, too oaky. New Lubéron venture: Verget du Sud. Follow closely.

Veuve Clicquot Yellow label NV; White Label DEMI-SEC NV; Gold Label 59 75 (since 1985 called Vintage Réserve: 85 **90** 93 95 96); Rosé Reserve 85 90 95 96 Historic CHAMPAGNE house of highest standing, now owned by LVMH. Full-bodied, almost rich: one of Champagne's surest things. Cellars at Reims. Luxury brands: La Grande Dame (**79 83** 85 90 95), new Rich Réserve (**89**) released 95 and La Grande Dame Rosé (90 95) in 97.

Veuve Devaux Premium CHAMP of powerful Union Auboise co-op in Bar-sur-Seine. Vg aged Grande Réserve NV, Oeil de Perdrix Rosé, and new Prestige Cuvée D.

Vidal-Fleury, J Rh ✶→✶✶ Long-established GUIGAL-owned shipper of top Rhône wines and grower of COTE-ROTIE. Steady quality. La Chatillonne top Côte-Rôtie.

Vieille Ferme, La S Rh r w ✶✶ Vg brand of COTES DU VENTOUX (red) and COTES DU LUBERON (white) made by the Perrins, owners of CH DE BEAUCASTEL Reliable.

Vieilles Vignes Old vines – therefore the best wine. Used by many, esp by BOLLINGER, DE VOGUE and CH FUISSE.

Vieux Télégraphe, Domaine du S Rh r w ✶✶✶ 78' **81'** 83 85 88 **89'** 90 93 **94' 95' 96' 97** 98' **99'** 00 01 A leader in vigorous, modern red CHATEAUNEUF-DU-PAPE, and tasty whites (fuller style since 90s), which age well in lesser yrs. New gd value 2nd wine: Vieux Mas des Papes. Second dom: de la Roquette, fruited wines. Owns GIGONDAS Dom des Pallières with US importer Kermit Lynch.

Vigne or vignoble Vineyard, vineyards. **Vigneron** Vinegrower.

Vin de l'année This year's wine. See Beaujolais, Beaujolais-Villages.

Vin Doux Naturel (VDN) Sweet wine fortified with wine alcohol, so the sweetness is natural, not the strength. The speciality of ROUSSILLON. based on GRENACHE or MUSCAT. A staple in French bars, but the top wines can be remarkable.

Vin de garde Wine that will improve with keeping. The serious stuff.

Vin Gris "Grey" wine is very pale pink, made of red grapes pressed before fermentation begins – unlike rosé, which ferments briefly before pressing. Oeil de Perdrix means much the same; so does "blush".

Vin Jaune Jura w ✶✶✶ Speciality of ARBOIS: odd yellow wine like fino sherry. Normally ready when bottled (after at least 6 yrs). Best is CH-CHALON.

Vin Nouveau See Beaujolais Nouveau.

Vin de Paille Wine from grapes dried on straw mats, consequently v sweet, like Italian passito. Esp in the JURA. See also Chave.

Vin de Pays Most dynamic category in France (140+). Zonal VDPs are best eg. Coteaux de l'Uzège, Côtes de Gascogne, Côtes de Thongue, amongst others.

Vin de Table Standard everyday table wine, not subject to particular regulations about grapes and origin. Choose VINS DE PAYS instead.

Vinsobres S Rh r (p w) ★ 95' 96 **98' 99'** 00 01' Contradictory name of gd village. Substantial reds, rounded and fruity, but many ordinary. Best incl Doms les Aussellons, Bicarelle, Charme-Armaud, Deurre, Jaume, du Moulin.

Viré-Clessé Burg w ★★ 99 00' **01** 02 New AC based around two of the best white-wine villages of MACON. Extrovert, exotic style esp A Bonhomme, CLOS du Chapitre, JADOT, Château de Viré, Merlin, and co-op.

Visan S Rh r p w ★ 95' 97 98' 99 **00** RHONE village for far better medium-weight reds than whites. Note: Dom des Grands Devers.

Viticulteur Wine-grower.

Vogüé, Comte Georges de ("Dom les Musigny") ★★★★ First-class 30-acre BONNES-MARES and MUSIGNY domaine at CHAMBOLLE-MUSIGNY. At best, esp since 90, the ultimate examples. Avoid most of the 80s.

Volnay Burg r ★★★ →★★★★ 85' 88' 89' 90' 91 93 **95** 96' **97** 98 99' 00 01 Village between POMMARD and MEURSAULT: often the best reds of the COTE DE BEAUNE, not dark or heavy but structured and silky. Best v'yds: Caillerets, Champans, CLOS des Chênes, Santenots, Taillepieds, etc. Best growers: D'ANGERVILLE, J M BOILLOT, HOSPICES DE BEAUNE, LAFARGE, LAFON, DE MONTILLE, POUSSE D'OR.

Volnay-Santenots Burg r ★★★ Excellent red wine from MEURSAULT is sold under this name. Indistinguishable from other PREMIER CRU VOLNAY. Best growers: AMPEAU, HOSPICES DE BEAUNE, LAFON, LEROY.

Vosne-Romanée Burg r ★★★→★★★★ 85' 88' 89' 90' **91** 93 **95** 96' **97** 98 99' 00 01 02 Village with Burgundy's GRANDest CRUS (ROMANEE-CONTI, LA TACHE etc). There are (or should be) no common wines in Vosne. Many good growers include Arnoux, Chevigny, DRC, ENGEL, GRIVOT, GROS, JAYER, LATOUR, LEROY, MEO-CAMUZET, Mongeard-Mugneret, Mugneret, RION.

Vougeot Burg r w ★★★ 90' **91** 93 95' 96' **97** 98 99' 00 01 02 Some village and premier cru red (and white) wines. See Clos de Vougeot. Exceptional Clos Blanc de Vougeot, white since 12th Century.

Vougeraie, Dom de la Burg r ★★→★★★ DOMAINE uniting all BOISSET's v'yd holdings. Good-value BOURGOGNE ROUGE up to exceptional MUSIGNY GRAND CRU.

Vouvray Lo w dr sw sp ★★→★★★★ 76' 82 83 **85' 86 88' 89'** 90' **93** 95' **96 97** 98 99 00 01 02 (SEC and DEMI-SEC) 4,350-acre AC just E of Tours: v variable wines, increasingly gd, reliable. Demi-sec is classic style but in great years MOELLEUX can be intensely sw, almost immortal. Gd, dry sp – look out for PETILLANT. Best producers: Allias, Champalou, Clos Baudoin, Dhoye-Deruet, Foreau, Fouquet, Ch Gaudrelle, HUET, Lemaire & Renard, Pinon, Vigneau-Chevreau.

Vranken, Champagne Ever more powerful CHAMP group created in 76 by Belgian marketing man. CHARD-led wines of gd quality. Leading brand Demoiselle. Acquired HEIDSIECK MONOPOLE in 96. Now Pommery, too.

Wolfberger Principal label of Eguisheim co-op. Exceptional quality for such a large-scale producer. V. important for CREMANT.

"Y" (pron: "ygrec") B'x **78' 79' 80' 85 86 88** 94 96 Intense dry wine produced occasionally at CH D'YQUEM. Most interesting with age.

Zind-Humbrecht, Domaine ★★★★ Outstanding 99-acre ALSACE estate in Wintzenheim, Thann, Turckheim. First-rate, single-vineyard wines (especially CLOS St-Urbain), and very fine from GRANDS CRUS from Rangen, Goldert, Brand, and Hengst. Very rich, ultra-conc'd style, sometimes at expense of elegance

Châteaux of Bordeaux

The following abbreviations
of regional names
are used in the text:

B'x	Bordeaux
E-Deux-Mers	Entre-Deux-Mers
H-Méd	Haut-Médoc
Mar	Margaux
Méd	Médoc
Pau	Pauillac
Pessac-L	Pessac-Léognan
Pom	Pomerol
St-Em	St-Emilion
St-Est	St-Estèphe
St-Jul	St-Julien
Saut	Sauternes

Heavier shaded
areas are the wine
growing regions.

Gironde

MEDOC

St-Estèphe

Pauillac

St-Julien

Côtes de
Blaye

Listrac

Margaux

Moulis

Côtes de
Bourg

HAUT-
MEDOC

Fronsac

Dronne

Isle

POMEROL

Lalande de Pomerol

St-Emilion Satellites

Libourne

Côtes de Castillon

ST-EMILION

Dordogne

Bordeaux

Premieres Côtes de
Bordeaux

Ste-Foy-
Bordeaux

PESSAC-
LEOGNAN

Garonne

ENTRE-
DEUX-MERS

GRAVES

Loupiac

Cérons

Côtes de Bordeaux/St-Macaire

BARSAC

Ste-Croix-du-Mont

SAUTERNES

Langon

Which Bordeaux vintages to drink now, and which to keep? There is little need or temptation to stock up on the most recent vintages now, either for drinking or investment, except for the more modest châteaux of 2000, which are consistently ripe and pleasing without inflated prices. There is plenty of wine to enjoy at all stages of maturity at similar or lower prices in the pipeline.

Anything older than 1982 is speculative: storage conditions will be decisive to its state of health. But 1982, a great vintage all round, does not look overpriced today. Nor do 1985 and 86 – the latter a classic Cabernet vintage and still a keeper for Médocs of quality. 1988 is relatively undervalued; 1989 fully valued but excellent for drinking or keeping. 1990 is a banker; an easy choice. No need to buy anything from 1991 to 1994, but 95 is an all-rounder beginning to be splendid drinking. Buy 1996s from the northern Médoc, 1997 all round for pleasant drinking soon, 1998s from the Right Bank, and 2000s as you need them. Leave "garage" wines to boy racers.

In case of doubt the term Left Bank is wine trade short-hand for the Médoc and Graves, lying on the west side of the north-flowing river Garonne and its estuary the Gironde. Right Bank means St-Emilion, Pomerol, Fronsac, and vineyards to the east.

In this listing we have picked out in colour the vintages which proprietors themselves may be serving this year as their first choices: their own wines in the state of maturity they prefer. Their choices, for older or younger wines or both, remind us that there are no absolutes – least of all in the glorious diversity of Bordeaux.

d'Agassac H-Méd r ★★ 82' **85' 86 88** 89' **90'** 93 94 **95 96 98** 99 00' 01 Sleeping Beauty 14th-C moated fort. 86 acres v nr Bordeaux suburbs. Wine popular in Holland. New owners since '96.

Andron-Blanquet St-Est r ★★ 82 85' **86** 88 89' **90** 91 93 **94 95** 96 98' 00'. Sister château to COS-LABORY. 40 acres. Toughish wines showing more charm lately.

Angélus St-Em r ★★★★ 85' 86 **87** 88 89' **90'** 92' 93 **94** 95 96 **97** 98' 99 00' 01 02 57-acre classed-growth on ST-EMILION COTES. A current star with some sumptuous wines. Promoted to Premier Grand Cru Classé status in '96.

d'Angludet Cantenac-Mar r ★★★ **82 83'** 85 86 **88' 89'** 90 **94 95** 96' **97'** 98' 00 01 02 75-acre cru bourgeois of classed-growth quality run by Benjamin SICHEL. Lively long-living MARGAUX of great style popular in Britain. Good value.

Archambeau Graves r w dr (sw) ★★ (r) 85 86 88 89 90 93 **94 95 96** 98 00 01 (w) **95** 96 **97 98 99** 00 01 Up-to-date 54-acre property at Illats. Vg fruity dry white; fragrant barrel-aged reds (¾ of v'yd).

d'Arche Saut w sw ★★ 83' **85** 86' **88' 89'** 90 95 96 97 98 99 01' 02 Classed-growth of 88 acres rejuvenated since '80. Modern methods. Rich juicy wines to follow with pleasure.

d'Arcins H-Méd r ★★ 90 **94 95 96** 98 00 185-acre Castel family property (Castelvin: famous VIN DE TABLE). Sister to n'bour Barreyres (160 acres).

Vintages shown in light type should only be opened now out of curiosity to gauge their future. Vintages shown in bold type are deemed (usually by their makers) to be ready for drinking. Remember though that the French tend to enjoy the vigour of young wines, and that many 88s, 89s, and 90s have at least another decade of development in front of them. Vintages marked thus' are regarded as particularly successful for the property in question. Vintages in colour are the first choice for 2004.

d'Armailhac Pau r ✭✭✭ 82' **85** 86' 88' 89 **90'** 93 **94 95'** 96' 98 99 00 01 02 Formerly CH MOUTON BARONNE PHILIPPE. Substantial fifth-growth under Rothschild ownership. 125 acres: wine much less rich and luscious than MOUTON ROTHSCHILD, but outstanding in its class.

l'Arrosée St-Em r ✭✭✭ 82 83 85' **86'** 88 89' **90' 92 93 94' 95 96 97** 98' 00 24-acre COTES estate. Name means diluted, but wine is top-flight: opulent, structured.

Ausone St-Em r ✭✭✭✭ 75 76 78' **79 82'** 83' **85 86' 88 89 90 93** 94 95' 96' 97' 98' 99 00' 01 02 Illustrious first-growth with 17 acres (about 2,500 cases); best position on the COTES with famous rock-hewn cellars. Priciest ST-EMILION, but for a long time behind CHEVAL BLANC or FIGEAC in performance. Second wine: La Chapelle d'Ausone. Now superb.

Bahans-Haut-Brion Pessac-L r ✭✭✭ NV and 82 **85** 86' 88 89' 90 93 **94 95** 96' **97** 98 99 00 01 02 The second wine of CH HAUT-BRION. Worthy of its noble origin; softly earthy yet intense.

Balestard-la-Tonnelle St-Em r ✭✭ **85 86' 88' 89 90'** 93 94 **95 96** 98' 00' 01 Historic 30-acre classéd-growth on the plateau. Big flavour and finesse.

de Barbe Côtes de Bourg r (w) ✭✭ **90 94 95 96 98** 99 00 01 The biggest (148 acres), best-known château of BOURG. Light, fruity Merlot.

Barde-Haut St-Em r ✭✭ 98 99 00 01 42-acre sister-property of CLOS L'EGLISE and HAUT-BERGEY. VALANDRAUD influence: opulent.

Baret Pessac-L r w ✭✭ (r) **85 86 88** 89' **90' 95 96** 98 00 Famous name recovered from a lull. Now run by BORIE-MANOUX. White well-made too.

Bastor-Lamontagne Saut w sw ✭✭ **85 86 88'** 89' **90' 95 96'** 97 98' 99 01 02 Large Bourgeois Preignac sister-château to CH BEAUREGARD. Classed-growth quality; excellent rich wines. Second label: Les Remparts de Bastor. Also Ch St-Robert at Pujols: red and white GRAVES. 10,000 cases.

Batailley Pau r ✭✭✭ **82' 83'** 85' **86 88'** 89' 90' 93 94 **95** 96 00 02 The bigger of the famous pair of fifth-growths (with HAUT-BATAILLEY) on the borders of PAUILLAC and ST-JULIEN. 110 acres. Fine, firm, strong-flavoured, and good value Pauillac, to age. Home of the Castéja family of BORIE-MANOUX.

Beaumont Cussac (Haut-Méd) r ✭✭ **82 85 86' 88 89' 90' 93'** 94 **95 96** 98' 00 01 200-acre+ Cru Bourgeois, well known in France for easily enjoyable wines from maturing vines. Second label: Ch Moulin d'Arvigny. 35,000 cases. In the same hands as CH BEYCHEVELLE.

Beauregard Pom r ✭✭✭ **85 86 88 89' 90' 94'** 95' 96' 97 98' 99 00' 01 42-acre vineyard; fine 17th century château near LA CONSEILLANTE. Top-rank rich wines. Advice from consultant Michel Rolland. Second label: Benjamin de Beauregard.

Beau-Séjour Bécot St-Em r ✭✭✭ **82'** 85 86' **88'** 89' 90' **94** 95' 96 97 98' 99 00' 01 02 Other half of BEAUSEJOUR-DUFFAU; 45 acres. Controversially demoted in class in '85 but properly re-promoted to 1er Grand Cru Classé in '96. The Bécots also own GRAND-PONTET. Now also la Gomerie: 1,000 cases, 100% Merlot, garagiste.

Beau-Site St-Est r ✭✭ 82 85 86' **88 89'** 90 **94 95 96** 98 00 55-acre Cru Bourgeois in same hands as CH BATAILLEY etc. Recent wines rather "easy" for ST-ESTEPHE.

Beauséjour-Duffau St-Em r ✭✭✭ 82 83 85 **86 88** 89' 90' 93' **94 95 96 97'** 98 99 00 01 Part of the old Beau-Séjour Premier Grand Cru estate on W slope of the COTES. 17 acres in old family hands; only 2,000+ cases of firm-structured, concentrated, even hedonistic wine.

de Bel-Air Lalande de Pom r ✭✭ **82'** 85 86 88' 89' 90 **94'** 95 96 **98** 00 The best-known estate of Lalande de Pomerol, just north of POMEROL. Similar wine. 37 acres.

Bel-Air Marquis d'Aligre Soussans-Mar r ★★ 82' 85 86 88 89 90 95 96 97 98' 00 01 Organically run Cru Bourgeois with 42 acres of old vines giving only 3,500 cases. Concentrated but supple; a sleeper.

Bel-Orme-Tronquoy-de-Lalande St-Seurin-de-Cadourne (H-Méd) r ★★ 85 86 88 89 90 94 95 96 97' 98' 00 01 60-acre Cru Bourgeois north of ST-ESTEPHE. Old vineyard previously known for tannic wines. More tempting since new management in 1997.

Belair St-Em r ★★★ 82' 83' 85' 86' 87 88' 89' 90' 94 95' 96 97 98 99 00' 01 02 Neighbour of AUSONE. Fine wine but simpler; less tightly wound. Also NV Roc-Blanquant (magnums only). Biodynamic approach since '98.

Belgrave St-Laurent r ★★ 82 85 86' 88 89 90' 94 95 96' 98' 00' 01 Fifth-growth well-managed by DOURTHE in ST-JULIEN'S back-country. 107 acres. Second label: Diane de Belgrave.

Belles-Graves Lalande de P r ★★ 82 85 86 88 93 94 95 96 99 00 01 Confusing name, but one of the reasons to watch LALANDE DE POMEROL.

Berliquet St-Em r ★★ 86 88 89' 90 91 93 94 95 96 97 98' 99 00' 01 23-acre Grand Cru Classé recently v well run.

Bernadotte H-Méd-r ★★ 98 99 00' 01 Small château managed by PICHON-LALANDE. One to watch.

Bertineau St-Vincent Lalande de P r ★★ 98 99 00' 01 10 acres owned by top oenologist Michel Rolland (see also Le Bon Pasteur).

Beychevelle St-Jul r ★★★ 82' 85 86' 88 89' 90' 93 94' 95 96 97 98 99 00 01 02 170-acre fourth-growth with historic mansion, owned by an insurance company; now also Suntory. Wine should have elegance and power, just below top-flight ST-JULIEN. Second wine: Amiral de Beychevelle.

Biston-Brillette Moulis r ★★ 95 97 98 00 01 02 Another attractive MOULIS wine. Making 7,000 cases.

le Bon Pasteur Pom r ★★★ 82' 85 86' 88 89' 90' 93 94' 95 96' 97 98' 99 00 Excellent small property on ST-EMILION boundary, owned by consultant oenologist Michel Rolland. Concentrated, even creamy wines can be virtually guaranteed.

Bonalgue Pom r ★★ 89 90 93 94 95 96' 97 98' 99 00 Ambitious little estate recently off-form. Les Hautes-Tuileries is sister château. Also manages CLOS DU CLOCHER in POMEROL.

Bonnet E-Deux-Mers r w ★★ (r) 90 94 95 96 97 98' 00 (w) DYA Owned by André Lurton. Big producer (600 acres!) of some of the best ENTRE-DEUX-MERS. Watch out for new Cuvée Prestige "Dominus" (2000).

le Boscq St-Est r ★★ 85 86 88 89' 90 93 95' 96' 97' 98 00 01 Leading Cru Bourgeois giving excellent value in tasty ST-EST.

le Bourdieu Vertheuil H-Méd r ★★ 82 85 86 88 89 90' 94 95 96 98 00 Vertheuil Cru Bourgeois with sister château Victoria (134 acres in all); ST-ESTEPHE-style wines.

Bourgneuf-Vayron Pom r ★★ 85' 86 88 89' 90 94 95' 96' 97 98' 99 00 01 22-acre v'yd on sandy gravel soil, its best wines with typically plummy POMEROL perfume. 5,000 cases.

Bouscaut Pessac-L r w ★★ (r) 82' 85 86' 88 89 90 94 95 96 98 00 01 (w) 96 97 98 99 00 01 Underperforming classed-growth at Cadaujac bought in '80 by Lucien Lurton of BRANE-CANTENAC etc. 75 acres red (largely Merlot); 15 white. Sophie Lurton is making steady improvements.

du Bousquet Côtes de Bourg r ★★ 85 86 88 89 90' 95 96 98 99 00 01 Reliable estate with 148 acres making attractive solid wine.

Boyd-Cantenac Mar r ★★★ 82' 85 86' 88 89 90 94' 95 96' 98' 00 44-acre third-growth often producing attractive wine, full of flavour, if not of third-growth class. Second wine: Jacques Boyd. See also CH POUGET.

Branaire St-Jul r ✹✹✹ 82' 85 86 88 89' 90' 93' 94 **95** 96 98 99 00 01 02 4-growth of 125 acres. Reliable source of smooth, typical ST-JULIEN. Second label: Duluc.

Brane-Cantenac Cantenac-Mar r ✹✹✹ **82'** 85 86' 88 **89** 90 **95 96** 98 99 00 01' 02 Big (211-acre) second-growth. At best rich, even gamey wines of strong character. Also owned by the Lurton family. Second label: Baron de Brane. Much improved from late 1990s.

du Breuil Cissac (H-Méd) r ✹✹ **89 90 93** 94 95 96 98 99 00 01 Historic château being restored by CISSAC's owners.

Brillette Moulis r ✹✹ **85' 86 88 89' 90** 95 96 **97** 98 99 00 02 70-acre Cru Bourgeois. Reliable and attractive. Second label: Berthault Brillette.

la Cabanne Pom r ✹✹ **82' 88' 89' 90'** 94' **95** 96 98' 00 Well-regarded 25-acre property. Recently modernized. Second wine: Dom de Compostelle. See also CH HAUT-MAILLET.

Cadet-Piola St-Em r ✹✹ 82 85' 86 **88** 89' **90 93' 94' 95** 96 **97** 98 99 00 01 Distinguished small property (17.5 acres) north of ST-EMILION town. 3,000 cases of tannic wine. FAURIE-DE-SOUCHARD: same owner; less robust.

Caillou Saut w sw ✹✹ **75 76** 79 81 **83 85** 86 **87** 88' **89'** 90' **95 96** 97 98 99 01 02 Well-run second-rank 37-acre BARSAC vineyard for firm fruity wine. Private CUVÉE (86 88 89' 97) is a top selection.

Calon-Ségur St-Est r ✹✹✹ 82' 85 86' 88' **89' 90' 93 94 95** 96' **97** 98 99 00' 01 Big (123-acre) third-growth; great historic reputation. Greater consistency since 1995. Second label: Marquis de Ségur.

Cambon La Pelouse H-Méd r ✹✹ **94 95** 96' 97 98' 99 00 01 02 Big accessible Cru Bourgeois. A sure bet for rich typical MEDOC.

Camensac St-Laurent (H-Méd) r ✹✹ **82'** 85 86' 88 **89 90 95** 96' **97'** 98' 00 01 149-acre fifth-growth. Quite lively if not exactly classic wines. Second label: La Closerie de Camensac.

Canon St-Em r ✹✹✹ 82' 85' 86 88' 89' 90' 93' **94 95** 96 97 98' 99 00 Famous first-classed-growth with 44-plus acres on plateau west of the town bought in 1996 by (Chanel) owners of RAUZAN-SEGLA. Conservative methods, the vineyard is being restructured. Steady progress. Second label: Clos J Kanon.

Canon-de-Brem Canon-Fronsac r ✹✹ **82' 85 86 88 89' 90** 94 95 **96** 98 99 00 01 One of the top FRONSAC vineyards for vigorous wine. Formerly a MOUIEX property now under new ownership (DE LA DAUPHINE). Massive recent investment. To watch.

Canon La Gaffelière St-Em r ✹✹✹ 82 85 86' 88' 89' 90' 93' **94' 95** 96 **97** 98' 99 00 01 02 47-acre classed-growth on the lower slopes of the COTES. Same ownership as CLOS DE L'ORATOIRE and LA MONDOTTE. Produces stylish, upfront, impressive wines.

Cantegril Graves r ✹✹ 94 95 **96 97** 98 99 00 Gd earthy red from CH DOISY-DAENE.

Cantemerle Macau (H-Méd) r ✹✹✹ 82 85 **88 89' 90 95** 96' **97 98'** 00 01 02 Romantic southern MEDOC estate, a château in a wood (sadly battered in 99 gales) with 150 acres of vines. Fifth-growth capable of great things. Second label: Les Allées de Cantemerle.

Cantenac-Brown Cantenac-Mar r ✹✹→✹✹✹ 82 85 86' 88 89 90' **94 95** 96 **97** 98 99 00 01 02 Formerly old-fashioned 77-acre third-growth. Now owned by AXA Millésimes (same as PICHON-LONGUEVILLE). Its investment is starting to pay off. Tannic wines. 2nd label: Canuet.

Cap de Mourlin St-Em r ✹✹ **82' 85 86 88 89 90** 93 94 **95** 96 97 98' 99 00 01 Well-known 37-acre property of the Cap-de-Mourlin family, also owners of CH BALESTARD and Château Roudier, MONTAGNE-ST-EMILION. Should be a rich tasty ST-EMILION.

Capbern-Gasqueton St-Est r ★★ 86 **88 89 90 94 95 96** 98 00 01 Good 85-acre Cru Bourgeois; same owner as CALON-SÉGUR.

Carbonnieux Pessac-L r w ★★★ 82 85 86' 88 **89' 90' 93 94 95** 96 98 99 00 Historic estate at LEOGNAN for sterling red and white. The whites, 65% Sauv (eg **92'** 94' 95 96 97 98 00 01 02), can have the structure to age 10 yrs. Ch'x Le Pape and Le Sartre are also in the family. Second label: La Tour-Léognan.

de Cardaillan Graves r ★★ **94** 95 96 98 99 00 The trusty red wine of the distinguished CHÂTEAU DE MALLE (SAUTERNES).

la Cardonne Blaignan (Méd) r ★★→★★★ **94** 95 **96** 97 **98** 99 00 02 Fairly large (125 acre) Cru Bourgeois of northern MEDOC.

de Carles Fronsac r ★★ 86 88 89 90 **94 95 96** 97' 98 99 00 01 Ancient château (named after Charlemagne). Steadily well-made quite juicy FRONSACS. Haut Carles is the top selection.

les Carmes-Haut-Brion Pessac-L r ★★★ 85 86 88' 89 90' **93'** 94 95 96 **97** 98 99 00 01 02 Small (11-acre) neighbour of HAUT-BRION with classed-growth standards. Old vintages show its potential. Produces 2,000 cases.

Caronne-Ste-Gemme St-Laurent (H-Méd) r ★★→★★★ **83** 85 86 89' 90 94' 95 96' 98 99 00 01 02 Cru Bourgeois (100 acres). Steady stylish quality repays patience. At minor CRU CLASSÉ level (esp 96).

Carsin Premières Côtes r w ★★ (r) **94 95 96 97** 98' 99 00 01 (w) **95 96 97 98** 99 00 01 Ambitious enterprise: Finnish-owned, Australian winemaker. Very attractive (especially "CUVEE Prestige" and white "Etiquette Grise"). To follow.

Carteau Côtes-Daugay St-Em r ★★ **85 88 89 90 94 95 96'** 97 **98'** 99 00 01 Emerging 5,000-case GRAND CRU; full-flavoured wines maturing fairly early.

Certan-Guiraud Pom r ★★ 82 83' **85 86 88 89' 90' 93' 94 95 96** 98 99 00 01 Small (17-acre) property. Has underperformed but was bought in '99 by J-P MOUEIX. Renamed Ch. Hosanna in 2000.

Certan-de-May Pom r ★★★ 82' 83' **85' 86 87 88' 89' 90' 94 95** 96' 98 00' 01 Tiny property (1,800 cases) with full-bodied, rich, tannic wine.

Chambert-Marbuzet St-Est r ★★→★★★ **82 85 86 88 89' 90'** 93 94' 95 96 97' 98 99 00 01 HAUT-MARBUZET's tiny (20-acre) sister château. Vg predominantly Cabernet, aged in new oak. M Duboscq likes his wine well hung.

Chantegrive Graves r w ★★ →★★★ 88 89 90 **94 95 96** 98' 99' 00 01 215-acre estate, half white, half red; modern GRAVES of very fair quality. CUVEE Caroline is top white selection (**93 94 95 96 97 98'** 99 00 01); top reds (**85 88** 89 90 **94 95** 96 98 99 00 01). Other labels incl Mayne-Lévêque, Mayne-d'Anice, Bon-Dieu-des-Vignes.

Chasse-Spleen Moulis r ★★★ 78' 82' 83' **85 86 88 89' 90'** 93 94 95 96 98 99 00 01 02 180-acre Cru Bourgeois at classed-growth level. Consistently good, often outstanding (eg **90'**), long-maturing wine. Second label: Ermitage de C-S. One of the surest things in Bordeaux. See also La Gurgue and Haut-Bages-Libéral.

Chauvin St Em r ★★ 88 89 90 **93** 94 95 **96** 98' 99 00 01 Steady performer; increasingly serious stuff. New vineyards purhased '98.

Cheval Blanc St-Em r ★★★★ 75' 76 78 79 82' 83' **85'** 86 88 89 90' 93 **94** 95 96' 97 98' 99 00' 01 02 This and AUSONE are the first growths of ST-EMILION. Until recent vintages, Cheval Blanc has been consistently richer, more full-blooded, intensely vigorous, and perfumed, from 100 acres. Delicious young; lasts a generation. For many *the* first choice in Bordeaux. Second wine: Le Petit Cheval.

Chevalier, Domaine de Pessac-L r w ★★★ 79 83' 85 86' 88' **89' 90'** 93 94' **95'** 96' 97 98' 99 00' 01 02 Superb estate of 94 acres at LEOGNAN. The red is stern at first, softly earthy with age. The white matures slowly and develops rich flavours (83' **85'** 87' 88 89 90' **92 93 94 95** 96' 97 98' 99 00

01 02). Second wine: Esprit de Chevalier. Also look out for Domaine de la Solitude, PESSAC-LEOGNAN.

Cissac Cissac-Médoc r ★★ **82' 83' 85 86' 88 89 90** 93 94' 95 96' 98 00 01 Pillar of the bourgeoisie. 80-acre Cru Bourgeois : steady record for tasty, very long-lived wine. New winery 00. Second wine: Les Reflets du Ch Cissac. Also, since 1987, CH DU BREUIL.

Citran Avensan (H-Méd) r ★★ **82 85 86 88 89' 90' 94'** 95 **96 97** 98 99 00 Cru Bourgeois of 178 acres, back in the possession of Villars-Merlaut family since 1996 after a Japanese interlude of dark, tannic wines. Much of the vineyard was replanted in 1999. Second label: Moulins de Citran. This is one to watch.

Clarke Listrac r (p w) ★★ **82** 85' **86' 88** 89' 90' 95 **96'** 97 **98'** 99 00 01 02 Huge (350-acre) Cru Bourgeois Rothschild development, incl visitor facilities and neighbouring Ch'x Malmaison and Peyrelebade. Also a dry white "Le Merle Blanc du Ch Clarke".

Clerc Milon Pau r ★★ 82' **85** 86' **88 89' 90'** 93 **94 95** 96' 97 98' 99 00 01 Once-forgotten fifth-growth bought by the late Baron Philippe de Rothschild in 70. Now 73 acres and a top performer, weightier than ARMAILHAC.

Climens Saut w sw ★★★★ **71'** 75' **76** 78 **79 80'** 83' **85'** 86' **88' 89 90'** 95 96 97' 98 99 01' 02 74-acre BARSAC classed-growth making some of the world's most stylish wine (but not v sweetest) for a good 10 yrs' maturing. (Occasional) second label: Les Cyprès. Owned by Berenice Lurton.

Clinet Pom r ★★★★ **82 83 85 86 88' 89'** 90' **93'** 94 95 96 97' 98' 99 00 01 02 17-acre property in central POMEROL making intense sumptuous wines from old vines. Since 88 one of the models for Pomerol. Since 98 owned by Groupe Jean Louis Laborde. 2nd label: Fleur de Clinet

Clos l'Eglise Pom r ★★★ **85 86 88 89** 90' **93 94 95 96 97** 98 99 00' 01 15-acre v'yd on one of the best sites in POMEROL. Fine wine with more depth since 98. M Rolland consults. The same family owns CH HAUT-BERGEY.

Clos Floridène Graves r w ★★ (r) 95 **96 97** 98' 99 00 01 (w) 93 **94 95** 96' 97 98' 99 00 01 A sure thing from one of B'x's most famous white winemakers, Denis Dubourdieu. Oak-fermented Sauv-Sém to keep 5 years; fruity red. See also CH REYNON. New winery 2000.

Clos Fourtet St-Em r ★★★ 82' 83 **85** 86 88 89 **90 94** 95 96 **97** 98 99 00 01 Well-placed 42-acre first-growth on the plateau, cellars almost in town. Back on form after a middling patch: Acquired by Philippe Cuvelier in January 2001. Second label: Dom de Martialis.

Clos Haut-Peyraguey Saut w sw ★★ **75 76 79 82** 83' **85 86' 88'** 89 90' **95'** 96 97 98 99 00 01' 02 Tiny production of excellent medium-rich wine. Haut-Bommes is the second label.

Clos des Jacobins St-Em r ★★ 82' 83' **85 86 88'** 89' **90'** 94 95 96 98 99 00 01 Well-known and well-run little (18-acre) classed-growth. New ownership from 2001; new creamy style. To watch.

Clos du Marquis St-Jul r ★★·★··★ 82 **85** 86' **88 89'** 90 **94 95** 96 **97** 98 99 00 01 The second wine of LEOVILLE-LAS-CASES, cut from the same cloth and regularly a match for many highly classed growths.

Clos de l'Oratoire St-Em r ★★ **90 94 95** 96 **97** 98 99 00 01 Serious performer on the NE slopes of ST-EM. Same stable as CANON-LA-GAFFELIÈRE and LA MONDOTTE but lighter than either.

Clos René Pom r ★★ 82' **85 86** 88 89 90 **94 95 96** 98 99 Leading château west of POMEROL. 38 acres. Increasingly concentrated wines. Alias Château Moulinet-Lasserre.

Clos Toumilon Graves r w ★★ 96 97 98 99 00 01 Little château in St-Pierre-de-Mons to note. Fresh and charming red and white.

la Closerie du Grand-Poujeaux Moulis r ★★ 85 86 88 **89** 90 **94' 95** 96 98' oo Small but respected middle-MEDOC property with emphatic wines. Also owners of neighbouring Ch'x Bel-Air-Lagrave and Haut-Franquet.

la Clotte St-Em r ★★**82 83'** 85 86 88 **89** 90' 93' 94 95' 96' 97 98' 99 oo' 01 Tiny COTES GRAND CRU CLASSÉ: pungent supple wine. Drink at owners' restaurant, Logis de la Cadène in ST-EM. Second label: Clos Bergat Bosson.

Colombier-Monpelou Pau r ★★ 86' 88 89 90' 94 95 96 97 98 99 oo Reliable small Cru Bourgeois; fair standard.

la Conseillante Pom r ★★★★ **70' 75' 81'** 82' 83 85 86 87 88 89 90' 93 94 **95'** 96' 97 98' 99 oo 01 29-acre historic property on the plateau between PÉTRUS and CHEVAL BLANC. Some of the noblest and most fragrant POMEROL, worthy of its superb position; drinks well young or old.

Corbin St-Em r ★★ 82' 83 85 86 88 89 90' **95** 96 98 99 oo 28-acre classed-growth. A cluster of Corbins occupy the plateau edge. Top vintages are v rich.

Corbin-Michotte St-Em r ★★ 82 85 88 89' 90 93 94' 95 96 97 98' 99 oo 01 Well-run modernized 19-acre property; generous, POMEROL-like wine. In same hands as Chx Calon, Cantelauze.

Cordeillan-Bages Pau r ★★ A mere 1,000 cases of rather lean PAUILLAC. Better known as a luxury wealth-spa for wine writers.

Cos d'Estournel St-Est r ★★★★ **82' 85' 86' 87 88' 89' 90'** 93' **94** 95 96' 97' 98' 99 oo 01 02 140-acre second-growth with eccentric chinoiserie chai. Most refined ST-EST and regularly one of best wines of the MEDOC. Second label: Les Pagodes de Cos. Managed by Jean-Guillaume Prats.

Cos-Labory St-Est r ★★ 82 85 86 87 88 89' 90' 93 94 95 96' 98' 99 oo 02 Little-known fifth-growth neighbour of COS-D'ESTOURNEL with 37 acres. Efforts since 1985 have raised it steadily to classed-growth form (especially since 1990). ANDRON-BLANQUET is sister château.

Coufran St-Seurin-de-Cadourne (H-Méd) r ★★**82' 85 86' 88 89 90 94 95 96' 97** 98 99 oo 01 Coufran and CH VERDIGNAN, in the extreme N of the HAUT-MEDOC, are co-owned. Coufran is mainly Merlot for supple wine. 148 acres. CH SOUDARS is another, smaller sister.

Couhins-Lurton Graves w ★★–★★★ 93 94 95 96 97' 98' 99 oo 01 Tiny quantity of fine oaky Sauvignon Blanc. Classed-growth château.

la Couspaude St Em r ★★★ 89 90 93 94 95 96 97 98 99 oo 01 Another to watch closely. Modern methods and full-flavoured wine.

Coutet Saut w SW ★★★ **71' 75'** 76 79 81' **83'** 85 86' **88' 89' 90'** (no 93 94) **95** 96 97 98' 99 01' 02 Traditional rival to CH CLIMENS; 91 acres in BARSAC. Usually slightly less rich; at its best equally fine. CUVÉE Madame is a v rich selection in the best vintages. A dry GRAVES is sold under the same name.

Couvent des Jacobins St-Em r ★★ **82' 85 86 87 88 89 90 94 95 96' 97** 98' 99 oo Well-known 22-acre vineyard on east edge of town. Among the best of its kind. Splendid cellars. Second label: Ch Beau-Mayne.

le Crock St-Est r ★★ 82 85 86 **88 89 90' 93 95** 96 97 98 99 oo 01 Outstanding Cru Bourgeois of 74 acres in the same family as CH LEOVILLE-POYFERRE. Among the best Crus Bourgeois of the commune.

La Croix Pom r ★★ 83 85' 86 88 89 90 93 94 95 96 97 98 99 oo 01 Well-reputed property of 32 acres. Appealing plummy POMEROL. Also La C-St-Georges, La C-Toulifaut, Castelot, Clos des Litanies, and HAUT-SARPE (St-Em).

la Croix-de-Gay Pom r ★★★ 85 86 88' **89 90** 93 94' **95 96** 98 99 oo 01 02 30 acres in best part of the commune. Recently on fine form. Has underground cellars (rare in POMEROL). LA FLEUR-DE-GAY is the best selection.

To decipher codes, please refer to "Key to symbols" on front flap of jacket, or to "How to use this book" on page 6.

la Croix du Casse Pom r ✶✶ 89 90 **93 94 95 96 97** 98 99 00 01 Up-and-coming property to look out for. Same owner as CLINET.

Croizet-Bages Pau r ✶✶ **82' 85 86 88** 89 **90' 95** 96' 98' 00 01 02 52-acre fifth-growth. Same owners as CH RAUZAN-GASSIES. The 98 may indicate better things to come.

Croque-Michotte St-Em r ✶✶ 82' **83 85 86** 88 89' 90' **94 95 96** 98 00 01 35-acre Grand Cru on the POMEROL border. Good steady wines but not grand enough to be classé.

de Cruzeau Pessac-L s r w ✶✶ (r) **86 88 89 90** 94 **95 96** 97 99 00 01 100-acre PESSAC-LEOGNAN v'yd recently developed by André Lurton of LA LOUVIERE etc. To try. Oak-fermented white keeps 2–5 years.

Dalem Fronsac r ✶✶ **85 86 88 89 90** 94 95 96' **97** 98' 99 00 01 Leading full-blooded FRONSAC. 36 acres: 85% Merlot.

Dassault St-Em r ✶✶ 82 **85 86** 88 **89** 90 94 95 **96** 97 98' 99 00 01 02 A consistent, early-maturing middle-weight GRAND CRU CLASSÉ. 58 acres. Could be more exciting.

de la Dauphine Fronsac r ✶✶ **85 86** 88 89' 90' 94 95 **96 98' 99** 00 01 Old star rejuvenated by J-P MOUEIX and sold to owners of CANON-DE-BREM in 00. New winery and cellars in 2002 – to watch.

Dauzac Labarde-Mar r ✶✶→✶✶✶ **82' 85 86** 88' 89' 90' 93' 94 **95** 96 98' 99 00 01 02 120-acre fifth-growth nr the river south of MARGAUX; underachiever for many years, now improving. New owner (insurance company) in 89; began to achieve in the 90s. Second wine: La Bastide Dauzac.

Desmirail Mar r ✶✶→✶✶✶ **82 85 86 88 89** 90 94 95' 96' 97 98 00 01 3rd-growth, now 45 acres. Wines for drinking fairly young, but higher ambitions.

Doisy-Daëne Barsac w (r) sw dr ✶✶✶ **76' 80 82 83** 85 86 88' 89' 90' **95 96** 97 98' 99 01 02 Forward-looking, even experimental, 34-acre estate producing a crisp oaky dry white and a red, CHATEAU CANTEGRIL, but above all renowned for its notably fine (and long-lived) sweet BARSAC. L'Extravagance (**90** 96 97 01 02) is a super-CUVEE.

Doisy-Dubroca Barsac w sw ✶✶ 75' 76 **78 79** 83 **85 86 88' 90' 95** 96 97 99 01 Tiny (8.5-acre) BARSAC classed-growth allied to CH CLIMENS.

Doisy-Védrines Saut w sw ✶✶✶ 75' 76' **79 80** 83' **85 86** 88' 89' **90 95 96** 97 98' 99 01 50-acre classed-growth at BARSAC, near CLIMENS and COUTET. Delicious, sturdy, rich: for keeping. A sure thing for many years.

la Dominique St-Em r ✶✶✶ **79 81 82' 83 86' 87** 88' 89' 90' 93 94 **95 96 97** 98 99 00 01 45-acre classed-growth for fruity, wines. Second label: St Paul de Dominique.

Ducluzeau Listrac r ✶✶ **82 85 86 88 89 90** 94 95 96' 00 01 Tiny sister property of DUCRU-BEAUCAILLOU. 10 acres, unusually 90% Merlot.

Ducru-Beaucaillou St-Jul r ✶✶✶✶ **61 66' 70' 75' 78' 81 82' 83' 85' 86'** 89 90 93 **94** 95 96' **97** 98 99 00' 01 02 Outstanding second-growth on excellent form; 120 acres overlooking the river. Classic cedar-scented claret suited to long ageing. See also GRAND-PUY-LACOSTE, HAUT-BATAILLEY, LALANDE-BORIE.

Duhart-Milon Rothschild Pau r ✶✶✶ 82' 85 **86 88 89 90 93 94 95** 96' 98 00' 01 02 Fourth-growth neighbour of LAFITE, under same management. Maturing vines; increasingly fine quality and reputation. 2000 is the best yet. 110 acres. Second label: Moulin de Duhart.

Duplessis Moulis r ✶✶ **82 85 86** 88' 89 90 93 95 96 98 00 01 CRU BOURGEOIS run by Marie Laure Lurton-Roux. Wines typical of MOULIS. See also VILLEGEORGE.

Durfort-Vivens Mar r ✶✶✶ **82' 85' 86 88' 89' 90** 94 95 96 98 99 00 01 02 Relatively small (49-acre) second-growth owned and being improved by Gonzague Lurton. Recent wines have structure (lots of Cab S) and class.

Dutruch Grand-Poujeaux Moulis r ★★ **82' 85 86 88 89 90 93** 94 95 96' 98' 99 00 01 One of the leaders of MOULIS making full-bodied and tannic wines.

de l'Eglise, Domaine Pom r ★★ 82' 85 86 **88 89 90 95 96** 98 99 00 Small property: stylish resonant wine distributed by BORIE-MANOUX.

l'Eglise-Clinet Pom r ★★★★ 82' 83' 84 85' 86 88' **89** 90' **93' 94** 95 96 97' 98' 99 00 01 11 acres. Ranked very near top; full, concentrated, fleshy wine. A château to follow, but expensive. 1,700 cases produced. Second label: La Petite Eglise.

l'Enclos Pom r ★★★ **82' 85 86 88** 89' 90' 93 94 **95** 96 98' 99 00 01 Excellent 26-acre property on west side of POMEROL. Usually big well-made long-flavoured wine.

l'Evangile Pom r ★★★★ **75'** 82' **83' 85'** 86 87 88' **89'** 90' 93 **95'** 96' **97** 98' 99 00 01 02 33 acres between PÉTRUS and CHEVAL BLANC. Deep-veined but elegant style in a POMEROL classic. Bought in 90 by Domaines (LAFITE) Rothschild. New equipment '00.

de Fargues Saut w sw ★★★ **70' 71' 75'** 76' 78 79 81 83 85' **86 88 89 90 95 96** 97 98 99' 01 25-acre v'yd by ruined château owned by Luc-Saluces of YQUEM fame. Fruity and extremely elegant wines, maturing earlier than Yquem.

Faurie-de-Souchard St-Em r ★★ **85 86 88** 89 90 93 **94 95 96** 98' 00 01 Small GRAND CRU CLASSÉ on the CÔTES. See also CH CADET-PIOLA.

de Ferrand St-Em r ★★ 85 86 88 89 90' 93' **94 95 96** 98 00 01 Big (75-acre) plateau estate. Rich oaky wines, with plenty of tannin.

Ferrande Graves r (w) ★★ **95** 96 98 00 Major estate at Castres: 100[+] acres. Easy enjoyable red and good white wine, at their best at 1–4 yrs.

Ferrière Mar r ★★→★★★ **89 90** 93 94 **95 96 97'** 98 99 00 01 02 In same capable hands as LA GURGUE and HAUT-BAGES-LIBERAL. New equipment '00.

Feytit-Clinet Pom r ★★ 82' 85' **86 90'** 94 95 96 97' 98 99 00 Little property. At best fine lightish wines. 00 owning Chasseuil family took back management from J-P MOUEIX.

Fieuzal Pessac-L r (w) ★★★ **82' 85' 86' 88 89 90' 93 94 95** 96' 97 98' 99 00 01 02 75-acre classed-growth at LEOGNAN. Finely made, memorable wines of both colours. Classic whites since '85 are 4–10-yr keepers. Ch Le Bonnat is sister château vinified at FIEUZAL.

Figeac St-Em r ★★★★ 70' 75 82' 83 85' 86' 88 89' 90' **94' 95' 96** 98 99 00 01 02 First-growth, 98-acre gravelly vineyard gives one of Bordeaux's most stylish, rich but elegant wines, lovely to drink relatively quickly but lasting indefinitely. Second label: Grangeneuve.

Filhot Saut w sw dr ★★ 82' 83' 85 86' **88' 88** 90 95 **96** 97 98 99 01 02 Second-rank classed-growth with splendid château, 148-acre vineyard. Lightish and rather simple (Sauvignon) sweet wines for fairly early drinking, a little dry, and red. Very good "Crème de Tête" (**90** extremely rich).

la Fleur St-Em r ★★ 82' **85 86 88** 89' 90' 94 95 96 98 00 01 16-acre CÔTES estate; deliciously fruity wines. Managed by J-P MOUEIX.

la Fleur-de-Gay Pom r ★★★ 1,000-case super-CUVÉE of CH LA CROIX DE GAY.

la Fleur-Pétrus Pom r ★★★★ 82 **83'** 85 86 87 88' 89' 90' 93 94 **95** 96' 97 98 99 00 01 32-acre vineyard flanking PÉTRUS with the same management. Exceedingly fine densely plummy wines; POMEROL at its most stylish (and expensive).

Fombrauge St-Em r ★★→★★★ 88' 89 90 **94' 95 96** 9800 01 120 acres at St-Christophe-des-Bardes, east of ST-EMILION; Mainstream St-Emilion making great efforts. Second label: Château Maurens. Magrez-Fombrauge is its "GARAGE" wine.

Fonbadet Pau r ★★ 85 86 88 89 90' **94 95** 96' 98' 00 01 Cru Bourgeois of solid reputation. 50 acres. Old vines; wine needs long bottle-age. Value.

BORDEAUX

Fonplégade St-Em r ★★ 82' 85 86 **88** 89 **90' 94 95 96** 98 00 48-acre GRAND CRU CLASSÉ on the COTES W of ST-EMILION. At best firm and long-lasting.

Fonréaud Listrac r ★★ **82' 83** 85' 86' 88 89 90 **94** 95 96 98 00 One of the bigger (96 acres) and better Crus Bourgeois of its area. Investment in 1998 and onwards. 5 acres of white: Le Cygne, barrel-fermented. See also CHÂTEAU LESTAGE.

Fonroque St-Em r ★★★ **75' 78 82 83' 85' 86 87 88 89' 90' 94 95 96** 98 00 01 48 acres on the plateau N of ST-EMILION. WAS J-P MOUEIX property until 00, now Alain Moueix. Major investment and organic ideas. Big deep dark wine: drink or (better) keep.

Fontenil Fronsac r ★★ 88 89 90 **94 95** 96 97 98 99' 00 01 A new FRONSAC leader started by Michel Rolland in 86. Dense, oaky, new-style.

Fontmarty Pom r ★★ **82 83 85 86 88' 89 90** 94 95' 96 98' 00 Small property owned by Bernard Moueix group (also TAILLEFER); 1,500 cases.

Forts de Latour Pau r ★★★ **70' 78' 81 82' 83 85 86 87 88 89' 90' 93 94** 95' 96' **97** 98 99 00 01 02 The (worthy) second wine of CH LATOUR; the authentic flavour in slightly lighter format. Until 1990 unique in being bottle-aged at least three years before release; now offered EN PRIMEUR.

Fourcas-Dupré Listrac r ★★ **82' 83' 85' 86'** 88 89' 90 94 95 96' 98' 99 00 01 02 Top-class 100-acre Cru Bourgeois making consistent wine in the tight LISTRAC style. To follow. Second label: Château Bellevue-Laffont. Complete renovation 2000.

Fourcas-Hosten Listrac r ★★ ···★★ **82' 83' 85** 86' **87** 88 89' 90' 94 **95' 96'** 98' 00 01 02 96-acre Cru Bourgeois often the best of its (underestimated) commune. Firm wine with a long life. New gear 98.

Franc-Mayne St-Em r ★★ 85 86 88 89' 90' 94 95 96 97 98' 99 00 01 18 acre-GRAND CRU CLASSÉ. Ambitious new owners 1996. Michel Rolland consults. To watch. Continuing renovation started 98.

de France Pessac-L r w ★★ (r) 89 **90' 95' 96' 98** 99 00 (w) **95 96 97** 98 99 01 Well-known GRAVES property (the name helps) with Michel Rolland consulting. Try a top vintage.

la Gaffelière St-Em r ★★★ **82' 83'** 85 86' 88' **89' 90' 94** 95 96 98' 99 00 01 61-acre first-growth at the foot of the COTES. Elegant, not rich wines. Re-equipped and improved since 1998.

Galius St-Em r ★★ 95 96 98 00 Oak-aged selection from ST-EMILION cooperative, to a high standard. Formerly Haut Quercus.

La Garde Pessac-L r w ★★ 90 **94** 95' 96' **97'** 98' 99 00 01 Substantial property of 120 acres owned by negociant CVBG-Dourthe; reliable red and improving. More Merlot planted 2000.

le Gay Pom r ★★★ **75' 76' 82' 83' 85 86 88 89' 90' 95** 96 97 98 99 00 01 Fine 14-acre vineyard on north edge of POMEROL. Same owner as CH LAFLEUR until 2002. Usually impressive tannic wines.

Gazin Pom r ★★★ **82 85 86 87'** 88 89' 90' 94' **95** 96 **97** 98' 99 00 01 02 Large property (for POMEROL): 58 acres recently shining. Second label: l'Hospitalet de Gazin.

Gilette Saut w sw ★★★ 49 53 **55 59 61 67 70** 75 76 78 79 81 Extraordinary small Preignac château stores its sumptuous wines in concrete vats to a great age. Only about 5,000 bottles of each. Château Les Justices is the sister château (**96** 97 99 01).

Giscours Labarde-Mar r ★★★ **70** 75' **78' 82** 85 88 89' 90 **94 95** 96' 98 99 00 01 02 Splendid 182-acre third-growth property south of CANTENAC. Excellent vigorous wine in 70s; 80s very wobbly; some revival during 90s esp under new owner since 1995, but should do better. Second labels: Château Cantelaude, Grand Goucsirs (!) and La Sirène de Giscours. Ch La Houringue is its baby sister.

du Glana St-Jul r ★★ **89 90 94** 95 96 97' 98 99 00 Big Cru Bourgeois. Undemanding; undramatic; value. Second wine: Château Sirène.

Gloria St-Jul r ★★ ·★★★ **82 85 86 88 89 90 95'** 96 98 99 00 01 Cru Bourgeois with wine of vigour. 110 acres. Recent return to long-maturing style. Second label: Peymartin.

la Gomerie See BEAUSÉJOUR-BÉCOT.

Grand Barrail Lamarzelle Figeac St-Em r ★★ **85 86 88 89 90 94 95 96** 98 00 48-acre property south of FIGEAC. Well-reputed and popular, if scarcely exciting.

Grand-Corbin-Despagne St-Em r ★★ ·★★★ **82' 83 85 88 89 90' 93 94 95** 96 97 98 99 00 01 One of the bigger and better GRANDS CRUS on CORBIN plateau. New generation in 93, determined to get reinstated as GCC – was demoted 96. Now fashionably thick wines. Also Ch Maison Blanche, MONTAGNE ST-EM.

Grand-Mayne St-Em r ★★★ **82 85 86 88 89' 90' 94 95** 96 97 98 99 00 01 02 40-acre GRAND CRU CLASSÉ on W COTES. Noble old château with wonderfully rich tasty wines recently.

Grand-Pontet St-Em r ★★★ **82' 86' 88 89' 93 94 95' 96 97** 98' 99 00 01 35 acres revitalized since 85. Quality improving.

Grand-Puy-Ducasse Pau r ★★★ **82' 85 86 88 89' 90 94** 95 96' 98' 99 00 01 02 Fifth-growth enlarged to 90 acres under expert management, but lacks the vigour of the next entry. Second label: Ch Artigues-Arnaud.

Grand-Puy-Lacoste Pau r ★★★ **70' 75 78' 79' 81' 82' 83 85' 86' 88' 89' 90' 93 94** 95 96' **97** 98 99 00 01 Leading fifth-growth famous for excellent full-bodied vigorous examples of PAUILLAC. 110 acres, owned by the Borie family (see Ducru-Beaucaillou). Second label: Lacoste-Borie.

Gravas Saut w sw ★★ **96 97** 01 Small BARSAC property; impressive, firm, sweet. NB CUVÉE Spéciale.

La Grave à Pomerol Pom r ★★★ **82' 85 86' 88** 89' 90 93 94 95 96 98' 00 01 Verdant château with small but first-class v'yd owned by CHRISTIAN MOUEIX. Beautifully structured POMEROL of medium richness.

Gressier-Grand-Poujeaux Moulis r ★★ ·★★★ **82 83' 85 86 88 89 90 94 95** 96 98 00 01 Vg Cru Bourgeois. Fine firm wine with good track record. Repays patient cellaring.

Greysac Méd r ★★ 95 96 00 02 Elegant 140-acre property. Easy, early maturing wines popular in US.

Gruaud-Larose St-Jul r ★★★★ **61 70 75 78' 82' 83' 85 86' 88' 89 90' 93** 95 96' 98 99 00 01 02 One of the biggest and best-loved second-growths. 189 acres. Smooth rich stylish claret, year after year; ages for 20⁺ years. Owned by Societé Bernard Taillan since 1997. Very good second wine: Sarget de Gruaud-Larose.

Guadet-St-Julien St-Em r ★★ 82 85 86 88 89 90' **94** 95 96' 98 00 01 Extremely well-made wines from v small GRAND CRU CLASSÉ.

Guiraud Saut w (r) sw (dr) ★★★ **79 81 83'** 85 86' 88' **89' 90' 95 96'** 97' 98 99 01' 02 Restored classed-growth of top quality. 250+ acres. At best excellent sweet wine of great finesse; also small amount of red and dry white.

la Gurgue Mar r ★★ **82 83' 85' 86 87 88 89' 90 94** 95' 96' 98 00 01 02 Small, well-placed 25-acre property, for MARGAUX of the fruitier sort. Same management as HAUT-BAGES-LIBERAL. Winery renovated '00.

Hanteillan Cissac r ★★ 95 96 98 00 01 Huge vineyard: very fair Cru Bourgeois, conscientiously made. Ch Laborde is the second label.

Haut-Bages Averous Pau r ★★ **82' 85' 86 88** 89' 90 94 **95 96** 98 99 00 The second wine of CH LYNCH BAGES. Should be tasty drinking.

Haut-Bages-Libéral Pau r ★★★ **82' 85 88 89** 90' 93 **94' 95** 96' 97' 98 99 00 01 Lesser-known fifth-growth of 70 acres (next to LATOUR) in same stable as LA GURGUE. Results are excellent, full of PAUILLAC vitality.

Haut-Bages-Monpelou Pauillac r ★★ **85 86 88** 89' 90 **94 95** 96 98 99 00 25-acre Cru Bourgeois stable-mate of CH BATAILLEY on former DUHART-MILON land. Good minor PAUILLAC.

Haut-Bailly Graves r ★★★ 82 83 85' **86 88' 89'** 90' 92 **93' 94 95** 96 **97** 98 99' 99' 00 01 02 70-acres+ at LEOGNAN American-owned since 98, but old family still directing. Since 79 some of the best savoury, round, intelligently made red GRAVES have regularly come from this château. Second label is La Parde de Haut-Bailly.

Haut-Batailley Pau r ★★★ **70'** 75' **78 82'** 83 85 86 88 89' 90' **95** 96' 97 98 99 00 Smaller part of divided fifth-growth BATAILLEY: 49 acres. Gentler than sister château GRAND-PUY-LACOSTE. Second wine: La Tour-d'Aspic.

Haut-Beauséjour St-Est r ★★ 95 97 98 99 00 01 Another Cru Bourgeois performing well. Owned by CHAMPAGNE house ROEDERER.

Haut-Bergey Pessac-L r ★★ 98 99 00 01 65 acres, largely Cab; fragrant delicate GRAVES. Also a little dry white. Completely renovated in the 90s. Same ownership as BARDE-HAUT and CLOS L'ÉGLISE.

Haut Bommes See Clos Haut-Peyraguey.

Haut-Brion Pessac (Graves) r (w) ★★★★ 59' 61' 66' 70' 71' 75' 76 78' 79' 81 82' **83'** 85' 86' **87** 88' 89' 90' **91 92 93** 94 95 96' 97 98' 99 00 01 02. The oldest great château of BORDEAUX and the only non-MEDOC first-growth of 1855. 108 acres. Deeply harmonious, never-aggressive wine with endless, honeyed, earthy complexity. Consistently great since 75. A little full dry white: 82 83 85 87 **88 89'** 90 **91 92 93 94 95** 96 97 98 99 00 01 02. See Bahans Haut-Brion, La Mission Haut-Brion, Laville-Haut-Brion.

Haut-Condissas Méd r ★★ 99 00 01 Aspiring new cru at Bégadan. To watch.

Haut Carles See CH. DE CARLES.

Haut-Maillet Pom r ★★ 98' 00 12-acre sister château of LA CABANNE. Well-made gentle wines.

Haut-Marbuzet St-Est r ★★→★★★ 82' 85' 86' 88 89' 90' 91 93' **94** 95 96' 97 98 99 00 01 The best of many good ST-ESTEPHE CRUS BOURGEOIS. Monsieur Dubosq has reassembled the ancient Dom de Marbuzet, in total 175 acres. Haut-M is 60% Merlot. Also owns CHAMBERT-MARBUZET, MACCARTHY, Tour de Marbuzet. New oak gives them a distinctive, if not subtle, style of great appeal.

Why do the Châteaux of Bordeaux have such a large section of this book devoted to them? Wine-lovers love to snipe at them and complain about their prices, but collectively they form by far the largest supply of high-quality wine on earth. A single typical Médoc château with 150 acres (some have far more) makes approximately 26,000 dozen bottles of identifiable wine each year – the production of two or three California boutique wineries. Moreover, between the extremes of plummy Pomerol, grainy Graves and tight, restrained Médocs – not to mention crisp dry whites and unctuous golden ones – Bordeaux offers a wider range of tastes than any other homogenous region.

The tendency over the last two decades has been to buy more land. Many classed-growths have expanded quite considerably since their classification in 1855. The majority have also raised their sights and invested their recent profits in better technology.

Haut-Pontet St-Em r ★★ 98 00 Reliable 12-acre v'yd of the COTES deserving its GRAND CRU status. 2,500 cases.

Haut-Sarpe St-Em r ★★ 82 83' 85 **86 88** 89 90' **93 94 95** 96 98 00 01 GRAND CRU CLASSÉ (6,000 cases) with elegant château and park, 70% Merlot. Same owner as CH LA CROIX, POMEROL.

Hortevie St-Jul r ★★ **90 95** 96 98 00 One of the few ST-JULIEN Crus Bourgeois. This tiny v'yd and its bigger sister TERREY-GROS-CAILLOU are shining examples. Now hand-harvesting only.

Hosanna Pom r ★★★★ 00 01 The new name for Moueix-owned CERTAN-GUIRAUD. Stellar ambitions.

Houissant St-Est r ★★ **90 95** 96 98 00 Typical robust well-balanced ST-ESTEPHE Cru Bourgeois also called Ch Leyssac; well-known in Denmark.

d'Issan Cantenac-Mar r ★★★ **85 86** 88 89 **90' 95** 96' **97** 98 99 00 01 Beautifully restored moated château nr the Gironde with 75-acre 3rd-growth v'yd; lightish, fragrant wines. 2nd label: Ch de Candale.

Kirwan Cantenac-Mar r ★★★ **82'** 85 **86 88** 89' **90'** 93' **94 95** 96 **97** 98 99 00 01 02 86-acre third-growth; from 97 majority owned by SCHRODER & SCHYLER. Michel Rolland advises. Mature vineyards now giving classy wines.

Labégorce Mar r ★★ **82' 85 86 88** 89' **90'** 94 95 96 98 99 00 01 02 Substantial 95-acre property N of MARGAUX; long-lived wines of true Margaux quality. Recent investment. Making every effort.

Labégorce-Zédé Mar r ★★ ★★★ 82' 83' 85 86' 88 **89'** 90' **93 94 95** 96' **97** 98 99 00 01 Cru Bourgeois on road N from MARGAUX. 62 acres. Typically delicate, fragrant, classic Same family as VIEUX-CH-CERTAN. Second label: Dom Zédé. Also 23 acres of AC Bordeaux: "Z".

Lacoste-Borie The second wine of CH GRAND-PUY-LACOSTE.

Lafaurie-Peyraguey Saut w sw ★★★ 78 82 83' **85** 86' 88' 89' 90' **95 96'** 97 98 99 01 02 Fine classed-growth of only 49 acres at Bommes, belonging to CORDIER. Now one of best buys in SAUTERNES. 2nd wine: La Chapelle de Lafaurie.

Lafite Rothschild Pau r ★★★★ **59 76' 78 79** 81' **82'** 83 85 **86' 87 88' 89' 90' 91 93** 94 95 96' **97** 98 99 00' 01 02 First-growth of famous elusive perfume and style, but never huge weight. Great vintages keep for decades. Recent vintages are well up to form. Amazing circular cellars. Joint ventures in Chile (88), California (89), Portugal (92). Second wine: Carruades de Lafite. 225 acres. Also owns CHATEAUX DUHART-MILON, L'EVANGILE, RIEUSSEC.

Lafleur Pom r ★★★★ 70' 75' 79' 82' **83** 85' **86' 88' 89' 90' 93 94** 95 96 97 98 99 00' 01 Superb 12-acre property. Resounding wine of the turbo-charged, tannic, less fleshy kind for long maturing and investment. Second wine: Les Pensées de Lafleur.

Lafleur-Gazin Pom r ★★ **82' 83 85' 86 88' 89 90 93** 94 **95** 96 98 00 Distinguished small J-P MOUEIX estate on the NE border of POMEROL.

Lafon-Rochet St-Est r ★★★ 70' 78 82 **83'** 85 86 88' 89' 90' **94 95** 96' **97** 98 00 01 02 Fourth-growth n'bour of COS D'ESTOURNEL, 110 acres. Gd hard full-bodied ST-ESTEPHE, slow to give. Same owner as CH PONTET-CANET. New equipment 98. Second label: Numéro 2. Renovation 00.

Lagrange Pom r ★★ **82' 83 85' 86 88** 89' 90' 94 95 96 98 00 01 20-acre vineyard in the centre of POMEROL run by the ubiquitous house of J-P MOUEIX. Rising profile for flavour/value.

Lagrange St-Jul r ★★★ 82 85' **86' 88' 89' 90'** 93 94 95 96 **97** 98 99 00 01 02 Formerly neglected third-growth inland from ST-JULIEN, bought by Suntory

('83). 280 acres now in tiptop condition with wines to match (and lots of oak). Second wine: Les Fiefs de Lagrange.

la Lagune Ludon (H-Méd) r ✦✦✦ 82' **83'** 85 86' 88' **89'** 90' **94 95** 96' 98 99 00 01 02 Ultra-modern 160-acre third-growth in southernmost MEDOC. Rich wines with marked oak and steady, high quality. Owned by CHAMPAGNE AYALA.

Lalande-Borie St-Jul r ✦✦ A baby brother of the great DUCRU-BEAUCAILLOU created from part of the former vineyard of CHÂTEAU LAGRANGE. Gracious, easy drinking wine.

de Lamarque Lamarque (H-Méd) r ✦✦ **82 85** 86' **88 89** 90' **94 95 96** 97 98 99 00 Splendid medieval fortress in central MEDOC. 113 acres giving admirable wine of high BOURGEOIS standard. Second wine: Donjon de L.

Lamothe Bergeron H-Méd r ✦✦ **88 89 90 93 94** 95 96' 98' 00 150 acres at CUSSAC making 25,000 cases of reliable claret. Run by GRAND-PUY-DUCASSE.

Lanessan Cussac (H-Méd) r ✦✦**78' 81 82 83** 85 86' 88' 89' 90' 93 94 95 96' 98 00 Distinguished 108-acre Cru Bourgeois just S of ST-JULIEN. Fine rather than burly but ages well. Same family owns Châteaux de Ste-Gemme, Lachesnaye, La Providence.

Langoa Barton St-Jul r ✦✦✦ 78' **82'** 83 85 86' 88' 89' 90' 93 **94'** 95 96 98 99 00 01 02 49-acre third-growth sister château to LEOVILLE-BARTON. V old Barton-family estate with impeccable standards and generous value. Second wine: Réserve de Léoville-Barton

Larcis-Ducasse St-Em r ✦✦ 85 86 **88' 89' 90'** 94 95 96 98' 00 Top property of St-Laurent, eastern neighbour of ST-EMILION, on COTES. 30 acres in a fine situation; wines could be better. New management from 2002 (PAVIE-MACQUIN and PUYGUERAUD).

Larmande St-Em r ✦✦✦ **82 83'** 85 86 88' **89'** 90' 93 94 95' 96 **97** 98' 00 02 Substantial 60-acre property. Replanted, re-equipped, and now making rich strikingly scented wine, silky in time. Second label: Ch des Templiers.

Laroque St-Em r ✦✦→✦✦✦ **82'** 85 86 **88** 89 90 **94** 95 96 97 98 99 00 01 Important 108-acre v'yd on the ST-EMILION COTES in St-Christophe. Promoted to GRAND CRU CLASSÉ in '96.

Larose-Trintaudon St-Laurent (H-Méd) r ✦✦ 89 90' **94'** 95 **96'** 98 00 01 02 The biggest v'yd in the MEDOC: 425 acres. Modern methods make reliable fruity and charming Cru Bourgeois wine to drink young. Second label: Larose St-Laurent. Special CUVÉE: Larose Perganson.

Laroze St-Em r ✦✦ 90' 94 95 **96'** 98' 99 00 Large v'yd (74 acres) on western COTES. Fairly light wines from sandy soils, more depth from 98; approachable when young.

Larrivet-Haut-Brion Pessac-L r (w) ✦✦ 82' 83 **85 86 87 88 89 90 94 95** 96' 98' 00 01 02 LEOGNAN property with perfectionist standards; Michel Rolland consulting. Also 500 cases of fine, barrel-fermented white (**93 94 95 96' 98'** 99 00 01 02). New plantings 99.

Lascombes Mar r (p) ✦✦✦ 70' **82** 83' 85 86 88' 89' 90' **95** 96' 98' 99 00 01 02 240-acre second-growth owned since 01 by an American pension fund. Wines have been wobbly but improvements in recent vintages. Second label: Ch Segonnes.

Latour Pau r ✦✦✦✦ **49 59 61 62 64 66** 70' **75' 78' 79 81** 82' **83** 85 86' 87 **88' 89' 90' 91' 92 93'** 94' 95' 96' 97 98 99 00 01 02 First-growth considered the grandest statement of the MEDOC. Profound, intense, almost immortal wines in great yrs; even weaker vintages have the characteristic note of terroir and run for many years. 150 acres sloping to R Gironde. Latour always needs 10 yrs to show its hand. British-owned from 63 to 93, now again in (private) French hands. New chai (03) will allow more precise selection. 2nd wine: LES FORTS DE LATOUR; 3rd, PAUILLAC.

Latour-Martillac Pessac-L r w ★★ (r) **82' 85' 86 88' 89** 90 93 94 95 96 98' 99 00 01 Small but serious property at Martillac. 10 acres of white grapes; 37 of black. The white can age admirably (94' **95** 96 97 98' 99 00 01 02).

Latour-à-Pomerol Pom r ★★★ **61' 70' 82** 83 85' **86 87** 88' 89' 90' 93 94 95 96 98' 99 00 01 Top growth of 19 acres under MOUEIX management. POMEROL of great power and perfume, yet also ravishing finesse.

des Laurets St-Em r ★★ **89' 90'** 94 95 **96** 98 00 01 Major property in PUISSEGUIN-ST-EMILION and MONTAGNE-ST-EMILION (to the east) with 160 acres of v'yd on the COTES (40,000 cases). Sterling wines sold by J-P MOUEIX.

La Louzette Listrac r ★★ 82 **85 86 88 89 90 95** 96 98 99 00 38-acre Cru Bourgeois, previously named Ch Bellegrave, making full-flavoured wine. Why the name change? There are about a dozen Bellegraves in B'x.

Laville-Haut-Brion Pessac-L w ★★★★ **85' 86 88** 89' **90 92 93' 94** 95' 96 97 98 99 00 01 02 A tiny production of the v best white GRAVES for long succulent maturing, made at CH LA MISSION-HAUT-BRION. The 89, 95, 96 are off the dial.

Médoc: the class system

The Médoc has 60 crus classés, ranked in 1855 in five classes. In a separate classification it has 335 Crus Bourgeois which, since an EU ruling of 1976, have had to drop rankings like Exceptionnel on their labels. The 2003 reclassification rearranged them into CB Exceptionnel (top), CB Supèrieur (middle) and plain CB (basic). This classification has legal force; CB status in the past merely required membership of the Syndicat des Crus Bourgeois. Apart from the first-growths, the five classes of 1855 are now hopelessly jumbled in quality, with some second-growths making wine of fifth-growth level and vice versa. They also overlap in quality with the top Crus Bourgeois. The French always do things logically.

Léoville Barton St-Jul r ★★★★ 78 **82' 83 85' 86' 88' 89' 90' 93'** 94' 95 96' 97 98 99 00 01 02 The 90-acre portion of the great second-growth LEOVILLE vineyard in Anglo-Irish hands of the Barton family for over 150 years. Powerful classic claret; traditional methods, very fair prices. Major investment raised already high standards to super-second. See also Langoa-Barton.

Léoville-Las-Cases St-Jul r ★★★★ 66' 75' 78' 79 81' **82' 83'** 84 85' 86' 87 **88 89'** 90' 91 93' 94 95 96 97 98 99 00 01 The largest LEOVILLE; 210 acres with daunting reputation. Elegant, complex, powerful, austere wines, for immortality. Second label CLOS DU MARQUIS also outstanding.

Léoville Poyferré St-Jul r ★★★ 82' 83' **85 86' 88 89' 90'** 94 95 96 98 99 00 01 02 For years the least outstanding of the LEOVILLES; high potential rarely realised. Michel Rolland consults here; things should be better. 156 acres. Second label: Ch Moulin-Riche .

Lestage Listrac r ★★ 86' 88 89' 90' **95 96** 98 00 130-acre Cru Bourgeois in same hands as CH FONREAUD. Light stylish wine, oak-aged since 85. Second wine: Ch Caroline. Also La Mouette (white).

Lilian Ladouys St-Est r ★★ 89 90 **94 95** 96 97 98 00 01 02 Created in the 80s: a 50-acre Cru Bourgeois with high ambitions and early promise. There have been problems, but early and recent wines are looking good.

Liot Barsac w sw ★★ 75' **76 82 83** 85 **86 88** 89' 90' **95 96** 97 98 99 01 Consistent fairly light golden wines from 50 acres. How they last!

Liversan St-Sauveur (H-Méd) r ★★ **82' 85 86'** 88' 89' 90' **93** 94 95 96 98 00 01 02 116-acre Cru Bourgeois inland from PAUILLAC. The Polignac family have had steadily high standards. Same owners as PATACHE D'AUX. 2nd wine: Ch Fonpiqueyre.

Livran Méd r ★★ 82' 86 88' 89' 90' **94' 95** 96 98 00 Big Cru Bourgeois at St-Germain in the N MEDOC. Consistent round wines (half Merlot).

Loudenne St-Yzans (Méd) r ★★ 82' 85 86' 88 89' **90 94 95** 96' 98 00 01 02 Beautiful riverside château owned by Gilbeys 1975–2000. New owners, and Michel Rolland is consulting, so wines are getting bigger, blacker and denser. Well-made Cru Bourgeois red and Sauvignon Blanc white from 155 acres. The new oak-scented white is best at 2–4 yrs (**95 96 97 98 99' 00** 01).

Loupiac-Gaudiet Loupiac w sw ★★ **85 86 88 89 90** 95 96 **97** 98' 99 01 A reliable source of good-value "almost-SAUTERNES", just across River Garonne.

la Louvière Pessac-L r w ★★★ (r) **82' 85 86'** 88' 89' 90' **94' 95** 96' **97** 98' 99 00 01 02 (w) **93' 94 95' 96' 97' 98' 99** 00 01 02 135-acre LEOGNAN estate with classical mansion restored by André Lurton. Excellent white and red of classed-growth standard. See also Bonnet, de Cruzeau, Couhins-Lurton, and de Rochemorin.

de Lussc St-Em r ★★ **85 86 88 89'** 90 94 95 96 **97** 98 99 00 One of the best estates in LUSSAC-ST-EMILION (to the NE). New technical methods 00.

Lynch-Bages Pau r (w) ★★★★ 59 61 70 **79** 82' **83' 84** 85' 86' 88' **89' 90' 91 94** 95 96 **97** 98 99 00 01 02 Always popular, now a regular star. 200 acres. Rich robust wine: deliciously dense, brambly; aspiring to greatness. See also Haut-Bages-Averous. From 90, intense oaky white – Blanc de Lynch-Bages. Same owners (Cazes family) as LES ORMES-DE-PEZ.

Lynch-Moussas Pau r ★★ 89 90' **94 95'** 96' **98** 00 01 02 Fifth-growth restored by the director of CH BATAILLEY. Could be on the up, at last.

Lyonnat Lussac-St-Em r ★★ **95 96 98** 00 01 120-acre estate; well-distributed reliable wine.

MacCarthy St-Est r ★★ The second label of CH CHAMBERT-MARBUZET.

Macquin-St-Georges St-Em r ★★ 89 90' **94 95 96 97** 98 **99** 00 01 Steady producer of delicious, not weighty, satellite ST-EMILION at ST-GEORGES.

Magdelaine St-Em r ★★★ 82' 83' **85 86** 88 89' 90' 93 94 **95** 96 **97** 98' 99 00 01 Leading COTES first-growth: 28 acres owned by J-P MOUEIX. Top-notch, Merlot-led wine; recently powerful and fine.

Magence Graves r w ★★ (r) 90 94 95 96 **98** 00 (w) 96 **97 98** 00 01 Go-ahead 93-acre property in S GRAVES. Sauv Bl-flavoured dry white and fruity red. Both age well 2–6 yrs.

Malartic-Lagravière Pessac-L r (w) ★★★ (r) **82' 85 86'** 88 89 90' **94 95** 96 98 99 00 01 (w) **93 94 95 96 97 98** 99 00 01 02 LEOGNAN classed-growth of 53 acres. Rich modern red wine since late 90s and a little long-ageing Sauv Bl white. New Belgian owner (96) M Rolland and D Dubourdieu now consulting. To watch.

Malescasse Lamarque (H-Méd) r ★★ **82 85 86 88 89 90** 93' **94 95'** 96 98 00 01 02 Renovated Cru Bourgeois with 100 well-situated acres. Second label: Le Tana de M. Wines steadily improving.

Malescot-St-Exupéry Mar r ★★★ 61 70 **82' 83' 86 88 89 90' 94 95** 96 **97** 98' 99 00 01 02 Third-growth of 59 acres returned to fine form in the 90s. Can be tough when young, eventually fragrant MARGAUX.

de Malle Saut w r sw dr ★★★ (w sw) **75 76 78 79 81' 82' 83 85 86' 88 89' 90' 94 95 96'** 97 98' 99 01 02 Beautiful Preignac château. 124 acres. Very good SAUTERNES; also M de Malle dr w. See also Château du Cardaillan.

Marbuzet St-Est r ★★ **85 86 88** 89 90 **93 94** 95' 96' 98 99 00 01 02 Second label of COS-D'ESTOURNEL until 94 when it became a Cru Bourgeois in its own right.

Margaux Mar r (w) ★★★★ 53 61' **78' 79** 80 **81' 82' 83'** 84 85' 86' 87 **88' 89' 90'** 91 **93'** 94 95' 96' **97'** 98' 99 00' 01' 02 First-growth (209 acres), the most seductive and fabulously perfumed of all in its frequent top vintages. Pavillon Rouge (**86 88 89 90' 93 94 95** 96 **97** 98 99 00 01 02) is second wine. Pavillon Blanc is best white (Sauv) of MEDOC: keep 5 yrs plus (**88 89 90 91 93 95 96 98** 99 00 02). Now under full Mentzelopoulos ownership again.

Marojallia Mar r ★★★ 99 00 01 New micro-château with 5 acres, looking for big prices for big, beefy, un-Margaux-like wines. 2nd wine Clos Margalaine.

Marquis-d'Alesme-Becker Mar r ★★ 85 86 88' 89 90 94 95 96 98 00 01 02 Tiny (17-acre) third-growth. An underperforming CRU CLASSÉ, once highly regarded. Potential here for classic MARGAUX.

Marquis de St-Estèphe St-Est r ★ The growers' co-op; bigger but not as interesting as formerly.

Marquis-de-Terme Mar r ★★ →★★★ 82 83' 85 86' 88' 89' 90' 95 96 97 98 99 00 01 02 Renovated fourth-growth of 84 acres. Fragrant, lean style has developed since 85, with more Cab S and more flesh.

Martinens Mar r ★★ 86 88 89 90 95 96 97 98 99 00 Worthy 75-acre Cru Bourgeois for the mayor of CANTENAC.

Maucaillou Moulis r ★★ 82 83' 85 86' 88' 89' 90' 94' 95 96 98' 00 01 02 130-acre Cru Bourgeois with good standards, property of DOURTHE family. Richly fruity Cap de Haut-Maucaillou is second wine.

Mazeyres Pom r ★★ 95 96' 97' 98' 99 00 01 Consistent, if not exciting lesser POMEROL. Better since 96. Alain Moueix manages. See Fonroque. 50 acres.

Méaume B'x Supérieur r ★★ 90 96 98 00 An Englishman's domaine, N of POMEROL. Solid reputation for vg daily claret to age 4–5 yrs. 7,500 cases.

Meyney St-Est r ★★ →★★★ 82' 85 86' 88' 89' 90' 94 95 96 98 00 01 02 Big (125-acre) riverside property in a superb situation; among many steady long-lived CRUS BOURGEOIS in ST-ESTEPHE. Owned by CORDIER. Second label: Prieur de Meyney.

Millet Graves r w (p) ★★ 98 00 Useful GRAVES. Second label, Clos Renon: drink young. Cuvée Henri: oak-aged white.

la Mission-Haut-Brion Pessac-L r ★★★★ 59' 61' 66' 75' 78' 82' 83 85' 86 88 89' 90' 93' 94' 95 96' 97 98' 99 00 01 02 N'bour and long-time rival to CH HAUT-BRION; since 84 in same hands. Consistently grand-scale full-blooded long maturing wine; even bigger than H-B and sometimes more impressive. 30 acres. 2nd label is La Chapelle de la Mission. White is LAVILLE-H-B.

Monbousquet St-Em r (w) ★★★ 82 85' 86 88' 89' 90' 93 94 95 96 97 98 99 00. A familiar old property on gravel revolutionized by new owner. Now super-rich, conc'd, and voluptuous wines. New owners also acquired PAVIE and PAVIE-DECESSE in 98.

Monbrison Arsac-Mar r ★★→★★★ 82 83 85 86 88' 89' 90 95 96' 97 98 99 00 01 A name to follow. High standards make it Margaux's most modish Cru Bourgeois. 4,000 cases and 2,000 of second label, Ch Cordet.

la Mondotte St-Em r ★★★→★★★★ 96' 97' 98 99 00 01 Intense garagiste wines from micro-property owned by Comte Stephen von Neipperg (CANON-LA GAFFELIERE, CLOS DE L'ORATOIRE).

Montrose St-Est r ★★★→★★★★ 61 70' 75' 82' 85 86' 88 89' 90' 91 93 94 95 96' 97 98 99 00 01 158-acre family-run second-growth famous for deeply coloured forceful old-style claret. Vintages 79–85 (except 82) were lighter, but recent Montrose is almost ST-EST'S answer to LATOUR. Second wine: La Dame de Montrose.

Moulin du Cadet St-Em r p ★★ 89' 90' 94 95 96 97 98 00 Little vineyard on the COTES, owned by J-P MOUEIX. Fragrant medium-bodied wines.

Moulin de la Rose St-Julien r ★★ 95 96 98 00 01 Tiny Cru Bourgeois; high standards. To watch.

Moulin Pey-Labrie Canon-Fronsac r ★★ 89 90 94 95 96 97 98' 99 00 01 Increasingly well-made drinker-friendly FRONSAC. To follow.

Moulin-St-Georges St-Em r ★★ 95 96 97 98 99 00 01 Stylish and rich wine.

Moulin-à-Vent Moulis r ★★ **82' 85' 86** 88 89 90' **94 95 96'** 98 00 60-acre property in the forefront of this booming AC. Lively forceful wine. LA TOUR-BLANCHE (MEDOC) has the same owners.

Moulinet Pom r ★★ **85 88 89' 90 95 96 98** 00 01 One of POMEROL'S bigger châteaux; 45 acres on lightish soil, wine lightish too.

Mouton Baronne Philippe See D'ARMAILHAC.

Mouton Rothschild Pau r (w) ★★★★ 59 61 62' 66' **70' 75'** 76 78 81 82' 83' 85' **86' 88' 89' 90'** 91 **93'** 94 95' 96 97 98' 99 00' 01 02 Officially a first-growth since 73, though in reality far longer. 175 acres (87% Cab S) can make majestic, rich wine, often MEDOC'S most opulent (also, from 91, superb white Aile d'Argent). Artists' labels and the world's greatest museum of art relating to wine. 2nd wine: Le Petit Mouton from 97. See also Opus One, Calif and Almaviva, Chile.

Nairac Saut w sw ★★ 76' 82 83' **85** 86' **88 89 90'** 95' **96** 97 98 99 01 01 Perfectionist BARSAC classed-growth. 2,000 cases of oak-fermented and -scented wine to lay down for a decade.

Nenin Pom r ★★★ **82 85'** 86 **88' 89 90 94' 95 96** 97 98 99 00 01 Well-known 66-acre estate, one of POMEROL'S biggest; on a (v necessary) but slow upswing since 85. CH LEOVILLE-LAS-CASES involvement since 1997.

Olivier Graves r w ★★★ (r) 82 86 **88 89'** 90' **95** 96 98 00 01 (w) 93 **94 95 96 97 98'** 00 01 90-acre classed-growth, surrounding a moated castle at LEOGNAN. 9,000 cases oaky red, 6,000 oaky white. Recent wines promise more charm.

les Ormes-de-Pez St-Est r ★★ →★★★ **82' 85 86'** 88 89' 90' 93 94 95 **96 97** 98 99 00 01 02 Outstanding 72-acre Cru Bourgeois owned by CH LYNCH-BAGES. Consistently one of the most likeable ST-ESTEPHES.

les Ormes-Sorbet Méd r ★★ 82' **85'** 86' 88 **89** 90' **94 95 96** 98' 99 00 01 10,000-case Couquèques producer of gd stylish r aged in new oak. A leader in N MEDOC. Second label: Ch de Conques.

Palmer Cantenac-Mar r ★★★★ **61'** 62 **66'** 70 **71'** 75' 76 78' 79' 81 82 83' **85 86'** 87 **88' 89 90 93 94 95** 96' 98' 99 00 01' 02. The star of CANTENAC: a third-growth occasionally outshining first-growths. Wine of power, flesh, delicacy, and much Merlot. 110 acres with Dutch, British (the SICHEL family), and French owners. Second wine: Alter Ego de Palmer (a steal for early drinking).

Pape Clément Pessac-L r (w) ★★★ →★★★★ **70 75'** 83 85 86' 88' 89' 90' 93' **94'** 95 96 97 98 99' 00 01 02 Ancient PESSAC v'yd; record of seductive, scented, not ponderous reds. Early 80s not so gd: dramatic quality (and more white) since 85. Ambitious new-wave direction and more concentration from 00. Watch v closely. Also Ch Poumey at Gradignan.

de Parenchère r (w) ★★ **98 99 00** 01 Steady supply of useful AC Ste-Foy Bordeaux and AC Bordeaux Supérieur from handsome château with 125 acres.

Patache d'Aux Bégadan (Méd) r ★★ 89' 90' **95 96 98 99** 00 01 90-acre Cru Bourgeois of the N MEDOC. Fragrant largely Cabernet wine with the earthy quality of its area. See also Ch Liversan.

Paveil-de-Luze Mar r ★★ **82' 85 86'** 88' 89' 90 **95** 96' 98 00 Old family estate at Soussans. Small but highly regarded. Investment 00.

Pavie St-Em r ★★★ **82' 83' 85 86 88' 89' 90' 94 95 96'** 98 99 00 01 Splendidly sited first-growth; 92 acres mid-slope on the COTES. Great track record. Bought by owners of CH MONBOUSQUET, along with adjacent PAVIE-DECESSE and La Clusière. This is new-wave St-Emilion: thick, intense, sweet, mid-Atlantic, and the subjct of heated debate.

Pavie-Decesse St-Em r ★★ **82 86 88 89 90 94 95 96** 97 98 99' 00 01 24 acres. Brother to the above and on form since 98.

Pavie-Macquin St-Em r ★★★ **85' 86 88 89'** 90' 93 **94 95** 96' **97** 98' 99 00' 01 Another PAVIE; this time the neighbours up the hill. 25-acre COTES vineyard East of ST-EMILION. Steadily fine organic winemaking by Nicolas Thienpont of CHÂTEAU PUYGUERAUD. Second label: Les Chênes.

Pavillon Rouge (Blanc) du Château Margaux See Ch Margaux.

Pedesclaux Pau r ★★ 82' 85 86 88 89' 90' 94 95' 96 98' 99 00 50-acre fifth-growth on the level of a Cru Bourgeois. Wines mostly go to Belgium. Second labels: Bellerose, Grand-Duroc-Milon.

Petit-Village Pom r ★★★ 75' 82' 83 85' 86 88 89' 90' 91 93 94' 95 96 97 98' 99 00 01 02 Top property revived. 26 acres; same owner (AXA) as CH PICHON-LONGUEVILLE since 89. Powerful plummy wine. Second wine: Le Jardin de Petit-Village.

Pétrus Pom r ★★★★ 61 62 64 66 67 70' 71' 73 75' 76 78 79' 81 82' 83 84 85' 86 87 88' 89' 90 93' 94 95' 96 97 98' 99 00 01 The (unofficial) first-growth of POMEROL: Merlot solo in excelsis. 28 acres of gravelly clay giving 5,000 cases of massively rich and concentrated wine, on allocation to the world's millionaires. Each vintage adds lustre (NB no 1991 produced).

Peyrabon St-Sauveur (H-Méd) r ★★ 98 99 00 Serious 132-acre Cru Bourgeois popular in the Low Countries. Also La Fleur-Peyrabon (only 12 acres).

Peyre-Labade Listrac r p ★ Second label of CH CLARKE. Investment 00.

Peyreau St-Em r ★★ 90 94 95 96 98 99' 00 Sister-château of CLOS DE L'ORATOIRE.

de Pez St-Est r ★★ ⇢★★★ 82' 85 86' 88 89 90' 93' 94 95' 96' 97 98' 99 00 01 02 Outstanding Cru Bourgeois of 60 acres. As reliable as any of the classed-growths of the village, though not so fine. Bought in 1995 by CHAMPAGNE house ROEDERER.

Phélan-Ségur St-Est r ★★ ⇢★★★ 88' 89' 90' 94 95 96' 97 98 99 00 01 02 Big and important Cru Bourgeois (125 acres): rivals the last as one of ST-ESTEPHE's best. From 86 has built up a strong reputation.

Pibran Pau r ★★ 88 89' 90' 94 95 96 98 99 00 01 Small Cru Bourgeois allied to PICHON-LONGUEVILLE. Should be classy wine with PAUILLAC drive.

Pichon-Longueville Comtesse de Lalande Pau r ★★★★ 61 62 66 70' 75' 76 78' 79' 80 81 82' 83 85' 86' 88' 89' 90' 93 94 95 96 97 98 99 00 01 Super-second-growth neighbour to CH LATOUR. 148 acres. Consistently among the very top performers; a long-lived, Merlot-marked wine of fabulous breed, even in lesser years. Second wine: Réserve de la Comtesse. Rivalry across the road (next entry) worth watching. Other property Ch Bernadotte.

Pichon-Longueville (formerly Baron de Pichon-Longueville) Pau r ★★★★ 82' 83 85 86' 88' 89' 90' 93 94' 95 96 98 99 00 01 02 77-acre second- growth. Since 1987 owned by AXA Insurance. Revitalized winemaking matches aggressive new buildings. Second label: Les Tourelles de Longueville

le Pin Pom r ★★★★ 82 83 85 86 88 89 90' 94 95 96 97 98' 99 00 01 The original of the new Bordeaux cult mini-crus. A mere 500 cases of Merlot, with same family behind it as VIEUX-CHÂTEAU-CERTAN (a much better buy). Almost as rich as its drinkers, but prices well beyond PÉTRUS are ridiculous.

de Pitray Castillon r ★★ 85 86 88 89 90 94 95 96' 98' 00 Large (77-acre) vineyard on CÔTES DE CASTILLON E of ST-EM. Flavoursome wines, once the best-known of the APPELLATION.

Plince Pom r ★★ 82 85 86 88 89' 90 93 94 95 96 98' 99 00 Reliable 20-acre property nr Libourne. Lightish wine from sandy soil.

la Pointe Pom r ★★ ⇢★★★ 89' 90' 94 95 96 97 98 99 00 01 Prominent 63-acre estate; wines recently plumper and more pleasing. LA SERRE is in same hands.

Pontac-Monplaisir Pessac-L r (w) ★★ 90 94 95 96 98 99 00 Offers useful white and fragrant red.

Pontet-Canet Pau r ★★★ 82' 85 86' 88 89' 90 93 94' 95 96' 97 98 99 00 01 02' 182-acre neighbour to MOUTON-ROTHSCHILD. Dragged its feet for many yrs. Owners (same as LAFON-ROCHET) have done better since 86. Old hard tannins were a turn-off. Distinctly made wines since late 1990s.

Potensac Méd r ✶✶ 82' 85' 86 88 89' 90' **94 95** 96 **97** 98 99 00 01 Biggest and best-known Cru Bourgeois of N MEDOC. Run and part-owned by Delon family. Class shows, in the form of rich, silky, balanced wines.

Pouget Mar r ✶✶ **82' 85 86 88 89 90 94** 95 96 98' 00 27-acre fourth-growth attached to BOYD-CANTENAC. Similar wines. New CHAI '00.

Poujeaux (Theil) Moulis r ✶✶ **82'** 85' 86 88' 88' 90' 90' 93' 94' 95' 96' 97 98 99 00 01 Family-run Cru Bourgeois of 120 acres, with CHASSE-SPLEEN and MAUCAILLOU the high-point of Moulis. 20,000-odd cases of characterful tannic and concentrated wine for a long life, year after year. Second label: La Salle de Poujeaux. Also Ch Arnauld.

Prieuré-Lichine Cantenac-Mar r ✶✶✶ **82' 83' 85 86' 88** 89' **90' 94'** 95 96 97 98' 99 00 01 02 143-acre fourth-growth brought to the fore by the late Alexis Lichine, now advised by Michel Rolland. Fragrant MARGAUX currently on fair form: to follow. Second wine: Clairefont. A good Bordeaux Blanc, too.

Puy-Blanquet St-Em r ✶✶ 82' 85 **86** 88 **89'** 90' 94 95 96 98 00 A major property in St-Etienne-de-Lisse, E of ST-EMILION, with 50 acres.

Smaller Bordeaux châteaux to watch for:
The detailed list of ch'x on these pages is limited to the prestigious classified parts of the Bordeaux region. But this huge v'yd at the Atlantic works on many levels. Standard Bordeaux AC wine is claret at its most basic – but it is still recognizable. The areas and representative châteaux listed below are an important resource; they are potentially distinct and worthwhile variations on the claret theme to be investigated and enjoyed.

Bordeaux Supérieur Chx Mouton, Penin, Bouillerot, de Seguin, Trocard
Canon-Fronsac Chx Barrabaque, Cassagne-Haut-Canon (La Truffière), Canon-de-Brem, La Fleur Caillou, Grand Renouil, Moulin-Pey-Labrie, Vraye-Canon-Boyer, du Gaby
Côtes de Bourg Chx Bujan, Brûlesécaille, Falfas, Fougas, Guerry, Haut-Maco, Mercier, Nodoz, Roc de Cambes, Rousset, Tayac Cuvée Prestige
Côtes de Castillon Chx d'Aiguilhe, de Belcier, Cap de Faugères, Cantegrive, La Clarière-Laithwaite,Clos l'Eglise, Côte Montpezat, Peyrou, Robin, Roque le Mayne, Ste-Colombe, Vieux Château Champs de Mars
Côtes de Francs Chx Les Charmes Godard, de Francs, Laclaverie, Lauriol, Marsau, La Prade, Puygueraud
Entre-Deux-Mers Chx de Fontenille, Launay, Moulin de Launay, Nardique la Gravière, Sainte-Marie, Tour de Mirambeau, Toutigeac, Turcaud
Fronsac Chx Dalem, Fontenil, Mayne-Vieil, Moulin-Haut-Laroque, La Rousselle, Tour du Moulin, Les Trois Croix, La Vieille Cure, Villars.
Lalande de Pomerol Chx Les Annereaux, La Croix-St-André, La Fleur de Boüiard, Garraud, Grand Ormeau, Haut Chaigneau, La Sergue Perron, Sergant, de Viaud
Lussac St-Emilion Chx de la Grenière, Mayne-Blanc, des Roches
Montagne St-Emilion Chx Calon, Faizeau, Maison Blanche, Roudier
Premières Côtes de Blaye Chx Bel Air la Royère, Bertinerie, Charron, Haut-Sociando, Jonqueyres, Loumède, Prieuré Malesan (formerly Pérenne), Roland-la-Garde, Segonzac, La Tonnelle, des Tourtes
Premières Côtes de Bordeaux Chx Carignan, Chelivette, Clos Ste-Anne, Fayau, Grand-Mouëys, Haux, du Juge, Jonchet, Lamothe de Haux, Pic, Plaisance, Puy Bardens, Reynon, Suau, Tanesse
Ste-Croix du Mont Chx Loubens, Lousteau-Vieil, du Mont, Pavillon, La Rame

Puygueraud Côtes de Francs r ★★ 88 **89' 90 95' 96** 97' 98 99 00 01 Leading château of this tiny AC. Wood-aged wines of surprising class. Château Laclaverie and Les Charmes-Godard follow the same lines. Special Cuvée George from 00. Same winemaker as CH PAVIE-MACQUIN (ST-EM).

Rabaud-Promis Saut w sw ★★ ⤍★★★ 83' 85 86' 87 **88' 89' 90 94 95 96** 97 98 99 01 02 74-acre classed-growth at Bommes. Since 1986 it has been near top rank. Rich stuff.

Rahoul Graves r w ★★ (r) **82 85 86 88 89'** 90' 94 **95 96** 98' 00 01 37-acre vineyard at Portets is still a sleeper despite long record of good red (80%) and very good (Sémillon) white (**94 95 96 97 98** 99 00 01).

Ramage-la-Bâtisse H-Méd r ★★ 89' 90 **95 96' 98** 00 Potentially outstanding Cru Bourgeois; 130 acres at ST-SAUVEUR, NORTH of PAUILLAC. Château Tourteran is second wine.

Rauzan-Gassies Mar r ★★ 88 89' 90' **95** 96 98 99 00 00 01 02 75-acre second-growth neighbour of the next that has long lagged behind it. Is something stirring?

Rauzan-Ségla Mar r ★★★★ **70' 82** 83' 85 **86' 88'** 89' **90' 94'** 95 96 **97** 98 99 00 01 02 106-acre second-growth famous for its fragrance; a great MÉDOC name back at the top. New owners in 94 (Chanel) have rebuilt the château and CHAIS. Second wine: Ségla. This should be the top second-growth of all. Ancient vintages can be superb and latest ones are splendid.

Raymond-Lafon Saut w sw ★★★ 75' 76 79 80' 82 83' 85 86' **88 89' 90' 95 96' 97** 98 99 01 Serious little SAUTERNES estate (44 acres) owned by YQUEM ex-manager. Splendid wines for ageing. Ranks among the very top Sauternes.

Rayne Vigneau Saut w sw ★★★ 76' 83 85 86' **88' 89 90'** 95 **96 97** 98 99 01 164-acre classed-growth at Bommes. Very good. Sweet wine and dry Rayne SEC.

Respide Médeville Graves w (r) ★★ (w) 90 **92' 93** 94 **95' 96'** 99 00 01 One of the better unclassified properties but current whites disappointing. Should be full-flavoured wines for ageing. (NB CUVÉE Kauffman.) Drink the reds at 4–6 years – longer for the better vintages.

Reynon Premières Côtes r w ★★ 100 acres for fragrant white from old Sauv vines (VIEILLES VIGNES) (98' 99 00 01); also serious red (**88' 89** 90 **94 95 96 97 98** 99 00 01). Second wine (red): Ch Reynon-Peyrat. From 96 very good Ch Reynon Cadillac liquoreux, too. See also CLOS FLORIDÈNE.

Reysson Vertheuil (H-Méd) r ★★ 95 96 00 Recently replanted 120-acre Cru Bourgeois; same owners as GRAND-PUY-DUCASSE.

Ricaud Loupiac w sw (r dr) ★★ **95 96 97** 99 01 Substantial grower of SAUTERNES-like age-worthy wine just across the river.

Rieussec Saut w sw ★★★★ 67 71' 75' 79 82 **83' 85 86' 88' 89' 90'** 95 96' 97' 98' 99 01 02 Worthy neighbour of CHATEAU D'YQUEM with 136 acres in Fargues, bought in 1984 by the (LAFITE) Rothschilds. Vinified in oak since 96. Fabulously opulent wine. Also producing a dry "R" and super-wine Crème de Tête.

Ripeau St-Em r ★★ **95** 98 00 01 Steady GRAND CRU CLASSÉ with the right idea in the centre of the plateau. 40 acres.

de la Rivière Fronsac r ★★ 85' 86 88' **89** 90 **94 95 96'** 97 98' 99 00 01 The biggest and most impressive FRONSAC property, with a Wagnerian castle and cellars. Formerly big tannic wines seem to have lightened recently. New winery 99 – Michel Rolland consults.

de Rochemorin Pessac-L r (w) ★★⤍★★★ 89' 90' 93 94 95 96 **97** 98' 99 00 01 An important restoration at Martillac by the Lurtons of CH LA LOUVIERE: 165 acres of maturing vines. Oaky whites to keep 4–5 yrs.

BORDEAUX

Rol Valentin St-Em r ★★★ 95 96 97 98 **99** 00 01 New 10-acre estate going for modestly massive style (& price) owned by former professional footballer.

Rouet Fronsac r ★★ **90** 95 96 98 **99** 00 Well-made, full of life and fruit.

Rouget Pom r ★★ 85' 86 88 89' 90 **93 94 95 97** 98' 00 01 Attractive old estate on the N edge of POMEROL. New owners are doing well. Track-record is for solid long-agers. To watch.

Royal St-Emilion Brand name of important, dynamic growers' coop. See Galius.

Ruat-Petit-Poujeaux Moulis r ★★ **95** 96 98 00 45-acre vineyard with local reputation for vigorous wine, keep for 5–6 years.

St-André-Corbin St-Em r ★★ **95** 96 **97** 98' **99** 00 01 54-acre estate in MONTAGNE- and ST-GEORGES-ST-EMILION: above-average wines.

St-Georges St-Georges-St-Em r ★★ 88' 89' 90' 94 95' 96' 98' 00 01 Noble 18th-C château overlooking the ST-EMILION plateau from the hill to the north. 125 acres (25% of St-Georges AC). Good wine sold direct to the public.

St-Georges-Côte-Pavie St-Em r ★★ 82 85' **86** 88' 89' 90' **94 95** 96' 98' 00 Perfectly placed little vineyard on the CÔTES. Run with dedication.

St-Pierre St-Jul r ★★★ 82' 85 86' 88' 89' 90' **93 94 95**' 96' **97** 98 99 00 01 Small (42-acre) fourth-growth. Very stylish and consistent classic ST-JULIEN.

de Sales Pom r ★★ 82' 85 86 88 89' **90'** 94 **95** 98 00 Biggest v'yd of POMEROL (116 acres), attached to grandest château. Never poetry: recently below form. Second labels: ch'x Chantalouette, du Delias.

Sansonnet St-Em r ★★ **99** 00 01 17 acres ambitiously run in the new St-Em style (rich, fat) since 1999.

Saransot-Dupré Listrac r (w) ★★ **86 88 89** 90 **95 96**' 98' 99 00 01 02 Small property performing tremendously well since 1986. Also one of LISTRAC's little band of whites.

Sénéjac H-Méd r (w) ★★ 82' 85 86' 88 89' 90' 94 **95** 96 98 99 00 01 60-acre Cru Bourgeois in S MEDOC recently bought by the same family as CH TALBOT. Tannic reds to age and unusual all-Sém white, also to age (**96 97 98** 99 00 01). Second label: Artigue de Sénéjac.

St-Emilion: the class system
St-Emilion has its own class system, revised every ten years, the last in 1996. At the top are two Premiers Grands Crus Classés "A": Châteaux Ausone and Cheval Blanc. Then come 11 Premiers Grands Crus Classés "B'. 55 châteaux were elected as Grands Crus Classés. To be considered for classification the ch'x must have obtained the AC St. Emilion Grand Cru certificate which is renewable every year.

---

la Serre St-Em r ★★ 82 85 86 88' 89 90 **94 95** 96 98 99 00 Small GRAND CRU, same owner as LA POINTE. Pleasant stylish wines.

Sigalas-Rabaud Saut w sw ★★★ 75 76' 80 82 83 85 86 88 89' **90' 95' 96'** 97' 98 99 01 02 The smaller part of the former RABAUD estate: 34 acres in Bommes run by CORDIER. At best very fragrant and lovely. Since 95 second wine: Le Cadet de Sigalas Rabaud.

Siran Labarde-Mar r ★★→★★★ 82' **83 85** 86 **88** 89' 90' **95** 96 98 99 00 77-acre property of passionate owner who resents lack of CLASSÉ rank. To follow for full-flavoured wines to age. Property is continually striving.

Smith-Haut-Lafitte Pessac-L r (w p) ★★★ (red) 82' 85 86 89' 90' 94 95 96 98 99 00 01 02 (white) **93 94** 95 96 97 98 99' 00 01 02 Classed-growth at Martillac: 122 acres (14 acres white). Ambitious owners (since 90) continue to spend hugely to spectacular effec,t incl a luxurious wine therapy (external!) clinic. Plans to take over Ch de Pommard in Burgundy now shelved. Second label: Les Hauts de Smith. Also look out for their Ch Cantelys, PESSAC-LEOGNAN.

Sociando-Mallet H-Méd r ★★★ **82' 85' 86'** 88' **89' 90' 94** 95 96' **97** 98 99 00 01 Splendid, widely followed CRU BOURGEOIS at St-Seurin. 65 acres. Conservative big-boned wines to lay down for years. Second wine: Demoiselles de Sociando.

Soudars H-Méd r ★★ **86 89 90 94 95 96' 98** 99 00 01 Sister to COUFRAN; recent Cru Bourgeois doing pretty well.

Soutard St-Em r ★★★ **82' 85' 86 88'** 89' **90'** 93 **94** 95 **96** 97 98' 99 00 01 Potentially excellent 48-acre classed-growth, 70% Merlot. Potent wines: can be long-lived to suit Anglo-Saxon drinking; also exciting when young to French palates. Forward-thinking viticultural practices. Second label: Clos de la Tonnelle.

Suduiraut Saut w sw ★★★★ 67 75 76' **78 79'** 81 82 83 85 86 88' 89' 90' 95 **96** 97 98 99 01 02 One of the best SAUTERNES, in its best vintages supremely luscious. 173 acres potentially are of top class. See Pichon-Longueville.

du Tailhas Pom r ★★ 89 90 **94 95** 96' 98' **99** 00 5,000 cases. POMEROL of the lighter kind, near FIGEAC.

Taillefer Pom r ★★ 82 85 86 88' 89 90 94 95' 96 98' **99** 00 28-acres on the edge of POMEROL in the Bernard Moueix family (see also FONTMARTY).

Talbot St-Jul r (w) ★★★ **78'** 82' 83' 85' 86' 88' 89' 90 **94 95** 96' 98' 99 00 01 02 Important 240-acre fourth-growth, for many years younger sister to GRUAUD-LAROSE. Wine similarly attractive: rich, consummately charming, reliable; gd value. Very good second label: Connétable Talbot. White: Caillou Blanc matures as well as a good GRAVES. Oenologist also oversees TOUR DE MONS.

Tayac Soussans-Mar r ★★ **95** 96 **98** 00 MARGAUX's biggest CRU BOURG. Reliable if not noteworthy.

de Terrefort-Quancard B'x r w ★ **98 99** 00 Huge producer of good-value wines at ST-ANDRE-DE-CUBZAC on the road to Paris. Very drinkable quality. 33,000 cases. Also Bordeaux Supérior: Ch Canada.

Terrey-Gros-Caillou St-Jul r ★★ 82' 86' 88 89 90 **94 95 96** 98 99 00 Sister château to HORTEVIE; at best, equally noteworthy and stylish.

du Tertre Arsac-Mar r ★★★ 82' 83' 85 86 88' 89' 90' **94** 95 96' 98' 99 00 01 02 Fifth-growth isolated S of MARGAUX. History of undervalued fragrant and fruity wines. Since 97, same owner as CH GISCOURS. To watch. New techniques and investment 00 have produced a really conc'd wine.

Tertre Daugay St-Em r ★★★ 82' 83' 85 86 88' 89' 90' 94 95 **96 97** 98 **99** 00 01 Small, spectacularly sited GRAND CRU CLASSÉ. Currently being restored to gd order. Potent and stylish wines. Same owner as CH LA GAFFELIÈRE.

Tertre-Rôteboeuf St-Em r ★★★★ 85 86 **88' 89' 90'** 93 94 95 **96 97** 98' 99 00 01 A cult star making concentrated, even dramatic, largely Merlot wine since 83. The prices are frightening. The roast beef of the name gives the right idea. Also COTE DE BOURG property, Roc de Cambes.

Thieuley E-Deux-Mers r p w ★★ Supplier of consistent quality red and white AC Bordeaux; fruity CLAIRET; oak-aged red and white cuveé Francis Courselle. Also owns Clos Ste-Anne in Premières Côtes de Bordeaux.

la Tour-Blanche Saut w (r) sw ★★ 83' 85 **86** 88' 89' **90'** 95 **96** 97 98 99 01 02 Historic leader of SAUTERNES, now a gov't wine college. Coasted in 70s; hit historic form again in 88.

La Tour-de-By Bégadan (Méd) r ★★ 82' 85' 86 88' 89' 90' **94 95** 96' 98 00 01 02 V well-run 182-acre Cru Bourgeois in N MÉDOC with a name for the most attractive sturdy wines of the area.

la Tour-Carnet St-Laurent (H-Méd) r ★★ 82 85 86 89' 90 **94'** 95 96 98 99 00 01 Fourth-growth with medieval fortress, long neglected. New ownership and investment from 2000. Richer wines with more polish since. Second wine: Sire de Comin.

BORDEAUX

la Tour Figeac St-Em r ★★ 82' 83 85 86 88 89' 90' 94' 95 96' 97' 98' 99 00 01 02 36-acre GRAND CRU CLASSÉ between CH FIGEAC, POMEROL. California-style ideas since 94. Biodynamic methods. Keep an eye on this.

la Tour Haut Brion Graves r ★★★ 85 88 89 90 94 95 96' 97 98' 99 00 01 02 Formerly second label of CH LA MISSION-HAUT-BRION. Up to 83, a plainer, v tannic wine. Now a separate 12-acre vineyard: wines stylish, to keep.

Tour Haut-Caussan Méd r ★★ 95 96 98 00 01 Ambitious 40-acre estate at Blaignan to watch for full firm wines.

Tour-du-Haut-Moulin Cussac (H-Méd) r ★★ 82' 85' 86' 88' 89' 90' 94 95 96 98 00 Conservative grower: intense Cru Bourgeois to mature.

la Tour de Mons Soussans-Mar r ★★ 82' 83 85 86 88 89 90' 94 95 96' 98' 99 00 01 Famous Cru Bourgeois of 87 acres, 3 centuries in the same family. A long dull patch but new (95) TALBOT-influence is returning to the old fragrant, vigorous, ageworthy style.

Tour-du-Pas-St-Georges St-Em r ★★ 86 88 89 90 94 95 96 97 98 99 00 01 Wine from 40 acres of ST-GEORGES-ST-EMILION made by BELAIR winemaker.

la Tour-du-Pin-Figeac St-Emilion r ★★ 98 00 26-acre GRAND CRU CLASSÉ worthy of restoration.

la Tour du Pin Figeac Moueix St-Em r ★★ 82 83 85 86 88' 89' 90' 94 95 96 98 00 Another 26-acre section of the same old property, owned by the Armand Moueix family. Splendid site; should be powerful wines.

Tour-St-Bonnet Méd r ★★ 86 89' 90' 95 96 98 99 00 Consistently well-made potent N MEDOC from St-Christoly. 100 acres.

Tournefeuille Lalande de Pom r ★★ 82' 83' 85 86 88 89 90' 94 95' 98' 99 00 01 Well-known Néac château. 43 acres. On the upswing since 1998 with new owners.

des Tours Mont-St-Em r ★★ 98 99 00 01 Spectacular château – modern 170-acre vineyard. Sound, easy wine.

Tronquoy-Lalande St-Est r ★★ 82' 85 86 88 89 90' 94 95 96 98 99 00 01 40-acre Cru Bourgeois: high-coloured wines to age, but no thrills. DOURTHE-distributed.

Troplong-Mondot St-Em r ★★★ 82' 83 85' 86 88' 89' 90' 94' 95 96' 97 98' 99 00' 01 75 acres well-sited on the CÔTES. One of ST-EM's hottest things. Second wine: Mondot.

Trotanoy Pom r ★★★★ 61' 70' 71' 75' 81 82' 85' 88 89 90' 93 94 95 96 97 98' 99 00 01 Potentially the second POMEROL, after PÉTRUS, from the same stable. Only 27 acres; but at best (eg 82) a glorious fleshy perfumed wine. Ten wobbly years since; now resurgence under J-P MOUEIX control.

Trottevieille St-Em r ★★★ 82' 85 86 89' 90 94 95 96 98 99 00 01 First-growth of 27 acres on the CÔTES. Dragged its feet for years. Same owners as BATAILLEY have raised its game.

le Tuquet Graves r w ★★ (r) 95 96' 98' 99 00 (w) 93 94 95 96 97 98' 99 00 Big estate at Beautiran. Light fruity red; the white is better. (CUVÉE Spéciale oak-aged.)

de Valandraud St-Em r ★★★★ 92 93 94 95 96 97 98 99 00 01 Leader among garagiste micro-wines fulfilling aspirations to glory. But silly prices for the sort of thick, vanilla-scented wine California can make. Vineyards expanded 98; better terroir now. Second and third wines available in even smaller quantities: Virginie and Axelle.

Valrose St-Est r ★★ A newcomer since '99, co-owned with CLINET. To watch.

Verdignan Méd r ★★ 86 89' 90 94 95' 96 98 99 00 01 Substantial Bourgeois sister to CH COUFRAN. More Cab than Coufran. 2nd label: Ch Plantey de la Croix.

la Vieille Cure Fronsac r ★★ 94 95 96 97 98 99 00 01 50-acre property, US-owned, leading the commune.

> **Vins de garage**
> The concept of garage wine started in Bordeaux as a joke; the name at least: production was so small that a garage was big enough to make it in. With small production went rarity; hence the chance of a high price. It is now stylistic. Garage wines are made with v small crops, preferably from old vines, and have the dark colour, thick texture, rich mouthfeel, andcoffee/vanilla/ chocolate flavours associated with toasted new oak. The current runners are massively concentrated in St-Emilion, where the stylistic change is becoming widely influential. Not all are over-priced. In **St Emilion** Andréas, Barde Haut, Clos Badon-Thunévin, Croix de Labrie, Clos St Martin, Le Fer, Ferrand-Lartigue, Magrez-Fombrauge, Gracia, Péby-Faugères, Quinault-l'Enclos, Rol Valentin, Le Dôme, La Gomerie, La Mondotte, Valandraud; in **Pomerol** Beau Soleil; in **Graves** Branon; in **Margaux** Marojallia; in **Côtes de Castillon** Domaine de l'A and Le Presbytère; in **Premières Côtes de Blaye** Gigault-Cuvée Viva; in **Entre-Deux-Mers** Balestard.

Vieux-Château-Certan Pom r ★★★★ 78 **79 81 82' 83'** 85 86' 88' **89 90'** 93 94 95' 96' 97 98' 99 00 01 Traditionally rated close to PÉTRUS in quality, but totally different in style; almost HAUT-BRION build. 34 acres. Same (Belgian) family owns LABEGORCE-ZEDE and tiny LE PIN.

Vieux Château St-André St-Em r ★★ 82' 85' 86 88' **89' 90' 93' 94' 95** 98 99 00 01 Small v'yd in MONTAGNE-ST-EM owned by winemaker of PÉTRUS until 2002. To follow. 2,500 cases.

Villegeorge Avensan (H-Méd) r ★★ 82 85 86 88 89 90 **94 95** 96' 98' 99 00 01 24-acre Cru Bourgeois north of MARGAUX. Enjoyable rather tannic wine. Sister-château: DUPLESSIS.

Villemaurine St-Em r ★★ 82' 85' 86 88 89 90 95 96 98 99 00 01 Small GRAND CRU CLASSÉ with splendid cellars well-sited on the CÔTES by the town. Firm wine with a high proportion of Cab. Also Chx du Cartillon, Timberlay.

Vray Croix de Gay Pom r ★★ 82' 85 86 88 89 **90 95 96** 98 00 Very small but ideally situated vineyard in the best part of POMEROL. Could do a lot better.

Yon-Figeac St-Em r ★★ 85 86 88 89 90 95 **96** 98 **99** 00 01 59-acre GRAND CRU for savoury supple wine at best.

d'Yquem Saut w sw (dr) ★★★★ 67' 70 **71' 75'** 76' 79 80' **81' 83'** 85 86' **88' 89'** 90' 93 94 95' 96 97 The world's most famous sweet-wine estate. 250 acres; only 500 bottles per acre of very strong intense, luscious wine, kept four years in barrel. Most vintages improve for 15 years+; some live 100 years+ in transcendent splendour. Sadly, after centuries in the Lur-Saluces family, in 1998 control was surrendered to Bernard Arnault of LVMH (see Cheval Blanc). Also makes dry YGREC ("Y").

Italy

More heavily shaded areas
are the wine growing regions

The following abbreviations
are used in the text:

Ab	Abruzzi	Pie	Piedmont
Ap	Apulia	Sar	Sardinia
Bas	Basilicata	Si	Sicily
Cal	Calabria	T-AA	Trentino-
Cam	Campania		Alto Adige
E-R	Emilia-Romagna	Tus	Tuscany
F-VG	Friuli-	Umb	Umbria
	Venezia Giulia	VdA	Valle d'Aosta
Lat	Latium	Ven	Veneto
Lig	Liguria		
Lom	Lombardy	fz	frizzante
Mar	Marches	pa	passito

VALLE
D'AOSTA

L Come

L Maggiore

Milan

LOMBAR

Turin O
PIEDMONT

Genoa O

LIGURIA

Ligurian Sea

Wine is central to the Italian way of life. The vine is cultivated in almost every region and province with a variety of intentions and results that only France can rival. Until recently in Italy, a meal without wine was virtually unthinkable.

Italy produces a massive 55 million hectolitres each year, making it, along with France, the dominant player on the world wine stage. Italians are now drinking less than they used to, but the wine they do drink is of higher quality. The long conflict in the national psyche between wine as a basic essential and as a pleasurable choice is resolving itself in favour of the latter. But tension remains, and nowhere so visibly as in the proliferation of wines with indecipherable names and few clear links to their *terroir*. Often of excellent quality and having a lasting impact on their region, they have generated constant complaint about the confusion they create.

The first Italian appellations (DOCs) were created in the 1960s. They were not designed to assure quality, simply to protect "tradition" – yields, varieties, viticulture, and ageing practices were absurdly proscriptive. Houses with greater ambition were forced to operate outside their appellations, thereby creating the parallel production system which exists to this day. If consumers are fazed when presented by the challenge of a very long list of names to memorize, there may be some consolation in the fact that never before have so many fantastic choices been available.

Italy's two most important regions, Piedmont and Tuscany, have long produced wines with unambiguous links to precise, easily identifiable zones. This is where the quality revolution began. Now it is spreading to other parts of the country: first to Soave and Friuli-Venezia Giulia, where an excessively technological approach had led to a dull standardization in white wines. But no longer. Central Italy – Umbria,

TRENTINO–
ALTO ADIGE
○ Bolzano
○ Trento
FRIULI–
VENEZIA
GIULIA
VENETO
L Garda
○ Verona
○ Trieste
○ Venice
Po
EMILIA–
ROMAGNA
● Bologna
● Florence
isa
TUSCANY
● Siena
Tiber
L Trasimeno
MARCHES
UMBRIA
L Bolsena
LATIUM
L Bracciano
ABRUZZI
○ Rome
MOLISE
CAMPANIA
○ Naples
APULIA
● Bari
BASILICATA
Táranto
Adriatic Sea

SARDINIA
○ Cagliari
Tyrrhenian Sea
CALABRIA

○ Paler mo
○ Réggio
SICILY

then the Marches – was next to feel the winds of change; then–Emilia-
Romagna, once known only for its abundance. And perhaps the most
encouraging sign of all is the Brussels-spnsored revolution bringing
quality and character to the South and the islands.

Italy, after a brief flirtation with international varieties, is also
returning to its native grapes. They include many original, ancient, and
individual kinds that have never, before the advent of modern
winemaking, had the airing they deserve.

Recent Vintages in Tuscany

2002 Cool August, frequent rains in September/October. Dilution and rot was widespread. Some decent wines from severe selections, nothing more.

2001 A scorching August, unusually cool in early Sept, then humid when warm weather returned. Some excellent wines but much irregularity.

2000 Very hot, dry, late summer/early autumn, one of earliest vintages in memory. Full, alcoholic wines, some impressive, some unbalanced.

1999 Shaping up as an excellent vintage in all major zones.

1998 Excessively hot and dry in August, stressed vines, then early October rains. Very good along the coast, irregular elsewhere.

1997 Virtually perfect summer and the early autumn weather; rich, round, full wines, one of the outstanding vintages of the entire post-war period.

Recent Vintages in Piedmont

2002 Cool, damp growing season, heavy rain in September/October and serious hail damage in Barolo. First off-vintage after 7 winners in a row.

2001 Classy and firm Nebbiolo and Barbera, other grapes less successful.

2000 Excellent Barolo, Barbaresco, Barbera. 5th sound vintage in a row.

1999 Balanced and elegant Barbaresco and Barolo, Barbera more spotty due to irregular end-of-season weather, lovely Dolcetto.

1998 Very good whites, excellent reds. For Barolo and Barbaresco, third fine vintage in a row after difficulties in 91, 92, and 94.

1997 Hot, dry summer and early autumn. Superlative Barbera; rich, round, and alcoholic; vg Barolo and Barbaresco with unusually soft tannins.

Abbazia Sant Anastasia ★★ →★★★ New Sicilian producer of excellent reds.

Abboccato Semi-sweet.

Aglianico del Vulture Bas DOC r dr (s/sw sp) ★★★ **90' 93' 94' 95** 97' 98 99 00 01 Among the best wines of S Italy. Ages well to rich aromas. Called VECCHIO after three, RISERVA after five years. Top growers: D'Angelo (also makes pure Aglianico IGT Canneto), Basilium, Cantina del Notaio, Elena Fucci, PATERNOSTER, Le Querce, Torre degli Svevi, and Sasso.

Alba Major wine city of PIEDMONT, on River Tanaro, SE of Turin.

Albana di Romagna E-R DOCG w dr s/sw (sp) ★★ →★★★ DYA Italy's first DOCG for white wine, though it was hard to see why. Albana is the (undistinguished) grape. AMABILE is usually better than dry. ZERBINA's botrytis-sweet PASSITO (Scacco Matto) is outstanding.

Alcamo Si DOC w ★ Soft whites and reds. Rapitalà, Ceuso are best brands.

Aleatico Red Muscat-flavoured grape for sweet, aromatic, often fortified wines, chiefly in the South. Aleatico di Puglia DOC (best grower is CANDIDO) is better and more famous than Aleatico di Gradoli (Latium) DOC. Good Aleatico from Falesco, v gd from Jacopo Banti in Val di Cornia.

Alessandria, Gianfranco ★★★ Small producer of high-level ALBA wines at Monteforte d'Alba, esp BAROLO San Giovanni, BARBERA Vittoria, DOLCETTO.

Alezio Ap DOC p (r) ★★. Salento DOC especially for full, flavourful reds and delicate rosés. The top growers are Guiseppe Calò with fine, barrel-aged NEGROAMARO Portulan and Michele Calò with Negroamaro IGT Spano.

Allegrini ★★★ Top-quality Veronese producer; outstanding single-vineyard IGT wines (Palazzo della Torre, Grola, and Poja), AMARONE, and RECIOTO.

Altare, Elio ★★★ Small producer of good, very modern BAROLO. Look for Barolo Arborina, LANGHE DOC Larigi (Barbera), La Villa (NEBBIOLO-Barbera), VDT L'Insieme (native PIEDMONT grapes plus Cab).

Alto Adige T-AA DOC r p w dr sw sp ★ →★★★ Alto Adige or SÜDTIROL DOC includes almost 50 types of wines: different grapes of different zones (incl varietals of VALLE ISARCO/EISACKTAL, TERLANO/TERLANER, Val Venosta/Vinschgau, AA STA MAGDALENA, AA Bozner Leiten, AA MERANESE DI COLLINA/Meraner).

Ama, Castello di, (Fattoria di Ama) ★★★ One of the best, most consistent modern CHIANTI CLASSICO estates, near Gaiole. La Casuccia and Bellavista: top single-v'yd wines. Gd IGTS, CHARD, MERLOT (L'Apparita), PINOT N (Il Chiuso).

Amabile Means semi-sweet, but usually sweeter than ABBOCCATO.

Amaro Bitter. When prominent on label, contents are not wine but "bitters".

> ### A Barole of honour
> The classic style: Borgogno, Brovia, Cavallotto, Aldo Conterno, Giovanni Conterno, Paolo Conterno, Fontanafredda, Bruno Giacosa, Bartolo Mascarello, Giuseppe Mascarello, Massolino, Prunotto, Renato Ratti, Giuseppe Rinaldi, Vietti. A promising new generation: Gianfranco Alessandria, Altare, Boglietti, Bongiovanni, Cabutto, Cappellano, M Chiarlo, Damilano, Conterno Fantino, Cordero di Montezemolo, Corino, Clerico, Ghisolfi, Ettore Germano, Elio Grasso, Silvio Grasso, Giovanni Manzone, Molino, Oberto, Parusso, Luigi Pira, Principiano, Rocche Costamagna, Rocche dei Manzoni, Revello, Sandrone, Scavino, Fratelli Seghesio, Vajra, Gianni Voerzio, Roberto Voerzio, many others.

Amarone della Valpolicella (formerly Recioto della Valpolicella Amarone) Ven DOC r ★★★ 85′ 86 **88′ 90′ 93 94 95′** 97′ 98′ 00 01 Dry version of RECIOTO DELLA V: from air-dried VALPOLICELLA grapes; concentrated, long-lived, v impressive from: Stefano Accordini, Serègo Aldeghieri, Alighieri, ALLEGRINI, Begali, BERTANI, BOSCAINI, BRUNELLI, BUSSOLA, Campagnola, CS Valpolicella, DAL FORNO, Guerrieri-Rizzardi, LE SALETTE, MASI, Mazzi, Novaia, QUINTARELLI, LE RAGOSE Villa Monteleone, Speri, TEDESCHI, Trabucchi, Viviani, ZENATO.

Ambra, Fattoria di ★★ Fine CARMIGNANO (Tusc) producer with two very good single-vineyard DOCG wines, Elzana and Vigne Alte.

Angelini, Tenimenti ★★→★★★ Owner of Val di Suga BRUNELLO estate in MONTALCINO, Tre Rose in MONTEPULCIANO, and San Leonino in CHIANTI CLASSICO.

Anselmi, Roberto ★★★ A leader in SOAVE with his single-vineyard Capitel Foscarino and exceptional sweet dessert RECIOTO i Capitelli, now both IGT.

Antinori, Marchesi L & P ★★→★★★★ V influential, long-est'd Florentine house of highest repute (mostly justified), owned by Piero A, sharing mng't with oenologist Renzo Cotarella. Famous for CHIANTI CLASSICO (esp, Tenute Marchese Antinori & Badia a Passignano), Umbrian (CASTELLO DELLA SALA) & PIEDMONT (PRUNOTTO) wines. Pioneer of new IGT, eg TIGNANELLO, SOLAIA (TUSCANY), CERVARO DELLA SALA (Umbria). Marchese Piero A was the "Voice of Italy" in wine circles in 70s & 80s. Expanding into S Tuscan MAREMMA, MONTEPULCIANO (La Braccesca), MONTALCINO, in PIEDMONT, in ASTI (for BARBERA), in FRANCIACORTA (Lombardy) & in APULIA ("Vigneti del Sud"). Very good DOC BOLGHERI Guardo al Tasso (Cab-Merlot). See Prunotto.

Apulia Puglia. Italy's heel, producing almost a 6th of Italian wine, mostly bottled in N Italy/France. Region to follow in increasing quality/value. Best DOC: CASTEL DEL MONTE, MANDURIA (PRIMITIVO DI), SALICE SALENTO. Producers: D'Alfonso del Sordo, ANTINORI, Botromagno, CANDIDO, Castel di Selva, Co-op Copertino, Co-op Due Palme, Conti Zecca, La Corte, D'Alfonso del Sordo, Fatalone, Felline, I Pástini, LEONE DE CASTRIS, Masseria Monaci, Masseria Pepe, Michele Calò, Pasquale Petrera, Pervini, RIVERA, Rubino, ROSA DEL GOLFO, Santa Lucia, Sinfarosa, TAURINO, Torre Quarto, Valle dell'Asso, VALLONE.

Aquileia F-VG DOC r w →→★★ (r) **95 96 97** 99′ 00 01 12 single-grape wines from around the town of Aquileia. Gd REFOSCO, SAUVIGNON. Denis Montanara is one to watch.

Argiolas, Antonio ★★→★★★★ Important SARDINIAN producer. High-level CANNONAU, NURAGUS, VERMENTINO, Bovale, and red IGT Turriga (★★★).

Arneis Pie w ★★ DYA Fairly gd white from nr ALBA: revival of an ancient grape to make fragrant light wine. DOC: ROERO Arneis, a zone NW of ALBA, normally better than LANGHE Arneis. Gd from Almondo, Ca' du Russ, Cascina Chicco, Correggia, BRUNO GIACOSA, Malvirà, Monchiero-Carbone, PRUNOTTO.

Assisi Umb r (w) ★→★★ DYA IGT ROSSO and BIANCO di Assisi: v attractive. Villa Fidelia particularly good.

Asti Major wine centre of PIEDMONT.

Asti Spumante Pie DOCG w sw sp ★→★★ NV Unfortunately, the big Asti houses are not remotely interested in making production of 80 million bottles better than routine. Despite its unique potential, Asti is a cheap, fairly proper product for supermarket shelves. Few producers care: WALTER BERA, Dogliotti-Caudrina, CASCINA FONDA, Vignaioli di Santo Stefano (see also Moscato d'Asti).

Avignonesi ★★★ Noble MONTEPULCIANO house; highly ambitious and v fine range: VINO NOBILE, blended red Grifi, CHARD, superlative VIN SANTO (★★★★).

Azienda agricola/agraria Estates – lge & sml – making wine from own grapes.

Azienda/casa vinicola Négociants making wine from bought-in & own grapes.

Azienda vitivinicola A (specialized) wine estate.

Badia a Coltibuono ★★★ Fine CHIANTI-maker in lovely old abbey at Gaiole with a restaurant and collection of old vintages. Best wine: IGT SANGIOVETO.

Badia di Morrona ★★→★★★ Nr Pisa (Tus). Gd CHIANTI, outstanding IGT N'Antia (Cab S-SANGIO), and IGT Vigna Alta (Sangio-Canaiolo).

Banfi (Castello or Villa) ★★→★★★ Space-age CANTINA of biggest US importer of Italian wine. Huge plantings at MONTALCINO, mostly SANGIO; also Syrah, PINOT N, Cab S, CHARD, SAUV, etc: part of a drive for quality plus quantity. BRUNELLO gd but "Poggio all'Oro" is ★★★. Centine is ROSSO DI M. In PIEDMONT also produces gd Banfi Brut, GAVI, BRACCHETTO D'ACQUI, PINOT GR. See also Eastern States US.

Barbaresco Pie DOCG r ★★→★★★★ 88' 89' 90' 93 95' 96' 97' 98' 99' 00 01 Neighbour of BAROLO; other great NEBBIOLO wine. Perhaps marginally less sturdy. At best palate-cleansing, deep, subtle, fine. At four years becomes RISERVA. Producers include Antichi PODERI di Gallina, Ca' del Baio, Piero Busso, Cascina Luisin, CERETTO, CIGLIUTI, Cortese, Fontanabianca, GAJA, BRUNO GIACOSA, MARCHESI DI GRESY, La Contea, MOCCAGATTA, Montaribaldi, Fiorenzo Nada, Giorgio Pelissero, Paitin, PIO CESARE, PRODUTTORI DEL B, PRUNOTTO, Roagna, Albino Rocca, BRUNO ROCCA, RIVETTI, Ronchi, Sottimano, Varaldo.

Barbatella, Cascina La ★★★ Top producer of BARBERA D'ASTI: excellent single-v'yard. VIGNA dell'Angelo and MONFERRATO Rosso Sonvico (Barbera-Cab).

Barbera d'Alba Pie DOC r ★★→★★★ 97' 98' 99 00 01 Tasty, fragrant red. Best age up to 7 years. Many excellent wines, often from fine producers of BAROLO and BARBARESCO. Top producers: Gianfranco Alessandria, Almondo, Cascina Chicco, ALDO CONTERNO, Giovanni CONTERNO, Corino, Correggia, Ghisolfi, ELIO GRASSO, Silvio Grasso, MANZONE, Massolino, OBERTO, PARUSSO, Pelissero, Gianmatteo Pira, Principiano, PRUNOTTO, Rivetti, Albino Rocca, Ro**u**cche Costamagna, SCAVINO, Vajra, VIETTI, ROBERTO VOERZIO.

Barbera d'Asti Pie DOC r ★★→★★★ 97 98' 99 00 For real BARBERA-lovers: Barbera alone, tangy and appetizing, drunk young or aged up to 7–10 years. Top growers: LA BARBATELLA, BAVA, BERA, Berta, BERTELLI, Alfiero Boffa, BRAIDA, Brema, Cantina Soc Vinchio e Vaglio, CHIARLO, Contratto, COPPO, HASTAE, Hohler, La Lune del Rospo, L'Arbiola, La Tenaglia, Marchesi Alfieri, Martinetti, La Morandina, PRUNOTTO, RIVETTI, Scrimaglio, Scagliola, VIETTI.

Barbera del Monferrato Pie DOC r ★→★★ DYA Easy-drinking Barbera from Alessandria and ASTI. Pleasant, slightly fizzy, sometimes sweetish. Delimited area is almost identical to BARBERA D'ASTI but style is simpler, less ambitious.

Barco Reale Tus DOC r ★★ 97 98 99 00 DOC for junior wine of CARMIGNANO; using the same grapes.

Bardolino Ven DOC r (p) ★→★★ DYA Pale, summery, sl bitter red from E shore of Lake Garda. Bardolino CHIARETTO: paler and lighter. Top makers: Cavalchina, Guerrieri-Rizzardi, MONTRESOR, Le Vigne di San Pietro, ZENATO, Zeni.

Barolo Pie DOCG r ★★★→★★★★ 89' 90' 93' 95' 96' 97' 98' 99' 00 01 Sml area S of ALBA with one of Italy's supreme reds: rich, tannic, alcoholic (min 13%), dry but wonderfully deep and fragrant (also crisp and clean) in the mouth. From NEBBIOLO grapes. Ages for up to 20–25 yrs (RISERVA after 5).

Barolo Chinato A dessert wine made from BAROLO DOCG, alcohol, sugar, herbs, spices, and Peruvian bark. Producers: Guilio Cocchi, Cappellano, Ceretto.

Basciano ★★ Producer of good DOCG CHIANTI RUFINA and IGT wines.

Bava ★★→★★★ Producer of vg BARBERA D'ASTI Piano Alto and Stradivarius, MONFERRATO BIANCO, BAROLO CHINATO; the Bava family controls the old firm Guilio Cocchi in Asti where they produce good sparkling METODO CLASSICO.

Bellavista ★★★ FRANCIACORTA estate with brisk SPUMANTE (Gran Cuvée Franciacorta is top). Also Satèn (a crémant-style sparkler). Terre di Franciacorta DOC and Sebino IGT Solesine (both Cab-MERLOT blends).

Bera, Walter ★★→★★★ Small estate nr BARBARESCO. V gd MOSCATO D'ASTI, ASTI, BARBERA D'ASTI, and LANGHE NEBBIOLO .

Berlucchi, Guido ★★★ Italy's biggest producer of sparkling METODO CLASSICO.

Bersano Historic wine house in Nizza MONFERRATO with BARBERA D'ASTI Generala, and BAROLO Badarina, most PIEDMONT DOC wines include BARBARESCO, MOSCATO D'ASTI, ASTI SPUMANTE.

Bertani ★★→★★★ Well-known, good-quality wines from VERONA, especially old-style AMARONE.

Bertelli ★★★ Superb wines from a family of medical researchers near ASTI, especially BARBERA D'ASTI, CHARD, Cabernet; very interesting experiments with SAUVIGNON, Sémillon, Nebbiolo, Syrah, Marsanne-Roussanne.

Bianco White.

Bianco di Custoza Ven DOC w (sp) ★→★★ DYA Twin of SOAVE from VERONA'S other side (W). Corte Sant'Arcadio, Le Tende, Le VIGNE di San Pietro, MONTRESOR all good.

Biondi-Santi ★★★★ The original producer of BRUNELLO DI MONTALCINO, from 45-acre Il Greppo estate. Absurd prices, but occasional old vintages are v fine.

Boca Pie DOC r ★★ 90' 95 96' 97' 98' 99 00 01 Another NEBBIOLO from N of PIEDMONT. Look for La Piane and Poderi ai Valloni (Vigneto Cristiana ★★★).

Boccadigabbia ★★★ Top Marches producer of IGT wines: SANGIO, Cab, PINOT N, CHARD. Proprietor Elvidio Alessandri also owns fine Villamagna estate in Rosso Piceno DOC.

Bolgheri Tus DOC r p w (sw) ★★★→★★★★ Ultra-modish recent region on the coast s of Livorno. Incl 7 types of wine: BIANCO, VERMENTINO, SAUVIGNON BLANC, ROSSO, ROSATO, VIN SANTO and Occhio di Pernice, plus top IGTS. Newish DOC Bolgheri Rosso: Cab-MERLOT-SANGIO blend. Top producers: Caccia al Piano: DOC Levia Gravia; Giovanni Chiapinni: DOC Guado de Gemoli; Enrico Santini: DOC Montepergoli; Le Macchiole: DOC Paleo, TOSCANA IGTS Scrio (Syrah), Messorio (MERLOT); ORNELLAIA: DOC Ornellaia, Toscana IGT Masseto (Merlot); SAN GUIDO: DOC SASSICAIA; ANTINORI: DOC Guado al Tasso; Meletti-Cavallari: DOC Grattamacco; Michele Satta: DOC Piastraia, Toscana IGT VIGNA al Cavaliere (SANGIO). Much new investment and forthcoming wines from GAJA (Ca' Marcanda)and Ambrogio Folonari.

Bolla ★★ Famous VERONA firm for VALPOLICELLA, AMARONE, SOAVE, etc. Top wines: Castellaro, Creso (red and white), Jago. And RECIOTO.

Bonarda Minor and confusing red grape or grapes (can be Croatina) widely grown in PIEDMONT, Lombardy, Emilia-Romagna, and blended with BARBERA.

Bonarda Lom DOC r ★★ 97 98 00 01 Soft, fresh FRIZZANTE from S of Pavia.

Borgo del Tiglio ★★★ FRIULI estate for one of NE Italy's top MERLOTS, ROSSO della Centa; also superior COLLIO CHARD, TOCAI, and BIANCO.

Boscaini Ven ★★ VERONA producer of VALPOLICELLA, AMARONE, SOAVE.

Boscarelli, Poderi ★★★ Small estate with very good VINO NOBILE DI MONTEPULCIANO, barrel-aged IGT Boscarelli, and good ROSSO DI M.

Brachetto d'Acqui Pie DOCG r sw (sp) ★★ DYA Sweet sparkling red with enticing Muscat scent. Can be much better than it sounds. Or dire.

Braida ★★★ The late Giacomo Bologna's estate; for top BARBERA D'ASTI (BRICCO dell'Uccellone, Bricco della Bigotta, Ai Suma).

Bramaterra Pie DOC r ★★ **96 97'** 98' 99' 00 01 Neighbour to GATTINARA. NEBBIOLO grapes predominate in a blend. Good producer: SELLA.

Breganze Ven DOC ★→★★★ (r) 97' 98 99 00 01 Catch-all for many varieties nr Vicenza. Cab and CHARD are best. Top producers: MACULAN, Miotti, Zonta.

Bricco Term for a hilltop (and by implication very good) vineyard in PIEDMONT.

Brindisi Ap DOC r ★★ **94 95 97** 99 00 01 Strong NEGROAMARO, especially from Vallone, Due Palme, Rubino, and forthcoming wines from Zonin.

Brolio, Castello di ★★→★★★ After a sad period under foreign ownership, the RICASOLI family has taken this legendary 900-yr-old estate in hand again. Results are heartening. Very good CHIANTI CLASSICO & IGT Casalferro (SANGIOVESE-Cab-merlot).

Brunelli ★★→★★★ Vg quality of AMARONE and RECIOTO.

Brunello di Montalcino Tus DOCG r ★★★→★★★★ 88' 90' **93 95'** 97' With BAROLO, Italy's most celebrated red: strong, full-bodied, high-flavoured, tannic and long-lived. Four years' ageing; after five becomes RISERVA. Quality ever-improving. Montalcino is 25 miles S of Siena.

> **Brunello di Montalcino to buy**
>
> Altesino, Argiano, Banfi, Barbi, Biondi-Santi, Campogiovanni, Canalicchio di Sopra, Caparzo, Casanova di Neri, Case Basse, Castelgiocondo, Castello di Camigliano, Castella di Argiano, Cerbaiona, Col d'Orcia, Costanti, Eredi Fuligni, Fanti-San Filippo, Gorelli, La Campana, La Fiorita, La Fuga, La Gerla, Lambardi, La Rasina, La Serena, La Torre, Lisini, Marroneto, Mastrojanni, Oliveto, Siro Pacenti, Franco Pacenti, Ciacci Piccolomini, Pieve di Santa Restituta, La Poderina, Poggio Antico, Poggione, Salvioni-Cerbaiola, Scopetone, Sesta, Talenti, Tiezzi, Valdicava, and Vitanza.

Bussola, Tommaso ★★★ Emerging leading prod of AMARONE & RECIOTO in VALPOLICELLA.

Ca' dei Frati ★★→★★★ The best producer of DOC LUGANA; and v gd w IGT Pratto (Sauv Bl/CHARD), sw Tre Filer, and r IGT Ronchedone (Cab-merl).

Ca' del Bosco ★★★ FRANCIACORTA estate; some of Italy's best sparklers (outstanding DOCG Annamaria Clementi ★★★★), vg CHARD, and excellent Cab blend (Maurizio Zanella), PINOT N (Pinèro).

Cacchiano, Castello di ★★★ First-rate CHIANTI CLASSICO estate at Gaiole, owned by Barone Giovanni RICASOLI-Firidolfi, cousin of the Brolio Ricasolis.

Cafaggio, Villa ★★★ Very reliable CHIANTI CLASSICO estate with excellent IGTS San Martino (SANGIO) and Cortaccio (Cab).

Calatrasi Sl ★★→★★★ Good producer of r and w IGT labels, esp D'Istinto line of better wines (Syrah, Nero d'Avola, SANGIO-MERLOT, Magnifico red blend).

Caldaro (Lago di Caldaro) T-AA DOC r ★ DYA Alias Kalterersee. Light, soft, bitter-almond SCHIAVA. From a huge area. CLASSICO – smaller area – is better.

Candido, F ★★★ Top grower of Salento, APULIA; gd reds: Duca d'Aragona, Cappello di Prete, SALICE SALENTINO; also gd dessert wine: ALEATICO DI PUGLIA.

Cannonau di Sardegna Sar DOC r (p) dr s/sw ★★ **95 96 97 98** 99 00 01 Cannonau (Grenache) is S's basic red grape. Ranges from v potent to fine and mellow: ARGIOLAS, CS di Jerzu, Giuseppe Gabbas, Dettori.

Cantalupo, Antichi Vigneti di ★★→★★★ Top GHEMME wines – especially single-vineyard Breclemae and Carellae.

Cantina Cellar or winery.

Cantina Sociale (CS) Cooperative winery.

Capannelle ★★★ Very good producer of IGT and CHIANTI CLASSICO nr Gaiole.

Capezzana, Tenuta di (or Villa) ★★★ The TUSCAN estate (W of Florence) of the Contini Bonacossi family. Gd CHIANTI Montalbano, excellent CARMIGNANO (esp Villa Capezzagna, Villa Tefiano). Also vg B'dx-style red, Ghiaie Della Furba.

Capichera ★★★ No 1 producer of VERMENTINO DI GALLURA, esp VENDEMMIA Tardiva. Now with excellent red Mantènghja from Carignano grapes.

Caprai ★★★ Widely copied, superb DOCG SAGRANTINO, very good DOC ROSSO DI MONTEFALCO. Highly rated.

Capri Cam DOC r p w ★→★★ Legendary island with widely abused name. Only interesting wines are from La Caprense.

Cartizze Famous, frequently too expensive and too sweet DOC PROSECCO of top sub-zone of Valdobbiadene.

Carema Pie DOC r ★★→★★★ 89' 90' 93 **95** 96' 97' 98 99' 00 01 Old speciality of N PIEDMONT. Best from Luigi Ferrando (or the CANTINA SOCIALE).

Carignano del Sulcis Sar DOC r p ★★→★★★ 90 91 93 94 **95 96 97** 98 99 00 01 Well-structured, age-worthy red. Best are Terre Brune and Rocca Rubia from CANTINA SOCIALE di SANTADI.

Carmignano Tus DOCG r ★★★ 90' 93 **94 95 96** 97' 98 99' 00 01 Region W of Florence. CHIANTI grapes plus 15% Cab S makes distinctive, reliable, even excellent rs. Best incl AMBRA, CAPEZZANA, Farnete, La Piaggia, Lo Locco.

Carpenè Malvolti Leading producer of classic PROSECCO and other sp wines at Conegliano, Veneto. Seen everywhere in Venice.

Carso F-VG DOC r w ★★→★★★ (r) **94 97** 99' 00 01 DOC nr Trieste incl good MALVASIA. Terrano del C is a REFOSCO red. Top grower: EDI KANTE.

Casanova di Neri ★★★ BRUNELLO DI MONTALCINO (and vg ROSSO DI M) from Neri family.

Cascina Fonda ★★★ Brothers Marco & Massimo Barbero have risen to top in MOSCATO D'ASTI DOC: look for VENDEMMIA Tardiva & METODO CLASSICO ASTI SPUMANTE.

Case Basse ★★★★ Pace-setter at MONTALCINO with sublime BRUNELLO and single-vineyard Brunello Intistieti.

Castel del Monte Ap DOC r p w ★★→★★★ (r) 93' **94 95 96** 97' 98 99 00 01 Dry, fresh, well-balanced southern wines. The red is RISERVA after 3 yrs. Rosé most widely known. Good Pietrabianca and excellent Bocca di Lupo from Vigneti del Sud (Antinori), v good Il Falcone and Cappellaccio Riserva from Rivera.

Castelgiocondo ★★★ FRESCOBALDI estate in MONTALCINO: very good BRUNELLO and IGT MERLOT Lamaïone.

Castell' in Villa ★★★ Very good CHIANTI CLASSICO estate.

Castellare ★★→★★★ Small but admired CHIANTI CLASSICO producer. First-rate SANGIO IGT I Sodi di San Niccoló and sprightly GOVERNO di Castellare: old-style CHIANTI updated. Also CHARD and good Cab Coniale.

Castello Castle. (See under name: eg Albola, Castello d'.)

Castello della Sala See Antinori.

Castello di Albola See Zonin.

Castelluccio ★★→★★★ Pioneering producer of quality SANGIO of Romagna: IGT RONCO dei Ciliegi and Ronco della Simia.

Caudrina-Dogliotti Romano ★★★ Top MOSCATO D'ASTI: La Galeisa and Caudrina.

Cavalleri ★★→★★★ Vg reliable FRANCIACORTA producer. Esp sparkling.

Cavicchioli ★→★★ Large Emilia-R producer of LAMBRUSCO and other sparkling: Lambrusco di Sorbara Vigna del Cristo is best. Also TERRE DI FRANCIACORTA

Ca'Vit (Cantina Viticoltori) Group of co-ops nr Trento. Wines incl MARZEMINO, Cab, PINOTS N, BL, GR, NOSIOLA. Top wines: Brune di Monte (r & w) & sp Graal.

Cecchi ★ →★★ Lge TUSCAN bottler, producer; La Gavina, Spargolo, CHIANTI CL RISERVA.

Cerasuolo Ab DOC p ★★ The ROSATO version of MONTEPULCIANO D'ABRUZZO.

Cerasuolo di Vittoria Si DOC p ★★ **97 98** 99 00 Garnet, full-bodied, aromatic (Frappato and Nero d'Avola grapes); can be interesting, esp from Valle dell'Acate and COS.

Ceretto ★★★ Very good grower of BARBARESCO (BRICCO Asili), BAROLO (Bricco Rocche, Brunate, Prapò), LANGHE Rosso Monsordo, and ARNEIS. Also very good METODO CLASSICO SPUMANTE La Bernardina.

Cervaro See Castello della Sala.

Chardonnay Permitted for several northern DOCs (eg T-AA, FRANCIACORTA, F-VG, PIEDMONT). Some of the best (eg from ANTINORI, CAPANNELLE, BOCCADIGABBIA, PLANETA, and REGALEALI) are still only IGT. Now being tried almost everywhere.

Chianti Tus DOCG r ★ →★★★ 95' **97'** 99' 00 01 Chianti Annata DYA The lively local wine of Florence and Siena. At best fresh, fruity, and tangy. Of the subdistricts, RUFINA (★★ →★★★) and COLLI Fiorentini (★ →★★★) can make CLASSICO-style RISERVAS. Montalbano, COLLI Senesi, Aretini, and Pisani: lighter wines. New subdistrict since 97 is Chianti Montespertoli; wines similar to Colli Fiorentini.

Chianti Classico Tus DOCG r ★★ →★★★★ 95' **97'** 99' 00 01 (Riserva and single-v'yd) 88' 90' 93 **95 97'** 99 00 Senior CHIANTI from central area. Its old, pale style is now rarer as top estates opt for darker, richer, firmer wines. Some are among the best wines of Italy, but too much Cabernet can spoil the style. Members of the CONSORZIO use the badge of a black rooster, but many top firms do not belong.

Chiarlo, Michele ★★ →★★★ Good PIEDMONT producer. (BAROLOS Cerequio and Cannubi, BARBERA D'ASTI, LANGHE, and MONFERRATO Rosso). Also BARBARESCO.

Chiaretto Rosé (the word means "claret") produced esp around Lake Garda. See Bardolino, Riviera del Garda.

Chionetti ★★ →★★★ Makes top DOLCETTO di Dogliani (look for Briccolero).

Cigliuti, Renato ★★★ Small high-quality estate for BARBARESCO and BARBERA D'ALBA.

Cinqueterre Lig DOC w dr sw pa ★★ Fragrant fruity white from precipitous coast nr La Spezia. PASSITO is known as SCIACCHETRA (★★ →★★★). Good from Co-op Agrícola di Cinqueterre, Forlini, and Cappellini.

Who makes really good Chianti Classico?

AMA, ANTINORI, Bossio, CACCHIANO, Capaccia, Carobbio, Castello di Brolio, Casa Emma, Casale dello Sparviero, Casaloste, Castel Ruggero, CASTELLARE, CASTELL'IN VILLA, LE CINCIOLE, Collelungo, Colombaio di Cencio, COLTIBUONO, Le Corti, Felsina, Le Filigare, FONTERUTOLI, FONTODI, ISOLE E OLENA, Lucignano, Le Macie, LA MASSA, Le Masse di San Leolino, MONSANTO, Giovanna Morganti, Nittardi, PALAZZINO, PANERETTA, Panzanello, Petroio-Lenzi, Poggerino, Poggiolino, Poggio al Sole, Querceto, QUERCIABELLA, RAMPOLLA, Riecine, Rocca di Montegrossi, Rodano, Ruffino, SAN FELICE, SAN GIUSTO, Selvole, Vecchie Terre di Montefili, VERRAZZANO, Villa Cafaggio, VOLPAIA.

Cirò Cal DOC r (p w) ★ →★★★ **95 96** 97 98 99 00 01 V strong r from Gaglioppo grapes; light fruity w (DYA). Best: LIBRANDI (Duca San Felice ★★★), San Francesco (Donna Madda, RONCO dei Quattroventi), Caparra & Siciliani.

Classico Term for wines from a restricted area within the limits of a DOC. By implication, and often in practice, the best of the district. Applied to sparkling wines it denotes the classic method (as for Champagne).

Clerico, Domenico ★★★ Constantly evolving PIEDMONT wines; the aim is for international flavour. Especially good for BAROLO.

Col d'Orcia ★★★ Top MONTALCINO estate. Best wine: BRUNELLO.

Colli Hills. Occurs in many wine names.

Colli Berici Ven DOC r p w ★★ 95 97 99 00 01 Hills S of Vicenza. Best wine is Cabernet. Top producer: Villa Dal Ferro.

Colli Bolognesi E-R DOC r w ★★ SW of Bologna, 8 wines, 5 varieties. TERRE ROSSE, the pioneer, now joined by Bonzara (★★★), Santarosa, Vallona.

Colli del Trasimeno Um DOC r w ★→★★★ (r) 97 98 99' 00 01 Lively white wines from near Perugia, but now more important reds as well. Best: Duca della Corgna, La Fioraia, Marella, Poggio Bertaio.

Colli Euganei Ven DOC r w dr s/sw (sp) ★→★★★ DYA DOC SW of Padua for 7 wines. Adequate red; white and sparkling are pleasant. Best producers: Vignalta, Ca' Lustra, Riolite, Speaia.

Colli Orientali del Friuli F-VG DOC r w dr sw ★★→★★★★ (r) 94 95 97 99' 00 01 Hills E of Udine. 20 wines (18 named after their grapes). Both w and r can be vg. Top growers: Bastianich, Castello di Buttrio, DORIGO, Dri, Fiore dei Lieri, Le Due Terre, Le Viarte, LE VIGNE DI ZAMÒ, LIVIO FELLUGA, Meroi, Miani, Midolini, Moschioni, Rosa Bosco, Rocca Bernarda, Ronchi di Manzano, Ronchi di Cialla, RONCO DEL GNEMIZ, SCHIOPETTO, Scubla, Specogna, Volpe Pasini, WALTER FILIPUTTI, Vigna Traverso.

Colli Piacentini E-R DOC r p w ★→★★★ DYA DOC incl traditional GUTTURNIO and Monterosso Val d'Arda among 11 types grown S of Piacenza. Good fizzy MALVASIA. Most wines FRIZZANTE. New French and local reds: La Stoppa, La Tosa, Montesissa, Mossi, Romagnoli, Solenghi.

Colline Novaresi Pie DOC r w ★→★★ DYA New DOC for old region in Novara province. 7 different wines: BIANCO, ROSSO, NEBBIOLO, BONARDA, Vespolina, Croatina, and BARBERA. Incl declassified BOCA, GHEMME, FARA, and SIZZANO.

Collio F-VG DOC r w ★★→★★★★ 97 99' 00 01 19 wines, 17 named after their grapes, nr Slovenian border. Vg whites, esp SAUV, PINOTS B and GR from: BORGO DEL TIGLIO, Il Carpino, CASTELLO di Spessa, Damijan, Edi Keber, MARCO FELLUGA, Fiegl, GRAVNER, La Castellada, LIVON, Primosic, Princic, Renato Keber, RONCO dei Tassi, RUSSIZ SUPERIORE, SCHIOPETTO, Aldo Polencic, Tercic, Terpin, Venica & Venica, VILLA RUSSIZ, Zuani.

Colterenzio CS (or Schreckbichl) T-AA ★★→★★★ No 1 ALTO ADIGE cooperative. Look for Cornell line of selections (CHARD, Gewürz, LAGREIN, PINOT NOIR. Schwarzhaus), Lafoa Cab S and Sauv Bl, Cornelius red and white blends.

Consorzio In Italy there are 2 types of association recognized by wine law. One is dedicated to the observance of DOC regulations (eg Consorzio Tutela del CHIANTI CLASSICO). The 2nd is to promote the wines of their members (eg Consorzio del Marchio Storico of Chianti Classico, previously Gallo Nero).

Conterno, Aldo ★★★★ Legendary grower of BAROLO, etc, at Monforte d'Alba. Very good CHARD Printanier and Bussiadoro, good Barbera d'Alba Conca Tre Pile. Best BAROLOS: Gran Bussia, Cicala, and Colonello. Langhe Nebbiolo Favot and Langhe Rosso Quartetto both very good.

Conterno, Giacomo ★★★★ Top grower of BAROLO, etc, at Monforte d'Alba. Monfortino BAROLO is long-aged, rare, outstanding.

Conterno-Fantino ★★★ 2 young families for vg BAROLO, etc, at Monforte d'Alba.

Contini, Attilio ★ ⋅★★★ Famous producer of VERNACCIA DI ORISTANO; best is vintage blend "Antico Gregori".

Contratto ★★ At Canelli (owned by GRAPPA-producing family Bocchino), produces very good BARBERA D'ASTI, SPUMANTE, ASTI (De Miranda), MOSCATO D'ASTI.

Copertino Ap DOC r (p) ★★ 95 97 99 00 01 Savoury, ageable, strong red of NEGROAMARO from the heel of Italy. Look for CANTINA SOCIALE'S RISERVA and Masseria Monaci, especially new barrel-aged Le Braci.

Coppo ★★ ⋅★★★ Ambitious producers of BARBERA D'ASTI (eg "Pomorosso"), CHARD.

Cordero di Montezemolo-Monfalletto ★★→★★★ Historic maker of gd BAROLO.

Cortese di Gavi See Gavi. (Cortese is the grape.)

Corzano & Paterno, Fattoria di ★★★ Dynamic CHIANTI COLLI Fiorentini estate. Very good RISERVA, red IGT Corzano, and outstanding VIN SANTO.

COS ★★→★★★ Small estate: three friends making top Sicilian wines.

Dal Forno, Romano ★★★★ Very high-quality VALPOLICELLA, AMARONE, and RECIOTO from perfectionist grower, bottling only best: 14,000 bottles from 20 acres.

Del Cerro, Fattoria ★★★ Estate with vg DOCG VINO NOBILE DI MONTEPULCIANO (especially RISERVA and Antica Chiusina, red IGTS Manero (SANGIO) and Poggio Golo (MERLOT). Controlled by insurance co SAI. Also owns: La Poderina (BRUNELLO DI MONTALCINO), Colpetrone (MONTEFALCO SAGRANTINO).

Denominazione di Origine Controllata (DOC) Means much the same as Appellation d'Origine Contrôlée (qv France).

Denominazione di Origine Controllata e Garantita (DOCG) Like DOC but with an official "guarantee" of origin shown by an officially numbered neck-label on the bottle indicating limited production.

Di Majo Norante ★★ →★★★ Lone star of Molise, south of Abruzzo with vg Biferno ROSSO, Molise Montepulciano, Ramitello Don Luigi, and AGLIANICO Contado, white blend Falanghina-Greco and Moscato Passiton Apianae.

DOC, DOCG See Denominazione di Origine Controllata (e Garantita).

Dogliotti Romano See Caudrina.

Dolce Sweet.

Dolceacqua See Rossese di Dolceacqua.

Dolcetto ★→★★★ PIEDMONT's earliest-ripening red grape, for very attractive everyday wines: dry, youthful, fruity, and fresh with deep-purple colour. Gives its name to several DOCS: D d'Acqui, D d'Asti, D delle Langhe Monregalesi (look for Barome Ricatti), D di Diano d'Alba (also Diano DOC), esp Alari, Bricco Maiolica, Cascina Flinion, and Fontanafredda. D di Dogliani (esp from CHIONETTI, San Fereolo, San Romano, Poderi Luigi Einaudi, Pecchenino, M & E Abbona, Gillardi), and D di Ovada (best from La Guardia, Rossi Contini). D d'Alba: ALESSANDRIA, ALTARE, AZELIA, Baudana, Brovia, Cabutto, Ca' Viola, CLERICO, ALDO CONTERNO, CONTERNO-FANTINO, Corino, Gastaldi, Germano, GRESY, MANZONE, GIUSEPPE MASCARELLO, Massolino, Mossio, OBERTO, Luigi Pira, Gianmatteo Pira, PRUNOTTO, Rocche Costamanga, Sandrone, SCAVINO, Schiavenza, Fratelli Seghesio, VAJRA, ROBERTO VOERIO.

Donnafugata Si r w ★★→★★★ Zesty Sicilian whites (best from VIGNA di Gabri). Also solid, improving reds, especially Tancredi and IGT Mille e Una Notte. Was VDT, now in DOC Contessa Entellina.

Dorigo, Girolamo ★★→★★★ G COLLI ORIENTALI producer for white Ronc di Juri VDT, CHARDONNAY, dessert PICOLIT, red Pignolo (★★★), REFOSCO, Schioppettino, and Monsclapade (Cab-MERLOT).

Duca Enrico See Duca di Salaparuta.

Duca di Salaparuta ★★ Vini Corvo. Popular Sicilian wines. Sound dry reds; pleasant soft whites. Excellent Duca Enrico (★★★) is one of Sicily's best reds. Valguarnera is premium oak-aged white.

Elba Tus r w (sp) ★→★★ DYA The island's white is very drinkable with fish. Try Acquabona. Napoléon in exile here loved the sweet red ALEATICO. Me too.

Enoteca Wine library; also wine shop or restaurant with extensive wine list. There are many, the impressive original being the Enoteca Italiana di Siena.

Eredi Fuligni ★★★ Vg producer of BRUNELLO and ROSSO DI MONTALCINO.

Est! Est!! Est!!! Lat DOC w dr s/sw ★ DYA Unextraordinary white from Montefiascone, n of Rome. Trades on its oddball name. See FALESCO.

Etna Si DOC r p w ★★ (r) **95 97** 98 99 00 Wine from volcanic slopes. Good producers: Benanti, Cambria, Bonaccorsi.

Falchini ★★★ Producer of good DOCG VERNACCIA DI SAN GIMIGNANO and some of the best reds of the area, eg VDT Campora (★★★) and BIANCO Selva d' Oro.

Falerno del Massico ★★→★★★ Cam DOC r w ★★ (r) 90 93 **94 95 97'** 98 99 00 01 As in Falernum, the best-known wine of ancient times. Times change. Elegant red from AGLIANICO, fruity white from Falanghina. Very good producer: VILLA MATILDE. Masseria Felice is a promising new face.

Falesco ★★→★★★ Latium estate, very good MERLOT Montiano (★★★), Cab Marciliano, good red IGT Vitiano, pleasurable DOC EST! EST!! EST!!!

Fara Pie DOC r ★★ 90 **95' 96' 97** 98 99 00 01 Good NEBBIOLO from Novara, N PIEDMONT. Fragrant; worth ageing; esp Dessilani's Caramino and Lochera.

Farnetella, Castello di ★★→★★★ Estate near MONTEPULCIANO where Giuseppe Mazzocolin of FELSINA makes gd SAUV and CHIANTI COLLI Senesi. Also vg PINOT N "Nero di Nubi" and Poggio Granoni (SANGIO-Syrah-Cab-MERLOT blend).

Faro Si DOC r ★★ 97 98 99 00 01 Quite interesting full-bodied red from Messina. Good producer: Palari.

Italy's DOCG wines: the complete list (guaranteed)

Albana di Romagna, Asti and Moscato d'Asti, Barbaresco, Bardolino Superiore, Barolo, Brachetto d'Acqui, Brunello di Montalcino, Carmignano, Chianti, Chianti Classico, Franciacorta, Gattinara, Gavi, Ghemme, Montefalco Sagrantino, Soave Recioto, Taurasi, Torgiano Rosso Riserva, Valtellina Superiore, Vermentino di Gallura, Vernaccia di San Gimignano, and Vino Nobile di Montepulciano.

Fattoria Central Italian term for an agricultural property, normally wine-producing, of a certain size.

Fazi-Battaglia ★★ Well-known prod of VERDICCHIO, etc. Le Moie & San Sisto are best Verdicchio selections. Owns Fassati (prod of VINO NOBILE DI MONTEPULCIANO).

Felluga, Livio ★★★ Substantial estate, consistently fine COLLI ORIENTALI DEL FRIULI wines, esp PINOT GR, SAUVIGNON, TOCAI, MERLOT, REFOSCO, PICOLIT.

Felluga, Marco ★★→★★★ Brother of L FELLUGA, owns *négociant* house bearing name plus RUSSIZ SUPERIORE in COLLIO DOC, Castello di Buttrio in COLLI ORIENTALI DOC.

Felsina-Berardenga ★★★ CHIANTI CLASSICO estate; famous RISERVA VIGNA Rancia, IGT Fontalloro; the regular Chianti Classico and RISERVA, although less fashionable and less expensive, are more traditional.

Ferrari ★★→★★★ Cellars making dry sparkling wines nr Trento DOC, TRENTINO-ALTO ADIGE. Giulio Ferrari RISERVA is best. Sizeable production, steadily improving quality.

Feudi di San Gregorio ★★★ Top DOCG TAURASI, DOC FIANO, Flangina, Greco di Tufo. Red IGT Serpico and Patrio (MERLOT), white IGT Campanaro.

Fiano di Avellino Cam w ★★→★★★ (DYA) Considered the best w of Campania, Can be intense, slightly honeyed, memorable. Best producers: Caggiano, COLLI di Lapio, FUEDI DI SAN GREGORIO, MASTROBERARDINO, Terradora.

Filiputti, Walter ★★→★★★ Since 1997, tenant of the vineyards of Abbazia di Rosazzo (owned by bishopric of Udine) again. Produces very good white and red COLLI ORIENTALI wines under the label "Walter Filiputti".

Florio The major volume producer of MARSALA, controlled by Illva-Saronno.

Folonari Ambrogio Folonari & son Giovanni have split off from RUFFINO to create own house. Will continue to make w and r Cabreo (a CHARD and a SANGIO-Cab), wines of NOZZOLE (incl Cab Pareto), VINO NOBILE DI MONTEPULCIANO Gracciano, new offerings from BOLGHERI and COLLI ORIENTALI DEL FRIULI.

Fontana Candida ★★→★★★ One of the biggest producers of FRASCATI. Single-v'yd Santa Teresa stands out. See also GIV.

Fontanafredda ★★→★★★ Historic producer of PIEDMONT wines on former royal estates, including single-vineyard BAROLOS and range of ALBA DOCS. Very good SPUMANTE Brut (esp ★★★ GATTINARA).

Fonterutoli ★★★ Historic CHIANTI CLASSICO estate of the Mazzei family at Castellina. Noted new selection CASTELLO di Fonterutoli (dark, oaky, fashionable Chianti), IGT Siepi (SANGIO-MERLOT). Mazzei also own Tenuta di Belguardo in MAREMMA, good MORELLINO DI SCANSANO.

Fontodi ★★★ Top Panzano CHIANTI CLASSICO estate for Chianti and RISERVA, (esp Riserva del Sorbo) vg red IGT Flaccianello, Case Via Pinot Nero, Case Va Syrah.

Foradori ★★★ Elizabetta F makes v best TEROLDEGO. Also oak-aged Teroldego Granato, red IGT Karanar, white IGT Myrto. New estate in TUSCAN Maremma.

Forteto della Luja ★★★ Lone star in LOAZZOLO; vg BARBERA-PINOT N "Le Grive".

Fossi, Enrico ★★★ High-level small estate in Signa, west of Florence, very fine SANGIOVESE, Cabernet, Syrah, Malbec, CHARDONNAY.

Franciacorta Lom DOCG w (p) sp ★★→★★★★ Small sp wine centre growing in quality and renown. Wines exclusively bottle-fermented. Top producers: BELLAVISTA, CA' DEL BOSCO, CAVALLERI, Gatti, UBERTI, Vezzoli, VILLA; also vg: Contadi Gastaldi, Cornaleto, Il Mosnel, Monte Rossa, Castellino, La Montina, Majolini, Monzio Compagnoni, Ricci Curbastri, Ronco Calino. For w and r, see Terre di Franciacorta.

Frascati Lat DOC w dr s/sw sw (sp) ★→★★ DYA Best-known wine of Roman hills: should be soft, limpid, golden, tasting of whole grapes. Most is disappointingly neutral today: look for Conte Zandotti, Villa Simone, or Santa Teresa from FONTANA CANDIDA. Sweet is known as Cannellino. The best place to drink it is from the jug in a *trattoria* in Rome.

Freisa Pie r dr s/sw sw (sp) ★★ DYA Usually v dry (except nr Turin), often FRIZZANTE red, said to taste of raspberries and roses. With enough acidity it can be highly appetizing, esp with salami. Gd wines from CIGLIUTI, Clerico, CONTERNO, COPPO, PARUSSO, Pecchenino, Pelissero, Sebaste, Trinchero, VAJRA, and VOERZIO.

Frescobaldi ★★→★★★★ Ancient noble family, leading CHIANTI RUFINA pioneer at NIPOZZANO, east of Florence. Also white POMINO and Cab (Mormoreto). See also Montesodi. Owner of CASTELGIOCONDO (★★★). From '97: joint TUSCAN venture with Mondavi of Calif nr MONTALCINO producing LUCE and Lucente. New vineyards in COLLIO DOC and MAREMMA.

Friuli-Venezia Giulia The NE region on the Slovenian border. Many wines; the DOCS ISONZO, COLLIO, and COLLI ORIENTALI include most of the best.

Frizzante (fz) Semi-sparkling. Used to describe wines such as LAMBRUSCO.

Gaja ★★★★ Old family firm at BARBARESCO under meteoric direction of Angelo Gaja. Top-quality – and price – wines, especially BARBARESCO (single v'yds SORÌ Tildin, Sorì San Lorenzo, Costa Russi), BAROLO Sperss. Trend-setting, excellent CHARD (Gaia & Rey), CAB Darmagi. Latest acquisition: Marengo-Marenda estate (BAROLO), commercial Gromis label, PIEVE DI SANTA RESTITUTA (BRUNELLO); recently planted v'yd, Ca, at BOLGHERI. Single-v'yd BARBARESCOS & BAROLO now marked LANGHE DOC.

Galardi ★★★ Producer of Terra di Lavoro, mind-boggling blend of AGLIANICO and Piedirosso, in northern Campania near FALERNO DEL MASSICO DOC.

Galestro Tus w ★ V light white from eponymous shaley soil in CHIANTI country.

Gambellara Ven DOC w dr s/sw (sp) ★ DYA Neighbour of SOAVE. Dry wine similar. Sweet (RECIOTO DI G), nicely fruity. Top producer: La Biancara.

Gancia Famous ASTI house also producing dry sparkling.

Garganega Principal white grape of SOAVE and GAMBELLARA.

Garofoli ★★ ·★★★ One of quality leaders in the Marches (nr Ancona). Notable style in VERDICCHIO Podium, Macrina, & Serra Fiorese. ROSSO CONERO Piancarda and very good Grosso Agontano.

Gattinara Pie DOCG r ★★★ 89' 90' **93 95 96'** 97' 98 99' 00 01 Very tasty BAROLO-type red (from NEBBIOLO, locally known as Spanna). Best are TRAVAGLINI (RISERVA), Antoniolo (single-v'yd wines). Others incl Bianchi, Nervi, SERGIO GATTINARA.

Gavi Pie DOCG w ★ ⭐★★★ DYA At (rare) best, subtle dry white of CORTESE grapes. LA SCOLCA is best-known, good from BANFI (esp Vigna Regale), Castellari Bergaglio, TERRE DA VINO Minaia. CASTELLO di Tassarolo, Villa Sparina, CHIARLO, PODERE Saulino, Cascina degli Ulivi, Broglia, La Giustiniana are also fair.

Geografico ★★ Co-op with rising-quality CHIANTI CLASSICO; good RISERVA "Montegiachi". IGTS Pulleraia and Ferraiolo.

Ghemme Pie DOCG r ★★ 89 90' **93 95 96** 97' 98 99 00 01 Neighbour of GATTINARA but not as gd. Best: Antichi Vigneti di Cantalupo and Rovellotti..

Giacosa, Bruno ★★ ⭐★★★ Inspired loner: outstanding BARBARESCO, BAROLO and PIEMONTE wines at Neive. Remarkable ARNEIS white and PINOT N sparkling.

Governo Old TUSCAN custom, enjoying mild revival, in which dried grapes or must are added to young wine to induce second fermentation and give a slight prickle – sometimes instead of using must concentrate to increase alcohol.

Gradi Degrees (of alcohol), ie per cent by volume.

Grappa Pungent and potent spirit made from grape pomace (skins, etc, after pressing), sometimes excellent. Best grappa comes from PIEDMONT (Ugo Marolo, Paolo Marolo, Distilleria Astigiana, Berta), Trentino (POJER & SANDRI, Pilzer, Giovanni Poli), Friuli (Nonino), Veneto (Carlo Gobetti, Vittorio Capovilla, Jacopo Poli), Tuscany (Nannoni), Sicily (Giovi).

Grasso, Elio ★★★ VERY good BAROLO (look for Runcot, Gavarini, and Casa Maté), full, barrel-aged BARBERA D'ALBA VIGNA Martina, DOLCETTO D'ALBA, and CHARDONNAY Educato, etc.

Grattamacco ★★ ⭐★★★ Pioneering producer near BOLGHERI, on TUSCAN coast. Very good DOC BOLGHERI red.

Grave del Friuli F-VG DOC r w ★ ⭐★★ (r) **94 95 97** 99 00 01 DOC covering 15 different wines, 14 named after their grapes, from central part of region. Good REFOSCO, MERLOT, and Cabernet. Best producers: Borgo Magredo, Di Leonardo, Le Fredis, Le Monde, Plozner, Vicentini-Orgnani, Villa Chiopris.

Gravner, Josko ★★★ Visionary COLLIO prod, leading drive for low yields, oak-ageing, age-worthy wines. Tirelessly self-critical in search of new concepts & methods.

Grechetto White grape, more flavour than the ubiquitous TREBBIANO, increasingly popular in Umbria.

Greco di Bianco Cal DOC w sw ★★ **97** 98 99 00 Original, smooth & fragrant sw wine from Italy's toe; worth ageing. Best from Ceratti. See Mantonico.

Greco di Tufo Cam DOC w (sp) ★★ ⭐★★★ (DYA) One the best whites from the S: fruity and slightly wild in flavour. Vg examples from Benito Ferrara, Feudi di San Gregorio, MASTROBERARDINO (Nuovaserra & Vignadangelo), Terradora.

Gresy, Marchesi de (Cisa Asinari) ★★★ Consistent LANGHE producer of fine BARBARESCO. Also vg Langhe Rosso, SAUV, CHARD, and MOSCATO D'ASTI.

Grevepesa CHIANTI CLASSICO co-op – quality now rising.

Grignolino d'Asti Pie DOC r ★ DYA Lively light red of PIEDMONT.

Gruppo Italiano Vini (GIV) Complex of co-ops and wineries incl BIGI, Conti Serristori, FOLONARI, FONTANA CANDIDA, LAMBERTI, Macchiavelli, MELINI, Negri, Santi and since 1997 controls Ca' Bianca (PIEDMONT) and Vignaioli di San Floriano (FRIULI). Now moving into South: recent investments in Sicily and Basilicata.

Guerrieri-Gonzaga ★★★ Top TRENTINO estate; esp San Leonardo (Cab-MERLOT).

Gutturnio dei Colli Piacentini E-R DOC r dr ★ ⭐★★ DYA BARBERA-BONARDA blend from the hills of Piacenza, often FRIZZANTE.

Haas, Franz ★★★ Very good ALTO ADIGE PINOT N, LAGREIN, IGT r and w blends.

Hastae ★★★ New Super-BARBERA from ASTI from group of producers: BRAIDA, CHIARLO, COPPO, PRUNOTTO, VIETTI.

Hofstätter ★★★ ALTO ADIGE producer of top PINOT NOIR. (look for S Urbano), LAGREIN, Cabernet-Petit Verdot, Gewürztraminer.

IGT (Indicazione Geografica Tipica) New category for quality wines unable to fit into DOC zones or regulations; replaces the anomaly of glamorous VDTS.

Ischia Cam DOC w (r) ★→★★ DYA Wine of the island off Naples. Top producer d'Ambra makes good DOC red Dedicato a Mario D'Ambra, IGT red Tenuta Montecorvo, IGT white Tenuta Frassitelli, and Piellero.

Isole e Olena ★★★ →★★★★ Top CHIANTI CLASSICO estate of great beauty with fine red IGT Cepparello. Very good VIN SANTO, Cab, CHARD, and L'Eremo Syrah.

An Italian choice for 2004

Barbaresco Santo Stefano Riserva 1998 Bruno Giacosa (Piedmont)
Langhe Nebbiolo Conteisa 1998 Angelo Gaja (Piedmont)
La Spinetta Oro 2000 Giorgio Rivetti (Piedmont)
Colli Orientali del Friuli Sauvignon 2001 Rosa Bosco (Friuli)
Isonzo Chardonnay Vie di Romans 2000 (Friuli)
Brunello di Montalcino Poggio Banale La Poverina 1997 (Tuscany)
Vino Nobile di Montalcino Salco Il Salcheto 1999 (Tuscany)
Montepulciano d'Abruzzo Pignotto 2001 Elio & Antonio Monti (Ab)
Taurasi Vigna Cinque Querce Salvatore 1998 Slavatore Molettieri (Cam)
Capichera Fermentino Vendemmia Tardiva 2001 (Sardinia)

Isonzo F-VG DOC r w ★★★ (r) **94 95** 97' 98 99 **00** 01 DOC covering 19 wines (17 varietals) in NE. Best white and MERLOT compare to COLLIO wines. Esp from Masut da Rive, LIS NERIS-PECORARI, Pierpaolo Pecorari, RONCO del Gelso, Borgo San Daniele, VIE DI ROMANS, Sant'Elena.

Jermann, Silvio ★★★ Family estate with vineyards in COLLIO and ISONZO: top white VDT, include white blend VINTAGE TUNINA, oak-aged Capo Martino, and CHARDONNAY "WHERE THE DREAMS NOW IS JUST WINE ..." (yes, really). Now joined by important red entry, Pignacoluse.

Kalterersee German (and local) name for LAGO DI CALDARO.

Kante, Edi ★★★ Leading light of CARSO; fine DOC CHARDONNAY, SAUVIGNON, MALVASIA; good red Terrano.

Lacryma (or Lacrima) Christi del Vesuvio Cam r p w dr (sw fz) ★→★★ DYA Famous but ordinary wines in great variety from Vesuvius. (DOC Vesuvio.) MASTROBERARDINO and Caputo wines suggest untapped quality.

Lageder, Alois ★★→★★★ Top Alto-Adige producer. Exciting wines include oak-aged CHARDONNAY and Cabernet Löwengang and Römigberg. Single-vineyard SAUVIGNON is Lehenhof, PINOT GRIGIO Benefizium Porer, PINOT NOIR Krafuss, Lagrein Lindenberg, TERLANO Tannhammer. Also owns Cason Hirschprunn for very good IGT red and white blends.

Lago di Caldaro See Caldaro.

Lagrein T-AA DOC r p ★★→★★★ **95' 96** 97' 98 99 00 01 A grape with a bitter twist. Good, fruity wine – at best very appetizing. The rosé: "Kretzer", the dark: "Dunkel". Best from Colterenzio co-op, Gries, HAAS, HOFSTÄTTER, LAGEDER, Laimburg, Josephus Mayr, Thomas Mayr, Muri Gries, NIEDERMAYR, Gojer, Niedrist estates, TERLANO co-op, St Magdalena.

La Massa ★★★ Highly rated new producer of vg CHIANTI CLASSICO; Giorgio Primo.

Lamberti ★★ Large producers of SOAVE, VALPOLICELLA, BARDOLINO, etc, at Lazise on the E shore of Lake Garda.

Lambrusco E-R DOC (or not) r p dr s/sw ★→★★ DYA Popular fizzy red, best-known in industrial s/sw version. Best is SECCO, traditional with second fermentation in bottle (with sediment). DOCS: L Grasparossa di Castelvetro, L Salamino di Santa Croce, L di Sorbara. Best from: Bellei, Caprari, Casali, CAVICCHIOLI, Graziani, Lini Oreste, Medici Ermete (especially Concerto), Rinaldo Rinaldini, Venturini Baldini.

La Morandina ★★★ Small family estate with top MOSCATO and BARBERA D'ASTI.

Langhe The hills of central PIEDMONT, home of BAROLO, BARBARESCO, etc. Has become name for recent DOC (r w ★★→★★★) for 8 different wines: ROSSO, BIANCO, NEBBIOLO, DOLCETTO, FREISA, ARNEIS, Favorita, and CHARDONNAY. Barolo and Barbaresco can now be declassified to DOC Langhe Nebbiolo.

La Scolca ★★ Famous GAVI estate for good Gavi and SPUMANTE.

Latisana F-VG DOC r w ★→★★ (r) **97' 99** 00 01 DOC for 13 varietal wines from 50 miles NE of Venice. Best wine is TOCAI FRIULANO.

Le Cinciole ★★★ DOCG CHIANTI CLASSICO (the best is RISERVA "Valle del Pozzo").

Le Fonti ★★★ Very good CHIANTI CLASSICO house in Poggibonsi; look for RISERVA and IGT Vito Arturo (SANGIO).

Le Macchiole ★★★ Outstanding red DOC BOLGHERI Paleo, TOSCANA IGTS Macchiole Rosso (Sangiovese-Cab Franc), Messorio (MERLOT), and Scrio (Syrah).

Le Pupille ★★★ Top producer of MORELLINO DI SCANSANO (look for Poggia Valente), excellent IGT Cab-MERLOT blend Saffredi.

Le Salette ★★→★★★ Small VALPOLICELLA producer: look for very good AMARONE Pergole Vece and RECIOTO Le Traversagne.

Le Vigne di Zamò ★★★ First-class FRIULI estate for PINOT BLANC, TOCAI, Pignolo, Cabernet, and MERLOT from vineyards in three areas of COLLI PRIENTALI DEL FRIULI DOC: Buttrio, MANZANO, Premariacco.

Leone de Castris ★★ Large, reliable producer to follow for APULIAN wines. Estate at SALICE SALENTO, near Lecce. Four Roses is one of Italy's best ROSATOS.

Lessona Pie DOC r ★★ 94 **95 96' 97'** 98 99 00 01 Soft, dry claret-like wine from Vercelli province. NEBBIOLO, Vespolina, BONARDA grapes. Best producer: SELLA.

Librandi ★★★ Top Calabria producer. Very good red CIRO (RISERVA Duca San Felice is ★★★) IGT Gravello (Cab-Gaglioppo blend), and Magno Megonio from Magliocco grape. New IGT from Efeso from Mantonico grape most impressive.

Liquoroso Means strong, usually sweet and always fortified.

Lis Neris ★★★ Top ISONZO estate with bevy of high-quality wines: CHARD, PINOT GR, SAUV, a MERLOT-based red, and lovely VDT dessert VERDUZZO.

Lisini ★★★ Historic small estate for some of the finest BRUNELLO.

Livon ★★→★★★ Substantial COLLIO producer, also some COLLI ORIENTALI wines like VERDUZZO. Expanded into the CHIANTI CLASSICO and Montefalco DOCGS.

Loazzolo Pie DOC w sw ★★★ 95 **96' 97'** 98' 99' 00 01 DOC for MOSCATO dessert wine from botrytized, air-dried grapes: expensive and sweet. From Forteto della Luja.

Locorotondo Ap DOC w (sp) ★ DYA Pleasantly fresh southern white.

Lugana Lom and Ven DOC w (sp) ★→★★ DYA Whites of S Lake Garda: can be fragrant, smooth, full of body and flavour. Good from CA' DEI FRATI, ZENATO.

Luce ★★★ Typically ambitious Mondavi (cf California) joint venture (launched 98) with FRESCOBALDI. SANGIO-MERLOT blend. Could become Italy's Opus One.

Lungarotti ★★→★★★ Leading prod of TORGIANO, with cellars, hotel, & museum nr Perugia. Gd IGT Sangiorgio (SANGIO-Cab), Il Vessillo, & Giubilante. See Torgiano.

Macchiavelli See Gruppo Italiano Vini.

Maculan ★★★ Excellent Cab (Fratta, Ferrata), CHARD (Ferrata), MERLOT (Marchesante), Torcolato (esp RISERVA Acininobili).

Malvasia Widely planted grape; chameleon-like: w or r, sp or still, strong or mild, sweet or dry, aromatic or rather neutral, often IGT, sometimes DOC.

Manduria (Primitivo di) Ap DOC r s/sw ★★→★★★ 95 96 97' 98 99 00 01 Dark red, naturally strong, sometimes sweet from nr Taranto. Good producers: Felline, Pervini, Sinfarosa, Masseria Pepe.

Mantonico Cal w dr sw fz ★★ **95** 97 99 00 01 Fruity deep-amber sweet wine from Reggio Calabria. Can age remarkably well. Ceratti's is good. Notable new dry version from LIBRANDI. See Greco di Bianco.

Manzone, Giovanni ★★★ Vg ALBA wines of much personality from Ciabot del Preve estate nr Manforte d'Alba, esp single-v'yard BAROLOS, BARBERA D'ALBA, DOLCETTO.

Marchesi di Barolo ★★ Important ALBA house: BAROLO, BARBARESCO, DOLCETTO D'ALBA, BARBERA, FREISA D'ASTI, and GAVI.

Maremma Southern coastal area of TUSCANY in provinces of Livorno & Grosseto. DOCS incl BOLGHERI & VAL DI CORNIA (Livorno), MONTEREGIO, MORELLINO DI SCANSANO, PARRINA, SOVANA (Grosseto). Now attracting much interest and new investments for high quality potential demonstrated by wines.

Marino Lat DOC w dr s/sw (sp) ★→★★ DYA A neighbour of FRASCATI with similar wine; often a better buy. Look for Di Mauro.

Marsala Si DOC br dr s/sw sw fz ★→★★★ NV Sicily's sherry-type wine, invented by the Woodhouse Bros from Liverpool in 1773; excellent apéritif or for dessert, but mostly used in the kitchen for zabaglione, etc. The dry ("virgin"), s'times made by the *solera* system, must be 5 yrs old. Top producers: FLORIO, Pellegrino, Rallo, VECCHIO SAMPERI, De Bartoli. Very special old vintages ★★★★.

Martini & Rossi Vermouth and sparkling-wine house now controlled by Bacardi group. (Has a fine wine-history museum in Pessione, nr Turin.)

Marzemino (Trentino) T-AA DOC r ★→★★ 99 00 01 Pleasant local red. Fruity, slightly bitter. Especially from Bossi Fedrigotti, CA'VIT, De Tarczal, E Spagnolli, Gaierhof, Longariva, Letrari, Simoncelli, Vallarom.

Mascarello The name of two top producers of BAROLO, etc: Bartolo M and Giuseppe M & Figli. Look for the latter's supreme BAROLO Monprivato.

Masi ★★→★★★ Well-known, conscientious, reliable VALPOLICELLA, AMARONE, RECIOTO, SOAVE, etc, incl fine r Campo Fiorin. Also very good barrel-aged r IGT Toar.

Mastroberardino ★★→★★★ Campania's historic house has split into two parts: M and Terredora, but with very few changes. Wines incl FIANO DI AVELLINO, GRECO DI TUFO, LACRYMA CHRISTI, TAURASI (look for Radici), IGT Avalon wines from Vesuvius, IGT Historia Naturalis, new top blend of AGLIANICO and Piedirosso.

Melini ★★ Long-est'd producers of CHIANTI CLASSICO at Poggibonsi. Good quality/price; look for single-v'yd C Classico Selvanella. Look for RISERVAS La Selvanella and Masovecchio.

Meranese di Collina T-AA DOC r ★ DYA Light red of Merano.

Merlot Adaptable red B'x grape widely grown in N (esp) and central Italy. Merlot DOCS: abundant. Best producers: BORGO DEL TIGLIO, LIVIO FELLUGA (Sossò), Miani, Radikon, VILLA RUSSIZ (De la Tour) in F-VG; Bonzara (Rocca di Bonacciara) in Emilia-Romagna; BOCCADIGABBIA in the Marches; FALESCO (Montiano) in Latium; PLANETA in Sicily; Feudi di San Gregorio (Patrio) in Campania; and TUSCAN Super-IGTS AMA (L'Apparita), FRESCOBALDI (Lampione), Macchiole (Messorio), ORNELLAIA (Masseto), Petrolo (Galatrona), RODANO (Lazzicante), San Giusto a Rentennano (La Ricolma), Tua Rita (Redigaffi).

Metodo classico or tradizionale Now mandatory terms to identify classic method sparkling wines. "Metodo Champenois" banned since 94 and now illegal. (See also Classico.)

Mezzacorona ★★ Huge TRENTINO co-op with gd DOC TEROLDEGO and MC sp Rotari.

Moccagatta ★★→★★★ Specialist in impressive single-v'yd BARBARESCO: Basarin, Bric Balin (★★★) and Vigna Cole. Also BARBERA D'ALBA and LANGHE.

Molino ★★★ Talented producer of elegant ALBA wines at La Morra; look for BAROLOS Gancia and Conca, BARBERA Gattere, DOLCETTO, and CHARD.

Monacesca, La ★★→★★★ Fine producer of VERDICCHIO DI MATELICA. Top wine: Mirus.

Moncaro ★★ Marches co-op: good VERDICCHIO DEI CASTELLI DI JESI.

Monferrato Pie DOC r w sw p ★★ Hills between River Po and Apennines and name of a new DOC; incl ROSSO, BIANCO, CHIARETTO, DOLCETTO, Casalese, FREISA, CORTESE.

Monica di Sardegna Sar DOC r ★→★★ DYA Monica is the grape of a light dry red.

Monsanto ★★★ Esteemed CHIANTI CLASSICO estate, especially for Il Poggio vineyard and IGTS Fabrizio Bianchi (SANGIO) and Nemo (Cabernet).

Montalcino Small town in province of Siena (TUSCANY), famous for concentrated, very expensive BRUNELLO and more approachable, better-value ROSSO DI M.

Montevertine ★★★ Radda estate and a leading force in renaissance of TUSCAN wine in the 1970s and 1980s. IGT Le Pergole Torte a pioneering example of small barrel-aged SANGIO. Also Sodaccio (Sangio plus Canaiolo).

Montecarlo Tus DOC w r ★★ DYA (w) White wine area nr Lucca in N TUSCANY: smooth neutral blend of TREBBIANO with range of better grapes. Applies to CHIANTI-style red, too. Good producers: Buonamico (red IGTS Cercatoja Rosso andFortino), Carmignani (very good red IGT "For Duke"), red IGT's of La Torre, Montechiari, Wandanna, Fattoria del Teso.

Montefalco (Rosso di) Umb DOC r ★★·★★★ 93 94 **95** 96 **97'** 98 99' 00 SANGIO-TREBBIANO-SAGRANTINO blend. For producers, see Montefalco Sagrantino.

Montefalco Sagrantino Umb DOCG r dr (sw) ★★★·★★★★ 90 91 **93 94 95' 96'** 97 98 99' 00 01 Strong interesting SECCO or sw PASSITO r from Sagrantino grapes only. Good from Benincasa, CAPRAI, Colpetrone, Scacciadiavoli, Terra di Trinci.

Montellori, Fattoria di ★★·★★★ TUSCAN producer making SANGIO-Cab IGT blend Castelrapiti, Cab-MERLOT blend Salamartano, white IGTs Montecupoli, a blend, and Sant'Amato (SAUV), MC SPUMANTE.

Montepulciano An important red grape of central-east Italy as well as the famous TUSCAN town (see next entries).

Montepulciano d'Abruzzo Ab DOC r p ★ ·★★★ 90 92 94 **95** 97' 98' 00 01 At best, one of Italy's tastiest reds, full of flavour and warmth, from Adriatic coast near Pescara. Best: VALENTINI, Barone Cornacchia, Nestore Bosco, Cataldi-Madonna, Feuduccio, Monti, Valori, Filomusi-Guelfi, Illuminati, Masciarelli, Montori, Nicodemi, Orlandi Contucci Ponno, Terre d'Aligi, Torre dei Beati, and La Valentina. Farnese is the big-value brand. See also Cerasuolo.

Montepulciano, Vino Nobile di See Vino Nobile di Montepulciano.

Monteregio Emerging DOC zone near Massa Marittima in MAREMMA, high-level SANGIOVESE and Cabernet wines from MORIS FARMS, Massa Vecchia, Caldane, Suveraia. New investors (incl ANTINORI) flocking in.

Montescudaio Tus DOC r w ★★ **95 97** 98 99 00 01 DOC between Pisa & Livorno; best are SANGIO or Sangio-Cab blends. Try Merlini, Poggio Gagliardo, Sorbaiano.

Montesodi Tus r ★★★ 90 **93 95** 97 99 01 Tip-top CHIANTI RUFINA RISERVA from FRESCOBALDI.

Montevetrano ★★★ Tiny Campania producer; superb IGT Montevetrano (Cabernet S- MERLOT-AGLIANICO).

Montresor ★★ VERONA wine house: good LUGANA, BIANCO DI CUSTOZA, VALPOLICELLA.

Morellino di Scansano Tus DOC r ★ ·★★★ 90' 93 94 **95 97** 98 99' 00 01 Local SANGIOVESE of the MAREMMA, the S TUSCAN coast. Cherry-red, should be lively and tasty young or matured. Belguardo, Colli dell'Uccellina, Fattorie LE PUPILLE, La Carletta, Lhosa, Malfatti, MORIS FARMS, Mantellasi, Banti, Poggio Argentiera, Poggiolungo, and Cantina di Scansano are producers to try.

Moris Farms ★★★ Good producer of MORELLINO DI SCANSANO nr Grosseto; look for RISERVA and IGT Avvoltore, a rich SANGIO-Cab-Syrah blend.

Moscadello di Montalcino Tus DOC w sw (sp) ★★ DYA. Revived traditional wine of MONTALCINO, once more important than BRUNELLO. Sweet, white fizz and sweet to high-octane MOSCATO PASSITO. Best producers: COL D'ORCIA, La Poderina, Poggio Salvi.

Moscato Fruitily fragrant ubiquitous grape for a diverse range of wines: sparkling or still, light or full-bodied, but always sweet.

Moscato d'Asti Pie DOCG w sp sw ★★ ·★★★ DYA Similar to DOCG ASTI, but usually better grapes; lower in alcohol, sweeter & fruitier, usually from small producers. Best DOCG MOSCATO from Bera Walter, Ca'd'Gal, CASCINA FONDA, Caudrina, Il Falcheto, Icardi, Marino, Marco Negri, La Morandina, Perrone, Rivetti, Saracco, Scagliola, Vignaioli di Sante Stefano, and Viticoltori Acquese.

Moscato Giallo Aromatic ALTO ADIGE grape made into irresistible dry white, esp LAGEDER, CS CALDARO.

Müller-Thurgau Variety of some interest in TRENTINO-ALTO ADIGE, Lavis, LAGEDER, POJER & SANDRI, Zeni, and FRIULI.

Murana, Salvatore ★★★ Vg MOSCATO di PANTELLERIA and PASSITO di P.

Muri Gries ★★ Vg producer of DOC ALTO ADIGE, best is DOC LAGREIN.

Nada, Fiorenzo ★★★ Fine producer of smooth, elegant DOCG BARBARESCO.

Nebbiolo The best red grape of PIEDMONT. Also the grape of VALTELLINA (Lombardy).

Nebbiolo d'Alba Pie DOC r dr (s/sw sp) ★★ 95 **96 97** 98 99 00 01 From ALBA (but not BAROLO, BARBARESCO). Often like lighter Barolo but more approachable. Best from Alario, BRICCO Maiolica, Cascina Chicco, La Contea, Correggia, De Marie, Fontatìnafredda, GIACOSA, Gianmatteo, Hillberg, MASCARELLO, PRUNOTTO, SANDRONE, VAL DI PRETE. See also Roero.

Negri See Gruppo Italiano Vini.

Negroamaro Literally "black bitter"; APULIAN red grape with high quality potential. See Alezio, Brindisi, Copertino, and Salice Salentino.

Niedermayr ★★★ Vg DOC ALTO ADIGE, esp LAGREIN, PINOT N. Gewürztraminer, SAUVIGNON, and IGT Euforius (LAGREIN-Cab) and Aureus (sweet white blend).

Niedrist, Ignaz ★★★ Small, gifted producer of white and red ALTO ADIGE wines (esp LAGREIN, PINOT NOIR, PINOT BLANC, RIESLING).

Nipozzano, Castello di ★★★ FRESCOBALDI estate in RUFINA east of Florence making MONTESODI CHIANTI. The most important outside the CLASSICO zone.

Nittardi ★★→★★★ Up-and-coming CHIANTI CLASSICO estate.

Nosiola (Trentino) T-AA DOC w dr sw ★ DYA Light fruity white from Nosiola grapes. Also good VIN SANTO. Best from Pravis, Castel Noarna, POJER & SANDRI, Giovanni Poli, Zeni.

Nozzole ★★→★★★ Famous estate now owned by AMBROGIO FOLONARI, in heart of CHIANTI CLASSICO, N of Greve. Also very good CABERNET Pareto.

Nuragus di Cagliari Sar DOC w ★★ DYA Lively Sardinian white.

Oberto, Andrea ★★ →★★★ Small La Morra prod: top BAROLO and BARBERA D'ALBA.

Oddero Pie ★★→★★★ Well-known La Morra estate for excellent BAROLO (look for Mondocco di Bussia, Rocche di Castiglione, and VIGNA Rionda).

Oltrepò Pavese Lom DOC r w d sw sp ★→★★★ DOC for 14 wines from Pavia province, mostly named after grapes. Stimes vg PINOT N & M SPUMANTE. Top growers incl Anteo, Barbacarlo, Casa Re, Frecciarossa, Le Fracce, La Versa co-op, Monsupello, Mazzolino, Ruiz de Cardenas, Travaglino, Vercesi del Castellazzo.

Ornellaia Tus ★★★★ Lodovico ANTINORI-founded estate near BOLGHERI on Tuscan coast, now owned by MONDAVI-FRESCOBALDI, with a long list of prestigious wines: excellent Bolgheri DOC Ornellaia, superb IGT Masseto (Merlot), v good Bolgheri DOC Le Serre Nuove and VDT Le Volte.

Orvieto Umb DOC w dr s/sw ★→★★★ DYA The classic Umbrian golden white, smooth, substantial; formerly v dull but recently more int, esp when sw. Orvieto CLASSICO is better. Only finest (eg Barberani, Co.Vi.O, Decugnano del Barbi, La Carraia, Palazzone, Vi.C.Or) age well. But see Castello della Sala.

Pacenti, Siro ★★★ Very international-style BRUNELLO and ROSSO DI MONTALCINO.

Pagadebit di Romagna E-R DOC w dr s/sw ★ DYA Pleasant traditional "payer of debts" from around Bertinoro.

Palazzino, Podere Il ★★★ Small estate with admirable CHIANTI CLASSICO including Grosso Sanese.

Paneretta, Castello della ★★★ To follow for very fine CHIANTI CLASSICO, IGTS Quatrrocentenario, Terrine.

Pancrazi, Marchese ★★→★★★ Estate nr Florence: some of Italy's top PINOT N.

Panizzi ★★→★★★ Makes top VERNACCIA DI SAN GIMIGNANO. Also CHIANTI COLLI Senesi.

Pantelleria Island off the Sicilian coast noted for MOSCATO, particularly PASSITO. Watch for Bukkaram, Donnafugata, Nuova Agricoltura.

Parrina Tus DOC r w ★★ Grand estate near the classy resorts of Argentario. Good w Ansonica, improving reds (SANGIOVESE-Cab and MERLOT) from MAREMMA.

Parusso ★★★ Marco and Tiziana Parusso make fine BAROLO (eg single-vineyard Bussia VIGNA Rocche and Bussia Vigna Munie), BARBERA D'ALBA and DOLCETTO, w LANGHE (SAUVIGNON).

Pasqua, Fratelli ★★ Good-level producer and bottler of VERONA wines: VALPOLICELLA, AMARONE, SOAVE. Also BARDOLINO and RECIOTO.

Passito (pa) Strong, mostly sw wine from grapes dried on the vine or indoors.

Paternoster ★★★ Top AGLIANICO DEL V producer esp Don Anselmo, Villa Rotondo.

Patriglione ★★★ Dense, strong r IGT (NEGROAMARO-MALVASIA Nera). See Taurino.

Piave Ven DOC r w ★★→★★ (r) **97** 99' 00 01 (w) DYA Flourishing DOC NW of Venice for 8 wines, 4 red and 4 white, named after their grapes. Cabernet, MERLOT, and RABOSO reds can all age. Good examples from Molon, Loredan Gasparini.

Picolit (Colli Orientali del Friuli) F-VG DOC w s/sw sw ★★→★★★★ **95 97** 99 00 Delicate sw wine; exaggerated reputation. A little like France's Jurançon. Ages up to 6 yrs, but v overpriced. Best: DORIGO, FELLUGA, Meroi, Specogna, VILLA RUSSIZ.

Piedmont (Piemonte) With TUSCANY, the most important Italian region for top-quality wine. Turin is the capital, ASTI and ALBA the wine centres. See Barbaresco, Barbera, Barolo, Dolcetto, Grignolino, Moscato, etc.

Piemonte Pie DOC r w p (sp) ★→★★ New all-PIEDMONT blanket-DOC incl BARBERA, BONARDA, BRACHETTO, CORTESE, GRIGNOLINO, CHARD, SPUMANTE, MOSCATO.

Pieropan ★★★ Outstanding SOAVE and RECIOTO: deserving its fame, esp Soave La Rocca and Calvarino, sweet PASSITO della ROCCA.

Pieve di Santa Restituta ★★★ Estate for admirable BRUNELLO DI MONTALCINO, esp Sugarile. Owned by GAJA.

Pigato Lig DOC w ★★ DOC under Riviera Ligure di Ponente. Often outclasses VERMENTINO as Liguria's finest white, with rich texture and structure. Good from: Bruna, COLLE dei Bardellini, Durin, Feipu, Foresti, Lupi, TERRE ROSSE, Vio.

Pinnochio p w sw ★ Popular in youth, famous for its nose.

Pinot Bianco (Pinot Bl) Popular grape in NE for many DOC wines, generally bland and dry. Best from ALTO ADIGE ★★ (top growers: Colterenzio, HOFSTÄTTER, LAGEDER, NIEDRIST, TERLANO, Termeno), COLLIO ★★→★★★ (very good from Renato Keber, Aldo Polencic, RUSSIZ SUPERIORE, SCHIOPETTO, VILLA RUSSIZ), and COLLI ORIENTALI ★★→★★★ (best from Zamò & Zamò). ISONZO ★★ (from Masut da Rive).

Pinot Grigio (Pinot Gr) Tasty, low-acid white grape popular in NE. Best from DOCS ALTO ADIGE (SAN MICHELE APPIANO, CALDARO, LAGEDER, Termeno) and COLLIO (Renato Keber, LIVON, Aldo Polencic, RUSSIZ SUPERIORE, Tercic, Terpin, Venica, VILLA RUSSIZ, SCHIOPETTO) COLLI ORIENTALI (LIVIO FELLUGA), and ISONZO (Borgo San Daniele, LIS NERIS, Masut da Rive, Pierpaolo Pecorari, VIE DI ROMANS).

Pinot Nero (Pinot Noir) Planted in much of NE Italy. DOC status in ALTO ADIGE (HAAS, Haderburg, Laimburg, NIEDERMAYR, Termeno co-op, Colterenzio co-op SAN MICHELE APPIANO CO-OP, Niedrist, HOFSTATTER, co-op Cortaccia, co-op Caldaro, NIEDERMAYR, LAGEDER) and in OLTREPO PAVESE (Frecciarossa, Ruiz de Cardenas). Promising trials elsewhere eg FRIULI (Masut da Riva), TUSCANY (Ama, FARNETELLA, FONTODI, Pancranzi), and on Mount Etna in SICILY. Also fine from several regions: TRENTINO (Lunelli, Maso Cantanghel, POJER & SANDRI), Lombardy (CA' DEL BOSCO, Ronco Calinoto), Umbria (ANTINORI), Marches (BOCCADIGABBIA).

Pio Cesare ★★→★★★ Long-est'd ALBA producer, esp for BAROLO, BARBARESCO.

Planeta ★★★ Top Sicilian estate: Segreta Bianco (Grecanico, Catarratto, CHARD), Segreta ROSSO (Nero d'Avola-MERLOT); outstanding Chard, Cab, Cometa (Fiano), Merlot, Santa Cecilia (Nero d'Avola).

Podere Small TUSCAN farm, once part of a big estate.

Poggio Antico (Montalcino) ★★★ Admirably consistent, top-level BRUNELLO.

Poggione, Tenuta Il ★★★ Very reliable estate for BRUNELLO, ROSSO DI MONTALCINO.

Pojer & Sandri ★★→★★★ Top TRENTINO producers: r and w, incl SPUMANTE.

Poliziano ★★★→★★★★ Montepulciano estate. Federico Carletti makes superior VINO NOBILE (especially Asinine), and superb IGT Le Stanze (Cab-MERLOT).

Pomino Tus DOC w r ★★★ r **95 97** 98 99' 01 Fine white, partly CHARD (esp Il Benefizio), a SANGIO-Cab-MERLOT-PINOT N blend. Esp from FRESCOBALDI & SELVAPIANA.

Primitivo Very good red grape of far South, identified with California's Zinfandel. See Manduria.

Produttori del Barbaresco ★★→★★★ Co-op & one of DOCG's most reliable producers. Often outstanding single-v'yd wines (Asili, Montestefano, Ovello, etc).

Prosecco Shorthand in wide use for a glass of dry fizz. But see next.

Prosecco di Conegliano-Valdobbiàdene Ven DOC w s/sw sp (dr) ★★ DYA W grape for light v dry sp wine. Slight fruity nose, the dry, nicely bitter, the sweet fruity; sweetest are called Superiore di Cartizze. CARPENE-MALVOLTI: best-known; also Adami, Bisol, Bortolin, Canevel, Case Bianche, Le Colture, Col Salice, Col Vetoraz, Gregoletto, Nino Franco, Ruggeri, Zardetto.

Prunotto, Alfredo ★★★→★★★★ Very serious ALBA company with top BARBARESCO, BAROLO, NEBBIOLO, BARBERA D'ALBA, etc. Since 1999 Prunotto (now controlled by ANTINORI) also produces BARBERA D'ASTI (look for Costamiole).

Puglia See Apulia.

Puiatti ★★ Reliable, important producer of COLLIO; also METODO CLASSICO SPUMANTE. Puiatti also owns a FATTORIA in CHIANTI CLASSICO (Casavecchia).

Querciabella ★★★ Leader in CHIANTI CLASSICO with fine RISERVA, excellent IGT Camartina (SANGIO-Cab), barrel-fermented white Batàr, new SANGIO-MERLOT.

Quintarelli, Giuseppe ★★★★ True artisan producer of VALPOLICELLA, RECIOTO, and AMARONE, at the top in both quality and price.

Raboso del Piave (now DOC) Ven r ★★ **95** 97 99' 00 01 Powerful, sharp, interesting country red; needs age. Look for Molon.

Ragose, Le ★★→★★★ Family estate, one of VALPOLICELLA'S best. AMARONE and RECIOTO top quality; Cabernet and VALPOLICELLA very good, too.

Rampolla, Castello dei ★★★ Fine estate in Panzano in CHIANTI CLASSICO, notable Cabernet-based wines Sammarco and IGT Alceo.

> **Recioto**
> Wine made of half-dried grapes. Speciality of Veneto since the days of the Venetian empire; has roots in classical Roman wine, Raeticus. Always sw; s'times sp (drink young). Sweet, concentrated, can be kept for a long time.

Recioto di Gambellara Ven DOC w sw (sp s/sw DYA) ★ Mostly half-sparkling and industrial. Best is strong and sweet. Look for La Biancara.

Recioto di Soave Ven DOCG w s/sw (sp) ★★★ **90 91 92 93 94 95** 97 98 99 00 01 SOAVE from selected half-dried grapes: sweet, fruity, slightly almondy; high alcohol. Outstanding from ANSELMI, Gini, Tamellini, and PIEROPAN.

Recioto della Valpolicella Ven DOC r s/sw (sp) ★★→★★★ **95 97** 98 00 Potentially excellent rich and tangy red. Very good from Stefano Accordini, ALLEGRINI, Serègo Alighieri, Baltieri, BOLLA, BRUNELLI, BUSSOLA, Castellani, DAL FORNO, LE RAGOSE, LE SALETTE, QUINTARELLI, Speri, TEDESCHI, Trabucchi, CS Valpolicella, Villa Bellini, Villa Monteleone, and Viviani.

Recioto della Valpolicella Amarone See Amarone.

Refosco r ★★→★★★ **95 96 97'** 99' 00 Interesting, full, dark, tannic red for ageing. Poss same grape as Mondeuse of Savoie. Best comes from F-VG DOC COLLI ORIENTALI, vg from LIVIO FELLUGA Miani, gd from Dorigo, Moschioni, Ronchi di Manzano, Venica, Denis Montanara in Aquileia DOC. Often good value.

Regaleali See Tasca d'Almerita.

Ribolla (Colli Orientali del Friuli and Collio) F-VG DOC w ★→★★ DYA Thin NE white. The best comes from COLLIO. Top estates: La Castellada, Damijan, Fliegl, GRAVNER, Il Carpino, Primosic, Radikon, Tercic, Terpin.

Ricasoli Famous TUSCAN family, "inventors" of CHIANTI, whose C CLASSICO is named after their BROLIO estate and castle.

Riecine Tus r ★★★ First-class CHIANTI CLASSICO estate at Gaiole, created by its late English owner, John Dunkley. Also fine IGT La Gioia SANGIO.

Riesling Used to mean Riesling Italico or Welschriesling. German (Rhine) Riesling now ascendant. Best: DOC ALTO ADIGE ★★ (esp HOFSTÄTTER, Laimburg Ignaz Niedrist, Kuenhof, co-op La Vis, Unterortl); DOC OLTREPO PAVESE LOM ★★ (excellent from RONCO del Gelso (DOC ISONZO). Vg from Le Vigne di San Pietro (Ven), JERMANN, Vajra (Pie).

Ripasso VALPOLICELLA re-fermented on AMARONE grape skins to make a more complex, longer-lived and fuller wine. First-class is MASI's Campo Fiorin.

Riserva Wine aged for a statutory period, usually in casks or barrels.

Riunite One of the world's largest co-op cellars, nr Reggio Emilia, producing huge quantities of LAMBRUSCO and other wines.

Rivera ★★→★★★ Reliable winemakers at Andria, near Bari (APULIA), with very good CASTEL DEL MONTE RISERVAS Il Falcone (★★★) and Cappellaccio. Also VIGNA al Monte label.

Rivetti, Giorgio (La Spinetta) ★★★→★★★★ Fine MOSCATO d'Asti, excellent BARBERA, interesting IGT Pin, series of top single-vineyard BARBARESCOS. Now owner of v'yards both in the BAROLO and the CHIANTI Colli Pisane DOCGS.

Riviera del Garda Bresciano Lom DOC w p r (sp) ★→★★ r **97** 99 00 01 Simple, sometimes charming cherry-pink CHIARETTO, neutral white from SW Garda. Esp from: Ca' dei Frati, Comincioli, Costaripa, Monte Cigogna.

Rocca, Bruno ★★★ Young producer with admirable BARBARESCO (Rabajà) and other ALBA wines.

Rocca delle Macìe ★★ Large CHIANTI CLASSICO winemaker near Castellina.

Rocche dei Manzoni ★★★ Modernist estate at Monforte d'Alba. Vg oaky BAROLO (esp VIGNA Big, Vigna d'la Roul, Cappella di Stefano, Pianpolvere), BRICCO Manzoni (pioneer BARBERA-NEBBIOLO blend), Valentino Brut.

Rodano ★★ Pozzesi family makes typical CHIANTI, both Annata and RISERVA, at Castellina and new, very good IGT Lazzicante (MERLOT).

Roero Pie DOC r ★★ **96 97'** 98' 99' 00 01 Evolving former drink-me-quick NEBBIOLO from Roeri hills nr ALBA. Can be delicious. Best: Almondo, Ca' Rossa, Cascina Chicco, Correggia, Funtanin, Malvirà, Monchiero-Carbone, Taliano, Val de Prete.

Roero Arneis See Arneis.

Ronco Term for a hillside vineyard in N Italy, esp FRIULI-VENEZIA GIULIA.

Ronco del Gnemiz ★★★ Small estate, very fine COLLI ORIENTALI DEL FRIULI.

Rosato Rosé.

Rosato del Salento Ap p ★★ DYA From near BRINDISI; can be strong, but often really juicy and good. See Copertino, Salice Salento for producers.

Rossese di Dolceacqua Lig DOC r ★★ DYA Quite rare, fragrant, light red of the Riviera. Good from Foresti, Giuncheo, Guglielmi, Lupi, Terre Bianche.

Rosso Red.

Rosso Cònero Mar DOC r ★★→★★★ **94 95** 97' 98 00 01 Some of the best MONTEPULCIANO (the grape, that is) reds of Italy, eg GAROFOLI's Grosso

Agontano, Moroder's RC Dorico, and Le Terrazze's Sassi Neri, Visioni of J. Also good from Fazi-Battaglia, Lanari, Leopardi Dittajuti, Malacari, Poggio Morelli, UMANI RONCHI.

Rosso di Montalcino Tus DOC r ★★→★★★ **97'** 99' 00 01 DOC for younger wines from BRUNELLO grapes. For growers see Brunello di Montalcino.

Rosso di Montepulciano Tus DOC r ★★ **97' 98'** 99' 00 Equivalent of the last for jnr VINO NOBILE. For growers see Vino Nobile di M. While ROSSO DI MONTALCINO is increasingly expensive, Rosso di Montepulciano stills offers value.

Rosso Piceno Mar DOC r ★★ **95 97'** 98' 00 01 Stylish Marches red from MONTEPULCIANO-SANGIO, SUPERIORE from classic zone nr Ascoli: Best incl: Boccadigabbia, Bucci, COLLI Ripani, Fonte della Luna, Forano, Laila, Le Caniette, Saladini Pilastri, Velenosi Ercole, Villamagna.

Rubesco ★★ The excellent popular red of LUNGAROTTI; see Torgiano.

Ruchè (also Rouchè or Rouchet) Rare old grape, French origin; fruity, fresh, rich-scented red wine (s/sw). Ruchè di Castagnole Monferrato is recent DOC; look for Borgogonno, Dezzani, Garetto. SCARPA's Rouchet Briccorosa: dry (★★★).

Ruffino ★→★★★ Outstanding CHIANTI merchant at Pontassieve, E of Florence. RISERVA Ducale & Santedame: best. Vg IGT CHARD Solatia, SANGIO-Cab Modus. Owns Lodola Nuova in MONTEPULCIANO for VINO NOBILE DI M, & Greppone Mazzi in MONTALCINO for BRUNELLO DI M. Excellent new SANGIO-Colorino blend Romitorio from Santedame estate. Recent purchase: Borgo Conventi estate in F-VG.

Rufina ★★★ Important subregion of CHIANTI in the hills E of Florence. Best wines from Basciano, CASTELLO del Trebbio, CASTELLO DI NIPOZZANO (FRESCOBALDI), Colognole, Frascole, SELVAPIANA, Tenuta Bossi, Travignoli.

Russiz Superiore (Collio) See Felluga, Marco.

Sagrantino di Montefalco See Montefalco.

Sala, Castello della ★★→★★★ ANTINORI estate at ORVIETO, Campogrande is the regular white. Top wine is Cervaro della Sala, oak-aged CHARD and GRECHETTO. Muffato della Sala is one of Italy's best botrytis wines. PINOT N also good.

Salice Salento Ap DOC r ★★→★★★ **93 94' 95** 97' **97'** 99 00 01 Resonant but clean and quenching red from NEGROAMARO grapes. RISERVA after 2 years. Top makers: CANDIDO, LEONE DE CASTRIS, Due Palme, TAURINO, Valle dell'Asso.

San Felice ★★→★★★ Picturesque CHIANTI resort/estate. Fine CLASSICO RISERVA Poggio ROSSO. Also red IGT Vigorello (SANGIO-Cab), BRUNELLO DI M Campogiovanni.

San Gimignano Famous TUSCAN city of towers & its dry w VERNACCIA. Also v fine r wines: Le Calcinaie, Cesani, Cusona, FALCHINI, La Rampa di Fugnano, Palagetto, Palagione, PARADISO.

San Giusto a Rentennano ★★★→★★★★ One of the best CHIANTI CLASSICO prods (★★★). Delicious but v rare VIN SANTO. Superb SANGIO IGT Percarlo (★★★★).

San Guido, Tenuta See Sassicaia.

San Leonardo ★★★ Top estate in TRENTINO with outstanding San Leonardo (Cabernet S) and good Trentino DOC MERLOT.

San Michele Appiano Top ALTO ADIGE co-op, look for Sanct Valentin (★★★) selections: CHADONNAY, PINOT GR, SAUV, Cabernet, PINOT N, Gewürztraminer.

Sandrone, Luciano ★★★ Exponent of new-style BAROLO vogue with vg Barolo Cannubi Boschi, Le Vigne, DOLCETTO, BARBERA D'ALBA, LANGHE ROSSO, and NEBBIOLO D'ALBA.

Sangiovese (Sangioveto) Principal red grape of central Italy. Top performance only in TUSCANY, where many forms incl CHIANTI, VINO NOBILE, BRUNELLO, MORELLINO, etc. V popular: S di Romagna (Emilia-Romagna DOC), a pleasant standard red. Very good from La Berta, Berti, Calonga, Drei Donà, Madonia, Poderi dei Nespoli, San Patrignano, Tre Monti, Zerbina, IGT RONCO dell Ginestre, Ronco della Simia from CASTELLUCCIO. Very good MONTEFALCO ROSSO and TORGIANO (Umbria), sometimes good from ROSSO PICENO (Marches).

Santa Maddalena (or St-Magdalener) T-AA DOC r ★→★★ DYA Typical SCHIAVA AA red, s'times lightish with bitter aftertaste or warm, smooth & fruity esp: CANTINA SOCIALE St-Magdalena (eg Huck am Bach), Gojer, Hans Rottensteiner (Premstallerhof), Heinrich Rottensteiner, Georg Ramoser, Josephus Mayr.

Santa Margherita Large Veneto (Portogruaro) merchants: Veneto (Torresella), A-A (Kettmeir), TUSCANY (Lamole di Lamole, Vistarenni), Lombardy (CA' DEL BOSCO).

Santadi ★★★ Consistently fine wines from SARDINIAN co-op, esp DOC CARIGNANO DEL SULCIS Grotta Rossa, TERRE BRUNE, ROCCA Rubia and IGT Baie Rosse (Carignano), Villa di Chiesa (VERMENTINO-CHARDONNAY).

Santi See Gruppo Italiano Vini.

Saracco, Paolo ★★★ Small estate with top MOSCATO D'ASTI.

Sardinia (Sardegna). Major potential, at times evidenced in excellent wines, eg TERRE BRUNE from SANTADI, Turriga from ARGIOLAS, Arbeskia and Dule from Gabbas, VERMENTINO of CAPICHERA, CANNONAU RISERVAS of Jerzu, and SELLA & MOSCA.

Sartarelli ★★★ One of top VERDICCHIO DEI CASTELLI DI JESI producers, (Tralivio), outstanding, rare Verdicchio VENDEMMIA Tardiva (Contrada Balciana).

Sassicaia Tus r ★★★★ 85' 88' 90' **93 95' 96** 97' 98 99' 01 One of the first Cabs, outstanding in 70s and 80s & extraordinarily influential, from the Tenuta San Guido of Incisa della Rocchetta family at BOLGHERI. Promoted from SUPER TUSCAN VDT to special sub-zone status in Bolgheri DOC in 1994. Quality wobbling now.

Satta, Michele ★★★ Vg DOC BOLGHERI, IGT red blend Piastraia.

Sauvignon Sauvignon Blanc is working well in the Northeast, best from DOCS ALTO ADIGE, COLLIO, COLLI ORIENTALI, ISONZO.

Savuto Cal DOC r p ★★ **95 97'** 98 99 00 01 Fragrant juicy red from the provinces of Cosenza and Catanzaro. Best producer is Odoardi.

Scarpa ★★→★★★ Old-fashioned house with BARBERA D'ASTI (La Bogliona), rare Rouchet (RUCHE), vg DOLCETTO, BAROLO, BARBARESCO.

Scavino, Paolo ★★★ Successful modern-style BAROLO producer. Sought-after single-v'yd wines: Bric del Fiasc, Cannubi, Carobric, and Rocche dell'Annunziata; also oak-aged BARBERA.

Schiava High-yielding red grape of TRENTINO-ALTO ADIGE, used for light reds such as LAGO DI CALDARO, SANTA MADDALENA, etc.

Schiopetto, Mario ★★★→★★★★ Legendary COLLIO pioneer with recent 25,000-case winery; vg DOC SAUV, PINOT BL, TOCAI, IGT blend Bl de Rosis, etc. Now also operating with customary elegance in COLLI ORIENTALI DEL FRIULI.

Sciacchetrà See Cinqueterre.

Secco Dry.

Sella & Mosca ★★ Major SARDINIAN grower & merchant with very pleasant white TORBATO & light, fruity VERMENTINO Cala Viola (DYA), g Alghero DOC Marchese di Villamarina (Cabernet Sauvignon) & Tanca Farrà (CANNONAU-Cab), interesting Port-like Anghelu Ruju. A safe bet.

Selvapiana ★★★ Top CHIANTI RUFINA estate. Best wines are RISERVA Bucerchiale and IGT Fornace. Also fine red DOC POMINO.

Sforzato See Valtellina.

Sicily Island in full creative ferment, both with native grapes (Nero d'Avola, Frappato, Inzolia, Grecanico) and international varieties. To watch: Benanti, Ceusi, Colosi, COS, Cottanera, Cusumano, De Bartoli, DONNAFUGATA, DUCA DI SALAPARUTA, Firriato, Fondo Antico, Gulfi-Ramada, Morgante, MURANA, Principe di Butera (ZONIN), PLANETA, Rapitalà, Santa Anastasia, SIV, Spadafora, TASCA D'ALMERITA, VECCHIO SAMPERI.

Sizzano Pie DOC r ★★ 90 **93 95 96' 97'** 98 99' 00 01 Full-bodied r from Sizzano, (Novara); mostly NEBBIOLO. Ages up to 10 years. Esp from: Bianchi, Dessilani.

Soave Ven DOC w ★→★★ DYA Famous Veronese w. Should be fresh, smooth, limpid. Standards rising (at last). Soave CLASSICO: at best intense fruit/mineral flavours. Esp PIEROPAN; also La Cappuccina, Fattori, Graney, Gini, Guerrieri-Rizzardi, Inama, Portinari, Pra, Tamellini, TEDESCHI, Ca' Rugate.

Solaia Tus r ★★★★ 85 88 90 **93 94 95 96** 97 98 99 00 01 V fine Bordeaux-style VDT of Cabernet Sauvignon and a little SANGIO from ANTINORI; first made in 78. Italy's best Cabernet in the 1990s and great wine by any standards.

Solopaca Cam DOC r w ★ **94 95 97** 99 00 Rather sharp red; soft, dry white from near Benevento. Some promise: especially Antica Masseria Venditti.

Sorì Term for a high S-, SE- or SW-oriented vineyard in PIEDMONT.

Sovana New MAREMMA DOC; inland nr Pitigliano, look for SANGIO, Ciliegiolo from Tenuta Roccaccia, Pitigliano, Ripa, Sassotondo, forthcoming Cab from ANTINORI.

Spanna Local name for NEBBIOLO in a variety of N PIEDMONT zones (BOCA, BRAMATERRA, FARA, GATTINARA, GHEMME, LESSONA, SIZZANO).

Sportoletti ★★★ Very good wines from Spello, near ASSISI in Umbria, esp Villa Fidelia BIANCO (CHARD-GRECHETTO) and Villa Fidelia ROSSO (MERLOT-Cab).

Spumante Sparkling, as in sweet ASTI or many gd dry wines, incl both METODO CLASSICO (best from TRENTINO, A ADIGE, FRANCIACORTA, PIEDMONT, OLTREPO PAVESE, some very good also from FRIULI and Veneto) and tank-made cheapos.

Stravecchio Very old.

Südtirol The local name of German-speaking ALTO ADIGE.

Supertuscans Term coined for innovative wines from TUSCANY, often involving pure SANGIOVESE or international varieties, barriques, and elevated prices.

Superiore Winewith more ageing than normal DOC and 0.5–1% more alcohol.

Tasca d'Almerita ★★★ Historic Sicilian producer owned by noble family (between Palermo and Caltanissetta to the SE). Good IGT red, white, and p Regaleali, very good Rosso, impressive CHARD and Cab.

Taurasi Cam DOCG r ★★★ **90' 93' 94' 95** 97' 98 99 00 01 The best Campanian red. Tannic when young. RISERVA after four years. Very gd from FEUDI DI SAN GREGORIO, Gaggiano, Mastrobeardino, Molettieri, good from Terredora.

Taurino, Cosimo ★★★ Tip-top producer of Salento-APULIA, vg SALICE SALENTO, VDT Notarpanoro, and IGT PATRIGLIONE ROSSO.

Tedeschi, Fratelli ★★→★★★ V reliable and vg producer of VALPOLICELLA, AMARONE, RECIOTO. Good Capitel San ROCCO red IGT.

Terlano T-AA w ★★→★★★ DYA Terlano DOC incorporated into ALTO ADIGE. AA Terlano DOC is applicable to 8 varietal whites, especially SAUV. Terlaner in German. Esp from CS Terlan, LAGEDER, NIEDERMAYR, NIEDRIST.

Teroldego Rotaliano T-AA DOC r p ★★→★★★ **95 97** 99 00 01 Attractive blackberry-scented r; slightly bitter aftertaste; can age v well. Esp FORADORI'S. Also good from CA'VIT, Dorigati, Endrizzi, MEZZACORONA'S RISERVA, & Zeni.

Terre Brune Sard r ★★★ Splendid earthy Carignano-Boveladda blend from SANTADI, a flag-carrier for SARDINIA.

Terre di Franciacorta Lom DOC r w ★★ **97** 99 00 01 Usually pleasant reds (blends of Cab, BARBERA, NEBBIOLO, MERLOT); quite fruity and balanced whites (CHARD, PINOTS). Best producers: see FRANCIACORTA DOCG.

Terre Rosse ★★ Pioneering small estate nr Bologna. Its Cab, CHARD, PINOT BL, RIES, even Viognier were trail-blazing wines for the region.

Terre da Vino ★→★★★ Association of 27 PIEDMONT co-ops and private estates incl most local DOCS. Best: Barbaresco La Casa in Collina, Barolo Podere Parussi, Barbera d'Asti La Luna e I Falò.

Terriccio ★★★ Estate S of Livorno: excellent IGT Lupicaia, vg IGT Tassinaia both Cab-MERLOT blends.

Tignanello Tus r ★★★→★★★★ 88 90 **93 95** 96 97 98 99 00 01 Pioneer and leader of international-style TUSCAN reds, made by ANTINORI. Needs bottle-age.

Tocai Mild, smooth w (no relation of Hungarian Tokay) of NE. DOC also in Ven and Lom (★→★★), but producers are most proud of it in F-VG (esp COLLIO and COLLI ORIENTALI): (★★→★★★). Best producers: Aldo Polencic, BORGO DEL TIGLIO, Borgo San Daniele, LE VIGNE DI ZAMO, LIVIO FELLUGA, Masut da Rive, Meroi, Mirani, Renato Keber, RONCO del Gelso, RONCO DI GNEMIZ, RUSSIZ SUPERIORE, SCHIOPETTO, Venica and Venica, VILLA RUSSIZ.

Torgiano Umb DOC r w p (sp) ★★ and **Torgiano , Rosso Riserva** Umb DOCG r ★★→★★★ 90 93 **94 95 97** 99 00 01 Good red from Umbria, resembles CHIANTI CL in style. RUBESCO: standard. RISERVA VIGNA Montecchi has been outstanding in vintages such as 75, 79, 85; keeps for many years.

Traminer Aromatico T-AA DOC w ★→★★★ DYA (German: Gewürztraminer) Delicate, aromatic, soft. Best from: various co-ops (Caldaro, Colterenzio, Prima & Nuova, SAN MICHELE APPIANO, TERLANO, Termeno) plus Abbazia di Novacella, HAAS, HOFSTÄTTER, Kuenhof, LAGEDER, Laimberg, NIEDERMAYR.

Trebbiano Principal white grape of TUSCANY, found all over Italy. Ugni Blanc in French. Sadly, a waste of good vineyard space, with very rare exceptions.

Trebbiano d'Abruzzo Ab DOC w ★→★★ DYA Gentle, neutral, slightly tannic white from region of Pescara. Best producer: VALENTINI (also MONTEPULCIANO D'A), but challenged by Masciarelli; Nicodemi, Valentina Valori very good as well.

Trentino T-AA DOC r w dr sw ★→★★★ DOC for 20 wines, mostly named after grapes. Best: CHARD, PINOT BL, MARZEMINO, TEROLDEGO. Region's capital is Trento.

Triacca ★★→★★★ Very good producer of VALTELLINA; also owns estates in TUSCANY (CHIANTI CLASSICO: La Madonnina; MONTEPULCIANO: Santavenere. All ★★).

Trinoro, Tenuta di ★★★ Isolated and exceptional Tuscan red wine estate (B'x varieties) in DOC Val d'Orcia between MONTEPULCIANO and MONTALCINO. Early vintages of Cab-Petit Verdot TRINORO are jaw-dropping.

Tuscany (Toscana) Italy's central wine region, incl DOCS CHIANTI, MONTALCINO, MONTEPULCIANO, etc, regional IGT Toscana and of course "SUPERTUSCANS".

Uberti ★★→★★★ Producer of DOCG FRANCIACORTA. Very good red and white Terre di Franciacorta.

Umani Ronchi ★★→★★★ Leading Marches merchant and grower, esp for VERDICCHIO (Casal di Serra, Plenio), ROSSO CONERO Cumaro white IGT Le Busche (Verdicchio-Chard), red IGT Pelago (Cab-MONTEPULCIANO-MERLOT).

Vajra, Giuseppe Domenico ★★★ Vg consistent BAROLO producer, especially for Barbera, BAROLO, DOLCETTO, LANGHE, etc. Also an interesting (not fizzy) FREISA.

Valcalepio Lom DOC r w ★→★★ From nr Bergamo. Pleasant red; lightly scented fresh white. Good from Brugherata, CASTELLO di Grumello, Monzio.

Val di Cornia Tus DOC r p w ★★→★★★ **95** 97 98 99 00 01 New DOC nr Livorno, competing in quality with BOLGHERI with many vg wines from SANGIO, Cabernet, MERLOT, MONTEPULCIANO. Look for: Jacopo Banti, Botrona, Bulichella, Il Bruschello, Incontri, Tua Rita (Redigaffi), Montepeloso (Gabbro, Nardo), Ambrosini, Petra, Le Pianacce, Villa Monte Rico, Russo, San Giusto, San Luigi, San Michele, Suveraia, Tenuta Vignale.

Valdadige T-AA DOC r w dr s/sw ★ Name for the simple wines of the ADIGE Valley – in German "Etschtaler".

Valentini, Edoardo ★★★ The grand tradition and, with Gianni Mascerelli, the best maker of MONTEPULCIANO and TREBBIANO D'ABRUZZO.

Valgella See Valtellina.

Valle d'Aosta VdA DOC r w p ★★ Regional DOC for more than 20 Alpine wines including Premetta, Fumin, Blanc de Morgex et de La Salle, Chambave, Nus Malvoisie, Arnad Montjovet, Torrette, Donnas, Enfer d'Arvier.

Valle Isarco (Eisacktal) T-AA DOC w ★★ DYA AA Valle Isarco DOC is applicable to 7 varietal wines made NE of Bolzano. Good Gewürz, MULLER-T, RIESLING, SILVANER. Top producers: CS Eisacktaler, Abbasid di Novacella, and Kuenhof.

Vallone ★★→★★★ Always better DOC BRINDISI and DOC SALICE SALENTO; outstanding, very concentrated red IGT from dried NEGROAMARO grapes (Gratticaia).

Valpolicella Ven DOC r ★ →★★★ (Superiore) 93 94 95 **97** 98 oo o1 (others) DYA Attractive r from nr VERONA; best young. Can be v light, but the best can be concentrated, complex and merit higher prices. Delicate nutty scent, slightly bitter taste, (none true of junk sold in big bottles). CLASSICO more restricted; SUPERIORE has 12% alcohol and 1 yr of age. Good esp from Stefano Accordino, Bertani, Brunelli, Tommaso Bussola, Michele Castellani, Guerrieri-Rizzardi, LE RAGOSE, LE SALETTE, MASI, Mazzi, Pasqua, Sant' Antonio, Speri, TEDESCHI, Tommasi, CS VALPOLICELLA Villa Monteleone, ZENATO. DAL FORNO and QUINTARELLI make the best (★★★). Interesting IGTS on the way to a new Valpolicella style: MASI'S Toar and Osar, ALLEGRINI'S La Grola, La Poja, Palazzo della Torre (★★★).

Valtellina Lom DOC r ★★ →★★★ 90 **95 96 97** 98 99' oo o1 DOC for tannic wines: mainly from Chiavennasca (NEBBIOLO) grapes in alpine Sondrio province, N Lombardy. Vg SUPERIORE (DOCG since '98) from Grumello, Inferno, Sassella, Valgella v'yds. Best: Caven Camuna, Conti Sertoli-Salis, Fay, Nera, Nino Negri, Rainoldi. Sforzato, TRIACCA, is most conc'd type of Valtellina; similar to AMARONE.

Vecchio Old.

Vecchio Samperi Si ★★★ MARSALA-like VDT from outstanding estate. Best is barrel-aged 30 years, not unlike amontillado sherry. The owner, Marco De Bartoli, also makes the best DOC Marsalas and a good dry Cattarato.

Vendemmia Harvest or vintage.

Verdicchio dei Castelli di Jesi Mar DOC w (sp) ★★ →★★★ DYA Ancient fresh pale w from nr Ancona, now fruity, well-structured, good-value. Also CLASSICO. Esp Bonci-Vallerosa, Brunori, Bucci, Casalfarneto, Cimarelli, Colonnara, Coroncino, Fonte della Luna, GAROFOLI, Laila, Lucangeli Aymerich di Laconi, Mancinelli, Monte Shiavo, Sta Barbara, SARTARELLI, UMANI RONCHI, FAZI-BATTAGLIA.

Verdicchio di Matelica Mar DOC w (sp) ★★→★★★ DYA Similar to above, smaller, less known, longer lasting. Esp Belisario, Bisci, San Biagio, La Monacesca.

Verduno Pie DOC r ★★ (DYA) Pale red with spicy perfume, from Pelaverga grape. Good producers: Alessandria, Castello di Verduno.

Verduzzo (Colli Orientali del Friuli) F-VG DOC w dr s/sw sw ★★→★★★ Full-bodied w from a native grape. Ramandolo is highly regarded sub-zone. Top makers: Dario Coos, DORIGO, Giovanni Dri. Superb sw VDT from LIS NERIS in ISONZO.

Verduzzo (del Piave) Ven DOC w ★ DYA A dull little white wine.

Vermentino Lig w ★★ DYA Best seafood w of Riviera, esp from Pietra Ligure and San Remo. DOC is Riviera Ligure di Ponente. See Pigato. Esp gd : Colle dei Bardellini, Durin, Lambruschi, La Rocca di San Niccolao, Lunae Bosoni, Lupi, Picedi Benettini. Also Tuscan coast: ANTINORI, SATTA, Tenuta Vignale.

Vermentino di Gallura Sar DOCG w ★★→★★★ DYA Soft, dry, strong white of N Sardinia. Esp from CS di Gallura, CS del Vermentino, Capichera.

Vernaccia di Oristano Sar DOC w dr (sw fz) ★→★★★ **71' 80'** 85' 86' 87 88 90' 91' 93' 94' 95' 97' 98 99 oo o1 Sardinian speciality, like light sherry, a touch bitter, full-bodied, and interesting. SUPERIORE with 15.5% alcohol and 3 yrs of age. Top producer: CONTINI.

Vernaccia di San Gimignano Tus DOCG w ★→★★ DYA Renaissance favourite, then ordinary tourist wine. Much recent improvement (renaissance even), now newly DOCG with tougher production laws. Best: Cusona, Cesani, FALCHINI, Fontaleoni, Le Calcinaie, Il Paradiso, Montenidoli, Palagetto, Palagione, PANIZZI, Rampa di Fugnano, TERUZZI E PUTHOD.

Verona Capital of the Veneto region (home of VALPOLICELLA, BARDOLINO, SOAVE, etc) and seat of Italy's splendid annual April Wine fair "Vinitaly".

Verrazzano, Castello di ★★→★★★ Vg CHIANTI CLASSICO estate near Greve.

Vicchiomaggio ★★→★★★ CHIANTI CLASSICO estate near Greve.

Vie di Romans ★★★ Gifted young producer Gianfranco Gallo has built up his father's ISONZO estate to top FRIULI status within a few years. Excellent

Isonzo CHARDONNAY Pinot Gris, SAUVIGNON BLANC, and white blend called Flors di Uis.

Vietti ★★★ Exemplary producer of characterful PIEDMONT wines, incl BAROLO, BARBARESCO, BARBERA D'ALBA & D'ASTI at Castiglione Falletto in Barolo region.

Vigna or vigneto A single vineyard (but unlike elsewhere, higher quality than that for generic DOC is not required in Italy).

Vignalta ★★→★★★ Top producer in COLLI EUGANEI near Padova (Veneto); very good COLLI Euganei Cab RISERVA and MERLOT-Cab "Gemola".

Vignamaggio ★★→★★★ Historic, beautiful, vg CHIANTI CLASSICO estate nr Greve.

Villa ★★→★★★ Top producer of DOCG FRANCIACORTA, also very good red DOC TERRE DI FRANCIACORTA (Gradoni).

Villa Matilde ★★★ Top Campania producer of IGT VIGNA Camarato, Eleusi PASSITO, Falerno ROSSO and BIANCO (Vigna Caracci).

Villa Russiz ★★★ Impressive white DOC COLLIO Goriziano: very good SAUVIGNON and MERLOT (esp "de la Tour" selections), PINOT BL, PINOT GRIS, TOCAI, CHARD.

Vin Santo or Vinsanto, Vin(o) Santo Term for certain strong sweet wines, esp in TUSCANY: usually PASSITO. Can be very fine both in Tuscany and TRENTINO.

Vin Santo Toscano Tus w s/sw ★→★★★ Aromatic, rich and smooth. Aged in very small barrels called *caratelli*. Can be as astonishing as expensive, but a good one is very rare and top producers are always short of it. Best from AVIGNONESI, CAPEZZANA, CORZANO & PATERNO, FELSINA, ISOLE E OLENA, SAN GIUSTO A RENTENNANO, ROCCA DI MONTEGROSSI, SAN GERVASIO, SELVAPIANA.

Vino da arrosto "Wine for roast meat" – ie, good, robust dry red.

Vino Nobile di Montepulciano Tus DOCG r ★★★ 90 93 **95' 97'** 98 99 00 01 Impressive SANGIO r with bouquet & style but often v tannic, now making its name & fortune. RISERVA after 3 yrs. Best estates incl AVIGNONESI, Bindella, BOSCARELLI, Canneto, Le Casalte, Fattoria del Cerro, Contucci, Dei, Fassati, Le Berne, La Bracesca, La Calonica, La Ciarliana, I Cipressi, Macchione, Nottola, Paterno, POLIZIANO, Romeo, Salcheto, Trerose, Valdipiatta, Vecchia Cantina (look for Briareo), Villa Sant'Anna. So far reasonably priced.

Vino novello Italy's equivalent of France's *primeurs* (as in Beaujolais).

Vino da tavola (vdt) "Table wine": the humblest class of Italian wine. No specific geographical or other claim to fame, but occasionally some excellent wines which do not fit into official categories. See IGT.

Vintage Tunina F-VG w ★★★ A notable blended white from JERMANN estate.

Vivaldi-Arunda ★★→★★★ Winemaker Josef Reiterer makes top SUDTIROL sp. Best: Extra Brut RISERVA, Cuvée Marianna.

Voerzio, Roberto ★★★→★★★★ Young BAROLO pace-setter. Top single v'yard BAROLOS: Brunate, Cerequio, Sarmassa, Serra; impressive BARBERA D'ALBA.

Volpaia, Castello di ★★→★★★ First-class CHIANTI CLASSICO estate at Radda. Elegant, rather light Chianti, IGT r Coltassala (SANGIO) & Balifico (Sangio-Cab).

VQPRD "Vini di Qualità Prodotti in Regione Delimitata" on DOC labels.

Zanella, Maurizio Creator of CA' DEL BOSCO. His name is on his top Cab-MERLOT blend, one of Italy's best.

Zenato Ven ★★→★★★ V reliable estate for VALPOLICELLA, SOAVE, AMARONE.

Zerbina, Fattoria ★★★ New leader in Romagna; best ALBANA DOCG to date (rich PASSITO: Scacco Matto), gd SANGIO; barrique-aged Sangio-Cab IGT "Marzieno".

Zibibbo Si w ★★ Local PANTELLERIA name for Muscat of Alexandria. Good producer: Murana.

Zonin ★→★★ One of Italy's biggest private estates, based at GAMBELLARA, with DOC and DOCG VALPOLICELLA, etc. Also found in ASTI, CHIANTI CLASSICO (Castello di Albola), SAN GIMIGNANO, FRIULI, Sicily and throughout Italy. Also now at Barboursville, Virginia (USA). Quality on the rise under chief winemaker Franco Giacosa.

Germany

More heavily shaded areas are the wine growing regions

The following abbreviations of regional names are used in the text:

Bad	Baden
Frank	Franken
M-M	Mittelmosel
M-S-R	Mosel-Saar-Ruwer
Na	Nahe
Rhg	Rheingau
Rhh	Rheinhessen
Pfz	Pfalz
Würt	Württemberg

German wines should be enjoying a worldwide boom today. New ideas, easier labelling on many wines, reasonable prices, and an unprecedented string of 15 good-to-great vintages are all in their favour. Yet in most places outside Germany they are still a hard sell. What is wrong? Pure, penetrating flavours and low-to-moderate alcohol should be ideal for modern tastes. Instead, Germany has everyone confused. Kabinett, Spätlese, and Auslese might all be sweet, dry, or in the middle. Their appellations might mean single vineyards, whole communes, or entire regions. This, and the failure to create excitement for their wines, is a turn-off for the average consumer.

This is a pivotal time in the politics of German wine. With the 2000 vintage two new designations were introduced nationally. "Classic" denotes dry wines from a single variety intended for good, everyday drinking; each region has put together its own list of eligible varieties. There is no limit on yield, but the vineyards must be identified in the spring before the harvest. "Selection" is intended as the top designation for dry wines; a limited range of varieties is allowed and the rules include a maximum yield and a blind tasting test. But the international impact of these new categories has been almost zero. The German craze for dry German wines is not shared by the cognoscenti abroad.

Other German wines are still classified according to grape ripeness levels. Most wines (like most from France) need sugar added before fermentation to make up for missing sunshine. But unlike in France, German wine from grapes ripe enough not to need extra sugar is made and sold as a separate product: *Qualitätswein mit Prädikat*, or QmP. Within this top category, natural sugar content is expressed by traditional terms in ascending order of ripeness: *Kabinett, Spätlese, Auslese, Eiswein, Beerenauslese, Trockenbeerenauslese*.

QbA (*Qualitätswein bestimmter Anbaugebiete*), the second level, is for wines that needed additional sugar. The third level, *Tafelwein*, like Italian *vino da tavola*, is free of restraints. Officially it is the lowest grade, but impatience with the outdated law can make it the logical resort for innovative producers who set their own high standards.

Though there is much more detail in the laws, this is the gist of the quality grading. It differs completely from other countries' systems in ignoring geographical differences. In theory, all any German vineyard has to do to make the best wine is to grow the ripest grapes – even of inferior varieties – which is patent nonsense.

The law does distinguish between degrees of geographical exactness – but in a way that just leads to confusion. In labelling "quality" wine, growers or merchants are given a choice. They can (and still generally do) label their best wines with the name of a single vineyard or *Einzellage*. Germany has about 2,600 *Einzellage* names. Obviously, only relatively few are famous enough to help sell the wine, so the 1971 law created a second class of vineyard name: the *Grosslage*. A *Grosslage* is a group of *Einzellagen* of supposedly similar character. Because there are fewer *Grosslage* names, and far more wine from each, they have the advantage of familiarity – a poor substitute for hard-earned fame. This is another law that should change.

Thirdly, growers or merchants may choose to sell their wine under a *Bereich* or regional name. To cope with demand for "Bernkasteler", "Niersteiner" or "Johannisberger" these famous names were made legal for large districts. "Bereich Johannisberg" covers the entire Rheingau: another avenue to consumer disappointment that should be closed.

Leading growers are now simplifying labels to avoid confusion and clutter. Many use the village name only, or indeed sell top wines under a brand name alone, as in Italy. Whatever they do, the consumer remains confused because the law is framed to protect the producer – and sadly, not the quality producer – nor, indeed, the consumer.

Nonetheless, make a vow to drink a fine German wine once a month at least. It will change your perception of purity and finesse, and make most Chardonnay taste gross.

Recent vintages

Mosel-Saar-Ruwer

Mosels (including Saar and Ruwer wines) are so attractive young that their keeping qualities are not often enough explored, and wines older than about 8 years are unusual. But well-made Riesling wines of *Kabinett* class gain from at least 5 years in bottle and often much more, *Spätlese* from 5 to 20, and *Auslese* and *Beerenauslese* anything from 10 to 30 years.

As a rule, in poor years the Saar and Ruwer make sharp, lean wines, but in the best years, above all with botrytis, they can surpass the whole world for elegance and thrilling, steely "breed".

2002 It is a small miracle how well the Riesling grapes survived one of the wettest harvests on record to give ripe, succulent and lively wines (mostly Kabinett and Spätlese) which will be v attractive drunk young or mature.

2001 Golden October resulted in the best Mosel Riesling since 90. Saar & Ruwer less exciting but still perfect balance. Lots of Spätlesen & Auslesen.

2000 Riesling stood up to harvest rain here better than most other places. Dominated by gd QbA and Kabinett. Auslesen rarer, but exciting.

1999 Excellent in Saar and Ruwer, lots of Auslesen; generally only good in the Mosel due to high yields. Best will both drink well young and will age.

1998 Riesling grapes came through a rainy autumn to give astonishingly good results in the Middle Mosel; the Saar and Ruwer were less lucky, with mostly QbA. Plenty of Eiswein.

1997 A generous vintage of consistently fruity, elegant wines from the entire region. Marvellous Auslesen in the Saar and Ruwer.

1996 A very variable vintage with fine Spätlesen and Auslesen from top sites, but only QbA and Tafelwein elsewhere. Many excellent Eisweins.

1995 Excellent vintage, mainly of Spätlesen and Auslesen of firm structure and long ageing potential. Try to resist drinking too early.

1994 Another vg vintage, mostly QmP with unexceptional QbA and Kabinett, but many Auslesen, BA, and TBA. Rich fruit and high acidity. Drinking well now but will keep.

1993 Small excellent vintage: lots of Auslesen/botrytis; nr perfect harmony. Ready to drink except top Auslesen.

1992 A very large crop. Mostly good QbA, but 30% QmP. To drink soon.

1991 A mixed vintage. Bad frost damage in the Saar and Ruwer, many tart QbA wines but also fine Spätlesen. To drink soon.

1990 Superb vintage, though small. Many QmP wines were the finest for 20 years. Try to resist drinking them all too soon.

1989 Large and often outstanding, with noble rot giving many Auslesen, etc. Saar wines best; the Mittelmosel overproduced, causing some dilution. Except for top Auslesen, ready to drink.

1988 Excellent vintage. Much ripe QmP, esp in the Mittelmosel. For long keeping. Lovely now but no hurry.

Fine older vintages: 76 71 69 64 59 53 49 45 37 34 21.

Rheinhessen, Nahe, Pfalz, Rheingau

Even the best wines can be drunk with pleasure when young, but Kabinett, Spätlese, and Auslese Riesling gain enormously in character by keeping for longer. Rheingau wines tend to be longest-lived, improving for 15 years or more, but best wines from the Nahe and Pfalz can last as long. Rheinhessen wines usually mature sooner, and dry Franken and Baden wines are generally best at 3–6 years. Rheingau and Nahe are the longest-living.

2002 Few challenge the best 2001s, but should prove v gd for both classic style Kab/Spät and for dry; balance looks very good. Pinot Noir is excellent.

2001 Though more erratic than in the Mosel, here, too, this was often an exciting vintage for both dry and classic styles; excellent balance.

2000 The further south, the more difficult was the harvest, the Pfalz catching worst of harvest rain. However, all regions have islands of excellence.

1999 Quality was average where yields were high, but for top growers an excellent vintage of rich, aromatic wines with lots of charm.

1998 Excellent: rich, balanced wines, many good Spätlesen and Auslesen with excellent ageing potential. Slow-maturing; many wines still a bit closed.

1997 Very clean, ripe grapes gave excellent QbA, Kabinett, Spätlese in dry and classic styles. Little botrytis, so Auslese and higher are rare.

1996 An excellent vintage, particularly in the Pfalz and the Rheingau with many fine Spätlesen that will benefit from long ageing. Great Eiswein.

1995 Rather variable, but some excellent Spätlesen and Auslesen maturing well – like the 90s. Weak in the Pfalz due to harvest rain.

1994 Good vintage, mostly QmP, with abundant fruit and firm structure. Some superb Auslesen, BA and TBA. Except for them, beginning to drink

1993 A small vintage of v good to excellent quality. Plenty of rich Spätlesen and Auslesen, which are just beginning to reach their peak.

1992 Very large vintage, would have been great but for October cold and rain. A third were QmP of rich, stylish quality. Most drinking well now.

1991 A good middling vintage, though light soils in the Pfalz suffered from drought. Some fine wines are emerging. Most drinking well.

1990 Small & exceptionally fine. High percentage QmP; will keep many years.

1989 Summer storms reduced crop in Rheingau. Vg quality elsewhere, up to Auslese level. Most wines mature, but no hurry to drink.

1983 Vg Rieslings, esp in the Rheingau and central Nahe. Generally about half QbA, but plenty of Spätlesen, now excellent to drink.

Fine older vintages: 76 71 69 64 59 53 49 45 37 34 21.

GERMANY

NB On the German vintage notation

Vintage notes after entries in the German section are given in a different form from those elsewhere, to show the style of the vintage as well as its quality. Three styles are indicated:

Bold type (eg **93**) indicates classic, super-ripe vintages with a high proportion of natural (QmP) wines, including Spätlesen and Auslesen.

Normal type (eg 92) indicates "normal" successful vintages with plenty of good wine but no great preponderance of sweeter wines.

Italic type (eg *91*) indicates cool vintages with generally poor ripeness but a fair proportion of reasonably successful wines, tending to be over-acidic. Few or no QmP wines, but correspondingly more selection in the QbA category. Such wines sometimes mature more favourably than expected.

Where no mention is made, the vintage is generally not recommended, or most of its wines have passed maturity.

Achkarren Bad w (r) ★★ Village on the KAISERSTUHL, known esp for GRAUBURGUNDER. First Class vineyard: Schlossberg. Wines generally best drunk during first five years. Good wines: DR HEGER and co-op (WG).

Ahr Ahr r ★→★★ 90 91 92 **93 94 95** 96 **97** 98 **99** 00 **01** 02 Traditional specialized red-wine area, south of Bonn. Light, at best elegant, SPÄTBURGUNDER, esp from Adeneuer, Deutzerhof, Kreuzberg, MEYER-NAKEL, Nelles, Stodden.

Amtliche Prüfungsnummer See Prüfungsnummer.

Anheuser, Paul Well-known NAHE grower (★) at BAD KREUZNACH.

APNr Abbreviation of AMTLICHE PRUFUNGSNUMMER.

Assmannshausen Rhg r ★→★★★ 76 89 **90** 92 93 *94* **95** 96 **97** 98 **99** 00 **01** 02 RHEINGAU village known for its usually pale, light SPÄTBURGUNDERS. Top wines: Spätlese Trocken. First Class vineyard: Höllenberg. Grosslagen: Steil and Burgweg. Growers including Johanninger, AUGUST KESSELER, Robert König, Hotel Krone, Von Mumm, and the STATE DOMAIN.

Auslese Wines from selective harvest of super-ripe bunches, the best affected by noble rot (*Edelfäule*) and correspondingly unctuous in flavour. Dry Auslesen are usually too alcoholic and clumsy for me.

Avelsbach M-S-R (Ruwer) w ★★★ 71 75 76 **83** 85 88 **89 90** 91 92 **93** 94 **95** 96 **97** *98* **99** 00 01 02 Village near TRIER. At (rare) best, lovely delicate wines. Esp BISCHÖFLICHE WEINGUTER, STAATLICHE WEINBAUDOMÄNE (see Staatsweingut). Grosslage: Römerlay.

Ayl M-S-R (Saar) w ★★★ 71 75 **76 83** 85 88 **89 90** 91 92 **93** 94 **95** 96 **97** *98* **99** 00 01 02 One of the best villages of the SAAR. First Class v'yd: Kupp. Grosslage: SCHARZBERG. Growers incl BISCHÖFLICHE WEINGUTER, Lauer, DR WAGNER.

Bacchus Modern, perfumed, often kitsch, grape. Best for KABINETT wines.

Bacharach ★ ·★★★ **83** 88 **89 90** *91* 92 **93** 94 95 96 97 **98** 99 00 **01** 02 Main wine town of MITTELRHEIN, in new BEREICH LORELEY. Racy, austere RIESLINGS, some v fine. First Class v'yards: Hahn, Posten, Wolfshöhle. Growers incl FRITZ BASTIAN, TONI JOST, Randolph Kauer, Helmut Mades, RATZENBERGER.

Bad Dürkheim Pfz w (r) ★→★★ 76 88 **89 90** *91 92* **93** 94 *95* **96 97 98** 99 00 01 02 Main town of MITTELHAARDT, with the world's biggest barrel and an ancient September wine festival, the *Würstmarkt* (sausage market). First Class v'yds: Michelsberg, Spielberg. Grosslagen: Feuerberg, Hochmess, Schenkenböhl. Growers: Kurt Darting, Fitz-Ritter, Karst, Pflüger, Karl Schäfer.

Bad Kreuznach Nahe w ★★→★★★ **76** 79 **83 85** 86 88 **89 90** *91* 92 **93** 94 95 96 **97** 98 99 00 01 **02** Pleasant spa town with fine vineyards. First Class: Brückes, Kahlenberg and Krötenpfuhl. Grosslage: Kronenberg. Growers incl ANHEUSER, Anton Finkenauer, Carl Finkenauer, VON PLETTENBERG.

Baden Huge SW area of scattered v'yds but rapidly growing reputation for substantial, generally dry but supple wines good with food. Fine Pinots, SPÄTBURGUNDER, RIES, GEWÜRZ. Best areas: KAISERSTUHL, ORTENAU.

Badische Bergstrasse/Kraichgau (Bereich) Widespread district of N BADEN. WEISSBURGUNDER and GRAUBURGUNDER make best wines.

Badischer Winzerkeller Germany's (and Europe's) biggest co-op, at BREISACH; 25,000 members with 12,000 acres, producing almost half of BADEN'S wine: dependably unambitious.

Badisches Frankenland See Tauberfranken.

Barriques Small new-oak casks arrived tentatively in Germany 20 years ago. Results are still rather mixed. Oak aromatics can add substance to the white Pinots, SPÄTBURGUNDER and LEMBERGER. But they ruin RIESLING.

Bassermann-Jordan ★★★ **76** 79 **81** 83 86 88 **89** 90 **96** 97 **98 99** 00 01 02 104-acre MITTELHAARDT family estate with many of the best v'yds in DEIDESHEIM, FORST, RUPPERTSBERG, etc. New (96) winemaker Ulrich Mell has put this historic estate back on top. Now one of the most dependable large estates.

Bastian, Weingut Fritz ★★ 14-acre BACHARACH estate. Racy austere RIESLINGS with MOSEL-like delicacy, best from the First Class Posten v'yd.

Becker, J B ★★→★★★ Dedicated family estate and brokerage house at WALLUF. 30 acres in ELTVILLE, MARTINSTHAL, Walluf. Specialist in dry RIESLING.

Beerenauslese Luscious sweet wine from exceptionally ripe individually selected berries, usually concentrated by noble rot. Rare, expensive.

Bensheim See Hessische Bergstrasse.

Bercher ★★★ KAISERSTUHL estate; 40 acres of white and red Pinots at Burkheim. Excellent Chardonnay, etc, and some of Germany's best SPÄTBURGUNDER.

Bernkastel M-M w ★→★★★★ 71 75 76 83 85 86 **88** 89 **90** 91 92 **93** 94 **95** 96 **97** 98 **99** 00 **01** 02 Top wine town of the MITTELMOSEL; the epitome of RIES. Great First Class vineyard: Doctor, 8 acres; First Class v'yds: Graben, Lay. Grosslagen: Badstube, Kurfürstlay. Top growers incl HERIBERT KERPEN, DR LOOSEN, Markus Molitor, DR PAULY-BERGWEILER, J J PRÜM, Studert-Prüm, THANISCH, WEGELER.

Bernkastel (Bereich) Wide area of deplorably dim quality and superficial flowery character. Mostly MÜLLER-T. Includes all the MITTELMOSEL. Avoid.

Biffar, Josef ★★ Important DEIDESHEIM estate. 40 acres (also WACHENHEIM) of RIES. Dependable classic wines.

Bingen Rhh w ★→★★★ **76** 83 85 88 **89 90** 91 92 **93** 94 95 96 **97** 98 99 00 01 02 Rhine/NAHE town; fine v'yds: First Class: Scharlachberg. Grosslage: St-Rochuskapelle. Best grower: Villa Sachsen.

Bingen (Bereich) District name for northwest RHEINHESSEN.

The Mosel-Saar-Ruwer, Germany's most dynamic region

Nowhere else in Germany are there so many exciting new producers to be discovered as in the Mosel-Saar-Ruwer. Perhaps this is the result of the special mentality of the *Moselaner* as much as the international interest in the elegant and subtly aromatic Rieslings that this archetypal cool-climate region produces. These are four names to watch for:

Clemens Busch Clemens and Rita Busch's organic estate in Pünderich is situated in one of the least well-known sections of the Mosel Valley and produces unusually powerful, dry Rieslings as well as great Auslese.

Martin Müllen Finally, the historic Mosel town of Traben-Trarbach has a producer whose wines live up to its architecture. Using 19th-century winemaking technology Müllen produces powerful and expressive wines.

Daniel Vollenweider A young Swiss who bought vines in the forgotten Mosel top site of Wolfer Goldgrube in 2000 and specializes in classic-style Spätlese and Auslese inspired by famous names of Middle Mosel.

Van Volxem An historic Saar estate brought back to life by owner Roman Niewodniczanski and winemaker Gernot Kollmann. Good classic Kabinett and Spätlese, but it is the v'yard-designated dry wines that stand out.

Bischöfliche Weingüter ★★→★★★ Famous Mosel-Saar-Ruwer estate at TRIER, a union of the cathedral property with two other charities, the Bischöfliche (Dom) Priesterseminar and the Bischöfliches Konvikt. 240 acres of top vineyards, especially in SAAR and RUWER. Recent vintages returning to former fine form.

Bocksbeutel Flask-shaped bottle used for FRANKEN wines.

Bodensee (Bereich) Idyllic district of S BADEN, on Lake Constance. Dry wines are best drunk within 5 years. Riesling-like MÜLLER-THURGAU a speciality.

Boppard ★→★★★ **76** 83 88 **90** 91 92 **93** 94 **95** 96 97 **98** 99 00 **01** 02 Important wine town of MITTELRHEIN where quality is rapidly improving. Best sites all in amphitheatre of vines called Bopparder Hamm. Growers: Heinrich Müller, August Perll, Weingart. Unbeatable value for money.

> **Warning notice: *Bereich***
> District within an *Anbaugebiet* (region). The word on a label should be
> treated as a flashing red light. Do not buy. See Introduction and under
> Bereich names, eg Bernkastel (Bereich).

Brauneberg M-M w ★★★★ 71 75 76 83 85 87 **88** 89 **90** 91 **92 93** 94 **95** 96 **97** 98
99 00 **01** 02 Top M-S-R village nr BERNKASTEL (750 acres), unbroken tradition
for excellent full-flavoured RIES – Grand Cru if anything on the Mosel is.
Great First Class vineyard: Juffer-SONNENUHR. First Class v'yd: Juffer. Grosslage:
Kurfürstlay. Growers: Bastgen, FRITZ HAAG, WILLI HAAG, Paulinshof, M F RICHTER.

Breisach Frontier town on Rhine near KAISERSTUHL. Seat of the largest German
co-op, the BADISCHER WINZERKELLER.

Breisgau (Bereich) Little-known BADEN district. Good reds and pink WEISSHERBST.

Breuer, Weingut Georg ★★ Family estate of 36 acres in RÜDESHEIM, a CHARTA
leader: 6 acres of Berg Schlossberg, also 12.5-acre monopole RAUENTHALER
Nonnenberg. Both have given superb quality, full-bodied dry Ries in recent
years. Also excellent Auslesen, BA, TBA since 1995.

Buhl, Reichsrat von ★★ Historic PFALZ family estate, returning to historic form as
of 94. 160 acres (DEIDESHEIM, FORST, RUPPERTSBERG...). Leased by Japanese firm.

Bundesweinprämierung The German State Wine Award, organized by DLG (see
below): gives great (*grosse*), silver or bronze medallion labels.

Bürgerspital zum Heiligen Geist ★★ Ancient charitable WÜRZBURG estate. 275
acres: W'bg, RANDERSACKER etc. Rich, dry wines, esp SILVANER, RIES; can be vg.

Bürklin-Wolf, Dr ★★★ Famous PFALZ family estate. 234 acres in FORST, DEIDESHEIM,
RUPPERTSBERG and WACHENHEIM including many First Class sites. The full-bodied
dry wines from these are often spectacular, but avoid the 99s.

Castell'sches Fürstlich Domänenamt ★–★★★ Historic 142-acre princely estate
in STEIGERWALD. SILVANER, RIESLANER. Back on form since 1999. Superb 2001s.

Chardonnay Now grown throughout Germany; plantings shot up to over 1800
acres. A few gd wines from recent vintages. Best growers: K H JOHNER, REBHOLZ.

Charta Organization of top RHEINGAU estates making forceful dry RIES to far
higher standards than dismally permissive laws require.

Christmann ★★★ 35-acre estate in Gimmeldingen (PFALZ) making rich dry RIES
from First Class v'yds, notably Königsbacher Idig. Impressive quality since 95.

Christoffel, J J ★★★ Tiny domain in ERDEN, ÜRZIG. Polished elegant RIESLING.

Clevner (or Klevner) Synonym in WÜRTTEMBERG for Blauer Frühburgunder red
grape, a mutation of Pinot Noir or Italian Chiavenna (early ripening black
Pinot). Confusingly also ORTENAU (BADEN) synonym for TRAMINER. Known as
Pinot Madeleine in Burgundy.

Crusius ★★★ 33-acre family estate at TRAISEN, NAHE. Vivid RIES from Bastei and
Rotenfels of Traisen and SCHLOSSBÖCKELHEIM. Top wines age v well. Also good
SEKT and freshly fruity SPÄTBURGUNDER dry rosé.

Deidesheim Pfz w (r) ★★–★★★★ 71 76 83 85 **88 89 90** 91 **92** 93 94 95 **96** 97 98
99 00 01 02 Largest top-quality village of the PFALZ (1,000 acres). Richly
flavoured lively wines. Also SEKT. First Class v'yds: Grainhübel, Hohenmorgen,
Kalkofen, Kieselberg, Langenmorgen, Leinhöhle. Grosslagen: Mariengarten,
Hofstück. Esp BASSERMANN-JORDAN, BIFFAR, V BUHL, BÜRKLIN-WOLF, DEINHARD, WOLF.

Deinhard In 97 the Wegeler family sold the 200-yr-old merchant house and SEKT
producer Deinhard to sp-wine giant Henkell-Söhnlein. But the splendid
Deinhard estates remain in family ownership (see WEGELER).

Deinhard, Dr ★★★ Fine 74-acre family estate: some of DEIDESHEIM's best v'yds.

Deutscher Tafelwein Officially the term for very humble German wines. Now,
confusingly the flag of convenience for some costly novelties as well (eg
BARRIQUE wines). The law will have to change, as it did in Italy.

Deutsches Weinsiegel A quality seal (ie neck label) for wines which have passed a statutory tasting test. Seals are: yellow for dry, green for medium-dry, red for medium-sweet. Means little; proves nothing.

Diel, Schlossgut ★★★ Fashionable 30-acre NAHE estate; made its name by ageing GRAUBURGUNDER and WEISSBURGUNDER in French BARRIQUES. But today its traditional RIESLING is among the finest of Nahe wines. Makes stunning AUSLESE and EISWEIN.

DLG (Deutsche Landwirtschaftgesellschaft) The German Agricultural Society at Frankfurt. Awards national medals for quality – far too generously.

Domäne German for "domain" or "estate". Sometimes used alone to mean the "State domain" (STAATSWEINGUT or Staatliche Weinbaudomäne).

Dönnhoff, Weingut Hermann ★★★★ 88 **89 90** 91 92 93 94 **95** 96 97 **98** 99 **00 01** 02 31-acre leading NAHE estate with exceptionally fine RIESLING from NIEDERHAUSEN, Oberhausen, SCHLOSSBÖCKELHEIM. Produces some of Germany's greatest wines.

Dornfelder New red grape making deep-coloured, usually rustic wines in PFALZ.

Durbach Baden w (r) ★★ ·★★★ ~~76-90~~ 93 94 95 **96** 97 **98 99** 00 01 Village with 775 acres of vineyards incl a handful of First Class sites. Top growers: A LAIBLE, H Männle, SCHLOSS STAUFENBERG, WOLFF METTERNICH. Choose their KLINGELBERGERS (RIESLING) and CLEVNERS (TRAMINER). Grosslage: Fürsteneck.

Edel Means "noble". *Edelfäule* means "noble rot".

Egon Müller zu Scharzhof ★★★★ 75 76 77 78 79 80 81 82 **83** 84 85 86 87 88 **89 90** 91 92 **93 94 95** 96 **97 98 99** 00 01 02 Top SAAR estate of 30 acres at WILTINGEN. Its rich and racy SCHARZHOFBERGER RIESLING in AUSLESEN vintages is among the world's greatest wines; best are given gold capsules. 93s, 95s, 97s, 99s, and 01s are sublime, honeyed, immortal. Le Gallais is a second estate in WILTINGER Braune Kupp.

Eiswein Dessert wine made from frozen grapes with the ice (ie water content) discarded, thus very concentrated in flavour, acidity and sugar – of BEERENAUSLESE ripeness or more. Alcohol content can be as low as 5.5%. Very expensive. Sometimes made as late as Jan/Feb of following year. 2002 looks to be the best Eiswein vintage since 1996, possibly since 1983.

Eitelsbach M-S-R (Ruwer) w ★★→★★★★ 71 75 **76** 83 85 **88 89 90** 91 92 **93** 94 95 96 **97 98 99** 00 01 02 RUWER village now part of TRIER, incl superb Great First Class KARTHAUSERHOFBERG vineyard site. Grosslage: Römerlay.

Elbe Important wine-river of eastern Germany. See Sachsen.

Elbling Grape introduced by the Romans, widely grown on upper MOSEL. Can be sharp and tasteless, but capable of real freshness and vitality in the best conditions (eg at Nittel or SCHLOSS THORN in the OBERMOSEL).

Eltville Rhg w ★★ ·★★★ 71 76 83 88 **89 90** 91 92 **93** 94 **95** 96 **97** 98 **99** 00 01 02 Major wine town with cellars of RHEINGAU STATE DOMAIN, FISCHER and VON SIMMERN estates. First Class v'yd: Sonnenberg. Grosslage: Steinmächer.

Enkirch M-M w ★★ ·★★★ 71 76 **85 88 89 90** 91 **93** 94 95 96 **97** 98 99 00 **01** 02 Little-known MITTELMOSEL village, often overlooked but with lovely light tasty wine. The best grower is Immich-Batterieberg.

Erbach Rhg w ★★★ 71 76 **83** 85 86 88 **89 90** 91 92 93 94 **95** 96 97 98 99 00 01 02 RHG area: big, perfumed, age-worthy wines, including First Class vineyards Hohenrain, MARCOBRUNN, Siegelsberg, Steinmorgen, Schlossberg. Major estates: SCHLOSS REINHARTSHAUSEN, Schloss, SCHÖNBORN. Also BECKER, JAKOB JUNG, KNYPHAUSEN, VON SIMMERN, etc. Not as good as it once was.

Erben Word meaning "heirs", often used on old-established estate labels.

To decipher codes, please refer to "Key to symbols" on front flap of jacket, or to "How to use this book" on page 6.

Erden M-M w ★★★ 71 75 76 83 85 88 89 90 *91* 92 **93** 94 **95** 96 **97 98** 99 *00* **01** 02 Village between Urzig and Kröv: noble, full-flavoured, vigorous wine (More herbal and mineral than the wines of nearby BERNKASTEL and WEHLEN but equally long-living). Great First Class v'yds: Prälat, Treppchen. Grosslage: Schwarzlay. Growers incl BISCHÖFLICHE WEINGÜTER, J J CHRISTOFFEL, DR LOOSEN, Meulenhof, Mönchhof, Peter Nicolay.

Erstes Gewächs Literally translates as "first growth". See box on p.152.

Erzeugerabfüllung Bottled by producer. Being replaced by "GUTSABFULLUNG", but only by estates. Co-ops will continue with Erzeugerabfüllung.

Germany's quality levels

The official range of qualities in ascending order are as follows:

1 Deutscher Tafelwein: sweetish light wine of no specified character. (From certain producers, can be very special.)

2 Landwein: dryish Tafelwein with some regional style.

3 Qualitätswein: dry or sweetish wine with sugar added before fermentation to increase its strength, but tested for quality and with distinct local and grape character.

4 Kabinett: dry or dryish natural (unsugared) wine of distinct personality and distinguishing lightness. Can occasionally be sublime.

5 Spätlese: stronger, often sweeter than Kabinett. Full-bodied. Today many top Spätlesen are *trocken* or completely dry.

6 Auslese: sweeter, sometimes stronger than Spätlese, often with honey-like flavours, intense and long. Occasionally dry and weighty.

7 Beerenauslese: v sweet and usually strong, intense; can be superb.

8 Eiswein: (Beeren- or Trockenbeerenauslese) concentrated, sharpish, and very sweet. Can be v fine or too extreme, unharmonious.

9 Trockenbeerenauslese: intensely sweet and aromatic; alcohol slight. Extraordinary and everlasting.

Escherndorf Frank w ★★→★★★ 76 83 **88** *89* **90** *91* **92 93** 94 *95* 96 97 98 **99** 00 **01** 02 Important wine town near WURZBURG. Similar tasty dry wine. First Class vineyard: Lump. Grosslage: Kirchberg. Growers incl JULIUSSPITAL, Egon Schäffer, Horst Sauer, Michael Fröhlich, Rainer Sauer.

Eser, Weingut August ★★ 20-acre RHEINGAU estate at OESTRICH. V'yds also in Hallgarten, RAUENTHAL (esp Gehrn, Rothenberg), WINKEL. Variable wines.

Faul, Fritz Prolific producer of MÜLLER-THURGAU under fashionable BEREICH label.

Filzen M-S-R (Saar) w ★★→★★★ 76 83 88 **89 90** 92 **93** 94 **95** 96 **97** 98 **99** 00 **01** 02 Small SAAR village near WILTINGEN. First Class vineyard: Pulchen. Grower to note: Piedmont.

Fischer Erben, Weingut ★★★ 18-acre RHEINGAU estate at ELTVILLE with high traditional standards. Long-lived classic wines.

Forschungsanstalt Geisenheim See Hessische Forschungsanstalt.

Forst Pfz w ★★→★★★★ **71** 76 **83** 85 89 90 *91* 92 **93** 94 *95* **96** 97 **98** 99 *00* 01 02 MITTELHAARDT village with 500 acres of Germany's best v'yds. Ripe, richly fragrant, full-bodied but subtle wines. First Class vineyards: Jesuitengarten, Kirchenstück, FREUNDSTÜCK, Pechstein, Ungeheuer. Grosslagen: Mariengarten, Schnep-fenflug. Top growers incl BASSERMANN-JORDAN, BURKLIN-WOLF, DR DEINHARD, G MOSBACHER, Eugen Müller, H Spindler, Werlé, J L WOLF.

Franken Franconia Region of distinctive dry wines, esp SILVANER, always bottled in round-bellied flasks (BOCKSBEUTEL). The centre is WURZBURG. Bereich names: MAINDREIECK, STEIGERWALD. Top producers: BURGERSPITAL, CASTELL'SCHES, FÜRST RUDOLF, JULIUSSPITAL, LÖWENSTEIN, Horst Sauer, WIRSCHING, etc.

Freiburg Baden w (r) ★→★★ DYA Wine centre in BREISGAU. Good GUTEDEL.

Friedrich-Wilhelm Gymnasium ★★ Important 82-acre charitable estate based in TRIER with v'yds in BERNKASTEL, GRAACH, OCKFEN, TRITTENHEIM, ZELTINGEN, etc, all M-S-R. Since 95 much improved after poor patch.

Fuhrmann See Pfeffingen.

Fürst Rudolf ★★★ Small estate in Bürgstadt making some of the best wines in FRANKEN, particularly Burgundian SPÄTBURGUNDER and oak-aged WEISSBURGUNDER.

Gallais Le See Egon Müller.

Geisenheim Rhg w ★★→★★★ **71 76 85** 88 **89 90** 91 92 **93** 94 95 **96** 97 98 **99** 00 01 02 Village famous for Germany's best-known wine school and very good aromatic wines. First Class vineyards: Kläuserweg, Rothenberg. Grosslagen: Burgweg, Erntebringer. Top growers: JOHANNISHOF, SCHLOSS SCHÖNBORN, WEGELER, VON ZWIERLEIN.

Gemeinde A commune or parish.

Gewürztraminer (or Traminer) Highly aromatic grape, speciality of Alsace, also impressive in Germany, especially in PFALZ, BADEN, SACHSEN, and WÜRTTEMBERG.

Gimmeldingen Pfz w ★★ **76 85** 88 **89 90** 91 **92 93** 94 95 96 97 98 99 00 00 **01** 02 Village just South of MITTELHAARDT. At best, rich succulent wines. Grosslage: Meerspinne. Growers incl: CHRISTMANN, MULLER-CATOIR.

Graach M-M w ★★★ **71 75 76 83 85** 88 89 **90** 91 92 **93** 94 95 96 **97 98 99** 00 **01** 02 Sml village between BERNKASTEL and WEHLEN. First Class v'yds: Domprobst, Himmelreich, Josephshofer. Grosslage: Münzlay. Many top growers: VON KESSELSTATT, DR LOOSEN, J J PRÜM, WILLI SCHAEFER, SELBACH-OSTER, DR WEINS-PRÜM.

Grans-Fassian ★★★ Fine 25-acre MOSEL estate at Leiwen. V'yds there and in TRITTENHEIM. EISWEIN a speciality. Dependable high quality since 95.

Grauburgunder Synonym of RULÄNDER or Pinot Gris: grape giving soft full-bodied wine. Best in BADEN and southern PFALZ.

Grosser Ring Group of top (VDP) MOSEL-SAAR-RUWER estates, whose annual September auction regularly sets world-record prices.

Grosslage See Introduction, pages 133–134.

Gunderloch ★★★→★★★★ 88 **89 90** 91 92 **93** 94 95 **96 97 98** 99 00 **01** 02 30-acre NACKENHEIM estate making some of the finest RIES on the entire Rhine, including spectacular BA/TBA. The undisputed number one in RHEINHESSEN. Also owns well-known Balbach estate in NIERSTEIN.

Guntrum, Louis ★★ Large (67-acre) family estate in NIERSTEIN, OPPENHEIM, etc. Good SILVANER and GEWÜRZTRAMINER as well as RIESLING.

Gutedel German name for the ancient Chasselas grape, used in S BADEN.

Gutsabfüllung Estate-bottled. Term for genuinely estate-bottled wines.

Gutsverwaltung Estate administration.

Haag, Weingut Fritz ★★★★ 69 70 **71** 72 73 74 **75 76** 77 78 **79** 80 81 82 **83** 84 **85** 86 87 **88** 89 **90** 91 92 93 94 **95** 96 97 98 99 00 00 **01** 02 Top estate in BRAUNEBERG run by Wilhelm Haag, president of GROSSER RING. MOSEL RIES of crystalline purity & racy brilliance for long ageing. Haag's son runs the SCHLOSS LIESER estate.

Haag, Weingut Willi ★★ 7-acre BRAUNEBERG estate. Full, old-style RIES. Some fine AUSLESE. Improving quality since 95.

Haart, Reinhold ★★★ The best estate in PIESPORT, and growing in repute. Refined, aromatic wines capable of long ageing.

Halbtrocken Medium-dry (literally "semi-dry"). Containing fewer than 18 but more than 9 grams per litre unfermented sugar. Popular category of wine intended for mealtimes, usually better balanced than TROCKEN.

Remember that vintage information for German wines is given in a different form from the ready/not ready distinction applying to other countries. Read the explanation at the bottom of page 137.

GERMANY

Hattenheim Rhg w ★★→★★★★ **71 76 83 89 90** 91 **92 93** 94 **95 96** 97 98 **99** 00 01 02 Superlative 500-acre wine town, though not all producers achieve its full potential. The First Class vineyards are Engelmannsberg, Mannberg, Pfaffenberg, Nussbrunnen, Wisselbrunnen, and most famously STEINBERG (ORTSTEIL). Grosslage: Deutelsberg. MARCOBRUNN: on ERBACH boundary. Estates include KNYPHAUSEN, RESS, SCHLOSS SCHÖNBORN, VON SIMMERN, STATE DOMAIN, etc.

Heldenmut, Weingut Ideal VDP member; organic PRÄDIKAT wines only.

Henkell See Deinhard.

Heger, Dr ★★★ Leading estate of BADEN with excellent dry WEISSBURGUNDER, GRAUBURGUNDER and powerful oak-aged SPÄTBURGUNDER reds.

Heilbronn Würt w r ★→★★ **89 90 93** 94 **96 97** 98 99 00 01 02 Wine town with many small growers and good co-op. Best are RIESLING and LEMBERGER. Seat of DLG competition. Top growers: Amalienhof, Drautz-Able, Schäfer-Heinrich.

Hessen, Prinz von ★★→★★★ Famous 75-acre estate in JOHANNISBERG, KIEDRICH, and WINKEL. Rapidly improving quality since 95 vintage.

Hessische Bergstrasse w ★★→★★★ **90** 91 **92 93** 94 95 96 **97** 98 **99** 00 01 02 Smallest wine region in western Germany (1,000 acres), N of Heidelberg. Pleasant RIES from STATE DOMAIN v'yds at BENSHEIM, Bergstrasser co-op, Heppenheim, Simon-Bürkle, and Stadt Bensheim.

Hessische Forschungsanstalt für Wein-Obst & Gartenbau Famous wine school and research establishment at GEISENHEIM, RHEINGAU. Good wines incl reds. The name on the label is Forschungsanstalt.

Heyl zu Herrnsheim ★★★ Leading 92-acre NIERSTEIN estate, 60% RIES. Since fine 96 v'tge owned by Ahr family. Dry RIES, SILVANER, W'BURGUNDER of classical elegance.

Heymann-Löwenstein ★★★ Young estate in Lower or "Terrace Mosel" with most consistent dry RIESLING in MOSEL-SAAR-RUWER and some remarkable AUSLESE and TBA. Spectacular wines in 2001. A rapidly rising star ↓

Hochgewächs Supposedly superior level of QBA RIES, esp in MOSEL-SAAR-RUWER.

Hochheim Rhg w ★★ ·★★★★ **71 75** 76 79 **83 85** 86 **88 89** 90 91 **92 93** 94 95 **96 97 98** 99 00 01 02 600-acre wine town 15 miles E of main RHEINGAU area, once thought of as best on Rhine. RHEINGAU-like wines with an earthy intensity, body, and fragrance of their own. First Class vineyards: Domdechaney, Hölle, Kirchenstück, Königin Viktoria Berg (12-acre monopoly of Hupfeld of OESTRICH). Grosslage: Daubhaus. Growers incl Hupfeld, FRANZ KUNSTLER, WJ SCHAEFER, SCHLOSS SCHÖNBORN, STAATSWEINGUT, WERNER.

Hock Traditional English term for Rhine wine, derived from HOCHHEIM.

Hoensbroech, Weingut Reichsgraf zu ★★ Top KRAICHGAU estate. 37 acres. Dry WEISSBURGUNDER, GRAUBURGUNDER, SILVANER, eg Michelfelder Himmelberg.

Hohenlohe-Oehringen, Weingut Fürst zu ★★ Noble 47-acre estate in Oehringen and WURTTEMBERG. Earthy bone-dry RIESLING and powerful reds from SPÄTBURGUNDER and LEMBERGER grapes.

Hövel, Weingut von ★★★ Very fine SAAR estate at OBERMOSEL (Hütte is 12-acre monopoly) and in SCHARZHOFBERG. Superb wines since 93.

Huber, Bernard ★★★ Rising star of Breisgau area of BADEN with powerful oak-aged SPÄTBURGUNDER reds and Burgundian-style WEISSBURGUNDER, CHARDONNAY.

Huxelrebe Modern aromatic grape variety, best for dessert wines.

Ihringen Bad r w ★ ·★★★ **86** 88 **89 90** 91 92 **93** 94 95 **96 97 98 99** 00 **01** 02 One of the best villages of the KAISERSTUHL, BADEN. Proud of its SPÄTBURGUNDER red, WEISSHERBST, and GRAUBURGUNDER. Top growers: DR HEGER, Stigler.

Ilbesheim Deutsches Weintor Pfz w (r) ★ ·★★ **90 93** 94 95 **96 97** 98 99 00 01 02 Vast growers co-op with solid reputation for quality.

Ingelheim Rhh r w ★★ **90** 92 **93** 94 95 96 **97** 98 **99** 00 01 **02** Town opposite RHEINGAU historically known for its SPÄTBURGUNDER. Few wines today live up to reputation. Top v'yds are Horn, Pares, Sonnenberg and Steinacker.

Iphofen Frank w ★★→★★★ 76 79 83 85 87 88 89 90 91 92 93 94 95 96 97 98 **99** 00 **01** 02 Village nr WURZBURG. Superb First Class v'yds: Julius-Echter-Berg, Kalb. Grosslage: Burgweg. Growers: JULIUSSPITAL, Ruck, WIRSCHING.

Jahrgang Year – as in "vintage".

Johannisberg Rhg w ★★→★★★★ 71 75 76 83 85 86 88 **89** 90 91 92 **93** 94 **95 96 97** 98 **99** 00 **01** 02 260-acre classic RHEINGAU village with superlative subtle RIES. First Class v'yds: Hölle, Klaus, SCHLOSS JOHANNISBERG. Grosslage: Erntebringer. Top growers: JOHANNISHOF, SCHLOSS JOHANNISBERG.

Johannisberg (Bereich) District name for the entire RHEINGAU. Avoid.

Johannishof ★★★ JOHANNISBERG family estate, aka HH Eser. 45 acres. RIESLINGS that justify the great Johannisberg name. Since 96 also fine RÜDESHEIM wines.

Johner, Karl-Heinz ★★★ Small BADEN estate at Bischoffingen, in the front line for New-World-style SPÄTBURGUNDER and oak-aged WEISSBURGUNDER.

Josephshöfer First Class v'yd at GRAACH, the sole property of VON KESSELSTATT.

Jost, Toni ★★★ Perhaps the top estate of the MITTELRHEIN. 25 acres, mainly RIES, in BACHARACH and also in the RHEINGAU.

Juliusspital ★★★ Ancient WÜRZBURG religious charity with 374 acres of top FRANKEN v'yds and many top wines. Look for its dry SILVANERS and RIES.

Kabinett The term for the lightest category of natural unsugared (QMP) wines. Low in alcohol (RIES averages 7–9%) but sometimes capable of sublime finesse. Drink young or with several yrs' age.

Kaiserstuhl (Bereich) One of the top BADEN districts, with notably warm climate and volcanic soil. Villages incl ACHKARREN, IHRINGEN. Grosslage: Vulkanfelsen.

Kallfelz, Albert ★★ Useful producer of fresh MOSELS at ZELL and Merl.

Kallstadt Pfz w (r) ★★→★★★ 76 83 85 88 89 90 92 93 94 **95 96** 97 98 99 00 **01** 02 Village of N MITTELHAARDT. Often underrated fine, rich, dry Riesling and Pinot. First Class vineyard: Saumagen. Grosslagen: Feuerberg, Kobnert. Growers incl Henninger, KOEHLER-RUPRECHT, Schüster.

Kammerpreismünze See Landespreismünze.

Kanzem M-S-R (Saar) w ★★★ 71 76 **88 89 90** 91 92 **93** 94 **95** 96 **97** 98 **99** 00 **01** 02 Small neighbour of WILTINGEN. First Class vineyard: Altenberg. Grosslage: SCHARZBERG. Growers incl Othegraven, Reverchon, J P Reinert.

Karlsmühle ★★★ Small estate with Lorenzhöfer monopoly site in RUWER making classic Ruwer RIES, also wines from First Class KASEL v'yds sold under Patheiger label. Consistently excellent quality since 94.

Karthäuserhofberg ★★★★ Top RUWER estate of 46 acres at Eitelsbach. Easily recognized by bottles with only a neck-label. Since 1993 estate has been back on top form. Also good TROCKEN wines.

Kasel M-S-R (Ruwer) w ★★ →★★★ 71 76 83 85 **88 89** 90 91 92 **93** 94 95 96 97 98 **99** 00 **01** 02 Stunning flowery Römerlay wines. First Class v'yds: Kehrnagel, Nies'chen. Top growers: KARLSMUHLE, VON KESSELSTATT, WEGELER.

Keller Wine cellar. **Kellerei** Winery (ie a big commercial bottler).

Kerner Modern aromatic grape variety, earlier ripening than RIES, of fair quality but without Riesling's inbuilt grace and harmony. Best in SACHSEN.

Kerpen, Weingut Heribert ★★ Small good estate in BERNKASTEL, GRAACH, WEHLEN.

Kesseler, Weingut August ★★★ 35-acre estate making the best SPÄTBURGUNDER reds in ASSMANNSHAUSEN. Also very good classic-style RIES.

Kesselstatt, von ★★★ The lgst private MOSEL estate, 650 yrs old. Now belongs to Reh family. Some 150 acres in GRAACH, KASEL, PIESPORT, WILTINGEN, etc, producing aromatic generously fruity MOSELS. Consistent high quality, often magnificent wines from JOSEPHSHÖFER monopoly v'yd and SCHARZHOFBERG.

Kesten M-M w ★ →★★★ 71 76 83 88 89 90 91 **92 93** 94 **95** 96 **97** 98 **99** 00 **01** 02 Neighbour of BRAUNEBERG. Best wines (from Paulinshofberg v'yd) similar. Grosslage: Kurfürstlay. Top growers: Bastgen, Kees-Kieren, PAULINSHOF.

Kiedrich Rhg w ★★→★★★★ **71 76 83** 89 **90** 91 **92 93 94** 95 **96** 97 **98 99** 00 01 02 Neighbour of RAUENTHAL; equally splendid and high-flavoured. First Class v'yds: Gräfenberg, Wasseros. Grosslage: Heiligenstock. Growers incl FISCHER, KNYPHAUSEN, Speicher-Schuth. R WEIL now top estate.

Klingelberger ORTENAU (BADEN) term for RIESLING, esp at DURBACH.

Kloster Eberbach Glorious 12th-C Cistercian abbey in HATTENHEIM forest. Monks planted STEINBERG, Germany's Clos de Vougeot. Now STATE DOMAIN-owned; HQ of German Wine Academy.

Klüsserath M-M w ★→★★★ **76 83 88 90** 91 92 **93** 94 **95** 96 97 **98 99** 00 **01** 02 Little-known MOSEL village whose winegrowers have joined forces to classify its top site, Brüderschaft. Growers: Bernhard Kirsten, FRIEDRICH-WILHELM-GYMNASIUM, Regnery.

Knyphausen, Weingut Freiherr zu ★★★ Noble 54-acre estate on former Cistercian land (see Kloster Eberbach) in ELTVILLE, ERBACH, HATTENHEIM, KIEDRICH and MARCOBRUNN. Classic RHEINGAU wines, many dry.

Koehler-Ruprecht ★★★★ **76** 77 *78* **79** 80 **81** 82 **83** 84 **85** 86 *87* **88 89 90** 91 92 **93** 94 95 **96 97 98** 99 00 **01** 02 Highly rated (25-acre) going from strength to strength; top KALLSTADT grower. V traditional w'making; v long-lived dry RIESLING from K Saumagen. Outstanding SPÄTBURGUNDER.

Kraichgau Small BADEN region S of Heidelberg. Top grower: HOENSBROECH.

Kröv M-M w ★→★★★ **88 90** 91 92 **93** 94 95 *96* **97 98** 99 *00* 01 Popular tourist resort famous for its Grosslage name: Nacktarsch, or "bare bottom". Be very careful. Best grower: Martin Müllen.

Künstler, Franz ★★★★ HOCHHEIM estate expanded in 1996 to 50 acres by purchase of well-known Aschrott estate. Superb dry RIESLING, esp from First Class Domdechaney, H Hölle, and Kirchenstück, also excellent AUSLESE.

Kuntz, Sybille ★★ M-S-R Successful protagonist of untypical dry MOSEL RIESLING of AUSLESE strength.

Laible, Weingut Andreas ★★★ 10-acre DURBACH estate. Fine sweet and dry RIES, SCHEUREBE, GEWÜRZ (First Class Plauelrain vineyard). Klingelberger can be utter joy. Superb quality since 1997.

Landespreismünze Prizes for quality at state, rather than national, level.

Landwein A category of better-quality TAFELWEIN (the grapes must be slightly riper) from 20 designated regions. It must be TROCKEN or HALBTROCKEN. Similar in intention to France's *vin de pays* but without the buzz.

Leitz, J ★★★ Fine little RÜDESHEIM family estate for elegant, dry RIES. A rising star.

Liebfraumilch

Much-abused name, once accounting for 50% of all German wine exports – to the detriment of Germany's better products. Legally defined as a QBA "of pleasant character" from RHEINHESSEN, PFALZ, NAHE, or RHEINGAU, of a blend with at least 51% RIESLING, SILVANER, KERNER, or MÜLLER-T. Most is mild, semi-sweet wine from Rheinhessen and the Pfalz. Rules now say it must have more than 18 grams per litre unfermented sugar. Its definition makes a mockery of the legal term Quality Wine. With sales falling fast everywhere, this category is in the process of disappearing.

Lemberger Red variety imported to Germany and Austria in the 18th century, from Hungary, where it is known as Kékfrankos. Blaufränkisch in Austria. Deep-coloured, moderately tannic wines; can be excellent. Or rosé.

Liebfrauenstift 26-acre v'yd in city of Worms; origin of LIEBFRAUMILCH.

Lieser M-M w ★★ **71 76 83 88 89 90** 91 92 **93** 94 **95** 96 **97** 98 **99** 00 **01** 02 Little-known neighbour of BERNKASTEL. Lighter wines. First Class v'yd: Niederberg-Helden. Grosslage: Kurfürstlay. Top grower: SCHLOSS LIESER.

Lingenfelder, Weingut ★★ Small innovative Grosskarlbach (PFALZ) estate: good dry and sweet SCHEUREBE, full-bodied RIES, etc.

Loewen, Carl ★★★ Top grower of Leiwen on MOSEL making ravishing AUSLESE from town's First Class Laurentiuslay site. Also fine EISWEIN.

Loosen, Weingut Dr ★★★★ 71 72 73 74 **75 76** 77 78 79 80 81 82 83 84 85 86 87 **88** 89 **90** 91 92 **93** 94 **95** 96 **97** 98 **99** 00 **01** Dynamic 24-acre St-Johannishof estate in BERNKASTEL, ERDEN, GRAACH, URZIG, WEHLEN. Deep intense RIESLINGS from old vines in great First Class vineyards. Also JL Wolf in the Pfalz since 1996. Superlative quality since 1990. Joint-venture Riesling in Washington State with Ch Ste Michele: Eroica (dry) first vintage 1999. A new joint venture with Jasper Hill (Australia) is being planned.

Lorch Rhg w (r) ★→★★ **71 76 83 85** 88 **89 90** 92 93 94 **95** 96 **97 98** 99 00 01 02 Extreme W of RHEINGAU. Some fine MITTELRHEIN-like RIESL. Best grower: von Kanitz.

Loreley (Bereich) New BEREICH name for RHEINBURGENGAU and BACHARACH.

Löwenstein, Fürst ★★★ Top FRANKEN estate. Excellent 01. 66 acres. Intense savoury SILVANER from Homberger Kallmuth, very dramatic slope. Also 45-acre Hallgarten estate long rented by SCHLOSS VOLLRADS, independent since 1997.

Maindreieck (Bereich) District name for central FRANKEN, incl WÜRZBURG.

Marcobrunn Historic RHEINGAU v'yd; one of Germany's very best. See Erbach.

Markgräflerland (Bereich) District S of FREIBURG, BADEN. Typical GUTEDEL wine can be delicious refreshment when drunk very young, but best wines are the BURGUNDERS: WEISS-, GRAU- and SPÄT-. Also SEKT.

Maximin Grünhaus M-S-R (Ruwer) w ★★★★ 71 75 76 79 83 85 86 **88 89 90** 91 **92 93** 94 **95** 96 97 **98** 99 00 01 02 Supreme RUWER estate of 80 acres at Mertesdorf. Wines of firm elegance and great subtlety to mature 20 yrs+.

Meyer-Näkel, Weingut ★★★ 15-acre AHR estate. Fine SPÄTBURGUNDERS in Dernau and Bad Neuenahr exemplify modern oak-aged German reds.

Mittelhaardt The north-central and best part of the PFALZ, incl DEIDESHEIM, FORST, RUPPERTSBERG, WACHENHEIM, largely planted with RIESLING.

Mittelhaardt-Deutsche Weinstrasse (Bereich) Name for N & central PFALZ.

Mittelmosel The central and best part of the MOSEL, incl BERNKASTEL, PIESPORT, WEHLEN, etc. Its top sites are (or should be) entirely RIESLING.

Mittelrhein Northern Rhine area of domestic importance (and great beauty), incl BACHARACH and BOPPARD. Some attractive steely RIESLING.

Morio-Muskat Stridently aromatic grape variety now on the decline.

Mosbacher, Weingut ★★★ Fine 23-acre estate for some of best dry and sweet RIES of FORST. Best wines are dry Grosses Gewachs.

Mosel The TAFELWEIN name of the area. All quality wines from the Mosel must be labelled MOSEL-SAAR-RUWER. (Moselle is the French – and English – spelling.)

Mosel-Saar-Ruwer (M-S-R) 26,000 acre QUALITÄTSWEIN region between TRIER and Koblenz; incl MITTELMOSEL, RUWER, and SAAR. The natural home of RIESLING.

Moselland, Winzergenossenschaft Huge M-S-R co-op, at BERNKASTEL, incl Saar-Winzerverein at WILTINGEN. Its 5,200 members produce 25% of M-S-R wines (incl classic method SEKT), but little above average.

Müller zu Scharzhof, Egon See Egon Müller.

Müller-Catoir, Weingut ★★★★ **76** 77 78 **79** 80 81 82 **83** 84 85 86 87 88 **89 90** 91 **92 93** 94 95 **96** 97 **98 99** 00 **01** 02 Outstanding 40-acre NEUSTADT estate. V aromatic powerful wines (RIESLING, SCHEUREBE, RIESLANER, GEWÜRZ, WEISSBURGUNDER, GRAUBURGUNDER, and MUSKATELLER). Consistent quality & gd value; dry/sweet equally impressive.

Müller-Thurgau Fruity, early ripening, usually low-acid grape; most common in PFALZ, RHEINHESSEN, NAHE, BADEN, and FRANKEN; increasingly planted in all areas, incl MOSEL. Should be banned from all top v'yds by law.

Münster Nahe w ★ ·★★★ 71 75 76 83 88 **89 90** 91 92 **93** 94 95 **96** 97 **98** 99 00 **01** 02 Best N NAHE village; fine delicate wines. First Class vineyards: Dautenpflänzer, Kapellenberg, Pittersberg. Grosslage: Schlosskapelle. Top growers: Kruger-Rumpf, Göttelmann.

Muskateller Ancient aromatic white grape with crisp acidity. A rarity in the PFALZ, BADEN, and WÜRTTEMBERG, where it is mostly made dry.

Nackenheim Rhh w · ·★★★★ **76** 83 **89 90** 91 92 **93** 94 95 **96 97 98** 99 00 **01** 02 NIERSTEIN n'bour also with top Rhine *terroir*; similar best wines (esp 1st-class Rothenberg). Grosslagen: Spiegelberg, Gutes Domtal. Top grower: GUNDERLOCH.

Nahe Tributary of the Rhine and high-quality wine region. Balanced, fresh, clean but full-bodied, even minerally wines; RIES best. BEREICH: NAHETAL.

Nahetal (Bereich) BEREICH name for amalgamated BAD KREUZNACH and SCHLOSS-BÖCKELHEIM districts.

Neckar The river with many of WÜRTTEMBERG's finest v'yds, mainly between STUTTGART and HEILBRONN.

Neef M-S-R w ★★ 71 76 83 **89 90** 91 92 **93** 94 **95** 96 **97** 98 99 00 **01** 02 Village of lower MOSEL with one fine v'yd: Frauenberg.

Neipperg, Graf von ★★★ Noble 70-acre estate in Schwaigern, WÜRTTEMBERG: elegant dry RIES and TRAMINER, and good reds, esp from LEMBERGER.

Neumagen-Dhron M-M w ★★ Fine neighbour of PIESPORT. Top grower is Heinz Schmitt.

Neustadt Central town of PFALZ with a famous wine school. Top growers: MÜLLER-CATOIR, Weegmüller.

Niederhausen Nahe w ★★·★★★★ 71 75 76 83 85 86 87 88 **89 90** 91 **93** 94 **95 96** 97 **98** 99 **00 01** 02 Neighbour of SCHLOSSBÖCKELHEIM. Graceful, powerful wines. First Class vineyards including Felsensteyer, Gutsverwaltung Niederhausen-Schlossböckleheim, Hermannsberg, Hermannshöhle. Grosslage: Burgweg. Esp from CRUSIUS, DÖNNHOFF, Hehner-Kilz.

Nierstein Rhh w ★·★★★★ 71 75 76 83 **85** 86 **88 89 90** 91 **92 93** 94 95 **96** 97 **98** 99 00 **01** 02 Famous but treacherous village name. 1,300 acres. Superb First-Class vineyards: Brüdersberg, Glöck, Heiligenbaum, Hipping, Oelberg, Orbel, Pettenthal. Grosslagen: Auflangen, Rehbach, Spiegelberg. Ripe, aromatic, elegant wines. Beware Grosslage Gutes Domtal: a supermarket deception now disappearing from shelves. Try GUNDERLOCH, GUNTRUM, HEYL ZU HERRNSHEIM, ST-ANTONY, GA SCHNEIDER, Strub, Wehrheim.

Nierstein (Bereich) Large E RHEINHESSEN district of ordinary quality.

Nierstein Winzergenossenschaft ★·★★ The leading NIERSTEIN CO-OP, with above-average standards. (Formerly traded under the name Rheinfront.)

Nobling New white grape: light fresh wine in BADEN, esp MARKGRÄFLERLAND.

Norheim Nahe w ★★·★★★ 71 76 79 **83** 88 **89 90** 91 **92 93** 94 **95** 96 **97 98** 99 00 **01** 02 Neighbour of NIEDERHAUSEN. First Class v'yds: Dellchen, Kafels, Kirschheck. Grosslage: Burgweg. Growers: DÖNNHOFF, CRUSIUS, Mathern.

Oberemmel M-S-R (Saar) w ★★·★★★ 71 75 76 83 **85** 88 **89 90** 91 92 **93** 94 **95** 96 **97** 98 99 00 **01** 02 Next village to WILTINGEN. V fine from 1st Class vineyard Hütte, etc. Grosslage: SCHARZBERG. Growers: VON HÖVEL, VON KESSELSTATT.

Obermosel (Bereich) District name for the upper MOSEL above TRIER. Wines from the ELBLING grape, generally uninspiring unless very young.

Ockfen M-S-R (Saar) w ★★·★★★ 71 75 76 83 86 87 **88 89 90** 91 92 **93** 94 **95** 96 **97 98 99** 00 01 02 Superb fragrant, austere wines. 1st-class vineyard: Bockstein. Grosslage: SCHARZBERG. Growers: DR FISCHER, WAGNER, ZILLIKEN.

Oechsle Scale for sugar content of grape juice (see page 272).

Oestrich Rhg w ★★→★★★ **71 75** 76 **83 88 89 90** *91* **92 93** 94 95 **96** 97 98 **99** 00 01 02 Big village; variable but some splendid RIES esp AUSLESE. 1st-class vineyards: Doosberg, Lenchen. Grosslage: Gottesthal. Top growers: AUGUST ESER, Peter Jakob Kühn, Querbach, Spreitzer, WEGELER.

Offene weine Wine by the glass: the way to order it in wine villages.

Oppenheim Rhh w ★-★★★ **76 83 88 89 90** *91* **92 93** 94 95 96 **97** 98 99 00 01 02 Town S of NIERSTEIN; spectacular 13th-C church. 1st-class Herrenberg and Sackträger v'yds: top wines. Grosslagen: Guldenmorgen, Krötenbrunnen. Growers including GUNTRUM, C KOCH, Kühling-Gillot. None of these, though, are realizing the full potential of these sites.

Ortenau (Bereich) District just south of Baden-Baden. Good KLINGELBERGER (RIES), SPÄTBURGUNDER and RULÄNDER. Top village: DURBACH.

Ortsteil Independent part of a community allowed to use its estate vineyard name without the village name, e.g. SCHLOSS JOHANNISBERG, STEINBERG.

Palatinate English for PFALZ.

Pauly-Bergweiler, Dr ★★★ Fine 31-acre BERNKASTEL estate. V'yds there and in WEHLEN, etc. Peter Nicolay wines from URZIG and ERDEN are usually best.

Perlwein Semi-sparkling wine.

Pfalz 56,000-acre v'yd region S of RHEINHESSEN (see Mittelhaardt and Südliche Weinstrasse). Warm climate: grapes ripen fully. The classics are rich wines, with TROCKEN and HALBTROCKEN increasingly fashionable and well-made. Biggest RIES area after M-S-R. Formerly known as the Rheinpfalz.

Pfeffingen, Weingut ★★★ Messrs Fuhrmann and Eymael make very good RIES and SCHEUREBE on 26 acres of UNGSTEIN. Back on fine form since 1999.

Piesport M-M w ★-★★★★ **71 75** 76 **83 88 89 90** 91 **92 93** 94 95 96 **97** 98 99 *00* 01 02 Tiny village with famous vine amphitheatre: at best glorious rich aromatic RIES. Great First Class v'yds: Goldtröpfchen & Domherr. Treppchen far inferior. Grosslage: Michelsberg (mainly MÜLLER-T; avoid). Esp Grans Fassian R HAART, Kurt Hain, KESSELSTATT, St Urbanshof, Weller-Lehnert.

Plettenberg, von ★★ 100-acre estate at BAD KREUZNACH. Mixed quality.

Portugieser Second-rate red-wine grape now often used for WEISSHERBST.

Prädikat Special attributes or qualities. See QmP.

Prinz, Fred Rhg w ★★ Best RIESLING in the village of Hallgarten.

Prüfungsnummer The official identifying test-number of a quality wine.

Prüm, J J ★★★★ **69** *70* **71** *72 73 74* **75** *76 77 78* **79** *80* 81 82 **83** *84* 85 **86** 87 **88 89 90** 91 *92 93* 94 **95** 96 **97** 98 **99** 00 **01** 02 Superlative and legendary 34-acre MOSEL estate in BERNKASTEL, GRAACH, WEHLEN, ZELTINGEN. Delicate but long-lived wines, especially in Wehlener SONNENUHR: 81' KABINETT is *still* young. Plain Prüm RIESLING is a bargain.

Qualitätswein bestimmter Anbaugebiete (QbA) The middle quality of German wine, with sugar added before fermentation (as in French chaptalization), but controlled as to areas, grapes, etc.

Qualitätswein mit Prädikat (QmP) Top category, for all wines ripe enough to be unsugared (KABINETT to TROCKENBEERENAUSLESE). See pages 133 and 141.

Randersacker Frank w ★★-★★★ 76 **83 88** 89 90 91 92 **93** 94 95 96 **97** **98 99** 00 01 02 Leading village for distinctive dry wine. First Class v'yds: Marsberg, Pfülben, Sonnenstuhl. Grosslage: Ewig Leben. Growers incl BURGERSPITAL, STAATLICHER HOFKELLER, JULIUSSPITAL, Robert Schmitt, Schmitt's Kinder.

Ratzenberger, Jochen ★★ 20-acre estate making racy dry and off-dry RIES in BACHARACH; best from First Class Posten and Steeger St-Jost v'yds.

Rauenthal Rhg w ★★★-★★★★ **71 75** 76 **83** 88 **89 90** *91* **92 93** 94 95 96 **97 98 99** 00 01 02 Supreme village: spicy complex wine. First Class v'yds: Baiken, Gehrn, Nonnenberg, Rothenberg, Wülfen. Grosslage: Steinmächer. Top grower: BREUER.

Rebholz ★★★ Top SÜDLICHE WEINSTRASSE estate for 50 years. Many varieties on 33 acres. Makes the best dry MUSKATELLER, GEWÜRZTRAMINER, CHARDONNAY (Burgundian style), and SPÄTBURGUNDER in Pfalz.

Ress, Balthasar ★★ R'GAU estate (74 good acres), cellars in HATTENHEIM. Also runs SCHLOSS REICHARTSHAUSEN. Variable quality; original artists' labels.

Restsüsse Unfermented grape sugar remaining in (or in cheap wines added to) wine to give it sweetness. TROCKEN wines have very little, if any.

Rheinburgengau (Bereich) District name for MITTELRHEIN v'yds around the Rhine Gorge. Wines with steely acidity needing time to mature.

Rheingau Best v'yd region of Rhine, W of Wiesbaden. 7,000 acres. Classic, substantial but subtle RIES, yet on the whole recently eclipsed by brilliance elsewhere. BEREICH name for whole region: JOHANNISBERG.

Rheinhessen Vast region (61,000 acres of v'yds) between Mainz and Worms, bordered by River NAHE, mostly second-rate, but includes top RIESLINGS from NACKENHEIM, NIERSTEIN, OPPENHEIM, etc.

Rheinhessen Silvaner (RS) New uniform label for earthy dry wines from SILVANER – designed to give a modern quality image to the region.

Rheinpfalz See Pfalz.

Rhodt SÜDLICHE WEINSTRASSE village: esp Rietburg co-op; agreeable fruity wines.

Richter, Weingut Max Ferd ★★★ Top 37-acre MITTELMOSEL family estate, at Mülheim. Fine barrel-aged RIES from First Class v'yds: BRAUNEBERG Juffer-SONNENUHR, GRAACH Domprobst, Mülheim (Helenenkloster), WEHLEN Sonnenuhr.

Regions to watch out for in the early 2000s

Mittelrhein had a string of poor vintages to contend with, but with 2001 it proves that it is capable of producing great classic Rieslings.

Rheinhessen is producing a wave of new-style, clean harmonious dry white wines that are often excellent value for money.

Saale-Unstrut has finally shaken off the legacy of its communist past and is starting to make some surprisingly full-bodied, supple dry whites.

Sachsen too, has overcome the same problems and is making sleeker and more aromatic dry whites than Saale-Unstrut.

Rieslaner Cross between SILVANER and RIES; makes fine AUSLESEN in FRANKEN, where most is grown. Also superb from MÜLLER-CATOIR.

Riesling The best German grape: fine, fragrant, fruity, long-lived. Only CHARDONNAY can compete as the world's best white grape.

Rosswein Rosé wine made from red grapes fermented without their skins.

Rüdesheim Rhg w ★★→★★★★ **71 75 76** 79 *81* 82 **83** 84 **85** 86 87 88 **89 90** 91 **92 93** 94 95 **96 97 98 99** 00 **01** 02 Rhine resort with First Class vineyards; the three best are called Rüdesheimer Berg-. Full-bodied wines, fine-flavoured, often remarkable in off years. Grosslage: Burgweg. Many of the top RHEINGAU estates own some Rüdesheim vineyards. Best growers: G BREUER, JOHANNISHOF, August Kesseler, J LEITZ, SCHLOSS SCHONBORN, STATE DOMAIN.

Ruländer Pinot Gris: now more commonly known as GRAUBURGUNDER.

Ruppertsberg Pfz w ★★→★★★ 89 **90** 91 92 **93** 94 *95* **96** 97 **98** 99 00 01 02 Southern village of MITTELHAARDT. First Class vineyards incl Hoheburg, Linsenbusch, Nussbein, Reiterpfad, Spiess. Grosslage: Hofstück. Growers incl BASSERMANN-JORDAN, BIFFAR, VON BUHL, BÜRKLIN-WOLF, DEINHARD.

Ruwer **76 83** 88 **89 90** 91 *92* 93 94 95 *96* **97** *98* **99** 00 **01** 02 Tributary of MOSEL nr TRIER. V fine, delicate but highly aromatic and well-structured wines. Villages incl EITELSBACH, KASEL, MERTESDORF.

Saale-Unstrut 92 93 94 95 *96* **97** 98 99 **00 01** 02 Region in former East Germany, 1,300 acres around confluence of these two rivers at Naumburg, near Leipzig.

The terraced vineyards of WEISSBURGUNDER, SILVANER, RIESLING, GEWÜRZTRAMINER, etc, and red PORTUGIESER have Cistercian origins. Quality leaders: Lützkendorf, Landesweingut Kloster Pforta, Pawis, Thüringer Weingut.

Saar 75 76 *77 78* 79 80 81 82 **83** *84* 85 86 *87* 88 **89 90** 91 *92* **93** 94 **95** *96* **97** *98* **99** 00 01 02 Hill-lined tributary of MOSEL south of RUWER. The most brilliant, austere, steely RIESLING of all. Villages include AYL, OCKFEN, Saarburg, SERRIG, WILTINGEN (SCHARZHOFBERG). Grosslage: SCHARZBERG. Many fine estates here.

Saar-Ruwer (Bereich) District covering these 2 regions.

Sachsen 93 94 *95 96* 97 98 99 **00 01** 02 Former East German region (900 acres) in ELBE Valley around Dresden and Meissen. MÜLLER-THURGAU dominant, but WEISSBURGUNDER, GRAUBURGUNDER, TRAMINER, RIESLING give dry wines with real character. Best growers: SCHLOSS PROSCHWITZ, Vincenz Richter, Klaus Seifert, Schloss Wackerbarth, Klaus Zimmerling.

St-Antony, Weingut ★★★ Excellent 57-acre estate. Rich, intense, dry and off-dry RIES from First Class v'yds of NIERSTEIN.

St-Ursula Well-known merchants at BINGEN.

Salm, Prinz zu Owner of SCHLOSS WALLHAUSEN in NAHE and Villa Sachsen in RHEINHESSEN. President of VDP.

Salwey, Weingut ★★★ Leading BADEN estate at Oberrotweil, especially for RIESLING, WEISSBURGUNDER and RULÄNDER.

Samtrot Red WÜRTTEMBERG grape. Makes Germany's closest shot at Beaujolais.

Schaefer, Willi ★★★ The finest grower of GRAACH (but only 5 acres).

Scharzberg Grosslage name of WILTINGEN and neighbours.

Scharzhofberg M-S-R (Saar) w ★★★★ **71** 75 76 83 88 **89 90** 91 *92* **93** 94 **95** *96* **97** *98* **99** 00 01 02 Superlative 67-acre SAAR v'yd: austerely beautiful wines, the perfection of RIESLING, best in AUSLESEN. Top estates: BISCHÖFLICHE WEINGÜTER, EGON MÜLLER, VON HÖVEL, VON KESSELSTATT, Van Volxem.

Schaumwein Sparkling wine.

Scheurebe Aromatic grape of high quality (and RIESLING parentage), esp used in PFALZ. Excellent for botrytis wine (BA, TBA).

Schillerwein Light red or rosé QBA; speciality of WÜRTTEMBERG (only).

Schloss Johannisberg Rhg w ★★★ 76 79 83 85 86 **88 89 90** 91 92 93 94 95 *96* 97 98 **99** 00 **01** Famous R'GAU estate of 86 acres owned by Princess Metternich and the Oetker family. The original Rhine first growth. Wines incl fine SPÄTLESE, KABINETT TROCKEN. Since 96 there has been a dramatic return to form. The 2001s are the best wines since 75 and 76.

Schloss Lieser ★★★ Small estate run by Thomas Haag, from FRITZ HAAG estate, making pure racy RIESLINGS from underrated v'yds of Lieser.

Schloss Proschwitz ★★ Resurrected princely estate at Meissen, leading former E Germany in quality, esp with dry WEISSBURGUNDER and GRAUBURGUNDER.

Schloss Reichartshausen 10-acre HATTENHEIM v'yd run by RESS.

Schloss Reinhartshausen ★★★ Fine 250-acre estate in ERBACH, HATTENHEIM, KIEDRICH, etc. Originally property of Prussian royal family, now in private hands. Model RHEINGAU RIESLING. The mansion beside the Rhine is now a luxury hotel. The last couple of vintages were nothing special.

Schloss Schönborn ★★★ One of biggest RHEINGAU estates, based at HATTENHEIM. Full-flavoured wines, variable, at best excellent. Also vg SEKT.

Schloss Neuweier ★★★ Leading producer of dry Riesling in Baden.

Schloss Thorn Ancient OBERMOSEL estate, remarkable ELBLING, RIES and castle.

Schloss Vollrads Rhg w ★★★ 71 76 83 85 88 **89** 90 *91 92* 93 94 95 96 97 **98 99** 00 01 02 One of the greatest historic Rheingau estates, owned by a bank since the sudden death of owner Erwein Count Matuschka in August 97. Since 98 vintage quality is much improved.

Schloss Wallhausen ★★ The 25-acre NAHE estate of the Prinz Zu Salm, one of Germany's oldest. 65% RIES. Very good TROCKEN. Very good quality since 97.

Schlossböckelheim Nahe w ★★→★★★★ 71 75 76 79 83 85 86 88 89 90 91 92 93 94 95 96 97 98 99 00 01 Village with top NAHE v'yds, including First Class Felsenberg, In den Felsen, Königsfels, Kupfergrube. Firm yet delicate wine. Grosslage: Burgweg. Top growers: CRUSIUS, DONNHOF, GUTSVERWALTUNG NIEDERHAUSEN-SCHLOSSBÖCKELHEIM.

Schneider, Weingut Georg Albrecht ★★ Impeccably run 32-acre estate. Classic off-dry and sweet RIES in NIERSTEIN, the best from Hipping VIneyard.

Erstes Gewächs

From 1st September 2000, the Rheingau's vineyard classification came into force and with it the designation "Erstes Gewächs" or "First Growth". It applies to wines produced according to strict rules (incl max yield and blind-tasting test). The weakness of the scheme is that the classification takes in just over 35% of the region's vineyards including some rather poor sites. The scheme is open for Spätburgunder and Riesling, which may be dry or sweet. So far, few Erstes Gewächs wines have been released.

Schoppenwein Café (or bar) wine: ie wine by the glass.

Schubert, von Owner of MAXIMIN GRUNHAUS.

Schwarzer Adler, Weingut ★★★ Franz Keller and his son Fritz make top BADEN dry GRAU-, WEISS-, and SPÄTBURGUNDER on 35 acres at Oberbergen.

Schweigen Pfz w r ★★ 89 90 91 92 93 94 95 96 97 98 99 00 01 02 Southern PFALZ village. Grosslage: Guttenberg. Best growers: Fritz Becker, especially for SPÄTBURGUNDER, Bernhart.

Sekt German (QBA) sparkling wine, best when the label specifies RIESLING, WEISS-BURGUNDER, or SPATBURGUNDER. Sekt BA is the same but comes from a specified area.

Selbach-Oster ★★★ 26-acre ZELTINGEN estate among MITTELMOSEL leaders.

Serrig M-S-R (Saar) w ★★→★★★ 71 75 76 83 85 88 89 90 91 93 94 95 96 97 98 99 00 01 02 Village giving steely wines, excellent in sunny years. First Class vineyards: Herrenburg, Saarstein, WÜRZBERG. Grosslage: SCHARZBERG. Top grower: SCHLOSS SAARSTEIN.

Silvaner Third most-planted German white grape variety, generally underrated; best examples in FRANKEN: the closest thing to Chablis in Germany. Worth looking for in RHEINHESSEN and KAISERSTUHL too.

Simmern, Langwerth von ★★★ Famous ELTVILLE family estate. Top v'yds: Baiken, Mannberg, MARCOBRUNN. After disappointing quality during the 90s back on form with 2001.

Sonnenuhr Sundial. Name of several vineyards, esp First Class one at WEHLEN.

Spätburgunder Pinot Noir: the best red-wine grape in Germany – esp in BADEN and WÜRTTEMBERG and increasingly PFALZ – generally improving quality, but most still underflavoured in spite of improved colour.

Spätlese Late harvest. One better (riper, with more alcohol, more substance and usually more sweetness) than KABINETT. Good examples age at least 5 years, often longer. TROCKEN Spätlesen can be very fine with food.

Staatlicher Hofkeller ★★★ The Bavarian STATE DOMAIN. 370 acres of the finest FRANKEN vineyards with spectacular cellars under the great baroque Residenz at WÜRZBURG.

Staatsweingut (or Staatliche Weinbaudomäne) The state wine estates or domains; esp KLOSTER EBERBACH, TRIER.

State Domain See Staatsweingut.

Steigerwald (Bereich) District name for E part of FRANKEN.

Steinberg Rhg w ★★★ **71 75 76** 79 **83** 86 88 89 **90** 91 92 **93** 94 **95** 96 97 98 **99** 00 **01** 02 Famous 79-acre HATTENHEIM walled v'yd, planted by Cistercians 700 yrs ago. Now owned by STATE DOMAIN, ELTVILLE. Some glorious wines; some sadly feeble.

Steinwein Wine from WÜRZBURG's best v'yd, Stein.

Südliche Weinstrasse (Bereich) District name for S PFALZ. Quality has improved tremendously in last 25 yrs. See Ilbesheim, Rebholz, Schweigen.

Tafelwein Table wine. The *vin ordinaire* of Germany. Frequently blended with other EU wines. But DEUTSCHER TAFELWEIN must come from Germany alone and may be excellent. (See also LANDWEIN.)

Tauberfranken (Bereich) New name for minor Badisches Frankenland BEREICH of N BADEN: FRANKEN-style wines.

Thanisch, Weingut Dr H ★★→★★★ BERNKASTEL estate, includes part of the Doctor vineyard. Could try harder.

Traben-Trarbach M-M w ★★ **76 83 88 89 90 93** 94 **95** 96 97 98 99 00 **01** 02 Major wine town of 800 acres, 87% of it RIESLING. Top vineyards: Ungsberg, Würzgarten. Grosslage: Schwarzlay. Top growers: Louis Klein, Martin Müller, and MAX FERD RICHTER.

Traisen Nahe w ★★★ **71 75 76** 79 **83 85** 86 87 **88 89 90** 91 92 **93** 94 **95 96** 97 98 99 00 **01** 02 Small village incl First Class Bastei and Rotenfels v'yds, capable of making RIES of concentration and class. Top grower: CRUSIUS.

Traminer See Gewürztraminer.

Trier M-S-R w ★★→★★★ Great wine city of Roman origin, on MOSEL, nr RUWER, now also incl AVELSBACH and EITELSBACH. Grosslage: Römerlay. Big Mosel charitable estates have cellars here among imposing Roman ruins.

Trittenheim M-M w ★★ **71 75 76 85 89 90** 91 92 **93 94 95** 96 97 98 99 00 **01** 02 Attractive S MITTELMOSEL light wines. Top v'yds were Altärchen, Apotheke, but now incl second-rate flat land: First Class v'yds are Felsenkopf, Leiterchen. Grosslage: Michelsberg (avoid). Growers incl E Clüsserath, Clüsserath-Weiler, GRANS-FASSIAN, Milz.

Trocken Dry. Trocken wines have max 9 grams per litre unfermented sugar. Some are austere, others (better) have more body & alcohol.

Trockenbeerenauslese Sweetest, most expensive category of German wine, extremely rare, with concentrated honey flavour. Made from selected shrivelled grapes affected by noble rot (botrytis). TBA for short. See also Edel. *Edelbeerenauslese* would be a less confusing name.

Trollinger Common {pale} red grape of WÜRTTEMBERG; locally v popular.

Ungstein Pfz w ★★ ★★★ **71 76 83 85 88 89 90** 91 92 **93** 94 95 **96** 97 98 **99 00 01** MITTELHAARDT village with fine harmonious wines. First Class v'yds: Herrenberg, Weilberg. Top growers: Darting, FITZ-RITTER, PFEFFINGEN, Pflüger, Karl Schäfer. Grosslagen: Honigsäckel, Kobnert.

Ürzig M-M w ★★★★ **71 75 76 83 88 89 90** 91 92 **93** 94 **95** 96 **97** 98 **99** 00 **01** 02 Village on red sandstone and red slate famous for firm, full, spicy wine unlike other MOSELS. First Class v'yd: Würzgarten. Grosslage: Schwarzlay. Growers incl J J CHRISTOFFEL, DR LOOSEN, Mönchhof, WEINS-PRUM.

Valckenberg, P J Major merchants and growers at Worms, with Madonna LIEBFRAUMILCH. Also dry RIES.

VDP Verband Deutscher Prädikats und Qualitätsweingüter. The pace-making association of premium growers. Look for their eagle insignia. President: Prinz Zu Salm.

Vereinigte Hospitien ★★→★★★ "United Hospices". Ancient charity at TRIER with large holdings in PIESPORT, SERRIG, TRIER, WILTINGEN, etc; wines recently well below their wonderful potential.

Verwaltung Administration (of property/estate etc).

Wachenheim Pfz w ★★★ →★★★★ 71 76 83 88 89 90 91 92 93 94 95 96 97 98 99 00 01 02 840 acres, including exceptionally fine RIESLING. First Class v'yds: Belz, Gerümpel, Goldbächel, Rechbächel, etc. Top growers: BÜRKLIN-WOLF, BIFFAR, WOLF. Grosslagen: Mariengarten, Schenkenböhl, Schnepfenflug.

Wagner, Dr ★★★ Saarburg estate. 20 acres of RIESLING. Many fine wines including TROCKEN.

Walluf Rhg w ★★★ 75 76 79 83 88 89 90 92 93 94 95 96 97 98 99 00 01 02 Neighbour of ELTVILLE; formerly Nieder- & Ober-Walluf. Underrated wines. First Class vineyard: Walkenberg. Grosslage: Steinmächer. Growers include BECKER, TONI JOST.

Walporzheim Ahrtal (Bereich) District name for the whole AHR Valley.

Wawern M-S-R (Saar) w ★★→★★★ 71 75 76 83 85 88 89 90 91 92 93 94 95 96 97 98 99 00 01 02 Small village, fine RIESLING. First Class vineyard: Herrenberg. Grosslage: SCHARZBERG.

Wegeler ★★ Important family estates in OESTRICH, MITTELHARDT, and BERNKASTEL. The Wegelers owned the merchant house of Deinhard until 1997.

Wehlen M-M w ★★★→★★★★ 71 75 76 83 85 86 88 89 90 91 92 93 94 95 96 97 98 99 00 01 Neighbour of BERNKASTEL with equally fine, somewhat richer wine. Location of great First Class vineyard: SONNENUHR. Grosslage: Münzlay. The top growers are: Heribert Kerpen DR LOOSEN, J J PRÜM, S A Prüm, Studert-Prüm, WEGELER, and WEINS-PRÜM.

Weil, Weingut Robert ★★★★ 71 76 83 84 85 86 87 88 89 90 91 92 93 94 95 96 97 98 99 00 01 02 Outstanding 145-acre estate in KIEDRICH; now owned by Suntory of Japan. Superb QMP, EISWEIN, BA, TBA; standard wines also vg since 92. Widely considered RHEINGAU's No 1.

Weinbaugebiet TAFELWEIN region: MOSEL, RHEIN, SAAR, etc. Different to the more familiar QbA regions.

Weingut Wine estate.

Weinkellerei Wine cellars or winery. See Keller.

Weins-Prüm, Dr ★★→★★★ Classic MITTELMOSEL estate; 12 acres at Wehlen. WEHLENER SONNENUHR is usually top wine.

Weinstrasse Wine road: a scenic route through v'yds. Germany has several.

Weintor, Deutsches See Schweigen.

Weissburgunder Pinot Blanc. Most reliable grape for TROCKEN wines: low acidity, high extract. Also much used for SEKT.

Weissherbst Usually a pale pink wine, QBA or above & occasionally BA, from a single variety. Speciality of BADEN, PFALZ, and WÜRTTEMBERG.

Werner, Domdechant ★★★ Family estate on best HOCHHEIM slopes: top wines excellent, others only fair.

Wiltingen M-S-R (Saar) w ★★→★★★★ 71 75 76 83 85 86 88 89 90 91 92 93 94 95 96 97 98 99 00 01 02 The centre of the SAAR. 790 acres. Beautifully subtle austere wine. Great First Class v'yd is SCHARZHOFBERG (ORTSTEIL); and First Class are Braune Kupp, Hölle. Grosslage (for the whole SAAR): SCHARZBERG. Top growers: EGON MÜLLER, LE GALLAIS, VON KESSELSTATT, Von Volxem, etc.

Winkel Rhg w ★★★ 71 75 76 83 88 89 90 91 92 93 94 95 96 97 98 99 00 01 02 Village famous for full fragrant wine. First Class vineyards incl Hasensprung, Jesuitengarten, SCHLOSS VOLLRADS, Schlossberg. Grosslagen: Erntebringer, Honigberg. Growers incl PRINZ VON HESSEN, Johannis of Wegelen, Von Mumm, BALTHASAR RESS, SCHLOSS SCHÖNBORN, etc.

Winningen M-S-R w ★★ Lower MOSEL town near Koblenz: unusually full RIES for region. First Class v'yds: Röttgen, Uhlen. Top growers: Heymann-Löwenstein, Knebel, Richard Richter.

Wintrich M-M w ★★→★★★ **71** 76 **83 88 89 90** 91 **92 93** 94 **95** 96 **97 98** 99 00 **01** 02 Neighbour of PIESPORT; similar wines. First Class vineyards: Ohligsberg. Grosslage: Kurfürstlay. Top grower: REINHOLD HAART.

Winzergenossenschaft (WG) Wine-growers' co-operative, often making sound and reasonably priced wine. Referred to in this text as "co-op".

Winzerverein The same as the above.

Wirsching, Hans ★★★ Estate in IPHOFEN and FRANKEN. Wines can be firm, elegant, and dry but quality is variable. 170 acres in 1st-class vineyards: Julius-Echter-Berg, Kalb, etc.

Wonnegau (Bereich) District name for S RHEINHESSEN.

Wolf ★★★ Formerly run-down estate in WACHENHEIM acquired by Ernst Loosen (see Dr Loosen) of Bernkastel. From first vintage (1996) PFALZ wines with a Mosel-like finesse, labelled along confusingly French lines. Strong dry Auslesen feature. Superb quality since 1998.

Wolff Metternich ★★ Noble DURBACH estate: some good RIESLING.

Württemberg 83 84 85 86 87 88 **89 90** 91 92 93 94 95 96 98 **99** 00 **01** 02 Vast S area, little known for wine outside Germany despite some very good RIES (esp NECKAR Valley) and frequently unrealized potential to make good reds: LEMBERGER, TROLLINGER, SAMTROT.

Würzburg Frank ★★→★★★★ **71** 76 **81 83** 85 86 **88 89** 90 91 92 **93** 94 96 **97** 98 99 00 **01** 02 Great baroque city on the Main, centre of FRANKEN wine: fine, full-bodied, dry. 1st-class v'yds: Abtsleite, Innere, Leiste, Stein. No Grosslage. See Maindreieck. Growers: BURGERSPITAL, JULIUSSPITAL, STAATLICHER HOFKELLER.

Zell M-S-R w ★→★★★ **76 83 88** 89 **90** 93 94 **95** 96 **97** 98 99 00 01 02 Best-known lower MOSEL village, esp for awful Grosslage: Schwarze Katz (Black Cat). RIESLING on steep slate gives aromatic wines. Top grower: KALLFELZ.

Zell (Bereich) District name for whole lower MOSEL from Zell to Koblenz.

Zeltingen M-M w ★★→★★★★ **71 75 76** 79 **83 85** 86 **88 89 90** 91 92 **93** 94 **95** 96 **97 98** 99 00 **01** 02 Top MOSEL village near WEHLEN. Lively crisp RIESLING. First Class vineyard: SONNENUHR. Grosslage: Münzlay. Top growers: Markus Molitor, J J PRÜM, SELBACH-OSTER.

Zilliken, Forstmeister Geltz ★★★ Former estate of Prussian royal forester with 25 acres at Saarburg and OCKFEN, SAAR. Racy, minerally RIESLINGS, incl superb AUSLESE, EISWEIN with excellent ageing potential.

Zwierlein, Freiherr von ★★ 55-acre family estate in GEISENHEIM. 100% RIES.

Luxembourg

Luxembourg has 3,285 acres of v'yds on limestone soils on the Moselle's left bank. High-yielding Elbling and Rivaner (Müller-T) vines dominate, but there are also significant acreages of Ries, Gewürz and (usually best) Auxerrois, Pinot Bl and Pinot Gr. These give light to medium-bodied (10.5–11.5%), dry, Alsace-like wines. The highly competent Vins Moselle co-op makes 70% of the total, including quantities of v fair fizz. Domaine et Tradition estates association, founded in 88, promotes quality from noble varieties. The following vintages were all good: 89 90 92 95; 97 outstanding, 98 average, 99 similar but softer, 00 poor, 2001 much better, 2002 looks gd for Pinot Noir. Best from: Aly Duhr et Fils, M Bastian, Caves Gales, Bernard Massard (surprisingly good Cuvée de l'Ecusson classic method sparkling), Clos Mon Vieux Moulin, Ch de Schengen, Sunnen-Hoffmann.

Spain & Portugal

More heavily shaded areas
are the wine growing regions

The following abbreviations are used in the text:

Amp	Ampurdán-Costa Brava
Alen	Alentejo
Bair	Bairrada
Bul	Bullas
Cos del S	Costers del Segre
El B	El Bierzo
Est	Estremadura
La M	La Mancha
Mont-M	Montilla-Moriles
Nav	Navarra
Pen	Penedès
Pri	Priorato
Rib del D	Ribera del Duero
Rib del G	Ribera del Guadiana
R Ala	Rioja Alavesa
R Alt	Rioja Alta
RB	Rioja Baja
Som	Somontano
Set	Setúbal
U-R	Utiel-Requena
VV	Vinhos Verdes
g	vino generoso
res	reserva

El Bierzo
Rias Ribeiro
Baixas Monterrei Valdeorras
RIOS DO MINHO TRAS-
Vinhos OS-MONTES
Verdes Douro
Douro
BEIRAS
Bairrada Dão
Mondego
Tagus
ESTREMADURA
RIBATEJO
Bucelas
Colares
Carcavelos Setúbal Ribera e
ALENTEJO
TERRAS
DO SADO
ALGARVE
Lagoa Tavira Condado
Lagos de Huelva
Portimão

MADEIRA (off west coast of Africa)

Spain and Portugal joined the EU (and, as far as most of their wine is concerned, the 20th century) only 19 years ago. Both made rapid progress, Euro-grants encouraging massive re-equipping. Ferment continues: splendid new wines continue to appear. But some makers are asking (and indeed getting) silly prices.

Currently in Spain (apart from the sherry country), the North, Rioja, Navarra, Galicia, Rueda, Catalonia, and Ribera del Duero hold most interest; those in Portugal (apart from the port vineyards and Madeira) are the Douro, Ribatejo, Alentejo, the central coast, and the North. In Portugal especially, newly delimited areas have successfully challenged old, traditional appellations. Portugal is now concentrating on its huge range of indigenous grape varieties, especially Touriga Nacional, Tinta Roriz, and Trincadeira. Many are still largely unknown elsewhere, and they are one of Portugal's greatest strengths.

The following list includes the best and most interesting makers, types, and regions of each country, whether legally delimited or not. Geographical references (see map above) are to demarcated regions (DOs and DOCs), autonomies, and provinces.

Sherry, Port, and Madeira have a separate chapter on page 176.

Spain

Recent vintages of the Spanish classics
Rioja

2002 Cold and drought affected development of the fruit, and yields in Rioja Alta and Alavesa were low. Quality is doubtful but wait and see.

2001 Smaller harvest and good-quality fruit. Excellent potential.

2000 Generally favourable conditions. Huge harvest, but abnormally high summer and autumn temperatures led to uneven quality.

1999 The worst April frost in memory delayed maturation, and summer rain resulted in mildew. Average.

1998 Biggest-ever vintage. Lack of sun and rain in the autumn delayed picking. V gd.

1997 Given little sun & much rain, the vintage was large and patchy. Average/poor.

1996 An unusually cold spring and cool summer resulted in well-structured but fairly immediate wines. Very good.

1995 Good alcoholic strength and acidity. Excellent.

1994 Textbook weather produced colour, backbone, and intensity but wines are thinning out earlier than expected. Very good.

1993 Few sunny days and little rain. Wines thin and short-lived. Poor.

1992 Rainiest October in 50 yrs produced great contrasts in quality according to date of picking. Attractive but immediate. Good.

Ribera del Duero

2002 Hot weather followed by heavy rain in late summer led to a large harvest, but with quality often below normal.

2001 April frost reduced the crop, otherwise an almost perfect growing season and quality is outstanding.

2000 Very large harvest but ripening was uneven. Some bodegas made spectacular wines; in general, good.

1999 Almost perfect weather and bumper harvest, but rainfall around harvest time resulted in lack of acidity. Very good.

1998 Torrential rain in early autumn and record grape prices. Good.

1997 Cool and wet with spring and summer frosts. Poor.

1996 Dry summer and autumn. Good acidity and long-lived reservas. Excellent.

1995 April frost. But later sun and warmth resulted in rich, structured wines. Excellent.

1994 Frost-free, benevolent year, but crop small. Very good.

1993 Dank and sodden. Most appalling vintage of the decade. Poor.

Navarra

2002 Torrential August rains affected the quality of wines from the south of the region; others are excellent.

2001 This promises to be an excellent year with big, ripe, well-balanced wines.

2000 Very dry year of prolific yields, calling for rigorous selection. Best wines are big and fleshy, with gd potential for ageing. Very gd.

1999 Most frost-afflicted vintage of decade with soaring grape prices. Wines promise to be well-structured and long-ageing. Excellent.

1998 Spring frosts but dry, hot summer. Well-structured wines with excellent colour and elegant aromas. Very good.

1997 Dank, overcast summer. Short-lived wines. Poor.

1996 Cold, wet summer. Wines spare, but notably fresh and aromatic with adequate acidity and concentration. Good.

1995 Very small crop due to major frost in April. Wines similar to those of 94, but longer-lived because of superior acidity. Excellent.

1994 Exceptionally hot, dry summer. Wines mostly peaked.

Penedès

2002 August rain ruined part of the crop; then a splendid September resulted n good quality.

2001 April frosts reduced the yield but warm, dry summer produced v good wines.

2000 Dry winter, some spring rain, and very dry summer. Perfect ripening of the grapes gave well-balanced wines. Very good.

1999 Dry summer but abundant harvest. Very good.

1998 Very good whites and excellent reds.

1997 Large harvest. Good white wines and very good reds.

1996 Heavy August rains resulted in a prolific harvest. Very good.

1995 Dry and mild winter. Summer alternately wet and hot. Very good.

1994 Another very dry year. Small, slow-ripening grapes. Very good.

1993 The driest of recent years. Harvest was scarce but good quality.

Abadia Retuerta Castilla y León r ★★★ 96 97 98 99 One of the most modern BODEGAS in Spain. Non-DO, but with top Bordeaux help is making exceptional Temp, Cab S, and Merlot with prices to match. Esp El Palomar 97.

Agapito Rico Jumilla r ★★★ 95 98 99 00 Young BODEGA making some of Spain's best VINOS JOVENES in the unlikely region of JUMILLA, esp 98 99 Carchelo wines (Syrah, Merlot, or Monastrell with Temp and Merlot) Also excellent CRIANZA.

Agramont See Príncipe de Viana, Bodegas.

Agrícola Falset-Marca Montsant r ★→★★ 98 Co-op bordering PRIORATO, making intensely fruity Castel de Falset. Avoid the fiercely astringent younger wines.

Albariño High-quality, aromatic white grape of GALICIA. Its wine is perhaps most highly regarded white. See Rías Baixas, Cervera, Gran Bazán, Pazo de Barrantes.

Alella r w (p) dr sw 93 94 95 96 97 99 ★★ Sml, demarcated region north of Barcelona. Pleasantly fruity wines. (See Marfil, Marqués de Alella, Parxet.)

Alicante r (w) ★ DO. Most wines still earthy and over-strong – with shining exceptions such as Syrah from Enrique Mendoza.

Alión Rib del D r ★★★ 95 96 99 Since discontinuing the 3-yr-old VALBUENA in 97, VEGA SICILIA has acquired this second BODEGA to make 100% Tempranillo; impressive results. Vigorous; good to mid-term keeping.

Allende, Finca R Ala r ★★★→★★★★ 96 97 98' 99 00 Much-praised newish (94) BODEGA: elegant, oak-aged Tempranillos. Vastly expensive Aurus (96 97): and single-estate Calvario (99').

Alvaro Palacios Pri r ★★★★ 93 94 95 96 98 99 00 Gifted emigré from RIOJA making some of the most expensive and fashionable red wine in Spain, incl Finca Dofi (98), L'Ermita (94), Les Terrasses. One of the few PRIORATOS to repay bottle-age.

Ampurdán, Cavas del Amp r w p ★→★★ Big-selling w Pescador, r Cazador.

Ampurdán-Costa Brava Amp r w p ★→★★ Demarcated region abutting Pyrenees. Mainly co-op-made rosés, reds. See also last entry.

Año Year: 4° Año (or Años) means 4 yrs old when bottled. Was common on labels, now largely discontinued in favour of vintages, or terms such as CRIANZA.

Arco Bodegas Unidas See Berberana, Bodegas.

Artadi See Cosecheros Alaveses.

Arzuaga, Bodegas Ribera del Duero r ★★★ 94 95 96 97 98 Architecturally spectacular new BODEGA with 370 acres aiming for luscious, modern wines.

Bach, Masía Pen r w p d sw res ★★→★★★ 94 95 96 97 98 99 Stately villa-winery nr SAN SADURNÍ DE NOYA, owned by CODORNÍU. Speciality is white Extrísimo, both sweet and oaky, and dry. Also good red RESERVAS.

Barbier, René Pen r w res ★★ 96 98 01 Owned by FREIXENET, known for fresh white Kraliner, red RB RESERVAS.

Barón de Ley RB r (w) res ★★★ 94 95 96 97 98 00' Newish RIOJA BODEGA linked with EL COTO: good single-estate wines.

Baso r w ★★ Brand name for reliable Garnacha from NAVARRA made by young winemaker TELMO RODRÍGUEZ, formerly of LA GRANJA REMELLURI.

Berberana, Bodegas R Alt r (w) res ★★ 95 97 99 Now part of ARCO BODEGAS UNIDAS, incorporating BERBERANA, MARQUÉS DE GRIÑON, MARQUES DE MONISTROL, MARQUÉS DE CACERES, Lagunilla, Vinícola del Mediterraneo, and Bodegas Hispano Argentinas. Fruity, full-bodied reds, but Berberana is increasingly selling its best wines as MARQUÉS DE GRIÑON.

Berceo, Bodegas R Alt r w p res ★★→★★★ 94 96 00 01 Cellar in HARO with good Gonzalo de Berceo GRAN RESERVA.

Beronia, Bodegas R Alt r w res ★★→★★★ 94 96 99 Small, modern BODEGA making reds in traditional, oaky style and fresh, modern whites. Owned by González-Byass (see page 179).

SPAIN

Bilbaínas, Bodegas R Alt r w (p) dr sw sp res ★★ 94 **95 96 97** Long-established makers of traditional Viña Pomal, lighter Viña Zaco, and Vendimia Especial RESERVAS. New owner CODORNÍU is introducing less-oaky, modern-style wines, eg. La Vicalanda RESERVA (95). White Monopole is a national standard. Good Royal Carlton CAVA.

Binissalem r w ★★ Best-known MALLORCA DO. See also Franja Roja.

Blanco White.

Bodega Spanish term for (i) a wineshop; (ii) a concern occupied in the making, blending and/or shipping of wine; and (iii) a cellar.

Bodegas de Crianza Castilla la Vieja Rueda w dr sp ★★→★★★ The Sanz family produce some of RUEDA'S liveliest whites under a variety of labels (eg PALACIO DE BORNOS) using Verdejo, Viura, and Sauv B. Reds include concentrated, oaky Almirantazgo de Castilla from VT. Medina del Campo and wines from new BODEGA in DO TORO.

Bodegas y Bebidas Part of Allied-Domecq, owns wineries all over Spain. Mainly mid-market brands. Also controls various prestigious firms, eg AGE, CAMPO VIEJO, MARQUÉS DEL PUERTO.

Bodegas y Viñedos del Jalón Calatayud r (w dr p) ★★ 99 00 01 Leading brands are the very drinkable Castillo Maluenda and Marqués de Aragón. Value. Scotswoman Pamela Geddes is making sophisticated Poema Garnacha and Garnacha Syrah wines and, on her own account, Spain's first sparkling red from Murcian Monastrell, La Pamelita.

Bornos, Palacio de Bornos Rueda w sp ★★★ 99 00 01 First-rate Sauv Bl and Verdejo wines. See BODEGAS DE CRIANZA CASTILLA LA VIEJA.

Bretón, Bodegas R Alt r res ★★★ 90 91 94 95 96 Respected Loriñon range and little-seen, expensive, conc'd Dominio de Conté (96) and Alba de Bretón (98).

Calatayud ★→★★ 94 97 98 99 00 01 Aragón DO (of 4): especially Garnacha. VINOS Y VIÑEDOS DE JALON holds sway.

Campillo, Bodegas R Ala r (p) res ★★★ 91 92 94 95 96 97 Affiliated with FAUSTINO MARTÍNEZ, a young BODEGA with good wines.

Campo Viejo, Bodegas R Alt r (w) res ★→★★★ 95 97 99 00 100% Tempranillo Alcorta; big, fruity red RESERVAS, especially Marqués de Villamagna. See Bodegas y Bebidas.

Can Rafols dels Caus Pen r p w ★★ 94 96 97 98 00 01 Young, small PENEDÈS BODEGA: own-estate, fruity Cabernet, pleasant Chard-Xarel-lo-Chenin; Gran Caus and less expensive Petit Caus ranges. Best red is Caus Lubis 100% Merlot (96).

Canary Islands (Islas) r w p g ★→★★ Until recently there were few wines of any quality other than dessert Malvasías (BODEGAS El Grifo and Bodegas Mozaga on Lanzarote). No fewer than 8 DOs have now been created, and modernized bodegas esp on TENERIFE are making better and lighter wines. The tourist trade may keep prices high, but the flavours have real interest. To investigate.

Caralt, Cavas Conde de Pen r w sp res ★★→★★★ CAVA wines from outpost of FREIXENET, esp good, vigorous Brut NV; also pleasant still wines.

Cariñena r (w p) ★ 91 92 93 96 98 99 00 01 Co-op-dominated DO: large-scale supplier of strong, everyday wine. Being invigorated and wines lightened.

Casa Castillo Jumilla r (w p) ★★→★★★ 98 99 Some of the best wines from JUMILLA made by Julia Roch e Hijos, incl fruity Monastrell (**01**), leaner Las Gravas (**00**), and deep Pie Franco (**99**) from vines unaffected by phylloxera.

Casa Gualda La Mancha r ★★→★★★ 99 00 01 Cencibel (Temp), Cab S, Crianza, and young Merlot (99) of unbeatable quality/value from the co-op Nuestra Sra de la Cabeza in Cuenca.

Casa de la Viña Valdepeñas r (w p) ★★ 98 99 00 BODEGAS Y BEBIDAS-owned estate, since 80s: sound and fruity Cencibel, CRIANZAS, and JOVENES (00).

Castaño, Bodegas Yecla (w dr) r res ★★ 98 99 00 Trail-blazer in remote YECLA making sound and pleasant blends of Monastrell with Cab S, Temp and Merlot under the names of Castaño, Colección, Hecula, and Pozuelo.

Castell de Remei Cos de S r w p ★★→★★★ 99 00 Historic v'yds/winery revived, re-equipped, replanted since 83. Best wines: Gotim Bru (Temp, Cab S, Merlot), new designer-style Oda (**98**), and top 1780.

Castellblanch Pen w sp ★★ PENEDÈS CAVA firm, owned by FREIXENET. Look for Brut Zero and Gran Castell GRAN RESERVAS.

Castillo de Monjardín Nav r w ★★→★★★ 94 95 96 97 **98** Newish winery making fragrant, oaky Chard Res (97) and vg reds and rosé, esp blends of Merlot (95).

Castillo de Ygay R Alt r w ★★★★ (r) 25 52 64 68 75 78 82 85 87 89 94 A legend. The 64 is still superb. See Marqués de Murrieta.

Castillo del Perelada, Caves Amp r w p res sp ★★→★★★ 94 **95** 98 99 01 Large range of both still wines and CAVA, including Chard, Sauv B, Cab S (esp Gran Claustro 94 95 96), and sparkling Gran Claustro extra brut.

Cataluña New DO covering the whole Catalan area. Wines may be registered as from one of the existing DOs or from the new global DO, but not from both.

Cava Official term for any classic-method Spanish sparkling wine, and the DO covering the areas up and down Spain where it is made.

Celler de Capçanes Montsant r ★★→★★★ 94 97 99 00 01 Large ex-co-op in MONTSANT with some of the best new-wave wine from the Tarragona area. Typical is the 99, meaty, concentrated and somewhat tannic.

Cenalsa See Príncipe de Viana, Bodegas.

Centro Españolas, Bodegas La M r w p ★★ 96 97 99 01 Large modern BODEGA best known for creditable red Allozo, 100% Tempranillo.

Cervera, Lagar de Rías Baixas w ★★★ DYA Maker of one of best Albariños: flowery and intensely fruity with subdued bubbles and a long finish.

Chacolí País Vasco w (r) ★→★★ DYA Alarmingly fresh, often sp wine from Basque coast; 2 DOs for all 700 acres. 9–11% alcohol. Best producers: Txomín Etxaníz (Guetaria), Aretxondo (Viscaya).

Chivite, Bodegas Julián Nav r w (p) dr sw res ★★★ 94 95 96 **97** 98 99 The biggest and best NAVARRA BODEGA. Now some of Spain's top reds, deep-flavoured, v long-lived; flowery, well-balanced white, esp Chivite Colección 125 (00), vg 00 rosé and superb Vendemia Tarde Moscatel, the best from Spain. See Gran Feudo.

Cigales r p ★→★★ 99 00 Recently demarcated region north of Valladolid, esp for light reds (traditionally known as Claretes – a term banned by the EU).

Clos Mogador Pri r ★★★→★★★★ 95 96 97 98 00' René Barbier produces first-rate new-wave Clos Mogador PRIORATO.

Over-hyped Priorato?

With their deep, black hues and bewitching noses, some new releases from this DO initially promised structural immortality with their use of oak and French varieties. But after a relatively short time in bottle, many have proved to be disappointing. Priorato's neighbours, Tarragona and Montsant, offer more affordable alternatives

---

Codorníu Pen w sp ★★→★★★ One of the two largest firms in SAN SADURNÍ DE NOYA making good CAVA: v high-tech, 10m bottles ageing in cellars. Mature Non Plus Ultra, fresh Anna de Codorníu or premium Jaume de Codorníu RESERVA. Also owns RAÍMAT, BILBAINAS.

Compañía Vinícola del Norte de España (CVNE) R Alt r w dr (p) ★★→★★★ 94 95 96 **97** 98 00 Famous RIOJA BODEGA. In spite of (or because of?) a revolutionary new vinification plant, young wines are less good than formerly, though some of the older Viña Real and Imperial RESERVAS are spectacular. See also CONTINO.

SPAIN

Con Class, Bodegas Rueda w dr ★★→★★★ DYA Despite the dreadful name exciting Verdejo/Viura and Sauv Bl from the Sanz family.

Conca de Barberà Pen w (r p) Catalan DO region growing Parellada grapes for making CAVA. But its best wines are the superb MILMANDA Chard and red Grans Muralles, both from TORRES.

Condado de Haza Rib del D r ★★★ 94 95 96 **97 98** oo' Pure, oak-aged Tinto Fino. Similar to PESQUERA but more consistent and better value.

Conde de Valdemar See Martínez-Bujanda.

Consejo Regulador Official organization for the control, promotion, and defence of a DENOMINACIÓN DE ORIGEN.

Contino R Ala r res ★★★ 94 95 96' 97 **98 99** oo Very fine single-v'yd red made by a subsidiary of COMPANIA VINICOLA DEL NORTE DE ESPANA. Look for 100% Graciano (94') and premium Viña del Olivo (96').

Cosecha Crop or vintage.

Cosecheros Alaveses R Ala r (w p) ★★★ 94 95 96 97 98 Up-and-coming former co-op, esp for gd, young, unoaked red Artadi, and Viñas de Gain, Viña El Pisón, Pagos Viejos RESERVAS.

Costers del Segre Cos del S r w p sp ★★→★★★ **92 95 96 97 98 99 00** Small demarcated area around the city of Lleida (Lérida), famous for the vineyards of RAÍMAT.

Costers del Siurana Pri r (sw) ★★★→★★★★ A star of Priorato. 94 95 96 97 98 99' Carlos Pastrana makes the prestigious Clos de l'Obac, Misere, and Usatges from Garnacha/Cab S, sometimes plus Syrah, Merlot, Tempranillo, and Cariñena. Wonderful sweet Dolç de l'Orbac.

CoViDes Pen r w p sp res ★★ **96 99** oo o1 Large former co-op; good Duc de Foix white and Cabernet Sauvignon, Cab Sauvignon-Tempranillo; also first-rate Duc de Foix CAVA.

Criado y embotellado por... Grown and bottled by...

Crianza Literally "nursing"; the ageing of wine. New or unaged wine is "sin crianza" or "joven" (young). Reds labelled "crianza" must be at least two years old (with one year in oak, in some areas six months), and must not be released before the third year.

Cumbrero See Montecillo, Bodegas.

Denominación de Origen (DO) Official wine region (see page 156).

Denominación de Origen Calificada (DOCa) Classification for wines of the highest quality; so far only RIOJA benefits (since 91).

Domecq R Ala r (w) res ★★→★★★ 94 95 **97 98** 99 RIOJA outpost of sherry firm. Inexpensive Viña Eguía CRIANZAS and excellent Marqués de Arienzo RESERVAS, fragrant and medium-bodied.

Don Darias/Don Hugo Alto Ebro r w ★ Huge-selling, modestly priced wines, v like Rioja, from undemarcated BODEGAS Vitorianas. Sound red and white.

Dulce Sweet.

El Bierzo El B DO since 90, N of León. **91 92 94 96 98 99 00** Top wine: Luna Berberida RESERVA (**98**).

El Coto, Bodegas R Ala r (w) res ★★★ 94 95 97 98 99 BODEGA best-known for light, soft, red El Coto and Coto de Imaz RESERVAS (**94**).

Elaborado y añejado por... Made and aged by...

Enate Somontano DO r w p res ★★★ 94 95 96 97 98 99 Good wines from SOMONTANO in the North: light, clean, fruity incl barrel-fermented Chard (o1) and Cab S blends (the CRIANZA is full and juicy). Wonderful oo Merlot.

Espumoso Sparkling (but see Cava).

Fariña, Bodegas Toro r w res ★★→★★★ 95 98 99 oo Best-known BODEGA of newish DO TORO: good, spicy reds. Gran Colegiata is cask-aged; Colegiata not. Young Primero. Recent vintages overpriced and disappointing.

Faustino, Bodegas R Ala r w (p) res ★★→★★★ 93 94 95 97 Long-established BODEGA, formerly F Martínez, with good reds. GRAN RESERVA is Faustino I. Top is Faustino de Autor (**95**)

Fillaboa, Granxa Rías Baixas w ★★★ DYA Small firm; delicately fruity ALBARIÑO.

A Spanish choice for 2004

Toro Albalá Don PX 75 Montilla-Moriles

Juvé y Camps Milesimé Brut 97 cava

Viñas de Vero Chardonnay 01 Somontano

Castillo de Monjardín Merlot Rosado 00 Navarra

Cooperativa de Utiel Castillo de Utiel Rosado 00 Utiel-Requena

Jean León Crianza Merlot 99 Penedès

Muga Torre Muga 94 Rioja Alta

Lan Viña Lanciano cum Laude 96 Rioja Alta

Vega de Toro Numancia 99 Toro

Mauro Vendimia Seleccionada 98 Non-DO

Franja Roja Binissalem-Mallorca r res ★★ 97 98 99 00 Best-known MALLORCA BODEGA at Binissalem making improving José L Ferrer wines especially Especial Miró (99).

Freixenet, Cavas Pen w sp ★★→★★★ Huge CAVA firm, rivalling CODORNÍU in size. Good sparklers, notably bargain Cordón Negro in black bottles, Brut Barroco, RESERVA Real, and Premium Cuvée DS. Also owns Gloria Ferrer in California, Champagne Henri Abelé (Reims), and a sparkling-wine plant in Mexico.

Galicia Rainy NW Spain: esp for fresh, aromatic but pricy whites, eg ALBARIÑO.

Generoso (g) Apéritif or dessert wine rich in alcohol.

Granbazán w dr ★★★ DYA Agro de Bazán produces a classic, fragrant ALBARIÑO with mouth-cleansing acidity.

Gran Feudo Nav w res ★★→★★★ 94 95 96 **98** 99 Brand name of fragrant white, refreshing rosé (01); soft, plummy red; the best-known wines from CHIVITE.

Gran Reserva See Reserva.

Gran Vas Pressurized tanks (French *cuves closes*) for making cheap sparkling wines; also used to describe this type of wine.

Grandes Bodegas Rib del Duero r ★★→★★★ 94 95 96 97 98 99 Reorganized and with own v'yards, this BODEGA (in notoriously pricey region) makes affordable, unoaked Marqués de Velilla. More intense CRIANZAS and RESERVAS are pricier.

Guelbenzu, Bodegas Non-DO r (w) res ★★→★★★ 98 99 00 01 Family estate in Navarra making conc'd, full-bodied reds: Azul, EVO, and top wine Lautus.

Guitán Godello Valdeorras w ★★★→★★★★ 00 01 Made by BODEGAS Tapada, these splendidly fruity, fragrant, and complex 100% Godello wines, rated among the top whites in Spain, typify renaissance of native grapes in GALICIA. The barrel-fermented type has the edge.

Gran Muralles See Torres.

Haro Wine centre of the RIOJA ALTA, a small but stylish old town.

Hill, Cavas Pen w r sp res ★★→★★★ 93 96 97 **98** 99 Old PENEDÈS firm: fresh dry w Blanc Cru, gd Gran Civet, and Gran Toc reds, first-rate young Masía Hill Tempranillo, and delicate RESERVA Oro Brut CAVA.

Iljalba, Viña R Alt r w dr p ★→★★★ 94 95 96 **98** 99 00 A newish BODEGA with a reputation for organically-made younger wines and a rare 100% Graciano.

Induvasa Jumilla r ★★ Up-and-coming winery making the attractive and attractively priced young Monastrell Taja.

Josep Anguera Beyme Montsant r ★★→★★★ 96 97 98 00 Small family firm on verges of PRIORATO making superior fruity Finca L'Argata wines from Syrah, Cab S, Garnacha, and Cariñena blends.

SPAIN

Joven (vino) Young, unoaked wine.

Jumilla r (w p) ★→★★★ 91 93 96 98 99 00 DO in mountains N of Murcia. Its traditionally overstrong wines are being lightened by earlier picking and better winemaking. The Monastrell grape can yield dark and fragrant wines to rival those of RIBERA DEL DUERO. See Agapito Rico and Casa Castillo.

Juvé y Camps Pen w sp ★★★ 97 98 99 Family firm. Top-quality CAVA, from free-run juice only, esp RESERVA de la Familia and Gran Juvé y Camps (98).

LAN, Bodegas R Alt r (p w) res ★★→★★★ 94 95 96 97 98 Huge modern BODEGA. Recently reorganized; making improved Lan, Lanciano, & premium Culmen de Lan (94').

Lanzarote Canary Island with v fair dry Malvasía, eg El Grifo.

Lar de Lares Rib del G r res ★★ 97 98 99 00 Meaty GRAN RESERVA from BODEGAS INVIOSA, in remote Extremadura (in SW). And younger, lighter Lar de Barros. Also good Bonaval CAVA.

León, Jean Pen r w res ★★★ 90 91 93 96 97 Small firm; TORRES-owned since 95. Gd oaky Chard (99). Earlier Cab was huge, repaid long ageing; lighter since 90. Also outstanding Merlot (97).

López de Heredia R Alt r w (p) dr sw res ★★→★★★ 42 47 54 57 61 64 68 70 73 78 81 87 93 94 97 Old-est'd HARO BODEGA: v long-lasting, v trad wines. Best are really old RESERVAS from 54 onwards; still marvellous 64s.

Los Llanos Valdepeñas r (p w) res ★★ 95 96 98 99 One of growing number of VALDEPEÑAS BODEGAS to age wine in oak. RESERVA, GRAN RESERVA; premium Pata Negra Gran Reserva: 100% Cencibel (Tempranillo). Clean, fruity w, Armonioso.

Malaga Almost nothing left, but see Telmo Rodriguez.

Mallorca Interesting things are happening on the island at last, incl fresh Chard (better unoaked), Merlot, Syrah, Cab S. Also traditional varieties and blends. Anima Negra, FRANCA ROJA, Herens de Ribas, Miguel Oliver, Pere Seda, Son Bordils, and Jaume Mesquida are leaders.

Mancha, La La M r w ★→★★ 92 93 94 96 97 98 99 00 Vast demarcated region N and NE of VALDEPEÑAS. Mainly white wines; the reds lack the liveliness of the best Valdepeñas but show signs of improvement. To watch.

Marqués de Alella Alella w (sp) ★★→★★★ 98 99 01 (DYA) Light, fragrant w ALELLA wines from PARXET, some Chard (incl barrel-fermented Allier). Also CAVA.

Marqués de Cáceres, Bodegas R Alt r p w res ★★★ 91 92 94 96 98 01 Good r RIOJAS made by modern French methods inc premium Gaudium (96); surprisingly light, fragrant w (DYA), barrel-fermented Antea (01), and sw Santinela.

Marqués de Griñón Non-DO r w ★★★ 94 95 96 97 98 99 Enterprising nobleman initiated v fine Cab, delicious (99) Syrah and Petit Verdot at his Dominio de Valdepusa nr Toledo, S of Madrid, not formerly known for wine. Fruity wines to drink fairly young. Also gd RIOJAS and Durius (00) r from RIB DEL DUERO area.

Marqués de Monistrol, Bodegas Pen p r sp dr sw res ★★→★★★ 92 94 95' 98 99 Old BODEGA now owned by ARCO. Reliable CAVAS. Fresh blends of Cab S, Merlot, and Tempranillo.

Marqués de Murrieta R Alt r p w res ★★★→★★★★ 25 42 50 52 54 60 68 70 75 78 87 89 94 95 96 97 99 Historic, revered BODEGA nr LOGRONO. Famous for r CASTILLO DE YGAY and old-style, oaky white. Magnificent premium Dalmau, a blend of Temp/Cab/Graciano (99).

Marqués de Riscal R Ala r (p w) res ★★★→★★★★ 91 92 94 95 96 97 Best-known RIOJA ALAVESA BODEGA. Fairly light, dry r. Old vintages: v fine, some more recent ones variable; now right back on form. Barón de Chirel, 50% Cab S (94' 95' 96') is magnificent. RUEDA w incl Sauv (00), oak-aged RESERVA Limousin (97).

Marqués de Vargas, Bodegas y Viñedos R Aly ★★★ 92 93 94 95 96 97 Spectacular newcomer making a RESERVA and a Privada (96' 97), both with magnificent concentration and balance.

Marqués del Puerto R Alt r (p w) res ★★→★★★ 94 95 **96 97** Small firm, was BODEGAS López Agos, now owned by Marie Brizard. Reliable.

Martínez-Bujanda R Ala r p w res ★★★ 90 91 92 93 94 95 **96 97** Refounded (85) family-run RIOJA BODEGA, remarkably equipped. Superb wines, incl fruity sin CRIANZA, irresistible ROSADO; noble Valdemar RESERVAS (95), 100% Garnacha, and splendid premium 100% Tempranillo single-v'yd Finca Valpiedra (94 96 97).

Mascaró, Antonio Pen r p w sp ★★→★★★ **90 91 92 93** 94 96 Top brandy maker, gd CAVA; fresh, lemony, dry white Viña Franca, and Anima Cab S.

Mas Martinet Pri r ★★★→★★★★ 94' 95' 96 97 98' 99 00' Maker of Clos Martinet and a pioneer of the exclusive boutique PRIORATOS.

Mauro, Bodegas nr Valladolid r ★★→★★★ **94** 95 96 97 98 99' Young BODEGA in Tudela del Duero; very good, round, fruity TINTO del País (Tempranillo) red and superb Vendimia Seleccionado (98). Not DO, as some of the fruit is from outside RIBERA del D. Now making excellent TORO San Roman (98).

Milmanda ★★★ Premium barrel-fermented Chardonnay from TORRES.

Montecillo, Bodegas R Alt r w (p) res ★★ 94 95 96 **97** RIOJA BODEGA owned by OSBORNE. Old GRAN RESERVAS are magnificent. Excellent CRIANZA **96**.

Montsant DO since 2001. Tiny new DO in an enclave of PRIORATO, sharing much in common with its wines.

SPAIN

Muga, Bodegas R Alt r (w sp) res ★★★ 91 94 95 96 99 Small family firm in HARO, known for some of RIOJA'S best strictly trad reds. Wines are light but highly aromatic, with long complex finish. Best is Prado Enea and now extraordinary concentrated Torre Muga (94' 95 96 98). Whites and CAVA less good. Fresh white Viura fermented in barrel (00).

Navajas, Bodegas R Alt r w res ★★→★★★ 94 95 96 **98** 99 00 Small firm: bargain reds, CRIANZAS, RESERVAS. Also excellent oak-aged white Viura (98 00)

Navarra Nav r p (w) ★★→★★★ 92 94 95 96 97 **98 99** 00 Demarcated region. Stylish Temp & Cabernet reds, increasingly rivalling RIOJAS in quality and trouncing many in value. See Chivite, Guelbenzu, Palacio de la Vega, Ochoa, Príncipe de Viana.

Nuestro Padre Jésus del Perdón, Co-op de La M r w ★→★★ 91 93 **94 96 98 99** 00 01 Bargain fresh white Lazarillo and more-than-drinkable Yuntero; 100% Cencibel (alias Tempranillo) and Cencibel-Cab S aged in oak.

Ochoa Nav r p w res ★★ →★★★ 91 92' 93 94 **96 97** 99 00' Small family BODEGA; excellent Moscatel (01), but better-known for well-made red and rosés, incl 100% Tempranillo and 100% Merlot (99).

Organic Wines Spain's most prestigious and longstanding producer is Albet i Noya in PENEDÈS, maker of good Chard, Temp, Cab S, and first-rate Syrah (97).

Pago de Carraovejas Rib del D r res ★★→★★★ 98 99 New estate; some of the region's most stylish, densely fruity TINTO Fino/Cabernet in minimal supply .

Palacio, Bodegas R Ala r p w res ★★★ 91 93 94' 95 96 **97 98** Good old BODEGA rescued from Seagram ownership. Very sound RESERVA Privada (94) and Cosme Palacio (95).

Palacio de Fefiñanes Rías Baixas w dr ★★★ DYA Oldest-est'd of the BODEGAS in RÍAS BAIXAS, now making excellent, modern-style ALBARIÑOS.

Palacio de la Vega Nav r p w res ★★→★★★ 93 95 96 97 98 00 New BODEGA with juicy Tempranillo JOVEN, Cab S, Merlot, and much promise. Good barrel-fermented Chardonnay (01).

Parxet Alella w p sp ★★→★★★ Excellent fresh, fruity, exuberant CAVA (only one produced in ALELLA): esp Brut Nature. Also elegant w ALELLA: MARQUÉS DE ALELLA.

Paternina, Bodegas R Alt r w (p) dr sw res ★→★★ Known for its standard red brand Banda Azul. Conde de los Andes label was fine, but the famous 78 is strictly for fans of oak/volatile acidity, and recent vintages, as of its other RIOJAS, are disappointing. Most consistent is Banda Dorada white (DYA).

Pazo Ribeiro r p w ★★ DYA Brand name of the RIBEIRO co-op, whose wines are akin to VINHOS VERDES. Rasping red is local favourite. Pleasant slightly fizzy Pazo whites are safer; white Viña Costeira and Amadeus have quality.

Pazo de Barrantes Rías Baixas w ★★★ DYA New ALBARIÑO from RIAS BAIXAS; estate owned by late Conde de Creixels de MURRIETA. Delicate, exotic, top-quality.

Pazo de Señorans Rías Baixas w dr ★★★ DYA Exceptionally fragrant wines from a BODEGA considered a benchmark of the DO.

Penedès Pen r w sp ★→★★★ 91 93 94 95 96 98 99 00 Demarcated region including Vilafranca del Penedès and SAN SADURNI DE NOYA. See also TORRES.

Pérez Pascuas Hermanos Rib del D r res ★★★ 91 92 94 95 96 97 99 00 Immaculate, tiny BODEGA. In Spain its fruity & complex r viña Pedrosa is rated one of the best.

Pesquera Rib del D r ★★★ 90 91 92 93 94 95' 96 97 99 00 Small quantities of RIBERA DEL D from Alejandro Fernández. Robert Parker once rated it level with finest B'x, and it has never forgotten. Also CONDADO DE HAZA.

Pingus, Dominio de Rib del D r ★★★ 00 Tempranillo-based (only 450 cases). Winemaker/owner: Peter Sisseck. Spain's answer to B'x's "garage" wines. Absurdly expensive, their keeping qualities being unknown.

Piqueras, Bodegas Almansa r (w dr p) ★★→★★★ 94 95 96 98 00 Family BODEGA. Some of LA MANCHA's best: Castillo de Almansa CRIANZA, Marius GRAN RESERVA.

Pirineos, Bodega Som w p r ★★→★★★ 96 97 98 99 00 Former co-op and SOMONTANO pioneer. Best: Montesierra range; oak-aged Señorío de Lazán RESERVA.

Príncipe de Viana, Bodegas Nav r w p ★★ 91 96 00 Large firm (formerly "Cenalsa"), blending and maturing co-op wines and shipping a range from NAVARRA, incl flowery, new-style white and fruity red Agramont.

Priorato Pri br r ★★★ 92 93 94 95 96 98 99 00 DO enclave of TARRAGONA, traditionally known for alcoholic RANCIO and huge-bodied, almost black r. At its brambly best, one of Spain's triumphs. COSTERS DE SIURANA, MAS MARTINET, and ROTLLAN TORRA rightly rank among Spain's stars. See page 160.

Raïmat Cos del S r w p sp ★★→★★★ (Cab) 94 95 96 97 98 99 Clean, structured wines from DO nr Lérida, planted by CODORNÍU with Cabernet, Chardonnay, other foreign vines. Good 100% Chardonnay CAVA. Value.

Rancio Describes any maderized (brown) white wine of nutty flavour.

Raventós i Blanc Pen w sp ★★→★★★ Excellent CAVA aimed at top of market, also fresh El Preludi white and 100% Chard.

Remelluri, La Granja R Ala w dr r res ★★★ 95 96 99 00 Small estate (since 70), making very good traditional red RIOJAS but future less certain after departure of Telmo Rodríguez. Avoid the disappointing 97.

Reserva (res) Good-quality wine matured for long periods. Red reservas must spend at least 1 year in cask and 2 in bottle; Gran Reservas 2 in cask and 3 in bottle. Thereafter many continue to mature for years.

Rías Baixas w ★★→★★★ 95 96 97 98 DYA NW DO embracing subzones Val do Salnés, O Rosal, and Condado do Tea, now for some of the best (and priciest) cold-fermented Spanish whites, mainly from ALBARIÑO grapes.

Ribera del Duero Rib del D 91 94 95 96 98 99 00 Fashionable, fast-expanding DO east of Valladolid, (the Duero becomes the Portuguese Douro). Excellent for TINTO Fino (Temp) rs. Many excellent wines, but high prices. See ARZUAGA, PAGO DE CARRAOVEJAS, PÉREZ PASCUAS, PESQUERA, TORREMILANOS, VEGA SICILIA. Also non-DO MAURO.

Rioja r p w sp ★★→★★★★★ 64 70 75 78 81 82 85 89 91 92 94 95 96 98 99 00 N upland region along River Ebro for many of Spain's best red table wines in scores of BODEGAS de exportación. Tempranillo predominates. Subdivided into the following 3 areas:

Rioja Alavesa N of the R Ebro, produces fine red wines, mostly light in body and colour but particularly aromatic.

> **Important note:**
> Most large Spanish wineries make a range of red, white, and rosé. The
> vintages at the top of an entry refer to the best of a BODEGA's red CRIANZAS
> and RESERVAS and are only a rough guide, since the vintages and degree of
> maturity may well vary from one wine to another. When individual wines
> are named in the text, preferred vintages are given in brackets.

Rioja Alta S of the R Ebro and W of LOGROÑO, grows most of the finest, best-balanced red and white wines; also some rosé.

Rioja Baja Stretching E from LOGROÑO, makes stouter red wines, often from Garnacha and high in alcohol, and often used for blending.

La Rioja Alta, Bodegas R Alt r w (p) dr (sw) res ★★★ 89 90 94 **95 96 98** Excellent RIOJAS, esp red RESERVA VIÑA Alberdi, velvety Ardanza RESERVA, lighter Araña Reserva, splendid Reserva 904, and marvellous Reserva 890 (82) – but the wines are not lasting as long as they used to.

Riojanas, Bodegas R Alt r (w p) res ★★→★★★ 88 89 94 95 96 97 98 Old BODEGA. Trad VIÑA Albina; big, mellow Monte Real RESERVAS (96).

Roda, Bodegas R Alt r ★★★ 92 94' 95' 96 98 99' Founded in 89 by a Catalan couple who decided that only in HARO could they make their dream wines. Superb and costly Roda I (which has the edge) and Roda II. New Cirsión (98').

Rosado Rosé.

Rotllan Torra Pri r (r&w sw) ★★★ 95 96 97 98 99 Premium Amadis, Balandra, sweet Amadis Dolç and Moscatel Reserva Especial PRIORATOS.

Rovellats Pen w p sp ★★→★★★ Small family firm making only good (and expensive) CAVAS, stocked in some of Spain's best restaurants.

Rueda br w ★★→★★★ **96 97 98 99 00** Sm, historic DO W of Valladolid. Traditional FLOR-growing, sherry-like wines up to 17% alcohol; now for fresh whites, esp MARQUÉS DE RISCAL. Secret weapon is the Verdejo grape.

Ruíz, Santiago Rías Baixas w ★★→★★★ DYA Small, prestigious RIAS BAIXAS CO, now owned by LAN: fresh, lemony ALBARIÑO, not quite up to former standards.

San Sadurní de Noya Pen w sp ★★→★★★ Town S of Barcelona, hollow with CAVA cellars. Standards can be v high, though the flavour (of Parellada and other grapes) never gets close to Champagne.

Sangría Cold-red wine cup traditionally made with citrus fruit, fizzy lemonade, ice, and brandy. But too often repulsive commercial fizz.

Scala Dei, Cellers de Pri r w p res ★★→★★★ 95 **96 98** 99 00 Original PRIORATO BODEGA owned by CODORNIU. Dark, powerful Garnacha. Cartoixa RESERVAS, conc, blackberry-rich young Negre.

Schenk, Bodegas Valencia r w p ★★ 99 Decent Estrella Moscatel, good Monastrell/Garnacha Cavas Murviedro, and Los Monteros. See also below.

Schenk, Bodegas U-R r w p dr ★→★★ 99 00 01 Reliable Las Lomas reds and fresh Bobal ROSADO.

Seco Dry.

Segura Viudas, Cavas Pen w sp ★★→★★★ CAVA from SAN SADURNI (FREIXENET-owned). Buy the Brut Vintage 98, Galimany 98 or esp RESERVA Heredad 98.

Solís, Félix Valdepeñas w dr p r ★★ 95 96 **97** 99 00 BODEGA in VALDEPEÑAS making sturdy, oak-aged reds, VIÑA Albali RESERVAS, and fresh white.

Somontano ★★→★★★ 91 94 95 96 98 99 00 01 (Som) Fashionable DO in Pyrenean foothills. Given the cool conditions, future could lie with whites and Pinot N. Best-known BODEGAS: old French-est'd Lalanne (esp Viña San Marcos r: Moristel-Tempranillo-Cab S; white Macabeo, Chard), Bodega PIRINEOS, new VIÑAS DEL VERO. Also Viñedos y CRIANZAS del Alto Aragón (excellent ENATE range).

Tarragona r w br dr sw ★→★★★ 95 96 97 98 99 00 01 Table wines from demarcated region (DO); previously of little note; now greatly improved.

SPAIN

Telmo Rodríguez, Compañia de Vinos r w ★★→★★★ HQ in Logroño, controlled ny gifted oenologist Telmo Rodríguez, formerly of REMELLURI. Excellent DO wines in Toro, Rueda, Navarra (see BASO), Alicante. His Molina Real 100% Moscatel from Malaga is exceptional.

Tenerife r w ★→★★ DYA Now 4 DOs; s'times much more than merely drinkable young wines. Best BODEGAS: Flores, Monje, Insulares (VIÑA Norte label).

Tinto Red.

Toro r ★★★ 90 91 93 94' 95 96 98 99 00 01 This increasingly fashionable DO 150 miles NW of Madrid still produces powerful, fairly basic reds. VEGA SICILIA has now built a BODEGA there; and spectacular wines like San Román from MAURO and Numanthia from Vega de Toro are already showing what the region can do. See also BODEGAS FARINA.

Torremilanos Rib del D r (p) res ★→★★★ 89 90 91 92 94 95 96 97 99 Label of BODEGAS Peñalba López, a fast-expanding family firm nr Aranda de Duero. TINTO Fino (Tempranillo) is smoother, more RIOJA-like than most.

Torres, Miguel Pen r w p dr s/sw res ★★→★★★★ 87 88 89 90 92 93 94 95 96 97 98 World-famous family company among the stars of the wine world. Makes most of the best PENEDÈS wines; a flagship for all Spain. Wines are flowery w VIÑA Sol (01), Green Label Fransola Sauv (01), Gran Viña Sol (00) Parellada, MILMANDA oak-fermented Chard (00), off-dry aromatic Esmeralda (01), Waltraud Ries (01), red Sangre de Toro, Gran Sangre de Toro (96 97), vg Mas la Plana Gran Coronas (Cabernet Sauvignon) RESERVAS (89 93 94 96 98), fresh, soft Atrium Merlot (00), and Viña Magdala Pinot. Mas Borrás (98): 100% Pinot Noir. Superb new Grans Muralles (98), full-bodied, made from native grapes including reintroduced Garot, is noble. Also in Chile, California, and China. The new Nerola wines, with DO Catalunya, are innovative blends of Mediterranean grapes.

Unión de Cosecheros de Labastida R Ala r p w dr ★→★★★ 89 94 95 96 97 98 99 00 Old-established and first-rate RIOJAN cooperative. Young, juicy Montebuna, good Solagüen CRIANZAS and RESERVAS and top Manuel Qintano reservas (95).

Utiel-Requena U-R r p (w) ★→★★ 92 93 94 98 99 00 01 Region W of VALENCIA. Sturdy reds and hyper-tannic wines for blending; also light, fragrant rosé.

Valbuena Rib del D r ★★★ 89 90 91 92 94 95' 97 Formerly made with the same grapes as VEGA SICILIA but sold when 5 yrs old. Best at about 10 yrs. Some preferred it to its elder brother. But see Alión.

Valdeorras Gal r w ★ →★★★ DO E of Orense. Fresh, dry wines; at best, Godellos are now rated among top white wines in Spain. See GUITÁN GODELLO.

Valdepeñas La M r (w) ★→★★ 90 91 95 96 98 99 00 Demarcated region nr Andalucían border. Mainly reds, high in alcohol but surprisingly soft in flavour. Best wines (eg LOS LLANOS, FELIX SOLIS, and CASA DE LA VIÑA) now oak-matured.

Valduero, Bodegas Rib del D r (w p) ★★→★★★ 90 91 95 96 98 Now more than 10 yrs old; growing reputation for well-made wine and vg-value RESERVAS.

Valencia r w ★ Demarcated region exporting vast quantities of clean and drinkable table wine; also refreshing whites, esp Moscatel.

Vega Sicilia Rib del D r res ★★★★ 53 60 62 64 66 68 70 73 75 76 80 81 82 83 85 86 89 90 Top Spanish wine: full, fruity, piquant, rare, and fascinating. Up to 16% alcohol; best at 12-15 yrs. RESERVA Especial: a blend, chiefly of 62 and 79 (!). Also VALBUENA, ALION. Also owns Oremus in Tokáji, Hungary.

Vendimia Vintage.

Viña Literally, a vineyard. But wines such as Tondonia (LOPEZ DE HEREDIA) are not necessarily made only with grapes from the v'yd named.

Viña Pedrosa See Pérez Pascuas.

Viñas del Vero Som w p r res ★★→★★★ 92 93 94 95 96 97 99' 01' SOMONTANO estate. Gd varietal wines: Chard, Ries, Gewürz. Best r Gran Vos (97 98).

Vinícola de Castilla La M r p w ★★ 89 **91** 95 96 **01'** One of largest LA MANCHA firms. Red and white Castillo de Alhambra are palatable. Top are Cab, Cencibel (Tempranillo), Señorío de Guadianeja GRAN RESERVAS.

Vinícola Navarra Nav r p w dr res ★★ 97 98 99 00 01' Old-est'd firm, now part of BODEGAS Y BEBIDAS, but still thoroughly traditional. Best wines Castillo de Javier, Las Campañas Garnacha 01.

Vino común/corriente Ordinary wine.

Yecla r w ★→★★ DO north of Murcia. Decent red from BODEGAS CASTAÑO.

Portugal

Recent vintages

2002 Challenging vintage with heavy rain during picking. Better in the South.

2001 Large vintage throughout. Those producers who undertook careful selection made very good wines.

2000 Small harvest in fine weather led to ripe-flavoured wines from all regions.

1999 Another small year with prospects dashed by rain during the vintage. Wines from the South better than the North.

1998 Tiny yields, potentially excellent wines in the North diluted by late September rain. Inland areas and the Alentejo fared better.

1997 A good year throughout the country. A healthy crop produced balanced, ripe-flavoured reds. Good red Bairrada.

Adega A cellar or winery.

Alenquer r w ★→★★ Aromatic wines from IPR just north of Lisbon. Good estate wines from QUINTAS DE PANCAS, CARNEIRO, and de Monte d'Oiro (Syrah).

Alentejo r (w) ★→★★★ **95 96** 97 98 99 00 01 Vast tract of SE Portugal with only sparse v'yds, over the R Tagus from Lisbon, but rapidly emerging potential for excellent wine and expanding v'yds. To date the great bulk has been co-op-made. Estate wines from CARTUXA, CORTES DE CIMA, HERDADE DE MOUCHÃO, JOÃO RAMOS, JOSE DE SOUSA, QUINTA DO CARMO (part Rothschild-owned), and ESPORAO have potency and style. Best co-ops are at BORBA, REDONDO, and REGUENGOS. Now classified as a DOC in its own right with BORBA, REDONDO, REGUENGOS, PORTALEGRE, EVORA, Granja-Amareleja, Vidigueira, and Moura entitled to their own sub-appellations. Also VINHO REGIONAL Alentejano.

Algarve r w ★ Wines of the holiday area are covered by DOCS Lagos, Tavira, Lagoa, and Portimão. Nothing special apart from the fact that Sir Cliff Richard has a vineyard nr Albufeira.

Aliança, Caves Bair r w sp res ★★ Large BAIRRADA-based firm making classic-method sparkling. Reds and whites incl good Bairrada wines and mature DÃOS. Also interests in ALENTEJO.

Alorna, Quinta do Ribatejo r w ★→★★ DYA Enterprising estate with a range of good varietals: CASTELÃO, TRINCADEIRA, and CABERNET SAUVIGNON.

Altano Douro 99 00 Good new red from the Symington family (DOW'S port). Look out for future releases.

Alvarinho White grape planted in the extreme north of Portugal making fragrant and attractive white wines. Known as ALBARIÑO in neighbouring Galicia.

Ameal, Quinta do VV w ★★★ DYA. One of best VVs available. 100% LOUREIRO.

Aragonez Successful red grape in ALENTEJO for varietal wines. See Tinta Roriz.

Arinto White grape best from central and S Portugal where it retains acidity and produces fragrant, crisp, dry, white wines.

Arruda r w ★ DOC in ESTREMADURA with large co-op.

SPAIN

Avaleda, Quinta da VV w ★→★★ DYA Reliable VINHO VERDES made on the Avaleda estate of the Guedes family. It is sold dry in Portugal but slightly sweet for export. There are also gd varietal wines from LOUREIRO, ALVARINHO, and Trajadura. Reds: Charamba (DOURO) and Aveleda (ESTREMADURA).

Azevedo, Quinta do VV w ★★ DYA Superior VINHO VERDE from SOGRAPE. 100% LOUREIRO grapes.

Vinos de Alta Expresión

Within the last few years a new generation of select and very pricey wines has appeared in Spain. The full potential of the grape is realized by using fruit from old vines, picking at the optimum point, hand sorting, and fermenting in small batches. Some examples: from Rioja; ALLENDE Aurus; ARTADI EI PISÓN; MARQUÉS DE RISCAL Barón de Chirel; REMÍREZ DE GANUZA; Cirsión; MUGA Torre Muga. From Conca de Barberà: TORRES Grans Muralles. From Priorato: CLOS MOGADOR reserva; ALVARO PALACIO Finca Dolfi. From Navarra: GUELBENZU Lautus. From Ribera del Duero; Vega Sicilia Unico. Expect to pay.

Bacalhoa, Quinta da Set r res ★★★ **97 98 99 00** Estate nr SETUBAL. Its fruity, reliable, mid-weight Cab is made by J P VINHOS.

Bairrada Bair r w sp ★→★★★ **90' 94 97 98 99** 00 DOC in central Portugal for solid (astringent) reds from the tricky Baga grape. Best wines: CASA DE SAIMA, LUIS PATO, and CAVES SÃO JOÃO will keep for years. Most white used by local sparkling-wine industry.

Barca Velha Douro r res ★★★★ 91' Portugal's most renowned red, made in very limited quantities in the high Douro by the port firm of FERREIRA (now owned by SOGRAPE). Powerful, resonant wine with deep bouquet, but facing increasing competition from other Douro reds. **52 54 58 64 65 66' 78 81 82 85 91' 95.** Second wine known as Reserva Ferreirinha.

Beiras ★→★★ VINHO REGIONAL including DÃO, BAIRRADA, and granite mountain ranges of central Portugal.

Beira Interior ★ DOC incorporating former IPRS of Castelo Rodrigo, Pinhel, and Cova da Beira. Huge potential from old vineyards.

Boavista, Quinta da Est ★★ DYA Large property near ALENQUER making increasingly good range of r and w: Palha Canas, Quinta das Sete Encostas, Espiga, and a Chard, Casa Santos Lima. Winemaker: José Neiva.

Borba Alen r ★→★★ Small DOC in central ALENTEJO; well-managed cooperative producing fruity reds.

Branco White.

Brejoeira, Palácio de VV w (r) ★★ The best-known ALVARINHO fom Portugal, facing increasingly stiff competition from neighbouring VINHO VERDE estates around Moncão.

Bright Brothers ★★ DYA Australian flying winemaker based in Portugal: interests as far-flung as Argentina, Sicily, and Spain. Range of well-made wines from DOURO, RIBATEJO, ESTREMADURA, and BEIRAS. See also Fiuza Bright.

Buçaco Beiras r w (p) res ★★★★ (r) **53 59 62 63 70 78 82 85 89 92** (w) **91 92 93** Recent vintages disappointing. Legendary speciality of the Palace Hotel at Buçaco near Coimbra, not seen elsewhere. An experience worth the journey. So are the palace and park.

Bucelas Est w ★★ Tiny demarcated region north of Lisbon in the hands of 3 producers. QUINTA da Romeira makes attractive wines from the ARINTO grape.

Cadaval, Casa Rib r w ★★ **97 98 99 00 01** Good varietal reds especially TRINCADEIRA. Also Pinot Noir and Cabernet Sauvignon.

Carcavelos Est br sw ★★★ Normally NV. Minute DOC W of Lisbon. Rare sweet apéritif or dessert wines average 19% alcohol and resemble honeyed MADEIRA. The only producer is now QUINTA dos Pesos, Caparide.

Carmo, Quinta do Alen r w res ★★ **87' 93** 94 96 97 98 Beautiful small ALENTEJO ADEGA, partly bought in 92 by Rothschilds (Lafite). 125 acres, plus cork forests. Fresh white, red better. 2nd wine: Dom Martinho.

Carneiro, Quinta do Alenquer r ★★ 98 99 00 w DYA New-wave estate; gd, mid-weight reds (PERIQUITA, Trincadeira Preta, TINTA RORIZ, and TOURIGA NACIONAL).

Cartaxo Ribatejo r w ★ District in RIBATEJO N of Lisbon, now a DOC area making everyday wines popular in the capital.

Cartuxa, Herdade de Alen ★★→★★★ r **90** 94 97 00' w DYA Vast estate near Evora (500 acres). Big reds especially Pera Manca (91 94 95 97), one of ALENTEJO's best (and most pricey); creamy whites. Also Foral de Evora, and Fundação Eugenio de Almeida.

Carvalhais, Quinta dos Dão ★★★ r 97 98 99 00 w DYA Excellent single-estate SOGRAPE wine. Gd r varietals (TOURIGA NACIONAL, Alfronchiero Preto) and w Encruzado.

Casal Branco, Quinta de Ribatejo r w ★★ Large family estate making good red and white wines. Best red: Falocoaria (97 98 99 00).

Casal García VV w ★★ DYA Big-selling VINHO VERDE, made at AVELEDA.

Casal Mendes VV w ★ DYA The VINHO VERDE from CAVES ALIANÇA.

Castelão The official name for PERIQUITA a grape planted throughout southern Portugal, but particularly in TERRAS DO SADO. Makes firm-flavoured, raspberryish reds which take on a tar-like quality with age. Also known as João de Santarem.

Chryseia Douro r ★★★→★★★★ 00 Bruno Prats from Bordeaux has come together with the Symington family to produce a dense yet elegant wine from port grapes. A star in the making.

Colares r ★★ Small DOC on the sandy coast W of Lisbon. Its antique-style, dark-red wines, rigid with tannin, are from ungrafted vines. They need ageing, but TOTB (the older the better) no longer. See Paulo da Silva.

Consumo (vinho) Ordinary wine.

Cortes de Cima r ★★★ 98 99 00 01 Estate nr Vidigueira (ALENTEJO) owned by Danish family. Gd reds from ARAGONEZ, TRINCADEIRA, PERIQUITA grapes. Chamine: 2nd label. Also Syrah bottled under Incognito label.

Côtto, Quinta do Douro r w res ★★★ r 98 99 00 w DYA Pioneer table wines from port country; vg red Grande Escolha (90 94 95 00) and also do Côtto are dense fruity, tannic, wines for long keeping. Also port.

Crasto, Quinta do Douro r dr sw ★★★ 98 99 00 01 Top estate nr Pinhão for port and excellent oak-aged reds. Excellent varietal wines (TOURIGA NACIONAL, TINTA RORIZ) and Reserva. Look out for Vinha do Ponte (98) and María Theresa (98) made from individual plots of old vines.

Dão r w res ★★→★★★ 96 97 98 99 00 01 DOC region round town of Viseu. Too many dull, earthy wines produced in the past but region is improving, if not rapidly with single QUINTAS making headway: solid reds of some subtlety with age; substantial, dry whites. Most sold under brand names. But see Roques, Maias, Saes, Fonte do Ouro, Terras Altas, Porta dos Cavalheiros, Grão Vasco, Duque de Viseu, etc.

DFJ Vinhos r w ★→★★ DYA Successful partnership making well-priced wines, mainly in RIBATEJO and ESTRAMADURA. Look out for these labels: Ramada (r, w), Segada (r, w), Manta Preta (r), and Grand'Arte (r, w).

DOC (Denominacão de Origem Controlada) Official wine region. There are now 27 in total, a number of mergers having taken place in recent years. See also IPR, Vinho Regional.

Doce (vinho) Sweet (wine).

Douro r w ★★→★★★★ 95 96 97 98 99 00 01 N river valley producing port and some of Portugal's most exciting table wines. Look for BARCA VELHA, QUINTA DO CÔTTO, REDOMA, & Symington's new wines (see ALTANO). Watch this space.

Duas Quintas Douro ★★★ r 98 99 00 w DYA Rich red from port shipper RAMOS PINTO. Very good Reserva (94 95 97 99).

Duque de Viseu Dão ★★★ r 99 00 01 w DYA High quality r DAO from SOGRAPE.

Entre Serras r w ★ DYA BEIRAS. Sound barrel-fermented Chard; soft light reds.

Esporão, Herdade do Alen w DYA r ★★→★★★ 98 99 00 01 Impressive estate owned by Finagra. Wines made (since 92) by Aussie David Baverstock: rich, ripe, gently oaked w; fruity, young r Alandra; superior r Esporão: one of ALENTEJO's best. Also Monte Velho gently oaked r, fruity w. Gd varietals: ARAGONEZ, TRINCADEIRA, Cab S.

Espumante Sparkling.

Esteva Douro r ★ DYA V drinkable DOURO red from port firm FERREIRA.

Estremadura ★ VINHO REGIONAL on Portugal's W coast, s'times called "Oeste". Large co-ops. Alta Mesa, Ramada, Portada: gd, inexpensive wines from local estates and co-ops. IPRS: Encostas d'Aire. DOCS: ALENQUER, ARRUDA, Obidos, TORRES VEDRAS.

Evel Douro r ★★→★★★ 99 00 Much-improved Douro wines from REAL VINICOLA. Worth looking out for the red Grande Escolha.

Fernão Pires White grape making ripe-flavoured, slightly spicy whites in RIBATEJO. (Known as María Gomes in BAIRRADA.)

Ferreira Douro r ★→★★★★ Port shipper making a range of good to VG red Douro wines: Esteva, Vinha Grande, Callabriga, Quinta de Leda, Reserva Ferreirinha and BARCA VELHA.

Fojo, Vinha da ★★★ r 96' 98 99 Prime DOURO QUINTA; foot-trodden, dense reds.

Fonseca, José María da Est r w dr sw sp res ★★→★★★ Venerable firm in Azeitão nr Lisbon. Huge range of wines incl established brands like Periquita, Pasmados, Quinta de Camerate, Garrafeiras and the famous dessert SETUBAL (Alambre). impressive range of red wines from new winery opened in 2001: Septimus, Vinya, Primum, and the Domingos Soares Franco Seleccao Privado. Top of range: Optimum. Also with interests in Dao (Terras Atlas), Alentejo (JOSE DE SOUSA and d'Avillez), Douro (Domini). LANCERS rosé is less distinguished, but Lancers Brut is a decent sp made by a continuous process of Russian invention.

Fonte do Ouro Dão ★★ r 98 99 00 w DYA Good, balanced red from well-run single estate. Also single QUINTA TOURIGA NATIONAL (97 98 00) under Boas Quintas label. Second wine: Quinta da Giesta.

Foz do Arouce, Quinta da Beiras r ★★ 96 97 98 99 w DYA Big, cask-aged red from heart of BEIRAS.

Franqueira, Quinta da VV w ★★ DYA Typically dry, fragrant VINHO VERDE made by Englishman Piers Gallie.

Fuiza Bright Ribatejo r w ★★ DYA Joint venture with Peter Bright (BRIGHT BROS). Good Chardonnay, Sauvignon Blanc, Merlot, and Cabernet Sauvignon.

Gaivosa, Quinta de Douro r ★ 95 97 99 00 Important estate near Regua. Deep, concentrated, cask-aged reds from port grapes. 2nd wine: QUINTA do Vale da Raposa (DYA) is lighter, fruity red. 3rd wine: Quinta da Estação (DYA).

Garrafeira Label term: merchant's "private reserve", aged for minimum of 2 yrs in cask and one in bottle, often much longer. Usually their best, though traditionally often of indeterminate origin. Now has to show origin on label.

Gatão VV w ★ DYA Standard BORGES & IRMÃO VINHO V; fragrant but sweetened.

Gazela VV w ★★ DYA Reliable VINHO VERDE made at Barcelos by SOGRAPE.

Generoso Apéritif or dessert wine rich in alcohol.

Grão Vasco Dão r w ★★ DYA One of the best and largest brands of DÃO, from a new high-tech ADEGA at Viseu. Fine red GARRAFEIRA; fresh, young white. Owned by SOGRAPE.

IPR Indicação de Proveniência Regulamentada.

José de Sousa Alen r res ★★→★★★★ 99 00 Small firm acquired by J M DA FONSECA. The most sophisticated of the full-bodied wines from ALENTEJO (solid, foot-trodden GARRAFEIRAS (**93 94 97 98**), although now slightly lighter in style), fermented in earthenware amphoras and aged in oak.

J P Vinhos Set r w sp res ★→★★★ An enterprising and well-equipped winery producing a wide range of well made reds including inexpensive JP, Serras de Azeito, QUINTA DA BACALHOA, TINTO DA ANFORA, So (Varietal Syrah) and JP Garrafeira. Also Cova da Ursa Chardonnay and SETUBEL dessert wine. Lorridos sparkling wine comes from ESTREMADURA.

Portuguese wines to look out for in 2004

Douro reds Redoma and Batuta from Niepoort, Quinta Vale do Meao, Vinha do Ponte and Maria Theresa from Quinta do Crasto, Chryseia from Prats/Symington
Alentejo reds Especially wines made from Trincadeira, Quinta do Mouro
Dão Single quinta esp. Carvalhas, Roques & Saes. Duque de Viseu (value)
Indigenous Varietals Touriga Nacional, Tinta Roriz/Aragonez, Trincadeira.
Syrah from Alentejo and Terras do Sado

Lancers Est p w sp ★ Sweet, carbonated rosé and sparkling white extensively shipped to the US by J M DA FONSECA. Also Lancers Espumante (sparkling).

Lagoalva, Quinta da r w ★★ 98 99 00 01 Important RIBATEJO property making good reds from local grapes and Syrah. Second label: Monte da Casta. Also good Chardonnay.

Loureiro Best VINHO VERDE grape variety after ALVARINHO: crisp, fragrant whites.

Madeira br dr sw ★★→★★★★ Portugal's Atlantic island making famous fortified dessert and apéritif wines. See pages 176-183.

Maduro (vinho) A mature table wine – as opposed to a VINHO VERDE.

Maias, Quinta das Dão ★★ r 99 00 01 W DYA New-wave QUINTA: reds to age.

Mateus Rosé Bair p (w) ★ World's biggest-selling, medium-dry, carbonated rosé, from SOGRAPE. Now made at Anadia in BAIRRADA.

Messias r w ★→★★ Large BAIRRADA-based firm; interests in DOURO (incl port). Old-school reds best.

Minho River between N Portugal and Spain – lends its name to a VINHO REGIONAL.

Monção N subregion of VINHO VERDE on River Minho: best wines from the ALVARINHO grape. See Palácio de Brejoeira.

Monte d'Oiro, Quinta do Estremadura r ★★★ 99 00 Estate owned by rich industrialist determined to make fine Syrah. Seems to be succeeding.

Morgadio de Torre VV w ★★ DYA Top VV from SOGRAPE. Largely ALVARINHO.

Mouchão, Herdade de Alen r res ★★★ 90 91 92 94 95 96 98 Perhaps top ALENTEJO estate, ruined in 1974 revolution; since replanted and fully recovered. Good, powerful second wine under the Dom Rafael label.

Mouro, Quinta do Alen r ★★★★ 98 99 00 Fabulous old-style reds, particularly the extracted oaky Cabernet. From near Estremoz.

Niepoort Douro r w ★★★→★★★★ Family port shipper making even better Douro wines. Redoma (r w p) 99 00; Batuta (r) 00; Charme (r) 00. Rs age very well.

Palmela ★→★★★ Terras do Sado r w Sandy soil IPR. Reds can be long-lived. Now a promising DOC incorporating the limestone hills of the Serra d'Arrabida and the sandy plains around the eponymous town. Reds from PERIQUITA can be long-lived. See PEGOS CLAROS. Very sucessful Cooperativa de Pegoes (best wine: Colheita Seleccionada).

Pancas, Quinta das Est r w res ★★ 97 98 99 00 w DYA Go-ahead estate nr ALENQUER. Dense Cab, balanced, oaked Chard. Outstanding TOURIGA NACIONAL Reserva (**95**) and vg dry white ARINTO: QUINTA de Dom Carlos.

Pato, Luís Bair r sp ★★→★★★ 95' 96 97 99 00 Top estate of BAIRRADA. Tannic reds incl tremendous QUINTA DE RIBEIRINHO and João Pato. 95 reds notable esp Quinta do Ribeirinho Pé Franco. Vinha Formal is Pato's fresh aromatic dry white. Although still technically within the Bairrada DOC, Pato has declassified all his wines to VINHO REGIONAL BEIRAS after disagreeing with the authorities. Also classic-method sparkling.

Pegos Claros r 95 96 98 99 00 Solid, traditionally made red from PALMELA area. Proof at last that PERIQUITA can make substantial wine.

Periquita The nickname for the CASTELÃO grape. Periquita is also a brand name for a successful red wine from JOSÉ MARIA DE FONSECA (DYA). Robust, old-style red bottled under Periquita Classico label (92 94 95).

Pires, João w DYA Fragrant, off-dry, Muscat-based wine from J P VINHOS.

Planalto Douro w ★★ DYA Good white wine from SOGRAPE.

Ponte de Lima, Cooperativa de VV r w ★ Maker of one of the best bone-dry red VINHOS VERDES, and first-rate dry and fruity white.

Porta dos Cavalheiros Dão ★★→★★★ 97 98 Traditional style red and white DÃO. The Reservas (with a cork label) can be exceptional (85 95 96).

Portalegre Alen r w ★→★★★ DOC on Spanish border. Strong, fragrant reds with potential to age. Alcoholic whites. Best red wine JOSÉ MARIA DA FONSECA'S full flavoured d'Avillez. Promising wines from local co-op.

Quinta Estate.

Ramos, João Portugal Alen r w DYA Vila Santa (99 00 01) and Marqués de Borba. Reservas of the latter fetch a high price.

Raposeira Douro w sp ★★ Well-known fizz made by the classic method at Lamego. Ask for the Bruto.

Real Companhia Vinícola ★★→★★★ Giant of the port trade (see page 181); also produces increasingly good range of DOURO wines: EVEL, QUINTA dos Aciprestes, Quinta de Cidro.

Redoma ★★★ r 98 99 00 w DYA Particularly good DOURO red and white from port shipper NIEPOORT. Red will age well. Also delicious rosé. See NIEPOORT.

Redondo Alen r w ★ DOC in heart of ALENTEJO with well-managed co-op. Roque Vale: leading estate.

Reguengos Alen r (w) res ★→★★★ Important DOC nr Spanish border. Incl JOSÉ DE SOUSA and ESPORÃO estates, plus large co-op for good reds.

Ribatejo r w The second-largest wine-producing region in Portugal now promoted to DOC with a number of sub-regions entitled to village appellations: ALMEIRIM, CARTAXO, CORUCHE, Chamusca, Tomar, Santarem. Midweight reds include a number made from international grapes: Cab S, Pinot N, Chard, and Sauv Bl. Also VINHO REGIONAL Ribatejano.

Ribeirinho, Quinta do See Luis Pato.

Roques, Quinta dos Dão r ★ 96 97 98 99 00 w DYA Promising estate for big, solid, oaked reds. Good varietal wines from TOURIGA NATIONAL, TINTA RORIZ, Tinta Cão, and Alfrocheiro Preto.

Roriz, Quinta de Douro r ★★★ 98 99 00 One of the great QUINTAS of the Douro, now making fine reds (and vintage port) with the Symingtons (DOW'S port etc).

Rosa, Quinta de la Douro r ★★ 98 99 00 01 Firm, oak-aged red from port v'yds. Reserva is especially worthwhile. Amarela: lighter 2nd wine.

Rosado Rosé.

Saes, Quinta de Dão r w ★★★ 97 98 99 00 01 Sml mountain v'yard making refined wines. QUINTA de Pellada also making gd wines under same ownership.

Saima, Casa de Bair r (w DYA) ★★★ 97 98 99 00 Small trad estate; big, longlasting, tannic reds (esp GARRAFEIRAS 91 95' 97') & some astounding whites.

Santar, Casa de Dão r ★★★ 98 99 00 Well-established estate now making welcome comeback. Reds much better than old-fashioned whites.

São Domingos, Comp dos Vinhos de Est r w ★ DYA Reds (Espiga, Palha-Canas), from estate managed by José Neiva.

São João, Caves Bair ★★→★★★ r 97 98 Res 95 w DYA Sm, traditional firm making top-class wines the old-fashioned way. Reds can age for decades. BAIRRADA: Frei João; DAO: Porta dos Cavaleiros. Poço do Lobo: well-structured Cab S.

Seco Dry.

Serradayres ★ DYA Everyday red and enjoying something of a comeback having been taken over by CAVES DOM TEODOSIO.

Setúbal Set br (r w) sw (dr) ★★★ Tiny demarcated region South of the River Tagus. Dessert wines made predominantly from the Moscatel (Muscat) grape. Two main producers: JOSE DA FONSECA and JP VINHOS.

Sezim, Casa de VV w ★★ DYA Beautiful estate making very good VINHO VERDES.

Silva, Antonio Bernardino Paulo da Colares r (w) res ★★ 89 90 92 His COLARES Chitas is one of the very few of these classics still made.

Sogrape ★→★★★★ Largest wine concern in the country, making VINHOS VERDES, DAO, BAIRRADA, ALENTEJO, MATEUS ROSE, and now owners of FERREIRA, SANDEMAN port, and OFFLEY port. See also BARCA VELHA.

Tamariz, Quinta do VV w ★ Fragrant VINHO VERDE from LOUREIRO grapes only.

Teodosio, Caves Dom r w Lge producer in the RIBATEJO now making a welcome comeback. Everyday wines under the SERRADAYRES label but delicious red from QUINTA de Almargem made from TRINCADEIRA grape.

Terras Altas Dão r w res ★ DYA Brand of r and w DÃO from JOSÉ MARIA DA FONSECA.

Terras do Sado VINHO REGIONAL covering sandy plains around Sado Estuary.

Tinta Roriz A major port grape (alias Tempranillo) making good DOURO table wines. It is increasingly planted for similarly full reds. AKA ARAGONEZ in ALENTEJO.

Tinto Red.

Tinto da Anfora Alen r ★★ 98 99 00 New heavyweight red: Tinto da Anfora Grande Escolha 99. Lighter wines: Montes das Anforas.

Torres Vedras ★ Est r w DOC N of Lisbon famous for Wellington's "lines". Major supplier of bulk wine; one of biggest co-ops in Portugal.

Touriga Nacional Top red grape used for port and DOURO table wines; now increasingly elsewhere, esp DÃO, ALENTEJO, ESTREMADURA.

Trás-os-Montes VINHO REGIONAL covering mountains of NE Portugal. Reds and whites from international grape varieties grown in the DOURO. Also IPRS: Chaves, Mirandes, Valpaços.

Trincadeira Vg red grape in ALENTEJO for spicy, single-varietal wines.

Tuella r w ★★ DYA Good-value DOURO red from COCKBURN.

Vale Meão, Quinta do Douro r ★★★★ 99 00 Once the source of the legendary BARCA VELHA, now making great wine in its own right.

Vallado ★★ r 98 99 00 (Reserva) 01 w DYA Family-owned DOURO estate; very good wines.

Van Zeller Cristiano Van Z (formerly owner of QUINTA DO NOVAL) is making excellent port under a new label, Vale da Miña, and Domini red with FONSECA.

Verde Green (see VINHOS VERDES).

Vidigueira Alen w r ★→★★ DOC for traditionally-made unmatured whites from volcanic soils and some plummy reds.

Vinho Regional Larger provincial wine region, with same status as French Vin de Pays: they are: ALGARVE, ALENTEJO, BEIRAS, ESTREMADURA, RIBATEJANO, MINHO, TRÁS-OS-MONTES, TERRAS DO SADO. See also DOC, IPR.

Vinhos Verdes VV w ★→★★★ r ★ DOC between R DOURO and N frontier, for "green wines" (white or red): made from grapes with high acidity and (originally) undergoing a secondary fermentation to leave them slightly sparkling. Today the fizz is usually just added CO_2. Ready for drinking in spring after harvest.

PORTUGAL

Sherry, Port, & Madeira

Sherry, port, and Madeira are the three classic fortified wines of Spain and Portugal – and the world. They are reinforced with alcohol up to 15.5% (for fino) and 22% (for vintage port).

Sherry is the most famous of Spanish fortified wines, and since 1996 its name has been legally recognized as belonging to Spain alone. Like other fortified wines, sherry has suffered a decline in popularity over recent years, but remains an excellent preliminary to a meal and of all thoroughbred wines is certainly the best value. And more people are now discovering sherry with food.

The port trade underwent a major restructuring in 2001 leaving three major players (Symingtons, Fladgate Partnership, and Sogrape) with ownership of most of the big names. The millennium saw the third small vintage in a row for port. Both 1998 and 1999 produced some good single-quinta wines and 2000 was declared a Vintage across the board; 2001 will produce some good single quinta wines.

In Madeira the relatively new *Colheita* or "harvest" wines are now starting to emerge onto the market. Bottled after 6 years in wood (as opposed to the minimum 20 years for "vintage" Madeira) and from a single year, they are intended to be more accessible. Sadly, people used to drinking vintage Madeira will find them pretty simple stuff.

Recent Declared Port Vintages

2000 A very fine vintage, universally declared. Rich, well-balanced wines for the long-term. Drink from 2015.

1997 Fine, potentially long-lasting wines with tannic backbone. Most shippers declared. Drink 2012 onwards.

1994 Outstanding vintage with ripe, fleshy fruit disguising underlying structure at the outset. Universal declaration. Drink 2010-2030.

1992 Favoured by a few (esp Taylor, Fonseca) over 91 . Niepoort declared both. Richer, more conc over 91. 92 could be the better year. Drink from 2008

1991 Favoured by most shippers (esp. Symingtons with Dow, Graham and Warre) over 92; classic, firm but a little lean in style. Drink from 2005.

1987 Dense wines for drinking over the medium-term but only a handful of shippers declared. Drink now – 2015.

1985 Universal declaration which looked good at the outset but has thrown up some disappointments in bottle. Now-2020 for the best wines.

1983 Fine, powerful wines with sinewy tannins. Most shippers declared. Now-2020+ (the best wines need keeping).

1982 Soft, rather simple, early maturing wines declared by a few shippers in preference to 1983. Drink up.

1980 Lovely fruit-driven wines, perfect to drink now and over the next 15 years. Most shippers declared.

1977 Big, ripe wines declared by all the major shippers except Cockburn, Martinez, and Noval. Drinking now, the best still have a long life ahead.

1975 Soft and early maturing. Drink up.

1970 Classic, tight-knit wines – only just reaching their peak. Now-2020+.

1966 Wines combine power & elegance with the best rivalling 1963. Now-2020+.

1963 Classic vintage, one of the best of the 20th century (with prices to match). Some bottle variation. Now; no need to keep them.

Abad, Tomás Small sherry BODEGA owned by LUSTAU. Vg light FINO.

Almacenista Individual matured but unblended sherry; usually dark, dry wines for connoisseurs. Often superb quality and value. See LUSTAU.

Alvear Mont-M g Lgst prod of vg sherry-like apéritif & sw wines in MONTILLA.

Barbadillo, Antonio Much the largest SANLÚCAR firm with a wide range of MANZANILLAS and sherries, including Muy Fina FINA, Solear MANZANILLA PASADA, austere Principe AMONTILLADO, Cuco dry OLOROSO, Eva Cream, and superb but vastly expensive Reliquia PALO CORTADO, OLOROSO SECO and PX. Also young Castillo de San Diego table wines, for some reason.

Barbeito One of the 5 indep't Madeira shipping firms, now Japanese-controlled. Wines incl 1995 Colheita, 1980 Verdelho (most recent), and 1834 Malvasia.

Barros Almeida Large, family-owned port house with several brands (incl Feist, Feuerheerd, KOPKE): excellent 20-yr-old TAWNY and many COLHEITAS.

Barros e Sousa Tiny, family-owned Madeira producer with lodges in centre of Funchal. Extremely fine but now rare vintages, plus gd 10-yr-old wines.

Blandy The top name of the MADEIRA WINE CO. Duke of Clarence Rich Madeira is the most famous wine. 10-yr-old reserves (VERDELHO, BUAL, MALMSEY, SERCIAL) are good. Many glorious old vintages (eg Malmsey 1978, Bual 1920, Sercial 1940, Bual 1958), though mostly nowadays at auctions. New COLHEITAS from 95. New 5-yr-old blend of Bual and Malvasia called "Alvada".

Blázquez DOMECQ-owned sherry BODEGA at PUERTO DE S MARIA. Outstanding FINO, Carta Blanca, v old SOLERA OLOROSO Extra; Carta Oro AMONTILLADO *al natural* (unsweetened).

Bobadilla Large JEREZ BODEGA recently bought by OSBORNE and best known for v dry Victoria FINO and Bobadilla 103 brandy, esp among Spanish connoisseurs.

Borges, H M Family co making full range. Recent vintages: SERCIAL 79 & BOAL 77.

Bual (Sometimes spelt Boal.) One of the best grapes of Madeira, making a soft, smoky, sweet wine, usually lighter and not as rich as MALMSEY. (See panel on page 183.)

Burmester Family port house now owned by cork giant Amorim, with fine, soft, sweet 20-yr-old TAWNY; also vg range of COLHEITAS and single-QUINTA: Quinta Nossa Sra do Carmo. Vintages: **70 77 80** 85 89 91 92 94 95 97 00.

Burdon English-founded sherry BODEGA owned by CABALLERO. Puerto FINO, Don Luis AMONTILLADO, and raisiny Heavenly Cream are top lines.

Sherry Styles

Fino The lightest, finest sherries. Completely dry, v pale, delicate but pungent. Fino should be drunk cool and fresh. Deteriorates rapidly once opened (use ½ bottles if poss). Eg GONZALEZ BYASS' TIO PEPE.

Manzanilla A pale dry wine (not strictly a sherry), often more delicate than a FINO, matured in the cooler maritime conditions of SANLUCAR DE BARRAMEDA (as opposed to JEREZ, which is inland). Eg HIDALGO'S La Gitana.

Amontillado A FINO aged in cask to become darker, more powerful, and pungent. Naturally dry wines. Eg LUSTAU'S ALMACENISTAS.

Oloroso Heavier, less brilliant than FINO when young, but matures to richness and pungency. Naturally dry, often sweetened for sale. Eg DOMECQ'S Rio Viejo.

Palo Cortado A rare style close to OLOROSO with some AMONTILLADO character. Dry but rich and soft – worth looking for. Eg DOMECQ'S Sibarita.

Cream Sherry Sweet style from OLOROSO. Eg HARVEY'S Bristol Cream.

Other styles Manzanilla Pasada – half way between a FINO and AMONTILLADO; Pale Cream – sweetened FINO; Amoroso, Brown Sherry, East India Sherry – variations on CREAM SHERRY.

Age dated Sherries Two new categories – **VOS** (Very Old Sherry more than 20 years) and **VORS** (Very Old Sherry more than 30 years). Also very expensive.

Caballero Important sherry shipper at PUERTO DE STA MARIA. Pavón FINO, Mayoral Cream OLOROSO, excellent BURDON sherries, PONCHE orange liqueur. Also owns LUSTAU.

Cálem Old port house; had fine reputation, but recent vintages not as gd. Vtges: **63 66 70 75 77** 80 83 91 94 97 00 Reliable light TAWNY; gd range of COLHEITAS: Sold in 98, but family still owns Quinta da Foz (**86 87**).

Churchill **82** 85 91 94 97 00 Port shipper founded in 1981 and already highly respected. Bought its own QUINTA in 1999/2000. Vg traditional LBV. Quinta da Agua Alta and Quinta da Gricha are Churchill's single-QUINTA ports: **87** 90 92. VG Aged white port too.

Cockburn British-owned (Allied-DOMECQ) port shipper with a range of gd wines incl v popular, fruity Special Res. Fine VINTAGE PORT from v'yds predominantly in the Douro Superior: sometimes deceptively forward when young but with great lasting power. Vintages: **63** 67 70 75 83 **85** 91 94 97 00. Good single quinta wines from Quinta dos Canais.

Colheita Vintage-dated port of a single yr, but aged at least 7 winters in wood: in effect a vintage TAWNY. The bottling date is also shown on label. Excellent examples from KOPKE, CALEM, NIEPOORT, Krohn, & C DA SILVA (Dalva). Colheita now also applies to a new category of Madeiras from a single year (see introductory paragraphs).

Cossart Gordon One-time leading Madeira shipper, founded 1745, with BLANDY now one of the two top-quality labels of the MADEIRA WINE CO. Wines slightly less rich than Blandy's. Best-known for Good Company Finest Medium Rich. Also 5-yr-old reserves, old vintages (latest 74) and SOLERAS (esp BUAL 1845). Malvasia Colheita 1989, older vintages include 1958 BUAL and 1908 BOAL plus old wines from 19th-century soleras.

Crasto, Quinta do Ports improving, esp LBV. Vtges: **85 87** 91 94 95 97 00.

Croft One of the oldest firms shipping VINTAGE PORT: since 1678; now part of the Fladgate partnership alongside Delaforce. Well-balanced vintage wines tend to mature early (since 66). Vintages: **63' 66 67** 70 **75 77 82 85** 91 94 00. Lighter Quinta da Roeda vintages: (**83 87**). "Distinction": most popular blend. Morgan: sml separate co (also DELAFORCE). Also produces sherry, and brandy popular in Portugal.

Croft Jerez Founded only in 1970 and recently bought by GONZÁLEZ-BYASS. One of the most successful sherry firms. Best-known for the sw Croft Original Pale Cream & drier Croft Particular. Also dry and elegant Delicado FINO and first-rate and moderately priced PALO CORTADO.

Crusted Term for vintage-style port, usually blended from several vintages. Bottled young and then aged so it throws a deposit, or "crust". Needs decanting.

Cruz Market leader among ports in France. (French take 40% of port exports.) Standard French-style TAWNY – not brilliant quality. Owned by La Martiniquaise.

Delaforce Port shipper also part of the Fladgate Partnership, is best-known in Germany. His Eminence's Choice is a v pleasant 10-yr-old TAWNY; VINTAGE CHARACTER is also good. Vintage wines are very fine, among the lighter kind: **55 58 60 63 66** 70' **75 77 82 85** 94 00.

Delgado, Zuleta Old-est'd SANLUCAR firm best-known for marvellous La Goya MANZANILLA PASADA.

Domecq Giant family-run sherry BODEGA at JEREZ, recently merged with Allied-Domecq, famous also for Fundador and other brandies. Double Century Original OLOROSO, its biggest brand, now replaced by Pedro Cream Sherry; La Ina is excellent FINO. Other famous wines incl Celebration Cream, Botaina (old AMONTILLADO) and magnificent Rio Viejo (v dry oloroso) and Capuchino (PALO CORTADO). Recently: a range of wonderful old SOLERA sherries (dry Sibarita oloroso, Amontillado 51-1a, and venerable PX). Also in RIOJA and Mexico.

Don Zoilo Makes luxury sherries, including velvety FINO. Now sold by BODEGAS INTERNACIONALES to the MEDINA group.

Douro The port country river, known in Spain as the Duero. All the best port comes from the spectacular Upper Douro. Port country divides into three, with the best coming from Cima Corgo and Douro Superior, both well upriver. Table wines are now important, too.

Dow Brand name of port house Silva and Cozens, celebrated bicentenary in 98, and belongs to Symington family alongside GRAHAM, WARRE, SMITH WOODHOUSE, GOULD CAMPBELL, QUARLES HARRIS, and QUINTA DO VESUVIO. Style deliberately slightly drier than other shippers in group. Vg range of ports incl single-QUINTA Bomfim (78 79 82 84 86 87 88 89 90 92 95 98) and outstanding v'tges: 63 66 70 **72** 75 77 80 83 85 91 94 97 00'. New v'yd: Quinta da Senhora da Ribeira 98 99.

Duff Gordon Sherry shipper best-known for El Cid AMONTILLADO. Gd FINO Feria; Niña Medium OLOROSO. OSBORNE-owned; name also 2nd label for Osborne's ports.

Ferreira One of the biggest Portuguese-owned port growers and shippers (since 1751). Largest-selling brand in P. Well-known for old TAWNIES and juicily sweet, relatively light vintages: **63 66 70 75 77 78 80 82** 85 87 91 94 95 9700. Also Doña Antónia Personal Reserve, splendidly rich tawny Duque de Bragança and occasional single-QUINTA wines from Quinta do Seixo.

Flor A floating yeast peculiar to FINO sherry and certain other wines that age slowly and tastily under its influence.

Fonseca Guimaraens British-owned port shipper with a stellar reputation; connected with TAYLOR'S. Robust, deeply coloured vintage wine, among the v best. Vintages: Fonseca 63' 66' 70 **75** 77 **80 83 85** 92 94' 97 00'; Fonseca Guimaraens 76' **78 82 84** 86 87 88 91 94 95 98. Quinta do Panascal is a single-QUINTA wine. Also delicious VINTAGE CHARACTER Bin 27.

Forrester Port shipper and owner of the famous QUINTA da Boa Vista, now owned by SOGRAPE. The vintage wines tend to be round, fat, and sweet, good for relatively early drinking. Baron de Forrester is vg TAWNY. Vintages: (Offley Forrester) **63 66 67 70 72 75** 77 **80 82** 83 85 87 89 94 95 97 00'.

Garvey Famous old sherry shipper at JEREZ, now owned by José María Ruiz Mateos. The finest wines are deep-flavoured FINO San Patricio, Tio Guillermo Dry AMONTILLADO, and Ochavico Dry OLOROSO. San Angelo Medium amontillado is the most popular. Also Bicentenary PALE CREAM.

González-Byass Enormous family-run sherry firm with most famous and one of v best FINO: TIO PEPE. Brands incl La Concha med AMONTILLADO, Elegante dry fino, new El Rocío MANZANILLA Fina, San Domingo Pale Cream, Nectar Cream, Alfonso sw OLOROSO. Amontillado del Duque, Matúsalem OLOROSO & Apóstoles PALO CORTADO on higher plane. Magnificent Millennium is choicest old olorosos. Also top-selling Soberano & exquisite Lepanto brandies.

Gould Campbell Port shipper belonging to the Symington family. Good-value vintage ports **70** 77 80 83 85 91 94 97 00.

Graham 63' 70 Port shipper famous for some of the richest, sweetest, and best of vintage ports, largely from its own Quinta dos Malvedos (76 78 79 80 82 84 86 87 88 94' 00'). Also excellent brands, incl Six Grapes RUBY, LBV, and 10- and 20-yr-old TAWNIES. Vintages: 63 66 70 **75** 77 80 83 85 91 94 97.

Gracia Hermanos Mont-M Firm within the same group as PEREZ BARQUERO and Compañía Vinícola del Sur making gd-quality MONTILLAS. Its labels incl María del Valle FINO, Montearruit AMONTILLADO, OLOROSO CREAM, and Dulce Viejo PX.

Guita, La Famous old SANLÚCAR BODEGA noted for particularly fine MANZANILLA PASADA.

Hartley & Gibson See Valdespino.

Harvey's Important sherry pillar of the Allied-DOMECQ empire, along with TERRY. World-famous Bristol shippers of Bristol Cream (sweet), Club AMONTILLADO and Bristol Dry (medium), Luncheon Dry and Bristol FINO (not v dry).

Henriques & Henriques Independent Madeira shipper, with wide range of well-structured, rich wines – 10-yr-olds are medal-winners. Outstanding 15-yr-old wines. Good, extra-dry apéritif Monte Seco, and v fine old reserves & vtges incl 1944 Sercial, 1934 Verdelho, 1957 BUAL and malmseys from 1954 1934 and 1900. The joke goes: "There are only 2 names in Madeira ..."

Henriques, Justino The largest Madeira shippers in bulk terms with a modern lodge outside Funchal. Good 10-yr-old and Vintage, eg. 1934 Verdelho.

Hidalgo, Vinícola Old family sherry firm in SANLUCAR DE BARRAMEDA Excellent pale MANZANILLA La Gitana, fine OLOROSO Seco, lovely soft, deep Jerez Cortado & 1st-rate new Pastrana MANZANILLA PASADA.

Jerez de la Frontera Centre of sherry industry, between Cádiz & Seville. "Sherry" is a corruption of the name, pronounced in Spanish "hereth". In French, Xérès.

Jordões, Casal dos One of few certified organic port producers – decent LBV.

Kopke The oldest port house, founded by a German in 1638. Now belongs to BARROS ALMEIDA. Fair-quality VINTAGE wines, but some excellent (70 **74 75 77 78 79 80 82** 83 85 87 89 91 94 97 00) and excellent COLHEITAS.

Krohn Small family-owned port shipper with an excellent range of COLHEITAS, some dating back to the 19th century.

Late-bottled vintage (LBV) Port from a single vintage kept in wood for twice as long as VINTAGE PORT (about 5 years), therefore lighter when bottled and ages more quickly. Don't expect miracles. "Traditional" (unfiltered) LBV now has to spend an extra 3 yrs in bottle to qualify (WARRE, SMITH WOODHOUSE, NIEPOORT, CHURCHILL, FERREIRA, NOVAL).

Leacock One of the oldest Madeira shippers, now a label of the MADEIRA WINE COMPANY. Basic St-John range is very fair; 10-year-old Special Reserve MALMSEY and 15-year-old BUAL are excellent. Older vintages also available: Bual 34, Verdelho 54.

Lustau One of the largest family-run sherry BODEGAS in JEREZ (now controlled by CABALLERO), making many wines for other shippers, but with a vg Dry Lustau range (esp FINO and OLOROSO) and Jerez Lustau PALO CORTADO. Pioneer shipper of excellent ALMACENISTA and "landed age" wines; AMONTILLADOS and olorosos aged in elegant bottles before shipping. See also Abad.

Madeira Wine Company Formed in 1913 by two firms as the Madeira Wine Association, subsequently to include all the British Madeira firms (26 in total) amalgamated to survive hard times. Remarkably, three generations later, the wines, though cellared together, preserve their house styles. BLANDY and COSSART GORDON are top labels. Now controlled by the Symington group (see Dow).

Malmsey The sweetest and richest form of Madeira; dark amber, rich, and honeyed yet with Madeira's unique sharp tang. Word is English corruption of "Malvasia" (or the Greek "Monemvasia") qv. See box on page 183.

Martinez Gassiot Port firm, subsidiary of COCKBURN, known esp for excellent rich, and pungent Directors 20-yr-old TAWNY, CRUSTED, and LBV. Vintages: **63 67 70 75 82** 85 87 91 94 97 00. Also VG single quinta wines from Quinta da Eira Velha.

Marqués del Real Tesoro Old firm with a spanking new BODEGA – the first in years. Recently acquired the historic firm of VALDESPINO. Tío Mateo is a very good FINO (now histamine-free!).

Miles Formerly Rutherford & Miles. Madeira shipper: Old Trinity House Medium Rich, etc. Latest vintage 78 Malvasia. Now a MADEIRA WINE CO label.

Medina, José Originally a SANLUCAR BODEGA, now a major exporter, especially to the Low Countries. Now owns Bodegas Internacionales and WILLIAMS & HUMBERT, also Pérez Megia and Luis Paez: probably the biggest sherry grower and shipper, with some 25% of total volume.

Port & Madeira to look out for in 2004

White Port Churchill

Good value Single Quinta Ports Dow's Quinta do Bomfim 87 and 95, Taylor's Quinta de Vargellas 88, Martinez Quinta da Eira Velha 92, Quinta da Cavadinha 95.

Outstanding Vintage Ports Fonseca 63, Taylor 63, Dow 66, Fonseca 66, Graham 70, W Smith Woodhouse 77, Graham 80

Five Year-Old Madeira Blandy's Alvada

Other Ports Warre's Bottle Matured 94 LBV, Dow's Crusted (bottled 99)

Vintage Madeiras Leacock 78 Malvasia, Pereira d'Oliveira Verdelho 66, Cossart Gordon Bual 58, Justino Henriques Verdelho 34, Justino Henriques Malmsey 33, Pereira d'Oliveira Bual 22.

Montecristo Mont-M Brand of big-selling MONTILLAS by Compañía Vinícola del Sur.

Montilla-Moriles Mont-M DO nr Córdoba. Not sherry, but close. Its soft FINO and AMONTILLADO and luscious PX contain 14–17.5% natural alcohol and remain unfortified. At best, singularly toothsome apéritifs.

Niepoort Sml (Dutch) family-run port house with long record of fine VTGES (**63 66 70' 75 77 78 80 82** 83 87 91 92 94 97 00') & exceptional COLHEITAS. Also produces excellent single-QUINTA port, Quinta do Passadouro (91).

Noval, Quinta do Historic port house now French (AXA) owned. Intensely fruity, structured, and elegant VINTAGE PORT; a few ungrafted vines at the QUINTA make small quantity of Nacional – extraordinarily dark, full, velvety, slow-maturing. Vg 20-yr-old TAWNY. V'tges: **63 66 67 70 75 78 82 85** 87 91 94 95 97' 00'. 2nd label: Silval Also "traditional" (unfiltered) LBV.

Offley Forrester See Forrester.

Osborne Huge Spanish firm producing sherry and quality port, incl FINO QUINTA, Coquinero dr AMONTILLADO, 10 RF (or Res Familiar) med OLOROSO. DUFF GORDON used as 2nd label for Osborne ports. Declared gd VINTAGE PORTS in 95, 97 00'. NB: range of v fine "Rare" sherries, top-quality numbered bottles.

Paternina, Federico Marcos Eguizabel from RIOJA acquired the sherry firm Diez-Merito, retaining three wines to be marketed under his Paternina label. FINO Imperial, Olorose, Victoria Regina, and Pedro Ximénez Vieja Solera.

Pereira d'Oliveira Vinhos Family-owned Madeira Co est'd 1850. Very good basic range as well as 5-& 10-year-olds; fine old reserve VERDELHO 1890, BUAL 1908, Malvasia 1895. 1987 Colheita Malvasia. Vintages: 1973 Verdelho, 1968 BOAL, 1922BOAL, 1900 Moscatel.

Pérez Barquero Mont-M. Another firm like GRACIA HERMANOS once part of Rumasa. Its excellent MONTILLAS incl Gran Barquero FINO, AMONTILLADO, and OLOROSO.

Poças Improving family port firm specializing in TAWNIES and COLHEITAS. Good LBV and Vintage (97 00'). Single quinta wines from QuintaSta Barbera.

Ponche An aromatic digestif made with old sherry and brandy, flavoured with herbs and presented in eye-catching silvered bottles. See CABALLERO, de SOTO.

Puerto de Santa María 2nd city & former port of sherry, with important BODEGAS.

PX Short for Pedro Ximénez, grape part sun-dried: used in JEREZ for sweetening wines.

Quarles Harris One of the oldest port houses, since 1680, now owned by the Symingtons (see Dow). Small quantities of LBV, mellow, and well-balanced. Vintages: **63 66** 70 **75** 77 80 **83** 85 91 94 97 00'.

Quinta Portuguese for "estate". Also traditionally used to denote VINTAGE PORTS which are usually (legislation says 100%) from estate's vineyards, made in good but not exceptional vintages. Now several excellent quintas produce wines from top vintages in their own right, especially VESUVIO, LA ROSA, Passadouro (see Niepoort).

SHERRY, PORT, & MADEIRA

Rainwater A fairly light, medium-dry blend of Madeira – traditional in US.

Ramos-Pinto Dynamic, small port house specializing in single-QUINTA TAWNIES of style, elegance. Vintages on sweeter side. Some, like 60 and 83, have developed well. Owned by Champagne house Louis Roederer.

Real Companhia Vinícola do Norte de Portugal Aka Royal Oporto Wine Co & Real Companhia Velha; large port house, with long political history. Many brands and several QUINTAS, including Quinta dos Carvalhas for TAWNIES and COLHEITAS. VINTAGE PORTS have been dismal, but 97 looks more promising. Some aged tawnies are good.

Rebello Valente See Robertson.

Régua Main town in Douro Valley, centre for port producers and growers.

Rosa, Quinta de la Fine single-QUINTA port from the Bergqvist family at PINHÃO. Recent return to traditional methods and stone *lagares*. Look for 85 88 90 91 92 94 95 96 97 98 00 vintages.

Royal Oporto See Real Companhia Vinícola do Norte de Portugal.

Rozès Port shipper owned by Champagne house Vranken. RUBY v popular in France; also TAWNY. Vintages: 63 66 67 77 83 85 87 91 94' 95 97 00.

Ruby Youngest (and cheapest) port style: simple, sweet, and red. The best are vigorous, full of flavour; others can be merely strong and rather thin.

Sanchez Romate Family firm in JEREZ since 1781. Best-known in Spanish-speaking world, esp for brandy Cardenal Mendoza. Good sherry: OLOROSO La Sacristía de Romate, PX Duquesa, AMONTILLADO NPU ("Non Plus Ultra").

Sandeman Large firm founded by Scot George Sandeman who set up twin establishments in Oporto and Jerez. Scrupulously-made sherries include Medium AMONTILLADO, Don FINO, and Armada CREAM. Also rare and exceptional Royal Esmerelda PALO CORTADO and dry and sweet Imperial Corregidor and Royal Ambrosante OLOROSOS. Founder's Reserve is its well-known VINTAGE CHARACTER; TAWNIES are much better. VINTAGE has been very patchy in recent years (**63 66 70 75 77 80 82 85** 94 97 00) Second label: Vau Vintage.

Sanlúcar de Barrameda Historic seaside sherry town (see MANZANILLA).

Santa Eufemia, Quinta de Family port estate with very good old tawnies.

Sercial Madeira grape for the driest of the island's wines – supreme apéritif (see panel above).

Silva, C da Port shipper owned by Ruiz Mateos of GARVEY fame. Mostly inexpensive RUBIES & TAWNIES, but good aged tawnies and outstanding COLHEITAS under Dalva label.

Smith Woodhouse Port firm founded 1784, now owned by Symingtons (see Dow). GOULD CAMPBELL is a subsidiary. Relatively light, easy wines including Old Lodge TAWNY, Lodge Res VINTAGE CHARACTER (widely sold in US). Vintages (very fine): **63 66** 70 **75** 77' 80 83 85 91 94 97 00'. Single-quinta wine: Madalena for secondary vintages.

Solera System used in making sherry. Consists of topping up progressively more mature barrels with slightly younger wine of same sort, the object being to attain continuity in final wine. Most sherries are blends of several solera wines. Used to be applied to Madeiras. Although no longer used there are many very fine old solera wines in bottle.

Soto, José de Best-known for inventing PONCHE, this family firm, which now belongs to the former owner of Rumasa, José María Ruiz Mateos, also makes a range of gd sherries, esp delicate FINO and a fuller-bodied MANZANILLA.

Tawny Style of port aged for many yrs in wood (VINTAGE PORT is aged in bottle) until tawny in colour. Many of the best are 20 yrs old. Low-price tawnies are blends of red and white ports. Taste the difference.

Taylor, Fladgate & Yeatman (Taylor's) Often considered the best of the port shippers, especially for full, rich, long-lived VINTAGE wine and TAWNIES of

Since 1993, Madeiras labelled Sercial, Verdelho, Bual, or Malmsey must be at least 85% from that grape variety. The majority, made using the chameleon Tinta Negra Mole grape, which purports to imitates each of these grape styles, may only be called Seco (Dry), Meio Seco (Medium Dry), Meio Doce (Medium Rich), or Doce (Rich) respectively. Meanwhile, replantá is building up supplies of the (rare) classic varieties.

stated age (40-year-old, 20-year-old, etc). Its Vargellas estate is said to give Taylor's distinctive scent of violets. Vintages: 63 66 70 **75** 77 80 83 85 92 94 97 00'. Quinta de Vargellas is shipped unblended in lesser years (**67 72 74 76 78 82 84 86 87 88** 91 95 98). Also now Terra Feita single-quinta wine (**82 86 87 88 91** 95 96).

Terry, SA Magnificent sherry BODEGA at PUERTO DE SANTA M, part of Allied-Domecq. Makers of Maruja MANZANILLA & range of popular brandies. Blending & bottling of all HARVEY's sherries at the vast modern El Pino plant.

Tío Pepe The most famous of FINO sherries (see González-Byass).

Toro Albalá, Bodegas Mont-M Family firm located in 20s power station & aptly making Eléctrico FINOS, AMONTILLADOS & a PX among the best in MONTILLA & Spain.

Valdespino Famous family BODEGA at JEREZ, recently taken over by José Ertévez of MARQUÉS DEL REAL TESORO. Owner of Inocente v'yd & making excellent aged FINO of that name. Tío Diego is its dry AMONTILLADO, Solera 1842 an OLOROSO, Don Tomás its best AMONTILLADO. Matador is the name of Valdespino's popular range. In US, its sherries rank second in sales volume & are still sold as "Hartley & Gibson".

Vale D Maria, Quinta do Estate in the Torto valley – good value vintage port.

Verdelho Madeira grape for medium-dry wines, pungent but without the searing austerity of SERCIAL (see panel above). Pleasant apéritif and good, all-purpose Madeira. Some glorious old VINTAGE wines.

Vesúvio, Quinta de Enormous 19th-C FERREIRA estate in the high DOURO. Owned by Symingtons. 130 acres planted. Esp **89 90 91 92** 94 95 97 98 99 00'.

Vila Nova de Gaia City on the south side of the River Douro from Oporto where the major port shippers mature their wines in "lodges".

Vintage Character Somewhat misleading term used for a gd-quality, full, and meaty port like a premium RUBY. Lacks the splendid "nose" of VINTAGE PORT.

Vintage Port The best port of exceptional vintages is bottled after only 2 yrs in wood and matures very slowly for up to 20 or more in bottle. Always leaves a heavy deposit and therefore needs decanting.

Warre Oldest of British port shippers (since 1670), owned by the Symington family (see DOW) since 1905. Fine, elegant, long-maturing vintage wines, good TAWNY, VINTAGE CHARACTER (Warrior), excellent LBV; 10 year old Otima has been huge sucess. Single-v'yard QUINTA da Cavadinha (**78 79 82 84 86 87 88 89 90** 92 95 98). Vintages: 63 66 70' **75** 77' 80 83 85 91 94 97 00'.

White Port Port made of white grapes, golden in colour. Formerly made sweet, now more often dry: NIEPOORT, CHURCHILL, BARROS. Often drunk with tonic water. Recommended wines are those with age. Choose equally well-aged tonic, or (preferably) drink them both straight.

Williams & Humbert Famous 1st-class sherry BODEGA, now owned by MEDINA group. a Dry Sack (med AMONTILLADO) is best-seller; Pando is an excellent FINO; Canasta CREAM & Walnut Brown are gd in their class; Dos Cortados is its famous dry, old PALO CORTADO. Also the famous Gran Duque de Alba brandy acquired from DIEZ-MERITO.

Wisdom & Warter Not a magic formula for free wine, but old BODEGA (controlled by GONZÁLEZ-B) with good sherries, esp AMONTILLADO Tizón & v rare SOLERA. Also FINO Olivar.

SHERRY, PORT, & MADEIRA

Switzerland

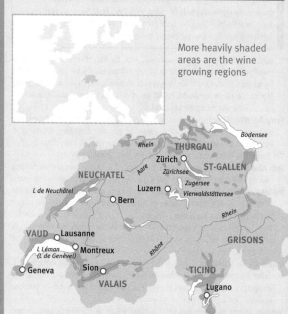

More heavily shaded areas are the wine growing regions

Rhein — Bodensee
THURGAU
Zürich
ST-GALLEN
NEUCHÂTEL
Aare — Zürichsee
Zugersee
L de Neuchâtel — Luzern — Vierwaldstättersee
Bern
Rhein
VAUD — Lausanne
L Léman (L de Genève) — Montreux
GRISONS
Rhône
Geneva — Sion
TICINO
VALAIS
Lugano

The high price of living, combined with cost-intensive wine production, means that Switzerland's wines find it difficult to compete on the world market and, in any case, are rarely seen outside the domestic arena. Those areas producing international style wines are Ticino (Merlot), Valais (Pinot Noir, Amigne, Arvigne), and Bündner Herrschaft (Pinot Noir). The most important vineyards (28,550 out of 37,280 a) are in French-speaking areas: along the south-facing slopes of the upper Rhône Valley (Valais) and Lake Geneva (Vaud). Wines from German-and Italian-speaking zones are treasured and mostly drunk locally. Wines are known by place, grape names, and legally controlled type names and tend to be drunk young. The Swiss cantonal and federal appellation system, set up in 1988, still governs wine production.

Aargau 00 01 02 Wine-growing canton in E Switz (976 a). Best for fragrant Müller-Thurgau and rich BLAUBURGUNDER.

Aigle Vaud r w ★★→★★★★ Well-known for elegant whites and supple reds.

Amigne Trad VALAIS white grape, esp of VETROZ. Full-bodied, tasty, often sweet. Best producer: André Fontannaz ★★ 00 01 02.

Ardon Valais r w ★★→★★★ Wine commune between SION and MARTIGNY.

Arvine Old VALAIS white grape (also "Petite Arvine"): dry and sweet, elegant, long-lasting wines with a salty finish. Best in SIERRE, SION, Granges, FULLY. Best producers: Benoît Dorsaz, René Faure et Fils ★★ **99** 00 01 02.

Auvernier NE r p w ★★→★★★ Old wine village on Lake NEUCHÂTEL and biggest wine-growing commune of the canton.

Basel Second-largest Swiss town and canton with many vines: divided into Basel-Stadt and Baselland. Best wines: Müller-Thurgau, BLAUBURGUNDER.

Beerliwein Originally wine of destemmed BLAUBURG'R (E). Today name for wine fermented on skins traditionally rather than SÜSSDRUCK. Drink young.

Bern Swiss capital and canton of same name. Vineyards in West (BIELERSEE: CHASSELAS, PINOT NOIR, white SPÉCIALITÉS) and East (Thunersee: BLAUBURGUNDER, Müller-Thurgau); 648 a. Prized by Germanic Swiss.

Recent vintages

2002 Not the best year for everybody. Stick to the best producers.

2001 Low yields but characteristic, full-bodied wines with ageing potential.

2000 4th good vintage in a row. One of the best for years for reds.

1999 Despite difficult weather, quality was vg, with remarkable fruit and colour (red wines). White have gd acidity.

1998 High-quality wines. Drink both reds and whites now.

Bielersee r p w ★→★★ 99 00 01 02 Wine region on N shore of the Bielersee (dry light CHASSELAS, PINOT N) and at the foot of Jolimont (SPÉCIALITÉS).

Blauburgunder German-Swiss name for PINOT N. (Aka Clevner.)

Bündner Herrschaft Grisons r p w ★★→★★★ Best German-Swiss region incl top villages: Fläsch, Jenins, Maienfeld, Malans. Serious BLAUB'R ripens esp well due to warm Föhn wind, cask-aged vg. Also CHARD, Müller-T, SPÉCIALITÉS. Best producers: Gantenbein ★★★ Davaz ★★, Fromm ★★★ 98 99 00 01 02.

Calamin Vaud w ★★→★★★ LAVAUX v'yds next to DEZALEY: lush, fragrant whites.

Chablais Vaud r w ★★→★★★ 99 01 02 Sunny wine region on right bank of Rhône and upper end of L GENEVA, incl VILLAGES: AIGLE, Bex, Ollon, VILLENEUVE, YVORNE. Robust, full-bodied reds and whites.

Chamoson Valais r w ★★→★★★ Largest VALAIS wine commune, esp for SYLVANER.

Chasselas (Gutedel) French cantons, top w grape: neutral flavour, takes on local character: elegant (GENEVA), refined, full (VAUD), exotic, racy (VALAIS), pétillant (lakes Bienne, NEUCHATEL, Murtensee). Only east of BASEL. Called FENDANT in VALAIS. 37% of Swiss wines are Chasselas.

Completer Native w grape, mostly used in GRISONS making aromatic, generous wines that keep well. Increasing experimentation. ("Complet" was a monk's final daily prayer, or "nightcap".) Best: Adolf Boner, Malans ★★ 99 00 **01.**

Cornalin ★★→★★★ 00 01 02 Local VALAIS speciality; dark spicy v strong red. Best: Salgesch, SIERRE, Conthey, Leytron, Leuk.

Côte, La Vaud r p w ★→★★★ Largest VAUD wine area between LAUSANNE and GENEVA (N shore of Lake). Whites with elegant finesse; fruity harmonious reds. Especially from MONT-SUR-ROLLE, Vinzel, Luins, FECHY, MORGES, etc.

Côtes de l'Orbe Vaud r p w ★→★★ N VAUD appellation between Lake NEUCHATEL and Lake GENEVA esp for light fruity reds.

Dézaley Vaud w (r) ★★→★★★ Celebrated LAVAUX v'yd on slopes above L GENEVA, once tended by Cistercian monks. Unusually potent CHASSELAS, develops esp after ageing. Red Dézaley is a GAMAY-PINOT N-MERLOT-Syrah rarity.

Dôle Valais r ★★→★★★ Appellation for PINOT N, more often a PINOT-dominated blend of PINOT NOIR and GAMAY (at least 85%) with other red varieties from the VALAIS: full, supple, often very good. Lightly pink Dôle Blanche is pressed immediately after harvest. Eg from MARTIGNY, SIERRE, SION, VETROZ, etc. 00 01 02.

Epesses Vaud w (r) ★★→★★★ 00 01 02 LAVAUX AC: supple, full-bodied whites.

Ermitage Alias the Marsanne grape; a VALAIS SPÉCIALITÉ. Concentrated, full-bodied dry white, s'times with residual sugar. Esp from FULLY, SION, Noble Contrée.

Féchy Vaud ★→★★ Famous appellation of LA CÔTE, esp elegant whites.

Federweisser German-Swiss name for white wine from BLAUBURGUNDER.

Fendant Valais w ★→★★★ VALAIS appellation for CHASSELAS. Wide range of wines. Better ones now use village names only (FULLY, SION, etc).

Flétri/Mi-flétri Late-harvested grapes for sw/slightly sw wine (respectively).

Fribourg Smallest French-Swiss wine canton (285 acres, nr Jura). Especially for CHASSELAS, PINOT N, GAMAY, SPÉCIALITÉS from VULLY, L Murten, S Lake NEUCHÂTEL.

Fully Valais r w ★★→★★★ Village nr MARTIGNY: excellent ERMITAGE and GAMAY. Best producer: Marie-Thérèse Chappaz ★★→★★★ **99 00 01 02**.

Gamay Beaujolais grape; abounds in French cantons. Mainly thin wine used in blends (SALVAGNIN, DÔLE). Gamay: 14% of grapes in Switzerland.

Geneva Capital, and French-Swiss wine canton; the third largest (3,370 acres). Key areas: Mandement, Entre Arve et Rhône, Entre Arve et Lac. Mostly CHASSELAS, GAMAY. Also Gamaret, Chard, PINOT, Muscat, and good Aligoté.

Gewurztraminer Grown in Switzerland as a spécialité variety esp in VALAIS. Best producer: Jean-Michel Novelle, Satigny 00 **01** 02.

Germanier, Jean-René VETROZ winemaker; Cayas (100% Syrah) ★★★ **97 98 99** 00 01; Mitis (sweet) ★★★ **97 98 99** 00.

Glacier, Vin du (Gletscherwein) Fabled oxidized wooded white from rare Rèze grape of Val d'Anniviers; offered by the thimbleful to visiting dignitaries. See also Visperterminen. Best producer: St Jodern-Kellerei ★ **00 01** 02.

Grand Cru Quality designation. Implication differs by canton: in VALAIS, GENEVA, and VAUD used where set requirements fulfilled.

Grisons (Graubünden) Mountain canton, mainly in German Switzerland (BÜNDNER HERRSCHAFT, Churer Rheintal; especially BLAUBURGUNDER) and partly south of Alps (Misox, especially MERLOT). 928 acres, primarily red, also Müller-Thurgau and SPÉCIALITÉS.

Heida (Païen) Old VALAIS white grape (Jura's Savagnin) for country wine of upper Valais (Visperterminen v'yds 1,000$^+$ m). Successful in lower VALAIS, too. Best producer: Josef-Marie Chanton ★★ **99 00 01** 02

Humagne Strong native white grape (VALAIS SPÉCIALITÉ). Humagne Rouge (unrelated, from Aosta Valley) also. Esp from CHAMOSON, LEYTRON, MARTIGNY.

Johannisberg Synomyn for SYLVANER in the VALAIS.

Landwein (Vin de pays) Trad light, easy white and esp red BLAUB'R from east.

Lausanne Capital of VAUD. No longer with v'yds in town area, but long-time owner of classics: Abbaye de Mont, Château Rochefort (LA CÔTE); Clos des Moines, Clos des Abbayes, Dom de Burignon (LAVAUX). Pricey.

Lavaux Vaud w (r) ★→★★★ DYA Scenic region on N shore of L GENEVA between Montreux and LAUSANNE. Delicate, refined whites, gd reds. Best: CALAMIN, Chardonne, DÉZALEY, EPESSES, Lutry, ST-SAPHORIN, VEVEY-MONTREUX, Villette.

Leytron Valais r w ★★→★★★ Commune nr SION/MARTIGNY, esp Le Grand Brûlé.

Malvoisie See Pinot Gris.

Martigny Valais r w ★★ Lower VALAIS commune esp for HUMAGNE ROUGE & Syrah.

Merlot Grown in Italian Switzerland (TICINO) since 1907 (after phylloxera destroyed local varieties): soft to very powerful wines. Also used with Cab.

Mont d'Or, Domaine du Valais w s/sw sw ★★→★★★ 00 **01** 02 Well-sited property nr SION: rich, conc'd demi-sec and sweet wines, notable SYLVANER.

Mont-sur-Rolle Vaud w (r) ★★ DYA Important appellation within LA CÔTE.

Morges Vaud r p w ★→★★ DYA Lgst LA CÔTE/VAUD AOC: CHASSELAS, fruity reds.

Neuchâtel City & canton **00 01** 02 V'yds (1,519 acres) from Lake N to BIELERSEE. CHASSELAS: fragrant, lively (sur lie, sp). Gd PINOT N (OEIL DE PERDRIX), PINOT GR, Chard. Best producer: Grillette Domaine de Cressier ★★.

Nostrano Word meaning "ours", applied to red wine of TICINO, made from native and Italian grapes (Bondola, Freisa, Bonarda, etc).

Oeil de Perdrix Pale PINOT rosé. DYA Esp NEUCHÂTEL's; also VALAIS, VAUD.

Pinot Blanc (Weissburgunder) New variety producing full-bodied, elegant wines.

Pinot Gris (Malvoisie) Widely planted white grape for dry and residually sweet wines. Makes v fine late-gathered wines in VALAIS (called Malvoisie).

Pinot Noir (Blauburgunder) Top red grape (31% of Swiss v'yds). Esp: BÜNDNER H, NEUCHÂTEL, VALAIS, ZÜRICH, THURGAU. Try: Philippe Constantin (Salgesch), Christian Hermann (Flàsch) ★★ **98** 99 00 01 02.

Rauschling Old white ZÜRICH grape; discreet fruit, elegant acidity (or sharp and dull).

Riesling (Petit Rhin) Mainly in the VALAIS. Excellent botrytis wines.

Riesling-Sylvaner Old name for Müller-THURGAU (top white of E; a SPÉCIALITÉ in W). Typically elegant wines with nutmeg aroma and some acidity. Best producers: Hermann Schwarzenbach, Daniel Marugg, Hans Weisendanger. All: ★★ 01 **02**.

St-Gallen E wine canton nr L Constance (553 acres). Esp for BLAUBURG'R (full-bodied), Müller-THURGAU, SPÉCIALITÉS. Incl Rhine Valley, Oberland, upper L ZÜRICH.

St-Saphorin Vaud w (r) ★★→★★★ 01 Famous LAVAUX AC for fine light whites.

Salvagnin Vaud r ★→★★ 00 GAMAY and/or PINOT N appellation. (See also DÔLE.)

Schaffhausen German-Swiss canton and wine town on River Rhine. Esp BLAUBURGUNDER; also some Müller-THURGAU and SPÉCIALITÉS.

Schenk Europe-wide wine giant, founded and based in Rolle (VAUD). Owns firms in Burgundy, Bordeaux, Germany, Italy, Spain.

Sierre Valais r w ★★→★★★ Sunny resort and famous wine town. Known for FENDANT, PINOT N, ERMITAGE, Malvoisie. Very good DÔLE.

Sion Valais r w ★★→★★★ Capital/wine centre of VALAIS. Esp FENDANT de Sion.

Sylvaner (Johannisberg, Gros Rhin) White grape esp in warm VALAIS v'yds. Heady, spicy: some with marked sweetness.

Spécialités (Spezialitäten) Wines of unusual grapes: vanishing local Gwäss, Himbertscha, Bondola, etc, ARVINE and AMIGNE, or modish Chenin Blanc, Sauv, Cabernet, Syrah. Eg VALAIS: 43 of its 47 varieties are considered spécialités.

Süssdruck Dry rosé/bright-red wine: grapes pressed before fermentation.

Thurgau German-Swiss canton beside Bodensee (678 acres). Wines from Thur Valley: Weinfelden, Seebach, Nussbaum, and Rhine. S shore of the Untersee. Typical: BLAUBURGUNDER, also gd RIES-SYLVANER (aka Müller-Thurgau: Dr Müller was born in the region). SPÉCIALITÉS incl Kerner, PINOT GR, Regent. Best producer: Hans Ulrich Kesselring ★★★ 98 99 **00 01** 02.

Ticino Italian-speaking S Switzerland (with Misox), growing mainly MERLOT (good from mountainous Sopraceneri region) and SPÉCIALITÉS. Trying Cab (oaked B'dx style), Sauv, Sém, Chard, Merlot white, and rosé. (2,347 acres.) Best producers: Luigi Zanini, Werner Stucky, Daniel Huber, Adriano Kaufmann, Christian Zündel. All: ★★★ 97 98 **99** 00 01.

Valais (Wallis) Rhône Valley from German-speaking upper-V to French lower-V. Largest and most varied wine canton in Switz (13,162 acres; source of 30% Swiss wine), now seeing a revival of quality, and ancient grapes. Near-perfect climatic conditions. Wide range: 47 grape varieties incl GAMAY, PINOT N, CHASSELAS, RIES, plus many SPÉCIALITÉS. Esp w; FLETRI/MI-FLETRI wines.

Vaud (Waadt) Fr Switz's 2ⁿᵈ-lgst wine canton incl CHABLAIS, LA CÔTE, LAVAUX, BONVILLARS, CÔTES DE L'ORBE, VULLY. CHASSELAS stronghold. Also GAMAY, PINOT N, etc.

Vétroz Valais w r ★★→★★★ Top village nr SION, esp famous for AMIGNE.

Vevey-Montreux Vaud r w ★★ Up-and-coming appellation of LAVAUX. Famous wine festival held about every 30 years.

Villeneuve Vaud w (r) ★★→★★★ Nr L Geneva: powerful yet refined whites.

Visperterminen Valais w (r) ★→★★ Upper VALAIS vineyards esp for SPÉCIALITÉS.

Vully Vaud w (r) ★→★★ Refreshing white from L Murten/FRIBOURG area.

Yvorne Vaud w (r) ★★ 01 **02** Top CHABLAIS AC for strong, fragrant wines.

Zürich Capital of largest German-speaking wine canton (same name). Mostly BLAUBURGUNDER; also PINOT GR, GEWÜRZ, and esp MÜLLER-T, RAUSCHLING (1,591 acres).

Austria

More heavily shaded areas are the wine growing regions

In less than 20 years Austria has emerged as a vigorous, innovative producer of dry white and dessert wines up to the very finest quality. Here red wines (20% of vineyards) are starting to make an international reputation, too. Strict laws, passed in 1985 and revised for the 1993 vintage, include curbs on yields (Germany: please copy) and impose higher levels of ripeness for each category than their German counterparts, reflecting the country's warmer climate. Many regional names, introduced under the 1985 law, are still unfamiliar outside Austria. All are worth trying; there are dramatic discoveries to be made.

Recent vintages

2002 Though Grüner Veltliner was hit by harvest rains, Riesling and the white Pinots did well. A difficult red wine vintage, but excellent dessert wines.

2001 Another top vintage for dry whites and very good for late-harvest wines. Red are more erratic.

2000 V Gd vintage in Lower Austria. Mixed in Styria due to harvest rains. In Burgenland, possibly the greatest vintage since 1945

1999 A great vintage whose dry white wines combine concentration and elegance. The best to date for the reds.

1998 A superb vintage for late-harvest wines, a very good one for the dry whites, but rather disappointing for reds.

1997 Very few late-harvest wines (wrong conditions for botrytis), but top dry whites and reds are rich and powerful.

1995 Rain threatened to ruin the harvest, but late pickers and dessert winemakers hit the jackpot.

Ausbruch PRÄDIKAT wine (v sweet) between Beerenauslese and Trockenbeeren-auslese in quality. Traditionally produced in RUST.

Ausg'steckt ("hung out") HEURIGEN are not open all year. To show potential visitors wine is being served, a green bush is hung up above the door.

Bergwein Legal designation for wines made from grapes grown on slopes with an incline of over 26%.

Blauburger Austrian red grape variety. A cross between BLAUER PORTUGIESER and BLAUFRÄNKISCH. Dark-coloured but light-bodied; simple wines.

Blauer Burgunder (Pinot Noir) A rarity, but on the increase. Vintages fluctuate greatly. Best in BURGENLAND, KAMPTAL and the THERMENREGION (from growers Achs, BRÜNDLMAYER, JOHANNESHOF, STIEGELMAR, UMATHUM, and WIENINGER).

Blauer Portugieser Light, fruity wines to drink slightly chilled when young. Mostly made for local consumption. Top producers: Fischer, Lust.

Blauer Wildbacher Red grape used to make SCHILCHER wines.

Blauer Zweigelt BLAUFRÄNKISCH-ST-LAURENT cross: high yields and rich colour. Lower yields and improved methods can produce some fine reds. Top producers: HEINRICH, Nittnaus, Pitnauer, Pöckl, UMATHUM.

Blaufränkisch (Lemberger in Germany, Kékfrankos in Hungary) Austria's red grape variety with the most potential, much planted in MITTELBURGENLAND: wines with good body, peppery acidity and a fruity taste of cherries. Often blended with CABERNET SAUVIGNON. Best from Gesellmann, HEINRICH, Iby, Igler, Krutzler, Nittnaus, E. TRIEBAUMER.

Bouvier Indigenous grape, generally producing light wines with low acidity but plenty of aroma, esp good for Beeren- and Trockenbeerenauslesen.

Bründlmayer, Willi r w sp ★★★→★★★★ 90 92 93 94 95 97 98 99 00 01 02 The leading LANGENLOIS-KAMPTAL estate. Very good wines: both local (RIES, GRUNER V) and international styles, incl CHARD and reds. Also Austria's best Sekt.

Burgenland Province and wine area (40,000 acres) in east next to Hungarian border. Warm climate. Ideal conditions, especially for botrytis wines near NEUSIEDLER SEE, also reds. Four wine regions: MITTELBURGENLAND, NEUSIEDLER SEE, NEUSIEDLERSEE-HÜGELLAND and SÜDBURGENLAND.

Buschenschank The same as HEURIGE; often a country cousin.

Cabernet Sauvignon Top producers are now giving up on Cab – too erratic.

Carnuntum r w Wine region since 94, E of VIENNA, bordered by the Danube to the north. Best producers: Glatzer, Pitnauer.

Chardonnay Increasingly grown, mainly oaked. Also trad in STYRIA as MORILLON (usually unoaked): strong fruit taste, lively acidity. Esp BRÜNDLMAYER, Loimer, Malat, POLZ, SATTLER, STIEGELMAR, TEMENT, VELICH, WIENINGER.

Deutschkreutz r (w) MITTELBURGENLAND red wine area, esp for BLAUFRÄNKISCH.

Donauland (Danube) w (r) Wine region since 1994, just west of VIENNA. Includes KLOSTERNEUBURG south of Danube and WAGRAM north of the river. Mainly whites, especially GRÜNER VELTLINER. Best producers include: Fritsch, Chorherren Klosterneuburg, Leth, Bernhard Ott, Wimmer-Czerny, R Zimmermann.

Dürnstein w Wine centre of the WACHAU with famous ruined castle. Mainly GRÜNER V, RIES. Top growers: FREIE WEINGÄRTNER WACHAU, KNOLL, PICHLER, Schmidl.

Eisenstadt r w dr sw Capital of BURGENLAND and historic seat of Esterházy family. Major producer: Esterházy.

Falkenstein w Wine centre in the eastern WEINVIERTEL nr Czech border. Good GRÜNER VELTLINER. Best producers: Jauk, Luckner, HEINRICH and Josef Salomon.

Federspiel Medium quality level of the VINEA WACHAU categories, roughly corresponding to Kabinett. Fruity, elegant, dry wines.

Feiler-Artinger r w sw ★★★→★★★★ 91 92 93 94 95 96 97 98 99 00 01 02 Considered the outstanding RUST estate. Top AUSBRUCH dessert wines since 93. Also good dry whites and increasingly exciting reds.

Freie Weingärtner Wachau w (r) ★★★ 92 93 94 95 96 97 98 99 00 02 Important and vg growers' co-op in DURNSTEIN. Excellent GRÜNER VELTLINER, RIES.

Gamlitz w Town in southern STYRIA. Growers incl Lackner-Tinnacher, SATTLER.

Gemischter Satz A blend of grapes (mostly white) grown, harvested, and vinified together. Traditional wine, still served in HEURIGEN.

Gobelsburg, Schloss ★★★ Renowned 86-acre estate in KAMPTAL revitalized since 1996, excellent dry RIESLING and GRÜNER VELTLINER.

Gols r w dr sw Largest BURGENLAND wine commune (N shore of NEUSIEDLER SEE). Best producers: Beck, HEINRICH, Leitner, A&H Nittnaus, Renner, STIEGELMAR.

Grüner Veltliner Austria's national w grape (over a third of v'yd area). Fruity, racy, lively young wines. Can be distinguished, age-worthy. Chardonnay, watch out! Best: BRÜNDLMAYER, FREIE WEING'R WACHAU, HIRTZBERGER, Högl, KNOLL, MANTLER, NEUMAYER, NIGL, NIKOLAIHOF, PFAFFL, F X PICHLER, PRAGER, Schmelz, Walzer.

G'spritzer Popular refreshing summer drink, usually white-wine-based; made sparkling by adding soda or mineral water. Esp in HEURIGEN.

Gumpoldskirchen w r dr sw Resort village S of VIENNA, famous for HEURIGEN. Centre of THERMENREGION. Distinctive, tasty, often sweet wines from ZIERFANDLER and ROTGIPFLER grapes. Best producers: Biegler, Schellmann.

Heinrich, Gernot r w dr sw ★★→★★★ 92 93 94 96 97 98 99 00 01 02 Young, modern estate in GOLS with Pannobile and (esp) red Gabarinza labels.

Heurige Wine of the most recent harvest, called "new wine" for one year, then classified as "old". Heurigen are wine houses where growers-cum-patrons serve wine by glass/bottle with simple local food – an institution, esp in VIENNA.

Hirtzberger, Franz w ★★★★ 90 93 94 95 96 97 98 99 00 01 02 Leading producer with 22 acres at SPITZ AN DER DONAU, WACHAU. Fine, dry RIES and GRÜNER VELTLINER.

Horitschon MITTELBURGENLAND region for reds. Best: Anton Iby, WIENINGER.

Illmitz w (r) dr sw SEEWINKEL region famous for Beeren- and Trockenbeerenauslesen. Best from KRACHER, Martin Haider, Helmut Lang, OPITZ.

Jamek, Josef w ★★★ 92 93 94 95 97 98 99 00 01 02 Well-known WACHAU estate and restaurant. Pioneer of dry whites since 50s. Recently back on top form.

Jurtschitsch/Sonnhof w (r) dr (sw) ★→★★ 92 93 94 95 97 98 99 00 01 02 Domaine run by three brothers: good whites (RIES, GRÜNER VELTLINER, CHARD).

Kamptal r w Wine region since '94, along R Kamp N of WACHAU. Top v'yds: LANGENLOIS, STRASS, Zöbing. Best growers: BRÜNDLMAYER, Dolle, Ehn, Schloss Gobelsburg, Hiedler, Hirsch, JURTSCHITSCH, Loimer, Topf.

Kattus ★→★★ Producer of traditional Sekt in VIENNA.

Klöch w W STYRIA wine town famous for Traminer. Best from Stürgkh.

Kloster Und Winetasting centre in restored monastery nr KREMS.

Klosterneuburg r w Main wine town of DONAULAND. Rich in tradition with a famous Benedictine monastery and a wine college founded in 1860. Best producers: Chorherren Klosterneuburg, Zimmermann.

KMW Abbreviation for "Klosterneuburger Mostwaage" (must level), the unit used in Austria to measure the sugar content in grape juice.

Knoll, Emmerich w ★★★★ 93 94 95 96 97 98 99 00 01 02 Traditional, highly regarded estate in LOIBEN, WACHAU, producing showpiece GRÜNER V & RIESLING.

Kollwentz-Römerhof w r dr (sw) ★★→★★★ 90 92 93 94 95 96 97 98 99 00 01 02 Innovative producer nr EISENSTADT: Sauvignon Bl, Eiswein, good reds.

Kracher, Alois w (r) dr (sw) ★★★★ 81 89 91 93 94 95 96 97 98 99 00 01 02 1st-class sml ILLMITZ producer; speciality: PRÄDIKATS (dessert wines), some barrique-aged (Nouvelle Vague), others not (Zwischen der Seen), gd reds since 97.

Krems w (r) dr (sw) Ancient town, W of VIENNA. Capital of KREMSTAL. Best from Forstreiter, NIGL, SALOMON, Weingut Stadt Krems, Walzer.

Kremstal w (r) Wine region since 94 esp for GRÜNER V and RIES. Top growers: Malat, MANTLER, NIGL, SALOMON, Weingut Stadt KREMS.

Langenlois r w Wine town and region in KAMPTAL with 5,000 acres. Best producers: BRÜNDLMAYER, Ehn, Hiedler, JURTSCHITSCH, Loimer.

Lenz Moser ★★→ Producer nr KREMS. LM III invented high-vine system. Also incl wines from Schlossweingut Malteser Ritterorden (wine estate of Knights of Malta): Mailberg (WEINVIERTEL), Klosterkeller Siegendorf (BURGENLAND).

Loiben w In lower, wider part of Danube Valley (WACHAU). Ideal conditions for RIES and GRÜNER V. Top: Alzinger, FREIE WEINGÄRTNER, KNOLL, F X PICHLER.

Mantler, Josef w ★★→★★★ 90 95 96 97 98 99 00 01 02 Leading estate in Gedersdorf nr KREMS. Very good traditional RIESLING, GRÜNER VELTLINER, CHARDONNAY, and rare Roter Veltliner (Malvasia).

Mayer, Franz w With 60 acres, the largest producer in VIENNA. Traditional jug wines (at picturesque HEURIGE Beethovenhaus – yes, he drank here), plus in contrast, excellent "older-vintage" (20 yrs) RIESLING and Traminer.

Messwein Mass wine: must have ecclesiastical approval (and natural must).

Mittelburgenland r (w) dr (sw) Wine region on Hungarian border protected by three hill ranges. Makes large quantities of red (especially BLAUFRÄNKISCH). Producers: Gesellmann, HEINRICH, Iby, Igler, P Kerschhaum, WEININGER.

Mörbisch r w d sw Wine town on the western shore of NEUSIEDLER SEE just north of the Hungarian border. The top grower is Schönberger.

Morillon Name given in STYRIA to CHARDONNAY.

Müller-Thurgau See Riesling-Sylvaner.

Muskat-Ottonel Grape for fragrant, often dry whites, interesting PRÄDIKATS.

Muskateller Rare aromatic grape for dry whites. Best from STYRIA and WACHAU. Top growers: Gross, HIRTZBERGER, Lackner-Tinnacher, F X PICHLER, POLZ, SATTLER.

Neuburger Indigenous white grape: nutty flavour; mainly in the WACHAU (elegant, flowery), in the THERMENREGION (mellow and ample-bodied), and in N BURGENLAND (strong, full). Best from Beck, FREIE WEINGÄRTNER, HIRTZBERGER.

Neumayer ★★★ 94 95 96 97 98 99 00 01 02 The Neumayer brothers make powerful, pithy, dry GRÜNER VELTLINER and RIESLING at the best estate in the new TRAISENTAL region.

Neusiedler See V shallow (max 1.8m deep) BURGENLAND lake on Hungarian border. Warm temperatures, autumn mists encourage botrytis. Gives name to wine regions of NEUSIEDLERSEE-HÜGELLAND and NEUSIEDLERSEE.

Neusiedlersee r w dr sw Region N and E of NEUSIEDLER SEE. Best growers: Achs, Beck, HEINRICH, KRACHER, Nittnaus, OPITZ, Pöckl, UMATHUM, VELICH.

Neusiedlersee-Hügelland r w dr sw Wine region W of NEUSIEDLER SEE based around OGGAU, RUST, and MORBISCH on the lake shores, and EISENSTADT in the foothills of the Leitha Mts. Best producers: FEILER-ARTINGER, KOLLWENTZ, Mad, Prieler, Schandl, Schönberger, Schröck, ERNST TRIEBAUMER, Wenzel.

Niederösterreich (Lower Austria) With 58% of Austria's v'yds: CARNUNTUM, DONAULAND, KAMPTAL, KREMSTAL, THERMENREGION, TRAISENTAL, WACHAU, WEINVIERTEL.

Nigl ★★★ w 92 93 94 95 96 97 98 99 00 01 02 Top grower of KREMSTAL making sophisticated dry RIESLING and GRÜNER VELTLINER capable of long ageing.

Nikolaihof w ★★★ 90 91 92 94 95 97 98 99 00 01 Estate built on Roman foundations. Superb RIESLING from Steiner Hund site, other wines v good and v traditional in style.

Nussdorf VIENNA district famous for HEURIGEN and vg Ried Nussberg.

Oggau Wine region on the W shore of NEUSIEDLER SEE.

Opitz, Willi ★★★ A tiny ILLMITZ estate specializing in late-harvest wines, including "Schilfmandl" and "Opitz One" from grapes dried on reeds from the NEUSIEDLER SEE.

Pfaffl ★★★ 90 93 94 95 96 97 98 99 00 01 02 WEINVIERTEL estate in Stretten nr VIENNA. Best-known for blended red "Excellence", but racy, dry GRÜNER VS are no less impressive. Recently took over nearby Schlossweingut Bockfliess.

AUSTRIA

Pichler, Franz Xavier w ★★★★ 90 92 93 94 95 96 97 98 99 00 01 02 Top WACHAU producer with very intense, rich RIESLING and GRÜNER V (esp Kellerberg). Widely recognized as Austria's No 1 grower for dry wines.

Polz, Erich and Walter w ★★★ 92 93 95 96 97 98 99 00 01 02 S STYRIAN (Weinstrasse) growers; esp Hochgrassnitzberg: Sauv, CHARD, Grauburgunder, WEISSBURGUNDER.

Prädikat, Prädikatswein Quality graded wines from Spätlese upwards (Spätlese, Auslese, Eiswein, Strohwein, Beerenauslese, AUSBRUCH, and Trockenbeerenauslese). See Germany, page 149.

Prager, Franz w ★★★★ 90 91 92 93 94 95 96 97 98 99 00 01 02 Together with JOSEF JAMEK, pioneer of top-quality WACHAU dry white. Now run by Anton Bodenstein; new RIESLING clones and great PRÄDIKAT wines.

Renomierte Weingüter Burgenland Assoc founded 95 by top BURGENLAND producers to promote region's top wines; incl KRACHER, TRIEBAUMER, UMATHUM.

Retz r w Important region in W WEINVIERTEL. Especially Weinbauschule Retz.

Ried Single v'yd.

Riesling On its own always means German RIESLING. WELSCHRIESLING (unrelated) is labelled as such. Top growers: Alzinger, BRÜNDLMAYER, FREIE W WACHAU, HIRTZBERGER, Högl, KNOLL, NIGL, NIKOLAIHOF, PFAFFL, F X PICHLER, PRAGER, SALOMON.

Riesling-Sylvaner Name (wrongly) used for Müller-T (about 10% of Austria's grapes). Müller-T is actually Riesling x Chasselas de Courtillier. Well, these things happen. Best producers: HIRTZBERGER, JURTSCHITSCH.

Rotgipfler Fragrant indigenous grape of THERMENREGION. With ZIERFANDLER, makes lively, interesting wine. Esp Biegler, Schellmann, Stadelmann.

Rust w r dr sw BURGENLAND region, famous since 17th C for dessert AUSBRUCH; now also for r and dry w. Esp from FEILER-ARTINGER, Schandl, Heidi Schröck, ERNST TRIEBAUMER, Paul Triebaumer, Wenzel. Cercle Ruster Ausbruch producers focus on powerful sw wines from a wide range of grapes. Standards already v high.

St-Laurent Traditional red-wine grape, potentially very gd, with cherry aroma, possibly related to Pinot N. Esp from Fischer, Mad, STIEGELMAR, UMATHUM.

Salomon-Undhof w ★★★ Very good producer of RIES, WEISSBURGUNDER, Traminer in KREMS. Excellent quality since 95.

Sattler, Willi w ★★–★★★ 92 93 94 95 96 97 98 99 00 01 02 Top S STYRIA grower. Esp for Sauv, MORILLON. Recent vintages less oaked, better balanced.

Schilcher Rosé wine from indigenous BLAUER WILDBACHER grapes (sharp, dry: high acidity). Speciality of W STYRIA. Try: Klug, Lukas, Reiterer, Strohmeier.

Schlumberger Largest sparkling winemaker in Austria (VIENNA); wine is bottle-fermented by unique "Méthode Schlumberger". Delicate and fruity.

Seewinkel ("Lake corner") Name given to the part of NEUSIEDLERSEE including Apetlon, ILLMITZ, and Podersdorf. Ideal conditions for botrytis.

Sepp Moser ★★★ 93 94 95 97 98 99 00 01 02 KREMSTAL estate (Rohrendorf) founded with original LENZ MOSER v'yds. Richly aromatic, elegant, dry RIES, GRÜNER V, CHARD, Sauv. Also good reds from Apetlon in Neusiedlersee region.

Servus w BURGENLAND everyday light and mild, dry white-wine brand.

Smaragd Highest-quality category of VINEA WACHAU, similar to dry Spätlese.

Spätrot-Rotgipfler Typical THERMENREGION (Spätrot and ROTGIPFLER) wine.

Spitz an der Donau w WACHAU cool microclimate: esp from Singerriedel v'yd. Top growers are: HIRTZBERGER, FREIE WEINGARTNER, Högl, Lagler.

Steinfeder VINEA WACHAU quality category for very light, fragrant, dry wines.

Stiegelmar, Georg w r dr sw ★–★★★ 93 95 96 97 98 99 00 01 02 GOLS grower: CHARD, Sauv Bl, red wine, and unusual specialities. Whites currently dull.

Strass w (r) Centre of KAMPTAL region for gd Qualität w wines. Best prods: Dolle, Topf.

Styria (Steiermark) Southernmost wine region of Austria. Prestigious dry whites. Incl SUDSTEIERMARK, SUD-OSTSTEIERMARK WESTSTEIERMARK (S, SE, W Styria).

Süd-Oststeiermark (SE Styria) w (r) STYRIAN region with islands of excellent vineyards. Best producers: Neumeister, Winkler-Hermaden.

Südburgenland r w Small S BURGENLAND wine region: good red wines. Best producers: Krutzler, Wachter, Wiesler.

Südsteiermark (S Styria) w Best wine region of STYRIA: makes v popular whites (MORILLON, MUSKATELLER, WELSCHRIESLING, and Sauv Blanc). Top producers: Gross, Lackner-Tinnacher, Muster, POLZ, Prünte, SATTLER, Skoff, TEMENT, Wohlmuth.

Tement, Manfred w ★★★ 90 92 93 94 97 98 99 00 01 02 Renowned estate on S STYRIA Weinstrasse for beautifully made, traditional "Steirisch Klassik" and gently oaked Sauv Bl & MORILLON from Ziereggsite. World-class.

Thermenregion r w dr sw Wine/hot-springs region, south of VIENNA. Indigenous grapes (eg ZIERFANDLER, ROTGIPFLER) and good reds from Baden, GUMPOLDSKIRCHEN Tattendorf, Traiskirchen areas. The top producers are: Alphart, Biegler, Fischer, Johanneshof, Schafler, Schellmann, Stadelmann.

Traditionsweingüter Assoc of KAMPTAL and KREMSTAL wine estates, committed to quality and v'yd classification. Incl BRÜNDLMAYER, Loimer, G Malat, NIGL, SALOMON.

Traisental New region: 1,750 acres just south of KREMS on Danube. Mostly dry whites in style similar to WACHAU. Top producer: NEUMAYER.

Triebaumer, Ernst r (w) dr sw ★★★ 90 92 93 94 95 97 98 99 00 01 02 RUST producer; some of Austria's best reds: BLAUFRÄNKISCH (Mariental), CAB-Merlot. Very good AUSBRUCH.

Umathum, Josef w r dr sw ★★★ 90 91 92 94 95 97 98 99 00 01 02 Distinguished NEUSIEDLERSEE producer for vg reds incl BLAUER BURGUNDER; also good whites.

Velich w sw BURGENLAND ★★★ Burgundian-style "Tiglat" CHARDONNAY (99 00) has 22 months in barrel and since 95 some of top PRÄDIKATS in the SEEWINKEL.

Vienna w (r) ("Wien" in German and on labels.) The Austrian capital is a wine region in its own right (1,500 v'yd acres in suburbs). Generally simple, lively wines, served in HEURIGEN: esp Bernreiter, MAYER, Schilling, WIENINGER.

Vinea Wachau WACHAU appellation started by winemakers in 83 with three categories of dry wine: STEINFEDER, FEDERSPIEL, and powerful SMARAGD.

Wachau w Danube wine region W of KREMS: some of Austria's best wines, incl RIES, GRÜNER V. Top producers: Alzinger, FREIE WEINGÄRTNER, HIRTZBERGER, Högl, JAMEK, KNOLL, NIKOLAIHOF, F X PICHLER, PRAGER.

Wagram r w Part of the Donauland wine region with loess terraces in DONAULAND. Best producers: Fritsch, Leth, Bernhard Ott, Wimmer-Czerny.

Weinviertel "Wine Quarter" w (r) Largest Austrian wine region, between Danube and Czech border. Mostly light, refreshing w, esp from Falkenstein, Poysdorf, RETZ. Best producers: Graf Mardegg, Hardegg, Jauk, Luckner, Lust, Malteser Ritterorden, PFAFFL, Schwarzböck, Taubenschuss, Zull.

Weissburgunder (Pinot Bl) Ubiquitous: good dry wines and PRÄDIKATS. Esp Beck, Fischer, Gross, HEINRICH, HIRTZBERGER, Lackner-Tinnacher, POLZ, TEMENT.

Welschriesling White grape, not related to RIESLING, grown in all wine regions: light, fragrant, young-drinking dry wines and good PRÄDIKATS.

Weststeiermark (West Styria) p Small Austrian wine region specializing in SCHILCHER. Esp from Klug, Lukas, Reiterer, Strohmeier.

Wien See Vienna.

Wieninger, Fritz w r ★★→★★★ 92 93 94 95 97 98 99 00 01 02 Very good VIENNA-Stammersdorf grower: HEURIGE, CHARD, BLAUER BURGUNDER reds; esp good GRÜNER VELTLINER and RIESLING.

Winzer Krems Wine-growers' cooperative in KREMS: dependable solid whites.

Zierfandler (Spätrot) White variety almost exclusive to the THERMENREGION. Blended with ROTGIPFLER: robust, lively, age-worthy wines. Best producers: Biegler, Schellmann, Stadelmann.

AUSTRIA

Central & Southeast Europe

More heavily shaded areas are the wine growing regions

Prague ○
CZECH REPUBLIC

Bratislava ○   Danub

Drava

Ljubljana ○
SLOVENIA   Zagreb ○
CROATIA   Sava

BOSNIA-
HERZEGOVINA

Split ○
Adriatic Sea   Sarajevo ○

Dubrovnik ○

To say that parts of this region are still in transition is an under-statement. But new regional autonomies and new statehoods are being followed in many cases by higher aspirations in winemaking.

In a few much-publicized cases this takes the form of international "flying winemakers" pitching their tents at vintage-time, usually to make wines acceptable to Western supermarkets from predictable grape varieties, occasionally to do far better. This affects indigenous winemaking, too – often with happy results, making fresher and fruitier wines of intriguingly different flavours.

The 15 years since Communism has witnessed the decline of state firms and the emergence of new family- and corporate-owned wineries. These are now establishing their winemaking styles and market positions with either fresh and fruity or more complex, aged wines. So far, Hungary, Bulgaria, Slovenia, and the Czech Republic have taken the lead in what has become an area to follow with fascination. The potential of other ex-Communist states has still to emerge, with Romania in particular catching up. But about Greece there is no doubt: the new age of wine has well and truly arrived.

In this section, references are arranged country by country, each shown on the map on this page. Included alongside regions are producers and other terms in the alphabetical listings.

Hungary

Hungary entered the Communist era with E Europe's finest and most individual wines. It emerged with traditions severely battered. The past 15 years have been revolutionary. Winemakers have invested capital and earnings into improving cellar equipment and procedures and expanding plantings of international grapes. The initial years of experiment have given way to proven winemaking techniques and definite wine styles.This is especially true for the reds of Villány, Szekszárd (the "z"s are silent), and Eger. Tokaji, the one undisputed great wine of Central European history, remains in full renaissance, and native grapes (only white) provide the backbone for the more traditional preference for fiery, hearty, full-bodied wines. 2000 is potentially one of the best vintages in the last 100 years.

Alföld Hungary's Great Plain: much everyday wine (mostly Western grapes) and some better. Incorporates 3 wine districts: HAJÓS-Baja, Csongrád, Kunság.

Aszár-Neszmély W wine district in NW Hung nr Danube. Native & western grapes.

Aszú Botrytis-shrivelled grapes and the sweet wine made from them, similar to Sauternes. Used to designate both wine and shrivelled berries.

Aszú Eszencia Tokaj br sw ★★★★ **57 63 93** 96 99 Second TOKAJ quality (see Eszencia). 7 PUTTS plus; shld be superb amber elixir, like celestial butterscotch.

Badacsony w dr sw ★★→★★★ Wine district on the N shore of Lake BALATON, home to the native variety KEKNYELU. The basalt soil can give rich, highly flavoured white wines; well-made Rieslings and SZURKEBARAT have fine mineral flavours. The leader is SZEREMLEY's Szent Orbán Winery.

Balaton Hungary's inland sea, Europe's lgst freshwater lake. Many gd wines take its name. The ending "i" (eg Balatoni, Egri) is equivalent of -er in Londoner.

Balatonboglár r w dr sw ★★→★★★ Progressive winery on S shore of Lake BALATON in Dél-Balaton region. Decent whites (Chard, Sémillon, Muscat). Also *cuve close* sp. Owned by Henkell & Söhnlein.

Bikavér Eger r ★ "Bull's Blood", historic red wine of EGER: at best full-b'd & well-balanced, highly variable in export version today. Now under supervision to protect identity & improve quality (see Eger). Mostly from KEKFRANKOS, Cab S & F, Kekoporto, & Merlot. Also made in SZEKSZARD.

Bock, József Family winemaker in VILLANY. Hearty reds, both varietal and blends.

Bor Wine. Vörös is red, Fehér is white, Asztali is table.

Dégenfeld, Grof Lrge Tokaj estate, traditional style wines plus dry Furmint.

Disznókö Important 1ˢᵗ-class Tokaj estate, owned by AXA (French co) since 92. V modern style, Sauternes-influenced wines of great refinement and vigour.

Edes Sweet wine (but not as luscious as ASZU).

Eger Eger district r w dr sw ★→★★★ Best-known red-wine centre of N Hung; Baroque city of cellars full of BIKAVER. Fresh w LEANYKA (perhaps its best product), OLASZRIZLING, Chard, Cab. Top prods: Vilmos Thummerer (consistent Bikaver), TIBOR GAL, Pók Tamás, Ostoros Bor, Béla Vincze, & potentially the huge Egervin.

Eszencia ★★★★ The fabulous quintessence of TOKAJI: intensely sw & aromatic from grapes wizened by botrytis. Properly grape juice of very low, if any, alcoholic strength, reputed to have miraculous properties: its sugar content can be over 750 grams per litre. In commerce, ASZU ESZENCIA takes its place.

Etyek-Buda Near Budapest. Source of modern standard wines, esp Chard, Sauv Bl, especially from HUNGAROVIN.

Ezerjó "Thousand blessings" Widespread traditional variety. At MOR, makes one of Hungary's top dry whites; great potential: fragrant with hint of grapefruit.

François President French-founded (1882) sparkling-wine producer at Budafok, nr Budapest. Vintage wine President is very drinkable.

Furmint The classic grape of TOKAJ, with great flavour, acidity, and fire, also grown for table wine at Lake BALATON and in SOMLO.

Gál, Tibor EGER winemaker for barrique-aged BIKAVER, also oaked GIA Chard.

Gere, Attila Family winemaker in VILLANY with good, forward-looking reds, esp oak-aged Cab S (93). Gere & Wenninger is another label (Cuvée Phoenix).

Gundel TOKAJ venture at MAD, making wines for famous Gundel's restaurant in Budapest. Also v'yds & cellar at EGER.

Hajós Pincék Alföld r ★ Charming village in S Hungary with 1,500 cellars. Mostly traditional, family production. Some quality lighter red wines can be found.

Hárslevelü "Linden-leaved" grape used at Debrö and as 2nd main grape of TOKAJ (cf Sém/Sauv in Sauternes). Gentle, mellow wine with a peach aroma.

Helvécia (Kecskemét) Historic ALFOLD cellars. V'yds ungrafted: phylloxera bugs cannot negotiate sandy soil. Whites and rosés modernist; reds traditional.

Hétszölö Noble first-growth 116-acre TOKAJ estate owned by Grands Millésimes de France and Japanese Suntory. Second label, from purchased grapes: Dessewffy. Fordítás is halfway to ASZÚ in style.

Hilltop Neszmély Winery in ASZAR-NESZMELY; Western-style wines, including Woodcutters White from homegrown Czerszegi Fuszeres hybrid.

Hungarovin Traders/prods with cellars at Budafok nr Budapest: Western varietals, also *cuve close*, transfer, & classic sp. Owner: German Sekt specialist Henkell.

János Arvay New TOKAJ cellar owned by former DISZNÓKO winemaker. First releases are awaited.

Kadarka Traditional red grape for vast quantities in S, but can produce ample flavour and interesting maturity (eg especially at SZEKSZARD and VILLANY) and considered by some an essential component of BIKAVER.

Kékburgundi German Spätburgunder: Pinot Noir.

Kecskemét Major town of the ALFOLD. Much everyday wine, some better.

Kékfrankos Hungarian for Blaufränkisch; reputedly related to Gamay. Good light or full-bodied reds, esp SOPRON. Used in BIKAVER at EGER.

Kéknyelü ("Blue stalk") High-flavoured, low-yielding white grape making the best and "stiffest" wine of Mt BADACSONY. It should be flowery and spicy stuff. Watch for top producer HUBA SZEREMLEY (aromatic and fruity whites).

Királyudvar Promising new TOKAJ cellar at TARCAL. Directed by ISTVAN SZEPSY.

Különleges Minöség Special quality: highest official grading.

Kunság Largest region in Great Plain. Gd KADARKA esp from Kiskörös.

Leányka ("Little girl") Old Hungarian white grape. Admirable, aromatic, light, dry wine. Királyleányka ("Royal") is a different variety and supposedly superior.

Mád Old commercial centre of the TOKAJ region. Growers incl GUNDEL, ROYAL TOKAJI, SZEPSY, József Monyok, Vince Gergely.

Mátraalja w (r) ★★ District in foothills of Mátra range in N, nr Gyöngyös (site of huge modernized winery) incl Debrö, Nagyrede. Promising, dry SZURKEBARAT, Chard, MUSKOTALY, Sauv Bl. French, Australian, and now German investment.

Mecsekalja S Hungary district, known for good whites of PECS, esp sparkling.

Megyer, Château TOKAJ estate bought by Jean-Louis Laborde, of Ch Clinet in Pomerol. Also owns CHÂTEAU PAJZOS. Megyer is the lighter wine. Quality is fair.

Mézes Mály In TARCAL. This & SZARVAS are historically the greatest v'yds of TOKAJ.

Minöségi Bor Quality wine. Hungary's appellation contrôlée.

Mór N Hungary w ★★→★★★ Region long-famous for fresh, dry EZERJO. Now also Riesling and Sauvignon. Wines now mostly exported.

Muskotály Muscat; usually Ottonel. Muscat Bl à Petits Grains is Muscat Lunel. Makes light, but long-lived, wine in TOKAJ and EGER. A little goes into the TOKAJI blend. V occasionally makes a wonderful ASZU wine solo.

Nagyburgundi Literally "great burgundy": indigenous grape often mistaken for KÉFRANKOS. Sound, solid wine, esp around VILLANY and SZEKSZARD.

Olaszrizling Hungarian name for the Italian Riesling or Welschriesling. Better examples can have a burnt-almond aroma.

Oremus Ancient TOKAJI v'yd of founding Rákóczi family, owned by owners of Spain's Vega Sicilia with HQ at Tolczva. 1st-rate ASZU. Also a lesser Tokaj grape.

Pajzos, Château B'x-owned Tokaj estate with some fine ASZÚ. See Ch Megyer.

Pécs Mecsek w (r) ★→★★ Major S wine city. Esp sp, OLASZRIZLING, Pinot Bl, etc.

Pinot Noir Normally means KÉKBURGUNDI.

Puttonyos Measure of sweetness in TOKAJI ASZU. A "puttony" is a 25-kilo measure, traditionally a hod of grapes. The number of "putts" per barrel (136 litres) of dry base wine or must determines the final richness of the wine, from 3 putts to 7. 3 is equal to 60 g of sugar per litre, 4:90, 5:120, 6:150. ASZU ESZENCIA must have at least 180. The measuring of residual sugar has replaced actual puttonyos. See Eszencia for the *really* sticky stuff.

Royal Tokáji Wine Co Pioneer Anglo-Danish-Hung venture at MAD. 200 acres, mainly 1st or 2nd growth. 1st wine (90) a revelation: 91 & (esp) 93 led renaissance of TOKAJI. 95, 99, 00 to follow. I have to declare an interest as a founder.

Siklós City in S Hungary; part of VILLANY-SIKLOS. Mainly sm producers, known for whites: esp HARSLEVELU. Ripe, fruity Chard: promising; also TRAMINI, OLASZRIZLING.

Somló N Hungary w ★★ Isolated small district N of BALATON: whites (formerly of high repute) from FURMINT & Juhfark (sheep's tail) varieties in both traditional barrel-fermented and fresh, fruity styles. Top prods incl Fekete, Inhauser.

Sopron W Hungary r ★★→★★★ Historic enclave S of Neusiedlersee (see Austria). Traditionally known for lighter reds like KEKFRANKOS and Austrian-style sweet wines but showing promise for whites such as Sauv Bl.

Szamorodni Word meaning "as it was born"; describes TOKAJI not sorted in the v'yd. Dry or (fairly) sw, depending upon proportion of ASZU grapes naturally present. Sold as an aperitif. In vintage TOKAJI Aszu yrs, the sw style can offer some Aszú character at much less cost. Dry Szamorodni is Hungary's sherry.

Száraz Dry, esp of TOKAJI SZAMARODNI.

Szarvas TOKAJI v'yd at Tarcal; one of top sites. Solely ownered by TOKAJI TRADING.

Szekszárd r ★★→★★★ District in south-central Hungary; some of country's top reds from Kékfrankos, Cab S & F, and Merlot. Also KADARKA which needs age (3–4 yrs); can also be botrytized ("Nemes Kadar"). Good organic BIKAVER and gd Chard and OLASZRIZLING, too. Quality wines are lighter, more delicate than those from VILLANY. Producers incl Vesztergombi, Peter Vida, Heimann.

St Ozbán See Szeremley.

Szepsy, István Legendary name and impeccable small production of long-ageing TOKAJI ASZU. A Szepsy ancestor helped to create the ASZÚ method in 17th-C.

Szeremley, Huba Leader in BADACSONY. Ries, SZURKEBARAT, KEKNYELU, ZEUSZ are modern models. Fine KEKFRANKOS from Tihány Peninsula. Szent Ozbánis another label.

Szürkebarát "Grey Friar": Pinot Gr. Key variety in TOKAJI, as well as a source of sw tourist wines from BALATON. But this is one of the best: wait for great dry wines.

Tarcal TOKAJ commune with 2 great first-growths and several gd prods.

Tiffán, Ede VILLANY grower producing full-bodied, oaked red wines.

Tokajbor New TOKAJ Cellar at Bodrogkeresztúr. To watch.

Tokaji Tokaj w dr sw ★★→★★★★ The ASZU is Hungary's famous liquorous sweet wine (since drca 1600), comparable to a highly aromatic, dramatically vital Sauternes with a searing finish, from hills in NE nr Ukraine border. Appellation covers 13,500 acres of the Tokajhegyalja. See Aszú, Eszencia, Furmint, Puttonyos, Szamorodni. Also dry table wine of character.

Tokaji Trading House The formerly state-owned TOKAJI CO, now reduced to 180 acres incl the magnificent Szarvas v'yd. Also called Crown Estates. Castle Island is the brand for dry wines. Quality improving.

Tramini Gewürztraminer, esp in SIKLOS.

Villány-Siklós Southern wine region named after its two main towns. Villány makes mostly reds, often gd quality Bordeaux styles. Siklós is mostly white. High-quality producers incl BOCK, ATTILA GERE, Günzer, Malatinsky, Molnár, Polgar, TIFFAN, Villány Borászat, and Vylyan.

Wille-Baumkauff, Márta Hungarian returnee goes MÁD with TOKAJ. Quality improves steadily.

Zemplen Ridge Or Zemplén Hegyhát. ISTVAN SZEPSY and Anthony Hwang of KIRÁLYUDVAR think there's a market for less conc'd Tokaji for younger drinkers. First vintage was 02. Couldn't they just dilute to taste?

Zéta A cross of Bouvier and FURMINT used by some in ASZU production, also as varietal with a pear/green-apple flavour, but production waning.

Zeusz Recent variety for aromatic sweet whites.

Bulgaria

2001 was the first vintage under the new "French style" Wine Law, which introduced detailed regulations in the 5 wine regions. The drive for higher standards has been reflected by the increased demand for quality wines.

The Danube Plain regions specialize in fruity whites and reds at Svishtov and Rousse, while further south, Lyaskovets, Pavlikeni, and Suhindol produce some well-balanced reds. The Black Sea region is particularly suitable for the production of fresh, dry, and fruity whites at Targovishte, Shumen, and Pomorie. The largest and most productive region is the Thracian Valley with constant high temperatures producing rich reds, especially at Haskovo, Iambol, Sliven, and Assenovgrad. Struma Valley in the southwest is the hottest region, producing substantial reds of great longevity at Damianitsa and Harsovo.

Foreign investment in the modernization of established wineries continues, while newcomers are bringing a welcome diversity to the wine scene.

Assenovgrad r ★★ 01 Main MAVRUD-producing cellar near PLOVDIV. Should age well.

Blueridge, Sliven r (w) ★★ Largest winery. CAB (00), MERLOT (01), Barrique good.

Boyar Estates Domaine Boyar merged with Vinprom ROUSSE to form one of largest companies in East and Central Europe, marketing worldwide under Domine Boyar, Blueridge, and Vinprom Rousse labels.

Burgas w p (r) ★→★★ Black Sea port and source of rosé (the speciality), easy whites and some good young reds.

Cabernet Sauvignon Dark, vigorous, fruity, v drinkable young; best quality ages well. Good examples: IAMBOL, SLIVEN, ROUSSE, SVISHTOV.

Chardonnay Was less successful than CABERNET. Gd results now from N & E. V dry, full-flavoured wine. Recent wines promising, esp SHUMEN, PRESLAV, & POMORIE.

Controliran Like DOCG and AOC. New wine law published in 2000.

Country Wines Regional wines (cf French Vins de Pays), often 2-variety blends.

Damianitza r ★★ MELNIK winery specializing in native Melnik grape. Also excellent MERLOTS such as Redark (01).

Danube River dividing Bulgaria and Romania. ROUSSE and SVISHTOV vineyards benefit from its proximity, esp for reds.

Dimiat The common native white grape, grown in the E towards the coast. Good examples from Blueridge (01) and Black Sea Gold.

Gamza Red grape (Kadarka of Hungary) with potential esp from N region DANUBE plain. PAVLIKENI, NOVO SELO, and PLEVEN are specialists.

Harsovo Struma Valley region, esp for MELNIK.

Haskovo r (w) ★★ Recently privatized winery (with v'yds) in Thracian Plain region specializing in MERLOT; STAMBOLOVO, and SAKAR are satellite wineries.

Iambol r w ★★→★★★ Winery in Thracian Plain specializing in CAB S & MERLOT.

Karlovo Town in the famous Valley of the Roses. Whites, especially MISKET.

Khan Krum Satellite cellar of PRESLAV, whites esp Reserve CHARD.

Lovico Suhindol r w Bulgaria's 1st co-op (1909). GAMZA, CAB, MERLOT blends.

Mavrud Grape variety and darkly plummy red from S Bulgaria, esp ASSENOVGRAD. Can mature 20 yrs[+]. Considered the country's best indigenous red variety.

Melnik Village in SW and highly prized grape. Dense red; locals say it can be carried in a handkerchief. Needs 5 yrs[+]; lasts 15. Also ripe age-worthy CAB.

Merlot Soft r variety mainly in HASKOVO in the S. Excellent examples: STAMBOLOVO, IAMBOL, Lyubimets, and Elhovo in the S; SHUMEN & SVISHTOV in the North.

Misket Mildly aromatic indigenous grape; the basis for most country whites.

Muscat Ottonel Normal Muscat grape, grown in E for mid-sweet, fruity white.

Novo Selo Good red GAMZA from the North.

Oriachovitza r ★★ Satellite of STARA ZAGORA. Thracian Plain area for CONTROLIRAN CAB and MERLOT. Rich, savoury red best at 4–5 yrs. Recently good RESERVE Cab.

Pamid The light, soft, everyday red of the Southeast and Northwest.

Pavlikeni r Specializes in MERLOT and CAB.

Peruschtitza r Winery nr PLOVDIV. Reds only, esp MAVRUD, CAB, & RUBIN grapes.

Pleven N cellar for PAMID, GAMZA, CAB. Also Bulgaria's wine-research station.

Plovdiv City in S region; source of gd CAB & MAVRUD. Most w'making at ASSENOVGRAD & PERUSCHTITZA. University's Food Technology Dept where most Bulg oenologists study.

Pomorie w (r) ★★ Black Sea winery in E, whites & reds, esp CHARD & MUSKAT.

Preslav w ★★ Well-known white cellar in Black Sea region. Also gd brandy.

Reserve Used on labels of selected and oak-aged wines. Whites for a minimum of two years and reds for at least three years in oak vats.

A Bulgarian choice for 2004

Red Iambol Merlot 2002, Vini Sliven Cabernet Sauvignon "Tweeda" 2002, Pomorie Black Sea Gold Merlot 2002.

White Vini Sliven Chard and Sauv Bl 2002, Pomorie Black Sea Gold Chard 2002.

Indigenous Blueridge Dimiat 2001, Assenovgrad Mavrud 2001.

Reserve Stambolovo Merlot Res 2000, Oriachovitza Cab Special Res 1997 and 1999, Domaine Boyar Iambol Royal Res Cab 1996, Svishtov Cab Gorchivka 1998.

Riesling Rhine Ries is grown, but most is Italian (Welschries) used for med & dr ws.

Rkatziteli One of the most widely grown grapes in the world, known as Rikat in Bulgaria. Widely used in dry and medium white-wine blends in NE.

Rousse w r Lge winery in N on the DANUBE. Merged with BOYAR ESTATES. Fresh, high-tech whites esp CHARD, SAUV BL. Gd reds, incl limited selection CAB (00).

Rubin Bulgarian cross (Nebbiolo x Syrah); often blended with CAB or MERLOT.

Sakar SE wine area for MERLOT, some of Bulgaria's best.

Sauvignon Blanc Grown in E and N Bulgaria esp at SHUMEN and TARGOVISHTE.

Shumen w r ★★ Black Sea region and winery (owned by BOYAR ESTATES), esp whites and New World-style reds. Barrique CHARD (01) and MERLOT (00).

Slaviantsi w (r) ★★ Mainly whites, especially MUSCAT, CHARD, MISKET, and Ugni Blanc. Recommended: Ashton Estate CHARD (01).

Sliven r (w) ★★ Big producing S region, esp for CAB, MERLOT & Pinot N (blended COUNTRY WINE), MISKET, & CHARD. Vini Sliven produces r & w. Promising barrique-aged Cab.

Stambolovo Satellite cellar of HASKOVO. MERLOT specialist.

Stara Zagora Thracian Plain winery: reds, esp CAB and MERLOT to RESERVE quality.

Sungurlare Satellite of SLAVIANTSI. MISKET noted for delicate fragrance. Also CHARD.

Svishtov r ★★ N region winery on DANUBE. Reds only, especially finely balanced CABERNET. Also good rosé Cabernet (01).

Targovishte w ★★ Winery in east. Quality CHARD (incl barrel-fermented) & SAUV BL.

Traminer Increasingly grown in Northeast. Fine whites with hints of spice.

Varna w ★ Black Sea coast region for whites, esp CHARD (buttery or unoaked), SAUV, DIMIAT, ALIGOTE, and UGNI BL (sometimes blended).

Croatia and The Balkans

Slovenia

Slovenia is scheduled to join the EU in May 2004. The traditional, conservative wine industry is wary of change but quality producers (growing in number since independence in 1991) will only benefit from access to a bigger market.

Slovenia is divided into 3 wine regions, subdivided into districts. The better ones are listed below. Wines are generally bottled by grape variety although many producers are pushing their signature blends. Vintages do not vary greatly, yet among the most recent, 1997 and 2000 are considered exceptional.

Barbara International Sparklers of all types and price. NV Barbara and Miha (both ★) are gd value, while No.1 vintage (★★★) is often Slovenia's best.

Bati ★★ Increasingly organic v'yd from VIPAVA. Top wine: Chard, others also vg.

Bjana ★★ Top producer of sparklers from GORIŠKA BRDA. Intense, full-bodied wines. Very popular in classier Ljubljana restaurants.

Cabernet Sauvignon Grown in PROMORSKI region, best in KOPER. Almost everybody in GORIŠKA BRDA and VIPAVA grows it. Decent quality.

Chardonnay Grown everywhere, generally gd, often unoaked, esp in PODRAVSKI.

Cviček Traditional pink blend of PODRAVSKI. Low alcohol, high acid. Decent quality from co-op KRŠKO, premium by Frelih (Cviček od fare).

Curin ★★ Legendary pioneer of private winegrowing from early 70's onwards. Varietal whites and PREDIKATS of very high standards.

Gorice Name for hills with vineyards, used with different geographical names to denote districts in PODRAVSKI region.

Goriška Brda Slovenian part of Collio. Many vg producers, among them Jakončič, Kabaj, Klinec, MOVIA, SIMČIČ, ŠČUREK etc. Slovenia's lgst co-op of the same name produces several brands: Bagueri ★★★ (esp Chard, Merlot), Quercus (Rebula, Tokaj) ★★, and low priced Villa Brici.

Haloze ★→★★★ Prestigious winery in Ptuj with a collection of vintages from 1917. Recent vintages less notable, but the 80s were fantastic (and still great value): look in particular for RENSKI RIZLING and TRAMINEC.

Izbor Auslese. **Jagodni izbor** Beerenauslese.

Joannes ★★ Fine winery nr Maribor. Crisp, well defined whites.

Kogl ★★★ Hilltop winery near Ormož tracing its history to 1542. Replanted in 1984. Whites are among Slovenia's best, either varietal (Solo) or Duo, Trio, and Quartet blends. MODRI PINOT (00). Exceptional long-lived PREDIKATS.

Kristančič Dušan ★★★ Top producer from GORIŠKA BRDA. Very strict low quantities, top Chardonnay and SIVI PINOT. Reds: ★★.

Koper PRIMORSKI coastal district, best-known for REFOŠK. SANTOMAS & VINAKOPER excel.

Kras PRIMORSKI district. Several gd TERAN producers. Incl Cotar, Lisjak Boris, RENČEL.

Kupljen Jože ★★ Quality dry wine pioneer near Ormož. One of Slovenia's first Pinot Ns labeled Modri Burgundec ★★★; in better years also POZNA TRGATEV.

Laški Rizling Italy's Welschriesling. Most planted variety, but now in decline.

Ledeno vino Icewine. Only in exceptional years and can be sublime.

Ljutomer Traditionally top wine district with neighbouring Ormož. Co-op called Ljutomerčan will definitely see better times, as the vineyards it encompasses are among Slovenia's best.

Malvazija Underrated variety in KOPER. Slightly bitter yet generous flavour goes very well with seafood. M by VINAKOPER is incredible value.

Merlot Planted widely in PRIMORSKI (except KRAS). Fairly gd, seldom outstanding.

Mlečnik ★★ Disciple of Italy's Joško Gravner from VIPAVA. The closest anyone in Slovenia comes to organics. Best-known for Chard, also for REBULA and Tokaj.

Modra frankinja Austria's Blaufränkisch. Fruity reds mostly in POSAVSKI region, best as Metliška črnina by the Metlika co-op in the Bela krajina district.

Modri pinot Pinot Noir. Recently planted in all regions, with mixed results.

Movia ★★→★★★★ Best-known Slovenian winery. Releases only mature vintages of top wines: Veliko Rdeče (r) after 6 years and Belo (w) after 4. Recently planted different varieties in one v'yd for white blend Turno. Varietals: look for REBULA and possibly Slovenia's finest MODRI PINOT. 2nd wine: Villa Marija.

Ormož ★★ Top wine district with Ljutomer. Co-op named Jeruzalem Ormož. Redefining image with premium brand Holermuos, and gd Muscat sparkler.

Podravski Traditionally most respected Slovenian region in the NE. Recent come back with aromatic whites and increasingly fine reds, mostly MODRI PINOT.

Posavski Conservative wine region in the SE, best known for CVIČEK.

Pozna trgatev Late harvest.

Predikat Wines made of botrytis-affected grapes with high sugar content. The term is taken from the German tradition and is used mostly in the PODRAVSKI region as POZNA TRGATEV, IZBOR, JAGODNI IZBOR, SUHI JAGODNI IZBOR, LEDENO VINO.

Primorski Region in the SW from the Adriatic to GORIŠKA BRDA. The most forward-looking Slovenian wine region for both reds and whites.

Radgonske gorice ★★→★★★ District nr Austrian border, and co-op home to Radgonska Penina, Slovenia's best known sparkler. Vintage Zlata (golden) is drier and fuller, also ages well, NV Srebrna (silver) often off-dry. Also very popular sweet TRAMINEC and blend Janževec.

Rebula Traditional white variety of GORIŠKA BRDA. Can be exceptional.

Refošk Italy's Refosco. Dark and acidic red, a local favourite. Top by SANTOMAS. In oaked and (better) unoaked versions.

Renčel ★★★★ Outstanding producer of TERAN (tiny quantities), also vg whites.

Renski Rizling Ries. PODRAVSKI. best: JOANNES, Jeruzalem ORMOŽ, KOGL, Skaza Anton.

Santomas ★★★ Producing high quality mature REFOŠK and international-style Cabernet. Premium brands are Antonius and Grande Cuvée.

Simčič Edi ★★★ Highly reputed GORIŠKA BRDA producer. In particular look for REBULA. All reserve bottlings are very refined and harmonious.

Simčič Marjan ★★★ GORIŠKA BRDA producer of v high standards (Chard and SIVI PINOT). REBULA based blend Teodor is outstanding. A particular gem is Sauv Bl.

Sivi Pinot Italy's Pinot Grigio. Not particularly fine but top names can be vg.

Sčurek ★★ Very reliable GORIŠKA BRDA producer (REBULA, Tokaj, Sauv Bl, Chard, Cab Franc). Red and white blends Stara brajda are ★★★.

Steyer ★★ Top name from RADGONSKE GORICE. Best known for TRAMINEC, recently also very good Chard, RENSKI RIZLING, SIVI PINOT.

Suhi jagodni izbor Trockenbeerenauslese. Extremely rare, notable by VINAG.

Sturm ★★→★★★ Long-established, yet lone star of the Bela Krajina district in POSAVSKI region. Red and white PREDIKATS, and also gd varietal wines.

Teran 100% REFOŠK from KRAS. Alongside CVIČEK most popular Slovenian wine.

Traminec Gewürztraminer, only in PODRAVSKI. Generally sw – also as PREDIKAT.

Valdhuber ★★★ Dry wine pioneers in PODRAVSKI. Top wine is (dry!) TRAMINEC.

Vinag ★★→★★★ One of lgst co-ops in the country with HQ and immense cellars in Maribor. Decent varietals and many older vintage PREDIKATS.

Vinakoper ★★★ Large co-op in KOPER. Many vg varietals: MALVAZIJA, CAB S REFOŠK. Premium: Capo d'Istria. Sw Muscat, and reworked r & w Capris blends.

Vinakras ★→★★★ Co-op producing decent quality TERAN in large quantities. Matured TERAN is branded Teranton and is v different from its younger cousin.

Vipava ★★→★★★ District in PRIMORSKI region. Many fine producers: BATIČ, Lisjak Radivoj, MLEČNIK, Sutor, Tilia. Co-op of same name with premium Lanthieri (formerly Vipava 1894).Traditional blend Vrtovčan and more recent one with intriguing name Kindermacher. Several decent varietals.

Croatia

Communism and civil war have not helped the wine industry of Croatia. The economic situation is improving but still tough. Foreign investment is not widespread. Wine areas are divided in two major regions: Kontinentalna (inland) and Primorska (coastal). There are many native varieties, especially in Dalmatia. In 2002 it was confirmed that Zinfandel/Primitivo originated from a native Dalmatian grape known locally as Crljenak. Most wine is consumed by Croats themselves.

Agrolaguna ★→★★ Co-op at Poreč, ISTRIA. Good r and w, esp Cabernet S.

Babič Dark, long-lived, native red from Primošten (DALMATIA). Can be excellent. Best by VINOPLOD. Picturesque v'yds protected by Unesco.

Badel ★→★★★ Big négociant and co-op. Wines from all over. Best are IVAN DOLAC, DINGAČ, GRAŠEVINA Daruvar, Rukatac Smokvica, Pošip Smokvica.

Bogdanuša Local white from island of HVAR. Look for Plančič.

Chardonnay Grown in KONTINENRALNA HRVATSKA and ISTRIA. Usually good.

Dalmacija-vino ★ Co-op at Split: range of DALMATIAN wines.

Dalmacija Dalmatia. The coast of Croatia, Zadar to Dubrovnik including islands. Home of many native varieties. Traditionally high in alcohol. Excellent reds, but whites are often old-fashioned and oxidized.

Dingač V'yd designation on PELJEŠAC'S steep southern slopes. Made from partially dried PLAVAC M producing full-bodied, jammy red, but emerging as robust dry red that supports oak and bottle ageing. Highly esteemed and expensive. Look for Bura, Kiridžija, Matuško, Miličić, Skaramuča.

Enjingi, Ivan ★★★ Producer of excellent w from Požega. Sivi Pinot, Graševina, Gewürz, botrytised wines. Interesting Zweigelt.

Graševina Local name for Welschriesling. Best from SLAVONIA. Look for Adžič, ENJINGI, KRAUTHAKER, Vinarija Daruvar, Djakova_ka vina, KUTJEVO.

Grk White native grape, speciality of island of Korcula, producing strong, sherry-like wine, and also a lighter, paler one. Look for Cebalo Branimir.

Grgič, Miljenko ★★★ Californian w'maker (Grgich Hills) returns to Croatian roots. Cellar on PELJESAC peninsula. Makes PLAVAC and POŠIP.

Hvar Island in middle Dalmatia. Some excellent reds from PLAVAC MALI grapes from steep southern slopes. Interesting whites and reds picked from plateau. Look for ZLATAN PLAVAC, IVAN DOLAC, Faros.

Istria N Adriatic peninsula. Gd MALVASIA, CHARD and Muscat. Look for Coronica, Degrassi, Kozlovič, MATOŠEVIČ, Ravalico. Also gd Merlot, Cab S, and TERAN.

Istravino (Ivex) ★ Co-op based in Rijeka. Known for its sparkler.

Ivan Dolac V'yd area on southern slopes of HVAR. Vg dry red from PLAVAC MALI.

Kontinentalna Hrvatska Inland Croatia (N). Mostly for w (GRAŠEVINA, Riesling, CHARD). Gd reds (Pinot Noir, Merlot) emerging.

Krauthaker, Vlado ★★★ Vg w from Kutjevo, esp CHARD & GRAŠEVINA. Reds ★★.

Kutjevo Town in SLAVONIJA and co-op ★★. Vg Gewürz, GRAŠEVINA and botrytis.

Malvazija Malvasia. Planted in ISTRIA. A pleiad of private producers made a shift from old-fashioned oxidized MALVASIAS to some vg crisp wines.

Maraština Strong herbal, dry DALMATIAN white, best from Lastovo.

Matoševič, Ivica ★★★ Small producer from ISTRIA. Look for CHARDONNAYS.

Miloš, Frano ★★ Producer from PELJEŠAC. Cult brand Stagnum (PLAVAC MALI).

Pelješac Beautiful peninsula and quality wine region in S DALMATIA. Some vg r PLAVAC MALI, but mostly overrated. See GRGRIČ, MILOŠ, POSTUP, DINGAČ.

Plančič ★★ Producer of interesting r and w on HVAR. Rare r Darnekuša.

Plavac Mali The best DALMATIAN r grape: wine of body, strength, and ageability. See DINGAČ, GRGČ, IVAN DOLAC, MILOŠ, POSTUP, ZLATAN OTOK.

Polu Semi... Polu-slatko is semi-sweet, polu-suho is semi-dry.

Postup V'yd designation on AC, just NW of DINGAČ. Med- to full-bodied red

Prošek Almost Port-like dessert wine from ISTRIA and DALMATIA: 15% abv.

Primorska Entire coastal Croatia including ISTRIA and DALMATIA inland.

Slavonija sub-region in N Croatia for whites. Try: ENJINGI, KRAUTHAKER, KUTJEVO.

Stolno vino Tablewine. Some very good wines are designated as this.

Teran Stout, highly acidic dark red of ISTRIA made from Refosco grape.

Vinoplod ★ Co-op from Sibenik in N DALMATIA. BABIČ ★★★

Vrhunsko vino New origin-based designation for top-quality wines.

Vugava Rare w of Vis (mid-DALMATIA). Linked to Viognier. Look for Lipanovič.

Zlatan otok ★★★ HVAR-based winery producing top-quality red from PLAVAC MALI branded Zlatan Plavac. Look for 99. Good w and p. Also vg PROŠEK.

Zlahtina W native from island of Krk. Look for Katunar, Toljanič.

Bosnia and Herzegovina

Blatina Ancient MOSTAR red grape and wine from pebbled W bank of Neretva.

Kameno Vino White wine of unique irrigated desert v'yd in Neretva Valley.

Mostar Means "old bridge". Was Herzegovina's Islamic-looking wine centre, but cellars destroyed during the civil war. Ljubuski and Citluk are rebuilding. Potentially admirable ZILAVKA white and BLATINA red.

Samotok Light, red (rosé/"ruzica") wine from run-off juice (and no pressing).

Zilavka The white grape of MOSTAR, potentially dry and pungent and memorably fruity with a faint flavour of apricots.

Serbia

Serbia has its own Prokupac grape; used alone it makes a light, fruity red, often blended with Pinot Noir or Gamay. Some Cab S and Merlot in Southeast

Montenegro

13 July State-run co-op; high-tech Italian kit, nr PODGORICA. VRANAC: high quality.

Crmnica Lakeside/coastal v'yds esp for Kadarka grape (see Macedonia).

Duklja Late-picked, semi-sweet version of VRANAC.

Krstac Montenegro's top white grape and wine; esp from CRMNICA.

Merlot Since 80: good, wood-aged results.

Vranac Local vigorous and abundant red grape and wine. Value.

Macedonia

Recommended wineries: Povardarie-Negotine, Bovin-Negotino for Cab Sauv, Merlot, Pinot N, and VRANEC. Lozar-Veles for Sauv Bl, Chard, and Zilavka.

Belan White Grenache. Makes neutral blended wine.

Kadarka Major red grape of Hungary; here closer to its origins around L Ohrid.

Kratosija Locally favoured red grape; sound wines with good potential.

Plovdina Native (S) grape for mild red, white; esp blended with tastier PROKUPAC.

Prokupac Serbian and Macedonian top red grape. Makes dark rosé (Ruzica) and full red of character, esp at Zupa. PLOVDINA often added for smoothness.

Rkatsiteli Russian (white) grape often used in blends.

Temjanika Grape for spicy, semi-sweet whites.

Teran Transferred from Istria, but Macedonia's version is less stylish.

Tikves Much-favoured hilly v'yd region (20,000 acres). Esp for pleasant, dark-red Kratosija; fresh, dry Smederevka – locally mixed with soda.

Traminac The Traminer. Also grown in Vojvodina and Slovenia.

Vardar Valley Brings the benefits of the Aegean Sea to inland v'yds.

Vranec Local name for Vranac of Montenegro (qv); indifferent quality.

Vrvno Vino Controlled origin designation for quality wines.

The Czech Republic and Slovakia

The Czech and Slovak republics had barely any tradition of exporting but good wines have emerged since 1989. 1997, 1999, & 2000 are outstanding vintages. Privatization and foreign investment and advice bode well for the future.

Moravia Favourite wines in Prague for variety and value. Vineyards situated along Danube tributaries. Many wines from Austrian border: similar grapes, Grüner V, Müller-T, Sauv, Traminer, St-Laurent, Pinot Noir, Pinot Blanc, Blauer Portugieser, Frankovka, Rhine Riesling, Vlassky Riesling; eg from **Mikros Mikulov** (vg Chardonnay 2000), **Znovin Satov** (modern, mostly white – grapes from local farms and co-ops), **Jaroslavice** (oak-aged reds), **Vinium** (since 1936, now privately-owned & advised by Australian winemakers: mostly white, also light, fruity reds, incl Moravia Hills Dry Red), **Vinne Sklepy Valtice** (Historic South Moravian château, now a privately owned co-op: clean, savoury white and aromatic red), & **Znojmo** (long-est'd, ideal limestone soil; local white grapes, sweetish prize-winning Pinot Gris from Sobes). **Other regions:** Prímetice (full, aromatic whites), Blatnice, Hustopece, sunny Pálava, Saldorf (esp Sauvignon bl, "Rynsky" Riesling), and Velké Pavlovice (vg Veltliner 1999 from Vinselekt). Moravia also has sparkling.

Bohemia Winemaking since 9th C. Same latitude and similar wines to eastern Germany. Best: N of Prague, in Elbe Valley, and (best-known) nr Melník (Ries, Ruländer, and Traminer predominate). Bohemia Sekt from Stary Plzenec is popular: tank-fermented (mostly) with grapes from SLOVAKIA and MORAVIA. Soare sparkling also growing. Also interesting Pinot N. Top wineries: **Lobkowitz** (at Melnik), **Roudnice, Litomerice, Karlstein**.

Slovakia V'yds now declining. Best in east n'bouring Hungary's Tokaj region. Hungarian and international varieties and a little Tokaj, too. Key districts: Malo-Karpatská Oblast (largest region, in foothills of the Little Carpathians, incl Ruländer, Ries, Traminer, Limberger, etc), Malá Trna, Nové Mesto, Skalice (small area, mainly reds), and (in Tatra foothills) Bratislava, Pezinok, Modra.

Romania

Romania has a long winemaking tradition, but potential for quality was wasted during decades of supplying the USSR with cheap sweet wine. Quantity is still the goal but modern equipment, foreign expertise, and a growing focus on vineyard management are seeing a fraction of Romania's vast potential realized. The full, soft reds from Dealul Mare (esp Pinot Noir) are gaining an excellent international reputation. Further capital investment, as well as consistency, is still needed.

Alba Iulia Area in cool TIRNAVE region of TRANSYLVANIA, known for aromatic and off-dry white (Italian RIES, FETEASCA, MUSKAT-OTTONEL), bottle-fermented sparkling.

Aligoté Pleasantly fresh white from 11,000 acres (2nd only to France).

Băbească Neagra Traditional red grape of the FOCSANI area, light body and colour. (Means "(black) grandmother grape".)

Banat Plain on border with Serbia. Workaday Italian RIES, SAUV BL, MUSKAT-OTTONEL, and local Ries de Banat; light red Cadarca, CABERNET, and Merlot.

Burgund Mare Name linked to Burgenland in (Austria) where grape is called Blaufränkisch (Kékfrankos in Hungary).

Buzau Hills Gd reds (CAB, Merlot, BURGUND M) from continuation of DEALUL MARE.

Cabernet Sauvignon Increasingly grown, esp at DEALUL MARE; dark, intense wines.

Carl Reh New German-owned 2.5m litre winery in Oprisor.

Carpathian Winery Dealul Mare. Excellent Pinot N. Try Telegraph Hill 2000.

ROMANIA

Chardonnay Some sweet styles but modern dry and oak-aged styles, esp from MURFATLAR and TRANSYLVANIA increasingly available.

Cotnari N region with warm microclimate and gd botrytis. Famous (rare) light sw w from GRASA, FETEASCA ALBA, TAMAIIOASA, and Francusa. Like v delicate Tokaj.

Crisana W region including historical MiniS area (since 15th C: reds, esp Cadarca, and crisp, white Mustoasa), Silvania (esp FETEASCA), Diosig, Valea lui Mihai.

Dealul Mare "The big hill". Important, up-to-date, well-sited area in SE Carpathian foothills. R's from FETEASCA NEAGRA, CAB, Merlot, PINOT N, etc. W's from TAMIIOASA. French investment. Look for Dionis label (fine reds).

Dobrogea Sunny, dry, Black Sea region. Incl MURFATLAR. Quality is good.

DOC New classification for higher-quality wines replacing VS, VSO.

DOCG (Was VSOC) Top-range wines. CMD: late-harvest, CMI: late-harvest with noble rot, CIB is from selected nobly rotten grapes (like Beerenauslese).

Drăgăşani Region on River Olt S of Carpathian Mtns, since Roman times. Traditional and modern grapes (esp Sauv Bl). Gd MUSKAT-OTTONEL, reds (CAB).

Fetească White grape with spicy, faintly Muscat aroma. Two types: F Alba (same as Hungary's Leányka, age-worthy and with better potential esp when carefully handled; base for sp and sw COTNARI) and F Regala (gd for sp).

Fetească Neagră Red Feteasca. Difficult to handle, but can give deep, full-bodied reds with gd character and ageing potential. "Black maiden grape".

Focsani Important MOLDAVIA region, incl Cotesti, Nicoresti, and Odobesti.

Grasă A form of the Hungarian Furmint grape grown in Romania and used in, among other wines, COTNARI. Prone to botrytis. Grasa means "fat".

Iaşi Region for fresh, acidic whites (F ALBA, also Welschries, ALIGOTE, spumante-style MUSKAT O): Bucium, Copu, Tomesti. Reds: Merlot, CAB; top BABEASCA.

Jidvei Winery in the cool Carpathians (TIRNAVE) among Romania's N-most V'yds. Good whites: FETEASCA, Furmint, RIES, SAUV BL.

Lechinta Transylvanian wine area. Wines noted for bouquet (local grapes).

Merlot Romania's workhorse grape. Most widely planted red.

Murfatlar V'yds nr Black Sea, 2nd-best botrytis conditions (see Cotnari): esp sweet CHARD, late-harvest CAB. Now also full, dry wines and sparkling.

Muscat Ottonel The E European Muscat, a speciality of Romania, esp in cool-climate TRANSYLVANIA and dry wines in MOLDAVIA.

Paulis Small estate cellar in town of same name. Oak-aged Merlot a treasure.

Perla Semi-sw speciality of TIRNAVE: Italian RIES, FETEASCA, and MUSKAT-OTTONEL.

Pinot Gris Widely grown in TRANSYLVANIA and MURFATLAR. Full, slightly aromatic wines, closer to Alsace than Italian Pinot Grigio in style.

Pinot Noir Grown in the South: can surprise with taste and character.

Prahova Winecellars Promising British venture (7 wineries in DEALUL MARE) using native and international grapes, incl Sangiovese. Try Pinot N 99.

Premiat Reliable range of higher-quality wines for export.

Riesling (Italian Riesling) Widely planted. Most poorly made, but has potential.

Sauvignon Blanc Often Romania's tastiest white, esp blended with FETEASCA.

Tămîîoasă Românească Traditional white grape known as "frankincense" for its exotic scent and flavour. Pungent sw wines often affected by botrytis.

Târnave Transylvanian region (Romania's coolest), known for its PERLA and FETEASCA REGALA. Dry aromatic wines (esp Pinot Gr, Gewürz) and sparkling.

Transylvania High central region. See Alba Iulia, Lechinta, Tîrnave.

Valea Călugărească "Valley of the Monks", part of DEALUL MARE. CABERNET, Merlot, & PINOT NOIR are admirable, as are Italian RIESLING & PINOT GRIS.

Vin de Masa Most basic wine classification – for local drinking only.

Vinexport Est'd 90, fast developing (80% of Romania's wine exports).

Vinterra Dutch/Romanian venture. Best wine is Merlot 99.

Vrancea Eastern region covering Panciu, Odobesti, Cotesti, and Nicoresti.

Greece

Since entry into the EC in 1981 Greece's antique wine industry has moved up a gear. Some is still fairly primitive, but a new system of appellations is in place, and recent years have seen an explosion of stylish and original wines. Well-made authentically Greek wines are worth seeking out and not only in Greece.

Agiorghitiko Widely planted NEMEA red-wine grape. Very high potential.

Agioritikos Medium whites and rosés from Agios Oros (Mt Athos), Halkidiki's monastic peninsula. Brand name for TSANTALIS.

Alpha Estate ★★ Modern estate in cooler-climate Amindeo. First wine the barrel-aged 2002 blend of Merlot, Syrah, and Xinomavro. To watch.

Antonopoulos ★★→★★★ Highly reputed producer: MANTINIA, Adoli Ghis, unoaked (01), nutty Chard (00), Cabernet-Nea Dris (**97 98 00 01**). New conc'd aromatic Gris de Noir (01). To watch.

Argyros ★★→★★★ Top SANTORINI producer with delicious (expensive) Vinsanto aged 20 yrs in cask. Current vintage: 84. Bone-dry white Ktima Argyos 01.

Boutari, J and Son ★→★★★ Merchants in NAOUSSA. Also wineries in GOUMENISSA, MANTINIA, on SANTORINI and CRETE. Broad range from all over Greece. New varietals: white oak-fermented Kallisti, MOSCOFILERO.

Calliga ★ KOURTAKIS-owned. Gd AGIORGHITIKO for Montenero and Rubis.

Cambas, Andrew ★ Brand owned by BOUTARI. Vg value Chard & Cab S.

Carras, Domaine ★★ Estate at Sithonia, Halkidiki with its own AC (Côtes de Meliton). Old Vine Syrah 98. Under new management since 2000.

Cava Legal term for cask-aged still w & r wine. Eg Cava BOUTARI (NAOUSSA-NEMEA).

Cephalonia (Kephalonia) Ionian island: good white ROBOLA and Muscat.

Creat-Olympias ★→★★ Emerging Cretan producer. Vg value fruity w Xerolithia. Improving juicy red Mirabelo and cask-aged red and white Creta-Nobile 01.

Crete Improving quality. Led by Alexakis, Ekonomou, Lyrarakis.

Emery ★→★★ An historic RHODES producer, specializing in local varieties: brand names Villare and GrandRose. Also gd-quality, trad-method sp wine.

Gaia ★★★ Top-quality NEMEA-based producer. Fruity Notios label. Leading Aghiorghitiko. Top wine Gaia Estate (**97 98 99 00 01**). Also unoaked and oaked Thalassitis from SANTORINI. Astonishing RETSINA Ritinitis Nobilis.

Gentilini ★★→★★★ Upmarket white ROBOLA from CEPHALONIA. New Syrah 01.

Gerovassiliou ★★★ Perfectionist miniature estate nr Salonika. New World-style Syrah-Merlot Ktima 01. Spicy Syrah 01.

Goumenissa (AC) **★→★★** Oaked red from MACEDONIA. Esp BOUTARI, Ktima Tatsis.

Hatzimichalis, Domaine ★ Small estate and merchant in Atalanti. Huge range. Greek and French varieties. Top wine: red CAVA.

Katsaros ★★→★★★ Sml winery of v high standards on Mt Olympus. Organic. Ktima has staying power. Cab-Merlot (00), supple Chard (02).

Kir-Yanni ★★→★★★ V'yds in Naoussa and at Amindeo – high quality. Vibrant w Samaropetra (02). Gd Syrah (00). Top Naoussa: Xinomavro Single V'yd (98).

Kouros ★ Reliable, well-marketed white PATRAS and red NEMEA from KOURTAKIS.

Kourtakis, D ★★ Athenian merchant with mild RETSINA and good, dark NEMEA.

Ktima Estate, farm. Term not exclusive to wine.

Nico Lazaridis ★★ Family estate in Drama, NE of Salonika. Spectacular post-modernist winery. Rich Merlot (01). Top wine: Magiko Vouno w (01) & r (98).

Lazaridis, Domaine Kostas r w p **★★→★★★** Not to be confused with NICO LAZARIDIS. High-quality Amethystos label. Top wine: unfiltered r CAVA (00).

Lemnos (AC) Aegean island: co-op dessert wines, deliciously fortified Muscat of Alexandria. New dry Muscats by Kyathos-Honas winery.

Macedonia Quality wine region in the North, for XINOMAVRO.

Malagousia Rediscovered perfumed white grape. Major producers CARRAS, GEROVASSILIOU (new single varietal in 2001 or blended with Assyrtiko), MATSA.

Mantinia (AC) PELOPONNESE region. Fresh, grapey MOSCOFILERO.

Matsa, Château ★★→★★★ Sml ATTICA prod exploiting native Greek varieties. Top wine: SAVATIANO Vieilles Vignes. Also stylish Laoutari & excellent MALAGOUSIA.

Mavrodaphne (AC) "Black laurel", and red grape. Cask-aged Port/recioto-like, concentrated red; fortified to 15–22%. Speciality of PATRAS, N PELOPONNESE.

Mercouri ★★→★★★ PELOPONNESE family estate. V fine Refosco, delicious RODITIS. New CAVA (00) Classy Refosco dal Penducolo rosso and MAVRODAPHNE blend.

Moscofilero Rose-scented high-quality, high-acid grape.

Naoussa (AC) r High-quality region for XYNOMAVRO. One of two Greek regions where a "cru" notion may soon develop. Excellent vintages include: 00 01.

Nemea (AC) r Region in E PELOPONNESE producing dark, spicy AGIORGHITIKO wines. Often also the backbone of many (not always Greek) blends. High Nemea merits its own appellation. Koutsi front-runner for cru status.

Oenoforos ★★ Gd PELOPONNESE producer. Leading RODITIS w Asprolithi. Elegant w Lagorthi. Fresh Chard, subtle Cab. Crisp Riesling (02) and fine Syrah (01).

Papaïoannou ★★→★★★ Top NEMEA grower. V classy red, incl Pinot N; flavourful, oaky w. Top wine: Ktima Papaioannou Palea Klimata (old vines) 97 98.

Patras (AC) White wine (based on RODITIS) and wine town facing the Ionian Sea. Home of MAVRODAPHNE. Rio-Patras (AC) sweet Muscat.

Peloponnese Mountainous southern land mass of mainland Greece, with half of the country's v'yds, incl NEMEA, MANTINIA, and PATRAS.

Rapsani Interesting oaked red from Mt Ossa. Rasping until rescued by TSANTALI.

Retsina Attica speciality white with Aleppo pine resin added; oddly appropriate with certain Greek food. Domestic consumption now waning.

Rhodes Easternmost island. Home to creamy (dry) ATHIRI white grape. Top wines include Caïr (co-op) Rodos 2400 and Emery's Villare. Also some sparkling.

Robola Gd-quality, lemony w grape, originating from speciality of Ionian isles.

Roditis White grape grown all over Greece. Good when yields are low.

Samos (AC) Island nr Turkey famed for sw, pale, golden Muscat. Especially (fortified) Anthemis, (sun-dried) Nectar. Rare old bottlings can be great.

Santorini Volcanic island N of CRETE: luscious, sweet Vinsanto (sun-dried grapes), mineral-laden, bone-dry white from fine Assyrtico grape. Oaked examples are gd. Top producers incl: ARGYROS, GAIA ,Sigalas. Hadjidakis is a new winery.

Savatiano White grape of retsina. Often considered dull, but see Ch Matsa.

Semeli, Château ★★ Estate near Athens. Good white and red, incl Nemea.

Skouras ★★ Innovative PELOPONNESE wines. Viognier (Cuvée Eclectic). Best wine: Megas Oenos red (99). Good high Nemea, Grande Cuvée (00).

Spiropoulos, Domaine ★★ Organic quality producer in MANTINIA. Improving oaky, red Porfyros (AGIORGHITIKO), Cab, Merlot). Sparkling Odi Panos has potential.

Strofilia-Katogi ★ Predominantly Greek varieties. Also Chard & Cab. Floral Traminer.

Tsantalis ★→★★ Merchant/producer at Agios Pavlos. Vineyards in NAOUSSA, Maronia, and RAPSANI. Wide range of country and AC wines. New Athonite wines, w Chromitsa Chardonnay-Athiri-Assyrtiko and r Metohi Limnio-Cab.

Tselepos ★★→★★★ Top-quality MANTINIA producer and Greece's best Gewürz (02). Fresh, oaky Chard. Solid Nemea (00). Very good Cab/Merlot (99). Stylish Merlot (00). Single v'yd Avlotolpi Cab (00), Kokinomylos Merlot (00).

Voyatzi Ktima ★★ Small estate near Kozani. Fat white Malvasia Aromatica (01). Top red: Ktima Voyatzi (01) Xynomavro and Cabernet S blend.

Xinomavro The tastiest of many indigenous Greek red grapes – though name means "acidic-black". Grown in the cooler North, it is the basis for NAOUSSA, GOUMENISSA, and Amindeo. High potential.

Zitsa Mountainous North. Epirus AC. Delicate Debina white, still or fizzy.

Cyprus

Cyprus's finest product is the historic sweet Commandaria – a watery version of which is often used as Communion wine in churches. For years "sherry" paid the bills and reds and whites were basic. Now upgrading has started. Soils are predominantly limestone and the vineyards are located in the foothills of the Troodos Mountains at altitudes of between 250 and 1,600 metres. The majority of the island's wine is produced by 4 organizations. Until recently, only 2 local grapes were grown; now another 12 have emerged, including the inevitable international favourites. In the past, wineries were located near the coastal ports for convenience in shipping. These are now being replaced by small regional wineries in vineyard areas. Significantly, Cyprus has never had phylloxera.

Afames Area on the south slopes of Troodos and a dry tangy r (MAVRO) from SODAP (major wine co-op at LIMASSOL).

Arsinoë Dry, delicate, fruity, dry white XYNISTERI from SODAP, named after an unfortunate female turned to stone by Aphrodite.

Commandaria Good-quality brown sweet wine since ancient times in hills N of LIMASSOL. Region limited to 14 villages; named after crusading order of knights. Made from sun-dried XYNISTERI and MAVRO grapes. Best (as old as 100 yrs) is superb: incredible sweetness, fragrance, concentration – a jewel to seek out. Most Commandaria is solera-matured and a limited quantity is now being exported.

Emva Brand name of well-made dry, medium, and cream Sherry-style wines.

ETKO One of 4 largest producers, based in LIMASSOL. 16 different wines. Best is Ino red, others include white: Nefel, red: Olympus, Cornaro Carignan, Cornaro Grenache, and Semeli.

Kalo Khorio Principal COMMANDARIA village, growing only XYNISTERI.

KEO Lgst, most go-ahead firm at LIMASSOL, also operates 3 wineries. Range incl Alkion, Aphrodite (dry XYNISTERI white), Bellapais (fizzy med-dry white and pink), Thisbe (med-dry white), Rosella (dry fragrant pink), Heritage (rich oaked dry red from MARATHEFTICO), Othello (solid dry red, best drunk at 3-4 yrs), Domaine d'Ahera (velvety, dry red). COMMANDARIA St John (sweet fortified). Standard KEO Dry White & Dry Red: vg value.

Kokkineli Deep-coloured, semi-sw rosé: the name is related to cochineal.

Laona The largest of the small regional wineries at Arsos, now owned by KEO. Good range, incl an oak-aged red and a fruity dry white.

Limassol Southern wine port. Home to all the large wineries.

Loel One of major prods. Reds incl Orpho Negro, Hermes, whites incl varietal PALOMINO and Ries, also COMMANDARIA Alasia (sweet fortified), and brandies.

Marathasa Region in the Troodos foothills.

Maratheftico Vines of superior quality make concentrated red wine of tannin, colour, close to Cab S; the future grape of Cyprus.

Mavro The black grape of Cyprus. Can produce quality if planted at high altitude; otherwise gives sound, acceptable wines.

Monte Roya Modern regional winery at Chryssoroyiatissa Monastery.

Muscat All major firms produce pleasant, low-price Muscats.

Opthalmo Black grape (red/rosé): lighter, sharper than MAVRO.

Palomino Soft dry white (LOEL, SODAP). Very drinkable ice-cold.

Pitsilia Region S of Mt Olympus. Some of best white and COMMANDARIA wines.

Semeli Good traditional red from ETKO. Best at 3–4 years old.

SODAP A co-op winery and one of the four largest producers. Wines incl: w: Arsino, Artemis, Danae; r: Afames, and varietal Carignan and Grenache. Also new range called Island Vines r & w – modern, fresh, inexpensive.

Xynisteri Native aromatic white grape of Cyprus, making delicate & fruity wines.

Asia, North Africa, & the Levant

Algeria As a combined result of Islam and the EC, once-massive vineyards continue to dwindle. Red, white, and esp rosé of some quality and power come from coastal hills of Tlemcen, Mascara (good red and white), Haut-Dahra (strong red, rosé), Zaccar, Tessala, Médéa, and Aïn-Bessem (Bouira can good). Sidi Brahim: drinkable red brand. These had VDQS status in French-colonial days. Cork is also produced.

China China's new enthusiasm for wine is unabated and national consumption increases each year. Investment is pouring in and traditional areas like Xinjiang are planting international varieties. Even in cold Heilongjiang there is a Canadian/Chinese joint venture planting vines for icewine. The regions are becoming more defined, with the Bohai Bay Area on the E coast accounting for roughly 50% of grape wine production. It is home to the premium areas of the Shandong Peninsular and the Tianjin Coast. The North Western Region, including the historical areas in Xinjiang and Gansu, has had an influx of foreign expertise and there is some impressive Cab S. Viticulture is expanding in the Shacheng District to the N of the Great Wall and in the Yellow River Area in Anhui and Henan provinces. Huadong (Shandong) continues to set new standards, esp with single vineyard wines from Chardonnay and Riesling. In Xinjiang, Lou Lou Winery in the Turpan Basin is showing promise with Cab S, Merlot, Chenin Blanc, and the local variety Bayiu. Other wineries to look for include the Suntime Group (Xinjiang) and the Lafang Castel-Changyu winery (Shandong), the largest winery in Asia.

India Tiny industry dominated by Ch Indage (70% of national total), SE of Bombay, with international recognition for Chard- & Pinot N-based sparklers: Omar Khayyám, Marquise de Pompadour (sweeter), and Celèbre (vintage). Still wines incl European varietals as well as blends incorporating local varieties. Labels are Chantilli, Soma, Riviera, & Vin Ballet. Grover is the other significant producer, S of Bangalore. Sula, NE of Bombay, is a new entrant.

Japan The wine industry is based in the central Honshu prefecture of Yamanashi, W of Tokyo. Nagano & Yamagata prefectures (N of Tokyo) and the northern island of Hokkaido are the other significant regions. The sentimental favourite of the Japanese is the Koshu grape, upon which the industry was founded. But 80% of the 55,000 acres under vine is planted with *V. labrusca* varieties or *V. labrusca*-based hybrids (eg Delaware, Kyoho, Campbell's Early Muscat, & Muscat Bailey A), mainly for the table but used by winemakers. Plantings of Chard, Cab S, Cab F, & Merlot have created a new de luxe market for Japanese wines; quality can be v high, but quantities are tiny (2,500 acres). To compensate for inappropriate varieties, tricky conditions and high costs, concentrates, must (even grapes) and bulk wine are imported and used for fermenting or blending locally. Labelling laws permit a small amount of genuine domestic wine to go a long way. Low-priced "domestic" wine has mostly imported content; even premium wines receive a boost. Five drinks giants account for two-thirds total production: Mercian, Suntory, Sapporo (Polaire), Manns, and Kyowa Hakko Kogyo (Ste-Neige). The most interesting (and expensive) wines are Mercian's Kikyogahara Merlot and Jyonohira Cab: real density and quality. Suntory also makes limited bottlings. Smaller operations making Koshu and/or European varieties incl Ch Lumière, Marufuji, Grace, Kizan, Katsunuma Jozo, Alps, Takeda, Okuizumo, and Kobe Wines. Tokachi Winery does interesting things with wild vines native to Hokkaido.

Morocco North Africa's best wine is produced from vineyards along the Atlantic coast (Rabat to Casablanca, light, fruity with a white – "Gris" – made from red grapes) and around Meknes and Fez (best-known). Vineyards have declined from 190,000 to 32,000 acres but big investment from French companies such as W'm Pitters & Castel is transforming the industry. Celliers de Meknes is the local leader but has now been joined by Cépages de Meknes, Cépages de Boulaouane, and SADAY in producing quality wines. Look for varietal reds and Sauvignon Blanc. Also L'Excellence de Bonassia (aged Cabernet-Merlot blend), Domaine de Sahari, or good-value Atlas Vineyards, and El Baraka.

Tunisia Now has 37,000 vineyard acres (there were 120,000 15 yrs ago). The speciality was sweet Muscats and light rosés. Some drinkable reds are now being produced. Coolest v'yds are on the coast. Selian is one to watch and Accademia del Sole, with investment from Sicily, better grape varieties and an Aussie winemaker, is making the best wine.

Turkey Most of Turkey's 1.5 million acres of v'yds produce table grapes; only 3% are for wine. Wines from Thrace, Anatolia, and the Aegean can be v drinkable. Many indigenous varieties: 60 are commercial – eg Emir, Narince (w) and Bogazkere, Oküzgözü (r), and used with Riesling, Sém, Pinot N, Grenache, Carignan, and Gamay. Trakya (Thrace) white (light Sém) and Buzbag (E Anatolian) red are well-known standards of state producer Tekel (21 state wineries). Diren, Doluca, Karmen, Kavaklidere, Taskobirlik are private firms; fair quality. Doluca's Villa Nevar from Thrace is well-made, as is Villa Doluca. Kavaklidere makes gd Primeurs (white Cankaya, red Yakut) from local grapes. Buzbag is Turkey's most original and striking wine.

The Old Russian Empire

The 12 CIS (Commonwealth of Independent States) countries of the former USSR now produce a total of only 3% of the world's wine. Improvements since the 1991 revolution are slow but some producers are producing interesting wines.

Ukraine (incl Crimea) 2nd-lgst wine-producing country in the CIS. Crimea's first-class dessert & fortified wines were revealed in 90 by the auction of old wines from the last Tsar's Massandra Collection, nr Yalta, where production continues. Classic brut sp from Novy Svet (founded 1890 by Prince Golitsyn, served at Tsar's coronation 1896 and Grand Prix Paris 1900. Reds: potential (eg Massandra's Alushta). Whites: Aligoté & Artmovskoe sp. To watch.

Georgia Possibly the oldest wine region of all. Antique methods such as fermentation in clay vats (*kveris*) still exist. Newer techniques used for exports (Mukuzani, Tsinandali); Reluctant to modernize. Kakheti (E): produces two-thirds of Georgia's wine, famed for big red (Saperavi), acceptable white (Tibaani, Rkatsiteli, Gurjaani). Kartli: central area. Foreign investors: Pernod Ricard big in Kakheti with GWS brand, US-owned Bagrationi has cheap, drinkable sp. Both widely exported. As equipment, techniques, attitudes evolve, Georgia could be an export hit.

Moldova The most important in size and potential. Wine generates a 3rd of Moldova's income. Wine regions are: Bugeac (most important, S), Nistrean, Codrean, Northern. Grapes incl Cab, Pinot Noir, Merlot, Saperavi (fruity), Ries, Chard, Pinot Gr, Aligoté, Rkatsiteli. Blends of Cabernet and Saperavi can be particularly good, like long-lived, old-fashioned red Bordeaux. Top wineries: Purkar, Cahul, Kazayak, Hincesti; also good: Cricova. Western and Antipodean (Penfolds since 1993) investment at Hincesti, and more recently by local company Vininvest, has brought modern, hygienic winemaking practices. Moldova's most modern-tasting wine: Ryman's Hincesti Chard is very good.

Most wineries are now privatised; progress has not been smooth, but worth following. Appellations are now in force. Cricova's cellars are an impressive tourist attraction with some 120 km of tunnels.

Russia Wine culture was never strong. Main region: Krasnodar on Northern Black Sea Coast, produces 80% of Russia's wine. Sw wines prevail, dry growing fast. Fair Cab, Merlot, Saperavi, Riesling, & Rkatsiteli (Anapa & Temruk); Vityazevo Winery (Anapa), Kagor (sw), and Pontiskoe (red); red sparkling Tsimlanskoye Shampanskoe (Rostov). Abrau Durso brut (also Prince Golitsyn): since 1896 classic sp (Aligoté, Chard, Cab F); Champagne-like climate; Muscats. Top prod: Fanagoria (Temruk): Merlot, Cab, Chard.

The Levant

Israel New vineyards with classic varieties and a focus on cool climate, high altitude regions like Upper Galilee and Golan Heights has transformed Israeli wines, as has modern technology and internationally trained winemakers.

Amphorae r w ★★ Powerful, full-bodied Cab S (oo) – new quality winery.

Barkan r w Israel's 2nd-lgst winery. Consistent Reserve Cab and Segal Chard.

Carmel r w sp No 1 producer and exporter. Private Collection Cab S and Ramat Arad Merlot best; "Vineyards Selected" wines good value. New boutique winery with Yatir vineyards very promising.

Castel Judean Hills r w ★★★ Small family estate in mountains west of Jerusalem producing characterful, complex Cab-Merlot (**96** 97 **98** 99'); outstanding Chard (oo). 2nd label Petit Castel.

Dalton Upper Galilee r w Best Israeli Sauv Bl; Merlot and Cab S also good.

Flam r ★ Fine, concentrated Merlot (oo). Young "Classico" is good value.

Galil Mountain Upper Galilee r w Forward, fruity reds are great value.

Margalit r ★ Deeply coloured, intense Special Reserve Cab S (**95** oo).

Recanati r w Produce Cab, Chard, Merlot; Reserve Chardonnay is best.

Saslove r w Res Cab has ageing potential; easy drinking "Aviv" full of flavour.

Soreq Tal Shahar Vineyard r Small estate. Recent Cabernets showing quality.

Tabor Lower Galilee r w Complex single vineyard Chardonnay.

Tishbi r w sp Family grower. Buttery Chard and improving Merlot.

Tzora r w Kibbutz winery. Good Sauv Bl. "Misty Hills" Cabernet S is best so far.

Yarden Golan Heights r w sp ★★→★★★ Leader in Israel's "wine awakening". Delicate multi-layered Cab S (**93 96** 97' 99); oaky barrel-ferm Chard. Rare de luxe Katzrin red Cab S-Merlot-Cab F (oo eagerly awaited). Gamla Cabernet (Bordeaux style) – excellent value.

Lebanon The small wine industry is based in Beka'a Valley, E of Beirut. The older wineries are heroic survivors of the civil war. There are some quality reds, made with French influence.

Ch Musar r (w) ★★★ Splendid and unique Cab S with Cinsault (**89 91 93** 94 95 96), has recently tasted stretched. Should improve with age. Lighter r Hochar Père et Fils (Cinsault and Cab). Also full-bodied, oaky white from indigenous grape, Obaideh.

Clos St Thomas r (w) Small winery. Ch St Thomas is soft, fruity, rounded red.

Kefraya r w ★★ Fragrant Ch Kefraya Comte de M, (**96** 97 98) – blend of Cab S, Mourvèdre, & Syrah. Also fresh rosé and luscious dessert, Lacrima d'Oro.

Kouroum de Kefraya r w New with extensive plans. As yet only simple wines.

Ksara r w ★ Est 1857 by Jesuits. New World style. Château Ksara (99) – spicy, aromatic Cab S, Reserve du Couvent – fruity red, gd value. Clean Chard.

Massaya r w French-Lebanese collaboration, incl top French names, challenging CH MUSAR. Cab S-Mourvèdre shows promise.

Wardy r w Promising winery. Good Chard & Sauv Bl. Red label Ch les Cedres.

England & Wales

Over two million bottles a year are now being made here from over 300 vineyards (2,000 acres). Although most are white and made from fruity German crosses, a number of interesting reds come from Pinot Noir and Dornfelder, as well as from a new variety, Rondo. Bottle-fermented sparkling wines, or "Bubbly", are also proving to be one of England's great successes, made of Chardonnay and Pinot Noir and closely modelled on Champagne. Since 1994, an EU-approved "Quality Wine Scheme" has been run by the UK Vineyards Association. Unfortunately, it is only open to vinifera varieties so growers of the (v worthy) Seyval Blanc (and other hybrids) may not apply. Two or three years bottle-age is usually a good idea. NB: Beware "British Wine" – neither British, nor indeed wine, and has nothing to do with the following.

Recent Vintages

2002 A reduced crop overall, but an Indian summer resulted in very ripe grapes. Reds and full-bodied (some oak-aged) whites will be excellent and sparkling wines potentially the best to date.

2001 Warmest year on record with quality wines made in many wineries. Bacchus wines are very spicy. Reds are good and will keep.

2000 Cool year with a wet harvest. Whites better than reds. Sp wines should be good. The best will keep, but many should be drunk within 2 yrs.

1999 Average yields and a warm summer helped most winemakers produce interesting wines, esp with varieties such as Bacchus and Seyval Bl.

1998 Overall, a warm year with a fine autumn. The west fared better than the east, where early frosts did some damage. Sp wines should be good.

Adgestone nr Sandown (Isle of Wight) 8a/3.2ha on chalky hill site. Est'd 68. Wines variable.

Astley Stourport-on-Severn (Worcestershire) 00 01 ★ 5 acres; some fair wines. Kerner and Severn Vale 99 and sparkling 98 recommended.

Barnsole (Kent) 98 ★ 3.4 acres Planted 1993 and now producing improving range of wines. Consistently awarded Quality and Regional Wine status.

Battle Wine Estate Battle (East Sussex) ★★ 33 acres New Zealand-trained winemaker. Wines of consistent quality.

Bearsted Maidstone (Kent) 98 ★→★★★ 4 acres Est'd 86. Sparkling now very good, especially 97 Brut. The Bacchus and Faberrebe are also good.

Beaulieu Abbey Brockenhurst (Hampshire) 01 ★ 1.5 acres. Est'd 58 on old monastic site. Now part of Beaulieu Estate. Fair sparkling.

Beeches Ross-on-Wye (Hertfordshire) Very small vineyard. Good dry white 01.

Beenleigh Manor Totnes (Devon) 00 ★→★★★ 0.3 acres. Vines grown under polythene tunnels. Makes award-winning oak-aged Cabernet/Merlot. Winner of Best Red Wine Trophy in 99 and 01.

Biddenden nr Tenterden (Kent) ★→★★ 20 acres. Planted 72: Ortega and Huxelrebe worth trying. Sparkling also v good. Gd cider & apple juice, too.

Bookers Bolney (W Sussex) 6 acres. Müller-T and others. Slowly improving.

Bothy Abingdon (Oxfordshire) 2.6 acres. New owners 02. Wines have been gd.

Boze Down Whitchurch-on-Thames (Oxfordshire) ★→★★ 5.4 acres Wide range of high-quality wines. Reds worth trying. Good website.

Breaky Bottom Lewes (E Sussex) ★★ 5.5 acres. Cult following. Gd, dry wines, esp Seyval Bl and 96 sp: gd and getting better. Older wines worth trying.

Camel Valley Bodmin (Cornwall) 99 00 01 ★→★★ 4.4 acres. Good quality, especially Cornwall Brut 99, rosé sparkling 99, and Bacchus 01. Excellent facilities and very welcoming to visitors. Worth a detour.

Carr Taylor Hastings (E Sussex) 21 acres. Est'd 73. Sparkling wines good. Now part of NEW WAVE WINES. Wines variable.

Carters Colchester (Essex) ★★ 4.2 acres. Variable. Bacchus 01 worth trying.

Chapel Down Tenterden (Kent) 00 01 ★→★★ Epoch Brut sp, Epoch red, Pinot Noir, Bacchus, Downland Oak are best wines. British Airways, House of Commons, and major multiples supplied. Now part of NEW WAVE WINES.

Chiddingstone Edenbridge (Kent) ★ 17 acres. Stress on dry wines, esp barrel-aged. Pinot Blanc and Chasselas worth trying.

Chilford Hall (Cambs) 98 99 ★ 18 acres. Est'd in 72. Wide range wines. Sparkling wines improving. "Aulric de Norsehide" is trophy winner. Vg visitor facilities.

Chiltern Valley Henley (Oxfordshire) 1 acre of vineyards high up on chalk plus grapes from local v'yds. Wines incl Old Luxters Dry Reserve. Good sp.

Coddington Ledbury (Herefordshire) 2.4 a. Est'd 85. Improving. Bacchus good.

Danebury Stockbridge (Hants) 5.3 acres. Auxerrois, Bacchus, etc. Improving. Gd sp.

Davenport Rotherfield (E Sussex) 98 99 ★→★★ Young winery: serious wines. Aus-trained winemaker. Organic from 2002. Sp coming on. Try Brut 98.

Denbies Dorking (Surrey) 99 00 ★→★★ 261 acres. (England's lgst v'yd). Impressive winery: worth a visit. Vg Riesling. Reds and sw recommended.

Eglantine Loughboro' (Leics) 3.3 acres. Madeleine Sylvaner sw wins medals.

Frithsden Hemel Hempstead (Herts) 2 acres. Ortega and Kerner worth trying.

Frome Valley Vineyard Bishops Frome (Herefordshire) 00 01 ★ 2.5 acres. Well-presented wines made at THREE CHOIRS. Schönburger worth trying.

Gifford's Hall Bury St-Edmunds (Suffolk) 9 acres. Interesting wines (incl oak-aged) and visitor facilities.

Glyndwr Vineyard Llanblethain (Wales) 3.4 acres. Mild conditions nr sea. Made at THREE CHOIRS. Notable sp and rs. Oldest commercial Welsh v'yard.

Great Stocks Billericay (Essex) 00 01 ★ 6.5 acres. Interesting wines including Regency and oak-aged Orion Fumé. Wines made at DAVENPORT.

Hale Valley Wendover (Bucks) 1.5 acres. Wines of interest. One to watch.

Halfpenny Green (Staffordshire) 15 acres. Esp gd Madeleine Angevine and sp.

Harden Farm (Kent) 12a/4.9ha Bacchus and Schönburger good.

Hendred (Berkshire) 6 acres. Planted in 71. Interesting Seyval & Mad. Angevine.

Hidden Spring Horsham (E Sussex) ★★ 7.5 acres. Wines consistently good, esp Sunset Rosé. Wines made at VALLEY.

Horton Estate (Dorset) 9 acres. Bacchus, Reichensteiner, reds. Showing promise.

Ickworth (Suffolk) 99 00 2 acres. Starting to win awards and be noticed.

La Mare Jersey (Channel Isl) Wines fair but improving; continued investment.

Lamberhurst (Kent) ★ 26 acres. Since 2000 part of NEW WAVE WINES. Fumé won "McNie Trophy" for best oaked wine in 2002. Wines made at CHAPEL DOWN.

Leeds Castle Maidstone (Kent) ★ 3.25 acres. Long-established. Müller-T and Seyval Blanc. Wines sold only at Castle outlets. Made at TENTERDEN.

Leventhorpe (Yorkshire) 5.5 acres. Most northerly commercial v'yd, planted 1986 and doing well with Mad Angevine, Mad Sylvaner, and Seyval Bl.

Llanerch S Glamorgan (Wales) 00 ★ 5.5 acres. Established 86. Wines sold under "Cariad label". Good rosé and sparkling especially 2000 vintage.

Meopham Valley (Kent) 99 4.75 acres. Est'd 1991. Starting to make interesting wines, especially Pinot Gris.

Mersea East Mersea (Essex) 97 ★→★★ 6.6 acres. Est'd 85, south-facing v'yd on scenic island. Consistently gd wines. Made at CHAPEL DOWN & VALLEY.

New Hall nr Maldon (Essex) 90 acres. on mixed farm. Vg Bacchus 00. Grape supplier to other wineries, incl CHAPEL DOWN, THREE CHOIRS, and VALLEY.

New Wave Wines Ltd ★→★★ Largest UK producer. INC CARR TAYLOR, CHAPEL DOWN, Curious Grape, LAMBERHURST, and TENTERDEN brands. Curious Grape Bacchus (Best Wine 2001) and Pinot Noir 99 (Best Wine and Best Varietal in 2002).

Northbrook Springs Bishops Waltham (Hampshire) ★★ 13 acres. Improving wines winning medals. Sp showing well. Supports Quality Wine scheme.

Nutbourne Pulborough (W Sussex) 00 ★★ 15 acres. Sussex Reserve 2000.

Nyetimber W Chiltington (W Sussex) 94 95 ★→★★★ 39 acres. Planted 88: Chard, Pinots N, & Meunier for classic sp. Showing the way forward for English sparklers. Blanc de Blancs 95 is excellent. New owners in 2001.

Penshurst Tunbridge Wells (Kent) 12 acres. Established 1972, including good Seyval Blanc and Müller-Thurgau. Fine, modern winery.

Plumpton College Lewes (E Sussex) Experimental vineyard attached to college running courses on viticulture and winemaking. Small winery; wines improving. Now rents Ditchling vineyard and supplies CHAPEL DOWN.

Priors Dean Alton (Hampshire) 0.9 acres. Seyval 98 gd. Wines made at VALLEY.

Ridge View Ditchling Common (E Sussex) 97 98 ★→★★★ 16 acres. Planted 95: Chard, Pinots N & Meunier for high quality sparkling. Cuvée Merret Cavendish 98 and NV Fitzrovia Rosé are vg: major awards in 2002.

Rosemary (Isle of Wight) 28 acres. IOW's lgst v'yd. Variable quality.

St Augustine's Aust (Gloucs) ★ Gd Mad Angevine. Wine made at THREE CHOIRS.

Sandhurst Cranbrook (Kent) ★★ 13.6 acres. High-quality Bacchus, red and sw wines. Wines made at TENTERDEN. Major grape supplier to CHAPEL DOWN.

Sedlescombe Organic Robertsbridge (East Sussex) 8 acres. UK's main organic v'yd. Range of wines with quite a following. Some of interest.

Sharpham Totnes (Devon) 99 00 ★→★★ 9.8 acres. Award-winning v'yd produces consistently gd wines. 99 Barrel-fermented & 2000 Estate Selection winners.

Shawsgate Framlingham (Suffolk) ★★★ 12.5 acres. Under new ownership (2000). Bacchus 2000 won Jack Ward Trophy.

Standen E Grinstead (W Sussex) 2.5 acres. Shows promise. Will specialize in sp.

Sugar Loaf (Wales) ★ 4 acres. Wines made at THREE CHOIRS. Award-winner.

Tenterden (Kent) ★★ 18.5 acres. Est'd 77. Consistently good including Estate Dry & Cinque Ports Classic. Part of NEW WAVE WINES.

Three Choirs (Glos) 99 00 ★→★★ 74 acres. Est'd 74. Estate Reserve Bacchus, Phoenix, and Siegerrebe are very good. English Nouveau is v popular and sparkling is good. UK's 2nd-lgst producer. Sparkling improving.

Tiltridge Upton-upon-Severn (Worcestershire) 99 1 acre. Small v'yd with good local following. Wines of interest. Elgar Dry sparkling very good.

Titchfield Titchfield (Hampshire) 1.25 acres. Planted 88. Good-quality wines made at THREE CHOIRS.

Valley Twyford (Berks) 98 99 00 ★→★★★ 20 acres. UK's most successful producer with serious range of quality wines. Oak-aged Fumé, Clocktower Pinot N, Ascot Sp worth trying. Makes for a large number of other v'y'ds.

Warden Abbey (Bedfordshire) 99 ★★ 5.6 acres. Planted in 86. Wines well made and regularly win prizes. Warden V'yd and sp wines recommended.

Webbsland Wickham (Hampshire) 98 99 7.4 acres. Established 1993. Wines improving, particularly the Pinot Noir.

Wickham Shedfield (Hampshire) 99 00 ★→★★ 18 acres. Since 84. Wines consistent, esp Vintage Selection 99 and Fumé 00. New owners in 2000.

Worthenbury Wrexham (Wales) 00 ★ 0.6 acre. Pinot Noir, Chardonnay, and Sauvignon Blanc produced under polythene.

Wroxeter Roman Shrewsbury (Shropshire) 6 acres on Roman site. Improving.

Wylye Valley Warminster (Wilts) ★ 8.8 acres. Planted 89. Wines winning awards.

Wyken Bury-St-Edmunds (Suffolk) 99 5 acres. Planted 88. 92 Auxerrois, Bacchus, and Kernling are good. Restaurant *vaut le voyage*.

North America

WASHINGTON
OREGON
CALIFORNIA
EASTERN STATES

California

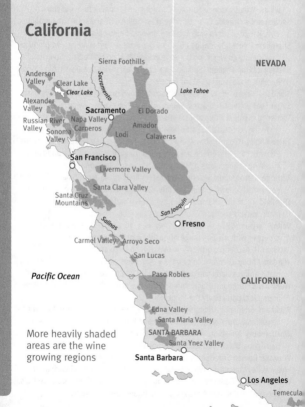

NEVADA

Sierra Foothills

Anderson Valley
Clear Lake
Clear Lake

Sacramento

Lake Tahoe

Alexander Valley

Russian River Valley
Napa Valley
Carneros
Sonoma Valley

Sacramento

El Dorado
Amador
Lodi
Calaveras

San Francisco

Livermore Valley

Santa Clara Valley

Santa Cruz Mountains

Salinas

San Joaquin

Carmel Valley   Arroyo Seco

San Lucas

Fresno

Pacific Ocean

Paso Robles

CALIFORNIA

Edna Valley

Santa Maria Valley

More heavily shaded areas are the wine growing regions

SANTA BARBARA

Santa Ynez Valley

Santa Barbara

Los Angeles

Temecula

The robust expansion of the California industry during the1990s started to crack a bit in 2002, then registered significant alarm in 2003 as the pond of surplus bulk wine continued to grow toward lake-sized proportions. Many factors made producers nervous – the fallout from events on 11th September 2001, the implosion of the dot.com bubble, the overall sluggish US economy – but per capita consumption in the US held fairly steady. The major downward influence on prices was a dramatic increase in supply as tens of thousands of new Central Valley plantings began bearing fruit.

As prices per ton for grapes began to fall from the extortionate levels of the late '90s, many of the smaller, more prestigious growers reasoned they should be able to get more for their crop as wine than as grapes. Many elected to build wineries or have some of their crop custom-crushed for their own label. Hence California has seen an explosion of new brands at a time when restaurants are struggling and distributors are consolidating. This boom-bust cycle has a strong historical precedent in the California wine industry. A single phase, from peak to peak, usually lasts ten to 12 years. Many of the labels being launched today will not live to see the next upswing in prices which may be six or seven years away. Meanwhile good buying opportunities abound for consumers.

US regulators approved a measure in 2003 which allows wine labels to make certain health benefit claims as long as they are accurate, documented, and not graphically emphasized. While this change does not herald an end to neo-prohibitionist pressures in the US, it was still greeted with joy by all US wine producers.

California remains a bastion of clean, fruit-driven, intensely ripe wines able to carry large amounts of hearty new oak. Elevated alcohol levels have been an unfortunate side effect from pursuing this course at some wineries, particularly with Zinfandel (red) which has enjoyed a considerable surge in the marketplace. The artistic advancement of Syrah has also been noteworthy throughout California.

The principal California vineyard areas

Central Coast

San Francisco Bay S to Santa Barbara, scattered with increasing wine activity.

Arroyo Grande & Edna Valley The largely maritime districts west of coastal mountains in San Luis Obispo County. Best known for lemony Chardonnay that matures elegantly. Also hosts CA's best Viognier and Pinot Bl.

Carmel Valley Coastal AVA Monterey County. Small production, better known for golf courses than wine. Some wonderful red Meritage.

Paso Robles Large, productive district east of coastal range in San Luis Obispo County. Long known for Zinfandel. Inexpensive land converted from alfalfa farms, attracting many major players. Soft Cabernet S, Syrah are the mainstays.

Salinas Valley 100-mile-long flat farming district, too cold for grapes at N on Monterey Bay, but hosts world's largest contiguous v'yd (San Bernabe) at S end. Fine, pineapple-scented CHARD; good nectarine-scented Riesling.

San Benito County Hot, rural county E of Monterey, inland of Gabilan Mountains.

Santa Barbara County Lgst, prestigious district 3 hrs drive from Los Angeles. Many celebrity owners. Lush, layered Pinot N and Chard; superb SYRAH in warmer E canyons; distinctive Sauvignon Blanc, Riesling in foggy west. Including Sta Maria & Santa Ynez AVAs.

South Coast

Los Angeles Megalopolis has a few hobbyist v'yds incl Malibu Canyon AVA, as well as 800 historic acres in Cucamonga AVA, with fine Grenache.

Temecula (Rancho California) In S California, 25 miles inland, halfway between San Diego and Riverside. Mainly whites. 2,000 acres of vines.

Ventura River watershed; productive agricultural district, with a few v'yds.

North Coast

Encompasses Lake, Mendocino, Napa, & Sonoma counties, all N of San Francisco.

Anderson Valley Cool coastal valley in Mendocino County makes America's best sparklers, excellent Gewurz, and rapidly improving PINOT N.

Lake County & Inland Mendocino County Warm to hot districts around Ukiah and SW shore of Clear Lake do very well with Zinfandel, Rhône varietals, Sauv Bl. Italian varieties advancing fast. Full-bodied Cab.

Napa Valley Best-known wine district just N of San Francisco Bay. With its relatively small size and large number of wineries (about 25% of those in CA), Napa's v'yd land has become more expensive than any outside Europe. Great diversity of soil, climate and topography in such a small area can produce a wide range of wines (esp Cab, Merlot, Sauv Bl) very well. A dozen AVAs incl, for example Oakville, Rutherford, Stags Leap, Mt Vedeer, and Carneros at the south end on the Bay (for Chard and Pinot N). Total nearly 40,000 acres. Has become an international gourmet destination with prices to match.

Northern Sonoma Warm districts (Alexander Valley, Dry Creek, Knights Valley) and cool ones such as Russian River. Healdsburg is the nexus for wine culture. Great Pinot N, Chard all along River Road & Westside Road from Healdsburg almost to Pacific Ocean. Superb Zin in Dry Creek. Lush, accessible Cab S from Alex. Valley.

Sonoma Valley & Carneros Separated from Napa Valley by 2,400 ft Mayacamus mountains. Carneros AVA at S end, bordering San Francisco Bay, is shared by both valleys, and coolest part of either, specialising in sp, Pinot N, Chard. Sonoma town square still feels rural.

Bay Area

Contra Costa County Historic growing district on N slope of Mt Diablo now succumbing to homes. Remaining old vines make fine Zins, red Rhônes.

Livermore Gravel soil on E of mountains defining San Francisco Bay. Urban pressure being relieved by creative planning. CA's best Semillon.

Santa Clara Valley Broad valley south of the Bay, once major wine district, now called Silicon Valley. Remnant areas like Hecker Pass can surprise today.

Santa Cruz Mountains Steep slopes separating S Bay from Pacific Ocean. Room for few v'yds but several top-class wineries (eg Ridge). Cold on the ocean side.

Central Valley

Lodi & The Delta Hydrological centre, from Sacramento to Stockton, is cooler than either the Northern or Southern halves of Central Valley. Clarkesburg in W does Ca's best Chenin; Lodi (E) backs on to Sierras with dense ZIN.

Sacramento Valley N half of Ca's agricultural centrepiece makes affordable Rhône varietals from the Dunnigan Hills AVA.

San Joaquin Valley Fertile and hot, the source of most of the jug, bag-in-a-box, and fortified dessert wines from the state. 300,000+ acres.

Sierra Foothills

Amador County Warm region famous for old ZIN vineyards producing jammy, intense wines with a signature metallic backnote. Top Rhône reds and Italian varietals are beginning to see good experimental results.

Calaveras County Southernmost of the premium Sierra Foothills districts and gateway to spectacular Yosemite National Park. Good CAB FR.

El Dorado County Cutting edge of high elevation viticulture in Ca with several vineyards at 3,000 ft. Two districts: one around Placerville has four of Ca's best wineries; second called Fairplay is charmingly eccentric.

Recent vintages

California's climate is not as consistent as its "land of sunshine" reputation suggests. Although grapes ripen regularly, they are often subject to spring frosts, sometimes a wet harvest-time and (too often) drought.

Wines from the San Joaquin Valley tend to be most consistent year by year. The vintage date on these, where there is one, is more important for telling the age of the wine than its character.

Vineyards in the Central Coast region have a different pattern of vintage quality from those in the North Coast or Sierra Foothills. Rain arrives later, rarely before mid-December, and is much less of a factor. The Central Coast vineyards, also have much cooler maritime mesoclimates. Grapes ripen more slowly and are harvested 3-6 weeks later than inland North Coast regions such as Napa. That said, the following vintage assessment relies most heavily on evaluation of Cabernets and Zinfandels from North Coast regions:

2002 Average winter rainfall and slightly delayed budbreak with some frost damage. Heavy rain in May, cool growing season but no rain until November. Average sized crop with every indication of superior quality.

2001 Little winter rain, sporadic heat in March, severe April frost, hottest May on record, and no rain until October. Excellent quality.

2000 Scares included a threatened storm from the south in early September, but damage was minimal. Biggest harvest on record. Okay quality.

1999 Very cold spring and summer created v late harvest, but absense of fall rain left crop unscathed. High natural acids and a hot Oct made for intensely flavoured and coloured wines. Crop size off by 10-40%. Outstanding quality.

1998 Erratic harvest stumbled into November. Wines are adequate to dismal.

1997 Huge crop, but strongly flavoured and showing v well at present. Favourite vintage on record for growers; well appreciated by consumers, too.

1996 Tiny crop, with lots of structure, lacks aromatic charm. Age is helping.

1995 Tiny crop, great vitality but slow to unfold. Good Zins, great Cabs. Best vintage for cellaring since 90.

1994 Mild growing season and dry, late harvest. Superb Zins, although a bit long in the tooth now; Cabs are supple, wonderful for drinking right now.

1993 Modest, plain-faced, serviceable year in the North Coast, but spectacular in the Sierra Foothills with conc'd Zins and refreshing acidity. Drink up.

1992 Oddly inconsistent. Some empty. Some flavourful and vital.

1991 Very late harvest; v large crop: 30-50% bigger than normal and twice the size of tiny '90. Wines are lean, racy, most European styled in years. Took a long time to develop in bottle.

1990 Picture-perfect California vintage and a small crop: wonderful development and strong collectors' value. Cabs magnificent at present.

1987 First year of a long drought. Cabernets and Zins very dark and extracted. Hard and uncompromising for a decade, they have now emerged to show some grace alongside the power. Best will last another five years.

1985 V cool vintage created a steel rod in the backbone. Bouquet development and balance make them very reliable today.

1984 Warm year. Showy early. In dotage now.

CALIFORNIA

1983 Warm year with El Niño rains at harvest. Never was much good.
1982 Cool year with El Niño rain at harvest. Risky today
1980 V cool growing season with a severe heat wave at harvest. Big wineries had trouble. Little wineries can often surprise today.

California wineries

Acacia Napa ★★★ (Chard) **99** 01 02 (Pinot N) **95** 99 01 Long-time specialist in durable, deep CARNEROS Chard & Pinot returning to single v'yd wines after a phylloxera-induced interlude of extra-oaky Reserves.

Alban Edna Valley ★★★ Pioneer planter of Rhône varieties, and benchmark for Viognier, in California. Estate model crisper than Central Coast version. Small quantities of excellent Grenache. Reva Syrah one of CA's best over last 4 yrs.

Alexander Valley Vineyards Sonoma ★★ Cabernet S most likely of 6 wines to live up to promise of fine vineyard. Whites quirky at best.

Anapamu and Rancho Zabaco ★★ Parts of the large Gallo operation made in Dry Creek. Anapamu is good Chardonnay sourced near Monterey; Rancho Zabaco is good. Zinfandel sourced in Mendocino.

Andrew Murray Sta Barbara ★★ **99** 00 01 Sml winery. Vineyards planted on slopes thus reducing yields. Good Syrah, great Roussanne.

Araujo Napa ★★★★ 95 97 99 01' Eisele v'yd, now an estate, its Cabernet as dark and tannic as when JOE PHELPS made it famous.

Arrowood Sonoma ★★→★★★ (Chard) **99** 01 02(Cab) 85 87 90 91 94 95 96 97 99 01Long-time CHATEAU ST JEAN winemaker Dick A on peak form with supple, ageworthy Cab S. Chard (esp Res) for oak-lovers. Sold to Mondavi '00.

Artesa Napa ★ Still wines made at the fabulously beautiful facility owned by, and formerly called, Cordorniu.

Artisans and Estates Collection of wineries & v'yds owned by Jess Jackson, of KENDALL-JACKSON fame. Each has its own winemaker, and expansion through acquisition since '88 has been meteoric. Highest end incls: HARTFORD COURT, Alexander Mtn Estates, MATANZAS CREEK, Stonestreet (SON), Kristone and CAMBRIA (ST BARB), CARDINALE and Lokoya (NAPA). Mid-range incls: La Crema, Edmeades, Robt Pepi, Bailey & Brock. Also has properties in Italy, Argentina, Australia and Chile and its own cooperage in France. No end appears to be in sight.

Atlas Peak Napa ★★ Allied-Domecq-owned winery previously focused on Sangiovese and Sangio-Cab Consenso, now much more on Cab, from Antinori-owned v'yds in east hills.

Au Bon Climat Sta Barbara ★★★ (Chard) 96 99 **01** 02 (Pinot N) **95** 99 01' Jim Clendenen listens to his private drummer: ultra-toasty Chard, flavourful Pinot N, light-hearted Pinot Bl. Vita Nova label for Bordeaux varieties, Podere dellos Olivos for Italianates. See also Qupé.

Babcock Vineyards Santa Barbara ★★★ Very cool location in western SANTA YNEZ VALLEY. Strong reputation for Pinot N and Chard; "Eleven Oaks" Sauv Bl is one of CA's better examples. New entry into Syrah is impressive.

Barnwood Sta Barbara ★★ **98** 99 01 Located in the remote NW corner of the county, but has purchased LAETITIA for presence on the coast. Gd value Cab.

Beaulieu Vineyard Napa ★★→★★★ (Cab) 58 65 73 78 85 90 91 95 97 99' UDV's crown jewel is, rightly, best known for ageable, American-oaked Georges de Latour Private Reserve Cabernet Sauvignon. CARNEROS Chardonnay worth a look. Commodity line is Beautour, experimental one Signet.

Benessere Napa ★★ One of top five Sangiovese from CA.

Benziger Family Winery Sonoma ★★ Called Benziger of Glen Ellen until Proprietors Reserve sold to UDV (then Heublein). Now all SONOMA grapes and dotty for oak across whole range.

Beringer-Blass Napa ★★→★★★ (Chard) 99 **00** 01 (Cab S) 87 90 91 **94** 95 97 99' Acquired in 2000 by Australia's Mildara-Blass (Fosters), this century-old winery pursues larger-than-life style from top of line (Reserve, single v'yd Cabs) to recently introduced commodity range called Beringer Founder's Estate (originally named Hudson Estate). Also owns CHATEAU ST-JEAN, CHATEAU SOUVERAIN, MERIDIAN, NAPA RIDGE, and STAG'S LEAP WINERY.

Bernardus Carmel Valley ★★★ Strong Meritage wines from densely planted hillside. In town high-end auberge includes top sommelier south of S Fran.

Biale Napa ★★ Small, ZIN specialist using mostly Napa fruit.

Boeger El Dorado ★★ Mostly estate wines. Attractive Merlot, Barbera, Zin; all less bold than many neighbours.

Bonaccorsi Sta Barbera ★★★ Very good Sanford and Benedict Vineyard Chardonnay from one of CA's top sommeliers.

Bonny Doon Sta Cruz Mtns ★★★ Mad punster Randall Grahm still resolutely Rhôneist with pink Vin Gris de Cigare and red Cigare Volant (94 **97** 99) in cigar-box 6-pack. Meditations now extend to Italianates, too. Also bargain Pacific Rim Riesling with a screw cap. Grown to 2000,000 cases in new Santa Cruz facility.

Briggs, August Napa ★★★ 99 00 Exceptional style with Pinot Noir and Zin.

Bruce, David Sta Cruz Mts ★★★ (Pinot) 95 97 **99** 00 Long-time source of eccentric bruiser (now moderated) Chardonnay. Pinot Noir (from own and SONOMA vines) is forte.

Pierce's Disease

This bacterial vine infection became a high profile issue in '00 when an energetic flying insect called the Glassy-winged Sharpshooter arrived borne on ornamental plants. Some districts were particularly hard hit, but despite hysterical press announcements even small growers in those areas soldiered on, fighting back with insect sprays and careful v'yard management. Spread of the problem has since proven to be slow. New research at UC Davis shows strong promise for techniques to ameliorate the problem over the next 5 yrs.

Buehler Napa ★★ (Cab S) **90** 91 94 95 97 99' 00 In E hills recently repositioned with upscale prices on unchanged estate Cab S, Zin and Russian River Chard.

Buena Vista Carneros ★★ (Chard) **99** 00 01 Has swapped an earlier taste-the-grapes style for one more heavily marked by winemaking: esp Chard.

Burgess Cellars Napa ★★ (Cab) **90** 95 97 99' Emphasis on dark weighty well-oaked reds; Cab rather plain-faced, but VS version ages well. Zin begins to be more outsized.

Bynum, Davis Sonoma ★★ (Pinot N) 95 **99** 00 Long-underrated but beginning to draw attention for characterful single vineyard wines, especially Pinot Ns from RRV.

Byron Vineyards Sta Barbara ★★ (Chard) 96 **99** 00 01' (Pinot) 95 97 **99** 00 Prospering under MONDAVI; estate PINOT N leads with CHARD not far behind.

Cain Cellars Napa ★★★ (Cain Five) 85 87 90 94 **95** 97 99' Stylish, supple Cain Five anchored in estate plantings of Cabernet S and four cousins on Spring Mtn; Cain Cuvée (declassified Cain Five) can rival the big brother. Monterey Sauvignon Musqué also fine.

Cafaro Napa ★★★ Winemaker label for sturdy-to-solid Cab and Merlot.

Cakebread Napa ★★ (Chard) 97 **99** 00 01 (Cab S) **85** 87 **90** 94 95 97 99' Now up to three bottlings of Cab: all hearty and heartily-oaked.

Calera San Benito ★★★ (Chard) 99 00 01 (Pinot) 95 96 97 **99** 00 Dry sunny chalky hills near Chalone lead to booming Rhône-weight estate Pinot Ns named after individual vineyard blocks (Reed, Selleck, Jensen). Also for perfumiest Viognier.

Callaway Temecula ★ (Chard) 00 01 Sourcing grapes outside home region for new fighting-varietal-priced coastal line.

Cambria Sta Barbara ★★ Part of KENDALL-JACKSON'S ARTISANS AND ESTATES group. Chard routinely toasty, Pinot N more enticing.

Canandaigua See Constellation.

Carmenet Sonoma ★★→★★★ (Cab S blend) 87 90 94 95 99' Fancifully named variations on ripe Cab (eg Moon Mountain, Dynamite, Vin de Garde) all from mountaintop vineyard. CHALONE-owned.

Carneros Creek Carneros ★→★★ (Pinot N) 95 96 97 **99** 00 Resolute explorer of climates and clones in CARNEROS offers 5 Pinots each yr: lightsome Fleur de Carneros; Côte de Carneros; darker, richer Estate; Reserve Francis Mahoney Estate. Single v'yd Las Brisas.

Castoro San Luis Obispo ★★ Paso Robles estate, as substantial as its wines (Cab S, Zin). Savvy winemaker Nils Udsen has a way with fresh fruit aromas. Nb nouveau wines. Zins: vg & value. Remainder of the line, esp Cab, reliable.

Caymus Napa ★★→★★★ (Cab S) 87 90 **91** 94 95 96 97 98 99' Dark quick-to-mature American-oaked Cab Special Selection: celebrated core. Lighter, basic bottling not far behind. Developing v'yds: MONTEREY, SONOMA for other varieties.

Chalk Hill Sonoma ★★ Large estate near Windsor, frequently changing styles for Chard, Sauv Bl, Cab. Now high-end single v'yd Pinot Gris and Merlot.

Chalone Monterey ★★★ (Chard) 95 **99** 00 Unique estate high in Gavilan Mts; source of flinty Chard and dark tannic Pinot N, both slow-to-open burgundy imitations (Pinot N can go 15 yrs). Pinot Bl and Chenin styled after Chard. Also owns ACACIA, CARMENET, EDNA VALLEY VINEYARD, Echelon Gavilan and Canoe Ridge (Washington). (Lafite) Rothschilds own major share.

Chappellet Napa ★★★ (Cab S) 69 78 87 90 94 95 97 99' Beautiful amphitheatrical hill vineyard. Always ageworthy Cab S has new grace-notes, esp Signature label. Chenin: a NAPA classic now touched with oak. Chardonnay gentle; easy Sangiovese too. Also very good Cabernet Franc, Merlot, Tocai Friulano, sweet Moelleux.

Château Montelena Napa ★★★ (Chard) 96 **99** 00 01'(Cab) 87 **90** 95 97 99' Understated ageworthy Chard, and Calistoga-Estate Cab modified after 90 vintage but still tannic and able to age long term.

Château Potelle Napa ★★ Expat French couple produce quietly impressive Chard (Reserve edition toastier) and vigorous Cabernet from MT VEEDER estate, outright aggressive VGS Zin from AMADOR.

Château St Jean Sonoma ★★→★★★ Style always bold, heady; more so since bought from Suntory in 96 by BERINGER owners. Known for single-v'yd Chards (Robert Young, Belle Terre); now reds are creating a stir.

Château Souverain Sonoma ★★ →★★★ (Cab S) 87 90 95 97 99' Top-of-the-line CARNEROS Chard, Alexander Valley Cab, and Dry Creek Valley Zin, all with lots of oak. So too basic SONOMA bottlings. Same owner as BERINGER.

Chimney Rock Napa ★★→★★★ (Cab S) **90** 94 95 97 99' Once racy Stags Leap District Cabernet now fleshier and driven more by cassis aroma due to sophisticated trellising. Nice meritage called Elevage.

Christopher Creek Sonoma ★★★ 97 **99** 00 Ownership by Fred Wasserman has seriously improved already admirable Syrah and Petite Sirah.

Cline Cellars Carneros ★★ Originally Contra Costa (important vineyards still there), now in SONOMA/CARNEROS and still dedicated mostly to husky Rhône Rangers (blends and varietals), eg Côtes d'Oakley, Mourvèdre.

Clos du Bois Sonoma ★★→★★★ (Chard) **99** 00 01 (Cab) **87** 90 94 95' 97 99' 00 Sizeable (400,000 case) Allied-Domecq firm at Healdsburg. Winemaker

Margaret Davenport hitting impressive stride with Cab S, Pinot N, Chard. Top are single-v'yd incl Cab Briarcrest, Chard Calcaire.

Clos Pegase Napa ★★ (Chard) **99** 00 01 (Cab S) 90 91 94 95 **97** 99' 00 Post-modernist winery-cum-museum (or vice versa) intelligently grows Chard in CARNEROS and Cab in Calistoga.

Clos du Val Napa ★★★ (Cab) 85 87 **90** 94 95 97 99' French-run. Elegant, reliable, aging candidates. Nice selection of older vintages available in Cabs and Sem/Sauv Bl blend too.

Cohn, B R Sonoma ★★→★★★ One-time SONOMA estate Cab S specialist now buying grapes as far afield as Paso Robles.

Constellation Huge NY firm, formerly known as Canandaigua, now No 2 to GALLO in California and long a power in bottom tier of market (Richard's Wild Irish Rose, Taylor California Cellars, etc). Lately reaching up, first tentatively with DUNNEWOOD, more aggressively with SIMI, now acquiring FRANCISCAN Estates along with ESTANCIA and MT VEEDER including '01 acquisition of RAVENSWOOD.

Corison Napa ★★★ (Cab) 90 94 95 97 99' Long-time winemaker at CHAPPELLET on her own making supple flavoursome Cabernet promising to age well.

Cosentino Napa ★★ (Meritage) 97 99' Irrepressible winemaker-owner always full-tilt. Results s'times odd, sometimes brilliant, never dull. Crystal Valley is widely distributed down-market brand.

Craig, Robert Napa ★★ Immodestly priced, these wines have a leaner, more Old World feel than most from CA, esp Affinity Cabernet Sauvignon.

Crocker-Starr St Helena ★★★ 97 99' Former winemaker from SPOTTSWOODE teamed up with the great-grandson of the Crocker who built the western part of the trans-continental railroad. A range of three Cabernet Franc based offerings. All are exceptional.

Cuvaison Napa ★★★ (Chard) 99 00 01 (Merlot) 95 **97** 98 99 00 Estate CARNEROS Chard steadily fine though fleshier, oakier than formerly. Recent estate Cab begins to outshine Merlot.

Dalla Valle Napa ★★★★ Hilly estate has become a cult classic with newly supple reds (Cab-based Maya, Sangio-based Pietre Rosso).

Darioush Napa ★★ Look for the opulent, lavishly oaked Cabernet.

Dehlinger Sonoma ★★★ (Pinot) **95** 97 **99** 00 01 Tom D focuses on ever-plummier estate Russian River Valley Pinot N, and rightly. Also Chard, Syrah.

Delectus Napa ★★★ 00' New producer making a fine Merlot from Stanton Vyd recalling past glory days of lushly textured Merlot in the Napa Valley.

DeLoach Vineyards Sonoma ★★★ (Chard) **99** 00 01' Fruit-rich Chardonnay ever the mainstay of reliable Russian River Valley winery. Gargantuan single-vineyard Zins (Papera, Pelletti) finding an audience.

Diamond Creek Napa ★★★★ (Cab S) 85 87 90 **94** 95 97 99' Austere, stunningly high-priced cult Cabs from hilly v'yd nr Calistoga go by names of vineyard blocks, eg Gravelly Meadow, Volcanic Hill. 3,000 cases.

Domaine Carneros Carneros ★★★ Showy US outpost of Taittinger in CARNEROS echoes austere style of its parent in Champagne. Vintage Blanc de Blancs the luxury cuvée. Still Pinot Noir also impressive.

Domaine Chandon Napa ★★ Maturing v'yds, maturing style, broadening range taking Moët & Chandon's California arm to new heights. Look esp for NV Reserve, Etoile Rosé. Still wines a recent addition.

Domaine Saint-Gregory Mendocino ★★ Companion label to Monte Volpe for wines from French grape varieties.

Domaine de la Terre Rouge Amador County ★★★ Former retailer is a Rhône specialist with a strong stable of growers. Syrah and Grenache are both tops. Zinfandels under Eastin label from old Fiddletown vineyards are also noteworthy.

CALIFORNIA

Dominus Napa ★★★★ 85 87 90 **96 97** 98 99' Christian Moueix of Pomerol is now sole owner of the fine Napanook vineyard and elegantly austere winery (98). Style, tannic at first, variable with vintages through mid-90s, now much more fruit-driven since move into own facility.

Dry Creek Vineyard Sonoma ★★ Large but unimpeachable source of dr tasty w, esp Chard & Fumé Blanc, but also Chenin Bl from Clarksburg. Cab S & Zin rather underrated.

Duckhorn Vineyards Napa ★★★ (Merlot) **90 95** 97 99' 00 Known for dark, tannic, almost plummy-ripe single-v'yd Merlots (esp Three Palms, and Cab-based blend Howell Mountain. Goldeneye PN made in Anderson Valley startled the marketplace with its atypical weight and intensity.

Dunn Vineyards Napa ★★★★ (Cab) 80 87 90 **94 95** 97 99' Owner-winemaker Randy Dunn makes dark, iconic Cab from Howell Mt which ages magnificently, slightly milder from valley floor. 4,000 cult cases.

California wines to try in 2004

Cedarville Mannered and elegant Syrah from elevated v'yd in El Dorado.
Duxoup Eccentric Dry Creek winery makes a richly fruity Charbono.
Edgewood Outgrowth of former Napa Co-op produces CA's top Malbec.
Kathryn Hall Wealthy Texan acquiring Napa v'yds debuts with great Cab.
Parras Former Jade Mtn owner now specializing in cool clime Nebbiolo.
Portfolio New cult Cab. Own label by Genevieve Janssens, Mondavi winemaker.
Salvestrin Long time St Helena grower debuts with ethereal, fine-grained Cab.
Testarossa Gutsy, dense style okay for Pinot Noir, but sinfully indulgent for whole roster of Central Coast Chards, esp Bien Nacido version from Sta Maria.
Voss Widely hailed Napa Sauvignon Blanc is both grassy and tropically exotic.

Dutton-Goldfield Western Sonoma Co ★★★ Adroitly crafted Burgundian varieties from several top sites by former K-J Pinot specialist.

Eberle Winery San Luis Obispo ★★ Burly ex-footballer makes Cab and Zin in his own image. Also look for their polar opposite: Muscat Canelli.

Edna Valley Vineyard San Luis Obispo ★★ (Chard) 99 00 01 Decidedly toasty Chard from a joint venture of local grower and CHALONE. Pinot N best drunk soon after vintage. 48,000 cases.

Edizione Pennino Napa ★★ Expensive; ZIN is the best item.

Estancia FRANCISCAN label for gd value MONTEREY Chard, Sauv, Pinot N, Cab S.

Eisele, Volker Chiles Valley, Napa ★★ Distinctively scented Cabs are noteworthy.

Etude Napa ★★★→★★★★ (Pinot N) **99** 00 Winemaker-owned cellar of highly respected consultant Tony Soter. V gd NAPA Cab overshadowed by burnished CARNEROS Pinot Noir. Engaging experiments in Pinots Blanc, Gris, and Meunier. Soter has moved to, and is opening a winery in, Oregon.

Far Niente Napa ★★★ (Chard) **99** 00 01 (Cab S) **94 95** 97 99' Opulence is the goal in both Cab S and Chard from luxury mid-NAPA estate.

Farrell, Gary Sonoma ★★★★ After yrs of sharing, maker of brilliant, ageworthy RRV Pinot N is building own cellar. Also excellent Merlot, Zin, ultra-toasty Chardonnay.

Ferrari-Carano Sonoma ★★ Ostentatious winery draws on far-flung estate vineyards to make range of broad wines well suited to property. New mountain v'yds for Italianate and Bd'x varieties producing leaner models.

Fess Parker Santa Barbara County ★★ Owned by actor who played Dan'l Boone on TV; son Eli is winemaker. Serviceable Chardonnay and Pinot N. Impressive Riesling. Very good Syrahs every vintage back to 1992.

Fetzer Mendocino ★★ 3M case, Brown-Forman owned. Consistently good value from least expensive range (Sundial, Valley Oaks) to most (Reserve).

Fiddlehead ★★★ Winemaker Kathy Joseph commutes between home/office nr Sacramento and 2 wineries where she contracts space: one in ARROYO GRANDE AVA, San Luis Obispo; the other in Oregon. Fine Sauv Bl & top-end Pinot N.

Fife Napa ★★★ Property in Mendocino's Redwood Valley supplements purchases from older vineyards in a long list of Zins and Rhonish reds.

Flowers Sonoma Coast ★★ Pinot Noir vineyard in closely watched mountains N and W of Russian River AVA. Good potential as prices moderate.

Firestone Sta Barbara ★★ (Chard) 99 00 01 (Merlot) **95 97** 99 00 Fine Chardonnay overshadows but does not outshine delicious Riesling.

Fisher Sonoma ★★ Hill-top SONOMA grapes for often-fine Chard; NAPA grapes dominate steady Cab. 10,000 cases.

Flora Springs Wine Co Napa ★★ (Chard) **99** 00 01 (Trilogy) **90 94 95** 97 99 Old stone cellar full of oak. So are wines, esp proprietory Sauvignon called Soliloquy, Cab blend called Trilogy, and varietal Sangiovese.

Fogarty, Thomas Sta Cruz Mts ★★ Famous heart surgeon with beautiful estate. Fine Gewurz from VENTANA sets the pace.

Folie à Deux Napa ★★ Valley doyen Richard Peterson and winemaker Scott Harvey have extraordinary Amador Zins and vastly underrated Napa Cabs.

Foppiano Sonoma ★★ Long-est'd wine family turns out fine reds (esp Petite Sirah, Zin) under family name. Whites labelled Fox Mountain.

Forman Napa ★★★ The winemaker who brought STERLING its first fame in the 70s now makes excellent Cab and Chard on his own. 15,000 cases.

Foxen Sta Barbara ★★★ (Pinot) 97 **99** 00 Tiny winery nestled between Santa Ynez & Santa Maria valleys. Always bold, frequently brilliant Pinot N.

Franciscan Vineyard Napa ★★★ (Cab) 85 87 90 **94** 95 97 99' Big v'yd at Oakville for stylish Cabernet, Zin, ultra-oaky Chard takes extra step with wild yeast fermentation. Austere Cab and red MERITAGE from Mt Veeder label.

Franzia San Joaquin ★ Penny-saver wines under Franzia, Corbett Canyon, Chas Shaw ('Two-Buck Chuck') and other labels. "Bottled in Ripon" is the tip off. Lgst bag-in-box producer.

Freemark Abbey Napa ★★★ (Chard) **99** 00 01 (Cab S) 85 87 **90 91 92** 94 **95** 97 99' Underrated today, but consistent for inexhaustible stylish Cabernet Sauvignons (esp single-vineyard Sycamore and Bosché) of great depth. Vg deliciously true-to-variety Chardonnay.

Frog's Leap Napa ★★→★★★ (Cab S) 87 90 94 95 97 99' Small winery, charming as its name (and T-shirts) and organic to boot. Lean racy Sauv, toasty Chard quite the reverse. Zin. Cabernet, Merlot all take to age.

Gabrielli Mendocino ★★ Essentially a winemaker label for gd value varietals from Ukiah region.

Gainey Vineyard, The Sta Barbara ★★ Pinot N leads the list but Chard, Sauv, Cab worth a look. 12,000 cases.

Gallo, E & J San Joaquin ★→★★ Having mastered the world of commodity wines (with eponymously labelled "Hearty Burgundy", "Pink Chablis", etc) this 40M-case family firm (the world's biggest) is now unleashing a blizzard of regional varietals under such names as Anapauma, Marcellina, Turning Leaf, Zabaco and more, some from Modesto, some via GALLO SONOMA.

Gallo Sonoma Sonoma ★★→★★★ (Chard) 99 00 01 (Cab S) 94 **95 97** 99 3 million cases facility run by third generation doing small single v'yd bottlings from Sonoma. Can be impressive at times.

Geyser Peak Sonoma ★★→★★★ Bought from Henry Trione in 1999 by distiller Jim Beam. Aussie winemaker Daryl Groom (who came when Penfolds was a partner) stays aboard, making good Chard, crackerjack Sauv and Syrah outright superior Reserve Alexandre.

Gloria Ferrer Carneros ★★ Original goal of Spain's Freixenet was nothing but classic sp. Now smoky CARNEROS Chardonnay and silky Pinot Noir from diverse clonal selection on equal footing, maybe in forefront.

Gott Amador Co ★★ Modestly priced Zin. All the berries and iron you can handle.

Greenwood Ridge Mendocino ★★ (Merlot) **97** 99' 01 Est'd specialist in racy ANDERSON VALLEY Riesling more recently appreciable for melony Sauv, herby Merlot. Pinot N begins to convince, too. 4,000 cases.

Grgich Hills Cellars Napa ★★★ (Chard) 95 96 97 98 99' 00 01 Winemaker Grgich and grower Hills join forces on pure Sauv, deftly oaked Chard long-ageing Cab, and – too little noticed – Spätlese-sweet Ries. Also plummy SONOMA Zin. Sauvignon Bl is a great ager, too. 60,000 cases.

Groth Vineyards Napa ★★→★★★ (Cab S) 85 87 90 **94** 95 97 99' Oakville estate challenges leaders among NAPA Cab & Sauv Bl. 85 Reserve Cab was Parker's first 100-pointer, for good or ill.

Guenoc Vineyards Lake County ★★ Ambitious winery/v'yd in its own AVA just North of NAPA county line. Property once Lillie Langtry's challenge to B'dx. Wines less over-oaked recently.

Gundlach-Bundschu Sonoma ★★ (Cab) 90 **94** 95 97 99' Pioneer name solidly revived by fifth generation. Versatile Rhinefarm v'yd signals memorably individual Gewurz, Merlot, Zin, Pinot N. 50,000 cases.

Hagafen Napa ★★ First and perhaps still the finest of the serious kosher producers. Especially Chard and Johannisberg Ries. 6,000 cases.

Handley Cellars Mendocino ★★ (Chard) **97** 99 01' Winemaker-owned. Excellent ANDERSON VALLEY Chard, Gewurz, plus (tiny lots) classic sp and Meunier. Also vg Dry Creek Valley Sauv, Chard from her family's vines.

Hanzell Sonoma ★★★ (Chard) 96 99' 00 01 The late founder revolutionized Calif Chards, Pinot Ns with French oak in late '50s. Three owners later, Hanzell produces classically ageworthy Chard. PN sometimes overripe and leathery.

Harlan Estate Napa ★★★★ Cab 94 **95** 97 99' Racy Cabs from small estate in hills W of Oakville earning their right to luxury prices.

Harrison E Mtns Napa ★★ 94 **95** 96 97' 99' 01' Nicely located near LONG VINEYARDS and the cult Cab of Bryant family. Predictably specializing in Cabernet.

Hartford Court Sonoma ★★★ Specialist in KENDALL JACKSON'S ARTISANS & ESTATES group shows promise with single v'yd Pinot Ns, tight coastal-grown Chard and wonderful old-vine Zins.

Hartwell Napa ★★★ High-end image, small producer with good Cab potential.

HDV Carneros 2000 was first release of a Chardonnay from grower Larry Hyde's vineyard in conjunction with Aubert de Villaine of Romanee Conti.

Heitz Napa ★★→★★★★ (Cab) **74 78 90** 91 97 99' On dark, deep-flavoured, minty Cab S from Martha's Vineyard (replanted 92) rests its fame. So it has since the 60s, when the individualist w'maker-owner (†2000) set new standards for his peers. Bella Oaks and newer Trailside V'yd rival but don't beat Martha.

Heller Estate Monterey ★★→★★★★ (Cab) 95 96 97 99 Some simple juicy (organic) Cabernets. Signature Cabernet is overweight but Chenin Bl is charming. Cachagua line is ★★.

Hendry Napa ★★ Long known as a grower on other labels; now making nice Cab and ZIN for self.

Hess Collection, The Napa ★★★ (Chard) 99 00 01(Cab S) **94 95** 97 99 A Swiss art collector's winery-cum-museum in former Mont La Salle winery of CHRISTIAN BROTHERS. Ever more impressive Mt Veeder Cabernet S. Chardonnay newly from American Canyon. 60,000 cases. More broadly sourced 300,000 case Hess Selection label gives very good value.

Hill Winery, William Napa ★★ Allied-Domecq property on the rise with subtle (for California) Chard; even more with flavourful, silky Cab.

Hobbs, Paul Sonoma Co ★★★ Excellent winemaker, well-known for consulting with Catena in Argentina, buying top Chardonnay grapes in Carneros, Cabernet Sauvignon in Napa, and Pinot Noir in Russian River for own label.

Hop Kiln Sonoma ★★ Source of sometimes startlingly fine "Valdiguie" (aka NAPA Gamay). Russian River Gewurz is full-flavoured and large-scale.

Husch Vineyards Mendocino ★★ Has ANDERSON VALLEY vineyard for often fine Pinot N, Ukiah one for sometimes good Sauv, Cab S.

Indian Springs Nevada County, Sierra Foothills ★★ Large 450 acre v'yd, wines made by consultant Jed Steele. Showing promise with Sangiovese.

Iron Horse Vineyards Sonoma ★★(★)Chard) 99 00 01 Substantial Russian River estate at its best with classic-method fizz that hovers between fine and bold. Chard can excel. Cab-Sangio from affiliated Alexander Valley property.

J Sonoma ★★★ Born part of JORDAN, now on its own in former PIPER-SONOMA cellars. Creamy classic-method Brut the foundation. Also still Pinot N.

Jade Mountain Napa After sale to Chalone, pursuing lofty goals using Rhône varieties, esp Syrah.

Jarvis Napa ★ Spectacular underground construction easily distracts from the modest quality of an expensive range, primarily B'x reds and Chardonnay.

Jekel Vineyards Monterey ★★ Ripe juicy Riesling used to be most noteworthy item. It remains reliable, but red B'dx blends from Sanctuary section of own v'yds have improved dramatically. Owned by Brown Forman.

Jessie's Grove Lodi ★★ Old Zin vines work well for farming family's new venture.

Jordan Sonoma ★★★ (Cab S) 87 90 94 95 97 99' Extravagant Alexander Valley estate models its Cabernet on supplest Bordeaux. And it lasts. Chard typical California-toasty.

Justin Paso Robles ★★★ Former investment banker with little auberge operation making impressive blended reds, esp. MERITAGE called Isoceles.

Kautz-Ironstone Lodi and Calaveras County ★★ Showplace destination in SIERRA FOOTHILLS grew to 300,000 cases in five years. Renovated bulk facility in Lodi to aid growth. Honestly priced broad range led by fine Cab Franc.

Karly Amador ★★ Among more ambitious sources of SIERRA FOOTHILLS Zin.

Keenan Winery, Robert Napa ★★ Winery on Spring Mountain: supple, restrained Cabernet, Merlot; also Chardonnay.

Kendall-Jackson Lake County ★★→★★★ Staggeringly successful style aimed at widest market: esp broadly sourced off-dry toasty Chardonnay. Even more noteworthy for the development of a diversity of wineries under the umbrella of ARTISANS & ESTATES.

Kenwood Vineyards Sonoma ★★ (Jack London Cab S) 87 **90** 95 97 98 99' Single-vineyard Cab, Zin (several) the high points. Sauv Bl is very reliable value. Recently the same owner as KORBEL.

Kirkland Ranch Napa ★★ Big cattle farm, also big winery. Strong Merlot

Kistler Vineyards Sonoma ★★★★ (Chard) 95 **96 97** 98 99' 00 01' Still chasing the Burgundian model of single vineyard Pinot Noir, most from Russian River (greatest successes), Chardonnays very toasty, buttery but with taut, sinewy structure which demands several years of bottle age.

Konigsgaard (and Arieta) Napa ★★★ Expensive, mailing list Chardonnay, Syrah and Cabernet Franc blend from former Newton winemaker with marketing by his musical friend Fritz Hatton, auctioneer and Christie's executive.

Korbel Sonoma ★★ Long-established classic-method sparkling specialist emphazises bold fruit flavours, intense fizz; Natural tops the line. Purchased by Anhauser-Busch.

Krug, Charles Napa ★→★★ (Cab S) **91 94** 95 **97** 98 99 Historically important winery with generally sound wines. Cabs at head of list. CK-Mondavi is relentlessly sweet commodity brand.

Kuleto Estate East Mtns, Napa First wines just being released. Cabernet S and Sangiovese well worth trying. Famous restaurant designer's property raises the bar several notches higher in a region where conspicuous excess is the norm.

Kunde Estate Sonoma ★★ (Chard) 99 Long-time large grower has emerged as solid producer with buttery Chard, flavourful Sauv (lightly touched with Viognier). Reds still finding a footing.

La Jota Napa ★★ Tannic Cab S from small estate on Howell Mountain.

Laetitia San Luis Obispo ★★ Now owned by BARNWOOD, concentrating on estate still wines. Pinot N scintillating, Pinot B maybe. Also Chardonnay.

Laird Napa ★★(★) Quickly getting recognized for full-bodied Chard.

Lambert Bridge Sonoma ★★ Revival of briefly defunct Dry Creek Valley winery so far more sound than exciting.

Lamborn Howell Mountain ★★ Excellent site. Wine produced at new facility gives concentrated, peppery Zins. Solid track record.

Landmark Sonoma ★★ (Chard) 99 00 01 Long-time Chard specialist now in the me-too toasty-buttery school. Overlook version offers value.

Lang & Reed Napa ★★ New. Specialist with Loire-style Cab Francs.

Latcham Fairplay, El Dorado County ★★ Making standard range with a standout Petite Sirah under Granite Springs label. Cab F is worth seeking.

Laurel Glen Sonoma ★★★ (Cab S) 90 91 94 **95** 97 99' Floral, well-etched Cab with a sense of place from steep vineyard in SONOMA Mtn sub-AVA. 5,000 cases. Counterpoint, Quintana, Terra Rossa, and Reds are good-value, higher-volume additional labels.

Lava Cap El Dorado ★★(★) Bold styles rule, a source of singularly understated, intriguing Zins and Cabs. Buys in grapes for very concentrated Petite Sirah blossoms around its 5th birthday.

Lawrence, Karl Napa ★★★ Tiny production of excellent Cabernet Sauvignon.

Lewis Napa ★★★ Purchased grapes & custom crush with consultant Paul Hobbes have done wonders with Merlot & Chard. Owned by Indy race car driver.

Livingston Moffett St Helena, Napa ★★ Noteworthy Cabs from mid-sized winery in good location. Stanley's Selection Cabernet Sauvignon matures well.

Lockwood Monterey ★★ Lge v'yd (1,650 acres) in S SALINAS VALLEY. Lockwood, Shale Creek labels virtually indistinguishable by style, but Lockwood ranges wider.

Lohr, J Central Coast ★→★★ Lge, wide-reaching firm at peak with PASO ROBLES Cab S Seven Oaks. Commodity line sub-titled Cypress.

Lolonis Mendocino ★★ Substantial grower at Ukiah with range of consistently attractive varietals from own vines.

Long Meadow W. Mtns Napa ★★ Beautiful new rammed earth winery and olive pressing facility with great potential. Cathy CORISON is winemaker.

Long Vineyards Napa ★★★ (Chard) 99 00 01 (Cab) 87 90 **91 94 95** 97 99' Tiny n'bour of CHAPPELLET: lush Chard, flavourful Cab, luxury prices.

Longoria Winery Santa Barbara (★★→★★★) Long-time GAINEY winemaker now on own, and brilliant with Pinot Noir.

Luna Napa ★★ Italianate theme executed by former NEWTON winemaker John Konigsgaard is erratic on Pinot Gr but has interesting Sangiovese in barrel.

Lynmar Russian River ★★★ Three vintages in a row of top flight Pinot Noir have launched this new venture. Quail Hill designation is almost a bargain at $30.

MacRostie Carneros ★★ Buttery Chard is flagship. Also well-oaked Merl, Pinot N.

Madroña El Dorado ★★ Loftiest v'yds in SIERRA FOOTHILLS, and high altitude pioneer. Reds a wrestling match between tannin and acid, but acidity suits the Riesling. Standard Riesbest after 6 years, Late Harvest super all the time.

Marcassin Sonoma Coast ★★★★ Cult consultant Helen Turley's own tiny label. Worth so much at auction that few ever drink it. Chardonnay is so densely concentrated, those who do taste it never forget.

Markham Napa ★★ (Merlot) **94 95 97** 98 99 01' Recently good to excellent, esp Merlot and Cab S grown in own v'yds. Sauv also to note.

Martinelli Russian River ★★★ Family growers from fog-shrouded western hills, famous for old-vine Jackass Hill V'yd Zin, Sought after small production of Pinot N and Chard made under Helen Turley's consulting eye.

Martini, Louis M Napa ★★ Long history making surprisingly ageworthy Reserve Cab S, Merlot, Zin and Barbera from fine v'yds (Monte Rosso, Los Vinedos, Glen Oaks, etc). Purchased by Gallo 2002.

Masson Vineyards Monterey ★ CONSTELLATION's supermarket label.

Matanzas Creek Sonoma (Chard) 99 (Merlot) **94 95** 97 **99** 01' Merlot and Chard seek to be CA's most expensive with controversial results. Winery sold in 2000 to ARTISANS & ESTATES.

Mayacamas Napa ★★ Pioneer boutique v'yd with rich Chard and firm (but no longer steel-hard) Cabernet. Some Sauvignon, Pinot. 5,000 cases.

McDowell Valley Vineyards Mendocino ★★ Grower-label for family with hearts set on Rhône varieties, esp ancient-vine Syrah and Grenache.

Meridian San Luis Obispo ★★ Fast-growing sibling to BERINGER making mark with single-vineyard EDNA VALLEY Chard, Paso Robles Syrah. Also STA BARBARA Chard, Pinot N, PASO ROBLES Cab S. 300,000 cases.

Meritage Name coined in Calif in the early 80's (rhymes with heritage), and then trademarked, to describe r or w made from blends of B'x varieties. Whites have been slow to catch on, but reds have transformed Calif thinking on Cabs.

Merry Edwards Russian River ★★(★) Superstar consultant has planted her own Pinot N v'yd in Russian River district. Top quality results since 97.

Merryvale Napa ★★ Oak aplenty in red, white MERITAGES, Chardonnay. Cab S more middle of the road.

Michael, Peter Sonoma ★★★(★) Partly Knights Valley estate-v'yd and partly bought-in Howell Mountain: larger-than-life, Frenchified Chard, Merlot, Cab.

Michel-Schlumberger Sonoma ★★ Reinvigorated Dry Creek Valley winery at its best with Cabernet Sauvignon.

Miner Napa ★★ Nicely balanced wines with a reputation for Merlot.

Mirassou Central Coast ★★ Fifth-generation grower and pioneer in MONTEREY (SALINAS) gets highest marks for Pinot Bl classic sp. Chard, Pinot worth a look.

Mondavi, Robert Napa ★★→★★★★ Brilliant innovator now applying lessons to varietals for every purse. From top: NAPA Valley Reserves (bold, prices to match), Napa Valley appellation series (eg CARNEROS Chard, Oakville Cabernet, etc), Napa Valley (basic production), Coastal Series (eg CENTRAL COAST Chard, NORTH COAST Zin etc), RM-Woodbridge (California appellation for basic production, also pricier "Twin Oaks" line). Also Famiglia di Robert Mondavi, OPUS ONE, BYRON, Caliterra (Chile), Luce and Ornelia (Italy), Vichon (France). Living memorial, institute devoted to wine, food and art called Copia opened in downtown Napa 01.

Monteviña Amador ★★ Owned by SUTTER HOME. Now turning more to Italian varieties (30 trial plantings) but hearty SIERRA Zin still the foundation stone. Top of line called Terra d'Oro.

Monticello Cellars Napa ★★ (Cab S) **87 90 94 95** 97 99 Basic line under Monticello label, reserves under Corley. Both include Chard, Cab S. Reserve Pinot is the most intriguing.

Morgan Monterey ★★★ Winemaker-owner. Top-end single vineyard PNs and Chards from v gd Santa Lucia Highlands vineyards. Esp fine unoaked Chard called Metallico.

Mount Eden Vineyards Sta Cruz Mts ★★→★★★ (Chard) **96 97** 98 99 Big expensive Chardonnay from old Martin Ray vineyards; gentler Edna Valley version. Also Pinot Noir, Cabernet.

Mueller Russian River ★★★ Very fine, relatively unknown Pinot Noir.

Mumm Napa Valley Napa ★★ G H Mumm-Seagram joint venture range incl cheery Blanc de Noirs, distinctive single-v'yd Winery Lake & opulent luxury DVX.

Murphy-Goode Sonoma ★★ Large Alexander V estate. Sauv, Merlot, Cab S to explore. Reserves lavishly oaked.

Nalle Sonoma ★★★ (Zin) 97 99 01' Winemaker-owned Dry Creek cellar getting to the very heart of Zin: wonderfully berryish young; that and more with age. 2,500 cases. Master of the claret style.

Navarro Vineyards Mendocino ★★→★★★ From ANDERSON VALLEY, splendidly ageworthy Chardonnay, perhaps the grandest Gewurztraminer in state. Even more special: late-harvest Riesling, Gewurztaminer. Pinot Noir not to be ignored. Only self-deprecating prices keep this from being cult favourite of big-shot collectors.

Nevada City Sierra Foothills ★★ Wide range of tourism-designed offerings distract from extraordinary Cab F. Winery is in the cultural capital of the mountains.

Newlan Yountville, Napa ★★ 99' Reliable producer in good location with fine value Cabernet Sauvignon (worth ageing in good vintages).

Newton Vineyards Napa ★★→★★★ (Cab S) 87 94 95 97 99' Luxurious estate growing more so; formerly ponderous style now reined back to the merely opulent for Chardonnay, Cabernet, Merlot.

Neyers Napa ★★★ Marketing man's label but super winemaking consultant Ehren Jordan, fine quality overall; great on Syrah.

Niebaum-Coppola Estate Napa ★★→★★★ (Rubicon)84 85 91 92 94 95 96 97' 98 99' Movie-man Coppola's luxuriously wayward hobby much invigorated since acquisition of Inglenook winery and 220-acre vineyard (but not name). Flagship Rubicon is wonderful but lower-end blends are uneven.

Ojai Ventura Co ★★★ Former Au Bon Climat partner Adam Tolmach on his own since early '90s makes wide range of excellent wines, esp Syrah.

Olivet Lane Sonoma ★ Brand made by Merry Edwards. Nice low oak Chard.

Opus One Napa ★★★★ (Cab S) 85 87 90 91 94 95 97' 99' Joint venture of R MONDAVI and Baronne Philippine de Rothschild. Spectacular winery; wines becoming brilliant. Mouton, watch out!

Pacific Echo Anderson Valley ★★ Formerly Scharffenberger, now Pommery-owned, sparkling wine. No longer sourced exclusively in Anderson Valley.

Pahlmeyer Napa ★★★ Cultish MERITAGE producer has 200 acres newly planted south of ATLAS PEAK. Merlot-dominated blend is reliable.

Paradigm Napa ★★★ Westside OAKVILLE vineyard has unlimited potential. Releases since mid-90s have competed with the valley's best.

Paraiso Springs Monterey ★★ Up-and-comer owned by v lge grower in Salinas.

Patz & Hall Napa ★★→★★★ Reputation for CARNEROS Chard from individual v'yds firmly established around crisp structure and opulent winemaking.

Pecota, Robert Napa ★★ Drink-young Cab, Sauv, Chard, Gamay.

Pedroncelli Sonoma ★★ Old-hand in Dry Creek. Reds incl single vineyard, too austere for easy enjoyment. Whites more agreeable.

Perry Creek Fairplay, El Dorado Co ★★ Wide range of tourist wines and cigar sales in tasting room obscure extraordinary accomplishments with Zin.

Phelps, Joseph Napa ★★★ (Cab S) 85 87 90 91 94 95 97 98 99' Deluxe winery, beautiful v'yd: impeccable standards. Very good Chardonnay, Cabernet S (esp Backus) and Cabernet-based Insignia. Also look for fine Rhône series under Vin du Mistral label.

Philips, R H Yolo, Sacramento Valley ★→★★ Pioneer in Dunnigan Hills NW of SACRAMENTO trying everything on huge property, succeeding best with Syrah, Viognier, and great value Chardonnay ★★ under TOASTED HEAD brand. Sold in 00 to Canada's VINCOR.

Pine Ridge Napa ★★→★★★ Gentlemanly commune-labelled Cabs are best (Rutherford, Stags Leap, etc), Merlot not bad either. Dry oak-aged Chenin Petite Vigne is intriguing. Winery changed hands in 2002.

Plumpjack Napa ★★ Good Cabernet from old Villa Mount Eden property of Gordon Getty. Made headlines by using screwcaps on three figure Cabernet sold to San Francisco high society.

Preston Sonoma ★★ One of Calif's pioneer "terroiristes" concentrating on wines best suited to his Dry Creek v'yds: esp Zin, Barbera, and Rhône varieties.

Pride Mountain Spring Mountain, Napa ★★★ Top hillside location contributes bright fruit characters to fine Bordeaux variety offerings.

Quady Winery San Joaquin ★★ Imaginative Madera Muscat dessert wines, incl celebrated orangey Essencia, rose-petal-flavoured Elysium, and Moscato d'Asti-like Electra. Starboard (a play on Port); name is better than the wine.

Quintessa Napa ★★★(★) Splendid new estate of Huneeus family, on Silverado Trail, linked to FRANCISCAN. Predictably very high standards.

Quivira Sonoma ★★ Sauvignon, Zinfandel, others, from Dry Creek Valley estate. More enamoured of oak than vineyard in recent vintages.

Qupé Sta Barbara ★★→★★★ Never-a-dull-moment cellar-mate of AU BON CLIMAT. Marsanne, Pinot Bl, Syrah are all well worth trying.

Rafanelli, A Sonoma ★★ (Cab) **90 94** 95 97' 99 (Zin) **97 99** 00 01' Hearty, fetchingly rustic Dry Creek Zin; Cab of striking intensity.

Ravenswood Sonoma ★★ Originally major critical success for (or despite) single-v'yd Zins of skull-rattling power.Purchased in 01 by CONSTELLATION.

Raymond Vineyards and Cellar Napa ★★ (Cab S) 87 90 94 95 **97** 99 Old NAPA family now with Japanese partners. Generations signifies well-oaked top-of-the-line Chard, Cab. Amberhill is consistent gd value commodity 2nd label

Renaissance N Yuba, Sierra Foothills ★★ Spotty track record and quasi-religious fervour of artistic community backing this ambitious wine venture. Question marks remain, but French-Israeli w'maker for last8 yrs has made remarkable strides. 3 vintages of miniscule production Roussanne is best seen in CA.

Renwood Amador ★★ An ultra-ambitious venture-capitalist expanding rapidly, but maintains rock-hard style of yesteryear. Several single v'yard bottlings of Zinfandel, Syrah, and Barbera as ripe and monumental as red wine can be. They KO all comers for a few years, but then begin to reveal raisin smells.

Ridge Sta Cruz Mts ★★★★ (Cab S) 85 87 90 **94 95 97** 99' Winery of highest repute among connoisseurs. Drawing from NAPA (York Creek) and its own mountain v'yd (Montebello) for conc'd Cabs, worthy of long maturing in bottle but needing less than formerly (NB 90 91 more approachable than 80). But power remains in SONOMA (Lytton Springs) and SAN LUIS OBISPO (Dusí) Zins and other red wines. Gentle Chardonnay.

Rios-Lovell Livermore ★★ New producer with good Zin and conc'd Petite Sirah.

Rochioli, J Sonoma ★★★(★) (Pinot N) **94** 95 96 **97** 98 99 Long-time Russian River grower making four distinct Pinot Noirs from sizeable v'yd long-celebrated under own, other labels. Also very good Sauvignon Blanc.

Roederer Estate Mendocino ★★★ ANDERSON VALLEY branch of Champagne house (est '88). Resonant house style apparent esp in luxury cuvée l'Ermitage. Still stuns the Champenois. 25,000 cases, poised to triple. Sold as Quartet in Europe.

Rombauer Vineyards Napa ★★ Well-oaked Chardonnay, dark Cabernet S (especially reserve-style Meilleur du Chai). Now also owner of the revived Hanns Kornell sparkling wine cellars and NAPA cellars.

Ross, Stephen SLO ★★ Pretty gd Pinot N mostly sourced from Santa Barb Co.

Rubissow-Sargent Mt Veeder, Napa ★★ Good quality, modestly priced Cab.

CALIFORNIA

Rudd Napa ★★ Contributor to Culinary Institute puts out solid Cab S and Chard.

St Amant Lodi ★★ Easternmost section of large LODI AVA, closest to AMADOR County: one of the most adroit at winemaking. Rhônes okay; Zins pretty gd.

St Clement Napa ★★→★★★ (Cab) 85 87 90 91 94 95 97 99' Japanese-owned; burlier, oakier style in recent v'tges of Sauv Bl, Cab, Merlot, CARNEROS Chard.

St Francis Sonoma ★★ (Merlot) 94 95 97 99 01' (Zin) 97 99 00' 01 Tasty Chardonnay (Reserve oakier). Merlot and Cabernet subtly aged in American oak. Massive, alcoholic Zin.

St-Supéry Napa ★★ French-owned (Skalli qv) and much activity since arrival of consulting winemaker Michel Rolland. Most grapes come from Dollarhide Ranch (Pope Valley) E of NAPA. Sauv Bl v crisp and flavourful given hot climate. Red MERITAGE doing quite well in tastings recently.

Saintsbury Carneros ★★★ (Chard) 97 99 00 01' (Pinot N) 97 99 00 01' Contends as AVA's finest and longest-lived Pinot Noir. Lighter Pinot Garnet and oaky Chard also vg. 60,000 cases.

Sanford Sta Barbara ★★★ (Pinot) 96 97 98 99 00 01 Bold to over-the-top, esp Barrel Select but never dull Chard, Pinot N. Intensely regional Sauv worth a look.

Santa Barbara Winery ★★ (Chard) 99 (Pinot N) 96 97 99' 00 01 Former jug-wine prod, now among leaders, esp for Res Chard, Pinot Noir. Also Sauv Bl, Riesl.

Sarah's Vineyard Hecker's Pass, Santa Clara Valley ★★★ Sold (01) by one of the most charmingly eccentric personalities in the industry. Marilyn Taylor made great wines. One of the best Merlots in CA from Radike Vyd near PASO ROBLES.

Sattui, V Napa ★★ King of direct-only sales (ie winery door or mail order). Lusty Cab, more refined Ries are the wines to seek.

Sausal Sonoma ★★ Lge-scale Alexander V estate noted for its Zin and Cabs.

Scherrer Sonoma ★★★ Ripe, CA-style Pinot Noir and Chardonnay from Russian River, as well as mouthfilling old-vine Zin from Alexander Valley.

Schramsberg Napa ★★★ One of CA's top sparkling producers for decades. Historic caves. Res: splendid; Bl de Noir outstanding (2–10 yrs). Luxury cuvée J Schram is America's Krug. Founder Jack Davies died '98: his family presses on.

Schug Cellars Carneros ★★ German-born & trained owner-winemaker dabbles in other types, but CARNEROS Chard, Pinot N are his main interests and wines.

Screaming Eagle Napa ★★★★ The new NAPA paradigm: Cabernet S grower + consulting oenologist = small lots of (delicious) cult wine at luxury prices.

Seavey Napa ★★(★) Tucked in the eastern hills. Makes big, ripe Cab. Mulberry scented Merlot on the way. Chard okay, but not the main attraction.

Sebastiani Sonoma ★→★★ Substantial old family firm working low end of market (August Sebastiani Country, Vendange, Talus) but able to compete above this price level, esp with Sonoma Cask. 4 million cases.

Seghesio Sonoma ★★ Concentrating now on superb, ageworthy Zins from own old v'yds in Alexander, Dry Creek valleys, but don't overlook smaller lots of Sangiovese Vitigno Toscano, Pinot N.

Sequoia Grove Napa ★★ NAPA Cabs (Napa, Estate): dark and firm. Chards recently firmer, fresher, longer-lasting.

Seven Hills San Luis Obispo ★★ V lge new Australian investment E of PASO ROBLES making generous Shiraz. Also co-operating with Paragon V'yds in Edna Valley for Chard and Pinot N. Aussie w'making tricks worth watching on Paso fruit.

Shafer Vineyards Napa ★★★ (Cab S) 90 94 95 97' 99 With '95, oak overshadows grape in single-v'yd Red Shoulder Ranch Chard (CARNEROS), & begins to in Hillside Select Cab S (Stags Leap District), Sangio-based Firebreak.

Siduri Sonoma ★★★ Borderline cult pricing on stable of noteworthy Pinot Noirs from expensive vyds, particularly Pisoni.

Sierra Vista El Dorado ★★(★) Dedicated Rhôneist in SIERRA FOOTHILLS. Dedicated "Rhônigade" at high elevation. Style elegant, mid-weight and fruit driven.

Five Star Res Syrah won a panel tasting in London over many top French and Australian wines. Zins vg. Bargain: Châteauneuf-style "Fleur de Montagne".

Signorello Napa ★★★ Fairly high-end Cabs and Chards, noteworthy Pinot Noir from Russian River, very good Semillon-Sauvignon blend is best value.

Silver Oak Napa/Sonoma ★★★ Separate wineries in NAPA and Alexander Valleys make Cabernet Sauv only. Owners have ridden extreme American-oaked style to pinnacle of critical acclaim.

Silverado Vineyards Napa ★★→★★★ (Cab S) 90 **94 95 97** 99 Showy hilltop Stags Leap District winery (Disney-owned); vineyards also elsewhere in NAPA. Consistently refined Cab, Chard, Sauvignon, Sangiovese.

Names to Look for in 2004

Baron Herzog Large kosher producer with esp fine Riesling from Monterey

Du Mol Excellent Burgundian varieties put out by top Bay Area wine retailer

JC Cellars Miniscule output, super intense wines by Rosenblum winemaker

Giannini Paoletti Couple of vintages in a row of stunning Napa Cabernet

Sunset San Fran hobbyists going pro with great values, esp Napa Barbera

---

Simi Sonoma ★★ After trimming lines to a select few, historic winery (under new owners) is back to making a wide range of varietals. Long-lived Cab S, vg Chard still the heart of the matter. Reserves (like so many) try too hard.

Sinskey Vineyards, Robert Napa ★★ Winery in Stags Leap, v'yds in CARNEROS for boldly oaked, firm Chard, Merlot, Pinot N.

Smith-Madrone Napa ★★ (Cab S) 95 **97** 99 Chard from Spring Mtn estate has had ups & downs; now up. Ries supports a nr-lost NAPA tradition. Drink Cabs early.

Sonoma-Cutrer Vineyards Sonoma ★★→★★★ (Chard) 97 99 00 01' Ultimate Chard specialist at somewhat diminished best with single-v'yd Les Pierres, Cutrer. FETZER owner Brown-Forman acquired 80% interest in 99.

Spencer Roloson ★★ Concentrated Zinfandels from Chiles Valley in Napa.

Spottswoode Napa ★★★ (Cab S) 87 **91** 94 95 97 99 Firm resonant luxury Cab from sm St Helena v'yd. Supple polished Sauv. 3,500 cases.

Stag's Leap Wine Cellars Napa ★★→★★★★ (Cask 23) **78** 84 87 90 **91** 94 **95** 97 99' Celebrated v'yd for silky, seductive Cabs (SLV, Fay, top-of-line Cask 23), Merlots; non-estate vg; also Chard, Sauv, Ries. 70,000 cases.

Staglin Napa ★★★ (Cab S) **90 94 95** 97 99 From sm Rutherford Bench v'yd designed by late André Tchelistcheff, consistently fine v silky Cab S & Sangio.

Steele Wines Lake ★★→★★★ Long-time K-J winemaker patrols whole coast for esp single v'yd Chards. Boldly oaked, pricey. 2nd label called Shooting Star.

Sterling Napa ★★→★★★ Scenic Seagram-owned winery; extensive v'yds and inexplicable ups & downs. Look for tart Sauv & firm basic bottling of Cab S.

Stony Hill Napa ★★★ (Chard) **93** 96 97 99 00 01' Hilly v'yd and winery for many of California's v best whites over past 30 yrs. Founder Fred McCrea died in 77, widow Eleanor in 91; son Peter carries on powerful tradition. Chard (both estate and non-estate SHV) is less steely, more fleshy than before. Oak-tinged Riesling and Gewurz are understated but ageworthy.

Storrs Santa Cruz ★★ Prize winning red MERITAGE, good Grenache, Petite Sirah worth a search, reliable Chardonnay.

Storybook Mountain Napa ★★★ NAPA's only dedicated Zin specialist makes taut Estate and Reserve wines from Calistoga vineyard.

Strong Vineyard, Rodney Sonoma ★★ (Cab) **90 94 95 97** 99 Formerly Sonoma V'yds; produces gd basic bottlings, better single-v'yd ones (Alexander's Crown Cab, Chalk Hill Chard, Charlotte's Home Sauv, River East Pinot N). Windsor name and facilities purchased in 2000 by Mildara-Blass from Aus for access to direct shipment program.

Sutter Home Napa ★ Famous for sw white Zin, heady AMADOR Zin. Branching out and reaching up with Signature Series and M Trinchero: mid-priced varietals.

Swan, Joseph Sonoma ★★ (Zin) **94 95 97** 99 00 01 The son-in-law of late Joe Swan makes equally ultra-bold Zin, Pinot Noir.

Swanson Napa ★★→★★★ (Cab S) **94 95** 97 99 Reds are the measure of the house, esp heartily oaked Cab, Sangio, Syrah.

Tablas Creek Paso Robles ★★★ Beaucastel owners challenge themselves with cuttings from their Châteauneuf vyds. All are happy with results.

Taft Street Sonoma ★★ After muddling along, has hit an impressive stride with esp good-value Russian River Chards, Merlots. 18,000 cases.

Talbott, R Monterey ★★ Wealthy owner doing well with big toasty Chards from Santa Lucia, Highlands, and CARMEL VALLEY AVAs.

Talley Vineyards San Luis Obispo ★★ Estate in Arroyo Grande (near SANTA BARBARA boundary) growing exceptional Pinot Noir. Chard too.

Tanner, Lane Santa Barbara ★★ (Pinot N) 93 94 **95 96 97** 98 99 Owner-winemaker with often superb single-v'yd Pinot Noirs (Bien Nacido, Sierra Madre Plateau). Drink immediately or keep. Now Syrah too.

Toasted Head Central Valley ★★ New brand from RH Philips. Really great buttered toast '00 Chard.

Torres Estate, Marimar Sonoma ★★★ (Chard) 93 94 **96 97** 99' 00 01 Sister of Catalan hero. Edgy Chard (ages magnificently), lovely Pinot N from RR Valley.

Trefethen Napa ★★★ (Chard) **93** 94 **95 96** 97 98 99 00 01' Respected family winery. Vg dry Ries, tense Chard for ageing (late-released Library wines show how well). Cab shows increasing depths. Lower priced wines labelled Eshcol.

Truchard Carneros ★★→★★★ From the warmer, inner-end of CARNEROS comes one of the flavoury, firmly built Merlots that give the AVA identity. Cabernet S Syrah even better.

Turley Napa ★★★ Former partner in FROG'S LEAP, now specializing in hefty, heady single vineyard Zin and Petite Sirah from old vines. Ehren Jordan is consultant. Purchased Pesenti in Paso Robles in 2001.

Turnbull Wine Cellars Napa ★★ Once extra-minty Cab now (95 96) more classical, restrained. New Sangio looks bright too. Estate faces MONDAVI winery.

Ventana Monterey ★★ '78 winery, showcase for owner's v'yds: watch for Chard and esp Sauv from Musqué clone.

Viader Napa ★★ (Cab blend) **94 95** 97 99 Argentine Delia Viader fled to Calif to do her own thing: dark Cab blend from estate in hills above St Helena.

Viansa Sonoma ★★ After obligatory Chard, Merlot, roster pays homage to Sam SEBASTIANI'S ancestors with blended, varietal Italianates including such rarities (for California) as Arneis, Dolcetto, Freisa.

Vino Noceto Amador ★★ Estate with true-to-type.

Von Strasser Diamond Mtn ★★★ Intense Cabs and a fine 100% Petit Verdot.

Wente Vineyards Livermore and Monterey ★★ Historic specialist in whites, esp LIVERMORE Sauv and Sem. MONTEREY sweet Riesling can be exceptional. A little classic sparkling. Also owns Concannon. 300,000 cases.

Wild Horse Winery San Luis Obispo ★★→★★★ (Pinot) 95 96 97 **99** 00 01' Owner-winemaker has a particular gift for Pinot Noir (mostly San Luis Obispo and STA BARBARA GRAPES). Also worthy Chard, Merlot.

Williams Selyem Sonoma ★★★ (Pinot) **90 92 93** 96 97 99 00 01' Intense smoky Russian River Pinot esp Rochioli and Allen vineyards. Now reaching to SONOMA coast, MENDOCINO, too. New majority owner (98) from NY having a little trouble holding the reins.

Young's Amador County ★★★ Small production of very fine Barbera and Zin.

York Creek Spring Mtn, Napa ★★★ Exceptional vineyard owned by Fritz Maytag, father of microbrew revolution in US. Sells to Ridge and now has own label.

Zaca Mesa Sta Barbara ★★ Turning away from Chardonnay and Pinot to concentrate on Rhône grapes (especially Marsanne and Syrah) and blends (Cuvée Z) grown on estate.

ZD Napa ★★ (Chard) 96 98 **99** oo o1' Lusty Chardonnay tattooed by American oak is ZD signature wine. Try it with lobster-corn soup. 18,000 cases.

The Pacific Northwest

The wine country of the Pacific Northwest spans three adjoining states Oregon has more than 15,000 acres of vines, concentrated in the Willamette Valley, south of Portland. Washington's 35,000 acres of vineyard are concentrated in the warmer, drier half of the state, east of the Cascade mountain range. Idaho's wine country lies just east of Washington's, along the Snake River.

The grapes of Burgundy and Alsace do well in Oregon; Dijon clones of Chardonnay and Pinot Noir promise earlier ripening, potentially more complex wines. Across the Columbia River in eastern Washington, the warmer, drier climate of the Columbia Valley allows thicker-skinned varieties (Merlot, Cab S, Cab F, and the hot new favourite, Syrah) to ripen well. These same varieties also grow well in the warmer southern appellations of Oregon, and in Idaho.

The largest wineries of the Pacific Northwest seem small in comparison to those in California. Most of the more than 460 wineries – a number that increases every year – produce fewer than 30,000 cases of wine annually, and many wineries make only 2,000 to 5,000 cases. Washington's Walla Walla Valley has recently been the most glamorous and rapidly-expanding appellation, growing from ten to 30 producers within a year and doubling vineyard plantings within the same period.

Recent Vintages

2002 Great expectations for wines with full expression and elegance.

2001 Lower acidity and less concentration than previous three years. Softer, earlier-drinking wines with strong varietal identity.

2000 Solid vintage. High yields, conc'd, structured wines. Now – 2010.

1999 Superb. Perfect growing season produced balanced wines. Now – 2008.

1998 Excellent throughout. Reduced yields and greater concentration in Oregon (now or soon) ; quantity and quality in Washington (hold).

Oregon

Abacela Vineyards Umpqua Valley ★★ 97 **98** 99' oo New producer; and one to watch: Tempranillo, Dolcetto, Cab Fr, and Syrah stand out.

Adelsheim Vineyard Yamhill County ★→★★ 91 92 93 **94 95 96** 97 **98** 99' Smoothly balanced Pinot N. New Dijon clone Chard, Ries, Pinots Gris, and Blanc: clean, bracing. Also fruity Merlot.

Amity Willamette ★ **97 98 99** oo Top Gewurz, Ries, Pinot Bl. Patchy Pinot N.

Andrew Rich (Tabula Rasa) Willamette ★ Small producer; wide range: Pinot N, Washington Cab S, Chenin-Sauv Bl, rosé and Gewurz ice wine.

Archery Summit Yamhill Co ★★★ 93 94 **95' 96** 97 **98'** 99' oo' Flashy sibling of NAPA winery Pine Ridge. V impressive oaky Pinot N.

Argyle Yamhill County ★→★★ (sp) 89 91 **93 94** 96 98 99' oo NW's best sp (incl NV), consistently well made. Also fine Ries, Chard, & high quality Pinot N.

Beaux Frères Yamhill County ★★ 91 **92 93 94** 95 96 97 98 99' oo Excellent, structured Pinot N; more finesse in recent yrs. Part-owned by Robert Parker Jr.

Bethel Heights Willamette ★★→★★★★ 91 92 93 **94 95** 96 **97 98** 99' Deftly made Pinot N from estate nr Salem. Also notable Chard, Pinot Bl, Pinot Gr.

Brick House Yamhill County ★★ 93 94 95 96 97 98 99' 00 Dynamic, organic property operated by former CBS news correspondent. V Burgundian style. Sml quantities of v gd Pinot N, Gamay, & barrel-ferm Chard.

Cameron Yamhill County ★→★★ 93 94 95 96 97 98' 99' Eclectic producer of Pinot N, Chard: some great, others conversation pieces. Vg Pinot Bl.

Chehalem Yamhill County ★→★★ 91 92 93 94 95 96 97 98 99' (w 00') Top quality Pinot N, Chard, Pinot Gr, Ries. Reserve Pinot N: collaborations with Burgundian winemaker Patrice Rion.

Cooper Mountain Willamette ★ Steadily increasing quality. Pinot N, Chard, Pinot Gr, Pinot Bl. Certified biodynamic vineyards.

Cristom N Willamette ★→★★ 92' 93 94 95 96 97 98' 99' 00' Delicious Pinot N and buttery-smooth Chard. Try the barrel-fermented Viognier.

Domaine Drouhin Willamette ★→★★★★ 91 92 93' 94 **95 96** 97 **98'** 99' 00' Superb estate-grown Pinot N from one of the first families of Burgundy. Laurène Reserve silky and elegant equally fine Chard 96 97 98 99'.

Domaine Serene Willamette ★★ 98' 99' 00 Big, jammy wines. Small production; look for Evenstead Reserve Pinot N; new Rockblock Syrah worth finding.

Elk Cove Vineyards Willamette ★ **98** 99' Quality range of wines featuring Pinot N, Pinot Gr, Chard, Ries. Excellent dessert wine Ultima.

Erath Vineyards Yamhill County ★ **93'** 94 95 96 97 98 99 00 V gd Chard, Pinot Gr, Gewurz, Pinot Bl. Esp lovely old Pinots 76 & Ries 76. New winemaker 2002.

Evesham Wood Nr Salem Willamette ★→★★ Sm family winery; fine Pinot N (91 92 93 94 95 96 97 98 99), Pinot Gris and dry Gewurz. Ltd production of Cuvée J in high demand. Newly organic vineyards.

Eyrie Vineyards, The Willamette ★→★★ Pioneer ('65) winery with Burgundian convictions. Older vintages of Pinot Noir are treasures (**75' 76'** 80 83 86 89 90); Chards and Pinot Gr: rich yet crisp. All wines age beautifully.

Firesteed ★ Large-volume producer of value-priced Pinot N and a fine DOC Barbera d'Asti (made in Italy).

Ken Wright Cellars Yamhill County ★★ 93 94 95 **96** 97 **98'** 99 01 Floral Pinot N that has a cult following. Also very gd Chard and Melon de Bourgogne.

King Estate S Willamette ★ 94 95 96 97 98 99' Huge beautiful NAPA-like estate. Very good Pinot Gris; Chard and Pinot N improving; fruit sourced from all over, including Cab S, Merlot, and Zinfandel. New estate wines top.

Lange Winery Yamhill County ★ 98 99' Small family winery; look for excellent reserve Pinot N; Pinot Gr is solid but Res reveals a heavy hand with oak.

Lemelson Yamhill County ★→★★ 99' new, well-financed operation producing well-structured fine wines.

Panther Creek Willamette ★→★★ 91 92 93 94' **95** 96 97 98' 99' Concentrated, meaty single v'yd Pinot N and pleasant Melon de Bourgogne. Purchased grapes from top v'yds, including Shea.

Patricia Green Cellars Yamhill County ★→★★ Wines of great pizazz and expression from former TORII MOR winemaker.

Ponzi Vineyards Willamette Valley ★→★★ 89 90 91 92 93 94 **95** 96 **96** 97 98' 99' Small winery almost in Portland, well-known for Pinot Gr, Chard, Pinot N. Well-made Arneis and Dolcetto.

Rex Hill Willamette ★ 91 92 93 94 **95** 96 97 98' 99' Excellent Pinot N, Pinot Gr and Chard from several N Willamette vineyards. Reserves are among Oregon's best; King's Ridge label is great value. New winemaker 2002.

St-Innocent Willamette ★ 98 99 Gaining reputation for big, delicious, forward Pinot N; pleasant but slightly bitter whites.

Sokol Blosser Willamette ★→★★ 93 **94** 95 **96** 97 98' 99 Much improved. Pinot N. NV Evolution notable.

Torii Mor Yamhill County ★→★★ 93 94 95 **96** 97 98' 99 Established Pinot N v'yd (planted 1977) in Dundee Hills; good Pinot Gr. Several gd single v'yd Pinot N bottlings. New winemaker in '00. First $100 bottle in Oregon.

Tyee S Willamette ★ Small, family-owned and -run winery is especially good with dry Gewurz, Riesling and Pinot Bl. Pinot N improving.

Willakenzie Estate Yamhill County ★→★★ 98' 99' 00 First wines released 1996; delicious Pinots Gris, Blanc, Chardonnay, Pinot Noir. Well-financed, state-of-the-art facility; French owner and new winemaker.

Willamette Valley Vineyards Willamette ★→★★ 94 95 96 97' 98' 99' Huge winery near Salem. Moderate – to very high-quality Chard, Ries, Pinot Noir. Amazing range from commercial to top flight. Also owns and produces vg Griffin Creek and Tualatin brands. New winemaker; needs watching.

Tracking down Northwest wines

Portland Wildwood (1221 NW 21st Avenue, tel 503-248-9663) The quintessential Northwest restaurant, with a dynamite Northwest wine list. Oregon Wines on Broadway (515 SW Broadway, tel 503-288-4655) Wine bar/shop with focus on Pinot Noir. Daily selections for tasting.

Dundee Ponzi Wine Bar (100 7th Street, tel 503-554-1500) A very attractive stop in the centre of wine country (45 mins from Portland). While the focus of wines to taste and buy is Ponzi's, you'll also find a broad selection of hard-to-find current releases from other top and "hot" producers.

Seattle McCarthy & Schiering Wine Merchants (2401-B Queen Anne Ave.N. tel 206-282-8500; 6500 Ravenna Ave. NE, tel 206-524-9500) Seattle's best wine shop, with a stellar line-up of top Northwest names. Owner Dan McCarthy is co-author of "A Pocket Guide to the Wines if Washington, Oregon & Idaho".

Walla Walla Grapefields (4 East Main St, tel 509-522-3993) Casual wine bar with simple food and a super selection of hard-to-find Walla Walla gems.

Washington & Idaho

Andrew Will Puget Sound (Washington) ★★→★★★ 89 90 91 92 **93 94 95** 96 97 **98'** 99' 00' Exceptional Cabernet S, Merlot and barrel-fermented Chard from best E Washington grapes. Fine Pinot Gris.

Arbor Crest Spokane ★→★★ New life from 99 when enologist daughter returned; tremendous talent just now showing in the wines.

Barnard Griffin Pasco, Columbia Valley (Washington) ★→★★ Sml producer: well-made Merlot, Chard (esp barrel-fermented), Sem, Sauv Bl. Top Syrah.

Bookwalter Columbia Valley ★ 00' Older estate with new life thanks to consultant Zelma Long. Rich, balanced wines, well-priced.

Canoe Ridge Walla Walla (Columbia Valley) ★ Owned by CHALONE (California). Impressive 93 94 95 96 **97 98** 99 Chard and Merlot. Fine Gewurz

Cayuse Walla Walla ★★ →★★★ **98'** 99' Striking Rhône-styles; a real taste of place.

Château Ste-Michelle Woodinville (Washington) ★→★★★★ Ubiquitous regional giant is Washington's largest winery; also owns COLUMBIA CREST, Northstar, Domaine Ste-Michelle and Snoqualmie. Major east Washington vineyard holdings, first-rate equipment and skilled winemakers keep wide range of varieties in front ranks. Vineyard-designated Cabernet, Merlot, and Chard. Successful ventures with Antinori (Col Solare) & Ernst Loosen (Eroica).

Chinook Wines Yakima Valley (Washington) ★ Owner-winemakers purchase local grapes for sturdy Chard, Sauv, Merlot, and Syrah. Look for Cab Franc.

Columbia Crest Columbia Valley ★ Separately run CH STE-MICHELLE label for delicious well-made top value wines. Cab, Merlot, Syrah & Sauv Bl best. V gd res wines.

Columbia Winery Woodinville ★ (Cab) 79 83 85 87 88 **89 90 91 92 93** 94 95 **96** 97 **98** 99 Pioneer (1962, as Associated Vintners) and still a leader. Balanced stylish understated single-v'yd wines, esp Syrah and Viognier.

DeLille Cellars Woodinville ★★→★★★ 92 93 94 95 96' 97 98' 99 Exciting winery for vg red B'dx blends: ageworthy Chaleur Estate, D2 (more forward, affordable). Excellent barrel fermented white (Sauv-Sem). Look out for new Syrah, Doyenne.

Dunham Cellars Walla Walla ★★ 95 96 **97** 98' 99 Young exciting wines from former L'ECOLE NO 41 (see below) assistant winemaker. Cabernets and Sem-Chardonnays all well extracted and elegant; lovely Syrah.

Gordon Brothers Columbia Valley ★ Tiny cellar; consistent, balanced Chard (Res 91), Merlot, Cab. Recently improving: new w'maker.

Hedges Cellars Yakima Valley ★→★★ Made its name exporting its wines to Europe and Scandinavia. Now boasts fine vineyard (Red Mountain), château-style winery, delicious Cab, Merlot, Sauv Bl.

Hogue Cellars, The Yakima Valley ★★ Large well-established producer known for excellent, good value wines, especially Ries, Chard, Merlot, Cab. Produces quintessential Washington Sauv Bl.

Indian Creek Idaho ★ 98 Top quality Pinot Noir.

Kiona Vineyards Yakima Valley ★ Solid Red Mountain producer since 1980. Very good quality/value Lemberger, Syrah, Cabernet Sauvignon.

Leonetti Walla Walla ★★★ 91 92 **93** 94 95 **96'** 97 98' 99' 00' The Washington estate in highest demand – a major collectable wine. Harmonious individual Cabernet: fine and big-boned. Merlot: bold, ageworthy.

L'Ecole No 41 Walla Walla ★→★★ 91 92 93 94 95 96' 97 98' 99' 00' Blockbuster reds (Merlot, Cabernet, and MERITAGE blend) with jammy, ageworthy fruit. Good barrel-fermented Semillon.

Matthews Cellars Woodinville ★→★★ 96' **97** 98' 99 Smaller producer of mouth-filling Bordeaux blends since 1993. New Sem worth hunting down.

McCrea Puget Sound ★ Small winery for gd Viognier, Syrah, and Grenache. Experiments with Rhône blends continue.

A choice of Pacific Northwest wines for 2004
Kiona Cabernet Red Mountain
Cayuse Syrah Walla Walla, Washington
Delille Blanc Columbia Valley, Washington
Custom Pinot Noir Oregon
Ponzi Arneis Oregon
Adelsheim Pinot Gris Oregon

Quilceda Creek Vintners Puget Sound ★★★ 87 88 89 90 91 **92 93** 94 95 96' 97 98' 99 Expertly crafted ripe well-oaked Cab S from Columbia Valley grapes is the speciality. Exceptional finesse and ageability. Winemaker is the nephew of the legendary André Tchelistcheff.

Reininger Walla Walla ★→★★ 99' Small, focused producer of top wines.

Rose Creek Vineyards S Idaho ★ Small family winery; good esp for Chard.

Ste Chapelle Caldwell (Idaho) Pleasant, forward Chard, Ries, Cab, Merlot, Syrah from local and E Washington v'yds. Attractive sparkling wine: good value and improving quality.

Vickers Vineyard Idaho ★ Lovely rich barrel-fermented Chardonnay.

Washington Hills Cellars/Apex Yakima ★ Solid line incl Sem, Fumé, Cab, Chard, Merlot, and late-harvest Ries, Gewurz. Apex label: higher quality.

Waterbrook Walla Walla ★ 89 90 91 92 93 94 95 96 97 98 99 Stylish, distinctive Chard, Sauv, Cab, Merlot from a winery that has hit its stride.

Woodward Canyon Walla Walla ★★ 90 91 **92 93 94 95 96** 97 98 99' 00' Quality-driven, loyally followed. Ripe, intense, but elegant Cab, Chard, and blends.

East of the Rockies

Producers in New York (there are now 170 in 9 AVAs) and other eastern states, as well as Ohio (90 in 5 AVAs) traditionally made wine from hardy native grapes and French-American hybrids. Today, consumer taste plus cellar and vineyard technology largely bypass these. Chardonnay, Riesling, and Cabernet Sauvignon are now firmly established. Pinot Noir is emerging with some notable results, and Cabernet Franc and Merlot appear overall to be the East's most promising red. There are some exciting early results with Viognier and Gewurztraminer. Progress, from Virginia to Ohio, is accelerating as the wines gain recognition outside their own immediate region.

Wineries and vineyards

Allegro ★★ 01 02 Pennsylvania. Worthy Chard, Cab.

Antony Road Has risen to the top in Finger Lakes. Fine Riesling and superb late-harvest VIGNOLES.

Bedell ★★★ 00 01 02 LONG ISLAND winery; excellent Merlot and Cab S.

Biltmore Estate ★★ 00 01 02 Largest of North Carolina's 22 wineries with Vanderbilt mansion, America's lgst. Chardonnay and sparkling.

Chaddsford ★★★ 99 **00 01** 02 Solid Pennsylvania producer since '82: especially for good Pinot Gris and B'dx-style red blend.

Chamard ★★ 00 01 02 Connecticut's best winery, owned by Tiffany chairman. Top Chard. AVA is Southeastern New England.

Clinton Vineyards ★★ 01 02 HUDSON R winery; clean dr SEYVAL & spirited sp Seyval.

Chalet Debonné Vineyards ★★ 00 01 Popular OHIO estate (in Lake Erie AVA): hybrids, eg CHAMBOURCIN and VIDAL; and *vinifera*, eg Chard, Ries, Pinot Gr.

Constellation NY based. Owns and operates wineries in California, Idaho, NY, and Washington State. 2002 sales hit $US863 million. 45 million 9-litre cases of wine produced annually. Full range of wines (250,000 cases).

Finger Lakes Beautiful upstate NY cool region, source of most of state's wines. Top wineries: ANTONY ROAD, Ch La Fayette Reneau, DR FRANK, FOX RUN, GLENORA, STANDING STONE, Swedish Hill, H WEIMER, Kings Ferry, Red Newt & Shalestone.

Firelands ★★ 01 02 Ohio estate in LAKE ERIE AVA, growing Chardonnay, Cab, Gewurz, Pinot Gris, Riesling sp and Pinot Noir.

Fox Run ★★★ 00 01 02 Gd example of new generation FINGER LAKES winemaking; some of the region's best Chard, Gewürtz, Ries, Pinot Noir, & B'x style red.

Frank, Dr Konstantin (Vinifera Wine Cellars) ★★★ 98 99 **00 01** 02 Influential winery. The late Dr F was a pioneer in growing European vines in the FINGER LAKES. Good Ries, Gewurz, Chard, Cab S, and Pinot N. Vg Chateau Frank sp.

Glenora Wine Cellars ★★ 01 02 FINGER LAKES producer of good sparkling wine, Chard and Ries Restaurant and inn with scenic lake views. Expanding empire includes two new wineries.

Hamptons, The (Aka South Fork) LONG ISLAND AVA. The top winery is moneyed WOLLFER ESTATE. Showcase Duck Walk is owned by PINDAR.

Hudson River Region America's oldest winegrowing district (17 producers) and NY's first AVA. Straddles the river, two hours' drive N of Manhattan.

Lake Erie Lgst grape-growing district in the eastern US; 25,000 acres along shore of Lake Erie, incl portions of New York, Pennsylvania & OHIO. 90% is

CONCORD (mostly used for commercial juice & jelly), generally from New York's Chautauqua County. Also name of a tri-state AVA: NY's sector has 8 wineries, Pennsylvania's 5 and Ohio's 26. Ohio's Harpersfield sets standards for quality.

Lamoreaux Landing ★★★ **00 01** 02 Stylish FINGER LAKES house: promising Chard, Ries, and Cab Franc from striking Greek-revival winery.

Lenz ★★★ **00 01** 02 Classy winery of NORTH FORK AVA. Fine austere Chard in the Chablis mode, also Gewurz, Merlot and sparkling Merlot.

Long Island Exciting wine region East of the Rockies and a hothouse of experimentation. Currently 3,000 acres, all *vinifera* (35% Merlot) and 3 AVAs (LONG ISLAND, NORTH FORK, THE HAMPTONS). Most of its 29 wineries are on the North Fork. Best varieties: Chard, Cab, F Merlot. A long growing season; almost frost-free. Promising new wineries incl: Leib, Martha Clara, Old Field (1st wine sold 2002), Sherwood House (Chard & Merlot), Raphael.

Michigan In addition to fine cool climate Ries, impressive Gewurz, Pinot N, and Cabernet F, are emerging; 32 commercial wineries and four AVAs. Best include St-Julien Wine Co, Ch Grand Traverse, Peninsula Cellars (esp dry Gewurz), and Tabor Hill. Mawby Vyds and Ch Chantal known for sparkling wine from Chard, Pinot Noir, and Pinot Meunier. Fenn Valley and Good Harbour have lge local following. Black Star Farms, a showplace with inn, creamery and distillery. Up and coming Dom Berrien.

Millbrook ★★★ **01** 02 Top HUDSON RIVER REGION winery. Dedicated viticulture and savvy marketing has lifted spiffy whitewashed Millbrook in big old barn into NY's firmament. Burgundian Chards: Cab F can be delicious.

North Fork LONG ISLAND AVA (of 3). Top wineries: Bedell, Macari, LENZ, PALMER, PAUMANOK, PELLEGRINI, PINDAR. 2.5 hrs' drive from Manhattan.

The Big Apple has local wines – where to find them:

No longer the rarity they once were, NY wines have finally gained a foothold in Manhattan restaurants. Among the top players offering local wines:

Le Bernardin 1er seafood restaurant offering fish-friendly East Coast wines.

Home Cosy Greenwich Village spot where New York wines complement "American Neighbourhood" cuisine.

Gramercy Tavern A cosy mix of urban chic and low-key charm.

Gustavino's Trendy sunlit space under the 59th Street Bridge.

Jean Georges Sophisticated favourite of NY gourmands – local wine offerings.

Judson Grill Contemporary market-based seasonal fare – serious wine list.

Four Seasons Venerable see-and-be-seen hotspot.

Zoe Eclectic contemporary American cuisine –strong wine list

Ohio 90 wineries, 5 AVAs, notably LAKE ERIE and Ohio Valley.

Palmer ★★★ **00 01** 02 Superior LONG ISLAND (N FORK) producer and byword in Darwinian metropolitan market. High profile due to perpetual-motion marketing. Tasty Chard, Sauv Bl and Chinon-like Cab F.

Paumanok ★★★ **00** 01 02 Rising fine LONG ISLAND (N FORK) winery; impressive Cab, Merlot, Ries, Chard, outstanding Chenin, savoury late-harvest Sauv.

Pellegrini ★★★ 98 **99 00 01** 02 One of LONG ISLAND's most enchantingly designed wineries (on NORTH FORK), opened 1993. Opulent Merlot, stylish Chardonnay, Bordeaux-like Cabernet. Inspired winemaking. Exceptionally flavourful wines.

Pindar Vineyards ★★★ **99 00 01** Lge 287-acre operation at NORTH FORK, LONG ISLAND (Island's lgst). Wide range of blends & popular varietals, incl Chard, Merlot, sp and esp good B'x-type red blend, Mythology. Popular tourist destination.

Red Newt ★★★ 01 02 Est'd 99 in Finger Lakes. Turns out top Chard, Ries, Cab F, Merlot, and B'x-inspired red blend. Popular bistro.

Sakonnet ★★ 00 01 02 Largest New England winery, based in Little Compton, Rhode Island (SE New Eng AVA). V drinkable wines incl Chard, VIDAL, dry Gewurz, Cab Fr and Pinot N. Delicious sp Brut cuvée.

Standing Stone ★★ 00 01 02 One of FINGER LAKES' finest wineries with very good Ries, Gewurz and Bordeaux-type blend.

Tomasello ★★ 00 01 02 Est'd New Jersey winery. Gd CHAMBOURCIN. Cab S & Merlot.

Unionville Vineyards ★★ 00 01 02 One of New Jersey's best wineries, est '93. Lovely Ries and good Cab/Merlot blend.

Wagner Vineyards ★★ 01 02 Famous FINGER LAKES winery. Barrel-fermented Chard, dry and sw Riesling and Icewine. Attracts many visitors.

Westport Rivers ★★ 01 02 Massachusetts house est'd '89. Good Chard and elegant sparkling. (Southeastern New England AVA.)

Wiemer, Hermann J ★★→★★★ 98' 99 00 01 02 Creative German-born FINGER LAKES winemaker. Outstanding Ries incl vg sp and "late harvest". Vg Chard.

Wolffer Estate ★★★ 00 01 02 In operation since '87, has come of age with modish Chard, Merlot and sparkling from German-born winemaker. Proof that gd wine can be made on LONG ISLAND's South Fork.

Wollersheim ★★ Wisconsin winery specializing in variations of Maréchal Foch. Prairie Fumé (Seyval Bl) is a commercial success.

Southern and central states

Virginia Emerging as important wine state since 72. 71 wineries (in 6 AVAs), 2146 (51% increase from 1995) acres of vineyards. Top whites include Chard, Pinot Gr, & Viognier. Best reds are Cab F, Merlot, & Cab S. Top producers include Barboursville, Breaux, Horton (Viognier, other Rhône-style wines), Ingleside Plantation, Jefferson (near Monticello), Linden, Piedmont, Prince Michael, Oakencroft, Rockbridge, Tarara, Whitehall, Williamsburg, and Villa Appalaccia. Exciting newcomers: Chrysalis, impressive Viognier & Valhalla.

Missouri A blossoming industry with 41 producers in 3 AVAs: Augusta (first in the US), Hermann, Ozark Highlands. In-state sales catching fire. Best wines are SEYVAL BLANC, VIDAL, Vignoles (sweet and dry versions). Top estate is Stone Hill, in Hermann (since 1847): rich red from NORTON grape variety; Hermannhof (1852) is drawing notice for the same. St James for both Vignoles and Norton; Mount Pleasant, in Augusta: rich "Port" and nice sparkling wine. To watch are Adam Puchta, Augusta Winery, Blumenhof, Les Bourgeois, Montelle, Röbler.

Maryland 11 wineries, 2 AVAs. Basignani makes good Cabernet S, Chardonnay, SEYVAL. Best-known Boordy Vineyards: good Seyval Chard, Cab and sparkling. Fiore's CHAMBOURCIN is interesting. Catoctin AVA: main Cabernet and Chardonnay area. Linganore is second AVA.

The Southwest and the Rockies

Texas

The fifth-largest wine producing state in the US has over 40 bonded wineries and 7 AVAs. Although Pierce's Disease is a concern, growth in wine production continues apace. The best wines compare well with California.

Becker Vineyards ★★★ Stonewall. Very good Merlot, Cabernet S, Chardonnay & Port-style wine. Viognier is promising.

La Buena Vida Vineyards ★ Tasting room in Grapevine (nr Dallas). Produces tables wines under brands of Springtown, Walnut Creek Cellars, and La Buena Vida. Very good Walnut Creek "Ports".

Blue Mountain Vineyards Fort Davis. Very good Cabernet Sauvignon.

Cap Rock ★★★ Nr Lubbock. Reliably good varietals: Cab S, Chard, Merlot. Well-crafted blends, especially Cabernet Royale.

Fall Creek Vineyards Texas Hill Country. Good Chardonnay and Riesling.

Hidden Springs Winery Pilot Point. Good Chard.

Llano Estacado ★★★ Nr Lubbock. The pioneer (since 76) continues on award-winning track with Chard (esp Cellar Select), Chenin Blanc, Riesling and Zinfandel. Very good blends, esp Signature Series and Viviano.

Messina Hof Wine Cellars ★★★ Nr Bryan. Very good boutique wines. Excellent Riesling, Chard (Private Reserve), Merlot and Cabernet S. Vg red and white Port-style wines. Now has restaurant and deluxe B&B.

Sister Creek Boerne. Boutique winery with vg Pinot Noir and Muscat Canelli.

Ste-Genevieve ★ Fort Stockton. Largest Texas winery, linked with Domaines Cordier (France). Well-made NV wines, esp Sauvignon Blanc. Now has premium label Escondido Valley wines, esp Chard, Cab S, and Syrah.

Spicewood Good Sauvignon Blanc and Chardonnay.

> The Southwest – and area to watch in 2004
>
> The Southwest, in a concerted effort to call attention to the unique wines of this area, has initiated regional events, such as the Southwest Vine & Wine Conference and the Southwest Wine Competition. Statewide festivals and local wine events have increased public awareness of the wines. Although drought conditions in 2002 in New Mexico led to some decline in grape production, overall wine quality has increased.

New Mexico, etc

New Mexico continues to show promise with more emphasis on *vinifera* grapes, though some French hybrids are still used (historic Mission grape is produced at Tularosa Winery). Over 30 wineries, 3 AVAs. Black Mesa: ★ Vg Cab S, Pinot Gr, Merlot; gd blends, esp Coyote (red). Casa Rondeña: ★★ Vg Cab F and Sauv Bl. Corrales: ★★ Gd blends and vg Cab S. Gruet: ★★★ Excellent sp and vg Chard and Pinot N. Jory: Vg Sauv Bl and Zin. La Chiripada: ★★ Vg Ries and blends, some with hybrids; good Port-style wine. La Querencia: ★–★★ new in 2002, winning medals with Lemberger, Cab F, and Chambourcin. Milagro V'yds: vg Chard and Cab S. Ponderosa Valley: ★★ vg Ries, gd Pinot N, Merlot and blends, esp Summer Sage and Jemez Red. Santa Fe V'yds: ★ Vg Sauv Bl and Merlot. La Viña: ★★ vg Chard and Zin; gd blends, esp Rojo Loco. St Clair, Blue Teal V'yds, Mademoiselle V'yds, DH Lescombes, and Santa Rita Cellars all under winemaker Florent Lescombes have a good variety of wines.

Colorado continues to focus on vinifera grapes, with over 600 acres planted, mostly on the Western Slope. Over 40 wineries & two AVAs. Carlson Cellars: ★★★ vg Gewurz & Ries. Canyon Wind: gd Chard & Merlot. Cottonwood Cellars: rich Cab S, gd Merlot & Chard. Garfield Estates: new with promising Merlot, Cab F, esp 2002. Grande River: ★★–★★★ vg Chard, esp Barrel Select 99. Gd Merlot, Sem, Syrah & Viognier. Plum Creek: ★ gd Chard & Merlot. Terror Creek: ★★ small with vg Pinot N, Ries, Gewurz. Trail Ridge: gd Gewurz & Ries.

Arizona progresses in overall quality and the number of wineries (now 10). Success with Rhône and Mediterranean grape varieties: Sangiovese, Syrah, Petite Sirah show promise. Callaghan V'yards: ★★ Excellent Tempranillo-based *Padres*, vg Syrah, Cab S and blends, esp Caitlin's selection Dos Cabezas: ★ Vg Cab S, Petite Sirah, Sangiovese. Kokopelli, Arizona's largest winery, makes sound, reasonably-priced wines. Echo Canyon emphasizes Rhône varietals.

Oklahoma has expanded to over 12 wineries. Tidal School V'yds and Stone Bluff Cellars. Utah continues to show promise but has limited wineries. Nevada's Pahrump Valley nr Las Vegas has vg Chard, Cab S, and Symphony.

Canada

British Colombia

This expanding and significant part of the Canadian wine industry has grown up since the 70s. The biggest concentration of wineries is in the splendid Okanagan Valley, 150 miles east of Vancouver, in climatic conditions not very different from eastern Washington. There are 50 wineries and 4 appellations (Okanagan Valley, Frasier Valley, Similkameen Valley, and Vancouver Island).

Burrowing Owl 98' 99 00 01 Excellent Chard and Pinot Gr; promising reds.

Calona Vineyards ★★ 99 00 01 02 Large winery. Gd Pinot Bl, Sem and Merlot.

Gray Monk ★★ 99 00 01 02 Gd Okanagan Auxerrois, Gewurz and Pinot Blanc.

Mission Hill ★→★★★ 99 00 01 02 Acclaimed Reserve Chard, Pinot Blanc.

Cedar Creek ★★★ 98 00 01 02 Outstanding Chard, Pinot Bl, Pinot N. Tapas-style restaurant.

Quails's Gate ★★ 98' 99 00 01 Chard, Chenin Bl, Pinot Noir, Riesling Icewine.

Sumac Ridge ★★ 98' 99 00 01 02 Gewurz, Sauv Bl, sp among region's best. Notable MERITAGE and Merlot. (Owned by VINCOR.)

Ontario

The main eastern Canada wine region, on Niagara Peninsula, Pelee Island and LAKE ERIE north shore: 75 wineries. three top-notch young wineries (Thirty Bench, Malivoire, Thirteenth Street) now raising the quality bar here. Riesling, Chardonnay, Cab F, even Pinot Noir show potential for longevity. Icewine is international flagship of region. Gewurztraminer and Pinot Gris showing promise. 2002 vintage generally stellar.

Andres 2nd-lgst Canadian winery. Owns HILLEBRAND and new Peller Estates.

Cave Spring Cellars ★★★ 00 01 ONTARIO boutique: sophisticated Chard, Ries, and Gamay. Big restaurant, popular tourist stop, 28-room inn.

Château des Charmes ★★★ 00 01 02 Show-place château-style ONTARIO winery. Fine Chard, Viognier, Cab, sparkling.

Henry of Pelham ★★★ 98 99 00 01 Elegant ONTARIO Chardonnay & Riesling; Cabernet/Merlot, distinctive Baco Noir, Icewine.

Hillebrand Estates ★→★★★ 98' 99 00 01 ONTARIO producer attracting attention with Ries, sp, and B'dx-style red blend. Handsome restaurant.

Inniskillin ★★★★ 98' 99 00 01 Important (VINCOR-owned) producer that spearheaded birth of modern ONTARIO wine industry. Skilful burgundy-style Chard & Pinot N & B'dx-style red. Vg Ries, Icewine (incl sp), Pinot Gr.

Konzelmann ★★★ Top Ries, Chard and Icewine.

Peninsula Ridge ★★★ Est. Ontario 2000, already showing good Chard, Merlot, icewine. Restaurant with panoramic view of Lake Ontario.

Vincor International ★→★★ 4th lgst co in N America. (California's RH PHILLIPS & Washington's HOGUE CELLARS). Premium wines; varietals, blends. Owns Jackson-Triggs, INNISKILLIN (Chard, Cab), Sumac Ridge (BC), Goundrey recently added.

Vineland Estates ★★★ 00 01 02 Gd ONTARIO producer; dry and semi-dry Ries, Gewurz much admired. VIDAL Icewine: good, Chard, Cab, Sauv bl, and B'dx-style red. Excellent restaurant & tasting room.

Vintners Quality Alliance Canada's appellation body, started in ONTARIO but now incl BRITISH COLUMBIA. Its rigid standards have rapidly raised respect and awareness of Canadian wines to high levels. VQA enacted into Ontario law in 2000.

Central & South America

More heavily shaded areas
are the wine growing regions

Chile

There is a widening gap in Chile between those wishing to produce world-class wines and those content to produce large quantities of something more modest. The ambitious wineries are lowering yields dramatically, developing hillside vineyards, often at high altitudes, and showing a much more sensitive touch in matters such as oak-ageing. Cabernet Sauvignon is still the most important grape variety, although it is increasingly being blended with Merlot, Cabernet Franc and Carmenère, the old Bordeaux grape that the Chileans misidentified as Merlot for many years. Syrah is also proving successful.

Most vineyards (virtually all irrigated, mostly ungrafted) lie in the 300-mile long Central Valley to the south of Santiago. Variations in growing conditions are usually based on altitude and proximity to sea breezes. Most regions are warm and therefore suited to red wines. However, white varieties are being grown successfully in valleys near the coast such as Casablanca, between Santiago and Valparaiso, Limarí (N of Casablanca), Leyda (S of Casablanca), as well as Bio-Bio in the South.

Recent vintages

Most wines are ready to drink on release, although the better reds improve for up to five years. Curiously, odd years have been best for reds in recent vintages.
2002 Good in Maipo and Aconcagua, more patchy further south due to rain.
2001 Near-perfect conditions, generally lower yields, very high quality.

2000 Large cool vintage. Gd v'yard managers made excellent aromatic wines.
1999 Low yields and drought produced conc'd but some slightly baked reds.
1998 Cool, El Niño-affected season; erratic ripening and high yields.
1997 Excellent warm vintage, produced small crop of aromatic, conc'd wines.

Aconcagua Nthnmost quality wine region. Incl CASABLANCA, Panquehue, Leyda.

Almaviva See Baron Philippe de Rothschild.

Antiyal ★★★ New MAIPO venture from Alvaro Espinoza, winemaker at VIÑA CARMEN making fine and complex red from organically grown fruit.

Baron Philippe de Rothschild ★★★→★★★★ B'x company making good Mapa varietal range, better Escudo Rojo red blend, and expensive but classy, claret-style Almaviva, the latter a MAIPO joint venture with CONCHA Y TORO.

Bío-Bío Sthnmost quality wine region. Wet. Potential for gd whites and Pinot N.

Calina, Viña ★★ Kendall-Jackson (see California) venture. Better reds (esp Selección de Las Lomas Cab S) than whites, with silky Elite Cab S the pick. El Caliz is good, intro-level range.

Caliterra ★★→★★★ Sister winery of ERRAZURIZ, now half-owned by Mondavi (California). Chard and Sauv Bl improving (more CASABLANCA grapes), reds becoming less one-dimensional. Reserva range. Vg new Arboleda wines (Cabernet S, Syrah, Carmenère, Merlot, Chardonnay) even better. Seña (★★★★) is Mondavi-inspired Cab S/Merlot/ Carmenère blend launched 97.

Cánepa, José ★★ Back on song after upheavals in mid-1990s; lemony Sémillon and spicy Zinfandel among the more unusual wines, juicy berry-ish Malbec and fragrant Syrah Reserve among the best.

Carmen, Viña ★★→★★★ MAIPO winery under same ownership as SANTA RITA. Ripe, fresh Special Res (CASABLANCA) Chardonnay and deliciously light Late-harvest MAIPO Sém top whites. Reds even better; esp RAPEL Merlots, Maipo Petite Sirah, and Cabs, esp Gold Reserve. Now does vg Maipo Syrah/Cabernet and has new organic range called Nativa.

Carta Vieja ★★ MAULE winery owned by one family for six generations. Reds, esp Cab and Merlot, better than whites, though Antigua Selección Chard is good.

Casa Lapostolle ★★★ Money from the family of Grand Marnier and winemaking advice from Bordeaux's Michel Rolland result in fine range across the board. Bordeaux-style Sauvignon is good, but the reds, led by stunning (but pricey) Merlot-based Clos Apalta, are even better.

Casablanca Cool-climate region between Santiago and coast. V little water: drip irrigation essential. Top-class Chard and Sauv; promising Merlot and Pinot N.

Casablanca, Viña ★★★ Sister winery to SANTA CAROLINA. Wines now made by Joseba Altuna of Guelbenzu (Spain). RAPEL and MAIPO fruit used for some reds but better wines, notably Merlot, Sauv, Chard, and Gewürz, come from Santa Isabel Estate in CASABLANCA. Look for new super-cuvée Fundo.

Casa Silva ★★ Colchagua estate offering pithy Classic Sémillon, spicy, chunky Reserva Merlot, and top-of-the-range Quinta Generación Red and White; the white is a v successful blend of Chardonnay, Sauvignon Gris, and Viognier.

Concha y Toro ★★★ Mammoth but quality-minded operation, good value. Top wines: increasingly subtle Amelia Chard (Casablanca); rich chocolatey Marqués de Casa Concha Merlot (Rapel); inky Don Melchor Cab (Rapel); and silky Terrunyo Pinot Noir (Casablanca). Impressive Winemaker Lot on some markets. Copper Range, Trio, Explorer and Casillero del Diablo (incl fine new Viognier) offer v gd value. See also Baron Philippe de Rothschild.

Cono Sur ★★→★★★ Chimbarongo winery owned by CONCHA Y TORO for very good Pinots (local and CASABLANCA fruit). Also dense, fruity Cabs, delicious Viognier and spicy Zinfandel. Top releases appear as "20 Barrels" selection. Also second label Isla Negra.

Cousiño Macul ★★→★★★ Long-est firm, sold part of historic Maipo estate to est new v'yds further S in Buin. Long-lived Antiguas Res Cab; top wine Finis Terrae (B'dx blend). Supple Merlot, old-fashioned, v dry Sém, Chard.

Domus ★★★ MAIPO single, v'yd venture making good Chard and vg Cab. Patrick Valette (see EL PRINCIPAL).

Echeverría ★★ Boutique Curicó (MAULE) winery producing intense, complex Reserve Cabs, v gd oaked and unoaked Chard and rapidly improving Sauv Bl.

Edwards, Luís Felipé ★★ Colchagua (RAPEL) winery; citrus Chard, silky Res Cab. Wines now made by an ex-Penfolds winemaker.

El Principal, Viña ★★★ Excellent Pirque (Maipo) estate making complex Bordeaux blends under guidance of Patrick Valette of Ch Berliquet in St Emilion. El Principal is top wine, Memorias impressive 2nd cuvée.

Errázuriz ★★★ Sole winery in Panquehue district of ACONCAGUA. First-class range, including complex, mealy Wild Ferment Chard (now partnered by a Pinot N); brooding Syrah; Chile's best Sangiovese; earthy, plummy Merlot; fine Cabs topped by Don Maximiano Reserve. Also fine newcomer Viñedo Chadwick (Cab S/Carmenère), 1st vintage 99. Also see Caliterra.

Falernia, Viña New (2001) winery in far north Elqui Valley where fruit flavours are extreme. So far Sauvignon Blanc and Merlot are very tasty.-

Floresta ★★→★★★★ Long-est'd MAIPO bodega improving steadily. Range in ascending quality: 120, Reserva, Medalla Real, new Florester (inc. fine red blends), Casa Real. Best: Casa Real Maipo Cab S, but Triple C (Cab S/Cab F/Carmenère) nearly as gd.

Fortuna, Viña La ★★ Old-est'd winery in Lontué Valley. Range of attractive varietal wines, esp chunky Malbec.

Francisco de Aguirre, Viña ★★ Promising Cabs S and F and Chard under the Palo Alto label from the northerly region of Valle de Limari.

Gracia de Chile ★★ Newcomer with v'yds from ACONCAGUA down to BIO-BIO. Cab S Reserva R is best; gd Pinot N and Chard. Plans for Mourvèdre and Syrah.

Haras de Pirque ★★ New estate in Pirque (MAIPO). Smoky, Graves-like Sauv Bl, stylish Chard, dense, fruity Cab S/Merlot.

Larose, Viña de ★ RAPEL venture by Médoc Ch Larose-Trintaudon under the Las Casas del Toqui and Viña Alamosa labels. Promising top-end Leyenda Chard and red blend.

Leyda, Viña ★★ Sole winery in Leyda (see intro), producing elegant Chard and lush Pinot N. Also decent Maipo Cab and Rapel Merlot.

Maipo Famous wine regionclose to Santiago. Chile's best Cabs often come from higher eastern sub-regions such as Pirque and Puente Alto.

Maule S'most region in Central Valley. Incl Claro, Loncomilla, Tutuven Valleys.

Montes ★★→★★★ Alpha Cab can be brilliant; Merlot, Syrah and Malbec also fine; Chardonnay vg. B'x blend Montes Alpha M is improving with each vintage, while new Folly Syrah outstanding; the best in Chile.

MontGras ★★→★★★ State-of-the-art Colchagua winery with fine ltd edition wines, incl Syrah and Zin, and high-class fleshy flagship Ninquen Cab Sauv.

Morande ★★ Vast range including César, Cinsault, Bouschet, and Carignan. "Limited Edition" used for top wines, including a spicy Syrah/Cabernet Sauvignon and inky Malbec. Good value.

Paul Bruno ★★ MAIPO joint venture of Paul Pontallier and Bruno Prats from B'x with Chilean Felipé de Solminihac. Flagship wine slowly improving as vines age. Also promising Sol de Sol Chardonnay from Bío-Bío.

Porta, Viña ★★ MAIPO winery under same ownership as Viña Gracia offering reliable range including supple, spicy Cab.

Rapel Central quality region divided into Colchagua and Cachapoal valleys. Source of great Merlot. Watch out for sub-region Marchihue in the future.

La Rosa, Viña ★★ Impressive RAPEL Chards, Merlots, Cabs under La Palmeria and Cornellana labels.

San Pedro ★★→★★★ Massive Curicó-based producer. Gato and 35 South (35 Sur on some markets) are reliable top-sellers. Best wines: Castillo de Molina and 1865 reds, and Cabo de Hornas Cabernet S.

Santa Carolina, Viña ★★→★★★ Historic *bodega*; increasingly impressive and complex wines. All MAIPO Reserve wines are good, including a rich, limey Sauv Bl. Barrica Selection range, incl earthy Carmenère and supple Syrah, is better still. New Cab S/Merlot/Syrah Trébol is complex and excellent value.

Santa Inés ★★ Successful small family winery in Isla de MAIPO making ripe, blackcurranty Legado de Armida Cab Sauv. Also labelled as De Martino.

Santa Mónica ★→★★★ Rancagua (RAPEL) winery; the best label is Tierra del Sol. Riesling, Sémillon, and Merlot under Santa Mónica label also gd.

Selentia ★★ New Chilean/Spanish venture making Chard and Cab S. Reserve special Cab S is fine, B'dx-like red.

Seña See Caliterra.

Tarapacá, Viña ★★ MAIPO winery improved after investment, but still inconsistent.

Terramater ★★ Wines from throughout Central Valley incl v gd Altum range.

Terranoble ★★→★★★ Talca winery specializing in grassy Sauv and light, peppery Merlot, range now expanded and incl v gd spicy Carmenère Gran Reserva.

Torreón de Paredes ★★ Attractive, crisp Chard, age-worthy Res Cab from this RAPEL *bodega*. Flagship Don Amedo Cab S could be better.

Torres, Miguel ★★★ Pioneering Curicó winery now back on form with fresh whites and gd reds, esp sturdy Manso del Velasco single-v'yd Cab and Cariñena-based Cordillera. See also Spain.

Undurraga ★★ Traditional MAIPO estate known for its Pinot. Top wines: Reserva Chard, refreshing, limey Gewürz; peachy Late Harvest Sém.

Valdivieso ★★ Major producer with new Lontué winery. Single-vineyard Cab F, Merlot, Malbec and NV blend Caballo Loco are pick of the range. Reserve bottlings also gd, but quality more erratic among the cheaper wines.

Vascos, Los ★★→★★★ Lafite-Rothschild venture making Cab S in B'x mould. Recent vintages show more fruit than earlier efforts. Top wine: Grande Réserve.

Veramonte ★★ CASABLANCA-based operation of Agustín Huneeus (formerly of California winery Franciscan); whites from Casablanca fruit, red from Central Valley grapes – all good. Top wine: Primus red blend.

Villard ★★ Sophisticated wines made by French-born Thierry Villard. Gd MAIPO reds, especially heady Merlot, Equis Cab S and CASABLANCA whites. Also v alluring Casablanca Pinot Noir.

Viu Manent ★★ Emerging Colchagua winery; best of fine range are plummy Cab S, exotic Merlot, dense, chewy Malbec. Look for Syrah in the future.

Argentina

The Argentine financial crisis has not helped the country's wine producers, and exports are actually falling. However, wine quality continues to improve. The cheaper reds are among the best value wines in the world, whilst higher-priced wines often embarrass those over the Andes in Chile. An international thumbprint is evident in many, but there are increasing numbers of new high-class small bodegas to wave the local flag.

Malbec remains the most successful grape variety. Decent Cabernet also exists, although many of the unblended versions can seem hollow. Syrah is beginning to show promise, as are Bonarda, Tempranillo, and Sangiovese. For whites, very fair Chardonnay and

CENTRAL & SOUTH AMERICA

Sauvignon Blanc exist, but the spicy Torrontés makes the most distinctive wines; not to everyone's taste.

The warm dry climate, watered by snow-melt from the Andes, makes grape-growing relatively easy. Vineyard conditions are determined more by altitude than latitude. Mendoza is the most important province, but conditions are far from uniform.

Recent vintages

As a general rule, whites and cheaper reds should be drunk as young as possible.

2002 A mostly dry, hail-free and not too warm vintage, resulting in the best wines for more than a decade.

2001 Quality is variable, but some very good reds.

2000 Rain at harvest and hail caused problems but some excellent reds from those who picked after the rain.

1999 A drought year. Some rich, full-bodied red wines.

1998 The El Niño vintage. Dilute and occasionally unripe reds but some are gd.

1997 Lge harvest affected by storms. Erratic quality – top reds show good fruit.

1996 Without the depth and class of 95 but best reds have good fruit. Drink up.

Achaval Ferrer ★★★→★★★★ MENDOZA. Super-concentrated Finca Altamira Malbec and Quimera Malb/CS/Merl Blend.

La Agrícola ★ Dynamic MENDOZA estate producing gd-value Santa Julia range, led by new blend "Magna" and better "Q" label (impressive Malb, Merl, Tempranillo). New Terra Organica organic wines: good but not great.

Alta Vista ★★★ French-owned MENDOZA venture specializing in Malbec. Dense, spicy Alto among best wines in the country.

Altos las Hormigas ★★★ Italian-owned Malbec specialist, wines made by consultant Alberto Antonini (ex-technical director of Italy's Antinori). Top wine: Viña las Hormigas.

Anubis ★★ New joint venture between Alberto Antonini and Susana Balbo making exciting juicy reds, esp Malbec.

Arizù, Leoncio ★★ Small MENDOZA (Maipù) bodega with three tiers of quality – Viña Paraiso, Luigi Bosca and Finca Los Nobles. high standards with esp gd Los Nobles Malbec/Verdot and Cabernet/Bouchet. Alberto Arizù Snr makes fine Petit Verdot, Malbec, and Nebbiolo under Viña Alicia label.

Balbi, Bodegas ★★ Allied-Domecq-owned San Raphael producer. Juicy Malbec, Chard, & delicious Syrah (red & rosé). Red blend Barbaro also v gd.

Bianchi, Valentin ★ San Rafael red specialist. Familia Bianchi (Cab S) is excellent flagship, while gd-value Elsa's Vineyard incl meaty Barbera. Pithy Sauv Bl.

Canale, Bodegas Humberto ★★ Premier Río Negro winery known for its Sauv Bl and Pinot N, but Merlot & Malbec (esp the Black River label) are the stars.

Catena ★★★ Argento, Alamos Ridge (both for gd-value Cab, Chard, Malbec), Catena (v good Cab, Chard, Malbec), Catena Alta (top Cab, Malbec, stunning Chard) and new flagship Nicolas Catena Zapata. Also new Cabernet/Malbec blend "Caro" made with the Rothschilds of Lafite, 1st vintage 2000.

Chandon, Bodegas ★→★★ Makers of Baron B and M Chandon sparklers under Moët & Chandon supervision; new promising Pinot N-Chard blend. Mostly sold on home market. Also see Terrazas.

Doña Paula ★ Luján de Cuyo estate owned by Santa Rita (see Chile) making dense, structured Malbec.

Esmerelda, Bodegas See CATENA.

Etchart ★★→★★★★ Pernod-Ricard owned, two wineries: SALTA and MENDOZA. Fresh, spicy Torrontés from Cafayate in SALTA, reds from both regions gd, topped by plummy Cafayate Cab S.

Fabre Montmayou ★★ French-owned Luján de Cuyo (MENDOZA) bodega; fine reds and advice from Michel Rolland of B'dx. Also decent Chard.

Finca La Anita ★★→★★★ MENDOZA estate making high-class reds, esp Syrah and Malb, and intriguing whites, among them Semillon and Tocai Friulano.

Finca Colomé ★★★ SALTA bodega now owned by California's Hess Collection turning out very Rhône-like Cab-Merlot blend.

Finca Flichman ★★ Old co: two wineries in MENDOZA now owned by Portugal's Sogrape. Varietal range topped by Private Res Cab S. Good-value Syrah. Top wine: Dedicato blend.

Finca El Retiro ★★ MENDOZA bodega making good Malbec Bonarda and Tempranillo. See Altos las Hormigas.

Lurton, Bodegas J & F ★→★★ MENDOZA venture of Jacques and François Lurton. Juicy, conc Piedra Negra Malbec heads range which also includes decent Pinot G, Malbec and Cab S.

Masi Tupungato ★★→★★★ MENDOZA enterprise for the well-known Valpolicella producer. Passo Doble is fine Ripasso-style Malbec/Corvino blend, Corbec is even better Amarone lookalike from Corvina and Malbec.

Mendoza Most important province for wine (over 70% of plantings). Best sub-regions: Agrelo, Tupungato, Luján de Cuyo, and Maipú.

Navarro Correas ★★ Good if sometimes over-oaked reds, esp Col Privada Cab S. Also reasonable whites, inc v oaky Chard and Deutz-inspired fizz.

Nieto Senetiner, Bodegas ★★ Luján de Cuyo-based bodega. Gd value under Valle de Vistalba label, plus recently introduced top-of-range Cadus reds.

Norton, Bodegas ★★★ Old bodega, now Austrian-owned. Gd whites & v gd reds, esp chunky, fruity Malbec and Privada blend (Mer-Cab S-Malbec).

Patagonia, Viña ★→★★ Owned by Concha y Toro of Chile, making gd-value if rather international Malbec, Syrah, Cab S, Merlot, Chard under Trivento label.

Peñaflor ★→★★★ Argentina's biggest wine co, reputedly the world's third lgst. Bulk wines for domestic market incl Andean Vineyards, Fond de Cave (Chard, Cab) labels and for finer wines, TRAPICHE.

Río Negro Promising new area in Patagonia.

Salentein, Bodegas ★★ Ambitious new Valle de Uco (MENDOZA) bodega, already succeeding with Cab S, Malb, Merlot and (under the Primus label) Pinot Noir. Entry-level wins appear as Finca El Portillo or La Pampa.

Salta Northerly province with the world's highest v'yds. Sub-region Cafayate renowned for Torrontés.

San Pedri de Yacochuya ★★★ SALTA collaboration between B'x consultant Michel Rolland and ETCHART, making stunning Yacochuya Malbec from old vines.

San Telmo ★★ Modern Seagram-owned winery making fresh, full-flavoured Chardonnay, Chenin Bl, Merlot, & esp Malbec, & Cab Cruz de Piedra-Maipú.

Santa Ana, Bodegas ★ Old-est'd family firm at Guaymallen, MENDOZA. Malbec Reserva is pick of a wide but rather uninspiring range.

Tacuil, Bodegas ★★★ New SALTA venture for Raul Davalos, former owner of Finca Colomé (qv). 33 de Davalos is excellent spicy Cab/Malb ecblend.

Terrazas ★★→★★★★ CHANDON enterprise for still table wines made from Malb, C/S, Chard, and (soon) Syrah. The three ranges are entry-level Alto (juicy Cabernet is the star), mid-price Reserva, and top-of-the-tree Gran Terrazas.

Torino, Michel ★★ A rapidly improving (and organic) Cafayate enterprise with particularly good Cabernet.

Trapiche ★★→★★★★ Premium label of PEÑAFLOR. Labels in ascending quality order are Astica, Trapiche (pick is Oak Cask Syrah), Fond de Cave (good Malb Reserva), Medalla (decent plummy Cab S), and fine if pricey red blend Iscay.

Viniterra ★→★★ Clean, modern wines under the Omnium, Bykos, and Viniterra labels. Watch out in future for Pinot G.

Vistalba, Viña y Cava ★★ See Nieto Senetiner.

Weinert, Bodegas ★→★★ The Malbec, Cabernet, and Cavas de Weinert blend (Cab-Merlot-Malbec) are among the best reds from Argentina.

Yacochuya ★★★ SALTA. Stunning Malbec from old vines.

Other Central & South American wines

Bolivia With a generally hot, humid climate, annual domestic consumption of just one bottle per capita, only 2,000 ha of grapes (most destined for fiery *aguardiente* brandy), and only ten wineries, this is not a major producing country. Even so, wines from **Vinos y Viñedos La Concepción**, especially the Cabernets, are good and show what is possible. The vineyards, 1,000 km south of La Paz, lie at altitudes of up to 2,800 m, making them the highest in the world.

Brazil New plantings of better grapes are transforming a big and booming industry with an increasing home market. International investments, esp in Rio Grande do Sul and Santana do Liuramento, esp from France (eg Moët & Chandon) and Italy (Martini & Rossi), are significant, and point to possible exports. The new sandy Frontera region (bordering Argentina and Uruguay) and Sierra Gaucha hills (Italian-style sparkling) are to watch. Exports are beginning. More than two crops a year are possible in some equatorial vineyards. Quality from these so far has been basic, but look out for fruits of a new project involving Portuguese winemaker Rui Reguinga. Of the wines that do leave Brazil, 95% are made by the massive **Vinicola Aurora (Bento Gonçalves)**. Look out for **Amazon** label.

Mexico Oldest Latin American wine industry is reviving, with investment from abroad (eg Freixenet, Martell, Domecq) and California influence via UC-Davis. Best in Baja California (85% of total), Querétaro, and on the Aguascalientes and Zacatecas plateaux. Top Baja C producers are **Casa de Piedra** (v impressive Tempranillo/Cab S), **L A Cetto** (Valle de Guadaloupe, the largest, especially for Cabernet, Nebbiolo, Petite Sirah), **Bodegas Santo Tomás** (now working with California's Wente Brothers to make Duetto, using grapes from both sides of the border), **Monte Xanic** (with Napa-award winning Cab), **Bodegas San Antonio**, & **Cavas de Valmar**. The premium Chardonnay and Cab S from Monterrey-based **Casa Madero** are also good. **Marqués de Aguayo** is the oldest (1593), now only for brandy.

Peru **Viña Tacama** near Ica (top wine region) exports some pleasant wines, esp the Gran Vino Blanco white; also Cab S and classic-method sparkling. Chincha, Moquegua, and Tacha regions are slowly making progress. But phylloxera is a serious problem.

Uruguay Uruguay's point of difference is Tannat, the rugged and tannic grape which, in SW France, is responsible for Madiran. Tannat by itself produces a sturdy, plummy red, better blended with more supple Merlot and Cab Franc. Beyond Tannat, a few producers offer decent Gewürz and Chard, while the promising De Lucca has some Roussanne and Syrah. Five different viticultural zones were established in 1992, but the name of the producer is the most important element. **Carrau/Castel Pujol** is among the most impressive wineries. Its Amat Gran Tradición 1752 and Las Violetas Reserva show Tannat at its most fragrant. Other wineries include **Bruzzone & Sciutto**, **Casa Filguera** (consultant is Patrick Valette – see Viña El Principal in Chile), **Castillo Viejo** (gd value Catamayor range), **Los Cerros de San Juan** (working with LVMH), **Dante Irurtia**, **Juanicó** (in joint venture with B'x Ch Pape-Clément), **Pisano**, **Carlos Pizzorno**, and **Stagnari**. Flying winemaker wines under the **Bright Brothers** label are also worth trying.

Australia

Heavier shaded areas are
the wine growing regions

The influence of Australia in the modern wine world is out of all proportion to the size of its vineyards. They represent less than 4% of global production, yet Australian wines, ideas, and names are on all wine-lovers' lips. In 16 years, its exports have grown from 8 to 445 million litres and the number of wineries has climbed to over 1,500. Even growers in the south of France listen to Australian winemakers. Australia has mastered easy-drinking wine and is making some of the world's very best.

Its classics are Shiraz, Semillon, and Riesling. In the 70s they were joined by Cabernet and Merlot, Chardonnay, and Pinot Noir. In the 90s, Sauvignon Blanc, Grenache, and Mourvèdre were rediscovered. Next seems to be Tempranillo. Cool fermentation and the use of new barrels accompanied a general move to cooler areas. For a while, excessive oak flavour was a common problem. Moderation is now the fashion – and sparkling wine of highly satisfactory quality is a new achievement.

Australia faces a major challenge in managing its own helter-skelter growth. Take-over battles and big company egos do not help. It has to find ways to more than double its exports over the next ten years without damaging its reputation. Chardonnay was its flag-bearer in the 80s and 90s; it is now betting on Shiraz doing the trick in the current decade. Old World and New World alike will not make things easy in a global market which is still contracting.

Recent vintages

New South Wales

2002 Heavy Feb rain caused problems in all but two areas. Riverina outstanding.

2001 Extreme summer heat and ill-timed rain set the tone; remarkably, Hunter Valley Semillon shone.

2000 A perfect growing season for the Hunter Valley, but dire for the rest of the state; extreme heat followed by vintage rain.

1999 Another Hunter success; rain when needed. Other regions variable.

1998 Good to excellent everywhere; good winter rain, warm, dry summer.

1997 Heavy rain bedeviled the Hunter; Mudgee, Orange, and Canberra all starred.

1996 Yields varied (frost, hail), but a perfect close to the season produced very good wine in most regions.

1995 Severe drought slashed yields and stressed fruit; good at best.

1994 Hunter heatwaves and fires followed by torrential rain didn't help; good red wines elsewhere, particularly Mudgee.

1993 Unusually cool, wet spring & summer diminished quality; excellent autumn saved Canberra and Hilltops.

1992 Continuation of the 1991 drought followed by brief vintage flooding soured Hunter, Mudgee, and Cowra; others fared rather better.

Victoria

2002 Extremely cool weather throughout led to often tiny yields, but wines of high quality.

2001 Did not escape the heat; a fair-to-good red vintage, whites more variable.

2000 Southern and central regions flourished in warm and dry conditions; terrific reds. Northeast poor; vintage rain.

1999 Utterly schizophrenic; Yarra disastrous (vtge rain); some other southern and central regions superb; northeast up and down.

1998 Drought and October frost did not spoil an outstanding year in all regions, particularly for Shiraz, Cabernet, Merlot.

1997 A cool, wet spring gave way to drought; low yields of very high-quality grapes, especially Pinot in the South.

1996 Extremely variable. Far southwest, Grampians, and Bendigo did well.

1995 Mostly disappointing; the summer too hot, the autumn too cool and wet. Grampians (magnificent) and Geelong were the principal exceptions.

1994 Unusually cool and largely dry growing season depressed yields, quality saved by a glorious Indian summer; good to excellent throughout.

1993 A wet winter, spring, and summer partially retrieved by an Indian summer and autumn, most notably in the cooler red-wine regions.

1992 Magnificent for Yarra; gd elsewhere, equable growing conditions.

South Australia

2002 Very cool weather led to much reduced yields in the South, and to a great Riverland vintage in both yield and quality. Fine Riesling again.

2001 Far better than 2000; winter rain helped combat the searing summer heat; Clare Valley Riesling an improbable success.

2000 The culmination of a four-year drought impacted on both yield and quality, the Limestone Coast zone faring the best.

1999 Continuing drought was perversely spoiled by ill-timed March rainfall; Limestone Coast and Clare reds the few bright spots.

1998 V dry year; low yields, overall quality of reds superb, esp S of Adelaide.

1997 On-again, off-again weather upset vines and vignerons alike, with the exception of Eden and Clare Valley Riesling. Yields down overall.

1996 Good winter/spring rain followed by a warm, dry summer; classic vintage, classic wines, succulent, and long-lived.

1995 Dry winter, frosty spring, and rainy summer reduced yields and quality, the low yields averting disaster.

1994 A long, cool, and dry growing season produced excellent white wines across the state, and elegant reds with above-average yields.

1993 The 2nd-wettest growing season on record promised disaster until a warm and dry March and below-average yields saved the day.

1992 A cool, dry year until vintage rain in all regions except McLaren Vale and Langhorne Creek spoiled what might have been a good vintage.

Western Australia

2002 For the Swan District, the best since 1984. In the South, up to four weeks late; quality is variable.

2001 Great Southern, the best vintage since 95; good elsewhere.

2000 Margaret River excellent; variation elsewhere, the Swan Valley ordinary.

1999 An outstanding vintage for Margaret River and Swan reds (best in over a decade) and pretty handy elsewhere, other than the Great Southern.

1998 The Swan Valley shone again, but the sun didn't elsewhere in the state in a rainy March and April.

1997 Wet winter and spring, perfect summer. Gd reds from Margaret River, gd Riesling from Great Southern. North was fried in Jan/Feb heatwave.

1996 The Swan Valley was cooked but the warm year was a blessing for Margaret River and Great Southern, with lovely Cabernet the pick.

1995 Very low yields were (partially) compensated for by wonderful quality in the South and Margaret River; the Swan average.

1994 A textbook vintage – perfect conditions for Great Southern (superb) and Margaret River. Swan Valley as per usual.

1993 A cool and wet spring and summer produced best white wines in the Swan Valley for decades, excellent whites elsewhere, and useful reds.

1992 A mild growing season, marred only by rain in the Swan Valley, produced good white and red wines in the South.

Adelaide Hills SA) Spearheaded by PETALUMA: cool, 450-m sites in Mt Lofty ranges.

Alkoomi Mt Barker r w ★★★ (Riesling) **94' 96'** 99 01 02 (Cab S) **93'** 94' 97 99 25-year veteran producing fine, steely RIESLING and potent, long-lived reds.

Allandale Hunter Valley r w ★★ Small winery without v'yds, buying selected local and Hilltops grapes. Quality can be good, esp CHARD.

Amberley Estate Margaret River r w ★★ Successful maker of a full range of regional styles with Chenin Blanc the commercial engine.

Angove's Riverland SA) r w (br) ★ →★★ Large, long-established MURRAY VALLEY family business. Good-value whites, especially CHARDONNAY.

Ashbrook Estate Margaret River r w ★★★ Minimum of fuss; consistently makes 8,000 cases of exemplary SEM, CHARD, SAUV, VERDELHO, and CAB S.

Ashton Hills Adelaide Hills r w (sp) ★★★ Fine, racy, long-lived RIES and compelling PINOT N crafted by Stephen George from 20 yr-old v'yds.

Bailey's NE Vic r w br ★★ Rich, old-fashioned reds of great character, especially SHIRAZ (formerly Hermitage), and magnificent dessert Muscat (★★★★) and "TOKAY". Part of BERINGER BLASS.

Balnaves of Coonawarra r w ★★★ Grape-grower since 75; winery since 96. Vg CHARD; excellent SHIRAZ, MERLOT, CAB S.

Bannockburn Geelong r w ★★★ (Chard) **96' 97'** 98' 00 02' (Pinot N) **94' 97** 99' 00 02' Intense, complex CHARDONNAY and PINOT NOIR made using Burgundian techniques. 8,000 cases.

AUSTRALIA

Banrock Station Riverland SA r w ★→★★ 3950 acre property on Murray River, 600 acre v'yd, owned by BRL HARDY producing impressive budget wines.

Barossa SA Aus's most important winery (but not v'yd) area; grapes from diverse sources make diverse wines. Local specialities: SHIRAZ, SEMILLON, GRENACHE, etc.

Barwang Hilltops r w ★★ Owned by MCWILLIAMS; Stylish estate wines.

Bass Phillip Gippsland Vic r ★★★→★★★★ (Pinot N) 94' **95 96'** 97' 98' oo' o2' Tiny amounts of stylish, eagerly sought PINOT NOIR in three quality grades; very Burgundian in style.

Beggar's Belief Chardonnay S Aus w Oak and sugar mixture responsible for the majority of recruits to the ABC club.

Bendigo Vic Widespread sml v'yds, some vg quality. Balgownie, JASPER HILL.

Beringer Blass Barossa r w (sp, sw, br) ★★★ (Cab blend) **90' 91' 93 94 96' 97** 98' oo Founded by BAROSSA'S ebullient German winemaker, Wolf Blass, now swallowed up by massive multinational. It is well-served by winemakers Wendy Stuckey (Ries) and Caroline Dunn (reds).

Best's Grampians r w ★★→★★★ (Shiraz) **91 92'** 93 94' 96 97' 98' 99' oo' Conservative old family winery; very good mid-weight reds, CHARD not half bad. Thomson Family SHIRAZ from 120-yr-old vines superb.

Big Rivers Zone NSW & Vic The continuation of South Australia's RIVERLAND including the Murray Darling Perricoota and Swan Hill Regions.

Botobolar Mudgee r w ★★ Marvellously eccentric little organic winery.

Bowen Estate Coonawarra r w ★★★ **90' 91' 94'** 96' 97 98' 99 o1 Sm winery; intense CAB, spicy SHIRAZ, both ripe and alcoholic.

Brand's of Coonawarra Coonawarra r w ★★★ **90' 91' 93** 94' 96' 97 98' 99 o1 Owned by MCWILLIAMS. Going from strength to strength esp with super-premium Stentiford's SHIRAZ and Patron's CAB.

Brangayne of Orange Orange r w ★★ Reflects potential of relatively new region. Wines of great finesse incl CHARD, SAUV, SHIRAZ, CAB-Merlot.

Bremerton Langhorne Creek r w ★★ Regularly produces attractively priced red wines with silky, soft mouth-feel and stacks of flavour.

BRL Hardy See Hardy's.

Brokenwood Hunter Valley r w ★★★ (Shiraz) 87' 91' **93'** 94' 95' 98' 99' Exciting CAB, SHIRAZ since 73 – Graveyard SHIRAZ outstanding. Cricket Pitch SEM-SAUV fuels growth; zooming to 70,000 cases. See also SEVILLE.

Brookland Valley Margaret River r w ★★→★★★ Superbly sited winery and restaurant doing great things, esp with SAUV. Half-share owned by BRL HARDY.

Brown Brothers King Valley r w dr br sp sw ★→★★★ (Noble Ries) **92'** 94' 96' 97 98 Old family firm, new ideas: wide range of delicate, single-grape wines, many from cool mountain districts. CHARD, RIES. Dry white Muscat outstanding. CAB blend is best red.

Buring, Leo Barossa r w ★★→★★★ (Ries) 75' 79' **84' 91' 92 94' 95 97** 99' oo o2' Old RIESLING specialist, now owned by SOUTHCORP. Great with age (even great age), esp releases under Leonay label.

Cabernet Sauvignon 29,573 ha, 257,223 tonnes. Grown in all wine regions, best in COONAWARRA. From herbaceous green pepper in coolest regions through blackcurrant and mulberry, to dark chocolate and redcurrant in warmer areas.

Campbells of Rutherglen NE Vic r br (w) ★★ Smooth ripe reds and gd dessert wines, the latter in youthful, fruity style other than Merchant Prince Muscat.

Canberra District NSW Both quality and quantity on the increase; altitude-dependent, site selection important.

Cape Mentelle Margaret River r w ★★★→★★★★ (Cab) **83' 90' 91'** 93' 94' 95' 96 99' oo Idiosyncratic robust CAB can be magnificent, CHARD even better; also Zin and very popular SAUV-SEM. David Hohnen also founded Cloudy Bay, NZ. LVMH Veuve Clicquot principal shareholder of both since 90.

Capel Vale Geographe WA r w ★★★ Steadily growing and v successful with good whites, incl RIES. Also top-end SHIRAZ and CABERNET.

Central Ranges Zone NSW Encompasses MUDGEE, ORANGE, and Cowra regions, expanding in high altitude, moderately cool to warm climates.

Chain of Ponds Adelaide Hills r w ★★ Impeccably made, full, flavoursome wines vinified by PENFOLDS. SEM, SAUV, CHARD to the fore. Elegant Amadeus CAB also gd.

Chalkers Crossing Hilltops r w ★★→★★★ New winery with French-trained Celine Rousseau making beautifully balanced wines.

Chambers' Rosewood NE Vic br (r w) ★★→★★★ Good cheap table and great dessert wines, esp traditional "TOKAY" and Muscat.

Wineries and regions to watch in early 2000s

Clare Valley S Australia	Brilliant 2002 Rieslings
Cullen Margaret River	Chardonnay and Merlot
De Bortoli Yarra Valley	Consistently delivers
Devil's Lair Margaret River	Vineyard expansion coming on-stream
Ferngrove Great Southern	400ha vineyards; huge potential
O'Leary Walker Clare Valley	Some hype, even more performance
Tasmania generally	Global warming is just the ticket
Taylors Clare Valley	Spectacular improvement
Tower Estate Hunter Valley	Len Evans's pride and joy

Chapel Hill McL Vale r w ★★★ (r) Now owned by Swiss Schmidheiny group with multinational wine interests including Napa's Cuvaison.

Chardonnay 21,724 ha, 256,328 tonnes. Best-known for fast-developing buttery, peachy, sometimes syrupy wines, but cooler regions produce more elegant, tightly structured, age-worthy examples. Oak, too, is now less heavy-handed than it used to be.

Charles Melton Barossa r w (sp) ★★★ Tiny winery with bold, luscious reds, esp Nine Popes, an old-vine GRENACHE and SHIRAZ blend.

Cheviot Bridge Central Vic High Country r w ★★ 50,000 cases. Export-orientated business, set up in 98 by industry veterans.

Clare Valley SA Small, high-quality area 90 miles north of Adelaide, best for RIESLING (glorious in 2002); also SHIRAZ and CABERNET.

Clarendon Hills Mclaren Vale (w) ★★★ Monumental (and expensive) reds from small parcels of contract grapes around Adelaide.

Coldstream Hills Yarra Valley r w (sp) ★★★ (Chard) 88' 92' **96' 97 98** 00' 02' (Pinot N) **91'** 92' **96' 97** 00' 02' (Cab S) 91' 92' 94 97' 98' 00' Est'd 1985 by wine critic James Halliday. Delicious PINOT N to drink young and Reserve to age lead Australia. Vg CHARD (esp Res wines), fruity CAB, and CAB-MERLOT, and (from 97) Merlot. Acquired by SOUTHCORP in 96; production much increased.

Coonawarra SA Southernmost and finest v'yds of state: most of Australia's best CAB, successful CHARDONNAY, RIESLING, and SHIRAZ. Newer arrivals include Murdock and Reschke.

Coriole McLaren Vale r w ★★→★★★ (Shiraz) **90' 91' 92** 94' 96' 98' 99' 00 To watch, especially for old-vine SHIRAZ Lloyd Reserve.

Craiglee Macedon Vic r w ★★★ (Shiraz) 86' **88' 90' 91' 92 93** 94' 97' 98' (00') Re-creation of famous 19th-C estate: fragrant, peppery SHIRAZ, CHARD.

Cranswick Estates Riverina r w ★ Large winery firmly aimed at export market with accent on value. Acquired by Evans and Tate 2002.

Croser See Petaluma.

Cullen Wines Margaret River r w ★★★ (Chard) **94' 96' 97** 98 99' 00' 01 (Cab S-Merlot) **90' 91'** 92' 93 94 95' 96' 97' 99' 00' Vanya Cullen makes strongly structured CAB-MERLOT (Australia's best), substantial but subtle SEM-SAUV, and bold CHARD: all real characters.

Dalwhinnie Pyrenees r w ✭✭✭ (Chard) **94' 98'** 99' 00' 02' (Reds) **92' 93** 94' 95' 97 98' 99' 00' 5,500-case producer of concentrated, rich CHARD, SHIRAZ, and CAB s, the best in PYRENEES.

d'Arenberg McLaren Vale r w (rsw br sp) ✭✭→✭✭✭ Old firm with new lease of life; sumptuous SHIRAZ and GRENACHE, fine CHARD with lots of new labels.

Deakin Estate Murray Darling r w ✭Part of Katnook group producing over 200,000 cases of very decent varietal table wines.

De Bortoli Griffith NSW r w dr sw (br) ✭→✭✭✭✭ (Noble Sem) 82' **87' 91' 94** 95' **96' 97'** 99' 00' Irrigation-area winery. Standard reds and whites but splendid, sweet, botrytized Sauternes-style Noble SEM. See also next entry.

De Bortoli Yarra Valley r w ✭✭→✭✭✭ (Chard) **96'** 97 **98** 99 00' 01' (Cab S) **92'** 94' **97** 98' 99 00' (02') YARRA VALLEY's largest producer. Main label is more than adequate; second label Gulf Station and third label Windy Peak vg value. 170,000 c/s.

Delatite Central Vic r w (sp) ✭✭ (Ries) **93'** 97' **99** 00 01 02 Winemaker Rosalind Ritchie makes appropriately willowy and feminine RIES, Gewürz, and CAB from this v cool mountainside v'yd.

Devil's Lair Margaret River r w ✭✭✭ 40.5 ha of estate vineyards for opulently concentrated CHARD and CAB-Merlot. Fifth Leg is trendy second label. Acquired by SOUTHCORP early 97.

Diamond Valley Yarra Valley r w ✭✭→✭✭✭ (Pinot) **96' 97 98'** 99' 00 02' Outstanding PINOT N in significant quantities; other wines good, esp CHARD.

Domaine Chandon Yarra Valley sp (r w) ✭✭✭ Classic sparkling wine from grapes grown in all the cooler wine regions of Australia, with strong support from French owner Champagne house Moët & Chandon. Successful in UK under GREEN POINT label.

Dominique Portet Yarra Valley r w ✭✭ After a 25-year career at Taltarni, now in his own winery for the first time. Much is expected.

Dromana Estate Mornington Peninsula r w ✭✭→✭✭✭ (Chard) **98' 99** 00' 01 02' Led energetically by Gary Crittenden: light, fragrant CAB, PINOT, CHARD; now taking Italian varieties (grown elsewhere) very seriously.

Evans Family Hunter Valley r w ✭✭✭ (Chard) **98' 99'** 00' 01 Excellent CHARD from small vineyard owned by family of Len Evans. Fermented in new oak. Repays cellaring. See also TOWER ESTATE.

Elderton Barossa r w (sp br) ✭✭ Old v'yds; flashy, rich, oaked CAB and SHIRAZ.

Evans and Tate Margaret River r w ✭✭✭ (Cab) **91' 92' 94** 95' 96' 99' 00 Fine, elegant SEM, CHARD, CAB, Merlot from MARGARET RIVER, Redbrook. Stock-exchange listing underpins continued growth.

Ferngrove Vineyards Great Southern r w ✭✭✭ Cattle farmer Murray Burton has established over 988 acres of vines since 97; great RIESLING.

Fox Creek Mclaren V r (w) ✭✭→✭✭✭ Produces 35,000 cases of flashy, full-flavoured wines.

Freycinet Tasmania r w (sp) ✭✭✭ (Pinot N) **88' 91' 94'** 97 98 00'01' (02') East-coast winery producing voluptuous, rich PINOT N, gd CHARDONNAY.

Gapsted Wines Alpine Valleys (Vic) r w ✭✭ Brand of large winery which crushes grapes for 50 growers.

Geelong Vic Once-famous area destroyed by phylloxera, re-established mid-1960s. Very cool, dry climate: firm table wines from good-quality grapes. Names incl BANNOCKBURN, SCOTCHMAN'S HILL.

Geoff Merrill McLaren Vale r w ✭✭ Ebullient maker of Geoff Merrill, Mt Hurtle, Cockatoo Ridge. A questing enthusiast; his best are excellent, others unashamedly mass-market oriented. TAHBILK own 50%.

Geoff Weaver Adelaide Hills r w ★★★ 20 acre estate at Lenswood. Very fine SAUV, CHARD, RIES, and CAB-Merlot blend. Marvellous label design.

Giaconda Central Vic r w ★★★ (Chard) 91 92' 93 94' 96' 97' 98 99' 00' (02') V sml fashionable winery near Beechworth; Australia's answer to Kistler, California. CHARD is considered by many to be the best in Australia – certainly the 96 is one of all time greats. PINOT N is very variable.

Goulburn Valley Vic Very old (TAHBILK) and relatively new (MITCHELTON) wineries in temperate mid-Victoria region; full-bodied table wines.

Goundrey Wines Great Southern WA r w ★★ Recent expansion has caused quality to become variable.

Grampians Vic Region previously known as Great Western. Temperate region in central W of state. High quality.

Granite Belt Qld High-altitude, (relatively) cool region just N of NSW border Esp spicy SHIRAZ and rich SEMILLON.

Grant Burge Barossa r w (sp sw br) ★★→★★★ 110,000 cases of silky-smooth reds and whites from the best grapes of Burge's large v'yd holdings.

Greenock Creek Barossa r ★★★ Soaring prices and iconic status for SHIRAZ thanks to Mr Parker and US buyers.

Great Southern WA Remote, cool area; FERNGROVE, GOUNDREY, and PLANTAGENET are the largest wineries.

Green Point r w See Domaine Chandon.

Grenache 2,528 ha, 26,280 tonnes. Produces thin wine if over-cropped but can do much better. Growing interest in old BAROSSA & MCLAREN VALE plantings.

Grosset Clare r w ★★★→★★★★ (Ries) 90' 92 93' 94' 95' 97' 99' 00' 01 02' (Gaia) 90' 91 92' 94' 95 96' 98' 99' 01 Fastidious winemaker. Foremost Aus RIES, lovely CHARD, PINOT N, and Gaia CAB-Merlot.

Hanging Rock Macedon (Vic) r w sp ★→★★★ (Shiraz) 90 91' 92' 97' 98' 99 00' Eclectic range: budget Picnic wines; huge Heathcote SHIRAZ; complex sparkling.

Hardy's McLaren Vale, Barossa, Keppoch, etc r w sp (rsw) ★★→★★★★ (Eileen Chard) 96' 97 98 99' 00 (01)("Vintage Port") 46' 51' 54' 56' 58' 75 77 82 84' 96' Historic company blending wines from several areas. Best are Eileen Hardy and Thomas Hardy series and (Australia's best) "Vintage Ports". REYNELLA's restored buildings are group HQ. 1992 merger with Berry-Renmano and public ownership (BRL HARDY) makes this Australia's 2nd-lgst wine co; now to be taken over?

Heggies Adelaide Hills r w dr (sw w) ★★ (Ries) 92 95 98 99 00 01' Vineyard at 500 m in eastern BAROSSA Ranges owned by S SMITH & SONS. The wines are separately marketed.

Henschke Barossa r w ★★★★ (Shiraz) 58' 61' 64' 67' 68' 80' 81' 84' 86'90' 90' 91' 93' 96' 98' (00') (Cab S) 78' 80' 85 86' 88 90' 91' 92 93 94 96' 98' 99 125-yr-old family business, perhaps Australia's best, known for delectable Hill of Grace (SHIRAZ) vg CAB and red blends and value whites, including Riesling. Lenswood v'yds on ADELAIDE HILLS add excitement.

Hollick Coonawarra r w (sp) ★★ (Cab-Merlot) 90 91' 92 93 96' 98' 99 Gd CHARDONNAY, RIESLING; much-followed reds, especially Ravenswood.

Houghton Swan Valley r w ★→★★★ The most famous old winery of WA. Soft, ripe Supreme is top-selling, age-worthy white; a national classic. Also excellent CABERNET, Verdelho. SHIRAZ, etc. sourced from MARGARET RIVER and GREAT SOUTHERN. See HARDY'S.

Howard Park Mount Barker and Margaret River r w ★★★ (Ries) 91 93 94' 95' 96' 97' 98' 99' (02) (Note: the oo and the o1 are not good, over-acidified.) (Cab S) 88 90' 92 93 94' 96' 98' 99' (02) Scented RIESLING, CHARDONNAY; spicy CABERNET SAUVIGNON. 2nd label: Madfish Bay, excellent value.

Hunter Valley NSW Great name in NSW. Broad, soft, earthy SHIRAZ and SEMILLON that live for 30 years. CABERNET not important; CHARDONNAY is.

Huntington Estate Mudgee r w ★★★ (Cab S) **91** 93 **94' 95' 96'** 97' 99' 00' Small winery; the best in MUDGEE. Fine CAB, vg SHIRAZ. Invariably underpriced.

Jasper Hill Bendigo r w ★★★→★★★★ (Shiraz) **83' 85' 86'** 90' **91' 92'** 94 96' 97' 98' 99' (00) Emily's Paddock SHIRAZ-Cab F blend and George's Paddock Shiraz from dry-land estate are intense, long-lived, much admired. BENDIGO's best.

Jim Barry Clare r w ★★→★★★ Some great vineyards provide good RIES, McCrae Wood SHIRAZ, and convincing Grange challenger The Armagh.

> **Regions: Geographical Indications**
> The process of formally defining the boundaries of the Zones, Regions, and Sub-regions, known compendiously as Geographic Indications (GIs), continues. These correspond to the French ACs and United States AVAs. It means every aspect of the labelling of Australian wines has a legal framework which, in all respects, complies with EC laws and requirements. The guarantee of quality comes through the mandatory analysis certificate for, and the tasting (by expert panels) of, each and every wine exported from Australia.

Katnook Estate Coonawarra r w (sp sw w) ★★★ (Cab S) **86** 90' 91' 92 93 97' 98' 99 Excellent and pricey CABERNET and CHARDONNAY; also RIESLING and SAUVIGNON.

Keith Tulloch Hunter r w ★★★ Ex-Rothbury winemaker fastidiously crafting elegant yet complex SEMILLION, SHIRAZ, etc.

King Valley Vic Important alpine region. 15,000 tonnes chiefly for purchasers outside the region, some wineries of its own.

Knappstein Wines Clare r w ★★→★★★ Reliable RIESLING, Fumé Blanc, CAB-Merlot, and Cab Franc wines. Owned by PETALUMA/Lion Nathan.

Knappstein Lenswood Vineyards r w ★★★ Estate now sole occupation of Tim KNAPPSTEIN making subtle SAUV BL and powerful CHARD, PINOT N.

Knight Granite Hills Macedon r w ★★→★★★ 30-yr-old family vineyard and winery has regained original class with fine, elegant RIES and spicy SHIRAZ.

Lake Breeze Langhorne Ck r (w) ★★ Long-term grape-growers turned winemakers producing succulently smooth SHIRAZ & CAB.

Lake's Folly Hunter Valley r w ★★★★ (Chard) **94 95 96** 97' 98 99' 00' 01 (Cab S) **69 81 89' 91** 93' 94 97' 98' 99 00' Small family winery founded by Max Lake, the pioneer of HUNTER CAB. New owners since 2000. CAB is v fine, complex. CHARD exciting and age-worthy.

Lamont Swan V r w ★★ Winery and superb restaurant owned by Corin Lamont (daughter of legendary Jack Mann) and husband. Delicious wines.

Lark Hill Canberra District r w ★★ Most consistent CANBERRA producer, making esp attractive RIES, pleasant CHARD, and surprising PINOT.

Leasingham Clare r w ★★→★★★ Important mid-sized quality winery bought by HARDY's in 87. Gd RIES, SEM, CHARD, and CAB-Malbec. Various labels.

Leeuwin Estate Margaret River r w ★★★★ (Chard) **82' 83' 85' 86** 87' **89 90 91 92' 94** 95' 96 97' 98 99' (00) Leading W Australia estate, lavishly equipped. Superb (and very expensive) CHARDONNAY; vg RIESLING, SAUVIGNON, and CAB.

Limestone Coast Zone SA Important zone including COONAWARRA, PADTHAWAY Wrattonbully, Mount Benson, Robe, Mountgambier, and Bordertown. Rapidly expanding in southeast South Australia.

Lindemans Originally Hunter Valley, now everywhere r w ★→★★★ (COONAWARRA Red) **86' 90' 91' 92** 96' 97 98' 99 01 One of the oldest firms, now a giant owned by SOUTHCORP. Vg CHARD and C'warra reds (eg Limestone Ridge, Pyrus).

Macedon and Sunbury Vic Two adjacent regions, Macedon at much higher elevation, Sunbury nr Melbourne airport. CRAIGLEE, HANGING ROCK, VIRGIN HILLS.

Margan Family Winemakers Hunter r w ★★ Highly successful winemaker including fascinating House of Certain Views brand.

Margaret River WA Temperate coastal area with superbly elegant wines 174 miles S of Perth. Australia's most vibrant tourist wine region.

M. Chapoutier Mount Benson (SA) r ★★ 40 ha biodynamic v'yd, planted to Rhône varieties plus CAB SAUV. Elegant reds from young vines.

McLaren Vale SA Historic region on the southern outskirts of Adelaide. Big alcoholic, flavoursome reds have great appeal to US market.

McWilliam's Hunter Valley and Riverina r w (sw br) ★→★★★ (Elizabeth Sem) 84' 86' **87' 89' 92** 93 **94' 95** 96 98 99' 00' Famous family of HUNTER VALLEY winemakers at Mount Pleasant: SHIRAZ & SEMILLON. Also pioneer in RIVERINA: CABERNET S & RIESLING. Recent show results demonstrate high standards. "Elizabeth" (sold at 5 years) and "Lovedale" (10 years) SEMILLONS: now Australia's best. Honest RIVERINA wines at low prices.

Merlot The darling of the new millennium; from 9,000 tonnes in 1996 to 104,423 tonnes in 2002. Grown everywhere, but shouldn't be.

Miramar Mudgee r w ★★ Some of MUDGEE's best white wines, especially CHARDONNAY; long-lived CABERNET and SHIRAZ.

Miranda Riverina r w (sww) ★→★★ Vineyards & wineries in RIVERINA, KING VALLEY and BAROSSA underpin continuing growth of this major producer.

Mitchell Clare r w ★★→★★★ (Ries) 90' 92 94' 95 00' 01' 02' Small family winery for excellent CAB and v stylish, dry Ries.

Mitchelton Goulburn Valley r w (sw w) ★★→★★★ Substantial winery, acquired by PETALUMA in 92. A wide range incl a vg wood-matured Marsanne, SHIRAZ; classic Blackwood Park RIES from GOULBURN VALLEY is one of Australia's v best-value wines. Many enterprising blends and labels.

Moorilla Estate Tasmania r w (sp) ★★★ (RIES) **91' 93 94'** 95' 97' 99 00' 01' Senior winery on outskirts of Hobart on Derwent River: vg RIESLING, Traminer, and CHARD; PINOT N now in the ascendant.

Mornington Peninsula Vic Exciting wines in new cool, coastal area 25 miles S of Melbourne. 2,470 acres. Wineries incl DROMANA, STONIERS, TEN MINS BY TRACTOR.

Morris NE Vic br (r w) ★★→★★★★ Old winery at Rutherglen for Australia's greatest dessert Muscats and "TOKAYS"; also recently very good low priced table wine.

Moss Wood Margaret River r w ★★★★ (Sem) **92' 94'** 95' 97' 98' 99 01 (Cab S) 86 87 **90' 91' 93** 95' 96 99' 00' To many, the best MARGARET RIVER winery (only 29 acres). SEM, CAB, PINOT N, and CHARD, all with rich fruit flavours, not unlike some of the top California wines.

Mount Langi Ghiran Grampians r w ★★★ (Shiraz) 86' 88 **90' 91 92** 93' 95 96' 98' 99' Especially for superb, rich, peppery, Rhône-like SHIRAZ, one of Australia's best cool-climate versions. Now owned by YERING STATION.

Mount Mary Yarra Valley r w ★★★★ (Pinot N) **92' 94 95 96'** 97' 98 99' 00' (02') (Cab S-Cab F-Merlot) **84' 85' 86' 88'** 90' 92' **93'** 94 95' 96' 97' 98' 99 (00') Dr John Middleton is a perfectionist making tiny amounts of suave CHARD, vivid PINOT N, and (best of all) CAB S-Cab F-Merlot: Australia's most B'x-like "claret". All will age impeccably.

Mountadam Barossa r w (sp) ★★★ (Chard) **92' 93 94' 96 97** 98' 99 01' High EDEN VALLEY winery of Adam Wynn. CHARD is rich, voluptuous, and long. Other labels include David Wynn, Eden Ridge. Acquired by CAPE MENTELLE 2000.

Mudgee NSW Small, isolated area 168 miles northwest of Sydney. Big reds surprisingly fine SEMILLON, and full CHARDONNAYS.

Murdock Coonawarra r ★★★ Long-term grapegrower now making classic CAB S.

Murray Valley SA, Vic & NSW Vast irrigated v'yds. Principally making "cask" table wines. 40% of total Australian wine production.

Nepenthe Adelaide Hills r w ★★→★★★ First winery to be built here for 10 years (since PETALUMA); severe restrictions apply in water-catchment zone. State-of-the-art kit, excellent v'yds, skilled winemaking: sophisticated wines especially SAUVIGNON, CHARDONNAY, SEMILLON.

Ninth Island See Piper's Brook

O'Leary Walker Wines Clare r w ★★★ Two whizz-kids have mid-life crisis, leave BERINGER BLASS to do their own thing – very well.

Orange NSW Cool-climate region giving lively Chard, Cab S, Merlot, Shiraz.

Orlando (Gramp's) Barossa r w sp (br sw w) ★★→★★★ (St Hugo Cab) **86' 88** 90' 96 98' 99 01 Great pioneering co, bought by management in 88 but now owned by Pernod-Ricard. Full range from huge-selling Jacob's Creek to excellent Jacaranda Ridge CAB S from COONAWARRA. See also Wyndham Estate.

Alpine Valleys Vic Geographically similar to KING VALLEY and similar use of grapes.

Padthaway SA Large vineyard area developed as overspill of COONAWARRA. Cool climate; good PINOT N is produced and excellent CHARD (esp LINDEMANS and HARDY'S), also Chard-Pinot N sparkling.

Palandri Wines Margaret River r w ★→★★ Massive public investment in 210 ha v'yds in Great Southern, 2,500-tonne winery, and relentless advertising.

Paringa Estate Mornington Peninsula r w ★★★ Maker of quite spectacular CHARD, PINOT N, and (late-picked) SHIRAZ winning innumerable trophies.

Parker Estate Coonawarra r ★★★ Small estate making v good CAB, esp Terra Rossa First Growth.

Pemberton WA Region between MARGARET RIVER and GREAT SOUTHERN; initial enthusiasm for PINOT NOIR replaced by Merlot and SHIRAZ.

Penfolds Originally Adelaide, now everywhere r w (sp br) ★★→★★★★ (Grange) 52' 53' 55' **62' 63' 66' 67** 71' **75 76 80 83 85 86' 88** 90' 91' 92 94' 95 96' 97 98' (Bin 707) **64** 66' 76' **78 80 83' 86' 88** 90' **91** 92 94' 96' 98' Ubiquitous and excellent: in BAROSSA VALLEY, CLARE, COONAWARRA, RIVERINA, etc. Consistently Australia's best red-wine company. Its Grange (was called "Hermitage") is deservedly ★★★★. P's Yattarna CHARD, the long-awaited "White Grange", released 98. Bin 707 CABERNET not far behind. Other bin-numbered wines (e.g. Kalimna Bin 28 Shiraz) can be outstanding, though prices are rising. Grandfather "Port" is often excellent.

Penley Estate Coonawarra r w ★★★ High-profile, no-expense-spared, newcomer winery: rich, textured, fruit-and-oak CAB; also SHIRAZ-Cab blend and CHARD.

Perth Hills WA Fledgling area 19 miles E of Perth with a larger number of growers on mild hillside sites.

Petaluma Adelaide Hills r w sp ★★★★ (Ries) 80' **82 84' 86' 87** 94' **96'** 97 99' 00' 01' 02' (Chard) 92' **94' 95' 96'** 00 (Cab S) 79' 86' **88' 90' 91' 93** 94' **95'** 97 98' 99 00' A rocket-like 80s success with COONAWARRA CAB, ADELAIDE HILLS CHARD, Croser CLARE VALLEY RIES, all processed at winery in Adelaide Hills. Driven by the fearsome intellect and energy of Brian Croser. Red wines richer from 88 on. New Tiers Chard challenges PENFOLDS' Yattarna and LEEUWIN ESTATE. Owns KNAPPSTEIN, MITCHELTON, Smithbrook, and STONIERS. Fell prey to Lion Nathan 2002.

Peter Lehmann Wines Barossa r w (sp br sw w) ★★→★★★ Defender of BAROSSA faith, with consistently well-priced wines in substantial quantities. NB Stonewell SHIRAZ (tastes of blackberries and rum) and dry RIES.

Pierro Margaret River r w ★★★ (Chard) **90' 94** 95' 96' 99' 00' 01' Highly rated producer of expensive, tangy SEM/SAUV BL, and v good barrel-fermented CHARD.

Piper's Brook Tasmania r w sp ★★★ (Ries) 84' 85 **87 89' 92 93' 94' 95'** 96' 98' 99' 00' 01' (Chard) **92' 93' 94'** 95' 97 99' 00' (02') Cool-area pioneer; vg RIES, PINOT N, restrained CHARD from Tamar Vly. Lovely labels. 2nd label: Ninth Island. Acquired HEEMSKERK, Rochecombe in 98; now controls 35% of Tasmanian wine industry. Founder Andrew Pirie left 2003 – its future is uncertain.

Pinot Noir 4,414 ha, 21,341 tonnes Mostly used in sparkling. Exciting wines from S Victoria, TASMANIA, and ADELAIDE HILLS; plantings are increasing.

Pirramimma McLaren V r w ★★ Low-profile, century-old family business with first-class v'yds making underpriced wines incl excellent Petit Verdot.

Plantagenet Mount Barker r w (sp) ★★★ (Cab S) **92' 93'** 94' 95' 98 99 The region's elder statesman: wide range of varieties, especially rich CHARD, SHIRAZ, and vibrant, potent CAB S.

Poets Corner Mudgee r w ★★ Reliable underrated producer of CHARDONNAY SHIRAZ, and CABERNET. Also Montrose and Henry Lawson labels.

Primo Estate Adelaide Plains r w dr (w sw) ★★★ Joe Grilli is a miracle-worker given the climate; successes incl very gd botrytized RIES, tangy Colombard, potent Joseph CAB-Merlot (aka Moda Amarone).

Pyrenees Vic Central Vic region producing rich, minty reds and some interesting whites, esp Fumé Bl.

Red Hill Estate Mornington Peninsula r w sp ★★→★★★ One of the larger and more important wineries; notably elegant wines.

Redman Coonawarra r ★→★★ The most famous old name in COONAWARRA; red-wine specialist: SHIRAZ, CAB S, Cab-Merlot. Wine fails to do justice to the quality of the vineyards.

Reynell McL Vale r rsw w ★★→★★★★ ("Vintage Port") **75'** 77' **82 87** 88 90 Historic winery serving as HQ for BRL HARDY group. Vg "Basket-pressed" red table wines, superb vintage "Port", now under Reynell label.

Reynold's Orange NSW r w ★★ Brand name for 2,224 acre/20,000-tonne Cabonne Winery, exporting 175,000 cases to US via JV with Sutter Home.

Richmond Grove Barossa r w ★→★★★ Master winemaker John Vickery produces great RIESLING at bargain prices; other wines are OK. Owned by Orlando Wyndham.

Riesling 3,962ha, 27,838 tonnes. Has a special place in the BAROSSA, EDEN and CLARE valleys. Usually made bone-dry; can be glorious with up to 20 years bottle-age. Newer botrytis Rieslings made sparingly but can be superb.

Riverina NSW Large-volume irrigated zone centred around Griffith; good-quality "cask" wines (especially white), great sweet, botrytized SEM. Watch for reduced yields and better quality.

Robert Channon Wines Granite Belt (Queensland) r w ★★ Lawyer turned vigneron has 17 acres of permanently netted, immaculately trained vineyard producing stunning VERDELHO (plus usual others).

Rockford Barossa r w sp ★★→★★★★ Small producer, wide range of thoroughly individual wines, often made from very old, low-yielding v'yds; reds best. Sparkling Black SHIRAZ has super-cult status.

Rosemount Estate Upper Hunter, McLaren Vale, Coonawarra r w (sp) ★★→★★★ Rich, Roxburgh CHARD, MCLAREN VALE Balmoral Syrah, MUDGEE Mountain Blue CABERNET-SHIRAZ, & COONAWARRA Cabernet lead the wide range, which gets better every year. Merged with SOUTHCORP March 01. Links with Mondavi, too.

Rosevears Estate N Tasmania r w ★★ Spectacularly sited winery/ restaurant complex by Tamar River. Wines incl CHARD, PINOT N, and CAB-Merlot under Rosevears and Notley Gorge labels.

Rothbury Estate Hunter Valley r w ★★ Fell prey to Fosters/MILDARA in 96 after long bitter fight by original founder Len EVANS (since departed). Has made long-lived SEM and SHIRAZ and rich, buttery, early-drinking COWRA CHARD to good effect. Old Evans fans should see Evans Family and TOWER.

Rutherglen and Glenrowan Vic Two of five regions in the Northeast Victorian Zone justly famous for weighty reds and magnificent, fortified dessert wines.

Rymill Coonawarra ★★ Descendants of John Riddoch carrying on the good work of the founder of COONAWARRA. Strong, dense SHIRAZ and CABERNET especially noteworthy.

St Hallett Barossa r w ★★★ (Old Block) **86' 88' 90'** 91' **92' 93'** 94' 95 96' 97 98' 99 Rejuvenated winery. 60⁺-yr-old vines give splendid Old Block SHIRAZ. Rest of range is smooth and stylish. Lion Nathan-owned.

St Sheila's SA p sw sp **36 22 38** Full-bodied fizzer. Ripper grog, too.

Saltram Barossa r w ★★→★★★ Mamre Brook (SHIRAZ, CAB, CHARD) and No 1 Shiraz are leaders. Metala is assoc Stonyfell label for Langhorne Creek Cab-Shiraz. A Beringer Blass brand.

Sandalford Swan Valley r w (br) ★→★★ Fine old winery with contrasting styles of r and w single-grape wines from SWAN and MARGARET RIVER areas. Sandalera is amazing long-aged sweet white.

Sauvignon Blanc 2,914 ha, 25,567 tonnes. Usually not as distinctive as in New Zealand, and made in many different styles, from bland to pungent.

Scotchman's Hill Geelong r w ★★ Newcomer making significant quantities of stylish PINOT N and good CHARD at modest prices.

Semillon 6,610 ha, 100,785 tonnes. Before the arrival of CHARD, Semillon was the HUNTER VALLEY'S answer to South Australia's RIESLING. Traditionally made without oak and extremely long-lived. Brief affair with oak terminated.

Seppelt Barossa, Grampians, Padthaway, etc. r w sp br (sw w) ★★★ (Shiraz) 56' 71' **85' 86' 90 91' 92** 93' 96' 97' 98' 99' Far-flung producers of Australia's most popular sparkling (Great Western Brut); also new range of Victoria-sourced table wines. Top sparkling is highly regarded "Salinger". Another part of SOUTHCORP, Australia's largest wine company.

Sevenhill Clare r w (br) ★★ Owned by the Jesuitical Manresa Society since 1851; consistently good wine; reds (esp SHIRAZ) can be outstanding.

Seville Estate Yarra Valley r w ★★★ (Shiraz) 76' 85' **88 91'** 94 97' 00' Tiny winery acq by BROKENWOOD 97; CHARD, SHIRAZ, PINOT N, CAB.

Shadowfax Vineyard Geelong Vic r w ★★ Stylish new winery, part of historic Werribee Park, also hotel based on 1880s Mansion. NB P Noir.

Shantell Yarra Valley r w ★★→★★★ Under-rated producer with 30 year-old vineyard. SEMILLON, CHARDONNAY, PINOT NOIR, CABERNET SAUVIGNON.

Shaw & Smith McLaren Vale w (r) ★★★ Trendy young venture of flying winemaker Martin Shaw and Australia's first MW, Michael Hill Smith. Crisp SAUV, vg unoaked CHARD, complex, barrel-ferm Reserve CHARD, new Mer.

Shiraz 37,031 ha, 326,866 tonnes. Hugely flexible: velvety/earthy in the HUNTER; spicy, peppery, and Rhône-like in central and S Victoria; and brambly, rum-sweet, and luscious in BAROSSA and environs (eg PENFOLDS' Grange).

Simon Gilbert Wines Mudgee r w ★★ AUS$10 million winery as major contract maker plus own wines in major focus for Central Ranges Zone.

Sirronet Queensland Coast r w ★★ 247-acre, striking 75,000-case winery, 200-seat restaurant. Biggest of many such new ventures.

Southcorp The giant of the industry; watch its shares: owns PENFOLDS, LINDEMANS, SEPPELT, Seaview, WYNNS, etc, and, from 2001, ROSEMOUNT.

Southern NSW Zone (NSW) incl CANBERRA, Gundagai, Hilltops, and Tumbarumba.

S Smith & Sons (alias Yalumba) Barossa r w sp br (sw w) ★★→★★★ Big, old family firm with considerable verve. Full spectrum of high-quality wines, including HILL-SMITH ESTATE. HEGGIES and YALUMBA Signature Reserve are best. Angas Brut, a good-value sparkling wine, and Oxford Landing CHARDONNAY are now world brands.

Stanton & Killeen Rutherglen br r ★★★ Grandson Chris Killeen has a modernist palate, and makes a great dry red and outstanding "Vintage Port" plus Muscat.

Stonehaven PADTHAWAY r w ★★ First large (AUS$20m) winery in PADTHAWAY region built by BRL HARDY servicing whole LIMESTONE COAST ZONE production.

Stonier Wines Mornington Peninsula r w ★★★ (Chard) **94' 95 97 98** 00' 01' 02 (Pinot) **94 95' 97** 99 00' 02' Has overtaken DROMANA ESTATE for pride of place on the Peninsula. CHARDONNAY, PINOT NOIR are consistently vg; Reserves outstanding. 70% owned by PETALUMA since 88.

Swan Valley WA Birthplace of wine in the west, N of Perth. Hot climate makes strong, low-acid table wines but gd dessert wines. Declining in importance.

Tahbilk Goulburn Valley r w ★★→★★★ (Marsanne) 79' **84' 88' 89'** 95 98' 99 00 01 02 (Shiraz) **80** 84' **86' 88** 91' 95' 97 98 99' 00 (Cab) **86' 88 90** 91' 92 94 95 97 98' 99 00' Beautiful historic family estate: reds for long ageing, also RIESLING and Marsanne. Reserve CAB outstanding; value for money ditto. Rare 1860 vines SHIRAZ, too.

Taltarni Grampians/Avoca r w (sp) ★★ Huge but balanced reds for very long ageing; good SAUV and Clover Hill (Tasmania) sparkling.

Tarrawarra Yarra Valley r w ★★★ (Chard) 92' **94' 97** 98' **00'** (02') (Pinot N) 92' 94' **96 97'** 98 00' (02') Multimillion-dollar investment with limited quantities of idiosyncratic, expensive CHARDONNAY and robust, long-lived PINOT NOIR. Tunnel Hill is the second label.

Tasmania Only 200,000 litres produced in 2002; tiny because of bad weather at flowering. Great potential for CHARD, PINOT N, RIES in cool climate.

Tatachilla McLaren V r w ★★→★★★ Merged with St Hallett in 2000 to form public-listed Banksia Wines; significant (250,000 case) production of nice white and vg reds to increase rapidly. Acquired by Lion Nathan in 2002.

Taylors Wines Clare r w ★★→★★★ 200,000 case production of much-improved RIES, SHIRAZ, CAB esp under St Andrew's label.

Ten Minutes by Tractor Mornington Peninsula r w ★★ Amusing name and sophisticated packaging links three family vineyards which are – yes, you've guessed. SAUVIGNON, CHARDONNAY, and PINOT NOIR are all good.

T'Gallant Mornington Peninsula w (r) ★★ Improbable name, avant garde labels for Aus's top Pinot Gris/Grigio producer; also fragrant unwooded CHARD.

Tower Estate r w ★★★→★★★★ Newest venture of Len EVANS (and financial partners) offering luxury convention facilities and portfolio of seven wines made from grapes grown in the best parts of Australia. Impressive.

Trentham Estate Murray Darling (r) w ★★ 50,000 c/s of family-grown & made sensibly priced wines from "boutique" winery on R Murray; gd restaurant, too.

Turkey Flat Barossa Valley r p ★★★ Icon producer of rosé, GRENACHE, SHIRAZ from core of 150-yr-old v'yd's. Top Stuff.

Tyrrell Hunter Valley r w ★★★ (Sem Vat 1) 77' **89' 90 94' 95' 96'** 98 99' 00' (Chard Vat 47) 73' **79' 92' 95' 97' 98'** 99' 00' 01 (Shiraz Vats) **73' 75' 79' 81' 87** 91' 92' **94' 96'** 97 98' 99' 00' Some of the best traditional HUNTER VLY wines, SHIRAZ and SEM. Pioneered CHARD with big, rich Vat 47 – still a classic. Also PINOT N.

Upper Hunter NSW Est'd in early 60s; irrigated vines (mainly whites), lighter and quicker developing than Lower Hunter's.

Vasse Felix Margaret River r w ★★★ (Cab S) **85 88 89** 91 **94 95'** 96' 97 99' With CULLEN, pioneer of the MARGARET RIVER. Elegant CAB, notable for mid-weight balance. Major expansion underway. Second label: Forest Hills (esp RIES, CHARD).

Verdelho Old white grape re-emerging in some light, aromatic wines and CHARD blends. Worth trying.

Virgin Hills Macedon Ranges r ★★★ 73' **74' 76' 81' 82 84 88** 91' **92'** 95 98' 00' Tiny supplies of one red (a CABERNET-SHIRAZ-Malbec blend) of legendary style and balance. Rapid ownership changes unsettling.

Voyager Estate Margaret River r w ★★★ 30,000 cases of estate-grown, rich, and powerful SEM, SAUV BL, CHARD, AND Cab-Merlot.

Wendouree Clare r ★★★★ **78 79 83** 86 89' 90' 91' 92 93 94' 96' 98' 99' (00) Treasured maker (tiny quantities) of some of Australia's most powerful and concentrated reds based on SHIRAZ, CABERNET S, MOURVEDRE, & Malbec; immensely long-lived.

Westfield Swan Valley w r ★→★★ John Kosovich's CAB, CHARD, and VERDELHO show particular finesse for a hot climate, but he is now developing a new v'yd in the much cooler PEMBERTON region.

Wirra Wirra McLaren Vale r w (sp sw w) ★★★ (Cab S) 86 90' **91' 92** 95 96' 97 98' 99 High-quality wines making a big impact. Angelus is superb, top-of-the-range CABERNET, ditto RSW SHIRAZ.

Wyndham Estate Mudgee NSW r w (sp) ★→★★ Aggressive, large HUNTER and MUDGEE group with brands: Craigmoor, Hunter Estate, MONTROSE, Richmond Grove, and Saxonvale. Acquired by ORLANDO in 90.

Wynns Coonawarra r w ★★★ (Shiraz) 55' **63 86' 88' 90'** 91' 93 **94'** 96' 98' 99 oo (Cab S) 57' 60' 62' **82' 85' 86'** 90' 91' **94'** 96' 97 98' 99' oo SOUTHCORP-owned COONAWARRA classic. RIES, CHARD, SHIRAZ, and CAB are all very good, especially John Riddoch Cab, and Michael Shiraz.

Yalumba See S Smith & Sons.

Yarra Burn Yarra Valley r w sp ★★→★★★ Estate making SEM, SAUV, CHARD, sparkling PINOT, Pinot N, CAB; acquired by BRL HARDY in 95, with changes now underway. Bastard Hill CHARD and PINOT N legitimate flag-bearers.

Yarra Ridge Yarra Valley r w ★★→★★★ Very successful CHARDONNAY, CABERNET, SAUVIGNON BLANC, PINOT NOIR, all with flavour and finesse at relatively modest prices. Owned by BERINGER BLASS.

Yarra Valley Superb historic area nr Melbourne. Growing emphasis on very successful PINOT NOIR and sparkling.

Yarra Yarra Yarra Valley r w ★★★ Recently increased from 2 ha to 7 ha giving greater access to SEM/SAUV and CAB S, each in classic Bordeaux style.

Yarra Yering Yarra Valley r w ★★★→★★★★ (Dry Reds) 81' 82' **83 84 85 90'** 91' 93' 94' 95 96' 97' 98 99' oo' Best-known Lilydale boutique winery. Esp racy, powerful PINOT N, deep, herby CAB (Dry Red No 1), and SHIRAZ (Dry Red No 2). Luscious, daring flavours in red and white. Also fortified "Port-Sorts" from the correct grapes.

Yellowglen Bendigo/Ballarat sp ★★ High-flying sparkling winemaker owned by BERINGER-BLASS. Recent improvement in quality, with top-end brands like Vintage Brut, Cuvée Victoria, and "Y".

Yeringberg Yarra Valley r w ★★★ (Marsanne) **91' 92 94'** 95 97 98 oo' o2' (Cab) 74 76 **79 80' 81' 84 86** 88' **90 91' 92** 93 94' 97' 98 99 oo' Dreamlike, historic estate still in the hands of the founding family, now again producing v high-quality Marsanne, Roussanne, CHARD, CAB, and PINOT N in minute quantities.

Yering Station/Yarrabank r w sp ★★★ Yarra Valley On site of Victoria's first v'yd; replanted after 80-yr gap. Extraordinary joint venture: Yering Station table wines (Reserve CHARDONNAY, PINOT NOIR, SHIRAZ); Yarrabank (especially fine sparkling wines for Champagne Devaux).

Zema Estate Coonawarra r ★★→★★★★ One of last bastions of hand pruning in COONAWARRA; silkily powerful, disarmingly straightforward reds.

Terroir in Australia

Terroir – the conjunction of soil, subsoil, slope, aspect, altitude, and all the elements of site climate – is as alive and well in Australia as it is anywhere else in the world. This vast continent offers a range of *terroirs* greater than any other country other than the US, sustaining the creation of styles ranging from the finest bottle-fermented sparkling wines to the richest fortified wines. But over the past five years, and into the future, there has been a move from warmer to cooler climates, and a progressive matching of *terroir* and variety. Thus Hunter Valley Semillon; Yarra Valley Pinot Noir; Coonawarra Cabernet Sauvignon; Barossa/McLaren Vale Grenache; Clare Valley, Riesling.

New Zealand

More heavily shaded areas
are the wine growing regions

Northland

Auckland
Auckland ○ Waiheke Island

Waikato

Gisborne

Hawke's
Bay

Wairarapa
(incl Martinborough)

Nelson **Nelson**
Nelso ○ ○ **Wellington**
Marlborough **Blenheim**

Canterbury Waipara
○ **Christchurch**

Central Otago

Tasman Sea ○ **Dunedin** Pacific Ocean

Since the mid-1980s, New Zealand has made its name for wines (mainly white) of a quality no-one had anticipated, well able to compete with those of Australia or California, or indeed France. In 1982, NZ exported 12,000 cases; in 2001, over 2.5 million. There are now over 45,000 vineyard acres.

White grapes still prevail though reds are catching up. The most extensively planted are Sauvignon Blanc and Chardonnay (covering over half of the national vineyard). Pinot Noir, Merlot, Cabernet Sauvignon are now well-established, with sizeable pockets of Riesling, Semillon, Pinot Gris (newly fashionable), Gewürztraminer, Cabernet Franc, Malbec, and Syrah. Intense fruit and crisp acidity are the hallmarks of New Zealand. Nowhere matches Marlborough Sauvignon for pungency. Chardonnay has shone throughout the country, and Riesling's stronghold is the South Island. Marlborough has also proved itself with fine fizz. Recent reds (esp Cabernet and Merlot-based) from the warmer Hawke's Bay and Auckland have at least equalled the best NZ whites in quality. Pinot Noir has now proved capable of wonderful wines in cooler Martinborough and the South Island.

Recent Vintages

2002 Bumper crop (50% heavier than previous record). Cloudy, wet summer, but a favourably warm, sunny, dry autumn. Outstanding Chard and variable reds in H Bay. Flavour dilution in some Marlb Sauvignon.

2001 V dry season in the South, wet in the North. Tiny crop in H Bay and Gisb. Marlb Sauv Bl of variable, often v gd quality. Pinot N excellent.

2000 Cool, wet spring and summer, saved by an Indian summer. Low yields. Aromatic whites – gd intensity and vigour. Pinot N better than Cab S.

1999 Promisingly dry and sunny summer, followed in the North by warm, wet autumn. Avge in Gisb and H Bay, but drier and better in Marlb.

1998 Widespread drought. Richly alcoholic wines with low acidity. Tropical fruit-flavoured Marlb Sauv Bl and powerful, conc'd H Bay reds.

Akarua Central Otago ★★ Large vineyard at Bannockburn, producing classy, exuberantly fruity Pinot Noir and flinty Chardonnay and Pinot Gris.

Allan Scott Marlborough ★★ Attract Ries, Chard, and Sauv Bl; top label Prestige.

Ata Rangi Martinborough ★★★ Small but highly respected winery. Outstanding Pinot N (**99 00** 01). Rich, conc'd Craighall Chardonnay. Increasingly impressive Cab/Merlot/Syrah blend "Célèbre".

Auckland (r) 96 **99** 00' 02 (w) **00'** 02 Lgst city in NZ. Henderson, Huapai, Kumeu, Matakana, Clevedon, Waiheke Island districts – top reds – nearby.

Babich Henderson (Auckland) ★★→★★★ Med-sized family firm, established 1916; quality, value. AUCK, H BAY, and MARLB v'yds. Rare premium wines: The Patriarch. Fine Irongate Chard (98' **99** 00'), Cab-Merlot (single v'yd).

Black Ridge Central Otago ★→★★ One of the world's southernmost wineries. Noted for rich soft Pinot N, also good Chard, Ries, and Gewürz.

Brancott Vineyards ★★→★★★ Brand used by MONTANA in US market.

Brookfield Hawke's Bay ★★→★★★ One of region's top v'yds: outstanding "gold label" Cab-Merlot; rich Chard, Pinot Noir, and Gewürz.

Cable Bay Waiheke Island ★★ Sizeable newcomer, first vintage 2002. Classy Waiheke CHARDONNAY and subtle, finely textured MARLB SAUVIGNON BLANC.

Cairnbrae Marlborough ★★ Recently bought by SACRED HILL; quality Sauvignon Blanc, Chardonnay, and Riesling.

Canterbury (r) 99' **00** 01' (w) 01' 02 NZ's 6th-largest wine region; v'yds at Waipara in N and nr Christchurch. Long dry summers favour Pinot N, Chard, Ries.

Canterbury House Waipara ★→★★ Sizeable North Canterbury winery, American-owned, with firm spicy Pinot N and flavoursome flinty Sauv, Ries, and Chard.

Carrick Central Otago ★★ Emerging Bannockburn winery with flinty, flavourful whites (Pinot Gris, Sauvignon Blanc, Chardonnay) and rich, velvety Pinot Noir.

Cellier Le Brun Marlborough ★★ Small winery: very gd bottle-fermented sp, esp vintage (96) and Bl de Blancs (96). Terrace Road table wines are solid.

Central Otago (r) 99' **01'** 02' (w) **01'** 02 Fast-expanding, cool, mountainous region in S of S Island. Ries, Pinot G promising; Pinot N rivals MARTINB's best.

Chard Farm Central Otago ★★ Good Chard, Ries, and perfumed silky Pinot N.

Church Road Hawke's Bay ★★→★★★ MONTANA winery. Wines include rich ripe Chard and elegant Cab S/Merlot. Top wines labelled Reserve; also prestige claret-style red, "Tom".

Clearview Hawke's Bay ★★→★★★ V small producer. Burly flavour-packed Res Chard; dark, rich Res Cab Franc, Res Merlot, and Old Olive Block (Cab blend).

Cloudy Bay Marlb ★★★ Founded by WA's Cape Mentelle; now owned by the vast LVMH group. Intense Sauv Bl & bold Chard were initially thrilling, now just v gd. Pelorus sp also impressive. Pinot N (**99'**) one of NZ's best.

Collard Brothers Auckland ★★ Long-est'd small family winery. Whites esp Rothesay Vineyard Chardonnay and Sauvignon Blanc.

Cooper's Creek Auckland ★★ Mid-sized producer. Excellent Swamp Reserve Chardonnay, MARLB Sauvignon Blanc.

Corbans Auckland ★→★★★ Est'd 1902, purchased by Montana in 2000. Key brands: Corbans (top wines: Cottage Block; Private Bin), Huntaway Res, STONELEIGH (MARLB), LONGRIDGE (H BAY), Robard & Butler. Top GISBORNE Chards, South Island Sauv Bl, Ries, & sp wines can be superb.

Craggy Range Hawke's Bay ★★→★★★ New winery with large v'yds in HAWKE'S BAY and MARTINBOROUGH. Immaculate Sauv Bl and Chard; complex, conc'd Merlot.

Cross Roads Hawke's Bay ★→★★ Sm winery. Satisfying Chard, Ries, Cab S, P Noir.

Delegat's Auckland ★★ Mid-sized family winery. V'yds at H BAY and MARLB. Proprietor's Reserve label dropped; replaced by Res label less oaky Chard, Merlot, and Cab S. OYSTER BAY brand: deep-flavoured MARLB Chard and Sauv Bl.

Deutz Auckland ★★★ Champagne co gives name and technical aid to fine sp from MARLB by MONTANA. NV: lively, yeasty, flinty; vintage bl de blancs: rich and creamy.

Domaine Georges Michel Marlborough ★→★★ French-owned, based at former Merlen winery. Stylish, full rounded Sauv Bl & crisp appley Chablis-like Chard.

Dry River Martinborough ★★★ Tiny winery. Penetrating, long-lived Chard, Ries, Pinot G (NZ's finest), Gewürz (ditto), powerful Pinot N (96' 97' **99**' 00' 00).

Esk Valley Hawke's Bay ★★→★★★ Now owned by VILLA MARIA. Some of NZ's most voluptuous Merlot-based reds (esp Res label 96' **98**' 99 00'), v gd dry Merlot rosé, Chenin Bl, satisfying Chards, and Sauv Bl.

Fairhall Downs Marlborough ★★ Rich vibrantly fruity whites, notably weighty, peachy, spicy Pinot Gr and scented, pure, deep-flavoured Sauv Bl.

Felton Road Central Otago ★★★ Star winery in warm Bannockburn area. Pinot N Block 3 and Ries outstanding; excellent Chard and regular Pinot N.

Firstland Waikato ★★ American-owned winery, previously De Redcliffe. Hotel du Vin attached. Gd MARLB whites and H BAY Chard. Improving H Bay reds.

Forrest Marlborough ★★ Small winery; fragrant, ripe Chard, Sauv Bl, and Ries; stylish H BAY Cornerstone Vineyard Cab-Merlot.

Framingham Marlborough ★★ Specializes in aromatic white wines, notably Ries (Classic Ries is slightly sw, intensely flavoured and zesty; Dry Ries even finer).

Fromm Marlborough ★★★ Small winery, Swiss-founded, focusing on very powerful red wines. Fine Pinot N, esp under Fromm Vineyard label.

Gibbston Valley Central Otago ★★ Pioneer winery with popular restaurant. Greatest strength Pinot N, esp fleshy firm Reserve (99' **00** 01). Racy local whites (Chard, Ries, Pinot Gr, Sauv Bl).

Giesen Estate Canterbury ★→★★ German family winery, now region's largest. Known for Ries, incl honey-sweet Late Harvest. Grapes now from CANTERBURY except Chard, Sauv Bl (MARLB). Reserve Pinot Noir especially good.

Gisborne (r) 98' 02' (w) 00' **02**' NZ's third-largest region. Strengths in Chard (typically fragrant, ripe and appealing in its youth), and Gewürz (highly-perfumed and peppery). Abundant rain and fertile soils ideal for heavy croppers, esp Müller-T. Reds typically light, but Merlot shows promise.

Goldwater Waiheke Island ★★★ Region's pioneer Cab S-Merlot (96 97 **99**' 00') still one of NZ's finest: Médoc-like concentration and structure. Also crisp, citrus Chard and pungent Sauv Bl, both grown in MARLB.

Greenhough Nelson ★★→★★★ One of region's top producers, with immaculate and deep-flavoured Ries, Sauv, Chard, and Pinot N. Top label: Hope Vineyard.

Grove Mill Marlborough ★★→★★★ Attractive whites, incl vibrant MARLB Chard; excellent Ries, Sauv, slightly sweet Pinot Gr.

A choice from New Zealand for 2004

Merlot Benfield & Delamere (01), CJ Pask (00), Matua Valley Ararimu (00)

Pinot Noir Ata Rangi, Daniel Schuster Omihi Hills (01), Fromm La Strada Fromm Vineyard (01), Mountford (01)

Chardonnay Coniglio Morton Estate (98), Te Awa Farm Frontier (00), Villa Maria Reserve Marlborough (01)

Sauvignon Blanc Mount Nelson (Marlb) (01), Palliser (02), Saint Clair Res (02)

Sparkling Nautilus Cuvée Marlborough NV, Lindauer Grandeur, Pelorus (98)

Sweet wines Dry River Late Harvest Craighall Riesling (02), Montana Virtu Noble Semillon, (98), Villa Maria Reserve Noble Riesling (01)

Hawke's Bay (r) 95' 98' 99 00 02 (w) 00' 02 NZ's 2nd-largest region. Long history of table-winemaking in sunny climate, shingly and heavier soils. Full, rich Cab S and Merlot-based reds in gd vintages; powerful Chard; rounded Sauv.

Highfield Marlborough ★★ After hesitant start, now Jap-owned with quality Ries, Chard, Sauv Bl, and Pinot N, and piercing, flinty, yeasty Elstree sp.

Huia Marlborough ★★ Mouth-filling, subtle wines that age well, incl savoury rounded Chard and perfumed well-spiced Gewürz.

Hunter's Marlborough ★★→★★★ Top name in intense, immaculate Sauv. Fine, delicate Chard. Excellent sp, Ries, Gewürz; light, elegant Pinot N.

Huthlee Hawke's Bay ★★ Small, low-profile winery with crisp zingy Sauv Bl and Pinot Gr and concentrated, claret-style reds (esp Merlot and Cab S-Merlot).

Isabel Estate Marlborough ★★★ Family estate with limey clay soil. Outstanding Pinot N, Sauv Bl, & Chard, all with impressive depth & finesse.

Jackson Estate Marlborough ★★→★★★ Large vineyard, no winery. Rich Sauv Bl, good Chard (esp weighty Res). Rich complex sp, gorgeous sw whites.

Kemblefield Hawke's Bay ★→★★ American-owned winery. Solid reds, buttery, ripely herbal, oak-aged Sauv Bl, soft, peppery Gewürz, and fleshy, lush Chard.

Kim Crawford Hawke's Bay ★★ Personal label of former COOPER'S CREEK winemaker, launched 96. Rich oaked GISBORNE Chard, robust, unwooded MARLB Chard, high-flavoured MARLB Sauv Bl, and vibrant supple HAWKE'S BAY Cab Fr.

Kumeu River Auckland ★★→★★★ AUCKLAND grapes, v rich, mealy Kumeu Chard (00'); single-v'yd Mate's Vineyard Chard even more opulent. Rest of range solid, including fresh, pure Pinot Gris and oaky, savoury Pinot Noir. Brajkovich is second label.

The best Pinot Noirs from New Zealand

Pinot Noir is the hot Kiwi red, yielding perfumed, supple, richly varietal wines in Martinborough and several South Island regions, notably Central Otago but also (recently) Marlborough. Quantities are small but rising swiftly, and the best are of exciting quality. Top labels include Ata Rangi, Martinborough Vineyard, Dry River, Palliser (all from Martinborough), Cloudy Bay, Felton Road Block 3, Fromm, Gibbston Valley Reserve, Kaituna Valley, Mt Difficulty, Neudorf, Pegasus Bay, and Seresin, Wither Hills .

Lake Chalice Marlborough ★★ Small producer with bold creamy-rich, softly-textured Chard and powerful Cab S and Merlot. Ries and Sauv Bl of good quality. Platinum is premium label.

Lawson's Dry Hills Marlborough ★★→★★★ Weighty wines with rich, intense flavours. Distinguished Sauv Bl (esp), Gewürz, and Ries.

Lincoln Auckland ★ Long-est'd family winery. Good value sound varietals: buttery GISBORNE Chard (President Selection).

Lindauer See MONTANA.

Linden Hawke's Bay ★→★★ Smallish producer with soft, buttery Chard, solid but not exciting Sauv, and smooth berryish Merlot, and Cab S.

Longridge Former CORBANS brand, now MONTANA-OWNED. Reliable, moderately priced H BAY wines, including citrus, lightly oaked CHARD.

Margrain Martinborough ★★ Small winery with firm, concentrated Chard, Ries, Pinot Gr, Merlot, and Pinot N, all of which reward bottle-age.

Marlborough (r) 99 00 01' 02 (w) 01 NZ's largest region. Sunny, warm days and cool nights give intense, crisp whites. Extraordinarily intense Sauv, from sharp, green capsicum to riper, tropical-fruit character. Fresh, limey Ries. High-quality sparkling. Too cool for Cab S, but Pinot N is highly promising.

Martinborough (r) 99' 00 01 (w) 00 01 02 Small, high-quality area in S WAIRARAPA (foot of North Island). Warm summers, dry autumns, gravelly soils.

Success with white grapes (Chardonnay, Sauvignon Blanc, Riesling, Gewürztraminer, Pinot Gris) but most renowned for sturdy, rich Pinot Noir.

Martinborough Vineyard Martinborough ★★★ Distinguished small winery; one of NZ's top Pinot N (99' **oo'** 01). Rich, biscuity Chard, intense Ries.

Matakana Estate Auckland ★★ Lgst producer in Matakana district. Since 1998, classy Chard, Pinot Gr, Sem, and Merlot/Cab blend. Volume label: Goldridge.

Matariki Hawke's Bay ★★→★★★ Stylish, conc'd w and r, extensive v'yds in stony Gimblett Road. Rich, ripe, oak-aged Sauv; robust, spicy Quintology red blend.

Matawhero Gisborne ★→★★★ Formerly NZ's top Gewürz specialist. Now has wide range (also Chard, Sauv Bl, Cab-Merlot) of varying but often gd quality.

Matua Valley Auckland ★★ →★★★ Highly rated mid-size winery with large estate v'yd, owned by Beringer Blass. Excellent oaked Matheson Sauv Bl. Top wines labelled Ararimu incl fat, savoury Chard, dark, rich Merlot-Cab S. Numerous attractive GISBORNE (esp Judd Chard), H BAY, and MARLB wines (Shingle Peak).

Mills Reef Bay of Plenty ★★→★★★ The Preston family produces impressive wines from H BAY grapes. Top Elspeth range incl lush, barrel-ferm'd Chard and dense, rich Bx-style reds. Middle-tier Reserve range also impressive. Two quality sparkling wines: Mills Reef and Charisma.

Millton Gisborne ★★→★★★ Region's top sm winery: mostly organic. Top med-sw Opou V'yd Ries. Soft, savoury Chard Opou V'yd. Robust complex dr Chenin Bl.

Mission Hawke's Bay ★→★★ NZ's oldest wine producer, est'd 1851, still run by Catholic Society of Mary. Solid varietals: sweetish, intensely perfumed Ries esp gd value. New Reserve range incl excellent Bordeaux-style reds, Semillon, Riesling, and Chardonnay.

Montana Auckland ★→★★★ NZ wine giant, over 50% market share after buying Corbans in 2000. Wineries in AUCKLAND, GISBORNE, H BAY (see CHURCH ROAD), and MARLB. Extensive co-owned v'yds. Famous for Marlb whites, incl top-value Sauv Bl, Ries, and Chard (new Reserve range esp good). Strength in sp, incl DEUTZ, and stylish, fine-value Lindauer. Elegant H BAY Church Road reds and quality Chard. Bought by UK-based Allied-Domecq in 2001.

Morton Estate Bay of Plenty ★★ Respected mid-size producer with v'yds in H BAY and MARLB. Refined, rich Black Label Chard one of NZ's best (**98'**), but mid-tier White Label Chard also gd. Brilliant Coniglio Chard is NZ's priciest.

Mount Riley Marlborough ★→★★ Fast-growing company with extensive v'yds and new winery. Beautifully balanced easy-drinking Chard; piercing Ries; punchy Sauv Bl and dark flavoursome Cab/Merlot. All good value.

Mt Difficulty Central Otago ★★★ New producer in relatively hot Bannockburn area. Powerful, firm, toasty Chard and v refined, intense Pinot N.

Muddy Water Waipara ★★ Small, high-quality producer since 96 with beautifully intense and poised Ries, refined, minerally Chard, & savoury, subtle Pinot N.

Nautilus Marlborough ★★ Small range of distributors Négociants (NZ), owned by S Smith & Son of Australia (cf Yalumba). Top wines incl Sauv Bl and fragrant, yeasty, smooth sp. Lower tier wines: Twin Islands.

Nelson (r) oo **o1'** o1' (w) o1' **o2** Small region west of MARLBOROUGH; similar climate but little wetter. Clay soils of Upper Moutere hills and silty Waimea Plains. Strengths in whites, esp Ries, Sauv Bl, Chard. Pinot N is best red.

Neudorf Nelson ★★★ One of NZ's top boutique wineries. Strapping, creamy-rich Chard, one of NZ's best (99' **oo** o1' o2'). Fine Pinot N, Sauv Bl, and Ries.

Nga Waka Martinborough ★★ Dry, steely whites of v high quality. Outstanding Sauv Bl; piercingly flavoured Ries; robust, savoury Chard.

Ngatarawa Hawke's Bay ★★→★★★ Med-sized. Top Alwyn Reserve range incl powerful Chard and strapping Cab S and Merlot. Mid-range Glazebrook.

Nobilo Auckland ★→★★ One of NZ's lgst wine companies. Acquired SELAKS 98; now owned by BRL Hardy. Early reputation for reds faded. Marlb Sauv: gd, sharply priced. Superior varietals labelled Icon. V gd Drylands Sauv Bl. Cheaper wines labelled Fernleaf and Fall Harvest.

Okahu Estate Northland ★→★★ NZ's northernmost winery, at Kaitaia. Hot, humid climate. Reds: stuffing and warm, ripe flavours. Kaz Shiraz 94 NZ's first gold-medal Shiraz. Savoury, complex Res Clifton Chard (multi-region blend).

Omaka Springs Marlborough ★ Small producer with solid Sauv Bl, Ries, Chard and Merlot. Reserve Chard and Pinot N more impressive.

Oyster Bay See DELEGAT'S.

Palliser Estate Martinborough ★★→★★★ One of the area's largest and best wineries. Superb tropical-fruit-flavoured Sauv Bl, excellent Chard, Ries, and Pinot N. Top wines: Palliser Estate; lower tier: Pencarrow.

Pask, C J Hawke's Bay ★★→★★★ Med-sized winery, extensive v'yds. Good to excellent Chard (esp Reserve). Cabernet S and Merlot-based reds fast improving, with rich, complex Reserve releases.

Pegasus Bay Waipara ★★→★★★ Small but distinguished range, notably taut cool-climate Chardonnay, lush complex oaked Sauv/Sem; and zingy, high-flavoured Ries. Cab S-based reds are region's finest. Pinot N lush and silky.

Peregrine Central Otago ★★ Emerging star with strikingly good debut Sauv Bl (98); steely, incisive Ries; fleshy, rich Pinot Gr and Gewürz.

Providence Auckland ★★★ Rare Merlot-based red from Matakana district. Perfumed, lush and silky, very high-priced.

Quartz Reef Central Otago ★★ Quality producer with weighty, flinty Pinot Gr; substantial rich Pinot N; yeasty, lingering,Champagne-like sp, Chauvet.

Rippon Vineyard Central Otago ★★ Stunning v'yd. Fine-scented, v fruity Pinot N and slowly evolving whites, incl steely, appley Chard.

Robard & Butler Former CORBANS brand, now MONTANA-owned. Low-priced varietals, often good value.

Rongopai Waikato ★→★★ Small winery, local, MARLBOROUGH, and GISBORNE fruit. Soft mouth-filling ripe Sauv Bl and Chard. Known for botrytized sw whites.

Sacred Hill Hawke's Bay ★★ Sound "Whitecliff" varietals; good, oaked Res Sauv Bl (Barrel Fermented and Sauvage). Gd Basket Press Cab S and Merlot-Cab. Powerful, creamy Rifleman's Reserve Chard v distinguished.

Saint Clair Marlborough ★★ Fast-growing export-led producer. Substantial vineyards. Fragrant, full Ries, Sauv Bl, easy Chard. Plummy, early-drinking Merlot. Rich, concentrated Reserve Sauv Blanc, Chardonnay, and Merlot.

St Helena Canterbury ★→★★ The region's oldest winery, founded near Christchurch in 78. Light, supple Pinot N (Res is bolder). Chard variable but gd in better vintages. Cheap, earthy, savoury Pinot Bl is fine value.

Seifried Estate Nelson ★→★★ Region's only medium-sized winery, founded by an Austrian. Known initially for well-priced Riesling and Gewürztraminer, but now also producing good-value, often excellent Sauvignon Blanc and Chardonnay. Light reds. Best wines labelled Winemaker's Collection.

Selaks ★→★★ Mid-size family firm bought by NOBILO 98. Sauvignon Blanc and Chardonnay are its strengths but the reds are plain.

Seresin Marlborough ★★→★★★ Est'd by expat NZ film producer Michael S. First vtge 96. Stylish, immaculate Sauv, Chard (esp Res), Pinot N and Gr, Ries, Noble Ries.

Sherwood Canterbury ★→★★ Tart austere Ries and Chard and two Pinot Ns, notably fresh, plummy, berryish Res model. Bold, peachy, nutty Res Chard.

Shingle Peak See MATUA VALLEY.

Sileni Hawke's Bay ★★ Major new winery (from 98) with extensive v'yds and v classy Merlot/Cab, Chard, and Sem.

Soljans Auckland ★ Long-est'd small family winery. Good, supple Pinotage.

Spy Valley Marlborough ★★ Fast-growing company with extensive vineyards, first vintage 2000. Especially good: Riesling. Gewürztraminer, Pinot Gris.

Stonecroft Hawke's Bay ★★→★★★ Small winery. Dark, concentrated Syrah, more Rhône than Australian. Also very good Cab/Syrah/Merlot blend ("Ruhanui"), Chardonnay, Gewürztraminer.

Stoneleigh Former CORBANS brand, now MONTANA-owned. Impressive MARLB whites and Pinot Noir, esp Rapaura Reserve.

Stonyridge Waiheke Island ★★★★ Boutique winery. Two Bordeaux-style reds: Larose exceptional (94' 96 97 99 00); Airfield is second label.

Te Awa Farm Hawke's Bay ★★ US-owned (since o2); lge estate v'yd. Classy Chard, Cab-Merl, and Merl: Boundary, Frontier, & larger vol Longlands labels.

Te Kairanga Martinborough ★★→★★★ One of district's larger wineries. Big, flinty Chard (Res: richer), perfumed, supple Pinot N (Res: complex, powerful).

Te Mata Hawke's Bay ★★★→★★★★ Prestigious winery. Fine, powerful Elston Chard; v good, oaked Cape Crest Sauv Bl; extremely stylish Coleraine Cab-Merlot (91' 95 98' 00'). Awatea Cab-Merlot (v gd): 2nd label, less new oak.

Te Motu Waiheke Island ★★ Top wine of Waiheke V'yds, owned by the Dunleavy and Buffalora families. Dark, concentrated, brambly red of very good quality, first vintage 93. Dunleavy Cab-Merlot is second label.

Torlesse Waipara ★→★★ Small, gd-value Canterbury producer of weighty conc'd Sauv Bl, fresh, flinty Ries and firm, toasty, citrus Chard.

Trinity Hill Hawke's Bay ★★ Part-owned by John Hancock (ex-MORTON ESTATE). Firm, conc'd reds since 96, and elegant Chard.

Unison Hawke's Bay ★★→★★★ Red-wine specialist with dark, spicy, flavour-crammed blends of Merlot, Cab, & Syrah. Selection label is oak-aged longest.

Vavasour Marlborough ★★ Based in Awatere Valley. Immaculate, intense Chard and Sauv Bl; promising Pinot N. Dashwood: second label.

Vidal Hawke's Bay ★★→★★★ Est 1905 by Spaniard, now part of VILLA MARIA. Reserves (Chard, Cab-Merlot) uniformly high standard. Other varietals gd.

Villa Maria Auckland ★★→★★★ One of NZ's three lgst wine companies incl VIDAL and ESK VALLEY. Owner: George Fistonich. Top range: Reserve (Noble Riesling NZ's most awarded sweet white); Cellar Selection: middle-tier (less oak); third-tier Private Bin wines can be excellent and top-value (esp Riesling, Sauvignon Blanc, Gewürztraminer). Brilliant track record in competitions.

Waipara Springs Canterbury ★★ Small producer with lively cool climate Ries, Sauv Bl, and Chard; reds promising.

Waipara West Canterbury ★★ Co-owned by London-based Kiwi wine distributor Paul Tutton. Finely scented lively Ries; freshly acidic, herbaceous Sauv; firm citrussy Chard, and increasingly ripe and substantial Pinot Noir.

Wairarapa NZ's 5th-largest wine region. See MARTINBOROUGH.

Wairau River Marlborough ★★ Intense Sauv Bl; succulent, toasty Chard.

Wellington Capital city and name of region; incl WAIRARAPA, Te Horo and MARTINB.

West Brook Auckland ★★ Long-est'd underrated, richly flavoured Chard, Sauv Bl and Ries. Top wines labelled Blue Ridge.

Whitehaven Marlborough ★★ Excellent wines: racy Ries, scented, delicate lively Sauv Bl, flavourful, easy Chard.

Wither Hills Marlborough ★★★ Vyd est by former DELEGAT's winemaker Brent Marris, sold to Lion Nathan o2. Exceptional Chard, Sauv Bl. Serious, conc, spicy Pinot N.

The best Sauvignon Blancs from New Zealand

Marlborough produces inimitably zesty and explosively flavoured Sauvignon Blancs, best drunk young (six to 18 months). Hawkes Bay's more robust, ripely herbaceous and rounded Sauvignons are less punchy, but better suited to barrel maturation. Classic labels include Brancott Estate, Cloudy Bay, Hunter's, Goldwater Dog Point, Grove Mill, Isabel, Lawson's Dry Hills, Montana, Palliser, Vavasour, Villa Maria Reserve, Seresin, Wither Hills.

South Africa

A younger, well-travelled, wine-savvy generation is taking charge in the Cape winelands. It has been little more than a decade since the country emerged from its enforced isolation and apartheid sanctions to encounter much-changed markets and fashions. Initially, the Cape's strong and long 350-year-old wine tradition slowed the transformation. The wine establishment had taken years to abandon its price-fixing powers and monopolistic production quotas. And, except for a small, independent minority, they were in denial about their rampant viruses and sloppy vineyard management. But all that is changing.

Pinotage is no longer regarded with such reverence. Today's movers take much more care over their vineyards – of all varieties. And the effort to grow first-rate fruit has the inevitable knock-on effect in the winery.

South Africa's rich wine diversity remains one of its great attractions. Its vineyards, clustered spectacularly around the mountains and coastlines of the southern tip of Africa, amid wild flora and fauna found nowhere else, are another. For a time, these will remain a plentiful source of sound, cheap (mainly white) supermarket wines. But the new-wave Cape winemakers are not aiming to hang about on the lower levels. Their sights are set much higher.

Recent Vintages

2002 Wet, mildewy start then a long heatwave in many districts; most top growers made reds of good colour and fruit (and generally less alchohol than 2001). Some excellent Sauvignon Blancs.

2001 Lower-than-avge yields, conc'd fruit: dry summer and winter. Should be among the best red vintages. Big wines, deep colours, should keep well.

2000 Difficult, 3rd successive year of high temps – many v'yd fires – then isolated hailstorms. General improvement in v'yd management yielded promising reds. Heat not ideal for crisp, fruity whites.

1999 Stop-start beginning played havoc with flowering, harming yields in early varieties. Prolonged heatwave prior to harvest pushed up alcohol; some massive, unbalanced wines, for long ageing.

1998 Searingly hot, dry vintage from outset, curtailing season. Low yields helped quality. Big, high-alcohol reds, for keeping.

1997 Longest, coolest season in decades, allowing for gradual ripening; finest red year of decade for growers not panicked by a few showers.

African Terroir Wines ★★ Big, Swiss-owned ST'BOSCH- and PAARL-BASED winery. Grapes sourced widely from around the Cape for several gd-value ranges. "Azania Range": Syrah (01), Chard; "Big Five Collection": gd Cab S, PINOTAGE, Merlot (all 01). Stars in "Out of Africa" range incl excellent Shiraz (01), Cab S, Chard. "Winds of Change" range has gd Sauv Bl.

Allesverloren r ★★ Among oldest family estate in Swartland W of Cape Town. Both Cab 99 and Shiraz oo less rugged than before. Long known for smooth, sweet Port-style (89 90, 93 **96** 97).

Anthony de Jager Wines r ★★★ PAARL-based Fairview Estate winemaker's own label; intriguing, much acclaimed, complex Shiraz-Viognier blend (**00**) named Homtini Shiraz.

Asara r w ST'BOSCH ★★ Old estate recently renamed (formerly Verdun); impressive makeover with finely oaked reds. Bell Tower Cab S. Merlot (97 98) is flagship. Outstanding Chenin Bl dessert botrytis.

Avontuur r w sw ★★ ST'BOSCH. Reputation for dense lemony Chard (oo), fruity res PINOTAGE (99 **00**). Gd sparkling Brut NV, from Pinot N/Chard. Barrel-aged, botrytis Riesling label, "Above Royalty" (99).

Axe Hill r sw ★★★ Outstanding tiny specialist producer of vintage Port style at Calitzdorp. Touriga National, Tinta B (**97** 98 99).

Backsberg r w sw ★→★★ Large PAARL estate undergoing renewal. Competitive pricing; loyal following for extensive range, incl outstanding cask-aged "Sydney Back" brandy from CHENIN.

Beaumont r w ★★ Walker Bay. Small, rustic, family-run winery with growing reputation for Rhône-style reds: Shiraz (oo 01); dense, dark Mourvèdre (99 01). Also gd PINOTAGE Res (99 00), Chard, and old vine CHENIN.

Bellingham r w ★→★★ Gd reds in "Spitz" range. Cab F (99), PINOTAGE (**99**), Shiraz (**98** 99 00). Popular whites (all DYA), esp Chard, Sauv Bl, and Chard/Sauv blend "Sauvenay".

Beyerskloof r ★★→★★★ STELLENBOSCH. Small specialist grower. Deep-flavoured Cab S-Merlot blend (95 97 98 99 00) and PINOTAGE (98 99 00 01).

Boekenhoutskloof r w ★★★ Franschhoek. Recently emerged as Cape star, with spicy, assertive Syrah (97 **98 99** 00) and acclaimed Cab S (97 **98** 99), also Sémillon. Gd-value 2nd label Porcupine Ridge.

Boland Kelder r w sw ★★ PAARL. Gd Cab S (**01**). Very full Shiraz Reserve (**01**). Gd, fortified white Muscadel desserts. Also powerful Pinotage (97 98 **01**).

Boplaas r w sw ★→★★ Estate in dry, hot Karoo. Earthy, deep Cape Vintage Reserve Port-style (**91 94 96** 97 99), fortified Muscadels and "Cape Tawny Port" NV.

Boschendal r w sp ★★ Cape's biggest estate near Franschhoek. Good whites, incl bold sparkling Chardonnay Res (01). Very good Shiraz (**97** 98 99 01). Also Bordeaux blend "Grand Reserve" (**97** 98 99), Merlot (**97 98** 99).

Bouchard-Finlayson r w ★★→★★★ Walker Bay. Leading Pinot Noir producer: Galpin Peak (**96 97** 99 00 01) & Tête de Cuvée (99 **01**). Excellent Chard sp "Missionvale" label, also Kaaimansgat (both 01 02). Vg Sauv Bl (DYA).

Buitenverwachting r w sp ★★★ Historic German-owned estate in Constantia suburbs of Cape Town. Always outstanding Sauvignon (01 **02** but generally DYA), Chardonnay (00 01 02), B'x blend "Christine" (95 96 **98** 99), Cabernet Sauvignon (95 **99**), Merlot (95 **99**).

Cabrière Estate ★★ Franschhoek. Gd NV sparklers under Pierre Jourdan label (Brut Sauvage, Chardonnay/Pinot Noir, and Belle Rosé Pinot Noir). Also fine Pinot Noir in some years (94 00).

Cap Classique, Méthode South African term for classic-method sp wine.

Cape Point Vineyards r w ★★ Cape Point. Atlantic on both sides of these v'yds on the Peninsula. Outstanding Sauv Bl (DYA) & Sauv/Sem (01). Gd Chard (01).

Cederberg Wines r w ★★→★★★ High Cape v'yds. Scintillating, fruity, crisp whites: Sauv Bl & Chenin Bl (00 01). Superb Cab-based blend "V Generations" (00).

Château Libertas Big-selling blend of mainly Cab S made by SFW.

Chenin Blanc Most widely planted grape; v adaptable. Sometimes vg; much upgrading by leading growers, incl with barrel-fermentation. Generally, short-lived as dry, fruity; often lasts better when sweet. Also called Steen.

Clos Malverne ★★ Small ST'BOSCH estate, with established reputation for PINOTAGE Res (97 **98 99** 00 00), Cab/Merlot/PINOTAGE blend "Auret" (**97** 98 99).

Constantia Once the world's most famous sweet Muscat-based wine (both red and white), from the Cape. See KLEIN CONSTANTIA.

Constantia Uitsig r w ★★ Chard Res. (01 02) Sem Res (99 00 01 02) (plus Cab S) from premium Constantia v'yds (with top restaurant of same name).

Cordoba r w ★★→★★★ Highly regarded winery/v'yds on Helderberg mountains, ST'BOSCH. Stylish Cab F-based claret blend – labelled Crescendo (**95 97** 98 99); plus ripe, rich Merlot (**95 96** 97 98).

Darling Cellars r w sw ★→★★ Atlantic Coast w of Cape Town, Onyx label tops large range, PINOTAGE, Shiraz, Grenache (01), also gd Cab S (**99**) and Shiraz (00). Good-value DC range.

De Toren r ★★★ ST'BOSCH. Among Cape's finest new labels, B'x blend Fusion V (**99** 00 01). Obssesive v'yd management and berry selection makes for elegance and complexity.

De Trafford Wines r w ★★★ ST'BOSCH. Exceptional small-scale artisanal – unfiltered, natural yeast fermentation B'x blend (**98** 99); Cab S (**97** 98 99 00 01); Shiraz (**98** 00 01), Merlot (00 01 02). Also dry CHENIN BL in oak (00), dessert CHENIN Vin de Paille (**98** 99 01).

De Wetshof w sw ★★ Robertson. Chardonnays of varying style – top are flagship barrel-selected Bateleur (00 **01 02**) and Finesse (**01** 02). Also Sauv Bl, Gewurz, Danie de Wet Rhine Ries, Edoloes (**99** 00). Bottles own-brand Chards for British supermarkets.

Delaire Winery r w ★★ High mountain v'yds at Helshoogte Pass above ST'BOSCH. Rich Chard (**99** 00 **01**), massive Cab Botmaskop (98 00 02), emphatic Merlot (**98** 00).

Delheim r w dr sw ★→★★★ Family winery, v'yds nr ST'BOSCH. Acclaimed Vera Cruz Shiraz (**98** 00 01); plummy Grand Res B'x blend (**96 97** 98 99). Gd Cab S (**97** 98 99 00); also Chard, Sauv, and sweet wines, outstanding botrytis Steen, Edelspatz (00).

Die Krans Estate ★→★★ Karoo semi-desert v'yds making rich, full Vintage Res Port style. Best **91 94 95** 97 99. Also traditional fortified sw r & w Muscadels.

Domaines Paradyskloof r w ★★★ Highly rated ST'BOSCH properties incl Vriesenhof, Talana Hill, and Paradyskloof labels. Run by Cape wine (and rugby) character, Jan Boland Coetzee. Winning approving notices with new Pinot N (00). Firmly structured B'x blend flagship Kallista (**93 94 95 97** 98 **99** 00), Cab (**94 95 97 98** 99), penetrating Pinotage (**97 98 99** 00). Gd Chard (98 99 00). Gd B'x blend Talana Hill (**99**) Chard (01).

Durbanville Hills r w ★★ Grapes from maritime-cooled vineyards. Fine reds: single v'yd Caapman Cab S/Merlot (**99**). Also premium Cabernet, Merlot, PINOTAGE, Shiraz (all **99 00**). Several gd Sauv Bl labels (DYA).

Edelkeur ★★★ Excellent, intensely sw, noble rot white from CHENIN BL by NEDERBURG – like all full-blown botrytis desserts, officially designated Noble Late Harvest.

Eikendal Vineyards r w sw ★→★★ Swiss-owned 100-acre vineyards, winery on Helderberg, ST'BOSCH. Merlot (**97 98 9 00**). Consistently gd Chard (**01 02**); Cab S Res (**94 96 99** 00).

Ernie Els r ★★★ SA's golfing great debuts with rich aromatic B'x blend (00) with fruit from Helderburg/ST'BOSCH v'yds. Made at Rust en Vrede.

Estate Wine Official term for wines grown and made (not necessarily bottled) exclusively on registered estates. Not a quality designation.

Fairview r w dr sw ★★→★★★ Cutting Edge Cape winery. Eclectic range of modern fruity styles. Top is Red Seal range incl three Shiraz labels: Solitude, Beacon Rock, Cyril Back (all **01**); two Pinotages: Primo, Amos (**00 01**); Pegleg Carignan (**01**); Akkerbos Chard; Oom Pegel Sem. Regular labels incl tasty Viognier (**98 99 00**). Successful with Rhône-style blends cheekily named Goats do Roam and Goat Roti.

A choice from South Africa for 2004

Cabernet Sauvignon Havana Hills, De Toren, Jordan, Cederberg V Generations, Springfield Méthod Ancienne, Graceland, Steytler Vision

Merlot Quoin Rock, De Trafford, Meinert, Overgaauw, Slaley, Morgenhof Reserve

Shiraz Anthony de Jager, Beaumont, Saxenburg, Vergelegen, Boekenhoutskloof, Neil Ellis, Gilga, Muratie

Pinotage Spice Route, Newton Johnson, Beyerskloof, Kaapzicht, Uiterwyk, Warwick

Pinot Noir Paul Cluver, Domaines Paradyskloof, WhaleHaven, Bouchard-Finalyson, Cabrière

Chardonnay Jordan, Constantia Uitsig, Kanu, Mulderbosch, Springfield, Buitenverwachting

Semillon Steenberg, Fairview, Bloemendal, Boekenhoutskloof

Sauvignon Blanc Cederberg, Cape Point, Villiera, Jordan, Klein Constantia, L'Avenir

Chenin Blanc Beaumont, Kanu, Cederberg, Ken Forrester, De Trafford

Dessert Asara, Ken Forrester Chenin Bl T, Kanu, De Trafford

Sparkling Desiderius (J.C. Le Roux), Villiera, Graham Beck Brut

---

Flagstone r w ★★ Cape Town. Enterprising Aussie-trained winemaker Best labels so far are The Berrio Sauv Bl (02), Longitude Shiraz/Merlot/PINOTAGE (**00**), Music Room Cabernet S (**00**).

Fleur du Cap r w sw ★→★★ Value range from giant producer Distell at ST'BOSCH, incl. Unfiltered Collection. Good Cab S. (**96 98** 00), Merlot (**96** 98 00), fine Gewurz, botrytis CHENIN, Chard (**00 01**), Gd Sauv Bl (DYA).

Gilga Wines r ★★→★★★ ST'BOSCH. A hit with intense spciy Syrah (98 00).

Glen Carlou r w ★★★ Top Cape winery, v'yds at PAARL, tie-up with Donald Hess of Napa, California (qv). Outstanding Chard Res (**98 99** 00 01); B'x blend Grand Classique (**95 97 98** 99); full Pinot N (**96 98 00** 01); Spicy Shiraz (**00** 01).

Graceland V'yds r ★★ST'BOSCH. V promising unfiltered Cab S (00), Merlot (99 00).

Graham Beck Winery r w sp ★★→★★★ Avant-garde ROBERTSON properties producing classy METHODE CAP CLASSIQUE bubblies: Brut RD NV; Blanc de Blancs – all Chardonnay (**93 96 97**); well-regarded Chard (**99 00 01**). Cult-status Shiraz The Ridge (**97 98 99** 00). Cornerstone Cab (**98** 99 01) and Old Road Pinotage (**98** 99 00). Also claret-style Estate Blend (99 00).

Grangehurst r ★★★ Small, top red specialist ST'BOSCH winery, buying in grapes. Outstanding Cape blend Nikela (97 98 99) – Cab S, PINOTAGE, Merlot. Good PINOTAGE (**95 97** 98) and conc'd Cab-Merlot (**95 96** 97 98).

Groot Constantia r w ★→★★ Historic gov't-owned estate near Cape Town. Superlative red & white Muscat desserts in early 19th century. Good Cab-Merlot Gouverneur's Reserve (94 95 97 99 00), PINOTAGE (**97 99** 00), Chard Reserve (**00 01**), sw Weisser (Rhine) Ries (98 99 01), also Port style and sparkling Chardonnay.

Hamilton Russell Vineyards r w ★★→★★★ Walker Bay. Cape's "burgundy" specialist estate at Hermanus. Fine Pinot Noir (**96 97 98 99** 00 01) and classy Chardonnay (**97 98 99 00** 01). Small yields, French-inspired vinification, careful barrelling.

Hartenberg r w ★→★★ ST'BOSCH. Respected producer of Shiraz (**93 95 96 97**); Merlot (**95 96 97** 00); Cab S (**94 96 97**). Zinfandel (**95** 97); Also Chard and sw Weisser (Rhine) Ries.

Havana Hills r w ★★→★★★ Durbanville. Top coastal winery behind Cape Town. Best are Bisweni and Reserve Du Plessis range, both with deep-flavoured Cab S/Merlot (**00** 01). Also Shiraz (**00** 01) and excellent Sauv Bl (**02**).

Hazendal r w ★→★★ Old ST'BOSCH estate. Russian-owned. Flagship is Cab/Shiraz (**97 98 99** 00). Also sparklers and PINOTAGE and CHENIN.

Hidden Valley r ★★★ Small Devon Valley, ST'BOSCH v'yd. Outstanding PINOTAGE (**96 97** 00). Classic Cab S (**99** 00).

J C le Roux sp ★→★★ ST'BOSCH. Gd, large sparkling-wine house. Top is Desiderius (96); also Pinot N (**98**); Blanc de blancs Chard, long – 5-9 yrs – maturation in bottle. Well-priced Pinot-Chard NV blend Pongràcz MÉTHODE CAP CLASSIQUE.

Jordan V'yds r w ★★★ ST'BOSCH. A Cape star. Excellent Chards (**99 00 01**) and Cab S blend named Cobbler's Hill (**97 98** 99); Cab S (**95 96 97** 98 99 00); Merlot (**99 00** 01); vg Sauv Bl (DYA) and barrel fermented Chenin Bl. California-trained husband-and-wife team, Gary & Cathy Jordan.

J P Bredell ★★ ST'BOSCH v'yds. Rich, dark, deep Vintage Res Port-style (Tinta Barocca and Souzão) (**91 95 97** 98). Also rich PINOTAGE (**96 98 99**), Merlot (98).

Kaapzicht Estate r w ★★→★★★ ST'BOSCH Regularly tops local listings with Steytler range PINOTAGE (**98 99** 00) and Vision blend – Pinotage, Cab S, Merlot (00); also well-crafted Cab S (**96 97** 98 99 00).

Kanonkop r ★★★ ST'BOSCH. Grand local status, international plaudits for friendlier, oak-finished PINOTAGE (**89 91 94 97 98** 99). Equally distinctive, emphatic B'x-style blend Paul Sauer (**89 91 94 95 97** 98 99). Individual, powerful Cab (**89 91 94 95 97** 98 99).

Kanu Wines r w sw ★★ ST'BOSCH. Prominent newcomer. Cab S Limited Release (**98** 99); Merlot (**98 99** 00); barrel-aged, new-style CHENIN BL; vg Chard (**99 00 01**); outstanding Sauv Bl (DYA); botrytis Harslevelü (99).

Ken Forrester Vineyards ★★ ST'BOSCH Helderberg producer (and restaurateur at 96 Winery Rd). Oustanding Chenins from 30+-year-old bush vines (**97 98** 00 01). Vg Sauv Bl (02). Botrytis Chenin (**00** 01). Unusual light-textured savoury blend, Grenache-Syrah (99 00).

Klein Constantia Estate r w sw ★★ →★★★ Standout neighbour of more historic Groot Constantia. Bold, crisp Sauvignon Blanc, DYA but can hang on for years. Solid Chardonnay (**97 98 99 00** 01); taut B'x-style blend Marlbrook (**94 95 96 97** 99); also Shiraz (**94 95 97 99** 00). From 1986, Vin de Constance revived 18th-century Constantia legend – mint-lime-coffee aromas – dessert from Muscat de Frontignan (**93 94 95 96** 97 98).

Kleine Zalze r w ★★ ST'BOSCH. Gd reds incl Cabernet S (**99** 00) and Merlot (**00**). Barrel-fermented CHENIN BL & Chard (**00 01**).

Kumala r w sp ★→★★Gd-value range by British-based Western Wines; biggest-selling Cape brand in UK (1.5 million cases p.a.). Sound Cab S and Merlot Reserves (**99 00 01**), Chard Brut, MÉTHODE CAP CLASSIQUE.

KWV International r w sw ★→★★★ PAARL. The Kooperatieve Wijnbouwers Vereniging, formerly SA's national wine co-op. Controlled Cape wine for most of the 20th century until controversial privatization 1997. Vast premises in PAARL, a range of gd-to-excellent wines, esp Cathedral Cellar reds, Cab S (**94 95 96 97 99**), Merlot (**94 95 96 97 98 99**), PINOTAGE (**94 95 96 97 99**), B'x blend Triptych (**94 95 96 97 98 99**), Shiraz (**96 97 98 99**), Chard (**00**). Regular KWV labels incl traditional blend of Shiraz, Merlot, Cab S called Roodeberg, legendary name in Cape wine (**96 97 98 99**); vast range of dry whites and others, incl Port styles Vintage Port (**97**), Millenium Vintage Port (**99**), and Full Ruby NV. KWV-run La Borie Estate Cab. S (**96 97 98** 01), luxurious, fortified dessert from PINOTAGE, Pineau de Laborie. Classic Chard/Pinot N bubbly (**96**).

La Motte r w ★★ Lavish Rupert family estate near Franschhoek. Lean, stylish reds: Bordeaux-style blend Millennium (**95 97 98 99**), good Shiraz (**95 96 97 98 99 00**).

L'Avenir ★★→★★★ Outstanding ST'BOSCH estate. Leading producer of PINOTAGE (**97 98 99 00 01**) and top, rich, sturdy Cape CHENIN BL (**99 00 01 02**); impressive Cab S (**95 97 99** 00), Chard (**00 01 02**), and Sauv Bl (DYA). Also Botrytis dessert Vin de Meurveur (**97 00**).

Landskroon Estate r w ★→★★ Solid, old (eight generations) family property in PAARL. Recently upgraded reds with Paul de Villiers Cab S (**99** 00); gd range of other Cab S and Merlot. Outstanding Port style (**96** 97 99).

Lanzerac r w ★★ ST'BOSCH Big new venture coming on stream from historic old v'yds (and grand hotel). Merlot (**99** 00) and Cab S (**98**) are best.

Le Bonheur Estate r w ★★ ST'BOSCH estate, fine, minerally B'x blend Prima (**95 96 97 98 99** 00). Cab S (**95 97 98**); big-bodied Sauv Bl (DYA).

Le Riche Wines r ★★→★★★ ST'BOSCH. Outstanding boutique wines, hand-crafted by respected Etienne le Riche: Cab S Res (**97 98 99 00 01**), Cab S (**97 99 00**), Merlot-Cab (**99 00 01**).

Long Mountain Wine ★→★★ Pernod-Ricard label, buying grapes from co-ops under peripatetic Aussie Robin Day and local Jacques Kruger. Well-priced Cabernet S, Ruby Cabernet, Cabernet S-Merlot Reserve, Chardonnay, CHENIN BLANC. Big presence in UK supermarkets.

L'Ormarins Estate r w sw ★★ One of two beautiful Rupert family estates nr Franschhoek. Best red is B'x blend Optima (**94 95 96 97** 98), Cab S (**91 94**).

Meerlust Estate r w ★★→★★★ ST'BOSCH. Prestigious old estate. Hannes Myburgh is 8th generation to own Meerlust. With Cape's only Italian winemaker, Friulian Giorgio Dalla Cia. Fine – stressing elegance over impact – Rubicon B'x blend (**91 92 95 97** 98 99); Merlot (**91 95 96 97** 99); Pinot N Res (**96 97 98** 99). Ripe, heavy Chard (**97 98 99 00** 01). Also lusty SA estate "grappa", from Cab S.

Meinert Wines r ★★ ST'BOSCH. Complex Cab S (**98** 00) and refined, silky Merlot (**98** 00) from Devon Valley vineyards. Owned by consultant Michael Meinert.

Morgenhof Estate r w sw ★★→★★★ French-owned ST'BOSCH estate on a roll. Outstanding Merlot Res (**98** 00), B'x blend Première Sélection (**95 96 97 98** 99), Cabernet S Res (**98**), Sauv Bl (DYA); Port style LBV (**95** 99), and Vintage (**98**). Gd, dry CHENIN BL.

Morgenster Estate r ★★★ ST'BOSCH. Serious new Italian investment. Kicking off with B'x blend Merlot, Cab S and F, for fine, elegant debut (**98 99** 00).

Mulderbosch Vineyards r w ★★★ ST'BOSCH. Penetrating unoaked Sauvignon Bl (DYA – but can last too) and oaked version (01); Chards, one oak-ferm (**98 99 00 01**), other fresh, unoaked (**98** 00). Very good barrel-fermented CHENIN Steen op Hout (**97 98 99** 00). Easy, B'x-style blend, Faithful Hound (**94 95 97** 98 00).

Muratie Estate r ★★ Old ST'BOSCH estate, revival began with B'x blend Ansela (**94 95 96** 97 98), gd Cab S (00). Pinot N (**97 98 00**). Sumptuous Vintage "Port" (98), ruby-style NV "Port" – all Portuguese varieties. Fortified Muscat Amber, with loyal following since 1925. Gd Chardonnay Isabella (**00 01**).

Nederburg r w p d sw s/sw sp ★→★★ Large PAARL winery (1 million cases pa; 50 different wines). Est'd 1937. Own grapes and suppliers. Gd Reserve Cab S (**97 98 99 00**), Cab-Merlot blend Edelrood (**97** 98); plus Chard, Sauv Bl, Ries, and sparklers. Small quantities Limited Vintage, Private Bins for auction, some outstanding – recently Private Bin PINOTAGE (**97 99** 00), plus botrytis desserts. Was 70s pioneer of botrytis sw wines. Stages Cape's biggest annual wine event, the Nederburg Auction. See also EDELKEUR.

Neethlingshof r w sw ★★ Large ST'BOSCH estate, many labels. Lord Neethling Cab S (**97 98 99**); Cab S (**94 96 97 98** 99); PINOTAGE (97 98); Shiraz (**95 96 97 98** 99); Chard (**00 01**); excellent Gewurz and blush Blanc de Noirs. Champion botrytis wines from Weisser Riesling.

Neil Ellis Wines r w ★★★ Among most-respected Cape names. Full, forthright wines from widely sourced grapes, vinified at Jonkershoek Valley, STELLENBOSCH. Quality-price tiering begins with top-flight Ries V'yd Selection Cab S (**97 98 99** 00), Shiraz (**97 98** 99 00). ST'BOSCH range: Cab S (**94 96 97** 99 00), PINOTAGE (**98 99 00**) Shiraz (**97 98 99**), Cab-Merlot (97 98 99). Always excellent Sauv Bl from various sites, sparkling Groenkloof (DYA), TWO full, bold Chards from ST'BOSCH and Elgin (00 01 02). Inglewood is value range.

Newton-Johnson Wines r w ★★→★★★ Sourcing grapes widely, supplemented by own harvests/labels: family-run winery at Walker Bay. Now joins small list of vg Cape Pinot Noirs with (**00** 01), Cab S (**98 99** 00), PINOTAGE (**98 00 01**), lemony Chard (**99 00 01**), intense Sauv Bl Sandstone (02) and regular Sauv Bl (DYA). Gd value Cape Bay labels.

Overgaauw Estate r w ★★ Old (since 1783) family estate near ST'BOSCH; excellent Merlot (**95 97 98 99** 01) and Bordeaux-style blend Tria Corda (**95 97** 98 **99** 01), very good Cabernet S (**95 97** 98 **99**). Also Cape Vintage (Port-style) (**88 89 90 97 98**), includes Touriga Nacional from 94 – South Africa's first. Good Chardonnay (01).

Paarl Town 30 miles northeast of Cape Town and the wine district around it.

Paul Cluver Estate r w ★★ Promising Pinot Noirs (**98** 00 01) from fashionable Elgin region, east of Cape Town. Also elegant Chard (**01**) and gd botrytis dessert and off-dry Rhine Weisser Riesling (**97 98 00 01** 02). Dependably stylish, aromatic off-dry Gewurz.

Pinotage S African red grape cross of Pinot N and Cinsault, "born" in 1926. Can be delicious – intriguing boiled-sweets, banana flavours, and has shown potential if carefully matured in oak. But coarse, estery flamboyance can dominate (and usually does).

Plaisir de Merle r w ★★ Grand, Distell-owned cellar, v'yds nr PAARL. Complex, delicious single v'yd Cab S Res (**99**); approachable regular Cab S (**95** 98 99), Merlot (**95 98 99** 00), also Chard and Sauv Bl (DYA).

Quoin Rock r w ★★★ New, lavish ST'BOSCH winery, v'yds aiming for cult status. Outstanding debut with rich, plush Merlot (01); elegant dry white flagship Oculus (01)– mainly Sauv Bl; also clean-cut Chard and Sauv Bl from own v'yds recently established at cooler, southerly Cape Agulhas region.

Radford-Dale r w ★★ New label to watch: Aussie Ben Radford teamed with Briton Alex Dale to source grapes for small-scale premium exports. Initial Merlot (**00** 01), Shiraz – unfiltered – (01), and Chard (00 01) well received.

Rickety Bridge r w ★★ Franschhoek. Vg Shiraz (**97 98** 00) and Cab S-Merlot flagship Paulinas Reserve (**96** 00). Also good Chard and Sem.

Robertson District Inland from Cape. Mainly dessert (notably Muscat) and white wines, determined effort now to increase red v'yds.

R&R at Fredericksburg Winery r w ★★→★★★ Top vineyards, cellar at Simondium, PAARL. International consultant Michel Rolland's influence evident in this joint venture between Rothschild and Rupert, two old French and S African wine families. Mellow soft Cab S & F with Merlot (**97 98 99** 00) named Baron Edmond since 98. Chard Baroness Nadine (98 99), deep-flavoured classic.

Rustenberg Wines r w ★★★→★★★★ Prestigious old ST'BOSCH estate, founded 300 yrs ago, making wine continuously for more than 100. Major cellar, v'yd revamp since mid-90s. Terrific flagship, single-v'yd Peter Barlow Cab S (**96 97 98 99** 01); Rustenberg B'x blend John X Merriman (**96 97 98 99** 00 01). Outstanding Chard Five Soldiers (**00 01 02**). Also top class 2nd label Brampton, Cab S-Merlot (**97 98 99 00** 00), plus Chard, Sauv Bl.

Rust en Vrede Estate r ★★★ Estate just E of STELLENBOSCH: best-known for strong, individual, mainly Cab S blend Rust en Vrede Estate Wine, superb in latest releases (**91 94 96 97 98** 99). Solid Cab S (**91 94 96 98 99**), Shiraz (**94 96 97** 98), also Merlot, Tinta Barroca.

Sadie Family Wines r ★★★ Swartland. Outstanding Shiraz-Mourvedre (00) appears set to become Cape benchmark. By star winemaker Eben Sadie.

Saxenburg Wines r w dr sw sp ★★→★★★ Swiss-owned ST'BOSCH vineyards and winery jointly run with the French Château Capion, specializing in Syrah/Shiraz. Distinctive, powerful Cape reds: (Private Collection = PC labels), Shiraz PC (**91 94 95 96 97 98 99** 00) & Shiraz Saxenburg Select (**98** 00). Robust, deep-flavoured PC PINOTAGE (**96 98 99 00** 00), PC Cab S (**91 92 94 95 97 98 00**). Also Merlot (**94 95 97 98 00**), plus Chardonnay, Sauvignon Bl, and sweet Gewurztraminer.

Seidelberg Estate r w ★★ PAARL. Promising start from major revamp of beautifully situated v'yds, (formerly De Leuwen Jagt) with Chardonnay (**99** 00), CHENIN BLANC (**01 02**), and Merlot (**99** 00).

Simonsig Estate r w sp sw ★★ Malan family winery at STELLENBOSCH; extensive range: Cabernet-Merlot Tiara (**91 94 95 97 98 99** 00). Frans Malan Reserve, mainly PINOTAGE with Merlot, Cab S (**98 99** 00), rich, Red Hill PINOTAGE (**99 00**), Syrah Res Merindol (**97 98 99**), very good Chard (**99 00 01**), dessert-style Gewurz. First – 30 yrs ago – Cape Méthode CAP CLASSIQUE, Kaapse Vonkel brut from Pinot N, Chard.

Simonsvlei International r w p sw sp ★ One of South Africa's best-known co-op cellars, just outside PAARL. Many tiers of quality, from Hercules Paragon (Merlot) to Mount Marble.

Spice Route Wine Company r w ★★→★★★ Malmesbury, fashionable West Coast region. V intense, dark, rich flagship Syrah (**98** 00), Merlot (**98** 99), PINOTAGE (**98 99** 00); full, barrel-ferm CHENIN BL (**99** 02).

Spier Cellars r w ★★ ST'BOSCH. A Wine Corp label. Expanding labels under premium Private Collection Cab S (**98** 00), Merlot (**98** 99). Promising new dry whites: Sem (01), Viognier (02), Chenin Bl (01) plus fresh Sauv Bl (01).

Springfield Estate Robertson ★★ Distinctive wines from whole-berry and wild yeast fermentation. Two vg softer style Cab S, unfiltered, unfined: Whole Berry (**98 99** 00) and Méthode Ancienne (98) crisp Sauv Bl (DYA), and rich, wild, yeast Chard under Méthode Ancienne (**98 99 00 01**).

Steenberg Vineyards r w ★★★ CONSTANTIA. Serious, elegant Merlot (**97 98 99 00**) and Merlot, Cab S, Shiraz blend Catharina (**97 99** 00); two consistently outstanding Sauv Bl. Flinty Res (**99 00 01** 02); fruitier gooseberry "Regular" label (**00 01 02**) two lasting Semillons (**00** 01 02), oaked and unoaked. Also gd sparkling brut 1682 NV Chard/Pinot N. Cape's only Nebbiolo (01).

Stellenbosch Oak-shaded university town, second oldest in SA, and demarcated wine district 30 miles E of Cape Town. Heart of the wine industry – the Napa of the Cape. Many top estates, especially for reds, tucked into mountain valleys and foothills; extensive wine routes, many restaurants.

Stellenbosch Farmers' Winery (SFW) World's fifth-largest winery, part of SA's biggest wine conglomerate Distell: equivalent of 14M cases pa. Range incl NEDERBURG; top is ZONNEBLOEM. Wide selection of mid-/low-price wines.

Stellenbosch Vineyards ★→★★ Big regional venture by some 150 growers merging forces (from former co-ops Welmoed, Eersterivier, Helderberg, Bottelary). Top range is Genesis Cab S (**00**), big, juicy Merlot (**99** 00), vg Shiraz (**97 98 99 00**), Chard (**99** 00); Kumkani label features excellent, tropical-fruit Sauv Bl plus gd value reds incl Shiraz (DYA). Gd-value wines, incl CHENIN-based dry white Versus.

Stellenryck Collection r w ★★ Gd BERGKELDER range. Cab S (**94** 98), Chard (**99 00** 01), Rhine Ries, Fumé Blanc.

Stellenzicht ★★ ST'BOSCH. Modern winery, neat mountainside v'yds. Vg Syrah (**94 95 97 98 99** 00), attractive B'x blend Stellenzicht (**94 95** 97 98 **99**), PINOTAGE (98 99), Semillon Res (**99 00** 01). Remarkable noble late-harvest botrytis dessert from Rhine Riesling (**96** 98). Golden Triangle range incl gd Cab S, Malbec, Pinotage, Shiraz.

Swartland Wine Cellar r w dr s/sw sw sp ★→★★ Vast range from hot, dry wheatland: big-selling, low-price; esp CHENIN and dry, off-dry, or sw. Gd Vintage Port style (**99**), and other fortified desserts from Muscat varieties.

Thelema Mountain Vineyards r w ★★★→★★★★ ST'BOSCH Winemaker Gyles Webb and Thelema, top international names for nearly a decade. Outstanding, individual (ripe berry/mint) reds; fresh, fruity, focused whites. Cab S (**91 92 93 94 95 97 98 99** 00), Merlot (**94 95 97 98** 99 00), ultra-rich Merlot Res (**99 00**). Chard (**93 97 98 99 00** 01), Sauv Bl (02). Individual, spicy, rich Chard named Ed's Reserve (**98 99 00**). Immaculate v'yds.

Tokara r w ST'BOSCH Ultra-modern winery exciting high expectations, not least because Gyles Webb (THELEMA) is in charge. Second label Zondernaam (no name) Sauv Bl (02) won best white in SAA airline tastings in 2003. First proprietary labels due 2004.

Twee Jonge Gezellen Estate w sw sp ★→★★ Old Tulbagh. In Krone family (18th-C founder). Méthode CAP CLASSIQUE Cuvée Krone Borealis Brut from Chard/Pinot.

Uiterwyk Estate r w ★★ Old estate SW of ST'BOSCH. De Waal is top range incl striking single-vineyard PINOTAGE Top of the Hill (**96** 97 00). Very good Cab S based blend, incl Pinotage (**94 96 97 98**), Shiraz (01). Also Viognier, Chard, Sauv Bl.

Veenwouden r ★★★ Immaculate family-run PAARL property owned by Geneva-based opera singer, Deon Van der Walt. Outstanding Merlot (**95 96 97 98 99** 00), and B'x blend Veenwouden Classic (**95 96 97 98** 99 00).

Vergelegen r w ★★★→★★★★ ST'BOSCH Helderberg. One of Cape's oldest wine farms, founded 1700, and currently hottest names, lifted by talented, outspoken winemaker André van Rensb rg, brilliant, complex, like his reds: Cab S (**97 98 99 00**), B'x blend flagship Vergelegen (**98 99 00**), Merlot (**98** 99 00), exceptional elegant, spicy Shiraz (01). Superb fresh, lemony Chard Res (**97 98** 99 00) and racy, exciting Sauv Bl Reserve. Schaapenberg (98 99 00 01 02). Cracker dessert: Noble Late Harvest Semillon (**98** 00).

Vergenoegd r w sw ★★ Old ST'BOSCH family estate. B'x blend (**94 95 97 98** 99 00), Cab S (**94 95** 98 00), Shiraz (**96 97 98** 00). Vintage "Port" (**93 94 95 96** 97).

Villiera Wines r w sp ★★→★★★ Big family-run ST'BOSCH winery with excellent quality range, including 4 MÉTHODE CAP CLASSIQUE bubblies: Brut Natural Chard, virtually organic; Tradition Brut and Tradition Brut Rosé (both NV), Monro Brut Première Cuvée (**95 96**) from Pinot Noir/Chard. Sound reds: B'x blend Cru Monro (**95 96 97 98 99** 00), unusual Merlot/Pinotage (**98** 00 01), Merlot Reserve (**98** 99), single-v'yd, spicy Shiraz (**99 00 01**). Top Bush Vine Sauv Bl (DYA), consistently good and good value, dry CHENIN BLANC, dessert botrytis Chenin Blanc (00), Port style (95 97).

Vredendal Cooperative r w dr sw ★ SA's largest co-op winery in warm Olifants River region. Improving reds, incl Shiraz Mt Maskam (98 99). Huge range, mostly white. Big exporter of various supermarket labels.

Warwick Estate r w ★★ ST'BOSCH. Consistently gd B'x blend Trilogy (**92 94 95 97 98** 99 00), individual Cab F (**94 95 97** 98 00). Top Old Bush Vine PINOTAGE (**95 96 97 98 99** 00) from 25-yr-old vines; red blend Three Cape Ladies, Cab S, Cab F, Pinotage (**97 98** 99). Vg Chard (**99 00** 01 02).

Waterford r w ★★ ST'BOSCH. Show-piece winery; Kevin Arnold Shiraz (**98** 99 00 01), Cab S (**99 00** 01). Vg Sauv Bl (DYA), Chard (00 01).

Welgemeend Estate r ★★ Boutique PAARL estate: B'x-style blend (**94 95 96 97 98** 00). Amade blend (**98** 00). Malbec based blend Duelle (96 97 98 00).

WhaleHaven Wines r w ★★ Walker Bay. Local reputation for Pinot Noir Oak Valley (**95 96 97 98 99** 00), cool-climate, limey crispness in Chard (**00 01**). Slightly fizzy pink, Baleine Noir.

Wine Corp Newly established (2000) umbrella group at ST'BOSCH, controlling SPIER CELLARS, Longridge, SAVANHA, Capelands.

Wine of Origin The Cape's appellation contrôlée, but without French crop-yield restrictions. Certifies the following: vintage, variety, region of origin.

Worcester Demarcated wine district round BREEDE and Hex river valleys, E of PAARL. Many co-op cellars. Mainly dessert wines, brandy, dry whites.

Zonnebloem r w sw ★★ (Cab S) SFW's top wines, with "Fine Art" range: Shiraz/Malbec (**01**), Cab S/Shiraz (**01**), Merlot (99 00 01), Shiraz (**99** 00). Gd regular range, including Cab S (94 95 98 99), Merlot (95 97 98), B'x blend Laureat (**91 93 94 96 97 98** 00), Shiraz (**96 97 98** 00), PINOTAGE (**95 98 99** 00), Sauv Bl (DYA), Chard (00 01 02). Blanc de Blancs is popular.

A little learning...

A few technical words

The jargon of laboratory analysis is often seen on back-labels. It creeps menacingly into newspapers and magazines. What does it mean? This hard-edged wine-talk, unsympathetic as it is to most lovers of wine, is very briefly explained below.

The most frequent technical references are to the ripeness of grapes at picking; the resultant alcohol and sugar content of the wine; various measures of its acidity; the sulphur dioxide used as a preservative; and occasionally the amount of "dry extract"– the sum of all the things that give wine its character. And about the barrels.

The **sugar** in wine is mainly glucose and fructose, with traces of arabinose, xylose and other sugars that are not fermentable by yeast, but can be attacked by bacteria. Each country has its own system for measuring the sugar content or ripeness of grapes, known in English as the **"must weight"**. The chart below relates the three principal ones (German, French, American) to each other, to specific gravity, and to the potential alcohol of the wine if all the sugar is fermented.

Sugar to alcohol: potential strength

Specific Gravity	°Oechsle	Baumé	Brix	% Potential Alcohol v/v
1.065	65	8.8	15.8	8.1
1.070	70	9.4	17.0	8.8
1.075	75	10.1	18.1	9.4
1.080	80	10.7	19.3	10.0
1.085	85	11.3	20.4	10.6
1.090	90	11.9	21.5	12.1
1.095	95	12.5	22.5	13.0
1.100	100	13.1	23.7	13.6
1.105	105	13.7	24.8	14.3
1.110	110	14.3	25.8	15.1
1.115	115	14.9	26.9	15.7
1.120	120	15.5	28.0	16.4

Residual sugar is the sugar left after fermentation has finished or been stopped, measured in grams per litre. A dry wine has virtually none.

Alcohol content (mainly ethyl alcohol) is expressed in percent by volume of the total liquid. (Also known as "degrees".) Table wines are usually between 11.5° and 13.5°, though up to 15° is increasingly seen.

Acidity is both fixed and volatile. **Fixed acidity** consists principally of tartaric, malic and citric acids, all found in the grape, and lactic and succinic acids, produced during fermentation. **Volatile acidity** consists mainly of acetic acid, which is rapidly formed by bacteria in the presence of oxygen. A small amount of volatile acidity is inevitable and even attractive. With a larger amount the wine becomes "pricked"– to use the Shakespearian term. It turns to vinegar. Acidity may be natural, in warm regions it may also be added.

Total acidity is fixed and volatile acidity combined. As a rule of thumb for a
well-balanced wine it should be in the region of one gram per thousand for
each 10° Oechsle (see above).

Barriques Too much of the flavour of many modern wines is added in the form of
oak; either from ageing and/or fermenting in barrels (the newer the barrel
the stronger the influence) or from the addition of oak chips or – at worst –
oak essence. Newcomers to wine can easily be beguiled by the vanilla-like
scent and flavour into thinking they have bought something luxurious rather
than something cosmetically flavoured. But barrels are expensive; real ones
are only used for wines with the inherent quality to benefit long-term.
French oak is classic and most expensive; especially that from the Allier, the
famous Tronçais forest, Burgundy, the Vosges, Nevers, and Limoges. Each
supposedly has a different flavour and influence – which can be altered by
"toasting" the inside to different degrees when the barrel is constructed.
American oak has a strong vanilla flavour. Baltic oak is more neutral.

Malolactic fermentation is often referred to as a secondary fermentation, and
can occur naturally or be induced. The process involves converting tart malic
acid into softer lactic acid. Unrelated to alcoholic fermentation, "la malo" can
add complexity and flavour to both red and white wines. In hotter climates
where natural acidity may be low canny operators avoid it.

Micro-oxygenation is a widely used technique that allows the wine controlled
contact with oxygen during maturation. This mimics the effect of barrel-
ageing, reduces the need for racking, and helps to stabilize the wine.

pH is a measure of the strength of the acidity: the lower the figure the more
acid. Wine usually ranges from pH 2.8 to 3.8. High pH can be a problem in
hot climates. Lower pH gives better colour, helps stop bacterial spoilage
and allows more of the SO_2 to be free and active as a preservative.

Sulphur dioxide (SO_2) is added to prevent oxidation and other accidents in
winemaking. Some of it combines with sugars etc and is **"bound"**. Only
the **"free" SO_2** is effective as a preservative. **Total SO_2** is controlled by
law according to the level of residual sugar: the more sugar, the more
SO_2 is needed.

Tannins are the focus of attention for red-winemakers intent on producing
softer, more approachable wines. Later picking, and picking by tannin
ripeness rather than sugar levels gives riper, silkier tannins.

Toast refers to the burning of the inside of the barrel. "High toast" gives
the wine caramel-like flavours.

Wines to drink now in an ideal world
(vintages in italics should be approached with circumspection)

Red Bordeaux
Top growths of 90, 89, 88, 86, 85, 83, 82, *78, 70, 66, 61, 59, 49, 47, 45*
Other crus classés of 96, 95, 90, 89, 86, 85, 82, *88, 70, 61*
Petits châteaux of 00, 98, 96, 95, *90, 89, 86*

Red Burgundy
Grands crus of 97, 96, 95, 93, 90, 89, 88, 85, *78, 71, 69, 64, 59*
Premiers crus of 98, 97, 96, 95, 93, 90, 89, 85
Village wines of 00, 99, 98, 97, 96, 95

White Burgundy
Grands crus of 98, 97, 96, 95, 92, 90, 89, *86, 85*

Premiers crus of 99, 98, 97, 96, 95, *93, 90, 89*
Village wines of 01, 00, 99, 98, 97, 96, 95

Rhône reds

Hermitage / top N Rhône reds of 98, 96, 95, 91, 90, 89, 88, 85, 83, 78, 61
Châteauneuf-du-Pape/Gigondas of 99, 98, 95, 94, 90, 89, *88, 85, 83*

Sauternes

Top growths of 96, 95, 90, 89, 88, 86, 85, 83, 81, 79, 76, 75, 71, 70, 67, 59, 55
Other wines of 99, 97, 96, 95, 90, 89, 88, 86, 85, 83

Alsace

Grands crus 99, 98, 96, 95, 94, 93, 90, 89, 88, 85, 83, *76, 67*
Standard wines of 01, 00, 99, 98, 97, 96, 95, 94, *90, 89, 88*

Sweet Loire wines

Top growths of 99, 97, 96, 95, 90, 89, 88, 86, 85, 78, 76, 75, *71, 64, 59, 47*

Champagne

Top wines of 96, 95, 93, 90, 89, 88, 86, 85, the v best of: *83, 82, 79, 75*

German wines

Sweet wines of 97, 96, 95, 94, 93, 90, 89, 88, 86, 85, 83, 76, 71, *59, 53*
Auslesen of 99, 98, 97, 95, 94, 93, 90, 89, 88, 86, *85, 83, 76, 71*
Spätlesen of 01, 00, 99, 98, 97, 96, 95, 94, 93, 92, 91, 90, 89, 88, *86, 85, 83, 76*
Kabinett and QbA wines of 01, 00, 99, 98, 97, 96, 95, 94, 93, 90

Italian wines

Top Tuscan reds of 97, 95, 93, 90, 88, *86, 85, 82*
Top Piedmont reds of 96, 95, 93, 90, 89, 88, 85, 82

Spanish wines

Top Rioja 96, 95, 94, 91, 90, *82, 70, 64*
Top Ribera del Duero 96, 95, 94, 91, 90, 89   Priorato 98, 96, 94

Austrian wines

Wachau Riesling and Grüner Veltliner 00, 98, 96, 95, 94, 93, 91

California wines

Top Cabs, Zins, Pinot N of 00, 99, 98, 97, 96, then (but not for Zins) 95, 94, 91,
90, then (but not Pinot N or Zins) 87, 86, 85
Top Chardonnays of 01, 00, 99, 98, 97, 96, 95, 94

Australian wines

Top Cabs, Shiraz, Pinot Noir of 98, 96, 94, 91, 90, then (but not Pinot Noir)
88, 86, 85, 84, 82, 80
Top Chardonnays of 01, 00, 99, 98, 97, 96, 95, 94, 92
Top Semillons & Rieslings of 01, 00, 99, 97, 95, 94, 93, 92, 90, *89, 88,*
(and possibly) *86, 84, 83*

New Zealand wines

Marlborough Sauvignon Blanc 02, 01,
Pinot Noir (Martinborough or South Island) 01, 00, 99, 97, 96
Hawkes Bay Cabernets 98, 95

South African wines

Stellenbosch Cabernet Sauvignon 98, 97, 95

Vintage Port 91, 85, 83, 82, 80, 77, 70, 66, 63, 55, 48, 45…

And the score is...

It seems that America and the rest of the world will never agree
about the idea of scoring wines. America is seemingly besotted
with the 100-point scale devised by Robert Parker, based on the
strange US school system in which 50 = 0. Arguments that taste
is too various, too subtle, too evanescent, too wonderful to be
reduced to a pseudo-scientific set of numbers fall on deaf ears.
Arguments that the accuracy implied by giving one wine a score
of 87 and another 88 is a chimera don't get much further.

America likes numbers (and so do salesmen) because they are
simpler than words. When it comes to words America likes
superlatives which, inconveniently, seldom give a true picture of a
wine. Figures have another advantage: computers can crunch them
like share prices, giving comfort to investors. But those who drink
wine for pleasure need a simple hedonistic measure.

The Johnson System

I offer a tried and tested alternative way of registering how much
you like a wine. The Johnson System reflects the enjoyment (or
lack of it) that each wine offered at the time it was drunk with
inescapable honesty. Here it is:

One sniff	the minimum score. Emphatically no thanks
One sip	one step up
Two sips	faint interest (or disbelief)
A half glass	slight hesitation
One glass	tolerance, even general approval

Individuals will vary in their scoring after this (they do with points
systems, too). You should assume that you are drinking without
compunction – without your host pressing you or the winemaker
glowering at you. But you have time and you are thirsty.

Two glasses	means you quite like it (or there is nothing else to drink);
Three glasses	you find it more than acceptable;
Four	it tickles your fancy;
One bottle	means satisfaction:
A second bottle	is the real thumbs up.
The steps grow higher now:	
A full dozen	means you are not going to miss out on this one...and so on.
	The logical top score in the Johnson System is, of course, the whole vineyard.

Quick reference vintage charts

These charts give a picture of the range of qualities made in the principal "classic" areas (every year has its relative successes and failures) and a guide to whether the wine is ready to drink or should be kept. Generalizations are unavoidable.

℘	drink up	Y	needs keeping
Ψ	can be drunk with pleasure now, but the better wines will continue to improve	⊼	avoid
		o	no good
		10	best

Vintage	Germany Rhine		Mosel		Italy Piedmont reds		Tuscan reds		Spain Rioja	
2002	7–8	Y	7–8	Y	5–6	Y	5–7	Y	6–7	Y
2001	7–9	Y	8–10	Y	6–8	Y	6–7	Y	7–9	Y
2000	5–8	Y	5–8	Y	8–9	Y	7–9	Ψ	7–8	Y
99	7–10	Ψ	7–10	Ψ	8–10	Y	8–10	Y	6–7	Ψ
98	6–9	Ψ	6–9	Ψ	8–10	Ψ	6–8	Ψ	7–8	Ψ
97	7–9	Ψ	7–10	Ψ	8–10	Ψ	8–10	Ψ	5–7	Ψ
96	7–9	Ψ	6–8	Ψ	7–9	Ψ	5–7	Ψ	7–9	Ψ
95	7–10	℘	8–10	Ψ	6–8	Ψ	5–8	Ψ	8–10	Ψ
94	5–7	Ψ	6–10	Ψ	4–6	℘	5–8	Ψ	8–10	℘
93	5–8	℘	6–9	Ψ	6–8	Ψ	5–7	℘	4–5	℘
92	5–9	℘	5–9	℘	2–5	⊼	2–5	⊼	6–8	℘
91	5–7	℘	5–7	℘	3–5	⊼	4–7	℘	7–9	℘
90	8–10	Ψ	8–10	Ψ	8–10	Ψ	8–10	Ψ	7–9	Ψ

Vintage	Australia Shiraz		Chardonnay		Champagne Vintage (97 = NV)		Port Vintage (97 = declared)	
2002	5–8	Ψ	5–8	Ψ	2002 7–9	Y	2002 N/A	Y
2001	6–8	Ψ	5–7	Ψ	2001 1–3		2001 6–7	Y
2000	6–8	Ψ	7–9	Ψ	2000 7–9	Y	2000 8–10	Y
99	7–9	℘	5–7	℘	99 6–8	Y	99 4–6	Y
98	7–9	Ψ	7–9	℘	98 5–7	Y	98 4–6	Y
97	6–8	Ψ	8–10	℘	97 5–7		97 8–10	Y
96	8–10	Ψ	4–7	℘	96 8–10	Ψ	96 4–6	Ψ
95	8–10	℘	3–5	⊼	95 7–9	Ψ	95 4–6	Ψ
94	6–8	℘	7–9	℘	94 2–4		94 8–9	Y
93	5–7	℘	5–7	℘	93 5–6	Ψ	93 2–5	Y
92	6–8	℘	6–8	℘	92 5–7	Ψ	92 8–9	Y
91	7–9	℘	7–9	℘	91 4–6	Ψ	91 8–9	Y

Vintage	California Cabernet		Chardonnay		New Zealand Red		White		S.Africa Red	
2002	6–8	Y	6–8	Ψ	6–8	Ψ	6–8	Ψ	6–8	Ψ
2001	6–8	Y	5–7	Ψ	5–7	Ψ	6–8	Ψ	6–8	Ψ
2000	6–7	Y	5–8	Ψ	6–8	Ψ	7–9	Ψ	4–6	℘
99	7–9	Y	5–8	Ψ	6–8	Ψ	7–9	℘	6–8	Ψ
98	4–7	Ψ	4–7	Ψ	7–9	Ψ	7–8	℘	7–9	Ψ

France

Vintage	Red Bordeaux		White Bordeaux		Alsace
	Médoc/Graves	Pom/St-Em	Sauternes & SW	Graves & dry	
2002	6-8	5-8	7-8	7-8	7-8
2001	6-8	7-8	8-10	7-9	6-8
2000	8-10	7-9	6-8	6-8	8-10
99	5-7	5-8	6-9	7-10	6-8
98	5-8	6-9	5-8	5-9	7-9
97	5-7	4-7	7-9	4-7	7-9
96	6-8	5-7	7-9	7-10	8-10
95	7-9	6-9	6-8	5-9	7-9
94	5-8	5-8	4-6	5-8	6-9
93	4-6	5-7	2-5	5-7	6-8
92	3-5	3-5	3-5	4-8	5-7
91	3-6	2-4	2-5	6-8	3-5
90	8-10	8-10	8-10	7-8	7-9
89	6-9	7-9	8-10	6-8	7-10
88	6-8	7-9	7-10	7-9	8-10
87	5-7	5-7	2-5	7-10	7-8
86	6-9	5-8	7-10	7-9	7-8
85	7-9	7-9	6-8	5-8	7-10

France continued

Vintage	Burgundy			Rhône	
	Côte d'Or red	Côte d'Or white	Chablis	Rhône (N)	Rhône (S)
2002	7-8	7-8	7-8	4-6	5-5
2001	6-8	7-9	6-8	7-8	7-9
2000	7-8	6-9	7-9	6-8	7-9
99	7-10	5-7	5-8	7-9	6-9
98	5-8	5-7	7-8	6-8	7-9
97	5-8	5-8	7-9	7-9	5-8
96	6-8	7-9	5-10	5-7	4-6
95	7-9	7-9	6-9	6-8	6-8
94	5-8	5-7	4-7	6-7	5-7
93	6-8	5-6	5-8	3-6	4-9
92	3-6	5-8	4-6	4-6	3-6
91	3-6	4-6	6-9	6-9	4-5
90	7-10	8-10	6-9	6-9	7-9

Beaujolais 02, 01, 00, 99 Crus will keep. **Mâcon-Villages** (white) Drink 01, 00, now or can wait. **Loire** (Sweet Anjou and Touraine) best recent vintages: 97, 96, 95, 93, 90, 89, 88, 85; Bourgueil, Chinon, Saumur-Champigny: 00, 99, 98, 97, 96, 95, 93, 90. **Upper Loire** (Sancerre, Pouilly-Fumé): 02, 00, 99, 98, 97 **Muscadet** 02, 01, 00, 99: DYA.

The right temperature

No single aspect of serving wine makes or mars it so easily as getting the temperature right. White wines almost invariably taste dull and insipid served warm and red wines have disappointingly little scent or flavour served cold. The chart below gives an indication of what is generally found to be the most satisfactory temperature for serving each class of wine.

	°F	°C	
	68	20	
	66	19	
Room temperature	64	18	Best red wines
	63	17	especially Bordeaux
Red burgundy	61	16	
	59	15	Chianti, Zinfandel
Best white burgundy			Côtes du Rhône
Port, Madeira	57	14	
	55	13	*Ordinaires*
	54	12	Lighter red wines
Ideal cellar Sherry	52	11	eg Beaujolais
	50	10	
Fino sherry, Tokaji Aszú	48	9	Rosés
Most dry white wines			Lambrusco
Champagne	46	8	
Domestic fridge	45	7	
	43	6	Most sweet white wines
	41	5	Sparkling wines
	39	4	
	37	3	
	35	2	
	33	1	
	32	0	

wine
catalogue

*The following titles are just a selection
from the Mitchell Beazley Wine List and
are available from all good bookstores.*

*To order direct from the publisher
in the UK call our Credit Card Hotline
number: 01903 828800*

*In the USA call Phaidon Press Inc
on 1877 Phaidon (toll-free)*

*In Canada call McArthur & Co
Publishing Ltd on 416 408 4007*

*Alternatively visit our website on
www.mitchell-beazley.com*

MITCHELL BEAZLEY

The Hugh Johnson List

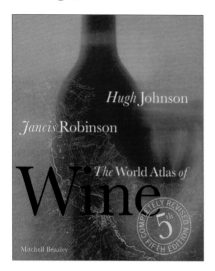

THE WORLD ATLAS OF WINE *5th Edition*
HUGH JOHNSON AND JANCIS ROBINSON

For this brand new extended edition of the best-selling *World Atlas of Wine*, Hugh Johnson has teamed up with Jancis Robinson to create the most comprehensive revision of the book so far. The maps, text, photographs, and illustrations have all been extensively updated, with additional pages dedicated to the fastest developing wine regions of the 1990s. In keeping with the *Atlas's* reputation for cartographic excellence, all the maps have been digitally updated and in some cases extended, and thirty new maps detail the vineyards in the wine world's emerging regions.

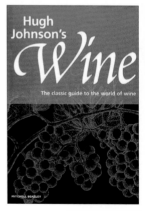

HUGH JOHNSON'S WINE
The classic guide to the world of wine
HUGH JOHNSON

For an accessible, all-round guide to the complex world of wine, *Hugh Johnson's Wine* covers everything from how wine is made to detailed tours of the wine regions, explaining what makes a "great" wine and how to select the right wine when dining out or entertaining at home.

THE WORLD ATLAS OF WINE
ISBN: 1 84000 332 4
£35 / US $50 / CN $70 Hardback 352 pages

HUGH JOHNSON'S WINE
ISBN: 0 85533 039 2
£14.99 / US $24.95 / CN $34.95
Hardback 272 pages

To order: **UK** 01903 828800 / **USA** 1877 Phaidon (toll-free)/**Canada** 416 408 4007 McArthur

HUGH JOHNSON'S WINE COMPANION
The Encyclopedia of Wines, Vineyards and Winemakers
5th Edition
HUGH JOHNSON

This new fifth edition is the most up-to-date, comprehensive, authoritative, and easy-to-use source of information on the world's wines and winemakers. It presents a unique approach to wine producers, combining detailed background information with practical advice on how to enjoy wine to the full. Extensively revised and updated by Stephen Brook, it leaves few questions about wine unanswered.

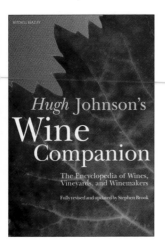

HUGH JOHNSON'S HOW TO ENJOY YOUR WINE
everything you need to know to get the most from wine
HUGH JOHNSON

Aimed at those who already enjoy a glass of wine, but who want to deepen their understanding of it. Hugh Johnson explains everything you need to know about handling wine in all social situations. With tips and guidance on all aspects of storing, serving, and tasting wine.

HUGH JOHNSON'S WINE COMPANION
ISBN: 1 85732 704 4
£30/US$40/CN$50 Hardback 592 pages

HUGH JOHNSON'S
HOW TO ENJOY YOUR WINE
ISBN: 1 84000 074 0
£9.99 Hardback 120 pages
*This edition not available from Phaidon/McArthur

To order: **UK 01903 828800** / **USA 1877 Phaidon (toll-free)/Canada 416 408 4007 McArthur**

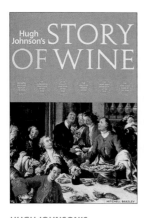

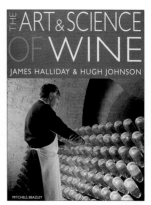

HUGH JOHNSON'S STORY OF WINE

HUGH JOHNSON

A fascinating examination of the history of wine written with all the characteristic wit and enthusiasm of Hugh Johnson, unveiling the cultural perspective of wine in enthralling episodes. Illustrated with 220 full-colour photographs, maps, and diagrams.

THE ART AND SCIENCE OF WINE

HUGH JOHNSON & JAMES HALLIDAY

An approachable guide to the process behind winemaking. Hugh Johnson and James Halliday examine how nature, art, and science combine to provide the infinite variety of the world's wines; from the vineyard, vatroom, and cellar to the bottle.

HUGH JOHNSON'S CELLAR BOOK

HUGH JOHNSON

Keep cellar records in order with this indispensable book. Useful tips on storing, opening, enjoying and recording wine. Followed by how to plan a cellar. The *Cellar Book* also includes space for personal notes.

HUGH JOHNSON'S CELLAR BOOK
ISBN: 1 84000 093 7
£19.99/US$29.95/CN$40
Hardback 224 pages

THE ART AND
SCIENCE OF WINE
ISBN: 1 85732 422 6
£15.99 Paperback
232 pages
*This edition not available
from Phaidon/McArthur

HUGH JOHNSON'S
STORY OF WINE
ISBN: 1 84000 120
£22.50/US$40/CN$60
Hardback 480 pages

HUGH JOHNSON'S CELLAR BOOK
ISBN: 1 84000 094
£80+ VAT/$120/ Special hardback,
leather bound edition, 224 pages

To order: **UK 01903 828800 / USA 1877 Phaidon (toll-free)/Canada 416 408 4007 McArthur**

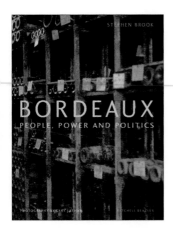

BORDEAUX
People, Power and Politics
STEPHEN BROOK

An incisive, no-holds barred exploration of Bordeaux as a wine culture. Stephen Brook looks at how Bordeaux's wines are produced, marketed and sold. The region's key winemakers are featured, and the power of the press, merchants, negociants and consumer over the wines, culture and economic health of the world's most famous wine region is also considered.

TUSCANY AND ITS WINES
HUGH JOHNSON
PHOTOGRAPHY BY ANDY KATZ

Tuscany and its Wines combines the inspirational writing of Hugh Johnson with the sparkling photography of Andy Katz. This is an irresistible portrait of Tuscany's culture, history, landscapes, people, foods and, above all, wines.

BORDEAUX
ISBN: 1 84000 363 4
£30/us$45/cn$60 Hardback 224 pages

TUSCANY AND ITS WINES
ISBN: 1 84000 274 3
£16.99 Hardback 144 pages
*This edition not available from Phaidon / McArthur

To order: **UK 01903 828800 / USA 1877 Phaidon (toll-free)/Canada 416 408 4007 McArthur**

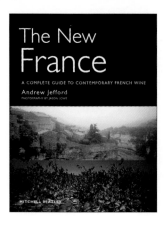

THE NEW FRANCE
ANDREW JEFFORD

This groundbreaking and authoritative book on French wine draws on painstaking research by leading wine writer Andrew Jefford, who has travelled extensively in each of France's fourteen wine regions to investigate the personalities and producers who have masterminded the resurgence of the French wine industry. Includes vintage charts and fifteen full-colour maps.

TOURING IN WINE COUNTRY
SERIES EDITOR HUGH JOHNSON

Each book in this best-selling series offers a comprehensive and inspirational guide to travelling in one of the world's top wine regions. Evocative descriptions of wine routes are accompanied by detailed maps showing the route and surrounding vineyards. Each title also includes the author's recommendations for hotels, restaurants, and producers.

BORDEAUX
ISBN: 1 84000 246 8

BURGUNDY
ISBN: 1 84000 245 X

NORTHWEST ITALY
ISBN: 1 85732 864 7

PROVENCE
ISBN: 1 84000 046 5

TUSCANY
ISBN: 1 84000 247 6

£12.99/us$19.95/cn$21.95
Paperback

THE NEW FRANCE
ISBN: 1 84000 410 X
£30/us$45/cn$70 Hardback 256 pages

To order: UK 01903 828800 / USA 1877 Phaidon (toll-free)/Canada 416 408 4007 McArthur

Mitchell Beazley Wine Guides

Mitchell Beazley relaunched its bestselling Wine Guides series, presenting each title with a new, clearer layout and boasting a more thorough update than ever before. The larger format has also been given a stylish new cover treatment.

WINE GUIDES
£9.99/US$14.95/CN$21.95 Hardback

WINES OF ITALY
BURTON ANDERSON
ISBN: 1 84000 553 X

WINES OF BORDEAUX
DAVID PEPPERCORN
ISBN: 1 84000 550 5

WINES OF CALIFORNIA
STEPHEN BROOK
ISBN: 1 84000 393 6

WINES OF AUSTRALIA
JAMES HALLIDAY
ISBN: 1 84000 708 7

WINES OF BURGUNDY
SERENA SUTCLIFFE
ISBN: 1 84000 709 5

WINES OF SPAIN
JAN READ
ISBN: 1 84000 710 9

MICHAEL BROADBENT'S WINETASTING
MICHAEL BROADBENT
ISBN: 1 84000 854 7

MICHAEL BROADBENT'S WINE VINTAGES
MICHAEL BROADBENT
ISBN: 1 84000 853 9

POCKET GUIDES
£8.99/US$14.95/CN$21.95 Hardback

FORTIFIED & SWEET WINES
JOHN RADFORD & STEPHEN BROOK
ISBN: 1 84000 248 4

WINES OF THE LOIRE, ALSACE AND THE
RHÔNE & OTHER FRENCH REGIONAL WINES
ROGER VOSS
ISBN: 1 84000 016 3

WINES OF NEW ZEALAND
MICHAEL COOPER
ISBN: 1 84000 020 1

CHAMPAGNE & SPARKLING WINE
MICHAEL EDWARDS
ISBN: 1 84000 077 5

SCOTCH WHISKY
CHARLES MACLEAN
ISBN: 1 84000 327 8

MICHAEL JACKSON'S POCKET BEER BOOK
MICHAEL JACKSON

This handy guide will keep beer lovers abreast of the world's best breweries and their beers.

MICHAEL JACKSON
ISBN: 1 84000 252 2
£8.99 Hardback 208 pages
*This edition not available from Phaidon/McArthur

To order: UK 01903 828800 / USA 1877 Phaidon (toll-free)/Canada 416 408 4007 McArthur